D0161792

BOLLINGEN SERIES LXV

ARCHETYPAL IMAGES IN GREEK RELIGION

Volume 2

C. Kerényi

DIONYSOS

Archetypal Image of Indestructible Life

TRANSLATED FROM THE GERMAN

BY *Ralph Manheim*

BOLLINGEN SERIES LXV · 2

PRINCETON UNIVERSITY PRESS

LIBRARY
McCORMICK THEOLOGICAL SEMINARY
1100 EAST 55th STREET
CHICAGO, ILLINOIS 60615

Copyright © 1976 by Princeton University Press

ALL RIGHTS RESERVED

THIS IS VOLUME TWO IN A GROUP OF STUDIES OF
ARCHETYPAL IMAGES IN GREEK RELIGION
WHICH CONSTITUTE THE SIXTY-FIFTH PUBLICATION
IN A SERIES SPONSORED BY
BOLLINGEN FOUNDATION

*Translated from the original manuscript of
the author.*

Library of Congress Catalogue Card Number: 78-166395
International Standard Book Number: 0-691-09863-8
MANUFACTURED IN THE UNITED STATES OF AMERICA
BY PRINCETON UNIVERSITY PRESS, PRINCETON, NEW JERSEY
DESIGN BASED ON ORIGINAL BY ANDOR BRAUN

Library of Congress Cataloging in Publication data will be
found on the last printed page of this book

BL
820
.B2
K4713

To

Gösta and Marie-Louise Säflund

Perhaps in this way we shall attain the high philosophical goal of perceiving how the divine life in man is joined in all innocence with animal life.

—GOETHE

CONTENTS

List of Illustrations   ix

Acknowledgments   xxii

Preface   xxiii

Introduction   xxxi

Part One: The Cretan Prelude

I Minoan Visions

The Spirit of Minoan Art   5
The Minoan Gesture   10
Visionary Crete   14
Transcendence in Nature   20
Artificially Induced Transcendence   22

II Light and Honey

Flaming New Year   29
The Preparation of Mead   35
The Awakening of the Bees   38
The Birth of Orion   41
Mythology of the Leather Sack   44

III The Cretan Core of the Dionysos Myth

Bull, Snake, Ivy, and Wine   52
Dionysian Names   68
Iakar and Iakchos   73
Zagreus   80
Ariadne   89

Part Two: The Greek Cult and Myth

iv   The Myths of Arrival

    From the History of Science   129
    The Forms of Arrival   139
    Arrivals in Attica   141
    The Arrival in Athens   160
    Myth of Arrival and Ancient Rite outside of Attica:
      Thebes and Delphi   175

v   Dionysos Trieterikos, God of the Two-Year Period

    Age and Continuity of the Trieteric Cult   189
    The Dialectic of the Two-Year Period   198
    Dionysos in Delphi   204
    The Mystical Sacrificial Rite   238
    The Enthronement   262

vi   The Dionysos of the Athenians and of His Worshipers
    in the Greek Mysteries

    The Thigh Birth and the Idol with the Mask   273
    The Dionysian Festivals of the Athenians   290
    The Beginnings of Tragedy in Attica   315
    The Birth and Transformation of Comedy in Athens   330
    The Greek Dionysian Religion of Late Antiquity   349

Abbreviations   391

List of Works Cited   393

Index   421

A Note on C. Kerényi   445

A Bibliography of C. Kerényi   447

Photographs are ascribed to the museums mentioned unless otherwise accredited. The following abbreviations refer to photographic sources:

DAIA   Deutsches archäologisches Institut, Athens.
DAIR   Deutsches archäologisches Institut, Rome.
H   Hirmer Fotoarchiv, Munich.
NYPL   New York Public Library

The illustrations are in a section following page 388.

1. *The Great Goddess on a mountain. Transcript of a seal from Knossos: reconstruction. From Arthur Evans, "The Palace of Knossos," BSA, VII (1900–1901), fig. 9.* P: *DAIR.*

2. *Bull game. Fresco from the palace of Knossos: reconstruction. Heraklion, Archaeological Museum.* P: *H.*

3A. *Capture of a wild bull. Detail of a Minoan ivory pyxis. Heraklion, Archaeological Museum. From S. Alexiou, Ὑστερομινωικοὶ τάφοι λιμένος Κνώσου (Athens, 1967).*

3B. *Transcript of 3A by T. Phanouraki.*

4. *Persephone with two companions and a flower, in a cup from the first palace at Phaistos. Heraklion, Archaeological Museum.* P: *Athens, Italian School of Archaeology.*

5. *Dancing women, in a "fruit bowl" from Phaistos: reconstruction. Heraklion, Archaeological Museum.* P: *Professor Doro Levi.*

6. *The cave of Eileithyia, near Amnisos. Detail of the interior.* P: *Paul Faure.*

7. *Man setting down a sacrifice in front of a mountain shrine, on a Minoan vase from Knossos. Heraklion, Archaeological Museum.* P: *Dr. Stylianos Alexiou.*

8. *Mountain shrine with goats and birds of prey, on a Minoan vase from Kato Zakros. Heraklion, Archaeological Museum.* P: *H.*

9. *Two male gesture figures among crocuses. Transcript of a drawing on a small Minoan amphora from the first palace at Phaistos. Heraklion, Archaeological Museum.* P: DAIR.

10. *Epiphany scene among flowers, on the seal disk of a gold ring from Isopata. Heraklion, Archaeological Museum.* P: H.

11. *Epiphany scene, on a gold ring from Knossos. Oxford, Ashmolean Museum.*

12. *Female figures in an epiphany scene, on a Minoan ring. Heraklion, Archaeological Museum.* P: H.

13. *Female figure with coiled snakes. Faience statuette from the palace of Knossos. Heraklion, Archaeological Museum.* P: H.

14. *Female figure holding snakes. Faience statuette from the palace of Knossos. Heraklion, Archaeological Museum.* P: H.

15. *Idol of a poppy goddess. Clay statuette from Gazi. Heraklion, Archaeological Museum.* P: H.

16. *The honey thieves, on an amphora from Vulci. London, British Museum.*

17. *Enthroned maenads with satyrs, on the other side of the Vulci amphora.*

18. *Hunt scenes and scorpion, on a black-figure vase by Nikosthenes. London, British Museum.*

19. *Youth bearing a rhyton. Fresco from the palace of Knossos. Heraklion, Archaeological Museum.* P: H.

20. *Bull's head rhyton from the fourth royal tomb of Mycenae. Athens, National Museum.*

21A/ 21B. *Sacrifice scenes. Late Minoan painted sarcophagus from Hagia Triada. Heraklion, Archaeological Museum.* P: H.

22A/ 22B. *Scenes of maenads with snakes, on a Tyrrhenian amphora. Paris, Louvre.*

23. *Silenus treading out grapes, on an Archaic vase decorated by the Amasis painter. Würzburg, Martin v. Wagner-Museum der Universität.*

24. *Mask between two goats. Transcript of a stone seal from a tomb near Phaistos. Heraklion, Archaeological Museum.* P: *DAIR.*

25. *A "lord of the wild beasts," on a Minoan seal from Kydonia. Oxford, Ashmolean Museum.*

26. *Youthful Dionysos in hunting boots, on a volute krater from Ceglie. Taranto, Museo Archeologico Nazionale.*

27. *Meander pattern on stairwells in the temple of Apollo at Didyma near Miletos.* P: *DAIR.*

28. *Pallas Athena, Theseus, and the Minotaur, on a bowl painted by Aison. Madrid, Museo Arqueologico Nacional.*

29. *Pallas Athena, Theseus, and the labyrinth, on a black-figure cup from the Akropolis in Athens. From B. Graef and E. Langlotz,* Die antiken Vasen von der Akropolis, I:iv *(Berlin, 1925), pl. 73.*

30. *Symbolic labyrinth, on an oil bottle from Attica. From Paul Wolters,* Archäologische Bemerkungen *(Munich, 1913), pl. I.*

31. *A late, complicated representation of the labyrinth, framed by meander patterns. Mosaic from a family tomb in Hadrumentum in North Africa.* P: *DAIR.*

32A. *The labyrinth fresco (as reconstructed by Evans) from the ground-floor corridor of the palace of Knossos.* P: *DAIR.*

32B. *The path in the labyrinth fresco. Drawing by Cornelia Kerényi.*

33. *Labyrinth graffito scratched into a tile on the left gable of the Parthenon, Athens.* P: *DAIR.*

34. *Labyrinth on a clay tablet from Pylos. From Mabel Lang, "The Palace of Nestor Excavations of 1957, Part II,"* AJA, LXII *(1958), pl. XLVI.*

35. *Ariadne's thread, on a seventh-century* B.C. *relief pithos. Basel, Antikenmuseum.*

36. *Dionysos, Ariadne, and Theseus, on a calyx krater. Taranto, Museo Archeologico Nazionale.*

37. *Dionysos accompanied by the three Horai. Transcript by Karl Reichhold of the painting on the François Vase, a krater by Ergotimos and Klitias. Florence, Museo Archeologico.* P: *DAIR.*

38. *Two maenads with a sacrificial animal, on a pyxis in the Archäologisches Institut, Heidelberg.* P: *DAIR.*

39A/ 39B. *Arrival of Dionysos, probably at the house of Semachos, on a sixth-century* B.C. *vase. Orvieto, Museo Archeologico.* P: *DAIR.*

40. *Arrival of Dionysos, accompanied by Hermes, perhaps at the house of Ikarios, on an Attic amphora from the circle of the Edinburgh painter. Agrigento, Museo Archeologico Nazionale.*

41. *Scene of the arrival of Dionysos, probably at the house of Ikarios. Orvieto, Museo Etrusco Faina.*

42A. *Athenian lady escorted to a festival by a silenus. Skyphos decorated by the Penelope painter. Berlin, Staatliche Museen.*

42B. *Girl swinging, pushed by a silenus, on the other side of the same skyphos.*

43. *Girl swinging. Terra cotta from Hagia Triada: reconstruction. Heraklion, Archaeological Museum.*

44. *Erigone mounting a chariot, with Dionysos in front of her, on an Attic krater. Palermo, Museo Archeologico Nazionale.*

45. *Maenad between Dionysos and a nude man, on the other side of the same krater.*

46. *Variation of the "goddess mounting her chariot" theme. Transcript of the painting on an Attic lekythos. From O. M. von Stackelberg,* Die Gräber der Hellenen *(Berlin, 1837), pl. XII 4.* P: *NYPL.*

47. *Dionysos mounting a chariot, about to leave Semele and ascend from the underworld. From Eduard Gerhard,* Etruskische und kampanische Vasenbilder *(Berlin, 1843), pl. 4.* P: *DAIR.*

48. *Dionysos, accompanied by two ithyphallic sileni, is received by a royal woman, on a neck amphora. Orvieto, Museo Etrusco Faina.* P: *DAIR.*

49. *Arrival of Dionysos on shipboard, accompanied by sileni and women, on an Attic amphora. Tarquinia, Museo Nazionale Tarquiniese.* P: *DAIR.*

50. *Variation of the "arrival of Dionysos on shipboard" theme, on an Attic amphora. Tarquinia, Museo Nazionale Tarquiniese.* P: *DAIR.*

51. *Dionysos on shipboard, on a cup from Vulci painted by Exekias. Munich.* P: *H. Koppermann.*

52A. *Dionysos on board a ship with a mule's head prow, on the inside of a black-figure Attic cup. Berlin, Staatliche Museen.*

52B. *Maenads riding on mules surrounding Dionysos, on the outside of the same cup.*

53. *Maenads arriving at a banquet on ithyphallic mules. Transcript of the painting on an Attic lekythos. From O. M. von Stackelberg,* Die Gräber der Hellenen *(Berlin, 1837), pl. XIV 5.* P: *NYPL.*

54A. *Dionysos with kantharos on an ithyphallic mule, on an Attic amphora. Museo Nazionale di Villa Giulia, Rome.* P: *DAIR.*

54B. *Ithyphallic mule dancing among drunken sileni. Fragment of an amphora, by the Amasis painter, that was found on Samos and lost. From Semni Karouzou,* The Amasis Painter *(Oxford, 1956), pl. XXX 2.* P: *NYPL.*

55. *Love play between mules with painted hides, on an Attic chous in Munich.* P: *DAIR.*

56A. *Dionysos in a ship car, on an Attic skyphos. Bologna, Museo Civico Archeologico.*

56B. *Transcript of 56A. From August Frickenhaus, "Der Schiffskarren,"* JDAI, *XXVII (1912), pl. III.*

57. *Dionysos in a ship car. Fragmentary skyphos in Athens. Transcript from B. Graef and E. Langlotz,* Die antiken Vasen von der Akropolis, *I:iv (Berlin, 1925), pl. 74.*

58. *Procession with sacrificial animal, on an Attic skyphos.* P: DAIR.

59A. *Dionysos in a ship car with a dog's head prow, on an Attic skyphos. London, British Museum.*

59B. *Transcript of 59A when the skyphos was in better condition.*

60. *Arrival of Dionysos and a companion at the house of Ikarios and Erigone with the she-dog Maira. Relief from the Bema of Phaidros. Athens, Ancient Theater.* P: DAIA.

61A. *Motley bull in procession, on a sixth-century Attic lekythos. London, British Museum.*

61B. *Procession led by a* salpinx. *Transcript of the painting on the same lekythos. From O. M. von Stackelberg,* Die Gräber der Hellenen *(Berlin, 1837), pl. XVI.* P: NYPL.

62. *Stone slab with traces of the tripod from the temple of Apollo, Delphi.* P: *P. Amandry.*

63. *Apollo sitting on a tripod and resting his feet on a* bathron. *Late fifth-century Attic votive relief. Athens, National Museum.*

64A–64D. *Scenes of preparations for a Dionysian sacrificial rite. Reliefs on a neo-Attic marble pedestal in the Vatican.* P: *Archivio Fotografio Vaticano.*

65A/ 65B. *The dying Semele, on a silver vessel from Pompeii (with transcript). Naples, Museo Civico Archeologico.*

66A–66E. *Scenes from the life of Dionysos. Relief on an ivory pyxis. Bologna, Museo Civico Archeologico.* P: *Stanzani.*

67. *Epiphany of the Divine Child out of a vine. Terra-cotta relief from a Roman building. London, British Museum.*

68. *Dancing satyrs and flute-playing maenad. Terra-cotta relief from a Roman building. Paris, Louvre.* P: *Alinari.*

69. *Satyr with mirror, and a dancing maenad. Terra-cotta relief from a Roman building. New York, The Metropolitan Museum of Art, Purchase, 1912.*

70. *Maenad with snake and satyr with panther. Terra-cotta relief from a Roman building. New York, The Metropolitan Museum of Art, Purchase, 1912.*

71. *The child in the* liknon, *swung by a maenad and a satyr. Terra-cotta relief from a Roman building. London, British Museum.*

72. *The uncovering of the phallus. Terra-cotta relief from a Roman building. Paris, Louvre.* P: *DAIR.*

73. *Birth of Dionysos from the thigh of Zeus, on an amphora by the Diosphos painter. Paris, Bibliothèque Nationale.*

74. *Birth of Dionysos from the thigh of Zeus, on a volute krater. Taranto, Museo Archeologico Nazionale.*

75. *Dionysos with his mystic alter ego, on a krater by the Altamura painter. Ferrara, Museo Archeologico Nazionale.* P: *H.*

76A. *Dionysos idol with an ithyphallic satyr and a maenad, on an Attic skyphos. Athens, National Museum.*

76B/ 76C. *Men bringing the hetaira and he-goat to the Dionysos idol seen in 76A.*

77. *Dance around the Dionysos idol in the Lenaion, on an Attic cup from Vulci by Makron. Berlin, Staatliche Museen.*

78. *Cult around the Dionysos idol in the Lenaion, on an Attic stamnos from Vulci. London, British Museum.*

79. *Marble mask of Dionysos from his temple in Ikarion. Athens, National Museum.*

80. *Kantharos in the right hand of the enthroned Dionysos from Ikarion. Athens, National Museum.*

81. *Torso of the enthroned Dionysos statue from Ikarion. Athens, National Museum.*

82A/ 82B. *Double mask of Dionysos worshiped by maenads, on an Attic lekythos. Athens, National Museum.*

83A–83C. *Variation of the theme in 82. Athens, National Museum.*

84. *Women ladling wine before the Dionysos idol in the Lenaion, on an Attic stamnos. Rome, Museo di Villa Giulia.* P: *Alinari.*

85. *Variation of 84 with dancing women, on an Attic stamnos. Naples, Museo Archeologico Nazionale.* P: *DAIR.*

86A. *The child Dionysos at the Lenaia, on an Attic stamnos. Warsaw, National Museum.*

86B. *Dionysian women with wine at the Lenaia, on the other side of the same stamnos.*

87A/87B. *Comic* phallophoriai, *on a black-figure Attic cup. Florence, Museo Archeologico.*

88A. *Sabazios and the Great Goddess of Asia Minor enthroned, on a krater painted by Polygnotos. Ferrara, Museo Archeologico Nazionale.* P: *H.*

88B–88D. *Ecstatic dance in honor of the divine pair seen in 88A.* P: *H.*

89. *Rite around a* liknon *containing an ivy-crowned mask, on a chous by the Eretria painter. Athens, Vlasto Collection.* P: *DAIR.*

90. *Attic deities, on a large Attic calyx krater by the Kekrops painter. Adolphseck, Schloss Fasanerie.* P: *DAIR.*

91. *Hermes and the winged souls of the dead beside a pithos, on an Attic lekythos of the fifth century. Jena University.* P: *Professor G. Zinserling.*

92A. *Singers of the dithyramb, on a fifth-century Attic krater. Copenhagen, National Museum.*

92B. *Cloaked man being abducted by two women with* thyrsoi, *on the other side of the same krater.*

93. *Children miming the rites on Choës Day, on an Attic chous. New York, The Metropolitan Museum of Art, Fletcher Fund, 1924.*

94. *Girl swinging over an open pithos, on an Attic hydria. Berlin, Staatliche Museen.*

95. *Swing game over an open pithos, on a chous by the Eretria painter. Athens, Vlasto Collection.* P: *DAIR.*

96. *Festive preparations of a distinguished woman, on a chous by the Meidias painter. New York, The Metropolitan Museum of Art, Gift of Samuel G. Ward, 1875.*

97A. *Athenian lady guided by a torchbearer in silenus costume and hunting boots, on a skyphos by Polygnotos, in the possession of Oskar Kokoschka.* P: *DAIR.*

97B. *A less distinguished couple, on the other side of the same skyphos.*

98. *Enthronement of a youth as Dionysos, on an Attic calyx krater of the Classical period. Copenhagen, National Museum.*

99. *Reception of a Mitrephoros at night, on an Attic chous. New York, The Metropolitan Museum of Art, Fletcher Fund, 1937.*

100. *Visit of Dionysos to Althaia, on an Attic krater. Tarquinia, Museo Nazionale Tarquiniese.* P: *DAIR.*

101. *Dionysian boys after death, on an Attic pitcher. Baltimore, Walters Art Gallery.*

102. *Boy playing with what appears to be a fawn, on an Attic chous, Boston, Museum of Fine Arts.*

103. *Figures of the month of Elaphebolion. Calendar frieze built into the Small Mitropolis in Athens.* P: DAIA.

104. *Archaic* komos *of men dressed as women, on an Attic cup. Amsterdam, Allard Pierson Museum.*

105. *Classic* komos *of men dressed as women, on an Attic krater. Cleveland, Museum of Art. Purchase, A. W. Ellenberger, Sr., Endowment Fund.*

106. *The* domina, *the door to the* cubiculum, *and the first figure of the preparations, from murals in the hall of preparations in the Villa dei Misteri, Pompeii.* P: DAIR.

107. *View of a rustic ritual scene, from murals in the* cubiculum *in the Villa dei Misteri, Pompeii.* P: *Alinari.*

108. *The adorning of the bride, from murals in the hall of preparations in the Villa dei Misteri, Pompeii.* P: *Alinari.*

109. *View of a fantastic ritual scene, from murals in the* cubiculum *in the Villa dei Misteri, Pompeii.* P: *Alinari.*

110A. *A boy, standing between two women, reading in preparation for his initiation, from murals in the hall of preparations in the Villa dei Misteri, Pompeii.* P: *Alinari.*

110B. *Pregnant young woman holding a tray* (left); *candidate bacchante running away* (right). *Continuation of* 110A. P: *Alinari.*

110C. *Initiation by mirroring the mask, and the divine pair. Continuation of* 110B. P: *Alinari.*

110D. *Before the uncovering of the phallus. Continuation of* 110C. P: *Alinari.*

110E. *The novice, initiates, and the initiated maenad. Continuation of* 110D. P: *Alinari.*

111. *View from the* cubiculum *into the hall of preparations. Villa dei Misteri, Pompeii.* P: *DAIR.*

112A. *Old silenus, from murals in the* cubiculum *in the Villa dei Misteri, Pompeii.* P: *DAIR.*

112B. *Young Dionysos, from murals in the* cubiculum *in the Villa dei Misteri, Pompeii.* P: *DAIR.*

112C/ 112D. *Dancing maenads, from murals in the* cubiculum *in the Villa dei Misteri, Pompeii.* P: *DAIR.*

112E. *Young satyr, from murals in the* cubiculum *in the Villa dei Misteri, Pompeii.* P: *Alinari.*

112F. *The* domina *holding a document, from murals in the* cubiculum *in the Villa dei Misteri, Pompeii.* P: *DAIR.*

113. *A drunken Dionysos being brought home at night by a silenus, on an Attic chous. Athens, National Museum.*

114. *A horned Dionysos as bridegroom in his Boukoleion, on a bell krater from Thurii, one of the Hope Vases.* P: *DAIR.*

115. *Deceased boys playing around a krater, on an Attic sarcophagus. Ostia, Museo Archeologico.* P: *DAIR.*

116. *Boy satyr with torch and* situla, *on an Italic chous. The University, Utrecht.*

117. *Dionysos and his beloved, served by a boy satyr, on an Italic chous. Brindisi, Museo Provinciale.* P: *DAIR.*

118. *Eros throws the ball to a hesitant woman, on an Italic krater with a Greek inscription. Naples, Museo Archeologico Nazionale.*

119. *A willing bride washing her hair, on an Italic bell krater. Lecce, Museo Provinciale.* P: *DAIR.*

120. *Bride with a mirror, preparing to go with Hermes, on an Italic krater. Lecce, Museo Provinciale.*

121. A deceased woman as a maenad led by Eros, on an Apulian amphora. Bonn, Antikensammlung. P: *Schafgans.*

122. Exodus to the Dionysian nuptials. Transcript of the painting on an Italic krater. Barletta, Museo Civico. P: *DAIR.*

123. Dionysos with a bell summoning a woman, on an Apulian krater. Ruvo, Museo Jatta. P: *DAIR.*

124. Youth with an egg before an Ariadne, on an Apulian bell krater. Lecce, Museo Provinciale. P: *DAIR.*

125. Ascension of an Ariadne, on an Apulian bowl. Ruvo, Museo Jatta. P: *DAIR.*

126. A Dionysos before a divine maenad, on an Apulian krater. Lecce, Museo Provinciale. P: *DAIR.*

127. Dionysian exodus, on an Apulian krater. Barletta, Museo Civico. P: *DAIR.*

128. Another version of the Dionysian exodus, on an Apulian krater. Bari, Museo Archeologico. P: *DAIR.*

129A/ 129B. The ways of initiation of a woman and a man, on the sides of an Apulian bowl, in the possession of an art dealer. P: *Lerch.*

130A–130E. Pictorial text of the initiation of a woman, on an Italic pointed amphora. Giessen, Antikensammlung.

130F. Transcript by Gudrun Haas of the continuous paintings in 130A–E.

131A/ 131B. Deceased woman as bride and maenad, on a skyphoid pyxis from Adernò, Sicily. Moscow, State Museum of Decorative Arts. P: *DAIR.*

132A–132C. Scenes of the initiation of Dionysos. Traces of murals in a tomb near Ostia. Ostia, Museo Archeologico. P: *DAIR.*

133. Scene from the initiation of a boy. Stucco ornament from La Farnesina in Rome. Museo Nazionale delle Terme. P: *Alinari.*

134. Scene from the initiation of a boy. Transcript of an ointment jar by Miss S. E. Chapman. Florence, Museo Archeologico. P: *DAIR.*

135. Scene from the initiation of a man. Terra-cotta relief. Hanover, Kestner Museum. P: *DAIR.*

136. Scene from the initiation of a maenad. Stucco relief from La Farnesina. Rome, Museo Nazionale delle Terme. P: *Alinari.*

137. The child Dionysos with his nurses. Lid frieze of a marble sarcophagus in Baltimore, Walters Art Gallery.

138. Scenes from the childhood of Dionysos, with preparation for the bath. Sarcophagus in Munich, Glyptothek. P: *Antikensammlungen, Munich.*

139. Further scenes from the childhood of Dionysos, with silenus beating a boy satyr. Sarcophagus in Rome, Museo Capitolino. P: *DAIR.*

140. Scenes showing the setting up of a Dionysian idol. Sarcophagus in Princeton, The Art Museum of Princeton University.

141. Dionysos and Ariadne on Naxos. Sarcophagus in Baltimore, Walters Art Gallery.

142. A later version of the childhood of Dionysos. Sarcophagus in Baltimore, Walters Art Gallery.

143. The domina and basket with snake. Villa dei Misteri, Pompeii. P: *DAIR.*

144. Dionysian cosmos. Sarcophagus in Salerno. P: *DAIR.*

145. Another version of the Dionysian cosmos. Sarcophagus in Rome, Museo Chiaramonti. P: *DAIR.*

146. Cosmos and zodiac, with the ascension of Dionysos and Ariadne. Terra-cotta disk found in Brindisi. Brindisi, Museo Provinciale. P: *DAIR.*

ACKNOWLEDGMENTS

For help in the preparation of the English edition, the publishers are indebted to Sarah George, Mary Manheim, and in particular Ruth Spiegel, who solved many problems, both scholarly and editorial.

Acknowledgment for the illustrations made available by institutions and persons is given in the list preceding. For help in collecting the photographs, the publishers are grateful to M. J. Abadie, Dr. Hans Peter Isler, Pamela Long, Dr. Hellmut Sichtermann, and Signora Magda Kerényi.

For permission to use quotations, acknowledgment is gratefully made as follows: to Random House, Inc., for quotations from *Basic Writings of Nietzsche*, translated and edited by Walter Kaufmann, and from *The Complete Greek Drama*, edited by Whitney J. Oates and Eugene O'Neill, Jr.; to Indiana University Press, for quotations from Walter F. Otto, *Dionysos: Myth and Cult*, translated by R. B. Palmer; to Penguin Books, Ltd., for a quotation from E. V. Rieu's translation of the Iliad; and to the New American Library, Inc., for a quotation from W. H. D. Rouse's translation of the Odyssey (Mentor Classics).

THE TIME for a definitive history of the religions of Europe (and of the descendants of Europeans on other continents) has not yet come. Our picture of the religions—especially the older religions—of our cultural sphere, of their transformations and influence, is still provisional. The enrichment of this over-all picture is a matter of concern not only to scholars but to all those who wish to gain greater awareness of the experience that is the content of a culture. The religious history of the European cultural sphere, even in its remote beginnings, is *our* religious history. It belongs to the history of our culture quite independently of how we as individuals may interpret it in the light of a religious denomination or philosophical conviction. No more than history in general can the history of religions be corrected in retrospect; and, unlike the tenets of a faith, it cannot be rejected. Even the rejection of a religion is an act that takes its place in the history of religions and adds to the sum of experience within our cultural sphere. A history of Western religion that took no account of Nietzsche or of atheism in general would meet the requirements neither of a modern science of religion nor of a comprehensive cultural history.

Nietzsche was a radical atheist, but at the same time he opposed a Greek god to Christ. In posing the alternatives "Dionysos or Christ," he selected—whether correctly or incorrectly—the god who struck him as compatible with his radical atheism. How did he come to do so? Though strange, his idea cannot have been totally unfounded. And once the "idea" made its appearance, it must be counted among the experiences that make up our culture. Regardless of whether it originated with Nietzsche or with the adepts of an ancient, unphilosophical Dionysian religion, it is a human experience. But what was behind the word

"Dionysos" when it was still the name of a god of an authentic historical religion? What light can be thrown on this question by the methods of cultural and religious history? In the "Self-Critique" with which Nietzsche prefaced his 1886 edition of *The Birth of Tragedy*, he wrote: "Even today virtually everything in this field [of the Dionysian] still remains to be discovered and dug up by philologists. Above all, the problem that there *is* a problem here—and that the Greeks, as long as we lack an answer to the question 'What is Dionysian?' remain as totally uncomprehended and unimaginable as ever."[1] This observation remains valid to this day, although we are obliged to transpose it. The Greeks themselves and their precursors on Crete will help us to understand that element in their culture which, once it is understood, will make the culture itself understandable. What Nietzsche said about the Greeks seems to find confirmation especially in regard to Minoan culture, which cannot be comprehended unless its Dionysian character is grasped.

No other god of the Greeks is as widely present in the monuments and nature of Greece and Italy, in the "sensuous" tradition of antiquity, as Dionysos.[2] We may almost say that the Dionysian element is omnipresent. The two characteristic products of Greek architecture of which we possess the greatest number of ruins or vestiges are the temple and the theater.[3] One of these, the theater, belonged to the domain of Dionysos. And of all the cultivated plants of antiquity, it is the vine that has survived most abundantly: it too was sacred to Dionysos and

1 "Attempt at a Self-Criticism," section 3; see *Basic Writings of Nietzsche*, p. 20. / For detailed information on footnote references, see the List of Works Cited.

2 Concerning the sensuous tradition, see the study "Unsinnliche und sinnliche Tradition" in Kerényi, *Apollon*, pp. 72–89.

3 See H. Kähler, *Der griechische Tempel*, p. 5.

bore witness to his presence. I first had this impression in 1931, the year in which the idea for this book was born. At that time it came to me that any account of the Dionysian religion must put the main accent not on intoxication but on the quiet, powerful, vegetative element which ultimately engulfed even the ancient theaters, as at Cumae. The image of that theater became for me a guiding symbol; another such symbol was the atmosphere of the vine, as elusive as the scent of its blossom.

With his *Dionysos: Mythos und Kultus*, Walter Friedrich Otto[4] anticipated my plan, which in any case was still far from maturity. In his monograph, Otto treated the material from a high spiritual point of view, primarily on the basis of the literary tradition, and attempted to appraise the experience expressed in that material. He did not portray the god as the bestower of a passing intoxication. Thus far Nietzsche had been followed by his friend Erwin Rohde and by most classical scholars and historians of religion. In Dionysos, Otto saw "creative madness," the irrational ground of the world. In this Otto was doubly influenced by Nietzsche: by his "Dionysian philosophy" and by his tragic fate, which however should have taught him that madness always calls for an *exact* diagnosis. Otto never gained the perspective on "Nietzsche" that would have enabled him to recognize the symptoms of Nietzsche's pathological state, his strange obsession with Ariadne,[5] for example. Nor did Otto ever gain awareness of the

---

4   W. F. Otto, *Dionysos: Mythos und Kultus* (Frankfurt, 1933) is referred to hereinafter in the English translation by R. B. Palmer.

5   See ch. IV at note 13. As to Nietzsche's illness, which may have been released by infection, but in which hereditary predisposition and archetypal components played the dominant role, see Kerényi, *Nietzsche an der Schöpfung seines Romans*, pp. 100–111; see also Kerényi, "Nietzsche zwischen Literatur- und Religionsgeschichte."

limited character of his own reaction to the ancient phenomenon: to the erotic feature of the Dionysian element he remained closed.

His book gave rise in 1935 to publication of my first thoughts about Dionysos,[6] which had come to me in a vineyard in southern Pannonia and on the Dalmatian island of Korčula. Otto's book, which accompanied me on my travels, was counterbalanced by observations of my own in the course of visits to a number of southern wine countries, and not last to Crete, but his book never lost its importance for me. The deciphering of the second Cretan linear script (Linear B) by Michael Ventris brought to light Dionysian names, including—in Pylos in the southern Peloponnese—the name of the god himself.[7] This confirmed Otto's view of the age of the cult in Greece. Dionysos must have been at home in Greek culture by the end of the second millennium B.C. at the latest.[8] As early as 1930, Charles Picard, the French archaeologist, took it for granted that Dionysos was one of the Greek gods of Cretan-Mycenaean origin.[9] Thus, there was an opportunity to begin the investigation of Dionysos' identity with the study of Minoan art.

I took this opportunity in my studies *Die Herkunft der Dionysosreligion,* "Dionysos le Crétois," and *Der frühe Dionysos.* These were the

---

6 "Gedanken über Dionysos." My first works on the subject, though not the beginning of my work in this field, were: "Satire und Satura" (1933); "Die orphische Seele" (first version, 1933; see now the essay "Pythagoras und Orpheus" in *Werke,* I, 37–46); *Dionysos und das Tragische in der Antigone,* a lecture delivered June 22, 1934, on the occasion of Walter F. Otto's sixtieth birthday. See also Kerényi, Preface to *Antigone* (1966).

7 Pylos Xa 102, confirmed as the name of the wine god by the context of an inscription (Pylos Xb 1419) discovered later; see in ch. III, the section on "Dionysian Names."

8 See Otto, *Dionysos: Myth and Cult,* p. 58.

9 See C. Picard, "Les Origines du polythéisme hellénique," pp. 94–97.

first steps toward the present book, which embodies the idea I had conceived in 1931. I have, however, been able to write it only by taking a dual view: that of a historian of religions who has devoted close attention to the traditional myths, cult actions, and festivals of the ancient world, and that of a historian of Greek and Minoan culture who has chosen to work on a *particular sphere* of life. I chose a sphere in which an essential element of the characteristic social existence that I understand by "culture" found its pure and adequate expression in religion. From the Mycenaean Age onward this was assuredly not the case in all religion, but only in that oldest stratum which was dominated by the archetypal image of that particular element: indestructible life. In relation to human existence, whose archetypal image I dealt with in *Prometheus*,[10] this is the *proteron*, the logically and chronologically earlier.

My point of view is that of a historian, and at the same time that of a rigorous thinker. By this I mean differentiated thinking about the concrete realities of human life. The summary thinking that has become dominant (under the influence of Sir James Frazer) in the study of the peoples of antiquity and in the study of Greek religion (especially under the influence of Martin P. Nilsson and Ludwig Deubner) cannot take these realities into account. True, when we consider them in all their concreteness, we are forced to admit that today the destruction of all life has become conceivable. Yes, conceivable, but not from the standpoint of life, only from that of history which, as we now know

---

10   *Prometheus: Das griechische Mythologem von der menschlichen Existenz* (1946); amplified editions: *Prometheus: Die menschliche Existenz in griechischer Deutung* (1959 and 1962), and *Prometheus: Archetypal Image of Human Existence* (1963).

on the strength of our own historical experience, may lead to universal destruction. According to the minimal definition of life current today, "assimilation and heredity (and their consequences: growth, reproduction, and evolution) . . . distinguish living from dead matter."[11] Because life includes heredity—otherwise it would not be life—it transcends the limits of the individual, mortal, living creature and proves in every individual case, regardless of whether or not the heredity is actually realized, indestructible. Life presupposes heredity and so possesses the seed of temporal infinity. The seed is present even if nothing springs from it. Thus, we are justified in speaking of "indestructible life," in finding its archetypal image in the monuments of religion, and in pointing to its value for religious man as a historical experience.

The distinction between infinite life and limited life is made in the Greek language by the two different words *zoë* and *bios*. Such a distinction was possible in Greece without the intervention of philosophy or even of reflection because language is the direct expression of experience. The present book deals with an experience still deeper than that of human existence, the subject of my *Prometheus*. A brief investigation of the meaning of the two Greek words for "life" may help to introduce the reader—whether or not he knows Greek—to this experience.

I should like to conclude this foreword with the final sentences of my "Gedanken über Dionysos" (1935): "Did the Greeks ever have such ideas about Dionysos as Otto's or these? They had it easier. For in myth and image, in visionary experience and ritual representation,

---

11 R. Schwyzer, "Facetten der Molekularbiologie," p. 5.

they possessed a *complete expression* of the essence of Dionysos. They had no need, as we do, to look for an intellectual formulation, which must always remain incomplete."

C. K.

Rome

October 1, 1967

The author wrote the foregoing preface upon the completion of Part One of his text. He finished writing Part Two and the notes in February 1969, and subsequently he read and approved the present translation. Professor Kerényi died in 1973.

Editor

Finite and Infinite Life in the Greek Language

THE INTERDEPENDENCE of thought and speech makes it clear that languages are not so much means of expressing truth that has already been established as means of discovering truth that was previously unknown. Their diversity is a diversity not of sounds and signs but of ways of looking at the world.[1]

Human experience does not always give rise immediately to ideas. It can be reflected in images or words without the mediation of ideas. Man reacted inwardly to his experience before he became a thinker. Prephilosophical insights and reactions to experience are taken over and further developed by thought, and this process is reflected in language. Thus there is a natural interdependence between thought and speech, which, if we disregard the world of science, still prevails in every living language and literature. Characteristically, the relationship between thought and speech is manifested in language and not in the ideas that subject and dominate language. Language itself can be wise and draw distinctions through which experience is raised to consciousness and made into a prephilosophical wisdom common to all those who speak that language.

A wide range of meaning is bound up with the Latin word *vita* and its Romance descendants, and with *life*, or German *Leben* and Scandinavian *liv* as well. In their everyday language the Greeks possessed two different words that have the same root as *vita* but present very different phonetic forms: *bios* (βίος) and *zoë* (ζωή). While the Greek

1 W. von Humboldt, "Über das vergleichende Sprachstudium," p. 27.

language was "in the making," these forms were produced by a phonetic development whose laws can be formulated with precision.[2] Both words have maintained themselves, a phenomenon made possible by an insight, a distinction of the kind referred to above. This insight and distinction are reflected in the Greek language, which we shall consult for an understanding of them before we enter the realm of images and visions.

Zoë, in Greek, has a different resonance from *bios*. Originally this difference did not spring from the phonetic form of the word *zoë*, and indeed we take the word "resonance" in a broad sense that goes beyond the acoustic. The words of a language carry certain overtones, corresponding to possible variations of the basic meaning, which sound in the ears of those who know the language intimately. The word *zoë* took on this resonance in an early period in the history of the Greek language: it "resounds" with the life of all living creatures. These are known in Greek as *zoön* (plural, *zoa*). The significance of *zoë* is life in general, without further characterization. When the word *bios* is uttered, something else resounds: the contours, as it were, the characteristic traits of a specified life, the outlines that distinguish one living thing from another. *Bios* carries the ring of "characterized life." Correspondingly, *bios* is in Greek the original word for "biography." This usage is its most characteristic application, but not an early one. *Bios* is attributed also to animals when their mode of existence is to be distinguished from that of the plants. To the plants the Greeks attributed only *physis*[3]—except when a mode of living was to be characterized,

2   F. O. Lindemann, "Grec βείομεν ἐρίων," pp. 99 ff.; see also the first version of this formulation in Kerényi, "Leben und Tod nach griechischer Auffassung," pp. 12 ff., which Lindemann had not seen.

3   Epikrates, the writer of comedies, fr. 11, line 14 (in Edmonds, *The Fragments of Attic Comedy*, II, 354).

and then they spoke of *phytou bios*, the "life of a plant."⁴ "A cowardly man lives the *bios* of a hare."⁵ The Greek who uttered these words looked upon the life of an animal—the hare—as a characteristic *life*, one of cowardice.

Once we become aware of the difference in meaning between *zoë* and *bios*, we discern it in the usage of so early a writer as Homer, but this should not be taken to mean that such usage was wholly conscious. In the present and imperfect tenses, which signify the unlimited course of life, *zen* is employed rather than *bioun*. In Homer the imperative *bioto* ("let him live," in opposition to "let the other die") or the second aorist *bionai* (also in contrast to "to die")⁶ is used as an intensive, attaching special weight to life as the limited life of one man. *Zoein*, the uncharacterized and not particularly emphasized state of enduring life, is often employed in Homer in parallel constructions signifying the minimum of life: "to live and see the sunlight," "to live and keep one's eyes open on earth," "to live and to be."⁷ For the gods it is easy to endure in life; accordingly, they are known as the *rheia zoöntes*, "those who live easily." But when one of them (Poseidon in the Iliad)⁸ wishes to assert his own mode of life in opposition to that of Zeus, he does so with the verb *beomai*, which is more closely related to *bios*.

The "life" with which modern biology concerns itself cannot be related to *bios*. The word *biologos* meant to the Greeks a mime who imitated the characteristic life of an individual and by his imitation made it appear still more characteristic. *Bios* does not stand in such a con-

4   Aristotle, *De generatione animalium* 736ʙ 13, in Ross, ed., vol. V.
5   Demosthenes XVIII (*De corona*), 263.
6   Iliad VIII 429, X 174, XV 511.
7   Iliad XXIV 558, I 88; Odyssey XXIV 263.
8   Iliad XV 194.

trast to *thanatos,* "death," as to exclude it. On the contrary, to a characteristic life belongs a characteristic death. This life is indeed characterized by the manner of its ceasing to be. A Greek locution expresses this in all succinctness: one who has died a characteristic death has "ended life with his own death."[9] It is *zoë* that presents an exclusive contrast to *thanatos.* From the Greek point of view modern biology should be called "zoology." *Zoë* is life considered without any further characterization and experienced without limitations. For the present-day student of the phenomenon "life," the fact that *zoë* is experienced without limitation is only one of its aspects, not the whole. Here again we cannot speak of a thoroughgoing identity, for, as we have said, *zoë* is the minimum of life with which biology first begins.

Zoë seldom if ever has contours, but it does contrast sharply with *thanatos.* What resounds surely and clearly in *zoë* is "non-death." It is something that does not even let death approach it. For this reason the possibility of equating *psyche* with *zoë,* the "soul" with "life," and of saying *psyche* for *zoë,* as is done in Homer,[10] was represented in Plato's *Phaedo* as a proof of the immortality of the soul.[11] A Greek definition of *zoë* is *chronos tou einai,*[12] "time of being," but not in the sense of an empty time into which the living creature enters and in which it remains until it dies. No, this "time of being" is to be taken as a continuous being which is framed in a *bios* as long as this *bios* endures—then it is termed "*zoë* of *bios*"[13]—or from which *bios* is removed like a part and assigned to one being or another. The part may be called "*bios* of *zoë.*"[14]

---

9 Diodorus Siculus XXXIX 18: ἰδίωι ἀπεβίω θανάτωι.

10 Iliad XXII 161.

11 *Phaedo* 105 DE.

12 Hesychios s.v. Ζωή.

13 Plato, *Timaeus* 44 C.

14 Plutarch, *Moralia* 114 D.

Plotinos called *zoë* the "time of the soul," during which the soul, in the course of its rebirths, moves on from one *bios* to another.[15] He was able to speak in this way because in the Greek language the words *zoë* and *bios,* each with its own special resonance, were already present: the one for not-characterized life–which, unless we wish to join the Greeks in calling it "time of being," we can only define as "not a non-life"–the other for characterized life. If I may employ an image for the relationship between them, which was formulated by language and not by philosophy, *zoë* is the thread upon which every individual *bios* is strung like a bead, and which, in contrast to *bios,* can be conceived of only as *endless.* Anyone wishing to speak in Greek of a "future life" could say *bios.*[16] Anyone who like Plutarch wished to express thoughts about the eternal life of a god[17] or to proclaim an "eternal life" had to employ *zoë,* as the Christians did with their *aionios zoë.*[18]

The Greek language clung to a not-characterized "life" that underlies every *bios* and stands in a very different relationship to death than does a "life" that includes death among its characteristics. The fact that *zoë* and *bios* do not have the same "resonance," and that "*bios* of *zoë*" and "*zoë* of *bios*" are not tautologies, is the linguistic expression of a very definite *experience.* This experience differs from the sum of experiences that constitute the *bios,* the content of each individual man's written or unwritten biography. The experience of life without characterization– of precisely that life which "resounded" for the Greeks in the word *zoë* –is, on the other hand, indescribable. It is not a product of abstractions

---

15 Plotinos, *Enneades* III 7 11, 43.   16 Diodorus Siculus VIII 15 1.

17 *De Iside et Osiride* 351 E.

18 See, for example, Matthew 19:16, Mark 10:17, Luke 18:18, John 3:36. For Jesus concerning himself, see John 11:25, 14:6.

at which we might arrive only by a logical exercise of thinking away all possible characterizations.

Actually we experience *zoë*, life without attributes, whether we conduct such an exercise or not. It is our simplest, most intimate and self-evident experience. When our life is threatened, the irreconcilable opposition between life and death is experienced in our fear and anguish. The limitation of life as *bios* can be experienced; its weakness as *zoë* can be experienced; and even the desire to cease to be can be experienced.[19] We might like to be without the experience of our actual *bios*, which is given to us with all its characteristics, or to be without experience in general. In the first case, we wish *zoë* to continue in another *bios*. In the second case, something would occur that has never been experienced. Being without experience, a cessation of experience, is no longer experience. *Zoë* is the very first experience; its beginning was probably very similar to the renewal of experience after a fainting spell. When we return from a state of non-experience, we cannot even remember an end that we might call our last experience.

Zoë does not admit of the experience of its own destruction: it is experienced without end, as infinite life. Herein it differs from all other experiences that come to us in *bios*, in finite life. This difference between life as *zoë* and life as *bios* can find a religious or a philosophical expression. Men even expect religion and philosophy to do away with this discrepancy between the experience of *bios* and the refusal of *zoë* to admit of its own destruction. The Greek language stops at the mere distinction between *zoë* and *bios*, but the distinction is clear and presupposes the experience of *infinite life*. As always, the Greek religion

19 See the epilogue to Kerényi, *The Religion of the Greeks and Romans*, pp. 261–79. The religious idea of non-existence is based on the experience of death, which is not canceled out by the experience of never-ending life.

points to figures and images that bring the secret close to man. Elements that in everyday speech, related to everyday events and needs, stand side by side and are often intermingled, are transposed into a pure time—festive time—and a pure place: the scene of events that are enacted not in the dimensions of space, but in a dimension of their own, an amplification of man, in which divine epiphanies are expected and striven for.

DIONYSOS:

Archetypal Image of Indestructible Life

Part One The Cretan Prelude

I. MINOAN VISIONS

The Spirit of Minoan Art

ANYONE who enters the Archaeological Museum of Heraklion in Crete encounters an abundance of the purest elements of a great prelude: the prelude to the history of religion in Europe. For a time these treasures remained mute, for they were seen only as astonishing works of art. They bore witness to the rich life of a people who were endowed with high artistic gifts but whose writing no one could read. It was long believed that even if we were able to decipher the written characters, the language would still be incomprehensible. The one thing which students felt certain of was that the men who had created and maintained this art were not Greeks and that they were separated from the Greeks by a downfall similar to if not even more catastrophic than that which separated pagan Rome from the Christianized Latin and Germanic peoples.

It was assumed that the Cretans, like the Romans, had left a cultural heritage and that those who came after did not fail to make use of it. But apart from the visible and tangible works that came to light after 1900 when Sir Arthur Evans began his excavations at Knossos, everything that was said of these pre-Greeks—they were termed "Minoans" after the mythical king of Crete—was mere hypothesis, abstract and indemonstrable. The works, however, provided a highly characteristic over-all picture which would have been intelligible even without words and has more important things to tell us about the Minoans than the meager account of the texts that have since been deciphered.

An outstanding authority, Nikolaos Platon, a Cretan who spent the greater part of his life in daily contact with these objects, has characterized them and the people who created them as follows. The Minoans "created a civilization whose characteristics were the love of life and nature, and an art strongly imbued with charm and elegance. Their objects of art were miniatures, worked with care and love; they chose carefully the material which they used and succeeded in creating masterpieces with it. They had a special inclination towards the picturesque and to painting, and even their miniature plastic work is elaborated in styles derived from painting. Motion is its ruling characteristic; the figures move with lovely grace, the decorative designs whirl and turn, and even the architectural composition is allied to the incessant movement becoming multiform and complex. The art is ruled by conventions, and yet it looks equally naturalistic. The secret life of nature is outspread in man's creation, which imbues it with a special charm and grace. A hymn to Nature as a Goddess seems to be heard from everywhere, a hymn of joy and life."[1]

The wisdom of this account resides in the fact that it concentrates on the most characteristic factor and is not subject to the modifications in matters of detail that are always possible in archaeology.[2] Platon starts from a concrete, but at the same time spiritual, element that lends Minoan art a specific atmosphere which is to be found nowhere else and which differs from the atmosphere characteristic of Greek art after the Geometric style became prevalent. The word "life" occurs

[1] N. Platon, *A Guide to the Archaeological Museum of Heraclion*, pp. 27 f.

[2] "We are assisting today in the radical transformation of all theories, even of the principles themselves, of the exact sciences: how could archaeology, which is the youngest—and, let us say frankly, the least objective—among the sciences remain immovable and untouchable?" D. Levi, "The Italian Excavations in Crete and the Earliest European Civilisation," p. 10.

three times in the short passage I have quoted. The word used in the original Greek text would have to be *zoë*, which lends itself to juxtaposition with *physis*, "nature," in the sense of plant life. "Love of life and nature" suggests not only the common element in these works of art, but also their manifest content—a content which can find direct expression only in art and which is evident in all these objects, whatever their immediate purpose. In calling this manifest content, perceptible to every viewer, the "spirit of Minoan art," I am not speaking of something abstract and have no need to prove that it is present. "Spirit" is openness and expansion of vision, a primordial experience of man. Openness and expansion arise naturally from a gift peculiar to man. They can take a definite direction; this we call a spiritual or cultural trend. On the strength of an evident direction, we can determine a characteristic spirit, in this case a spirit oriented toward life and nature, stressing them, bringing them out, and setting them before the eye.

In the passage cited above, Platon connected the very marked spirit of Minoan art with a particular deity, the only deity who, it was safe to assume, was a very special object of worship to the Minoans: the Great Goddess. A reliable portrait of her on the peak of a mountain appears on a seal from Knossos [1].[3] In the background we discern a mountain sanctuary; and facing the goddess is a male figure looking up at her and greeting her. The mountain is flanked by two lions. It has not been possible to discover a Minoan name for the goddess, unless the Greek name already occurred among the Minoans. Her rela-

---

3 Fragmentary prints of this seal were preserved in the great palace under the remains of the "small Columnar Shrine," an edifice which, according to Evans' reconstruction, had a column in the middle (*Palace of Minos*, II, 804–10). In view of its situation it may be regarded as the central shrine of the entire palace.

tionship to wild nature was, however, as evident as that of a corresponding goddess in Greek mythology: Rhea, the Great Mother of
the gods. The Great Goddess did not possess a significant cult site of
her own on the Greek continent. At Knossos the foundations of her
temple were shown to travelers in the Greek period.[4] These remains
demonstrate that this divine figure lived on among the Greeks.

The correspondence between the worship of this goddess and the
spirit of Minoan art provides Platon's characterization with its central
idea, which Platon himself wished to express with a certain restraint.
He did not wish to say openly—though under the impact of his over-all
view he came very close to it—that the art of the Minoans bore witness
to the omnipotence in Crete of a single deity, a Great Goddess, who is
manifested with varying attributes in the monuments. For, though
undeniable, this correspondence does not justify us in identifying the
characteristic spirit of this art exclusively with a mother religion, with
the cult of a single ruling goddess. From no ancient monuments is it
possible to draw inferences that would exclude the presence of something that is not represented. "The struggle with death, a familiar
theme in prehistoric cultures, is not here discernible," says Platon.[5]
The struggle with death *was* represented on Mycenaean tombs, and it
may be mere chance that tombstones with similar representations have
not been found in the Minoan sphere. But ancient art was never unre-
stricted in its choice of subject matter. It is not possible to draw a
dividing line between religious awe and artistic taste: the principle of
selection may have been determined by both at once and not by religion alone.

4   Diodorus Siculus V 66 1; identified by Evans (*Palace of Minos*, II, 6–7)
with the foundations of a Greek temple between the propylaia and the central
courtyard of the palace of Knossos.
5   *A Guide*, p. 28.

Even if this art did not express everything, it was *all expression*: the expression of a characteristic relation to the world, which runs unchanging through the manifestations of Minoan art and religion. The Minoan artist saw the world primarily in its plant and animal aspects—and very differently from the Christian artist, or from the Greek artist of the Geometric period and on. The attention of the Christians and Greeks was focused on anthropomorphic, spiritual gods. Small wonder that the Cretan eye saw other gods; these gods were, in a manner of speaking, the spirits, or the divine spirit, of the world of plants and animals. The sea roundabout adorned the wonderful Minoan vases not with Nereids but with polyps and nautili, and the murals with dolphins and flying fishes. It is possible that the Minoans looked upon two giant polyps—a male and a female—as the epiphanies of the divine rulers of the watery depths. Their marriage may have been the precursor of the marriage between Poseidon and Amphitrite.[6] Votive offerings at the shrine of a goddess found near the present-day village of Piskokephalo in eastern Crete[7] show that a scarablike dusk beetle, *Rhinoceros oryctes*, announced and accompanied a divine *parousia*, the presence of a goddess.

The Minoan artists bring us to a world of plants and animals, in which gods, coming from the sky, appear on mountain tops, beneath flowers. What was their view of man?

6   J. Wiesner, "Die Hochzeit des Polypus," pp. 35–51.
7   S. Alexiou, *Guide to the Archaeological Museum of Heraclion*, p. 80 (case 123).

The Minoan Gesture

ONCE AGAIN let us consult a modern, objective observer, a woman who studied the art monuments of Greece and those of the Near East with like dedication and was open to their special language—the language of art. "Cretan civilization is unhistorical not only in the sense that the modern historian happens to be unable to write an articulate account of its past, a record in which events and personalities have name and character, but because it lacked the desire for monumental statement, pictorial or otherwise. We find no interest in single human achievement, no need to emphasize, to rescue its significance."[8] Still more important is the following observation: "Cretan art ignored the terrifying distance between the human and the transcendent which may tempt man to seek a refuge in abstraction and to create a form for the significant remote from space and time; it equally ignored the glory and futility of single human acts, time-bound, space-bound. In Crete artists did not give substance to the world of the dead through an abstract of the world of the living, nor did they immortalize proud deeds or state a humble claim for divine attention in the temples of the gods. Here and here alone [in contrast to Egypt and the Near East] the human bid for timelessness was disregarded in the most complete acceptance of the grace of life the world has ever known. For life means movement and the beauty of movement was woven in the intricate web of living forms which we call 'scenes of nature'; was revealed in human-bodies acting their serious games, inspired by a

8   H. A. Groenewegen-Frankfort, *Arrest and Movement*, p. 186.

transcendent presence, acting in freedom and restraint, unpurposeful as cyclic time itself."[9]

Minoan art fully justifies this negative characterization—negative from the standpoint of man as the center, as the vehicle of his own historical and non-historical glory, but not from the standpoint of the deity, whose presence it demands and requires. Man is always on the edge of this epiphany of the spirit—the spirit or spirits of life and nature—if not face to face with it. In this view an intimation of the godhead could be manifested not only in a swarm of insects, in birds, or in the beasts of the sea, but also in a human gesture, and it could in turn determine man's gestures.

For in Minoan art man is never without gesture, although figures standing or sitting gestureless are known to us in the art of the ancient Orient and Greece. There are cult gestures everywhere, but it is something else again when gesture becomes an essential element, a characteristic, of the general view communicated by art. Here I am speaking not of cult gestures side by side with other equally characteristic gestures of simple human existence, but of *the* gesture which time and time again, in different forms of movement, represents the identical situation of man: his non-central position which demands an "opposite" and can be understood only as an "opposite."

This non-central position of man was confirmed by the deciphering of the Cretan writing. Even among the Mycenaeans, writing did not serve for self-perpetuation, for they too, for all their monumental edifices, scorned to put inscriptions on their tombs.[10] If, as the Mycenaeans most probably did,[11] the Minoans possessed an epic poetry that

---

9 Ibid., p. 216.
10 See Kerényi, *The Heroes of the Greeks*, pp. 8 f.
11 See Kerényi, "Im Nestor-palast von Pylos," *Werke*, II, 265.

complemented the statement of their art, it would not invalidate the testimony of the Minoan gesture that reveals man in a wholly religious situation: not oriented solely toward himself and his fellow men, but determined by something other, something outside himself, caught up in an atmosphere of festival as in an enchanted world.

The most dangerous of all Minoan gestures is to be seen in the bull game as represented in paintings and sculptured figures. Here the body is shown in free acrobatic movement. The player seizes the horns, lets himself be thrown upward by the bull, turns one or more somersaults in the air, and lands behind the animal which is running away [2].[12] The gesture grows out of the game, but game and body are a single indivisible gesture, free and at the same time controlled, which can well be said to have been "inspired by a transcendent presence." The bull game was a repetition of the original capture of the wild bull before the days of domestication [3A/3B].[13] From it developed the acrobatic art of the Minoan *toreros*. Such repetition and art require a religious inspiration, without which a festive game cannot come into being. For the Minoan bull game was clearly a festive game. In honor of whom? The Great Goddess of nature and life? Nikolaos Platon drew this inference from his interpretation of Minoan art.[14] In his view, the goddess was the divine onlooker, the "opposite," though this does not exclude the possibility of a divine presence in the game itself, especially

12   In this fresco from the small courtyard of the east wing of the palace of Knossos, three movements in the game are represented by three players, two girls and a young man, who execute the movements successively. An ivory figure reproduced in Marinatos and Hirmer, *Crete and Mycenae*, pl. 97, also shows the movement.

13   The scene appears on the ivory box published by S. Alexiou in Ὑστερο-μινωικοὶ τάφοι λιμένος Κνώσου, figs. 30–33.

14   N. Platon, "Sir Arthur Evans and the Creto-Mycenaean Bullfights," p. 93.

in the bull, an exemplary manifestation of the deity in Crete. Not only the human onlookers but also the Minoan *toreros*, who risked their lives with an art never equaled by their Spanish successors, are mere marginal figures in the drama they are performing.

It is somewhat different with the dance, the most universal gesture, in which man is all gesture. On a Minoan cup from the oldest palace of Phaistos, two girls are seen dancing around a goddess who approaches a flower springing up from the ground [4];[15] in another, three women are dancing, the one in the middle being perhaps a goddess [5]. Other figures—all women—are visible on the rim or on the disk that forms the base of the vessel. They are probably not divine beings, but since those on the rim are bowing low, it cannot be doubted that this vessel too was used in the cult; it presupposes a "transcendent presence" in the dance itself. Inspired gesture raises man to the sphere of the gods and the dance does still more. In the dance, gods can be made present; the greatest deity can be drawn into the midst of the dancers. The two women of the first vase, standing on either side of the snake goddess, raising their hands in circular movements, and admiring the flower, are no less goddesses than the central figure. The dance figure unites gods and men on the same level.

In such dances, the distance between "opposites" is annulled. But elsewhere it is present: plainly so on the Knossos seal showing the Great Goddess on a mountain top, bare-bosomed and holding out her staff like a shepherd's crook over the heads of the lions which flank her [1]. The man who holds his hand before his forehead—to judge by his size he is a superhuman being—is greeting her. Here the distance is manifest: on one side is the epiphany, and on the other, the beholder.

15   See the explanation in Kerényi, *Eleusis*, pp. xix f.; and "Die Blume der Persephone," pp. 29 f.

This is the situation of a vision such as assuredly occurred in the world surrounding Minoan art. Such visions constituted a dimension above the visible dimensions of nature. The "Minoan gesture"—an element as characteristic of Minoan culture as the spirit of Minoan art—points to such a dimension.

Visionary Crete

IN ACCOUNTS of ancient religions too little attention has been paid to the visionary faculty.[16] Visionary power does not seem to have been equally distributed among men; it was more abundant in ancient times and has steadily become rarer. Historians of religion have as a rule tended to ignore it unless their attention was called to it by explicit testimony. We find such testimony in the statements of the mystics of all times. But since mystics are exceptions in all religions and since historians of religion have no visions, our thinking in this matter ordinarily revolves around these two extremes: the positive experience of the mystics and the negative experience of the historians of religion

16   F. Matz, in "Göttererscheinungen und Kultbild im minoischen Kreta," has devoted a thorough archaeological investigation to this phenomenon of the Minoan religion. His findings, which are in every way positive, are rendered unclear by his unfortunate choice of the term *Epiphanienglaube* ("epiphanic faith"). Visionary capacity produces not "epiphanic faith," but epiphanies, nor does it necessarily involve ecstasy. Matz exaggerates the importance in the Minoan religion of ecstasy, for which the monuments do not provide adequate support. According to him, "essential elements of the Dionysos religion are present in prehistoric Crete," but from the name "Dionysos" he draws inferences only for the Mycenaean Greeks and not for the Minoan culture. He did not succeed in clarifying the relationships. We arrived at our largely similar conclusions independently of one another.

and all present-day non-mystics. We find little explicit testimony concerning what lies between the two extremes, although without such intermediate phenomena—the light, hovering visions of persons of moderate visionary endowment—a religion possessed of a living mythology would be unthinkable.

An indication that men in general are capable of such visions is supplied, for example, by the Indian coming-of-age ritual, which required all youths to fast and remain in the woods until they saw visions. We may seem to have drawn on a source remote from our subject, but all cultures have the same human *nature* as their basis though all cultures do not take the same attitude toward the capacity for visions. In the accounts of the religions of the forest Indians of North America, we find detailed indications of the type of visions that were demanded. They were waking dreams, which were expected to be sharper, more intense, and more striking than the dreams of sleep. An authority on the American Indians writes: "Visions are held to be 'real'; they represent actual contact with the superhuman, whereas dreams do not necessarily do so." And he quotes a saying of the Indians: "In visions there is something sacred, less so in dreams."[17]

Homer may perfectly well have been thinking of visions of this kind when in the Odyssey he described the epiphanies of Artemis on high mountains: "She looked like Artemis, when bow in hand she comes down from the mountains, over lofty Taÿgetos or Erymanthos, to hunt the boars and fleet-footed deer: round about her the nymphs make sport, those daughters of Zeus who frequent her countryside; and her mother is proud indeed, for she lifts head and brow above all the troop, and she is pre-eminent where all are beautiful. So shone the fresh

---

17 W. Müller, *Die Religionen der Waldlandindianer Nordamerikas*, p. 57, citing Wm. Whitman, *The Oto*, p. 85.

young maiden among her girls."[18] The myth of the gods is divine epiphany in the medium of language. It is not localized in the same way as visions. It can be related wherever its language is spoken. A vision always has as its setting a definite place, the place where it occurred. Its explicit localization bears witness to the visionary character of the myth cited above. This localization is a heritage of vision in myth and in all the tales that embody it, that is, in mythology.

Vision and myth, epiphany and mythology, influenced and engendered one another and gave rise to cult images. But in man's relation to the gods, epiphany has a priority grounded in the immediacy of every true vision. Visions and language are equally fundamental, and both are presuppositions of the mythological tale. In Crete visions are especially important. Cretan mythology has not come down to us in its own language. What we know of it through the Greeks is very meager, although there were numerous small shrines in Minoan Crete. How numerous has become known only recently, and we are not yet able to establish sure correspondences between the few old Cretan names preserved by Greek mythology and the figures known to us from art. According to Greek mythology, the snake goddess and the two dancing girls around the flower on the Phaistos cup [4] can only be Persephone and two companions.[19] The exact correspondence, however, is a surprising novelty, which perhaps for that exact reason was not immediately noticed. For whom are we to take the man looking across at the goddess on the mountain top on the Knossos gem? He is experiencing an epiphany.

This is not, however, the only indication that the large island was especially conducive to visions. The ridges and peaks of the high Cretan

18 Odyssey VI 102–9 (W. H. D. Rouse translation, p. 71).
19 See note 15, above, and [1].

mountains, situated between the Aegean and Libyan seas, were an ideal scene for epiphanies: a world of light and a Minoan cult scene. The subterranean world, the world of caves, was also a place of the Minoan cult, which seems to have been practiced more on the heights and in the depths than in the great palaces. These palaces appear in certain respects to be the forerunners of the Greek temples, especially of those that exceeded the modest proportions of small sanctuaries. The palaces were characteristic of the style of Minoan culture and probably were sacred in their totality, though only certain rooms were employed in the cult and these were not always distinguished by a central or otherwise prominent position. With their complex structure and several stories, the palaces—this is evident at least at Knossos— seem to reproduce the Cretan cosmos, the true scene of the Minoan cult. On the upper floors we find several rooms each with a single round column in the center, a column broadening toward the top, as— to cite a simple example—in the so-called temple tomb near the palace of Knossos. The religious implications of this column cannot be doubted, and indeed it presents an obvious analogy to a mythical view of the heavens.[20] Such cult rooms both in the palace and in the tomb correspond to other cult rooms with posts in the middle; the column above is, as it were, a continuation of the post. The dividing line can be drawn between the upper and lower rooms, between column and pillar, corresponding to the imaginary line that divides the cosmos of the Cretans into a higher and lower cult world.

We must also look into the inside of Cretan nature, into some of the many limestone caves that make up the lower world. They seem to

20 Kerényi and Sichtermann, "Zeitlose Schieferbauten der Insel Andros," pp. 33 f.; Kerényi, "Die andriotische Säule," *Werke*, III. According to Evans (note 3, above), the small central shrine of the palace of Knossos shows the same type.

be innumerable. More than three hundred have already been explored[21] in addition to those cult grottoes that have become famous. It is certain that the accidental human forms of the stalactites and stalagmites not only aroused the imagination of the ancients as they do of modern archaeologists, but also inspired visions that transformed the stalactite formations into divine figures. It cannot be established with certainty what those who visited Eileithyia in her cave near Amnisos, the harbor of Knossos, thought they saw there; but whatever they saw, they repeated the vision that had made the stalagmites into objects of the goddess' cult.

By the name Eileithyia, which the Odyssey mentions in connection with this grotto, the Greeks designated a goddess who presided over births and who presumably governed everything connected with the life of women even more in Minoan than in Greek times. A cult site of this goddess was a place dedicated to the origin of life. Two round enclosures are built into the cave. In front of them a very low stalagmite shaped like a navel might be regarded as a kind of altar. In the first enclosure stands a stalagmite suggesting two goddesses joined at the back [6].[22] The archaic art of Crete also bears witness to a dual Eileithyia.[23] In the second, inner, and more important enclosure there

21 See P. Faure, *Fonctions des cavernes crétoises.*

22 [6] is after Faure, *Fonctions*, pl. VII 5. / I speak from firsthand observation, supported by S. Marinatos' report of his excavation, "Τὸ σπέος τῆς Εἰλειθυίας," pp. 100 f. Other "interpretations" are those of N. Platon, "Περὶ τῆς ἐν Κρήτηι λατρείας τῶν σταλακτίτων," pp. 164 ff.; and Faure, *Fonctions*, p. 84. They are utterly free— as though there had been no myth to guide and determine the artist's imagination.

23 See, for example, the ivory relief in the Cretan style of the seventh century, in New York, published by G. Richter, "An Ivory Relief in the Metropolitan Museum of Art," pp. 261 ff. F. Matz came closest to the right interpretation in "Arge und Opis," pp. 1 ff. One of the two women is "released" and therefore

rises a solitary stalagmite. Phalli do not appear in Minoan works of high artistry. Here is one provided by nature. A masculine cult object is unmistakably present in the midst of this feminine sanctuary. Such emphasis on a natural phenomenon suggests insight and recognition among the visitors, whose visionary power no doubt helped to make the cave into a cult site. Statuettes—now in the Archaeological Museum of Heraklion—of mating couples from the cave sanctuary of Inatos on the southern coast of Crete leave no doubt as to the extreme concreteness of the Cretan view of the origin of life.

The heights, which stimulated the visionary power in a different way and in a still higher degree, also had their numerous sanctuaries, which we must include in our view of Cretan nature if we wish to form a conception of the island in the Minoan period. Before the erection of buildings, these sites of vision and worship were probably unmarked or marked only with stones. The list of mountain sites where traces of sanctuaries have been found has grown impressively.[24] It will grow still longer when the almost inaccessible mountain country of western Crete has been explored. Shrines that were built in such places are visible in works of art. The Knossos seal [1] showing the epiphany of the Great Goddess on the mountain top has a simplified picture of a temple corresponding to the human figure looking upward on the same plane. Thus, we know of these mountain shrines not only from the vestiges that have been preserved but from naturalistic rep-

---

"releasing"; the other is "bound" and therefore "binding." They represent the two aspects of the goddess of childbearing. This reliably identifies the two figures as Eileithyia. Matz and others give her wrong names.

24 According to the compendious report of P. Faure, "Cavernes et sites aux deux extrémités de la Crète," pp. 493 ff.; and N. Platon, Τὸ Ἱερὸν Μαζᾶ καὶ τὰ μινωικὰ Ἱερὰ Κορυφῆς," pp. 119 ff.

resentations in works of art. On a Minoan vase [7][25] a man sets a basket with sacrificial offerings down on a round rock in front of a shrine. To what unbelievable heights these offerings had to be carried is clearly shown. The woods are on the slopes below. The holy site hovers amid the crags above the tree line. The most perfect representation [8][26] of such a shrine shows how, in the absence of people, it is occupied by the *agrimi*, the wild mountain goats of Crete, and by birds of prey.

Transcendence in Nature

THE MINOAN gesture presupposes the possibility of epiphanies produced and made credible by a visionary capacity. The gesture brings transcendence into nature. Cretan nature itself promoted the visionary capacity, and assuredly not only on the heights and in the depths. It would be a mistake to suppose that country sanctuaries existed only on mountain peaks. The visionary capacity was also stimulated and satisfied by Minoan art, which provoked a preliminary state, followed by another in which transcendence was induced by more violent means.

How a gesture can open up the dimension of vision as an additional dimension of nature is shown by a drawing on a small amphora from the oldest palace of Phaistos [9].[27] Two figures with upraised hands appear among crocuses. They are characterized only by this gesture. We may justifiably call them male gesture figures; to us they are nothing else. This gesture is well known to us from ancient Oriental art as

25 Published by S. Alexiou, Νέα παράστασις λατρείας ἐπὶ μινωϊκοῦ ἀναγλύφου ἀγγείου, pp. 346 ff.

26 Published by N. Platon, "Kato Zakros," p. 174, fig. 187.

27 Published by D. Levi, "Attività della Scuola Archeologica Italiana di Atene nell'anno 1955," p. 254, fig. 33.

a gesture of worship.[28] Who is being worshiped? What god has appeared to these figures? Or are the gesture figures themselves gods? An epiphany is enacted in a field of crocuses which to us evokes no name. For the Minoans it was a very different matter: to them this epiphany was familiar. They recognized it, either in the gesture figures or in some larger figure, whose worshipers or perhaps companions were these little male beings.

A true gesture is always an excerpt; its representation is an instant view of a movement. Minoan art succeeded in combining hints of transcendence with the utmost naturalness in representing scenes whose character is unmistakable. The seal disk of a golden ring from Isopata near Knossos shows a scene full of musical movement [10]. The movement starts from above, from the dimension of divine epiphanies. An epiphany occurs among flowers. Two snakes strangely animate the background; they are situated so high up that conceivably they belong to the divine world. A single great eye, somewhat lower down than the snakes—the eye of an observer from another, more likely lower than upper, world—lends the whole image a special depth. Someone is looking on. Two of the four large female figures are epiphanies of goddesses. A small, fifth, female figure, hovering in the air behind the four larger ones, indicates that they come from an upper region. She raises one hand, while the goddess striding before her, as though descending in a spiral, raises both hands. This is the gesture of epiphany. It is answered by the upraised hands of the remaining two large female figures. It would be inadequate to call this a gesture of worship. Their gesture is an answer not only to the epiphany, but to the gesture of epiphany.

Unlike the gestures of ritual, from which original vision is absent,

28 S. Alexiou, Ἡ μινωϊκὴ θεὰ μεθ᾽ ὑψωμένων χειρῶν, pp. 250 ff.

the gestures in the visionary experience of an epiphany are authentic, not repeated gestures. In the representations they are not always quite the same, and their meaning is not always quite clear. On a gold ring from Knossos[29] a woman with her hand half-open greets a small male apparition which floats down from a country sanctuary [11].[30] On another ring two female figures greet each other with upraised hands [12]. One figure is nude, half-kneeling before a column indicating the sanctuary; the other, clothed, is arriving. Perhaps this latter figure with her dog or baboon is appearing to the other. If both women were goddesses, the epiphany gesture of the one and the responding gesture of the other were gestures of mutual greeting, and Cretan mythology has preserved the gestures. To us it is a mythology of images that speak for themselves. Thus, the faience statuettes from the palace of Knossos—female figures with bare breasts and outstretched or half-raised outspread hands bearing snakes, which in some cases are coiled around an arm [13, 14]—leave no room for doubt. It is uncertain only whether they represent a priestess or a goddess. By the gesture we recognize not the representative but the divinity. "Thus do I appear," says the gesture.

Artificially Induced Transcendence

THE FEMALE idols of the Late Minoan period are rigid, but with their upraised hands they say the same thing as the statuettes from Knossos. They bear witness to the fact that vision and epiphany, an additional dimension amplifying the world of nature, were still a need of the

29 From the subterranean treasure rooms which may have contained the objects from the main chapel of the palace of Knossos.

30 [11] is after V. E. G. Kenna, *Cretan Seals*, pl. X 250.

Cretans at a time when not only their artistic ability but also their visionary capacity had dwindled. The human nature in which this need was rooted cannot have changed very appreciably. The artistic decadence revealed by clay statues of this type is unmistakable. They are busts of extremely primitive workmanship on bell-shaped bases. Five such statuettes were found in a country sanctuary near the village of Gazi west of Heraklion.[31] On their heads they bear various attributes showing what goddess was intended.

The largest of these five female idols with epiphany gestures bears three poppy heads as head ornament and attribute. The stems are inserted behind her diadem [15].[32] The clay tablets that have been deciphered testify to the fact that poppies were widely cultivated both on Crete and in Pylos in the Late Minoan period. The use of the poppy head as an ideogram in these account books leaves no room for doubt. The yield of poppies mentioned is so enormous that students long suspected that the figures referred to grain rather than poppies.[33] Here we must take note of a little-known feature of Minoan culture, at least in its late period.

> *For the Greeks Demeter was still a poppy goddess,*
> *Bearing sheaves and poppies in both hands.*[34]

If in the Linear B script her name signified "poppy fields," conclusions must be drawn regarding the food of the Cretans. Poppy seed with honey is highly nutritious and not narcotic. In ancient as in modern Greece, poppy-seed cakes were baked on festive occasions.[35] Poppy

31   S. Alexiou, Ἡ μινωϊκὴ θεὰ μεθ᾽ ὑψωμένων χειρῶν, pp. 188 ff.
32   The height of the statuette is 77.5 cm.
33   Ventris and Chadwick, *Documents in Mycenaean Greek*, p. 35.
34   Theokritos VII 157.
35   Athenaios XIV 648 A; K. I. Kakoure, *Death and Resurrection*, p. 31.

heads appear among the symbols pointing to the Eleusinian Mysteries[36] or at least to the preparations for them. The ears of grain which in abbreviated form expressed the attained goal of the Mysteries are just as much in evidence. Nothing in the tradition suggests that the poppy had held as profound a significance in Eleusis as the grain. Still, the poppy may have performed a similar function, for example, that of evoking the image of the queen of the underworld. Nor is its use in the Eleusinian cakes, if not in the Eleusinian potion, the *kykeon*, to be excluded. This is uncertain. It seems probable that the Great Mother Goddess, who bore the names Rhea and Demeter, brought the poppy with her from her Cretan cult to Eleusis, and it is certain that in the Cretan cult sphere, opium was prepared from poppies.

The making of opium from poppies requires a special procedure. A pharmacobotanist discovered that the poppies on the head of the goddess figurine found in Gazi [15] reveal incisions which the artist colored more deeply than the rest of the flower to make them plainly visible.[37] This is a most significant discovery, because opium is obtained through such incisions. The coloring of the incisions was a way of displaying one of the goddess' gifts to her worshipers. They were reminded of experiences that they owed to her. This is concrete evidence that should not be blurred by vague reference to "medicines" (*pharmaka*) or to an unspecified ecstasy connected with the gifts of this goddess. What she bestowed through opium cannot have been essentially different in the Late Minoan period from today. What was it?

Here we find ourselves in the realm of pharmacological experience, and a large body of literature to which this specific experience has

36   See Kerényi, *Eleusis*, pp. 55, 74 f., 142 f., 184.

37   P. G. Kritikos and S. P. Papadaki, "The History of the Poppy and of Opium," p. 23.

given rise in recent times is at our disposal. This literature is far from unequivocal. The dosage, the mixture, and the form in which opium is taken can vary exceedingly, as can the mental states of those who have taken it, the reliability of their accounts, and the value of reports by outside observers. Nevertheless, some of these accounts seem significant in view of the archaeological observations disclosing a visionary element in the monuments of the Minoan religion. Opium induces much more than just sleep and dreams. The Greeks related that the Cretan Epimenides slept in a cave for fifty-seven years and thereby became a philosopher. They looked upon his wisdom as a miracle, not as an artificially induced state.[38] If this legend preserves a memory of the Late Minoan consumption of opium, it also shows that the knowledge of the actual effect of the *pharmakon* vanished with the Minoan culture. The Odyssey (IV 220) speaks of an Egyptian *pharmakon* against suffering and anger. Its effect seems comparable to the great euphoria that is an initial effect of opium; there is no mention of sleep.

Thus, we may turn to the modern classics on opium, from which I shall cite a few of the passages least conditioned by our own culture and closest to the atmosphere of Minoan art. "The ocean with its eternal breathing, on which however a great stillness brooded, symbolized my mind and the mood that then governed it . . . a festive peace. Here . . . all unrest gave way to a halcyon serenity."[39] These are De Quincey's words, quoted by Baudelaire. Baudelaire himself, in "Le Poison" (*Les Fleurs de Mal*), speaks of extending, not shattering, the limits of nature:

38 Diogenes Laertius I 109.

39 C. Baudelaire, *Les Paradis artificiels*, pp. 119–20: "L'Océan, avec sa respiration éternelle, mais couvé par un vaste calme, personnifiait mon esprit et l'influence qui le gouvernait alors . . . un repos ferie . . . et cependant toutes les inquiétudes étaient aplanies par un calme alcyonien."

> *Opium enlarges the boundless,*
> *Extends the unlimited,*
> *Gives greater depth to time . . .*[40]

Others, however, have spoken of a "world in which 'one can hear the walk of an insect on the ground, the bruising of a flower.' "[41] According to Cocteau, "opium is the only vegetable substance that communicates the vegetable state to us."[42]

It may be presumed that toward the end of the Late Minoan period, opium stimulated the visionary faculty and aroused visions which had earlier been obtained without opium. For a time, an artificially induced experience of transcendence in nature was able to replace the original experience. In the history of religions, periods of "strong medicine" usually occur when the simpler methods no longer suffice.[43] This development may be observed among the North American Indians. Originally mere fasting sufficed to induce visions. It was only in the decadent period of Indian culture that recourse was taken to peyotl, or mescalin. Earlier it was unnecessary.[44] This powerful drug had not always been an element in the style of Indian life, but it helped to maintain this style.

The same was true of opium in the Late Minoan period. It was

---

40 Baudelaire, *Les Fleurs du Mal*, XLIX, 6–8 (*Oeuvres complètes*, I, 80).

41 See E. Schneider, *Coleridge, Opium and Kubla Khan*, pp. 41 and 312–13, note 27, citing M. H. Abrams, *The Milk of Paradise* (pp. 4, 63).

42 J. Cocteau, "L'Opium," *Oeuvres complètes*, X, 113: "L'opium est la seule substance végétale qui nous communique l'état végétal"—or at least what the French poet understands by "vegetable state."

43 Kerényi, "Mescalin-Perioden der Religionsgeschichte," pp. 201–203.

44 See C. Mellen, "Reflections of a Peyote Eater," p. 65: "At the very moment when the entire traditional fabric of the tribe was rendered useless [after defeat by the United States in the Indian Wars of the 1870's] peyote was first used."

consonant with the style of Minoan culture and helped to preserve it. When Minoan culture came to an end, the use of opium died out. This culture was characterized by an atmosphere which in the end required such "strong medicine." The style of Minoan *bios* is discernible in what I have called the "spirit" of Minoan art. This spirit is perfectly conceivable without opium.

In his *Handbuch der Archäologie der Kunst*, Karl Otfried Müller (a classical philologist and mythologist whose methodic work in the first half of the nineteenth century also influenced archaeology) characterized the atmosphere of the Dionysian creations of Greek art in terms that call to mind the mural paintings in Cretan palaces, whose existence he could not have suspected: "Nature overpowering the mind and hurrying it out of a clear self-consciousness (whose most perfect symbol is wine) lies at the basis of all Dionysian creations. The cycle of Dionysian forms, which constitutes as it were a peculiar and distinct Olympus, represents this nature-life with its effects on the human mind, conceived in different stages, sometimes in nobler, sometimes in less noble shapes; in Dionysos himself the purest blossom is unfolded, combined with an *afflatus* which arouses the soul without destroying the tranquil play of feelings."[45]

In dealing with the Dionysian phenomenon, we must from the very start take a position that makes possible a truly comprehensive view. Otherwise—as has almost always been the case up to now—our picture will be restricted to certain forms of Dionysian ecstasy that were favored in Greek art from the second half of the sixth century on.[46]

---

45 Leitch translation, p. 488, of K. O. Müller, *Handbuch der Archäologie der Kunst* (see there p. 594).

46 See M. W. Edwards, "Representation of Maenads on Archaic Red-Figure Vases," pp. 78 ff.

Minoan art as a whole was characterized as follows by Bernhard Schweitzer in 1926: "It is a form of world-experience, one of those great fundamental forms of man's confrontation with the things that we call 'mystical' and whose specific nature can only be characterized by the catchword 'Dionysian.' "

Even then Schweitzer raised the question: "Do the roots of what has been termed Dionysian in the temperament of the Greeks reach back to ancient Crete?"[47] The resemblance between the atmosphere of the general picture drawn by Karl Otfried Müller and that of Minoan art as characterized by Bernhard Schweitzer is striking enough. A perspective is opening with unmistakable lines; it would be tempting to follow them even if the name of the god had not emerged in Pylos, in the same cultural sphere, toward the end of the second millennium B.C., and even if we had become aware of the Dionysian atmosphere only in the art of Minoan Crete.

47   B. Schweitzer, "Altkretische Kunst," pp. 311 f.

II. LIGHT AND HONEY

Flaming New Year

A STUDY of the Dionysian atmosphere becomes more concrete when we are able to attach it to the calendar. Feast days have always had an atmosphere of their own, an element that is hard to frame in words. They possessed such an atmosphere before art took it up, appropriated it, as it were, and preserved it in its more sublimated form. Dionysian art did this with the Dionysian atmosphere. But what has come down to us of the Minoan calendar of feast days? We must content ourselves with the little that we know from the Greek tradition.

It seems strange to us that of the four cardinal points of the solar year—the two solstices and two equinoxes—the summer solstice should have been chosen as the beginning of the year. With it begins the hottest period of the year. The days begin to grow shorter, the nights, longer. Men yearn for the night. A year beginning at this time seems understandable in Egypt alone of all Mediterranean countries.[1] After falling to its low point in May, the Nile begins to rise visibly in June. This would be a fresh beginning for the earth even if the skies revealed nothing new. For nine centuries the first rising of the Nile coincided with the rise of Sirius at dawn. Until far into the first millennium B.C., this took place on July 19th of the Julian calendar. According to the observations of a Greek astronomer of the second century B.C.,[2] Sirius rose at dawn, at the latitude of Rhodes, some thirty days after the summer solstice.

1 E. Meyer, *Geschichte des Altertums*, I:2, 107.
2 Hipparchos, *Hipparchi in Arati et Eudoxi Phaenomena commentarii* II 1 18.

29

Leading religious and political sites in Greece, such as Olympia,[3] Delphi, Athens, and Epidauros,[4] chose the month of the early rising of Sirius as the first month of the year. This calendar would be exceedingly strange if the Greeks had not inherited it from an earlier culture that possessed closer ties with Egypt than did Greece in the historical period. The connecting link could only have been the Minoan culture. Careful calculation has shown that the orientation of the palaces on Crete was determined by Sirius.[5] Sirius also determined an annual rite reported from the Greek period of the island. The rite's mythological interpretation, which must be later than the rite itself, is an evident example of old Cretan tradition.[6] The core of the story can be traced back to earlier times, but our record of it comes from the Roman Imperial Age.[7] This record is to be found in a story entitled "Thieves" in a collection of miraculous tales based on a prior, but not very ancient, work on the "origin of the birds." To quote the story: "In Crete, it is said, there is a cave of bees. There, according to the myth, Rhea gave birth to Zeus, and a religious commandment [*hosion*] decrees that no one, neither god nor man, may enter. At a certain time each year a great fiery glow is seen emerging from the cave. According to the myth, this occurs when the blood remaining from the birth of Zeus runs over. The cave is inhabited by sacred bees, the nurses of Zeus." It is further related that four foolhardy men wished to gather the honey of these bees. They put on bronze armor, scooped up some of the honey, and saw the "swaddling clothes of Zeus." Thereupon their armor cracked and fell from their bodies. Zeus was angry and

3 L. Weniger, "Das Hochfest des Zeus in Olympia," pp. 14 ff.
4 E. Bischoff, "Kalender," col. 1569.
5 S. Marinatos, "Zur Orientierung der minoischen Architektur," pp. 197 ff.
6 M. P. Nilsson, *Geschichte der griechischen Religion*, I, 321.
7 Antoninus Liberalis, Μεταμορφώσεων συναγωγή XIX.

raised his thunderbolt against them, but the goddess of fate and Themis, goddess of the rule of nature, restrained Zeus. For it would have been contrary to the *hosion* if anyone had died in this cave. The four honey thieves were transformed into birds.

The antiquity of the core of this tale is attested by a vase painting from the sixth century B.C. [16].[8] It shows nude men attacked by enormous bees. There are four men as in the story, and their armor must have fallen off, for it is inconceivable that they would have approached the bees naked. The other side of the vessel, an amphora, shows two enthroned maenads with satyrs [17]. This scene belongs to the Dionysian sphere; consequently the punishment of the honey thieves must have occurred not far from the realm of Dionysos. He was said to have invented honey,[9] and the ground on which his handmaidens, the maenads, danced was said to have flowed with milk, wine, and the "nectar of bees."[10] It was also said that honey dripped from the thyrsos staffs that the maenads carried.[11] Before the feeding of the infant Dionysos, a privilege of his non-animal, sacred nurses, his lips were sprinkled with honey.[12]

Before they were domesticated, bees had often been found in caves. With their sweet food they were the most natural nurses for a Divine Child who was born and then kept hidden in a cave. The archetypal situation that nature offered was taken into the Greek myth of Zeus. The bees offered men the essential sweetness of pure existence—the existence of infants in the womb. However, the true place of the flar-

---

8   See the *Catalogue of the Greek and Etruscan Vases in the British Museum*, II, pp. 123 ff., no. B 177; A. B. Cook, *Zeus*, II, pl. XLII.

9   Ovid, *Fasti* III 736.

10   Euripides, *Bacchae* 142; see also H. Usener, *Kleine Schriften*, IV, 398 ff.

11   Euripides, *Bacchae* 711.

12   Apollonius Rhodius, *Argonautica* IV 1136.

ing up or "lighting up" of the great celestial god of the Greeks was the sky. "Zeus" means "lighting up" and only later came to mean "he who illumines."[13] Where the story of his birth was told on the Greek mainland—and this was the case on Mt. Lykaion in Arcadia—the event was not associated with a cave or any place belonging to Eileithyia, the goddess of human birth.[14] He was born under the open sky, in a thicket, says the poet Kallimachos, who observes that this place was forbidden to child-bearing human and animal mothers. If a living creature, human or animal, set foot there, he ceased to cast a shadow.[15] If anyone went there by mistake, he did not die, any more than the honey thieves died, but he was permitted to live no more than one more year.[16] He was stoned or "looked upon as a deer," which probably meant that he incurred the fate of hunted game.[17] This place was one of absolute light, and it was certainly not the sacred precinct excavated on Mt. Lykaion. Here sacrifices were offered. Worthy of Zeus was another site, a place of supernatural existence that could only be experienced in visions. It is no more possible to doubt that the Greeks had this experience than that other Mediterranean peoples had the related experience of timeless being and beatitude.[18]

"Zeus" was the Greek interpretation of the Divine Child whose birth was related on Crete. For the Cretans the divine birth flared up

13 H. Zimmermann, "Das ursprüngliche Geschlecht von *dies*," pp. 79 ff.; P. Kretschmer, "Dyaus, Ζεύς, Diespiter und die Abstrakta im Indogermanischen," pp. 101 ff., in conjunction with Kerényi, *Griechische Grundbegriffe*, pp. 25 ff. Also see Kerényi, *Zeus and Hera: Archetypal Image of Father, Husband, and Wife*, ch. I.
14 Kallimachos, *Hymni* I 10–14.
15 Scholium on Kallimachos, *Hymni* I 12–13.
16 Pausanias VIII 38 6.
17 Plutarch, *Quaestiones Graecae* 300 c.
18 See Kerényi, *Niobe*, pp. 185 ff.

from dark depths. It was more the bursting forth of life than the flaring up of a more spiritual, pure light. The story of the birth of Zeus was adduced to explain the event underlying the story of the honey thieves. A point of contact was supplied by the assonance between *ekzein* ("to overflow") and the name "Zeus," but it is highly unlikely that the whole incident—the overflowing of the blood in the cave—was invented purely for the sake of a pun (*zein–Zeus*). Before the myth of Zeus could be adduced to interpret it, the event must have occurred.

The words of the story, "at a certain time" and "each year," form an incomplete indication of the date. It is not necessary to specify which of the known Cretan cult-grottoes was intended as the cave in which Zeus was born. A mysterylike cult was long preserved in the Idaean Cave,[19] and the term for a secret cult—*aporrhetos thysia*—has come down to us in connection with the Dictaean Cave.[20] Only chosen persons had access to a secret rite. The text of the "Thieves" story expresses this by saying that a "religious commandment" (*hosion*) barred access to the cave.[21] Those who enacted the ceremonies were the only exception. The secrecy went so far that the very existence of any exception was denied. Only what could not be denied—the great fiery glow emerging from the cave—was openly avowed, indeed, recorded on the calendar. In a purely formal sense the situation is the same as in the Mysteries of Eleusis;[22] there too the fire could not be kept secret. In Crete a mythological explanation, consecrated in the calendar, was given for the cult fire, whose glow emerged from the cave: namely, that at exactly that time the blood that had been preserved

19 Euripides, fr. 472 in Nauck, *TGF*.
20 See Agothokles of Babylon, in Athenaios III 378 A.
21 "Neither man nor god" is a universal expression of totality.
22 See Kerényi, *Eleusis*, p. 82.

in the cave after the birth of Zeus "overflowed" or "attained the high point of fermentation." This latter translation is provided by the fact that *zein* also means to ferment.

Thus, we must ask what the cave contained that could "overflow" or "attain the high point of fermentation." The "divine blood" in the story clearly refers to the honey, the abundance of which attracted the thieves to the cave. The importance of honey in the Minoan cult is attested by texts written in the Linear B script. It was considered a possession of the gods, theft of which exposed the thieves to punishment. The light bursting forth from the cave and the honey were not necessarily inventions of the storyteller. More likely they were the traditional, concrete foundation of the miraculous tale of the punished honey thieves. According to Homer, no ordinary blood flowed in the veins of the gods, but ichor.[23] Ichor is not red blood but a paler liquid resembling buttermilk or whey or the watery component of the body fluids. Greek physicians use the word in their writings,[24] as does Aristotle in describing the amniotic fluid.[25] Through the story of the "blood" left over after the birth of Zeus, the honey—whose presence in the cave could have been perfectly natural—was, not unnaturally, interpreted as divine amniotic fluid.

But how are we to understand the movement, the "overflowing," of the honey, and with what time of year is this occurrence to be related? Honey does not ferment in the comb. It ferments when mixed with water and exposed to heat, and in antiquity this occurred most often at the time of the early rising of Sirius. The fiery glow erupting from

23 Iliad V 340: ἰχώρ, οἷος πέρ τε ῥέει μακάρεσσι θεοῖσιν.
24 According to Liddell and Scott, *A Greek-English Lexicon*, the word was *serum*.
25 *Historia animalium* 586b 32.

the cave signified a festive rite, in which an intoxicating beverage—not yet wine, but mead—played a part.

The Preparation of Mead

HONEY HAS served mankind as food since the Old Stone Age. A dark-red rock painting in the cave of Araña near Bicorp in Spain shows the precursors of the "honey thieves" climbing tall trees in order to rob the bees.[26] The different methods of obtaining honey: directly from flowers,[27] from wild bees, and by the domestication of bees, would provide a special system of dating, varying with the region and people. The common—archetypal and biologically grounded—factor is that in addition to nourishment (it seems unlikely that men have ever lived on honey alone) *zoë* seeks sweetness and finds an intensification in it. A further intensification was provided by the making of an intoxicating drink from honey; though it is more correct to speak of euphoria than of intoxication, for it is hard to say where drunkenness sets in and can be recognized as a special state, distinct from euphoria. The bees were the first source of what men later obtained from the vine.

This sequence is reflected in Greek mythology. Dionysos obtained his place in the genealogy of the gods after Kronos and Zeus. According to Orphic doctrine, wine was among his last gifts.[28] The Orphists

26 M. Ebert, ed., *Reallexikon der Vorgeschichte*, VII, pl. 113; see also H. M. Ransome, *The Sacred Bee in Ancient Times and Folklore*, pp. 19 ff.

27 See Strabo XVI 4 17, concerning the Troglodytes, the cave dwellers of southern Arabia, who made mead for their chiefs. "The use of honey is familiar to savages, even when they do not obtain it from bees," writes Frazer in reference to Ovid, *Fasti* III 736. Citing B. Spencer and F. J. Gillen, *The Arunta*, I, 23, 159–62, Frazer relates how honey is derived from ants in Australia.

28 O. Kern, ed., *Orphicorum fragmenta*, fr. 116.

favored archaic versions of the stories of the gods,[29] and they preserved a tale about the cruel guile of Zeus who surprised his father Kronos, when he was drunk on the honey of wild bees, and castrated him.[30] This tale indicates the Orphic poet's incomplete knowledge of the archaic reality, for otherwise Kronos would first have invented mead and then gotten drunk on it. But honey in itself possessed a mythological significance: it was the drink of the Golden Age and the food of the gods.[31] Ovid, who wrote that "Bacchus invented honey,"[32] was not as careful as the Orphic poets and the Greek cult before them in distinguishing the different stages in the history of human food.

The original Greek words for "to be drunk" and "to make drunk" are *methyein* and *methyskein*. Rarer and later is *oinoun* (from *oinos*, "wine") meaning "to intoxicate with wine." Echoes of *methy* signify "honey" not only in a number of Indo-European languages, but also in a common Indo-European–Finno-Ugric stratum; for example, Finnish *mesi, metinen*, and Hungarian *mez*. German *Met* and English "mead" signify "honey beer," and these words have exact parallels in the Norse languages. In Greek, *methy* remained "intoxicating drink" and was used even for the beer of the Egyptians.[33] The claim that the mead made in Phrygia was the most celebrated in antiquity indicates that Phrygia had learned the art of winegrowing relatively late:[34] later than Greece, where no region boasted of producing an especially good *hydromeli*.

29 See Kerényi, "Die Schichten der Mythologie und ihre Erforschung," pp. 637 ff.; and "Miti sul concepimento di Dioniso," pp. 1 ff.

30 O. Kern, ed., *Orphicorum fragmenta*, fr. 154.

31 See Kerényi, *Niobe*, p. 197, and "Die Herrin des Labyrinthes," *Werke*, II, 266 ff.

32 Ovid, *Fasti* III 736.

33 Aischylos, *The Suppliant Women* 953: ἐκ κριθῶν μέθυ.

34 Pliny, *Natural History* XIV 113: "nusquam laudatius quam in Phrygia."

In the Greek cult, however, mead retained its precedence over wine for a long time. The chronological order is reflected in the instructions in the Odyssey for the sacrifice to the dead: "First with *melikratos*, then with sweet wine."[35] *Melikratos* means not only a mixture of honey and milk,[36] but also, as Hippokrates and Aristotle bear witness, the beverage later known as *hydromeli*.[37] Aristotle combated the superstitious but originally no doubt religious opinion that the role of the figures three to three in the mixture contributed to making the drink more healthful, arguing that its healthfulness increased with its water content. A recipe recorded by Pliny the Elder[38] also mentions the sacred number three and in addition takes account of the time element. "Heavenly water," as Pliny calls rain water,[39] should be kept until the fifth year and mixed with honey. This long lapse of time corresponds to the *pentaeteris*, or five-year cycle, governing the great Greek festivals, including the Olympic Games. It would be difficult to find a reason for this five-year period other than the traditional cycle on which the calendar of Greek feast days had probably been based since the Mycenaean Age.[40]

"The wiser people," Pliny continues, "boil the water down to two-thirds, add one-third of old honey, and let the mixture stand in the sun for forty days at the time of the early rising of Sirius [*canis ortu in sole habent*]." On one point Pliny is assuredly either inaccurate or incomplete. In the extreme heat of that season, the mixture could not possibly have been exposed to the sun in an open vessel. It would have evapo-

---

35 Odyssey X 519: πρῶτα μελικρήτωι, μετέπειτα δὲ ἡδέϊ οἴνωι.

36 This is expressly pointed out, as in Euripides, *Orestes*: μελίκρατον γά-
λακτος.

37 Hippokrates, *Aphorisms* V 41; Aristotle, *Metaphysics* XIV 1092b.

38 *Natural History* XIV 113.

39 Ibid., XXXI 69: "ex imbre puro."

40 G. Thomson, "The Greek Calendar," pp. 63 ff.

rated. Pliny does not name the type of vessel, probably because it was self-evident to his contemporaries. The only possible type was a kind of *askos*, a sack of animal hide that could be tied at the neck. Such sacks were watertight, but not airtight, and offered room for the "movement," the fermentation, of the liquid. Pliny adds that some people plugged (*obturant*) the vessel on the tenth day when the overflow (*diffusa*) set in. The learned Roman was not familiar with the relation of mead-making to the *pentaeteris* and to the occurrences in the heavens. He attached no religious, but only a practical, significance to his recipe. Nevertheless he speaks of brewing at a particular time of year, the period of the greatest heat, as though it were a fixed tradition. It is clear that the fermentation process was to culminate on a definite date, which is expressly given as the first day of the year of Sirius (*canis ortus*).

The Awakening of the Bees

IN LATE antiquity a strange, mythical formula or recipe was associated with this formerly very significant date of the first day of the Sirius year. It would seem to have been another way of lending a mythical significance to mead. The equation of honey with divine blood was an accommodation to the mythology of the Greek god of heaven, the myth of the "lighting up" expressed in the name of Zeus. In this case, however, it was not only by accommodation but also directly that a natural phenomenon inspired a myth of *zoë*, a statement concerning life which shows its indestructibility in fermentation, that is, even in decay. A link seems to have been perceived between fermentation and decay.

This myth's claim to truth was so great that it provided the basis for a practical formula.

This formula was said to have first been devised by Aristaios, who has been characterized as "a figure in Greek religious history, concerning whom we have only a fragmentary and dispersed tradition. From this tradition, however, the former importance of this god, who belonged to a very old and original stage of development, can be gathered."[41] His place in the history of culture is determined by his relation to honey. He was said to have imparted the use of the beehive to man[42] and was looked upon as the inventor of the mixture of honey and wine.[43] Thus, he belongs to a period of Mediterranean culture which was marked by the domestication of bees, rather than the exploitation of wild bees, and a period in which the vine was already cultivated. According to a tradition of the island of Keos, Aristaios was related in two ways to the season of the greatest heat. He had allegedly decreed that the early rising of Sirius be greeted both "with weapons" and with a sacrifice, but at the same time he had caused the *etesiai*, the trade winds, to blow, in order to attenuate the destructive power of the dangerous star.[44] In the later, Olympian religion, this sacrifice was also rendered to Zeus Ikmaios, the god of moisture, who sent the winds. Aristaios preceded that religion, and it was he who, after his bees died, used a peculiar method to awaken them.

The learned authors on agriculture and apiculture, such as Varro and Columella among the Romans, did not wish to discuss the practicability of this method—evidently because that would have been to call the myth into doubt. Varro refers to an epigram by the Greek poet Ar-

---

41 F. Hiller von Gaertringen, "Aristaios," col. 852.

42 Diodorus Siculus IV 81 2.   43 Pliny, *Natural History* XIV 5.

44 Apollonius Rhodius, *Argonautica* II 520–27 with scholium.

chelaos and to an old poem entitled *Bougonia*, "Birth from a Heifer."[45] Columella invokes the authority of Demokritos and of the Carthaginian Mago.[46] He also cites Virgil, who in the fourth book of his *Georgics* relates the mythical occurrence.[47] According to Columella, Demokritos, Mago, and Virgil concurred in mentioning the early rising of Sirius. This was a time in which not only the heady fermented mead but also bees could be made. At least *one* bovine had to be sacrificed for the purpose. A text by Cassianus Bassus, a late author on the same subject, shows that the bovine had to be transformed into a sealed skin.[48] Even apart from its relation to the calendar, the process shows a cosmic orientation, which reveals its origin in an ancient rite.

According to Virgil, Aristaios sacrificed four bulls and four cows. He let the bodies lie for nine days; then bees swarmed from the entrails which had become liquid.[49] Here the number four surely has a cosmic significance. It corresponds to the four cardinal points. Cassianus Bassus mentions it in the same connection. According to his instructions—which constitute the first description of an ancient Mediterranean cube-shaped house—a cubical structure should be built with a door and three windows, each turned toward one of the four cardinal points. In this house a thirty-month-old bovine must be killed with a club, so that no blood flows and the entrails grow soft. All the openings of the body must be sealed. The animal is transformed into a sack

45   Varro, *De re rustica* III 16 4.
46   Columella, *De re rustica* IX 14 6.
47   Virgil, *Georgics* IV 538–58; for indication of the time, see IV 425–28.
48   *Geoponica sive Cassii Bassi scholasticia de re rustica eclogae* XV 2 22–29.
49   In his edition of *The Fasti of Ovid* (II, 158), Frazer attempts to explain the belief in such a miracle by analogy with the natural appearance of "drone-flies" in the corpses of animals. In this case a natural phenomenon provided the basis for a myth of *zoë*.

containing its own fluids. After four weeks and ten days—roughly forty days, as in the traditional brewing of mead—grapelike clusters of bees fill the hut. All that remains of the bovine is the horns, the bones, and the skin. The natural phenomenon ushering in a great festival for the early rising of Sirius, an ancient New Year's festival, was raised to the level of a myth of *zoë*: an awakening of bees from a dead animal.

The Birth of Orion

RELATED to this tale is a version of the story of the birth of Orion, both the constellation still known by that name and at the same time an ancient mythical figure for whom it was not hard to find a place in the mythology of the Greeks. In the season that for the Greeks began with the early rising of Sirius, Orion, the great hunter, had already been visible in the heavens for months. Sirius was his dog. (In Chapter III we shall have more to say concerning this situation in the heavens.) In this variant of the story of his birth, as well as in a version of his removal to the heavens, Orion is related to Crete. Here again we run into puns, as is common among late mythographers when they try to explain old myths. And here again there is no reason to suppose that the stories were invented for the sake of the puns. The contrary is true. The Cretan story of Orion's birth was explained by the assonance between *Oarion*, a form of "Orion," and *oaristes*, "interlocutor." In Homer, Minos was an "interlocutor of the great Zeus."[50] Orion was said to be a son of Poseidon and Euryale, a daughter of Minos,[51] who to judge by

50   Odyssey XIX 179; Eustathius, *Commentarii ad Homeri Odysseam* 1535.
51   Eratosthenes, *Catasterismorum reliquiae* XXXII.

her name must have been a goddess of the "wide sea" (*eureia hals*).[52]
Thus, the hunter in the sky arose from the sea, as befits a constellation.
The other, exceedingly ancient link between Orion and Crete rested
in the story that his death and removal to the sky had been caused by
the bite of a scorpion.[53] The link with the scorpion is also an ancient
star legend suggested by the positions of the constellations: the as-
cendancy of the sign of Scorpio during the setting of Orion.[54] This myth
is presupposed in a black-figure vase of Nikosthenes [18].[55] The painting shows a hare hunt that must be related to Orion the hunter, because
under the net, between two snakes, is a giant scorpion.

In a second version of the story of Orion's birth, he was born from
the seed of the gods in a sack made from a bull's hide, and a pun is
employed to explain how divine seed could be gathered in such a sack.[56]
This version is connected with the village of Hyria near Tanagra in
Boeotia and with its hero Hyrieus. Hyrieus was childless, and the gods,
who had stopped at his house for the night, promised him a son who
would be born in a sack. To this end they let their seed flow into the
sack: *ourein* and "Orion" are thus connected in a pun. Originally, however, it was honey that played the role of the life substance in an animal hide. The name "Hyria" is connected with bees and with Crete.
According to Hesychios, *hyron* was a Cretan word for "swarm of bees"

52 See Kerényi, *The Gods of the Greeks*, p. 49 (Pelican edn., p. 43).
53 Eratosthenes, *Catasterismorum reliquiae* XXXII. According to another
version, the scorpion sting occurred on Chios: Aratos, *Phaenomena* 637–44.
54 Aratos, *Phaenomena* 636 with scholium.
55 See the *Catalogue of the Greek and Etruscan Vases in the British Museum*, II, p. 298, no. B 678; *Archäologische Zeitung*, XXXIX (1881), pl. 5; and
also Kerényi, "Il dio cacciatore," pp. 7 ff.
56 Scholium A on Iliad XVIII 489; Ovid, *Fasti* 499–500; Servius' commentary on *Aeneid* I 535; scholium on Nicander, *Theriaca* 15; see also Kerényi,
The Gods of the Greeks, p. 202 (Pelican edn., p. 178).

and "beehive." "Hyria" means "place of apiculture." It is a frequent place name. According to Herodotos, a "Hyria," also called "Ouria," was founded by Cretans in Apulia.[57] The place outside of Crete where Orion was born from a sealed animal skin is connected with Crete by its name, and the story becomes comprehensible only through the significance of this Cretan name.

A common inference can be drawn from the three traditions discussed in this chapter: the instructions for the brewing of mead at the time of the early rising of Sirius, the formula for awakening bees from a bovine transformed into a sack, and the story of the birth of Orion from a sack of animal hide. The three strange traditions all are explained by the ritual brewing of mead at the time of the early rising of Sirius, which in a large area marked the beginning of the year. Egypt, important localities in Greece, and Minoan Crete were included in this area. Such a ceremony accounts for the report that on a certain night of the year light burst forth from a Cretan grotto and that at the same time the mead overflowed. This was probably the night preceding New Year's Day, and the light was probably the torchlight of a mystery rite performed in the cave. In the non-Cretan documents cited, the episode is not linked with a cave, but there were many other places where such a connection also existed. Localities bearing the name "Korykos" or derivatives of *korykos* provide a kind of fossil evidence pointing to such a ceremony in a grotto. According to Hesychios, *korykos* means a "leather sack."[58]

57   Herodotos VII 170; see also Strabo VI 3 6, and Pliny, *Natural History* IV 54. On Hyria near Tanagra, see Strabo IX 2 12; on Hyria by Mt. Korykos, see Stephen of Byzantium s.v. Ὑρία.

58   Hesychios s.v. Κώρυκος: Θυλάκιον. ἔστι δὲ δερμάτινον ἀγγεῖον ὅμοιον ἀσκῶι.

Mythology of the Leather Sack

IN PERFORMING their sacrilegious deed, the honey thieves caught sight of the "swaddling clothes of Zeus."[59] Thereupon the bronze of their armor burst. The forbidden vision completed their offense against the *hosion*. The notion that swaddling clothes were kept in the cave fits in with the conceptions of Greek mythology. We know that in Greece *tainiai*, or narrow bands, were used to adorn sacred persons and objects, while in Minoan Crete broader bands knotted into bows indicated a high degree of holiness. Such emblems of the holiness of the place may well have been interpreted as swaddling clothes. They were, however, mere trappings. In Greek mythology we find frequent mention of the object to which they probably belonged: the *liknon*, a winnow-shaped basket, in which divine as well as mortal babies were kept. According to the Homeric Hymn to Hermes, the infant Hermes lay in his swaddling clothes in the Kyllenian grotto.[60] In his *Hymn to Zeus*, Kallimachos combines several Cretan traditions: the goddess Adrasteia lays the infant Zeus in a golden *liknon*, her goat suckles him, and in lieu of milk he is given honey.[61] A third example is that of Dionysos. As Liknites—"he in the *liknon*"—he was "awakened" by the Dionysian women in a cave on Mt. Parnassos, high over Delphi.[62] The awakening took the form of a mysterious ceremony: only the designation of the god as "Liknites" shows that the *liknon* was his "container." A

59 Antoninus Liberalis XIX 2: τὰ τοῦ Διὸς εἶδον σπάργανα.
60 The Homeric Hymn to Hermes 150–51.
61 Kallimachos, *Hymnus in Jovem* 40–41.
62 Plutarch, *De Iside et Osiride* 365 A. See also in ch. V, below, the section on "Dionysos in Delphi."

larger "container," the cave that housed the *liknon*, was said "to gleam with a golden radiance at certain times"[63]—evidently the torchlight of the nocturnal rite of Dionysos. A Delphic hymn speaks of this festival.[64] The name of the grotto, however, carries no intimation of a *liknon*, which in the Greek view would have been a fit receptacle for a Divine Child. The cave was called *Korykion antron*, "cave of the leather sack" —the most famous of all those places in and outside the Greek world that were named after the *korykos*, the container for liquids used in fermenting honey and, as we have seen, associated with a Cretan cave of Zeus.

"Korykos" was the name of the extreme western promontory on the north coast of Crete.[65] It could be reached from Kydonia, a city possessing an attested Dionysos cult and standing in a special relationship to Teos,[66] a Dionysian city in Asia Minor where periodic wine miracles were performed.[67] Across from Teos there was a high mountain also called "Korykos."[68] Nothing further is recorded concerning either these promontories or a seaport by the same name in Lykia, situated near a mountain and city of Olympos.[69] But much is told of the Cilician Korykos, a mountain, a seaport, and a cave.[70] Ancient geographers and

63 Antigonus Carystius, *Historiae mirabiles* CXXVII 141 (in Westermann, ed., p. 91).

64 Aristonous Corinthius, *Hymnus in Apollinem* I B 37 (in Diehl, *Anth. lyr.* [1st edn., II, 300]).

65 Strabo VIII 5 1.

66 M. Guarducci, *Inscriptiones Creticae* II, X 2.

67 Diodorus Siculus III 66.

68 The Homeric Hymn to Apollo 39; Hekataios, fr. 231, in Jacoby, *FGrHist*, I. Livy XXXVII 12 10 refers to it as "Corycus Pelorus."

69 Strabo XIV 3 8.

70 *Ibid.*, 5 5; Pomponius Mela, *De chorographia* I 13 71–76. For a description drawn from the accounts of modern travelers, see J. G. Frazer, *The Golden Bough*, IV : 1, 153 ff.

modern travelers have admired two large grottoes in the vicinity of this seaport, which in Turkish bears the name of "Korgos."[71] These grottoes seem to be crater-shaped fissures like the Pozzo di Santulla, the "well of Italy" near Collepardo in the mountains of the Hernici. Pomponius Mela, the Roman geographer, clearly brings out the Dionysian character of one of the caves: anyone entering the inner grottoes, he relates, hears the cymbals, Bacchic instruments, of an invisible divine procession. In Mela's time, the first century A.D., the other, darker fissure was associated with the story of a leather sack brought there by Typhon, the adversary of Zeus.[72] This distinction between the caves has little significance for the myth, which had its home in a far larger area than the caves of Korgos. The story reaches across the sea to Syria, bearing witness to a period in which the two coasts had gods and myths in common. The oldest variations of the mythological theme involving a leather sack are to be found among the Hittites, in whose empire a "Greater Cilicia" (a name which in a later day only the narrow coastal strip retained) probably played a leading role.[73]

According to the Greek source, the battle between the dragon Typhon, or Typhoeus, and Zeus took place on the Cilician coast of Asia Minor and on the slopes of Mt. Kasion near Ugarit, whose culture has come to light on the hill of Ras Shamra in Syria.[74] The Hittites told a similar story about a fight between Illuyankas, a snakelike monster, and their weather god. In the very fragmentary Hittite variants, there is no express mention of a leather sack, but only of the organs that were torn off the vanquished weather god, hidden, and finally given

71   F. Beaufort, *Karamania*, p. 238.
72   Pomponius Mela I 13 76.
73   See J. Garstang, *The Hittite Empire*, p. 167.
74   See Kerényi, *The Gods of the Greeks*, p. 27 (Pelican edn., p. 23).

back to him. Illuyankas took away the god's heart and eyes.[75] The fight in which this monster defeated the weather god does not necessarily require the use of a leather sack, nor does the sacred happening—the preservation and awakening, in which a container such as a leather sack does figure—necessarily involve a battle. This battle was a separate theme, which in Cilicia and Syria and probably among the Hittites as well was connected with the other, more sacred theme. A striking feature of the later version of the Hittite myth is that the heart and eyes of the weather god were recovered only in the second generation through the marriage of the weather god's son to the daughter of Illuyankas.

"The weather god," so the story runs, "instructs his son: 'When you go to the house of your wife, demand of them [my] heart and [my] eyes.' When he went there and demanded the heart of them, they gave it to him. Afterward he also demanded the eyes. When he had been restored to his previous form, he went out to the sea to do battle." This time the weather god defeated the dragon. But the Hittite text—perhaps by chance, or perhaps by design—does not tell us where Illuyankas and his daughter had hidden the heart and eyes. We do, however, learn this from the Cilician version, transmitted by a Greek author, in which Zeus replaces the Oriental god of sky and weather.[76] Here he fights the dragon first with his lightning bolts, then in close combat with a sickle-shaped sword, a divine weapon native to that region.[77]

On Mt. Kasion the tide of battle turns. The dragon wrests the sickle from Zeus and severs the tendons—*neura*—of his hands and feet. Then he carries him on his shoulders across the sea to Cilicia. "Arrived there,"

75 G. Furlani, *La Religione degli Hittiti*, p. 88; see also A. Goetze, *Kleinasien*, p. 140, from which quotations are taken.

76 Apollodoros, *Bibliotheca* I 6 3.

77 W. Staudacher, "Die Trennung von Himmel und Erde," p. 69.

the story goes, "he left him in the *Korykion antron*; he did the same with the tendons, which he hid in a bearskin." Thus, he had not only "severed" the tendons, as the Greek narrator supposed or wished to suppose, but from the defeated god's body removed something that was kept in a bearskin, i.e. a leather sack. *Neuron* in Greek—like *nervus* in Latin—can signify the male sex organ despite the plural, which here may be employed as a veil. That in this case the sack is a bearskin is not only a rare archaic feature, but also a partial revelation of the container's purpose. All people living among bears (which was the case in certain regions of Asia Minor as long as they remained wooded; later the bears withdrew to the Caucasus) were bound to know of the close relationship between bears and *honey*. The bear is the "honey-eating animal," par excellence. So he is termed in the Slavic languages with a composite word[78] which in Hungarian takes the form *medve* and means only "bear."

In the Cilician version the dragoness Delphyne guards Zeus and his severed "tendons." Hermes and Aigipan, the "goat Pan," steal the "tendons" and reunite them with Zeus; thus he is made whole again and defeats the dragon. In connection with Delphi, a tradition was preserved to the effect that a son of the Delphic dragon, called Python in this instance, was named "Aix," or "goat."[79] This name, like "Aigipan," suggests a member of the Python family. But another name for the Delphic dragon was "Typhon," and both a male and a female dragon are mentioned in the stories. There was enmity between the dragoness Delphyne and Apollo.[80] In the Delphic fight with the dragon, the god is not defeated but appears only as a victor. At Delphi the only

78   Old Church Slavic *medvědĭ.*
79   Plutarch, *Quaestiones Graecae* 295 c.
80   See Kerényi, *The Gods of the Greeks*, p. 136 (Pelican edn., p. 121).

temporarily defeated god could be Dionysos, since his tomb was shown in the innermost sanctuary, near the "golden Apollo."[81] Parts of him allegedly rested here, and his heart probably was thought to be in the cauldron from which the oracle issued. Holy men, the Hosioi, performed a secret sacrifice in the temple, while the holy women, the Thyiades, were awakening Liknites in the cave.[82] There seems to be a connection between the fight motif and the action in the *Korykion antron*, the victory of the one god and the awakening of the other. It is striking enough that the Delphic dragon possessed a family and that this feature was also present among the Hittites. Originally, the two actions no doubt were part of one and the same fight with the dragon. What happened in the *Korykion antron* proved that a god had only temporarily lost his powers and was therefore unconquerable. In Delphi as elsewhere, Dionysos took the place of an older vision of indestructible life, which in a sense *he already was*, although in relation to honey rather than wine. In the same context, the Homeric Hymn to Hermes speaks of three aged prophetic women, from whom Apollo learned the art of prophesy, as three bees,[83] and it calls the Pythia, the Apollonian prophetess herself, the "Delphic bee."[84]

We must assume that north of Crete, from Syria and Cilicia to Delphi, and especially on Crete itself, there were cult grottoes in which an intoxicating drink was prepared from honey on a particular festive

81   Philochoros, fr. 7, in Jacoby, *FGrHist*, III, B, p. 100, and the commentary in III, B (Supplement), ii, pp. 189–90; cf. Pausanias X 24 4–5. It was assumed that the tomb of Dionysos was a βάθρον—a base or step—under the tripod. (See also in ch. V, below, the section on "Dionysos in Delphi.")

82   Plutarch, *De Iside et Osiride* 365 C. Plutarch mentions τὰ τοῦ Διονύσου λείψανα in 365 A.

83   The Homeric Hymn to Hermes 552–59.

84   Pindar, *Pythia* IV 60.

occasion. To judge by Pliny's instructions for the making of mead and by the mythological formula for the making of bees, it would seem likely that this rite was performed over a period of forty days ending with a New Year's festival at the time of the early rising of Sirius. The relative chronology of honey and wine argues that the festival was older than viticulture in Crete, Greece, and Asia Minor.

Crete would seem to have chronological priority over the northern countries by reason of its geographic position and its early ties with Egypt. Only the time of year, and not the localization of the rite in a cave, can be traced back to Lower Egypt, the region with the earliest commercial ties to Crete. The question as to whether or not the rite was held at the same time of year in Asia Minor and Syria must remain open. It appears that the connection between the two themes—the fight with the dragon and the rite in which the leather sack figured—was made in Asia Minor and that this amplified "mythology of the leather sack" reached Delphi from the east. This does not exclude the possibility that the rite itself came to Delphi from Crete: the tradition that Cretan priests took part in the Delphic cult still survives in the Homeric Hymn to Apollo.[85] But it is also possible that the rite came to Crete from the surrounding regions, perhaps as early as the third millennium B.C., before the onset of the Middle Minoan period when the Minoan high culture with its palaces came into being.

Our inquiry up to now has been a kind of excavation. Where we found traces of Dionysos, they did not belong to the deepest stratum. The secret of life suggested by honey and its fermentation possessed religious forms that passed into the religion of Dionysos but were also temporarily taken into the religion of Zeus. The difference resides

85   The Homeric Hymn to Apollo 388–96, 516–23.

in the fact that the dividing line between the religion of Zeus and that older religion is more distinct and more relevant to the character of the god than is the dividing line between the Dionysos religion and the older cults and myths of indestructible life: often in the latter case only a chronological sequence can be established. When we say "in the third millennium" or "in the second millennium," we have no more than a relative chronology in mind. The most tangible feature of this chronology is that the palace culture of Crete was already related to viticulture. A kind of symbolic transformation in cultural and religious history is expressed in the fact that grape seeds, the seeds of the *vitis vinifera Mediterranea*, were found in the excavation of the oldest palace of Phaistos.[86]

86   D. Levi, "The Italian Excavations in Crete and the Earliest European Civilisation"; on the chronology, see his *The Recent Excavations at Phaistos*, p. 14.

III. THE CRETAN CORE
OF THE DIONYSOS MYTH

Bull, Snake, Ivy, and Wine

THE DIONYSOS religion ushered in the cult of life under the signs of "vision" and "honey," but not only under these signs, nor any more exclusively under the third, "wine." The presence of the Dionysian religion is to be recognized by the concurrence of several signs. Thus, its characteristic atmosphere is concretized, but not in any one festival. Such signs are the elements of a differentiated myth, which could be embodied in several festivals. The over-all Dionysian impression made by Minoan art can be broken down into concrete elements which are present in the same combination only in the Dionysian religion of known, historic times. To the Greeks, Dionysos was pre-eminently a wine god, a bull god, and a god of women. A fourth element, the snake, was borne by the bacchantes, as it was by less agitated goddesses or priestesses in the Minoan culture. Wine and bull, women and snakes even form special, lesser "syndromes"—to employ a medical expression deriving from the Greek physicians.[1] They are the symptoms, as it were, of an acute Dionysian state which *zoë* created for itself. For Greek culture, this was the Dionysos myth; for the Minoan culture, before the arrival of the Greeks, it was the myth of a god called by another name, but assuredly a more comprehensive and less clearly defined god than the one recognized in the fermenting mead. To this the rich drinking and libation vessels ornamented with bull's heads bear witness.

---

1 See Galen, *Ad Glauconem de medendi methodo* I (in Kühn, ed., XI, 59).

For a long time our understanding of the Minoan culture as a whole was obstructed by the assumption of its discoverer that the "chief drink" of the Minoans was beer. With this a dividing line was drawn between the Greeks and the Minoans; the Minoans were thus moved closer to the Philistines who assuredly possessed vessels for beer brewing.[2] In 1900 Sir Arthur Evans, excavating near the palace of Knossos, unearthed vessels adorned with ears of barley in relief. He inferred that a kind of beer had preceded wine on Crete.[3] The small size of the vessels on which this view was based argues rather that they were used for that other barley drink—consumption of which was a requirement for participation in the Mysteries of Eleusis[4]—in ceremonies which allegedly were performed without secrecy at Knossos.[5] In certain palaces, however, magnificent wine vessels were manufactured and used,[6] especially enormous rhyta, artificial drinking horns, which presuppose great wine ceremonies. One example, borne in a procession, was as tall as the entire torso of the youth who carried it [19].

A special type of rhyton takes the form of a whole bull's head [20][7].

2 See Ventris and Chadwick, *Documents in Mycenaean Greek*, p. 131.
3 A. Evans, *Palace of Minos*, I, 415; IV, 637 f.
4 See Kerényi, *Eleusis*, pp. 177–80.
5 Diodorus Siculus V 77 3.
6 Many more of these were found in the course of N. Platon's excavations at Kato Zakros in 1961. See his Τὸ ἔργον *1963*, pp. 167 ff.

7 The silver and gold rhyton shown in [20] is the best preserved example. There are also several of this type in the Heraklion Museum, among them the fine piece from Knossos shown in Marinatos and Hirmer, *Crete and Mycenae*, pl. 98. A still more beautiful piece was found at Kato Zakros; see N. Platon, Τὸ ἔργον *1963*, p. 175, fig. 188. Fragments of a piece with a spotted bull's head (a rosettelike spot near the eye) from the oldest palace of Phaistos have been published by D. Levi, "Attività della Scuola Archeologica Italiana di Atene nell'anno 1955," pl. III D.

It is inconceivable that these vessels served other than ritual purposes. When the wine poured from the little round hole of the rhyton as from the mouth of a bull, something happened which to the Minoans seemed particularly appropriate. They used the heads of various animals as wine vessels, but in certain ritual moments, it seems, the animal bestowing the wine had to be a bull. It was no doubt appropriate in the same sense when the Minoans gave a bull the name of "Oinops," *wo-no-qo-so*, "wine-colored," as is twice attested along with other names for bulls on tablets from Knossos.[8] This epithet for a bull also occurs twice in Homer, for whom undoubtedly it was already a set traditional formula.[9] For it is not so very natural that bulls should be "wine-colored."

It is quite possible, however, that these animals, to whom the name "Oinops" was given, had been selected for the wine god on the strength of certain special characteristics and had been reared with special care. On the Late Minoan painted sarcophagus from Hagia Triada we see two spotted calves, of different colors, borne in the arms as gifts for the dead [21A]. On the other side of the sarcophagus a bull is being prepared for sacrifice [21B]. The large, motley animal lies bound on the sacrificial altar. One and a half millennia later, it was related how in the Arcadian village of Kynaithai, at the winter festival of Dionysos, the men carried a bull—which they had chosen through divine inspiration—in their arms to the sanctuary.[10] On the island of Tenedos a cow with calf was cared for like a pregnant woman and then like a woman in childbed, for the benefit of Dionysos, who was known there as the

8   L. A. Stella, *La civiltà micenea nei documenti contemporanei*, p. 166; Ventris and Chadwick, *Documents*, p. 130.

9   Iliad XIII 703, Odyssey XIII 32. It appears also as the name of the father of a righteous onlooker at the sacrifice, in Odyssey XXI 144; and as an epithet for Dionysos himself, in *Anthologia Palatina* VI 44 5.

10   Pausanias VIII 19 2.

"god who crushes men."[11] When the calf was born, hunting boots such as the god often wore were put on it, and it was then sacrificed in place of a child, who was none other than the child Dionysos. The identity of the god with the calf and the bull is demonstrated in Greece by epithets such as *Bougenes*, "cow's son," and "worthy bull," who was expected to come to the Dionysian women "with riotous bull's foot."[12]

Homer knew of the ecstatic cult that the women devoted to Dionysos, and when he makes Zeus himself say that the son of Semele had been born for the joy of man, he was surely thinking of wine.[13] But Homer also knew of the ambivalent power of wine,[14] and with his clear vision of the Olympian gods he was bound to be a reticent witness in the Dionysian sphere, where animals, plants, and wine appear in material identity with the god. The Minoan expression of this identity is the use of a bull's head as a wine vessel. There is no sharp dividing line between the Minoan expression of this sphere and what we learn of the archaic Dionysos cult from Greek testimonies: in Crete another god was worshiped in a complicated ritual characterized by the role of the bull; in Greece it was Dionysos! The Minoan monuments and the Greek texts are mutually complementary. The picture that unfolds before us comprises elements which appear in Minoan art and others which are found in the tradition of continental Greece. When we combine them, they form a meaningful whole.

The Minoan palaces had their vineyards. The unifying line in this

11 For this epithet, see Aelian, *De natura animalium* XII 34, and below, ch. V, note 4.

12 Plutarch, *Quaestiones Graecae* 299 B. See also below, in ch. IV, the section on "The Arrival in Athens," and ch. V at notes 3, 4.

13 Iliad VI 132–35, 389, XXII 461, and XIV 325; see also W. F. Otto, *Dionysos: Myth and Cult*, pp. 53 ff.

14 Iliad VI 265.

picture, the Dionysian element in the art monuments, was made apparent by the excavation of a Minoan vineyard dating from the apogee of Minoan culture.[15] It is situated in the region of Vathypetro, some three miles south of the since-discovered palace of Archanes. The excavations at Kato Zakros in 1961 soon brought to light a *villa rustica* for wine.[16] The character of Minoan Crete as a great wine country was fully revealed in these years. It seems more than likely that viticulture came to Greece from Crete.[17] Though it is hard to draw a horizontal dividing line between the Minoan cult characterized by the bull and wine, on the one hand, and the Greek Dionysos religion on the other, it is equally difficult to draw a vertical dividing line setting off the migration of viticulture from that of the Dionysos cult.

Still a limitation and differentiation are necessary. For it is by no means certain that viticulture came to Greece only from Crete or by only one route. It should also be asked, What kind of viticulture came from Crete? The Minoan hieroglyph for wine, an ideogram in Linear B, is similar to the Egyptian hieroglyph with the same meaning, and the latter bears witness to a very highly developed viticulture.[18] It recalls that form of grape arbor which is represented on a picture of the wine harvest at the time of the Eighteenth Dynasty (1580–1314 B.C.).[19] Clay seals bearing the inscription "Vineyard of the royal palace" have been found in the tombs of the kings of the First and Second Dynasties

---

15 S. Marinatos, Ἀνασκαφαὶ ἐν Βαθυπέτρωι Κρήτης, p. 592. See also other accounts in the same periodical, *Praktika*, from 1949 on (1951, pp. 100 ff.). For a general view of the site in its present state, see Marinatos and Hirmer, p. 53, pl. XXI.

16 N. Platon, Τὸ ἔργον *1961*, pp. 221 ff.

17 Stella, *La civiltà micenea*, p. 173.

18 Ventris and Chadwick, *Documents*, pp. 35, 130.

19 A. Erman, *Aegypten und aegyptisches Leben im Altertum*, p. 227, fig. 72.

(3000–2778 B.C.).[20] Libyan wine jugs in the tombs of the First Dynasty seem to indicate that this type of viticulture originated in western North Africa, perhaps in the region investigated by Henri Lhote.[21] The vine had traveled a long way since the discovery of the wild grape as a source of joy!

It is possible that this itinerary through Egypt was not the only one, and that there also was a shorter route from the wild grapevine to the vineyards of the Minoan palaces. Among the Greeks the grapevine was called *hemeris*, the "tame,"[22] because they knew how grapes grew in the woods. There the plant could develop into a thick tree. From such a tree the Argonauts allegedly carved the cult image of the Great Goddess Rhea on Mt. Dindymon in Asia Minor.[23] The Dionysian epic of Nonnos, written toward the end of pagan antiquity, narrates an ancient myth about the invention of viticulture, unrelated to the rest of the story and indeed in contradiction to it. In the myth, the wild grapevine and the snake play a part, and at the same time the connection with Rhea is stressed. In response to an oracle of the goddess, Dionysos learned the use of grapes from a snake. Thereupon he invented the most primitive method of making wine: by trampling the grapes in a hollow rock. This took place at a time when the Great

20 Ibid., p. 228.

21 A. Herrmann, "Nysa," col. 1655; H. Lhote, *The Search for the Tassili Frescoes.*

22 Odyssey V 69.

23 Apollonius Rhodius, *Argonautica* I 1116–39. A statue of Jupiter in Populonia—it may, however, be presumed to have represented an archaic Fufluns (Dionysos) as city deity—is mentioned by Pliny, *Natural History* XIV 1, who tells us that it was carved "from a single vine." He speaks also of other uses, not exclusively "Dionysian," to which giant vine plants were put. / Here we are speaking of "syndromes" that may have a significance, never suggesting an exclusive interpretation.

Mother was rearing the child Dionysos in her Cybelean cave. The story Nonnos relates may very well be Asia Minor's myth of the origin of viticulture, but it has a possible significance for Crete insofar as it shows that the vine may have come to Crete from Asia Minor, where it still grew wild in the nineteenth century.[24] Accordingly, the myth is cited here.

"Once upon a time fruitful Olympian ichor fell down from heaven and produced the potion of Bacchic wine, when the fruit of its vintage grew among the rocks selfgrown, untended. It was not yet named grapevine; but among the bushes, wild and luxuriant with many-twining parsley clusters, a plant grew which had in it good winestuff to make wine, being full to bursting with its burden of dewy juice. There was a great orchard of it springing up in rows, where bunch by bunch the grapes swung swaying and reddening in disorder. They ripened together, one letting its halfgrown nursery increase with different shades of purple upon the fruit, one spotted with white, in colour like foam; some of golden hue crowded thick neighbour on neighbour, others with dark bloom all over like pitch—and the wineteeming foliage intoxicated all the olives with their glorious fruit which grew beside them. Others were silvery white, but a dark mist newly made and selfsped seemed to be penetrating the unripe berries, bringing plump fruitage to the laden clusters. The twining growth of the fruit crowned the opposite pine, shading its own sheltered growth by its mass of twigs, and delighted the heart of Pan; the pine swayed by Boreas brought her branches near the bunches of grapes, and shook her fragrant leafage soaked in the blood. A serpent twisted his curving backbone about the tree, and sucked a strong draught of nectar trickling from the fruit;

24 The wild vine was seen in Trebizond by J. P. Fallmerayer (*Fragmente aus dem Orient*, p. 94).

when he had milked the Bacchic potation with his ugly jaws, the draught of the vine turned and trickled out of his throat, reddening the creature's beard with purple drops.

"The hillranging god marvelled, as he saw the snake and his chin dabbled with trickling wine; the speckled snake saw Euios, and went coiling away with his spotty scales and plunged into a deep hole in the rock hard by. When Bacchos saw the grapes with a bellyful of red juice, he bethought him of an oracle which prophetic Rheia had spoken long ago. He dug into the rock, he hollowed out a pit in the stone with the sharp prongs of his earth-burrowing pick, he smoothed the sides of the deepening hole and made an excavation like a winepress; then he made his sharp thyrsus into the cunning shape of the later sickle with curved edge, and reaped the newgrown grapes.

"A band of Satyrs was with him: one stooped to gather the clusters, one received them into an empty vessel as they were cut, one pulled off the masses of green leaves from the bibulous fruit and threw away the rubbish. Another without thyrsus or sharpened steel crouched bending forwards and spying for grapes, and put out his right hand towards the branches to pluck the fruit at the ends of the tangled vine, then Bacchos spread the fruitage in the pit he had dug, first heaping the grapes in the middle of the excavation, then arranging them in layers side by side like cornheaps on the threshing-floor, spread out the whole length of the hole. When he had got all into the hollowed place and filled it up to the brim, he trod the grapes with dancing steps. The Satyrs also, shaking their hair madly in the wind, learnt from Dionysos how to do the like. They pulled tight the dappled skins of fawns over the shoulder, they shouted the song of Bacchos sounding tongue with tongue, crushing the fruit with many a skip of the foot, crying 'Euoi!' The wine spurted up in the grapefilled hollow, the runlets were empurpled; pressed by the alternating tread the fruit bubbled out red juice with white foam. They scooped it up with oxhorns, instead of cups which had not yet been seen, so that ever after the cup of mixed wine took this divine name of Winehorn."[25]

The last lines contain a pun, which creates a connection between the "mixed" (*kerannymenos*) wine and the "bull's horn" (*keras*) as the original vessel for drinking wine. At the core of this richly elaborated myth, in which the poet even recalls the rhyta, it is not easy to separate the Cretan elements from those originating in Asia Minor. The Minoan mountain goddess was none other than Rhea (or Rheia). The snake, which led the boy Dionysos, living in the sphere of the goddess, to the enjoyment of the grape, was a mythical snake. In the Dionysos cult, the maenads of the late period used harmless snakes as a barbaric adornment of their bacchantic dress—as is first related concerning Olympias, the mother of Alexander the Great.[26] This was not always the case. We know through Andromachos, a specialist in poisons and Nero's private physician,[27] that the poisonous snakes— *echidnai*, "vipers"—that were torn to pieces in the cult of Dionysos could be caught with the least danger at the time of the early rising

25 Nonnos XII 293–362 (in Rouse, ed., I 418–23).

26 Plutarch, *Alexander* II 6. Such snakes were conspicuously displayed in the Dionysian procession of Ptolemaios Philadelphos described by Kallixeinos of Rhodes, according to Athenaios V 198 ε. This harmless variety of snake, the ὄφις παρείας, was taken over from the cult of Sabazios, in which it was probably used at an even earlier date. See Demosthenes XVIII (*De corona*), 260 [315].

27 Cited by Galen, *De antidotis* I 8 (in Kühn, ed., XIV, 45). Andromachos was a Cretan, as is stressed by Galen in *Ad Pisonem de theriaca* I (in Kühn, ed., XIV, 211), probably an authentic work despite the opinion of Hermann Diels, whom I formerly followed (see Kerényi, *Werke*, I, 397, note 408; cf. *RE*, XX:2, 1802). Andromachos was not from Pergamon, as Nilsson, *Geschichte*, I, 579, contends.

of the Pleiades.²⁸ This corresponds roughly to the first Thursday in May, when nowadays in Cocullo, a village in the Abruzzi, the *serpari*, or snake catchers, offer up living vipers to St. Dominic. According to Andromachos, gravid snakes had to be spared, which fits in with a principle of the Dionysian religion that embryos must not be harmed. The older representations of maenads on vase paintings show clearly that their snakes were dangerous but could—at least for a short time— be tamed [22A/ 22B].²⁹ Here we encounter a familiarity with snakes that is certainly prehistoric in origin. It never became characteristic for Europe and its great religions, but in some cases proved amazingly tenacious, as the example of Cocullo shows. In the Dionysian religion this familiarity had a special significance. The snake is a phenomenon of life, in which the association of life with coldness, slipperiness, mobility, and often deadly peril, makes a highly ambivalent impression.³⁰ Among the Minoans and the Greeks, women celebrants carried snakes in their hands. We have also seen that the snake could enter into a mythological context with a grape-laden vine. Of the two characteristic plants of the Dionysian religion—ivy and the vine—it was the former, "colder" plant that suggested a kinship with the snake; thus, a snake was twined into the ivy wreaths of the maenads.³¹ The

28   The ninth of May according to the Julian calendar; J. G. Frazer, *The Fasti of Ovid*, IV, 73.

29   In the painting on the Tyrrhenian amphora (Louvre E 831) in [22A/ 22B], one snake appears attacking, and another snake is held in the hand of a maenad. This is the oldest known representation of maenads. (W. M. Edwards, "Representation of Maenads," p. 80, note 17, has characterized it as the "first strikingly maenadic scene.") See J. D. Beazley, *Attic Black-Figure Vase-Painters*, p. 103, no. 108; E. Pottier, *Vases antiques du Louvre*, p. 7.

30   In this connection I quoted in *Asklepios* (p. 13) D. H. Lawrence, who says in *Apocalypse* (p. 160) that "a rustle in the grass can startle the toughest 'modern' to depths he has no control over."

31   Plutarch, *Alexander* II 6 (ἐκ τοῦ κιττοῦ) hints at it.

maenads tore the snakes to pieces as they did the other animals they carried in their hands. They also tore the ivy wreaths,[32] perhaps instead of the snakes.

The ivy motif is in general far more frequent than the vine motif in Greek art and in the Etruscan art that derives from it. Why should this be? The problem is still more radical in Minoan art where, amid the many plant designs occurring in murals and vase paintings, not a single example of the vine has been found to this day. But ivy is frequent, both in representations of nature and in stylized form as an ornament. Sir Arthur Evans was impressed by this fact, in which he found a testimony to the Minoan religion. Concerning the so-called House of Frescoes at Knossos he writes: "Among the designs depicted on the frescoes a special place must be reserved for what may be not inaptly termed the 'sacral ivy.' . . . Trailing sprays of this mystic plant, identical in all details, recur in the analogous frescoes from Hagia Triada. The outline of the leaves and the serpentine course of the central stem taken in connection with the character of the flowers sufficiently demonstrate that we have here an intentional assimilation with ivy. Yet the plant that we see here was a natural growth of no terrestrial region."[33] Thus, in the eyes of the great excavator, the ivy decoration became a kind of mystic flora. In its stylization he saw a similarity to the papyrus blossom and looked to the Nile delta for its religious meaning. This, Sir Arthur thought, was how the Minoans conceived of the vegetation on the Isle of the Blessed.

The connection between ivy and Dionysos is more firmly established. It is a significant fact that in Greece the wine god never bore

32 Plutarch, *Quaestiones Romanae* 291 A.
33 A. Evans, *Palace of Minos*, II, 478, and pl. X. On the frescoes from Hagia Triada, see R. Matton, *La Crète antique*, pls. XII 27 and XVI 36.

the name or epithet "Ampelos," "vine," but in Attica was called "Kis-sos," "ivy."[34] Ivy can, moreover, be interpreted as a term both concealing and hinting at the vine, and it bears the poetic epithet "Oinops" or "Oinopos,"[35] in which its connection with Dionysos as the wine god is boldly manifested. In a classical passage of his *Dionysos*, Walter F. Otto shows the parallel between the two plants and how they complement one another: "The vine and the ivy are like siblings who have developed in opposite directions and yet cannot deny their relationship. Both undergo an amazing metamorphosis. In the cool season of the year the vine lies as though dead and in its dryness resembles a useless stump until the moment when it feels the renewed heat of the sun and blossoms forth in a riot of green and with a fiery elixir without compare.

"What happens to the ivy is no less remarkable. Its cycle of growth gives evidence of a duality which is quite capable of suggesting the two-fold nature of Dionysos. First it puts out the so-called shade-seeking shoots, the scandent tendrils with the well-known lobed leaves. Later, however, a second kind of shoot appears which grows upright and turns toward the light. The leaves are formed completely differently, and now the plant produces flowers and berries. Like Dionysos, it could well be called the 'twice-born.' But the way in which it produces its flowers and fruit is both strikingly similar to and yet startlingly different from that found in the vine. It blooms, namely, in the autumn, when the grapes of the vine are harvested. And it produces its fruit in spring. Between its blooming and its fruiting lies the time of Dionysos' epiphany in the winter months. Thus, after its shoots have opened out and up, it shows its reverence, as it were, to the god of the

---

34 Pausanias I 31 6.
35 Sophokles, *Oedipus at Colonus* 675.

ecstatic winter festivals as a plant transformed with a new spring growth. But even without this metamorphosis it is an adornment of winter.

"While the vine of Dionysos needs as much light and heat from the sun as it can get, the ivy of Dionysos has surprisingly little need for light and warmth, and grows green and fresh in the shade and in the cold, too. In the middle of winter when the riotous festivals are celebrated, it spreads its jagged leaves out boldly over the forest floor or climbs up the tree trunks precisely as if it wished to welcome the god and dance around him as the maenads do. It has been compared to the snake, and the cold nature ascribed both to it and to the snake has been advanced as a reason for their belonging to Dionysos. The way in which it creeps over the ground or winds itself around trees can really suggest the snakes which the wild women accompanying Dionysos wind around their hair or hold in their hands."[36]

The growth of the ivy presents only soothing, comforting features. A special aspect of life is here disclosed: its least warm, almost uncanny aspect, also presented by the snake. Such is *zoë* reduced to itself, yet forever reproducing itself. In the ivy it is present not as meaning but as reality: not as the meaning of a symbol or as an allegory for abstract ideas, but concrete and reassuring despite its inedible bitter fruit. The sweet fruits are borne by the vine, which with its slow, spreading growth is capable of imparting the greatest restfulness, and with its rapidly fermenting juice of arousing the greatest unrest, a life so warm and intense that one living thing inflicts upon another that which is the irreconcilable opposite of life: death. Such were the images evoked by

36 Otto, *Dionysos: Myth and Cult*, pp. 153–55. On the association of snakes and ivy with Dionysos because of their cold natures, see Plutarch, *Quaestiones conviviales* 653 A.

vine leaves and vine, grape and grape harvest. Minoan art, especially in the atmosphere of the palaces, avoided the representation of these images as much as possible, perhaps—as it now appears—entirely.

The oldest account of a wine harvest in European literature carries a note of grief. In Homer, Hephaistos adorned the shield of Achilles with a picture of a wine harvest.[37] The vineyard is surrounded by a trench and a fence. A single path leads through them to the vines, which stand in rows supported by stakes. At the time of the wine harvest the carriers, all young girls and boys, are striding down the path, carrying baskets full of sweet grapes. A boy walks among them with a lyre, singing the *linos*, the song of lamentation. They accompany him in dance steps, with songs and cries. This is no expression of sentimentalism, but a rite based on a myth. As in Minoan Crete and present-day Greece, the next step was assuredly performed indoors. Here the *lenos*—later called *pateterion*—was set up for treading the grapes. In his description of the happy life of the Phaiakians in the Odyssey, Homer mentions the act of pressing, in which probably, as in Egypt, the mash of treaded grapeskins was put into sacks and wrung out with a device called a *tropeion* in Greek.[38] Here again, Homer makes no mention of treading. In *Works and Days*, Hesiod also passes over the treading of the grapes. He indicates the time of the wine harvest, describes in detail the making of sweet wine from dried

37 Iliad XVIII 561–72.

38 See Odyssey VII 125. The word τροπήιον, the correct reading, appears in Hipponax (in Diehl, *Anth. lyr.*, fr. 53) in the same fragment in which the sack is mentioned. The wringing occurs in the "Shield of Herakles," attributed to Hesiod, *Carmina* 301. The earliest mention of treading, as far as I am able to determine, is in Ananios, a sixth-century satiric poet; see Diehl, fr. 5, line 4. In his *Natural History*, Pliny says expressly of the making of the *diachyton* (Italian *passito*): "octavo die calcatis." On the wine harvest, see Hesiod, *Works and Days* 609–614.

grapes, but stops before the pressing, whether performed by treading or with the help of a *tropeion*.

The silence of Greek literature concerning the simple wine press —the *lenos* or *pateterion*—runs through the entire Classical period. This may be accidental, but is none the less striking in view of the constant presence in Greek life of one or another phase of wine-making. Archaic vase painting introduces superhuman beings, sileni or satyrs, as wine pressers [23],[39] and they remain the indispensable performers of this act in ancient art down to the end of antiquity—except when they are replaced by Erotes, or cupids, likewise divine beings.[40] In the Dionysian procession of Ptolemaios Philadelphos about 275 B.C., an enormous wagon bore a *lenos* in which sixty satyrs supervised by a silenus treaded out the grapes. The sweet juice ran out into the street and the wine pressers sang the *melos epilenion*, the song of the *lenos*.[41] We learn the content of such a song from a later scholarly note: it was "a song to the wine press which, like the wine press itself, involved the dismemberment of Dionysos."[42] It is stressed that this was a peasant song.[43] In a list of melodies played on the flute, various laments are

39 See S. Karouzou, *The Amasis Painter*, pl. XXIX. For a black-figure vase in Leningrad, see G. Bendinelli, *La vite e il vino*, p. 45, fig. 86; for later examples, see Bendinelli, p. 126, figs. 172–73; p. 204, figs. 251–53; p. 214, fig. 264.

40 See G. Rodenwaldt, "Der Klinensarkophag von S. Lorenzo," p. 174, fig. 50, for a Roman sarcophagus with many examples of Erotes engaged in the wine harvest. When in the latest monuments—see, for example, Bendinelli, p. 246, fig. 299, or pl. X—the treaders have in their hands the crooked staff of the shepherds and hare hunters, this remains an indication of the satyr costume.

41 See Kallixeinos of Rhodes, quoted in Athenaios V 199 A.

42 Scholium on Clement of Alexandria, *Protrepticus* I 2 2: περιεῖχεν τὸν τοῦ Διονύσου σπαραγμόν.

43 Ibid., ἀγροικικὴ ᾠδή. See Anakreon, fr. 57, in Diehl, *Anth. lyr.*: πατοῦσιν σταφυλήν . . . ἐπιληνίοισιν ὕμνοις.

followed by the *epilenion aulema*, the "flute melody to the wine press."[44]
The note of lamentation in Homer's song on the grape harvest is understandable if so sad a thing as the dismemberment of a god was
involved. Cornutus, the tutor of the Roman poet Persius, tells us that
the wine treaders invoked the god by various names, such as "Bakchos" and "Euios."[45] Reference to these scenes was made at the Second
Council of Constantinople, the Trullianum, in the year 691 A.D. Until
that date the wine treaders still cried out "Dionysos," but this was now
forbidden.[46] The council ordered that instead, whenever a load of
grapes was brought in, the treaders should cry "Kyrie eleison." At this
time the grape treaders still wore masks[47]—probably the masks of satyrs
and sileni. It is the proceedings of this council that first explained
the artistic representations which throughout antiquity showed satyrs
and sileni in the role of wine treaders: they were indeed wine treaders
in disguise.

One of the constellations that the Egyptians saw in the heavens
was a "bloodthirsty wine press."[48] The Lord spoke to Isaiah: "I have
trodden the wine press alone, and of the people there was none. For
I will tread them in mine anger and trample them in my fury. And
their blood shall be sprinkled upon my garments, and I will stain all
my raiment."[49] These are images that carry us far away from the
Greeks and yet remain close to the original Dionysos myth and Minoan

44 Pollux IV 55.
45 Cornutus, *Theologiae graecae compendium* XXIX.
46 μὴ τὸ τοῦ βδελυκτοῦ Διονύσου ὄνομα τοὺς τὴν σταφυλὴν ἐκθλίβοντας ἐν τοῖς ληνοῖς
ἐπιβοᾶν, cited by P. Koukoules, Βυζαντινῶν βίος καὶ πολιτισμός, p. 293.
47 Koukoules quotes: προσωπίδας φοροῦντες. Conversely, a Bacchic festival
with thyrsos and wreath of ivy is represented as a wine harvest—*simulacrum
vindemiae*—by Tacitus, *Annales* XI 31.
48 See S. Schott, "Das blutrünstige Keltergerät," pp. 93 ff.
49 Isaiah 63:2.

Crete. This forms the bridge between Egypt and Greece. Everything that was here enacted was a prologue only in respect to historical Greece; otherwise it was an interlude in which not only Egypt but also the Orient participated. Certain elements of the Dionysian religion that appear in this interlude may, like viticulture, have been present to the east and south of Crete either earlier or at the same time. In Crete they made their appearance in a new style characteristic of a new and original culture.

Dionysian Names

S T Y L I S T I C considerations and most particularly the conspicuous presence or absence of certain objects in works of art would suggest connections between the Minoan culture and the Dionysian religion, even if such connections were not attested by the texts. For the present the texts are exceedingly meager, consisting of little more than names. First of all, on a tablet found in the palace of Nestor on the mainland at Pylos, which lies within the sphere of Minoan culture, we find the name of the god all by itself in the genitive: *di-wo-nu-so-jo*, "Dionysoio."[50] The clay tablet is broken off after the word. What probably followed was an indication of measure. The text may then have run: "Of [that which is of] Dionysos, so and so much." On a second tablet stands *di-wo-nu-so-jo* as a payment to a man, *tu-ni-jo*; again the line, probably containing an indication of measure, is broken off. On the other side, another payment is recorded, a payment of something that is still incomprehensible: *no-pe-ne-o[* to *wo-no-wa-ti-si*, that is, *oinoatisi*, "women

50 Pylos Xa 102.

of Oinoa." In both tablets "that which is of Dionysos" can hardly refer to anything but wine. The place name "Oinoa" probably still carried the original meaning of the word: "place of wine." Employed as a name for places or rivers, the word occurs at least twenty times, with different endings, in Greece.[51] Women thus identified were in all likelihood Dionysian women, such as those who later on in Greece formed special corporations—in Athens the fourteen Gerairai, in Elis the Sixteen Women, and in Delphi the Thyiades. Another short text from Pylos speaks of one "Eleuther, son of Zeus" to whom oxen were sacrificed.[52] "Eleuther," or "Eleutheros," corresponding to the *Liber pater* of the Romans, can only be Dionysos, especially as he is expressly termed the son of Zeus. This text, originating on the Greek mainland in the thirteenth century B.C. when the palace of Nestor was in its heyday, already bears witness to the Dionysian religion and to the well-known lineage of the god.

On Crete similar testimony is provided by "Pentheus," written *pe-te-u* on a tablet found in Knossos.[53] Among the attested names of the Greeks, no other corresponds to this spelling. The bearers of Dionysian names at Knossos were men mentioned in connection with various religious functions along with persons whose names have no visible religious significance. Proper names at all times give rise to problems that cannot be solved through knowledge of the language alone. As a rule one must also know the religion and mythology prevailing at the time when the names were given. How could we understand why cer-

---

51 Pylos Xb 1419: *di-wo-nu-so-jo*[. . . / *tu-ni-jo*[. . . / / *no-pe-ne-o*[. . . / *wo-no-wa-ti-si*[. . . ; see J. Puhvel, "Eleuther and Oinoatis: Dionysiac Data from Mycenaean Greece," p. 168.

52 Pylos Cn 3.1–2: *jo-i-je-si me-za-na e-re-u-te-re di-wi-je-we qu-o*; see Puhvel, p. 164.

53 Knossos As 603.

tain girls were given the name "Dolores" if we did not know that they were probably born on the day of *Mater dolorosa*, which in Spanish is also called *Dolores*. This name is intended to place them under the special protection of the Mother of God. Without knowledge of the life of Christ, the name would be utterly incomprehensible. Such is the case with the Cretan name "Pentheus," which embraces *penthos* and *dolores* and signifies a person who, for some reason, is called "full of suffering."

The name "Pentheus" presupposes the myth of a god who suffers for a time but then triumphs over suffering. Only on the strength of such a divine tale could a man bear such a name. It is in the myth of Dionysos that such names as "Pentheus" and "Megapenthes"—"he of great suffering"—occur later on, in Greece.[54] In the versions of the myth that have come down to us, Pentheus and Megapenthes were adversaries of the god who inflicted suffering on him and were in turn punished with suffering. Originally the "man of suffering"—Pentheus or Megapenthes—was the god himself. There were probably differences between the Dionysian religion of the Late Minoan period, in which the name Pentheus originated, and that of the era of Greek tragedy, in which Pentheus appears on the stage as the punished persecutor of the god. These differences would be due not to the essence of the Dionysian religion but to the relationship between man and the gods. Among the Greeks of the historic period, no names were given that would have gone as far as those of the Minoan period in relating a

54 On Pentheus, see Kerényi, *The Gods of the Greeks*, pp. 262 f. (Pelican edn., p. 231). On Megapenthes, see Kerényi, *The Heroes of the Greeks*, pp. 54, 55, 81. According to Homer, Megapenthes was the name of one of Menelaos' sons. In his name the son bore his father's "great sorrow," for Menelaos had no son by Helen; Megapenthes was born of a slave woman (Odyssey IV 11–12). See Kerényi, *The Gods of the Greeks*, pp. 250 ff.

man to a god. The core of the myth that the Greeks found in the Cretan palaces did not change, but changes did occur in the tales that adapted the myth to later times.

The suffering embraced in the name "Pentheus" belongs to the prehistory of Greek tragedy.[55] The prehistory of comedy in Greece includes Phales, a divine figure who was carried about in processions in honor of Dionysos and celebrated in song as his friend and companion.[56] The phallus, exciting image of excited *zoë*, has often been termed a "fertility symbol." This extreme abstraction misses the concrete character of the object carried about in wooden replica. A live snake never produces the effect of a mere symbol, nor did this image, even if women and young girls looked upon it with chaste reserve. *Phallagogiai* or *phallophoriai*, as the festive processions with great phalli were called, are nowhere to be seen in the art of the Minoans or Mycenaeans. Whether Phales occurs among their proper names, as Michael Ventris at first believed, is not certain,[57] but other, similar names are attested with certainty. For example, a shepherd in Pylos was named *sa-ni-io*, probably "Sannion," a word with the same meaning as "Phales,"[58] while at Knossos we find *si-ra-no*, "Silanos,"[59] a name given to the phallic, half-animal, half-human beings, the sileni, companions of Dionysos imitated in Greece by human dancers.

The absence of representations of this kind on the walls of the

55 Kerényi, "Die Bacchantinnen des Euripides," *Werke*, II, 283 f.

56 Aristophanes, *Acharnians* 236.

57 The written form of the name would be *pa-re*, which Ventris read as "Phales" in his 1953 *Glossary*. In the third edition of *The Knossos Tablets* (edited by Chadwick and Killen), *pe-re* is read in one place and the reading in the other place has never been certain.

58 Pylos An 5.6 and Cn 4.3. See O. Landau, *Mykenisch-griechische Personennamen*, p. 189, on σάννιον αἰδοῖον.

59 Knossos V 466.1. See Landau, p. 257.

palaces can be explained by the restraint and stylistic laws of art. Images and objects less decent than the familiar objects of high Minoan art are not lacking[60] but, like the cruder representations of later periods, they play a peripheral role and show little art in their execution.[61] A popular scene otherwise unknown to us is skillfully depicted on a steatite vessel from the Late Minoan palace of Hagia Triada, which can be dated at roughly 1500 B.C. The scene is of a procession with implements, probably pitchforks, which were used for beating the trees in the olive harvest. In its own sphere—not of wine but of oil —this procession may be compared with the *komos*, a Dionysian procession,[62] but the musical instrument held by one of the leaders of the procession is of Egyptian origin. It is a sistrum, proof that borrowings from Egypt were possible in this sphere also.

According to Herodotos, the *phallophoriai* originated in Egypt.[63] Melampous, the soothsayer and priest—with whom Megapenthes, the persecutor of Dionysos in Argos, was compelled to share his kingdom[64] and who, to judge by this legend, belonged to the Mycenaean period— introduced the phalli into Greece as a characteristic component of the

60 P. Demargne, "Deux représentations de la déesse Minoenne dans la nécropole de Mallia," pp. 305 ff.

61 These include perhaps some twenty phalluslike objects which were preserved at Knossos in front of the palace, in a pit by the "royal loggia," possibly as votive offerings. Half of a "horn of consecration" such as adorned the Minoan shrines lay beside them. I owe these details to Professor Nikolaos Platon, who dates the objects at roughly 2000–1700 B.C.

62 J. Forsdyke, "The 'Harvester' Vase of Hagia Triada," p. 8. Marinatos thought of an olive harvest (or threshing, which is certainly wrong); see his comment to pls. 103–5 in Marinatos and Hirmer, *Crete and Mycenae*, where the vessel is reproduced.

63 Herodotos II 48 2. See the Egyptian parallels in A. Wiedmann, *Herodots zweites Buch mit sachlichen Erläuterungen*, pp. 233 ff.

64 See Kerényi, *The Heroes of the Greeks*, p. 295.

cult of the god whose exegete he was.[65] In the Egyptian processions that Herodotos compares with the Greek *phallophoriai* the women carried such statues, which were themselves immobile and moved only their disproportionately large phalli. This was done by means of a mechanism built into the figures. The name "Sannion" expresses this motion: translated, it signifies "the wagging one."[66] Herodotos skips over Crete which may well have been the intermediate link for this procession as well as for the calendar based on the rising of Sirius. Two Minoan proper names, at least one of which must be regarded as Dionysian, are attributable to the importance of this star.

Iakar and Iakchos

WHEN IN EGYPT the early rising of Sirius became the beginning of the year, the approach of a better season could be foreseen by the first swelling of the Nile. Yet this was also the time of the most dangerous heat: a highly ambivalent season! The same was true in Crete and Greece (with the exception that there was no Nile). The heat was obviously evil, and so was the star with whose appearance it began. But in a mysterious way the season was also good. In Greek it was called *opora*, a word that is not easy to translate because it means not only the season but its fruits as well. Homer knew Sirius as "Orion's dog." As *Alpha canis* it belongs to the great hunter whose gigantic figure had already dominated the heavens for months and would continue to do so for several months more until, stung by the celestial scorpion,

---

65 Herodotos II 49: ὁ ἐξηγησάμενος τοῦ Διονύσου τό τε ὄνομα καὶ τὴν πομπὴν τοῦ φαλλοῦ.

66 From σαίνειν.

it sank below the horizon.⁶⁷ The full ambivalence of Sirius is expressed by a metaphor in the twenty-second book of the Iliad. As Achilles ran, "the bronze on his breast flashed out like the star that comes to us in autumn, outshining all its fellows in the evening sky—they call it Orion's Dog, and though it is the brightest of all stars it bodes no good, bringing much fever, as it does, to us poor wretches."⁶⁸

Opora, whose star is Sirius according to Homer,⁶⁹ does not exactly coincide with the autumn when Sirius rises for the first time at dusk. The season extends some fifty days from the second half of July to the middle of September, when, according to Hesiod, the situation of Orion in the center of the sky and the early rising of Arcturus give the signal for the wine harvest.⁷⁰ In his *Laws*, Plato mentions two gifts of this season: treasures that could be stored (namely, fruits), and something more sublime and less easily stored (*athesauriston*)—Dionysian joy.⁷¹ According to Pindar, the "pure light of high summer" (*hagnon phengos oporas*)⁷² is Dionysian, or perhaps it is even Dionysos himself.

67 See "Flaming New Year," at the beginning of ch. II, above.
68 Iliad XXII 26–31 (E. V. Rieu translation, Penguin edn., pp. 397–98).
69 Iliad XXII 26: ὀπώρης. ἀστὴν ὀπωρινός is the phrase in Iliad V 5.
70 *Works and Days* 609–11.
71 Plato, *Laws* VIII 844 D: τὴν παιδιὰν Διονυσίαδα ἀθησαύριστον.
72 See Bowra, *Pindari Carmina*, fr. 140:

> δενδρέων δὲ νομὸν Διώ-
> νυσος πολυγαθὴς αὐξάνοι,
> ἀγνὸν φέγγος ὀπώρας.

The last line permits two interpretations. *Hagnon phengos oporas* can be in apposition to Dionysos, in which case the god himself is the "pure light of high summer"; or it can be in apposition to δενδρέων νομόν, the orchards which Dionysos is expected to make grow, in which case the "pure light of late summer" is created by Dionysos. In either case, directly or indirectly, the light comes from him.

A vase painter of the fifth century[73] wrote next to the childlike figure of the god emerging from the thigh of Zeus: *Dios phos*, "light of Zeus." This light was originally the light of Sirius and the gift promised by the verdant vineyards, a gift of the ambivalent star.

Before Dionysos as wine god came to them from the south, the Greeks seem to have contented themselves with a mythical king as inventor of the vine and with Sirius as the actual giver. From that time on the vine possessed a myth of its origin: because of the star's movements in the sky, the discovery of the vine was related to Orion's dog. The home of this myth was Aitolia in the western part of the Greek mainland, bordering the territory of the western Locrians, mountainous regions far removed from Crete.[74] Hekataios of Miletos, the Ionian historian, transforms the myth into a genealogical tale.[75] A wild hunter (this quality is expressed by the name "Orestheus," "man of the mountains," which presents an assonance with "Orion"), a son of Deukalion, the first man, comes to Aitolia in search of a kingdom. His she-dog gives birth to a stick. He buries the stick, probably because it is an abortion. It soon turns out to be the first vine, a gift of the celestial dog, the dog of Orion, who may be recognized in the wild hunter. After the event Orestheus names his son "Phytios," "planter." *His* son in turn was named "Oineus," after *oine*, "vine." In another form of the myth

73   The so-called Diosphos painter. See C. H. E. Haspels, *Attic Black-Figured Lekythoi*, p. 96, with Beazley's explanatory remark about the vase painting and inscription. In his *Attic Black-Figure Vase-Painters*, p. 509, no. 120, Beazley points out a false interpretation given by H. Fuhrmann in "Athamas," pp. 111 ff. A correct classification as the oldest example of a representation of the birth of the god from the thigh of Zeus is to be found in A. D. Trendall, "A Volute Krater at Taranto," pp. 175–76 and pl. IX.

74   Strabo IX 4 10.

75   Hekataios, fr. 8, in Jacoby, *FGrHist*; Kerényi, *The Heroes of the Greeks*, pp. 113 f.

which obviously draws on the Dionysian religion, a he-goat disappears at intervals from the herds of Oineus and returns sated. The king has a shepherd with a name similar to that of the hunter in the older tale.[76] This shepherd finds out that the goat has been eating from a grape-laden vine, and thus Oineus becomes the first man to make wine of these grapes. In all the tales, however, it is clear that wine cannot be made without instruction from Dionysos! The god visits the king, or more correctly Queen Althaia, as in Athens each year he visited the wife of the bearer of the king's name, the *archon basileus*. Oineus had respectfully withdrawn and thus received the wine as a gift indeed.[77] In the myth's simpler, assuredly original form preserved among the Locrians, there is no mention of a special wine hero named "Oineus," but only of the hunter Orestheus and his dog. From the stick that he buried, sprang, in the form of branches—*ozoi*—not only the grape but also men, the Ozolian Locrians.[78]

Only gradually did this myth develop into a purely Dionysian sacred history. The name "Orestheus" and a common hunter were perhaps substituted for Orion only by Hekataios or shortly before his time. According to the story of Orion's birth (his emergence from a leather sack), Orion belonged to the age of honey. His relation to wine was not nearly as definite and well ordered as that of Dionysos. At the court on Chios of King Oinopion, who was probably a wine-inventor hero similar to Oineus and only later was made into a son of Dionysos, Orion behaved like a being of the primordial age still unfamiliar with wine, and he fell victim to it. As punishment for the wild actions per-

76 In *Mythographi Vaticani*, I, 87, this shepherd is named "Orista"; in Servius (who quotes Probos) *Commentarii in Vergilium Georgica* II 1, he is named "Staphylus" after σταφυλή, "grape."

77 Hyginus, *Fabulae* 129. 78 Pausanias X 38 1.

formed in his drunken state, he was blinded by Oinopion.[79] Aristaios, who belongs to the next cultural stage, that between honey and wine, commanded that on Keos the rising of Sirius be greeted with a dance of warriors, but at the same time he did everything possible to attenuate the harmful influence of the dog star.[80] In Egypt still another special measure was taken to this effect, and Minoan Crete also seems to have participated in this protective magic.

At Knossos we find the name *i-wa-ko*, whose Greek reading can be "Iakos," "Iachos," or "Iakchos"; at Knossos and Pylos it often takes the form of *i-wa-ka*.[81] "Iakar," a name for Sirius that seems utterly alien to the Greek language, may not really have been so foreign.[82] An Egyptian story can be cited in connection with the Minoan names "Iakar" and "Iakchos."[83] "Iachen" or "Iachim" was the name of a wise and pious man in Egypt who allegedly lived under King Senyes.[84] This man may also have been a divine figure. He was said to have softened the fiery power of Sirius at its early rising and thus to have wiped out the epidemics that raged at that time. After his death he was buried in a temple tomb, and when the appropriate sacrificial rites had been completed the priests took fire from his altar and carried it about, apparently in a magic ritual directed against the destructive fire of the star.

Through Dionysos this fire was transformed into the "pure light of high summer." In the person of the son of the god of heaven, it was

79   See Kerényi, *The Gods of the Greeks*, p. 202 (Pelican edn., p. 178).

80   See above, in ch. II, the section on "The Awakening of the Bees."

81   For *i-wa-ko*, see Knossos tablet As 1516.18. For *i-wa-ka*, see Knossos V 60.2, Uf 120; Pylos Jn 310, Ub 1317.

82   ’Ιακάρ· ὁ κύων ἀστήρ.

83   See *Suidae Lexicon*, II, 616, line 2; Aelian, fr. 105.

84   This king is otherwise unknown. See H. Kees ("Senyes," col. 1541), who remarks that "this story surely goes back to an Egyptian source."

received as the "light of Zeus." Hesychios defines the Greek word *iachron*—an adjective known to us only from his lexicon—as "bathed in a soft Zeus-light," further described by Hesychios as "εὐδιεινόν." Such light was placed, quite concretely, in the hand of a divine figure regarded as a double for Dionysos. This figure's name, which comes from the same root as the two Minoan proper names cited above,[85] probably took its definitive form "Iakchos" from the insistent cry with which it was repeated in the processions. There can be no question of a deification of the cry alone. For the Greeks, Iakchos had *two* characteristics: his name was called loudly in endless repetition, and he was a torchbearer.[86] In the figure of Iakchos, Dionysos' connection with light and fire was preserved. "Fire is a Dionysian weapon," says Lucian.[87] The bacchantes were capable of carrying fire in their hair.[88] In the *Antigone* of Sophokles the chorus calls on Dionysos, "who leads the round of the fire-spraying stars," to cure the sick city of Thebes. It might have invoked a true star in the sky in such terms, but it invokes him as "Iakchos, keeper of treasures" (*tamian Iakchon*)—keeper of the annual Dionysian treasures, which he confers.[89]

Dionysos brought this aspect with him from his Minoan origins, from the days of his connection with the flaming onset of the Sirius year. In Athens the procession in which a statue of the torch-bearing Iakchos was borne was held at the end of the *opora*; it ushered in the great Mysteries of Eleusis, in which, at the time of the wine harvest, a Divine Child was born in the underworld.[90] The loudly invoked Iak-

---

85 Their phonetic form distinguishes them from the Homeric ἰαχή, ἰάχω, later also ἰαχέω, originally also with ν in the first syllable.

86 As can be seen in reliefs from the Athenian agora.

87 *Bacchus* III.

88 Euripides, *Bacchae* 757–58.

89 Sophokles, *Antigone* 1146–52.

90 See Kerényi, *Eleusis*, pp. 62–64.

chos was the "light-bringing star of the nocturnal mysteries." So Aristophanes calls him in the *Frogs*, where he puts the procession on the stage in somewhat modified form as a procession of the blessed dead in Elysium.[91] From the first century B.C. we have a statement (the credibility of which is discussed below, in the section on "Ariadne") to the effect that the same Mysteries which in Eleusis only the initiates were permitted to behold, were at Knossos performed in the sight of all.[92] Even in Athens the procession with the statue of Iakchos and the cries of his name could not be kept wholly secret. More than a thousand years elapsed between the appearance of the Minoan name and the first-century statement referred to above. The period during which the divine name *pa-ya-vo* (Greek *paiaon*) appeared at Knossos and the cry of *paian* resounded at Delphi and throughout Greece was no shorter, although it was richer in testimonies, beginning with Homer.[93]

91   The text (*Frogs* 340–42) should be read as follows:

ἔγειρει φλογέας λαμπάδας ἐν χερσὶ τινάσσων—
     ″Ιακχ᾽ ὦ ″Ιακχε—
νυκτέρου τελετῆς φωσφόρος ἀστήρ.

Kindles the flaming torches, brandishing one in each hand,
     Iakchos, O Iakchos!
The light-bringing star of the nocturnal mysteries.

The middle line is a *versus intercalatus*, a refrain, syntactically independent both of the preceding and of the following line, whereas these other two lines are connected. Accordingly I read ἔγειρει instead of ἔγειρε. After ἐν χερσί, γὰρ ἥκει was added by way of explanation. This confirms the third person.

The chief difference in the processions was probably that in this one described by Aristophanes, Iakchos was called but not carried along, as he was from Athens to Eleusis. From line 340 on, the participants believed that he appeared before them. In line 350, σὺ δὲ λαμπάδι is addressed to the leader of the chorus, one of the blessed (μάκαρ), not to Iakchos.

92   See Kerényi, *Eleusis*, p. 8.
93   See Kerényi, *Asklepios*, pp. XVII–XVIII, 81–82.

Zagreus

A FURTHER PROBE into the history of Minoan and Greek culture carries us back to the days of primitive hunters. Two objects pertaining to the historical Dionysos cult, the mask and the goat, appear on a stone seal in a tomb near Phaistos: the mask is a manifestation of the god, and the goat (a characteristic sacrificial animal of the Dionysian religion) is his substitute. In the center, between two large goats, the cut stone shows a human face which differs from other faces in small Minoan monuments [24].[94] It is unmistakably a mask, a precursor of the archaic Dionysos masks known to us from vase paintings and statuary.[95] It is reasonable to include the seal among the monuments of the Dionysian religion.[96] The connecting link is provided by the wooden masks that were used in the Dionysos cult, either worn by dancers or hung on a pole or tree in the center of the rite. The *zoë* that is present in all living creatures became a spiritual reality as man opened himself to it, perceiving it in a kind of *second sight*. Man did not form a concept or idea of *zoë*. He experienced its immediate nearness in the animal. To those who did not wear them, the masks communicated a strangely ambivalent experience of *zoë* as uncannily near and at the same time remote. Such was the impression made by the god himself when he was only a face. He appeared to man with human features: more immediate

94   See L. Savignoni, "Scavi e scoperte nella necropoli di Phaestos," p. 622, fig. 96, also pl. IX. Cf. p. 623: "nello spazio centrale una testa umana con orecchi larghi e mento prominente." The seal is dated to approximately 1400–1300 B.C.

95   See below, in ch. VI, the section on "The Thigh Birth and the Idol with the Mask."

96   T. B. L. Webster, *From Mycenae to Homer*, p. 50.

than *zoë* in all other forms and yet lifeless, as though removed from every living thing.

Many stones carved by the Minoans represent fantastic beings which cannot, or can no longer, belong to the world of life: beings composed of both animal and human elements or equipped with wings that in nature do not grow from such bodies. This use of wings—an indication that the limits of nature were surpassed in an additional, purely visionary dimension—extends to the early Archaic art of the Greeks. Sometimes it characterizes all the participants in a mythological scene as divine.[97] On a Minoan gem from Kydonia, however, a ruler of at least part of the world of living things appears without wings: he is unmistakably a "lord of the wild beasts" [25].[98] His relationship to the two lions flanking him is clearly expressed in his gesture—he rests his hands on the heads of the erect animals. This type of figure was later provided with wings and as "Oriental Dionysos" was taken from the Near East into Hellenistic art.[99] This fact and the Greek name of a similar deity, "Zagreus," who was connected with the Orphic myth of Dionysos, make it seem highly probable that on the Kydonia seal we have a representation of the Cretan Dionysos. The god holds fast the lions, two living beasts of prey, with his bare hands.

97 See the representation of the birth of a god from the head of a goddess on a seventh-century pithos. Discovery and partial publication by N. M. Kontoleon, in *Kykladika*, II (1956), fig. 5; and *Kretika Chronika*, XV–XVI (1961–62), Part 1, pl. LI 1.

98 Concerning this find, Evans (in *JHS*, XXI, 1901, p. 164) wrote: "Discovered in the immediate neighbourhood of Canea, on or near the site of the ancient Kydonia." See also V. E. G. Kenna, *Cretan Seals*, pl. XVIII 9P.

99 See E. Langlotz, "Dionysos," p. 177, figs. 11, 12; C. Picard, "Dionysos Psilax," pp. 317 ff.; B. Segall, "Sculpture from Arabia Felix," pp. 212 ff., pl. LIX 2; *AM*, LI (1926), pl. XIX.

He tames them, as it were, by a "laying on" of hands. He draws them into his sphere of influence and holds them captive.

In Greek, a hunter who catches living animals is called *zagreus*. Later Greek scholars interpret the name as "great hunter" by analogy with *zatheos*, "thoroughly divine."[100] But the Ionian word *zagre*,[101] signifying "pit for the capture of live animals," proves that the name contains within it the root of *zoë* and *zoön*, "life" and "living thing." An exact translation of "Zagreus" would be "catcher of game." *Sa-ke-re-u* occurs as a proper name at Pylos in various grammatical forms—once as the name of a priest.[102] It seems plausible to render it as "Zagreus,"[103] although the script possessed a special sign for *za–*. A priest of Dionysos at Pylos, who in his sacerdotal capacity takes the name of his god and imitates him as a hunter who catches live animals, seems perfectly conceivable.

Crete was a great hunting ground before the introduction of viticulture and remained one after the vineyards died out. Divine hunters and huntresses played a prominent role in Cretan mythology. Orion was hunting on Crete when he threatened to exterminate all the animals on earth and when the earth for this reason sent the scorpion against him.[104] A Cretan huntress was Britomartis, daughter of Zeus, an Artemis-like goddess who probably had her name—which means "the sweet virgin"—as an epithet. Minos pursued her for nine months,[105] assuredly as a hunter. In the furrows of a thrice-plowed field, Demeter

---

100 *Etymologicum Gudianum* s.v. Ζαγρεύς.

101 In Hesychios the ending is Ionic: Ζάγρη, βόθρος, λάπαθον.

102 Pylos tablets Ea 56, 304, 756 (*i-je-re-wo*), 776.

103 L. A. Stella, "La religione greca nei testi micenei," p. 34.

104 See above, in ch. III, the beginning of the section on "Iakar and Iakchos."

105 See Kerényi, *The Gods of the Greeks*, pp. 147 f. (Pelican edn., p. 131).

gave herself to a hunter by the name of "Iasion" or "Iasios."[106] As the greatest among these Cretan hunters we must count the one called "Zagreus," because his characteristic was the catching of game. Where he is first mentioned in Greek literature, he is spoken of as the highest of all the gods. The line comes from the *Alkmeonis*, an epic written in the sixth century if not earlier:

πότνια Γῆι Ζαγρεῦ τε Θεῶν πανυπέρτατε πάντων

Mistress earth and Zagreus who art above all other gods![107]

An invocation thus connecting Zagreus with the earth goddess Gaia and placing him above all the gods must mean that the author regarded him as one of the greatest gods of the Greek religion: probably the supreme god of heaven (as the counterpart of Mother Earth), Father Zeus, or the other Zeus, the Zeus of the underworld. Just this is twice attested by Aischylos, once in a tragedy and once in a satire, both of which survive only in fragments. The one bears witness to the identity of Zagreus with Plouton, or Hades, the Zeus of the underworld; the other, to his identity with Plouton's son in the underworld.[108] On Crete, Dionysos was looked upon as the son of Zeus and Persephone,[109] and for that reason he was also called "Chthonios," "the subterranean," and "Zagreus."[110]

We may justifiably ask, Why was this great mythical hunter, who in Greece became a mysterious god of the underworld, a capturer of

106   Ibid., p. 113 (Pelican edn., p. 99).

107   See G. Kinkel, ed., *Epicorum Graecorum fragmenta*, fr. 3.

108   Nauck, *TGF*, frs. 5, 228.

109   Diodorus Siculus V 75 4; Firmicus Maternus, *De errore profanarum religionum* VI 5.

110   *Etymologicum Magnum* s.v. Ζαγρεύς. See also Kallimachos, frs. 43, 117.

wild animals and not a killer? What are the implications of "capturing alive"? What threatens those who are captured alive, if they are not divine maidens like Britomartis, or the Pleiades who were hunted by Orion and finally transformed into stars?[111] On a bronze shield from the Greek period of Crete,[112] carried in cult dances performed in honor of the Divine Child in the Idaean Cave and found in the excavation of that cave, we see the "lord of the wild beasts" with a different gesture from that on the gem from Kydonia. Under the influence of Assyrian art, he is represented here with a beard, but what interests us most is that he is stepping on the head of a bull and seems to be holding up and rending a lion. In this instance a lion is torn to pieces, but on Crete that could also be the fate of a bull. The bull games of the Cretans were a continuation of the bull capture, enacted in the form of a drama. It seems hardly credible that in a wild Dionysos cult such powerful animals should have been torn to pieces alive by the teeth of the participants and devoured raw, but we have express testimony showing that this monstrous rite occurred in a feast of Dionysos repeated every two years.[113] Even later the god retained epithets such as "Omestes"[114] and "Omadios,"[115] signifying "eater of raw flesh." In a chorus of his tragedy *Cretan Men*, Euripides speaks of the performance in the Idaean Cave of rites in which raw meat was eaten.[116] Thus, the purpose of the

111   See Kerényi, *The Gods of the Greeks*, p. 201 (Pelican edn., p. 178).

112   From the eighth century, according to E. Kunze, *Kretische Bronze-reliefs*, p. 247 and pl. 49. S. Benton dates it somewhat later in "The Date of the Cretan Shields," pp. 52 ff.

113   Firmicus Maternus, *De errore* VI 5.

114   Plutarch, *Themistocles* XIII, *De cohibenda ira* XIII.

115   Porphyry, *De abstinentia* II 55; Alkaios, fr. 129 (in Lobel and Page, *Poetarum Lesbiorum Fragmenta*); Quandt, *Orphei hymni* XXX 5, LII 7.

116   Nauck, *TGF*, fr. 472; see now R. Cantarella, *Euripide, I Cretesi*, pp. 23 ff.

"catching alive" evidently lay in the rending of the captive animals and the devouring of their raw flesh.

Euripides calls the god to whom the cave belongs "Zeus Idaios." Yet it is not of Zeus but only of Dionysos that we may say: "No single Greek god even approaches Dionysos in the horror of his epithets, which bear witness to a savagery that is absolutely without mercy." Having made this observation, Walter Otto asks: "Where does this put us? Surely there can be no further doubt that this puts us into death's sphere."[117] Seen in the history of civilization, it is the sphere of a society of wild hunters, who on certain occasions identified themselves with beasts of prey. These occasions, their "feast days," must be regarded as realizations of aggressive, murderous life. Crete must have had cult societies of this type both before and, in certain forms, simultaneously with its high palace culture. The modern literature has cited similar phenomena among the Arabs of Africa.[118] A noteworthy analogy is provided by the religious societies of the Aissaoua in Morocco. Among their various groups it is the panther- and lion-men who must acquire the same attitude toward living flesh as the animals with which they identify themselves.[119] This may be regarded not as an emanation of the Greek Dionysian religion[120] but rather as a migration or survival of a prehistoric rite. It is conceivable that this rite originated in pre-Hellenic Crete, where, in any case, the cruel cult underwent a decisive transformation.

117   Otto, *Dionysos*, p. 113.
118   J. E. Harrison, *Prolegomena to the Study of Greek Religion*, pp. 485 ff., citing the account of Nilus (in Migne, *Patrologia Graeca*); H. Jeanmaire, *Dionysos*, pp. 259 ff., citing René Bruel, *Essai sur la confrérie religieuse des Aissâoua au Maroc*; E. R. Dodds, *The Greeks and the Irrational*, p. 276, quoting Ernest Thesiger's account of a Tangierian rite.
119   Jeanmaire, *Dionysos*, pp. 259 f.
120   R. Eisler, "Nachleben dionysischer Mysterienriten," pp. 172–83.

To judge by Euripides' picture, the cause of the transformation would seem to have been that the mysteries of Zagreus were taken into the higher Zeus religion. In *Cretan Men*, Euripides' tragedy dealing with the birth of the Minotaur and the fate of Pasiphaë, the chorus consists of consecrated priests of the Idaean Zeus, who have come from their cypress-wood temple, erected in the cypress woods. Clad all in white, they avoid all contact with birth or death and they abstain from meat. Then they confer initiation, which also signifies purification, upon those who have eaten red meat.[121] This, according to the text, they do by means of the "thunders of the nocturnal Zagreus,"[122] who in this connection can only stand for a "nocturnal Zeus." We know that in a very late period, the initiation in the Idaean Cave was performed with a "thunderstone," *keraunia lithos*.[123] The "catching alive" and the "eating of raw flesh" are the preliminary phases of an initiation whose highest degree has been attained by the pure, white-clad priests who no longer eat meat. These early phases—the catching and the eating—must have seemed base and uncanny from the standpoint of the Zeus religion, but it is unlikely that this mystery cult came into being on their account. Elsewhere the Zeus religion is not related to any special need for purity or to the sparing of life. The transformation occurred when the very god whose example led men to "capture alive" was recognized in the animal caught alive and eaten raw—the bull, according to the attested Cretan rite. In the bull god—worshiped as

121 ὁσιωθείς; in Nauck, *TGF* (p. 505), fr. 472, line 15. See also line 12: Τοὺς [τὰς τ'] ὠμοφάγους δαίτας τελέσας. This interpretation is supported by Hesychios: Ὠμοφάγου δαίτας, τὰς τὰ ὠμὰ κρέα μερίζοντας καὶ ἐσθίοντας.

122 νυκτιπόλου Ζαγρέως βροντάς (line 11, in which the accusative is an accusative of content, attaching to τελέσας, line 12).

123 Porphyry, *Vita Pythagorae* XVII; E. Platakis, Τὸ 'Ιδαῖον ἄντρον, p. 48, note 44.

Dionysos in Greece, but also as Zeus on Crete—the hunter god, Zagreus, was recognized.

Greek scholars who tried to explain the origin of their gods denied that Dionysos could have had an anthropomorphic origin.[124] It is indeed hard to believe that the Dionysian religion originated in the vision of a god with the form of a man. A single human form would not have been a vision of *zoë*. It does seem reasonably evident, however, that the figure of a great hunter who captured live animals would have contributed to such a vision. The Greek scholars who denied the anthropomorphic origin of the gods were *physiologoi*, "explainers of nature." To their minds Dionysos' origin was simply the development of the grape, the origin of wine. Yet this origin, too, was presided over by the image of Orion, the wild hunter in the sky, an image pertaining to the age when hunting was the chief occupation of man.

The net used in catching animals alive played a more prominent part in Cretan-Mycenaean art and in Cretan mythology than any other instrument of the hunt. The wild bull—the *Bos primigenius*—was caught in a net,[125] and Britomartis, the divine maiden, jumped into a net from a steep cliff in the Dikte mountains.[126] She was also called "Diktynna," and this name was certainly formed from the word *diktys*, "net." It is no longer known whether the wild goats of the high mountains in Crete, the *agrimi*, were once caught in nets. In the Dionysos cult, in which the game captured alive was eaten raw, animals easy to catch and

124 Diodorus Siculus III 62 2: γένεσιν μὲν τούτου ἀνθρωπόμορφον μηδὲ γεγονέναι τὸ παράπαν.

125 Representations on a golden cup from Vaphio and a gold seal from Rutsi near Pylos, in Marinatos and Hirmer, *Crete and Mycenae*, pls. 179 and 209 (at the bottom). See also S. Marinatos, Θέατρα καὶ θεάματα τοῦ Μεσογειακοῦ Πολιτισμοῦ, pp. 180 ff.

126 See Kerényi, *The Gods of the Greeks*, p. 147 (Pelican edn., pp. 130 f.).

tear apart always served as sacrificial animals: in the end fawns were replaced by common kids. In the sky Orion is a hunter of hares; the hare was seen in the constellation under his feet.[127] In an illustration of the didactic astronomical poem of Aratos, Orion is equipped for hare-hunting with a *pedum* or *lagobolon*, a crooked staff, and with an animal skin:[128] stunned with the staff, the hare ran into the net and was caught alive in the skin. On a Roman sarcophagus adorned with Greek compositions, a young hunter god, a cult image parallel to the bearded Dionysos, holds in his hand a *pedum* and an object that can safely be identified as a net.[129] Here we have a non-mystical Dionysos-Zagreus.

We may ask, How did the maenad catch the live hare which she presents to Dionysos in a vase painting by the Amasis painter? Presumably she caught it in the retinue of a hunter who was once named Orion. For her, however, he was not the giant, but the youthful god in hunting boots, a vision of Dionysos [26][130] that became widespread in Greece some time later than the sixth-century vase from Ceglie depicting him thus. The Homeric Hymn to Dionysos tells us how his divine presence spread through the forest and mountains after he had

127 Aratos, *Phaenomena* 338–39.

128 Codex Vossianus, Lat. qto., 79; G. Thiele, *Antike Himmelsbilder*, p. 128, fig. 45; O. Höfer, "Orion," col. 1027.

129 Rome, Museo Nazionale della Terme, no. 106429 (= no. 94 in R. Paribeni's 1932 catalogue, no. 64 in S. Aurigemma's 1946 catalogue). See also Kerényi, "Il dio cacciatore," p. 131.

130 See A. D. Trendall, *Frühitaliotische Vasen*, pl. XXIV. In the representation of the so-called Bema of Phaidros in the Theater of Dionysos in Athens, the shoes (*cothurni*) are particularly conspicuous. See J. N. Svoronos, *Das Athener Nationalmuseum*, I, pl. LXII (at the bottom). They have been mistakenly interpreted as signs of the Thracian origin of the god, for example by C. Picard, "Les reliefs dits de la 'Visite chez Ikarios,'" p. 138. Dionysos did not come to Attica from the north but from the south, across the sea.

been reared by his nurses. In the forest and mountains he was not wreathed with vine leaves but with ivy and laurel.[131] In the hymn, his nurses are nymphs and the poet does not tell us that they too became hunting maenads. The bacchantes of Euripides are the pack with which the god hunts.[132] He hunted his enemy Pentheus "like a hare"—we read in the *Eumenides* of Aischylos[133]—and put him to death by rending.

Ariadne

> "Who knows . . . what Ariadne is?"
>
> —NIETZSCHE

ON A TABLET found in Knossos a great female figure of the Dionysian cycle appears with an inscription of few words including no name. And yet she was the first divine personage from Greek mythology to be immediately recognized in Crete. On the small clay tablet was written:

> *pa-si-te-o-i / me-ri*
> *da-pu-ri-to-jo / po-ti-ni-ja me-ri*[134]

There is no doubt about the Greek transliteration; therefore the translation is certain. The first word of the second line, it is true, discloses

---

131   The Homeric Hymn to Dionysos XXVI 7–9.

132   *Bacchae* 731: κύνες. 1189: ὁ Βάκχιος κυναγέτας σοφός. 1192: ἀγρεύς. 1146: ξυνκύναγος, ξυνεργάτης ἄγρας. See also Kerényi, *The Gods of the Greeks*, p. 262 (Pelican edn., p. 230).

133   *Eumenides* 26; see also Otto, *Dionysos*, p. 109.

134   Knossos Gg 702.2.

phonetic peculiarities deviating from later Greek, but they do not change the meaning:

πᾶσι θεοῖς μέλι . . .

λαβυρίνθοιο ποτνίαι μέλι . . .

To all the gods honey . . .
To the mistress of the labyrinth honey . . .

After both lines the amount of honey is indicated with a picture of a vessel. The quantity is the same for "all the gods" as for the "mistress of the labyrinth." She must have been a Great Goddess. Her high rank confirms the meaning of the labyrinth in this context as well as in countless other unwritten texts—pictorial representations and dances —which have been known throughout the world since early antiquity.[135]

The meander is the figure of a labyrinth in linear form. In the third to second centuries B.C., we find the figure and the word unmistakably related. The meander is impressively used in a monument at Didyma near Miletos, and in an inscription (a table of building costs) connected with it, the word *labyrinthos* is repeatedly used for the structure.[136] The structure recurs in two stairwells, one at either side of the entrance to the great hall of the temple of Apollo at Didyma; they house winding stairways leading up to the roof terrace of the temple

---

135 See Kerényi, "Labyrinth-Studien," *Werke*, I, 226–73, in which the mythological idea is developed. (First version: "Labyrinthos: Der Linienreflex einer mythologischen Idee" [1941], pp. 3–29. This was the first mention in the literature on the labyrinth of this highly instructive Ceramese example.) More about the development of the idea in the dance may be found in "Vom Labyrinthos zum Syrtos. Gedanken über den griechischen Tanz," *Werke*, I, 274–83. Additional documentation will be found below.

136 See A. Rehm, *Didyma: Die Inschriften*, s.v. λαβύρινθος in the index.

[27].[137] Theodor Wiegand, the archaeologist who completed the excavation, wrote that each section of stairs had its own horizontal marble ceiling. "One such ceiling is fully preserved. It bears a meander pattern in relief, nine meters long and roughly 10.20 meters wide, painted blue in the hollows; brightly colored rosette patterns filled the innermost squares and the whole rested on wall blocks bordered with cymatia painted red and blue."[138] Wiegand declares that these meander patterns were "symbolic" in significance and cites Paul Wolters, another great archaeologist, who had proved, on the basis of Attic vase paintings, that the meander in the representation of the Minotaur legend was employed as a "symbolic indication of the labyrinth."[139]

The use of the word "symbolic" may be misleading. Symbols demand an interpretation, whereas in all these examples the meander itself is an explanatory sign that was understood immediately. The winding stairways leading to the temple terrace were characterized as labyrinths by the meander pattern. Here we have at least two elements clarifying the nature of the labyrinth: the staircase is a spiral, a winding path, and this path leads upward. Of the painted vases that Wolters cites from the fifth and sixth centuries, three are particularly instructive. The painter Aison's bowl shows Theseus dragging the Minotaur out from the background with the help of the goddess Athena [28].[140] The meander appears not only in the vertical stripe surrounding the labyrinth in the background, but also on the Ionic columns of a vestibule evidently built in front of the labyrinth. On a black-figure cup

137   H. Knackfuss, *Didyma: Die Baubeschreibung*, pp. 79 ff.; pl. 85, F 327.

138   For Wiegand's description, see his *Sechster vorläufiger Bericht über Ausgrabungen in Milet und Didyma*, p. 75.

139   P. Wolters, *Darstellungen des Labyrinths*, pp. 113–32; *Archäologische Bemerkungen*, pp. 3–21.

140   J. D. Beazley, *Attic Red-Figure Vase-Painters*, p. 1174, no. 1.

from the Athenian Akropolis, the structure suggesting the labyrinth is adorned with running spirals in addition to the meander pattern: they form a sculptural correspondence to the meander [29].[141] A small oil bottle from Attica [30] shows (as do other examples) how little it took to suggest a labyrinth when the artist did not wish to draw its ground plan, which in meander or spiral pattern would have had to continue ad infinitum.[142] The artist simply drew a kind of gate or stele and on it painted the labyrinth sign. This idea was probably taken from a stage design using a meander pattern on an altar to indicate the labyrinth.[143] By the signs—the meander or running spiral— the audience recognized what the structure was supposed to represent.

At almost exactly the same time that the latest representatives of this type of labyrinth were being painted—by the vase painter Aison, for example—Sokrates, in the dialogue that Plato brought out under the title *Euthydemus*, speaks (at 291 B) of the labyrinth and describes it as a figure whose most easily recognized feature is an endlessly repeated meander or spiral line: "Then it seemed like falling into a labyrinth; we thought we were at the finish, but our way bent round and we found ourselves as it were back at the beginning, and just as far from that which we were seeking at first." When a dancer follows a spiral—whose angular equivalent is precisely the meander—he returns to his starting point. Both the spiral and the meander are to be taken

141   Wolters, *Darstellungen des Labyrinths*, pl. III; B. Graef and E. Langlotz, *Die antiken Vasen von der Akropolis zu Athen*, I:iv, pl. 73 (no. 1280).

142   When meanders or spirals are used as signs, a more detailed classification is not essential. For the bottle, see Wolters, *Archäologische Bemerkungen*, pl. I (reproduced here in [30]). For some other examples, in addition to those already mentioned, see Graef and Langlotz, no. 1314A; and Wolters, *Darstellungen des Labyrinths*, pl. II.

143   R. Eilmann, *Labyrinthos*, pp. 60 f.; Haspels, *Attic Black-Figured Lekythoi*, p. 179, no. 2.

as paths on which one involuntarily goes back to the beginning. Thus, the present-day notion of a labyrinth as a place where one can lose one's way must be set aside. It is a confusing path, hard to follow without a thread, but, provided one is not devoured at the mid-point, it leads surely, despite twists and turns, back to the beginning.

In Plato's *Phaedo*, Sokrates alludes to an image of the underworld that was characterized by many twists and turns but also by intersections. It was "labyrinthine" in the present acceptance of the word, a meaning which began to predominate even in antiquity. The "circuits" in Plato's texts were later even changed to "threefold paths."[144] In an account probably originating with Plutarch, the circuits became "arduous wanderings,"[145] but at the same time a way of initiation. The experiences of those initiated into the Mysteries of Eleusis were merged in literature with a labyrinthine journey to the underworld.[146] In the sanctuary of Eleusis there was not enough room for such wanderings but at most, during the archaic period, for round dances outside the temple. These ceased to be essential components of the Mysteries when, after the Persian invasion, the temple was surrounded with a protective wall that cut across the dance area.[147] Regardless of whether there were labyrinthine dances at Eleusis or whether the picture of processions in the underworld is based on a still older and not purely Eleusinian tradition,[148] the end of the dance was good. The labyrinth suggested

144 Plato, *Phaedo* 108 A: the path to Hades ἔοικε σχίσεις τε καὶ περιόδους πολλὰς ἔχειν. For "threefold paths," see Proklos, *In Platonis Rem publicam commentarii* II 85 6: τριόδους. / For the *Euthydemus* passage quoted above in the text, see *The Collected Dialogues*, p. 404.

145 Stobaeus, *Anthologium* V 1089 16: πλάναι τὰ πρῶτα καὶ περιδρομαὶ κοπώδεις.

146 See Kerényi, *Eleusis*, p. 204, note 65.   147 Ibid., pp. 70–72.

148 The most likely explanation is a tradition of Cretan origin transmitted by Orphic writings.

by meanders and spirals was a place of processions and not of hope-
lessness, even though it was a place of death.

When closed the labyrinth was indeed a place of death. Figure and
word never wholly lost their funereal character, which was connected
with the legend of the Minotaur, the bull-headed, man-eating monster.
This is explicitly stated in the inscription on a mosaic representation
of the labyrinth in a family tomb in the North African city of Hadrumentum: *Hic inclusus vitam perdit*, "He who is confined here loses his
life." The picture is a late, complicated representation of the labyrinth:
in the center is the dying Minotaur, and outside the entrance sits
Theseus' ship [31].[149] On both sides the labyrinth is framed by meander
patterns which indicate, in the ancient manner, the possibility of entering and leaving. In this connection it seems worthwhile to quote
Sophokles. In a lost tragedy he calls the labyrinth *achanes*.[150] The word
was later explained as "roofless," which may have something to do
with the fact that at Knossos a roofless dancing ground was spoken of
as a "labyrinth."[151] Yet the philosopher Parmenides, a contemporary
of Sophokles, used this term for an entrance with open doors.[152] And
there is nothing in the legend of Theseus to suggest that in entering the
labyrinth the hero broke open the gate that is mentioned. The meander
and spiral lines point to an open labyrinth which—if one turned at the
center—was a passage to the light.

A corridor on the ground floor of the palace of Knossos was adorned

149 Académie des Inscriptions et Belles-Lettres (Paris), *Comptes Rendus
des Séances*, 4th Ser., XX (1892), 319; L. Foucher, *Inventaire des Mosaïques*,
p. 76. For the inscription, see *CIL* VIII 10510.

150 Pearson, *The Fragments of Sophocles*, III, 141, fr. 1030.

151 Phrynichos, *Praeparatio Sophistica* s.v. Ἀχανές (in Bekker, *Anecdota
Graeca*, I, 28, 27–28).

152 H. Diels, *Die Fragmente der Vorsokratiker*, 28 [18] B 1 18.

with a fresco in the vestiges of which Sir Arthur Evans discovered, and reconstructed, a complex meander pattern that ran in not only one direction. The lines were dark red on a pale yellow background, and they were broken after the innermost turn [32A],[153] in contrast to the running and much interwoven spirals decorating other walls.[154] Like most Cretan art, the spiral decoration so frequent on Minoan walls must be interpreted as directly relating to *zoë*, which suffers no interruption and permeates all things. In the meander pattern of this lower corridor fresco the path was represented not by the lines but by the broad intervals. One who follows the direction of the intervals—on the fresco—will not be diverted from the path by the interruptions, but, as his eye moves onward, will proceed through more and more meander patterns [32B]. In the fresco it is no longer possible to discover an entrance or exit to the system as a whole. The explanation of the labyrinth is Evans' own. The analogies that he discovered in Egypt, especially on a steatite tablet from Memphis,[155] are significant connecting links between Minoan Crete and the land of the pharaohs. Evans also noted a similarity to the stairwells of Didyma but did not follow this analogy far enough. The corridor at Knossos leads toward the most important source of the palace's light: a courtyard framed in seven columns.[156] This situation tells us what *da-pu-ri-to-jo* meant to the Minoans: "a way to the light."

It meant a particular, often executed linear construction forming a delimited but not closed place or area, such as that suggested by the locution "mistress of the labyrinth." We may think of this con-

153 Evans, *Palace of Minos*, I, 356–59, fig. 256.
154 See ibid., Index (1936), s.v. Spirals, in conjunction with Kerényi, "Labyrinth-Studien," *Werke*, I, 226 ff.
155 Evans, *Palace of Minos*, I, 359, fig. 258c; cf. p. 122, fig. 91.
156 J. D. S. Pendlebury, *A Handbook to the Palace of Minos*, p. 50.

struction as an ingenious composition of endless spirals or meanders (depending on whether the drawing is round or angular) on a delimited surface. There resulted a classical picture of this procession, which originally led by way of concentric circles and surprising turns to the *decisive turn* in the center, where one was obliged to rotate on one's own axis in order to continue the circuit. The straight lines were easier to draw, and so the rounded form was early changed into the angular form.[157] The question as to whether the entire construction was invented in one place from which it radiated out over the whole world or whether, like the solution to a geometrical problem, it was discovered in several places, might be answered in both ways. In any case, the invention may have originated in Minoan Crete.

As in the case of the meander pattern, so also in the case of this so-called "Knossion,"[158] the firm relationship between figure and word may be regarded as the starting point of a path that surely leads back to Crete. A late, playful example is a drawing scribbled on the wall of a house in Pompeii. Above and beside the drawing stand the words: *labyrinthus / hic habitat / Min / otaurus.*[159] The drawing is angular, executed with a rather uncertain hand, as though someone were trying to show that he was capable of doing it. Greek coins from Knossos

157 How it can be constructed with the help of a certain trick may be learned from J. L. Heller, "A Labyrinth from Pylos?" pp. 57–62. He proceeds—as he had already done in his earlier work "Labyrinth or Troy Town?" pp. 123–39—from the mistaken assumption that a labyrinth *must* be a "true maze" in which people lose their way, and he therefore does not regard the construction as a labyrinth. This view is confuted by the staircases of Didyma and the corridor fresco of Knossos, as well as by the concordance of the Pompeian graffito with the Greek coins from Knossos.

158 The word seems to be employed by goldsmiths. I borrow it from a specialist in that field.

159 *CIL* IV 2331, and pl. XXXVIII 1.

bear the figure relatively late, but still early enough to prove that the invention of this construction was regarded there as national property. The angular form makes its first appearance on the coins from the fourth century B.C., and only later, on those from the second century B.C., does the rounded form appear, as though in an effort to recall the dance figure.[160] As movement—not of dancers, to be sure, but of riders—the same figure is attested in Etruria by the drawing on a small seventh-century B.C. vase, a wine pitcher from Tragliatella.[161] When the Parthenon was roofed, roughly between 450 and 400 B.C., the angular figure was scratched into a tile on the left gable "by a playful hand" [33].[162] Here we find further proof that the sign was regarded as a good omen and appropriate to the higher region into which a temple roof juts.

Playfully, and assuredly more as a sign of good fortune than of bad, the Knossion was drawn as early as 1300 B.C. on a soft clay tablet at Pylos [34].[163] A palace scribe who took delivery of animals was amusing himself with it when goats were handed over to him by various persons. In his warm hand, the figure, already scratched into the tablet, was somewhat compressed. Thus, as a mere toy, or at most as a superstitious game, the figure existed at the end of a cultural period begin-

160   For the angular form, see W. Wroth, *Catalogue of the Greek Coins of Crete*, pl. V 12, pl. VI 3 11–18; and J. N. Svoronos, *Numismatique de la Crète Ancienne*, I, pl. V 19 and 22, pl. VI 1–9 and 15–16. For the rounded form, see Wroth, pl. VI 5; Svoronos, pl. VI 18.

161   On the wine pitcher of Tragliatella, where *truia* as the name of the labyrinth may be read on the coils, see W. Helbig, *Führer*, pp. 341 ff. Accordingly, in my "Labyrinth-Studien," I termed this type of labyrinth drawing the "Tragliatella type."

162   E. Buschor, *Die Tondächer der Akropolis*, I, 45; see also Heller, *AJA*, LXV (1961), pl. XXXIII 10.

163   Pylos Cn 1287. See M. Lang, "The Palace of Nestor Excavations of 1957, Part II," pp. 183, 190, and pl. XLVI (reproduced here in [34]).

ning in Crete and also embracing Pylos. The honey offering given to the "mistress of the labyrinth" carries the style of a much earlier period: that stage in which Minoan culture was still in contact with an "age of honey." In the history of civilization, honey offerings and dances go hand in hand as forms of myth and cult, even when they survive in a mature high culture. This culture preserved them from its own beginnings. The intervals in the Knossion, which, if it was a dance figure, must originally have been rounded, were the paths of the dancers who honored the "mistress of the labyrinth" with their movements. The dancing ground, on which the figure of the dance was drawn, represented the great realm of the mistress.

For the dancing ground Homer is our source, but I believe we have another in the small clay tablet from Knossos. In the Iliad (XVIII 590–93), the dancing ground that Hephaistos "with rich and varied art" (*poikille*) incised on Achilles' shield is compared with the one Daidalos built at Knossos for Ariadne. Ariadne is described as a girl "with beautiful braids of hair," an ornamental epithet that Homer confers more often on goddesses than on common girls. According to the Odyssey (XI 321–22), Ariadne was a daughter of the "evil-plotting Minos"—an epithet that presupposes the labyrinth as a place of death. Ariadne, the king's daughter, was mortal, since she was killed by Artemis. She committed the sin of following Theseus, the foreign prince. Homer knew the story of how the hero and his band of seven youths and seven maidens were rescued by means of the famous thread, which is held in the hand in executing the difficult dance figure [35].[164] The thread was a gift of Ariadne, and it was she who saved Theseus from the

164 This can be seen on the relief pithos from the seventh century B.C. shown in [35]. For text concerning it, see Kerényi, "Vom Labyrinthos zum Syrtos," *Werke*, I, 274–88.

labyrinth. Even in this story, which has become so human, Ariadne discloses a close relationship, such as only the Minoan "mistress of the labyrinth" could have had, to both aspects of the labyrinth: the home of the Minotaur and the scene of the winding and unwinding dance. In the legend the Great Goddess has become a king's daughter, but there can be no doubt as to her identity. In the Greek period of the island she bore a name—although, as we shall soon see, she also had others—that is not a name at all but only an epithet and an indication of her nature. "Ariadne" is a Cretan-Greek form for "Arihagne," the "utterly pure," from the adjective *adnon* for *hagnon*.[165]

Still another mythical name, "Daidalos"—which likewise was not originally a proper name—is connected with the two aspects of the labyrinth: prison and dance ground. According to Homer, Daidalos built the dance ground for Ariadne with consummate skill (*eskese*). The word *daidallein*, synonymous with *poikillein*, might have been used for this skillful building—a tautology if the master's name was given. For the entire Greek tradition Daidalos was the builder of the Minotaur's house, in which Daidalos himself was later confined and from which he escaped through his invention of flying.[166] According to a tale that Sophokles used in a tragedy, Daidalos solved a difficult problem connected with the spiral: he drew a thread through the convolutions of a snail shell.[167] This he did by fastening the thread to an ant which proceeded to crawl through the shell. This story, the style of which shows it to be one of a number of picaresque tales older than

165 Hesychios s.v. Ἀδνόν. This cannot be a late invention, because the transition from *dn* to *gn* occurs; at most it represents a "hypercorrect pronunciation," according to H. Frisk, *Griechisches etymologisches Wörterbuch*, I, 21.

166 See Kerényi, *The Heroes of the Greeks*, p. 231.

167 Pearson, *The Fragments of Sophocles*, II, 3 ff.

Homer,[168] is based on the original form of the labyrinth. For Homer there were many *daidala*, even apart from Daidalos. Every skillfully performed piece of workmanship was a *daidalon*. This adjective, applied to objects made with skill, preceded the other forms of the word. The masculine and feminine, *daidalos* and *daidale*, are derived from it, since the word connotes a characteristic of a thing, or rather of many things, of all *daidala*. "Daidalos" and "Daidale," as names respectively of a mythical master and a goddess, were not early divine names. They were products of a living mythology, but not of the earliest Mediterranean mythology or that which the Greeks had brought with them to Greece.

There was a community whose members called themselves "Daidalidai," "descendants of Daidalos," and they probably observed a cult of the hero Daidalos. Yet it does not seem likely that Knossos, at the time of the stone tablet showing a derivative of the word but not necessarily of the name, had a shrine of Daidalos. The tablet is a register of oil deliveries; on it is written *da-da-re-jo-de*.[169] Two transliterations are possible: *Daidaleionde* and *Daidaleonde*.[170] The first would presuppose a kind of cult site devoted to Daidalos, whereas the second does not require this unlikely assumption. "Into the Daidaleon" as the designation of a place need not derive from the proper name "Daidalos," but could come from the simple adjective *daidalon*. "Daidaleon" might also signify an artificially or artistically constructed place, an edifice that was only later attributed to the Athenian architect. It was either the house of the Minotaur or a dance ground. It is doubtful that anyone

---

168   J. Toepffer, *Attische Genealogie*, pp. 165 ff.

169   Knossos Fp 1.3; see Ventris and Chadwick, *Documents*, pp. 305–307.

170   On Δαιδάλεόν δε see Kerényi, "Möglicher Sinn von *di-wo-nu-so-jo* und *da-da-re-jo-de*," pp. 1021–26.

ever saw a prisonlike building attributed to Daidalos, but it is not impossible.[171] It is more likely that the ruins of the palace of Knossos or
one of the numerous Cretan caves was interpreted—as has been done
by certain modern observers[172]—as the labyrinth of the Theseus legend.
The only alternative would be a dance ground, a place for cult dances
erected on a solid foundation,[173] to which the contributions of oil were
delivered.

The mistress whose realm this edifice represented in abbreviation,
as it were, stood in a strange relationship to Dionysos. For Homer,
Ariadne was something more than a daughter of Minos who followed
Theseus to Athens and was killed by Artemis (Odyssey XI 321–25).
This occurred on the little island of Dia, within sight of Crete, at the
behest of Dionysos (line 325):

$$\Delta ί η ι \ ἐ ν \ ἀ μ φ ι ρ ύ τ η ι \ \Delta ι ο ν ύ σ ο υ \ μ α ρ τ υ ρ ί η ι σ ι ν.$$

The word *martyriai* means that Dionysos called upon Artemis—as
men call a god or the gods to witness when wrong is done them—to
see what was happening. When Artemis saw Ariadne fleeing with the
stranger, she punished her with death. Ariadne's flight had been a
break with the sphere of power in which Dionysos was the great god,
above even the "mistress of the labyrinth." Ariadne belonged to Dionysos, as maiden or wife. If her flight had not also been a sin against the
feminine sphere, Artemis would not have been summoned. The question arises, What was Ariadne? What do we know of her and what did

171   The report of Philostratos, *De vita Apollonii Tyanei* IV 34 is legendary,
and even if it were not, we have no way of knowing what was shown at Knossos
as a labyrinth in the first century A.D. Possibly it was a dance ground.

172   Faure, *Fonctions*, pp. 166 ff.

173   Evans discovered the representation of such a dance ground in a fresco
of the palace of Knossos; see *Palace of Minos*, II, 23, 8; III, 66 f., and pl. XVIII.

her thread lead to?, if we penetrate to the core of the traditions which the Athenian, humanized version of her mythology cannot entirely conceal. These traditions prevailed south of Athens, and Ariadne's thread would seem to lead to the very heart of the Cretan religion.

The Attic hero mythology observed the boundaries of the special divine realm that came to Athens from the south. From that realm Theseus was not permitted to bring anything that was not in full radiance. According to one tradition, Theseus abandoned Ariadne because he was consumed with love for Aigle,[174] a girl whose name means "light." According to another tradition, he later married Ariadne's sister Phaidra from Crete,[175] who (at least according to her name) glittered brightly. According to Kleidemos, the Athenian historian, Theseus made peace with Ariadne when, after the reigns of Minos and his son, she became queen of Crete[176]—a humanized version of the fact that the "mistress of the labyrinth" was the true divine queen of Crete. According to the tradition of the Oschophoria, a feast of the ripe grapes held in the seaport of Phaleron, Theseus was the first to celebrate this Dionysian rite of thanksgiving in honor of the gods who had protected him on his flight from Greece. Athena and Dionysos protected Theseus from the danger of fully mastering Ariadne and taking her home as his wife [36].[177] Dionysos and Ariadne, who was also thanked,[178] released him from their sphere. This sphere was present wherever death

174 Plutarch, *Theseus* XX 2.
175 Plutarch, *Theseus* XXVIII 1; Diodorus Siculus IV 62 1.
176 Plutarch, *Theseus* XXVIII 1; Kleidemos, fr. 17, in Jacoby, *FGrHist*.
177 This is shown by such vase paintings as those on the hydria of the Syleus painter, Berlin F 2179, in Kerényi, *The Gods of the Greeks*, pl. XVIB; on a calyx krater in Syracuse by the Kadmos painter (in Beazley, *Attic Red-Figure*, p. 1184, no. 4); and on a calyx krater in Taranto (see [36]).
178 Plutarch, *Theseus* XXIII 4: Διονύσωι καὶ Ἀριάδνηι χαριζόμενοι (after Demon, the Athenian historiographer, fr. 6, in Jacoby, *FGrHist*).

and the tomb were elements in the cult of Ariadne. A tomb of Ariadne was shown in Argos: in reality, no doubt it was an altar where offerings were made to her as a subterranean goddess. The place itself was a subterranean sanctuary of Dionysos Kresios,[179] whose name—"Dionysos the Cretan"—says clearly that we are in the sphere of the Cretan Dionysian religion.

Homer largely shared the attitude of the Athenians toward this sharply delimited sphere.[180] According to the lines he devotes to Ariadne in the vision of departed heroines in the Odyssey (XI 321–25), she was the unfaithful betrothed of a god. These lines should be interpreted as follows: "The god must have had a claim on Ariadne, for the story corresponds exactly with the story of the death of Koronis, who was also shot by Artemis, and this at Apollo's instigation because she had betrayed the god with a mortal lover. . . . Koronis dies even before she gives birth to Asklepios, but Ariadne, according to the legend of her Cyprian cult, is said to have died in childbirth."[181] The parallel can be carried still further. Though according to her name she was a "dark crow-virgin," Koronis had another aspect. She also bore the name "Aigle," like the daughter of Panopeus (the "all-seeing," a second Orion).[182] Theseus loved Aigle so passionately that he left Ariadne for her.

On the strength of these parallels, and also on other grounds, we may assume that in one aspect of her being Ariadne was a dark goddess. Among the Greeks the epithet "utterly pure" was attached preeminently to Persephone, the queen of the underworld, although other

179   Pausanias II 23 8.
180   It has been noted that in this passage on Ariadne, Homer actually uses the name "Dionysos" in Attic form (Odyssey XI 325).
181   See Otto, *Dionysos*, p. 57; before him, L. Preller, *Ausgewählte Aufsätze*, p. 294.
182   *Anthologia Palatina* VII 578; R. Hanslik, "Panopeus," col. 649.

goddesses also were termed *hagne*. What seems significant here is the intensive contained in the first part of the name. A similarly accented attribute completed Ariadne's character and provided another aspect. The Cretans also called her "Aridela," "the utterly clear,"[183] just as they also called Koronis "Aigle." She could appear "utterly clear" in the heavens. The lunar character of Ariadne can no more be doubted than that of the crow-virgin, mother of Asklepios, who was able to shine like light. In the case of Koronis this view is supported by the fact that in her mythologem the crow was originally white and then turned to black—a widespread mythological expression for the darkening of the moon.[184] In the case of Ariadne signs on coins suggest a connection with the moon.

Coins from Knossos dating from the fifth century B.C. on show a strange labyrinth design: it consists of four meander patterns joined like the wings of a windmill or the four arms of a cross. The center is not always filled, as though the makers of the coins were uncertain as to how much it was permissible to say about the core and content of the labyrinth. In the oldest pieces of this type, the reverse of the coin, which was on top in the printing process, shows the Minotaur in *Knielaufschema*, while the obverse has a rosette at the center of the four meanders.[185] The Minotaur was soon replaced by the head of a goddess, usually crowned with a wreath of grain.[186] Anywhere else she must have been named Persephone or Demeter, and perhaps she bore

---

183 Hesychios has Ἀριδήλαν, according to the best codex and in the correct alphabetical order. This was replaced by an arbitrary conjecture in Kurt Latte's 1953 edition of Hesychios.

184 See Kerényi, *Asklepios*, p. 93; p. 124, note 16.

185 Wroth, *Greek Coins of Crete*, pl. IV 7; Svoronos, *Numismatique*, pl. IV 23–25.

186 Wroth, pl. IV 10–13; Svoronos, pl. IV 1–11.

one of these names at Knossos as well—but it is certain that she was also Ariadne, mistress of the labyrinth, for her head was framed in a running square meander pattern suggestive of the labyrinth.[187] The same framing was done to a bull's head.[188] This sign language is plain. To the labyrinth belonged its mistress or the Minotaur—or both. The connection between Ariadne on one face of the coin and the labyrinth sign on the other is made still clearer when the meander quaternion embraces a sickle moon.[189] This sign has no other implication in the myth whose abbreviations appear on coins from Knossos. It is a small view of the nocturnal world on the face of the coin that lay downward in the printing process and is, as it were, oriented downward: a totality that came into being through the combination of the four meander patterns with the round surface of the coin.[190] This view of the world became still more complete when astronomical signs were added beside the four meander patterns: one or two sickle moons—one waxing and one waning—and in the middle, inside the labyrinth, a star.[191] "Minotauros," "the bull of Minos," was not a true name. For the inhabitant of the labyrinth the names "Asterios" and "Asterion" have come down to us, both synonymous with *aster*, "star."[192] They also became names of the first Cretan king, who received Europa, the beloved of the bull-formed Zeus.[193] No Greek myth attaches to these names. No luminous aspect of the Minotaur was accepted by the Greeks outside of Knossos, but the Knossos coins bear witness to a star in the laby-

187 Svoronos, pl. IV 34.
188 Wroth, pl. V 1; Svoronos, pl. V 1.
189 Wroth, pl. IV 12; Svoronos, pl. V 2.
190 See Kerényi, "Arethusa," *Werke*, I, 210 ff.
191 Wroth, pl. IV 13; Svoronos, pl. V 3, 4, 7.
192 Asterios: Apollodoros, *Bibliotheca* III 1 4. Asterion: Pausanias II 31 1.
193 Scholium on Homer, Iliad XII 292; Apollodoros, *Bibliotheca* III 1 2.

rinth, to the lunar nature of Ariadne, and to an identity which justifies us in regarding "Persephone" as a possible name for the "mistress of the labyrinth," and not just because of her attribute of utter purity.

The parallel with Koronis, who gave birth to a god—Asklepios, who flared up[194] and healed but was also surrounded with darkness—has led us to the mythologem of the birth of Dionysos. The Cyprian myth is the strangest among the stories of the death of Ariadne, stranger than either that of Homer, in which Artemis kills her, or another in which she hangs herself in Crete and in this way suffers a gruesome Artemis-like death. (One of the goddess' names was "Artemis Apanchomene," "hanged Artemis.")[195] In the Cyprian version, Ariadne's death in childbirth forms the core of a twofold parallelism: one with the death of Koronis, who was already lying on the pyre when Apollo took his son, the little Asklepios, out of her womb,[196] and the other with the premature labor of Semele, who, set on fire by Zeus' lightning, gave birth to Dionysos in the seventh month of her pregnancy.[197] Ariadne did not give birth, but was buried with the child in her womb by the women of Amathus in a sacred grove, which from then on belonged to her as Ariadne Aphrodite.[198] Outside of Crete she took the form of the Great Goddess of love. In the Athenian view it was Aphrodite who helped

194   See Kerényi, *Asklepios*, p. 41.

195   Plutarch, *Theseus* XX 1; Otto, *Dionysos*, p. 188. See further ch. IV, at note 79.

196   Pindar, *Pythia* III 38–44; see also Kerényi, *The Gods of the Greeks*, p. 144 (Pelican edn., p. 127).

197   Ovid, *Metamorphoses* III 308–12; Hyginus, *Fabulae* 179. Concerning the seven months, see Diodorus Siculus I 23 4; Lucian, *Dialogi deorum* XII (IX) 2. This story was encountered in the folklore of Thrace by R. M. Dawkins, "The Modern Carnival in Thrace," p. 196. The tale is decisive because there was also a mythological tradition concerning the premature birth of Apollo, whose sacred number was seven.

198   Plutarch, *Theseus* XX 3–4, citing the historian Paion of Amathos.

Theseus out of the labyrinth,[199] but it is not quite clear whether she guided Ariadne by her power or whether the hero met the goddess embodied in the queen's daughter. On Delos, however, a legend was preserved to the effect that Ariadne—evidently representing Aphrodite—gave Theseus a statue of the goddess and that the figure of the labyrinth was danced by the rescued youths and maidens as this statue was being set up.[200] Thus, even when she was honored by the labyrinth dance outside of Crete, the "mistress of the labyrinth" always remained within the sphere of the Cretan Dionysos. She carried her child with her into the underworld. Was she "a mortal Aphrodite"[201] who died with her unborn child? This would be rather more than the humanization of a myth; it would be a realistic invention which, though pointless, had become a cult legend, a myth! Ariadne not only mirrored Great Goddesses like Artemis, Aphrodite, and Persephone,[202] she *was* Persephone and Ariadne in one person. It may be supposed that she gave birth in the underworld, and we are entitled to inquire after the child.

Both Koronis and Ariadne were former Great Goddesses who became earthly women. A proof of this is that they bear two names, which mortal girls do not. Semele, whose name is Phrygian and in Phrygia belonged to a goddess of the underworld,[203] may have experienced a still more far-reaching humanization. Her myth is the Theban version of the birth of Dionysos and contains the significant motif of *birth in*

---

199   Plutarch, *Theseus* XVIII 2.   200   Ibid., XXI 1.
201   Otto, *Dionysos*, p. 185.   202   Ibid., p. 184.
203   See P. Kretschmer, "Semele und Dionysos," pp. 17 ff. Kretschmer's only mistake was to suppose that "Semele" signified "earth goddess" in the same massive sense signified by "Ge." In formation the name "Semele" was an adjective similar to *chthamale* and in the myth of Dionysos must be rendered "Chthonia." See Kerényi, "Miti sul concepimento di Dioniso," pp. 1 ff.

death as clearly as does the story of Koronis. Here it is connected with the no less important motif, characteristic of Dionysos, of premature birth. The god of *zoë* was the only one among the gods who came into the world as an embryo, as a being whose first movement in the womb was the most direct manifestation of life, something which only women can experience. If Ariadne gave birth and her child did not remain in the underworld, this too was a premature birth in a sense. It is certain that in some form of the Cyprian myth her child was not nameless. In myth there is no such thing as pregnancy without birth, and the child never remained unnamed, regardless of whether it was to belong to the mythology of the gods or that of the heroes. In the various tales, Ariadne gave birth to various Dionysian children. She even bore Theseus a child, and this was the extreme humanization—in fact, the utter secularization—of the myth.[204] All these children were distinctly earthly beings, in some way connected with viticulture, as for example was Staphylos, "the grape." None of them was subterranean. A birth in death is something that must be termed "mystic" in the ancient sense, since the Mysteries of Eleusis revolved around such a birth.[205] How much more "mystical" it was if Ariadne was impregnated by Dionysos, as Koronis was by Apollo, and if, like Semele, she gave birth to Dionysos! Such a widening of the "ancient mystic" realm must be taken into consideration.

The Homeric version of the death of Ariadne becomes fully comprehensible only if there was between her and Dionysos the closest relationship possible between man and woman. Artemis, who punishes women for their lost virginity with labor pains and the danger of death

204 Plutarch, *Theseus* XXI 1, after Ion, the poet of Chios who carried on the Athenian tradition.
205 See Kerényi, *Eleusis*, pp. 93 f.

in childbirth, appeared when Ariadne, who in Greek mythology was before all other women the woman of Dionysos, was about to escape from his sphere and cease to be his possession. Consequently, in his *Theogony*, Hesiod, correcting Homer, tells us of the mercy of Zeus, who granted Ariadne immortality and eternal youth.[206] In Euripides' *Hippolytus*, Ariadne's sister Phaidra calls her "wretched" (*talaina*) because for love of Theseus she had sinned against her father and brother, Minos and Minotauros, and yet she is the "wife of Dionysos."[207] It is *this* attribute, which for Homer was the explanation of her death, that became the solution of the dramatic involvement in the later, universally known myth. For the entire ancient world, which had forgotten the original Cretan myth, the marriage of Dionysos and Ariadne was the fulfillment and apotheosis of an earthly woman. Theseus abandoned Ariadne on a small island, little more than a rock, while she was sleeping, and Dionysos merely awakened her from a deep sleep. From the god she received the wreath that gleams in the heavens as the "wreath of Ariadne," the corona borealis.[208] Like the journey to the heavens following marriage, this transfer of the wreath to the sky is a vestige of Ariadne's original connection with the heavens. Not in all the stories, however, did she receive the wreath on the island of Dia where Dionysos found her.[209] In one version the wreath was the price for which Ariadne allowed herself to be seduced by Dionysos, and the

206   Hesiod, *Theogony* 947–49.

207   Euripides, *Hippolytus* 339.

208   This is true even if a poet—Aratos in *Phaenomena* 71 2—takes account of Homer and employs an ambiguous turn of phrase: σῆμα ἀποιχομένης Ἀριάδνης. (In the version of Germanicus [72], it is: tunc illi Bacchus thalami memor addit honorem.)

209   Hyginus, *Astronomica* II 5. According to the poem that Hyginus used as a source, all the gods appeared at the wedding on Dia. Aphrodite's gift was the wreath with the hours.

wreath already gleamed in the labyrinth.[210] The memory of a Cretan marriage is preserved by the orator Himerios (fifth century A.D.), who drew on an unknown author. "In Cretan caves," he tells us—and perhaps this latest account preserves the earliest version of the story— "Dionysos took Ariadne to wife."[211]

The love of Zeus for Semele is radically humanized. In an older version of the story of the birth of Dionysos, Persephone is seduced by her own father. This version appeared until late antiquity in the didactic poems of the Orphics, but in the first century B.C. the historian Diodorus Siculus states expressly that this was the Cretan version. The vacillation between Persephone and Demeter, preserved in Diodorus, corresponds to the equally vacillating iconography of the Knossos coins, which show a Demeter-like head of Persephone in connection with the labyrinth.[212] Here we have an allusion to the so-called Orphic story of the god's birth, known to us as the birth of Zagreus. This myth seems to differ from the Theban myth of the god's birth even in the person of the mother. Elsewhere the Cretan Dionysos was characterized by his relation to Ariadne; here we find an equally characteristic relation to Persephone, goddess of the underworld. This would be known to us even without the testimony of Diodorus and even if it were not made clear by the content and style of the myth.

According to the Cretan historians whom Diodorus follows, Dionysos was first and foremost the wine god and was born on Crete to Zeus and Persephone. Diodorus adds that it was Dionysos who, according to the tradition of the Orphic mysteries, was torn to pieces by the Ti-

210 Epimenides, in Diels, *Die Fragmente der Vorsokratiker*, 3 [68] B 24; Hyginus, *Astronomica* II 5.
211 Himerios, *Orationes* IX 5.
212 See above, ch. III, at notes 186, 187.

tans.²¹³ Another passage makes it clear that the Cretans cited by Diodorus sometimes called Dionysos' mother "Persephone" and sometimes
"Demeter."²¹⁴ The myth itself is in an excerpt from a lost Orphic
theogony, cited by Athenagoras, the Christian Apologist.²¹⁵ The seduction of Persephone by her father who came to her in the form of a
snake is mentioned by Ovid in the *Metamorphoses*, at the end of a list
of Zeus' love stories. "In the form of a glittering serpent [he deceived]
the daughter of Deo," *varius Deoida serpens*.²¹⁶ These three words contain two of the three earliest elements of the original myth, the two
that are absolutely archaic: incest and the snake.²¹⁷ Deo—Demeter as
mystery goddess—replaced the third element which is archaic only in
a relative sense, that is, in relation to the religious history of Greece.
The other two motifs are archaic everywhere and at all times, regardless of context. Throughout Greek mythology Demeter is one of Zeus'
wives, the mother of Persephone,²¹⁸ but nowhere is there a corresponding mythologem—a story connected with a cult—about their marriage.
Demeter's marital relation with Poseidon, concerning which there is a
mythologem,²¹⁹ was fundamental to her person; her connection with
Zeus was not. Here she takes the place of Rhea, in both qualities of
the Minoan Great Goddess: first as mother, then as wife. The Orphic

213   Diodorus Siculus V 75 4.   214   Ibid., III 64 1.
215   Athenagoras, *Libellus pro Christianis* 20; Orpheus, fr. 58, in O. Kern,
ed., *Orphicorum fragmenta*.
216   Ovid, *Metamorphoses* VI 117. *Varius* is the translation of αἴολος, which
could also be interpreted as ποίκιλος but more likely signifies the swift movement
of the snake. "Deo" is the mystical name of Demeter.
217   See Kerényi, "Miti sul concepimento di Dioniso," pp. 1 ff., and "Die
Schichten der Mythologie und ihre Erforschung," pp. 637 ff.
218   Hesiod, *Theogony* 912.
219   Pausanias VIII 25 5; see also Kerényi, *The Gods of the Greeks*, p. 185
(Pelican edn., p. 163).

theogony preserved this historically probable event: "After becoming the mother of Zeus, she who was formerly Rhea / became Demeter. . . ."[220]

Along with the absolutely archaic elements, Athenagoras, who likes to dwell on the incestuous dealings of the old gods, preserves the one element that is only relatively archaic: the mother-daughter relationship between Rhea and Persephone. He does not intercalate Demeter as daughter of Rhea and mother of Persephone (by Zeus). Vestiges of the original relationship were also preserved in the best Greek tradition, in the Homeric Hymn to Demeter and in Euripides.[221] In Athenagoras we read: "Since his mother Rhea forbade the marriage he desired [Zeus with Rhea], he pursued her. After she had turned herself into a serpent, he did likewise and, entwining her in a so-called Herakleotic knot, entered into union with her. The sign of this form of union is the staff of Hermes. Afterward he entered into union with their daughter Persephone [daughter of Rhea and Zeus] by taking the form of a serpent and raping her. She bore him Dionysos."

The Orphic author from whom the Christian Apologist takes the myth (no doubt coarsening its style) is the source of the interpolated learned remarks about the Herakleotic knot and the two snakes on the staff of Hermes. These scholarly notes show that the author was working with ready-made material. He tries to explain the unfamiliar by the familiar: the form of the union between Zeus and Rhea by the "Herakleotic knot"—with which his readers had apparently been made familiar by wrestling exercises in the palaestra—and by the staff of

220 Orpheus, fr. 145, in O. Kern, ed., *Orphicorum fragmenta.*
221 The Homeric Hymn to Demeter 469; Euripides, *Helen* 1307. See also Kerényi, *Eleusis*, p. 44. / For the Athenagoras passage cited in what follows, see *Libellus pro Christianis* 20.

Hermes. With this example, to be sure, he shows the characteristic Orphic taste for the archaic, a taste to which we also owe the story of the mead of Kronos. The source of this highly archaic ready-made material can be stated with certainty: Minoan Crete.

Three elements of the tradition that lead us to Crete are: the cult of Rhea, the characteristic role of the snake in the religion of the Minoan period, and the express testimony that Persephone conceived and gave birth to Dionysos on Crete. The uncertainty as to the names of the gods further increases our certainty that this was a Cretan myth. In the Minoan period Rhea's husband could scarcely have been named "Zeus," and her son could scarcely have borne a name containing the element "Dio–." The names are not decisive; in a later phase of the Minoan religion they may have been substituted for other names. We also do not know whether the true name of Ariadne and Aridela on Crete was the same as that of the underworld goddess of Attica, that is, "Persephone." Even in Olympia, Zeus took the place of a snake god.[222] The Cretans of the Greek period spoke of a Zeus of their own, stressing the Cretan mythologem of his birth by the use of the epithet "Kretogenes," "he who was born in Crete."[223] By this they meant the god born in a Cretan setting that included the cave. If we drop the Greek names "Zeus" and "Dionysos," there remains the great anonymous snake god who, according to the late testimony of Himerios, held his marriage "in Cretan caves."

Less archaic than the seduction by a snake was the universally known myth of the rape of Persephone. "Hades," "Plouton," or the

222 He was given the cover name "Sosipolis," "savior of the city"; see Pausanias VI 20 2–3. See also L. R. Farnell, *The Cults of the Greek States*, II, 612.

223 Evidence is the inscription in Latos, in H. Collitz and F. Bechtel, *Sammlung der griechischen Dialekt-inschriften*, III, no. 5075, 74.

"subterranean Zeus" were only cover names for the ravisher. Fundamentally he too was a great anonymous god. To the version in which the scene of the rape was Sicily, Nonnos in his *Dionysiaka* appended an account of the snake marriage.[224] Demeter leaves Crete with her virgin daughter Persephone and hides her in a cave near the spring of Kyane. Thither comes Zeus, the bridegroom in the form of a snake:

> . . . *through marriage with this heavenly dragon*
> *Persephone's womb became fruitful, prepared*
> *To give birth to Zagreus, the horned infant.*

Aischylos bears witness to the contradictory identity of Zagreus, on the one hand with a "subterranean Zeus," on the other with his subterranean son. "Zagreus," "he who captures alive," was also a cover name, a circumlocution for a great god, in fact the greatest god of all time. He visits his hidden daughter in a cave, and she bears him to himself as his own son. The "mystic" feature which we have presupposed in the relationship between Dionysos and Ariadne here appears in an archaic myth in which generation and birth never go beyond the same couple. Taking his mother or daughter to wife, the son or husband begets a mystic child who in turn will court only his mother. To such involvements the snake figure is more appropriate than any other. It is the most naked form of *zoë* absolutely reduced to itself. Rhea, the Great Mother, assumes it for the original generation of her son, but this form is eminently suited to a male, a son and husband, who forces his way uninterruptedly down through the generations of mothers and daughters—the generations of living beings—and so discloses his continuity just as *zoë* does. Individual snakes were ritually torn

224 Nonnos VI 120–65.

to pieces, but *the* snake, the genus as a whole, was indestructibly present, bearing witness to the indestructibility of life in what was, in a manner of speaking, its lowest form.

Here we have recaptured the first act of a mythical drama that must be assigned to Minoan Crete and discloses a style more ancient than the culture of the palaces. The child in whose birth this first act culminates is horned; the bull, either as such or in a partly human form, dominates the second act. The ritual form of this act, the rending of a bull or some other horned sacrificial animal, most often a he-goat, became a Dionysian sacrifice. This sacrificial act, with all the details representing the indestructibility of life amid destruction, can be reconstructed: it gave rise to Greek tragedy and remained throughout antiquity the least striking, but most universal, of Dionysian rites.[225] A similar ceremony probably was performed in Minoan Crete. Two essential elements permit this assumption: that we have it on good authority that unlikely as it may seem a whole bull was torn to pieces at a feast of Dionysos held every second year; and that this was regarded as a characteristic Cretan sacrifice.[226] Representations of bulls or cows play a prominent part in Cretan art, as do three other motifs that have already been discussed: woman, snake, and drinking horn with the bull's head. It has been argued that the bull cannot have represented a bull god on Crete because in most representations the bull is too passive to embody a god. In this connection, seals are of paramount interest. About them it has been observed that "there are not a few which are among the most beautiful of their kind. They represent

225 See the section on "The Mystical Sacrificial Rite" in ch. V, below. See also Kerényi, *Der frühe Dionysos*, pp. 33 ff., and *Streifzüge*, pp. 53 ff.

226 On the Cretan rite of tearing a live bull apart, see above, ch. III, at note 113.

the bull in his peaceful existence, striding, grazing and resting, in extreme danger, pursued by beasts of prey, attacked, torn to pieces, and, finally, in the throes of death."[227] This is precisely what happened in the great Dionysian sacrifice, where the sacrificial animal represented a suffering, dismembered god.

The birth of a bull child, whose fate was no different from that of a sacrificial animal, was taken over by Greek hero mythology as an element of the all-too-human story of the Cretan king's daughter and her mother. In Greek mythology Hera and Hebe, but more especially the "two goddesses of Eleusis," were also mother-daughter dualities, in which the daughter was merely a detached half and younger repetition of the mother. In Eleusis the two goddesses were named "Demeter" and "Kore," or, to call the daughter by a more secret name, "Demeter" and "Persephone." Originally they were undoubtedly "Rhea" and "Persephone." As the Persephone of the original Cretan myth, Ariadne must surely have been the daughter of Rhea. It was only in the humanized version of the myth that she acquired Pasiphaë as a mother. Here again we have a mother-daughter duality in the Greek style; like Hera and Hebe or Demeter and Persephone, the two were almost or wholly identical. The name *Pasi-phaë* is just as transparent as *Ari-dela* and means "she who shines for all," which can be said only of the full moon in the sky.

The snake marriage was discarded, replaced by love for the bull. It was an extraordinarily beautiful bull,[228] but it was an animal, not merely—as in the case of Zeus who assumed the form of a bull in order to seduce Europa—a god in disguise! The identity of *zoë* in the

227   F. Matz, "Minoischer Stiergott?" pp. 220 f. / On the mother-daughter duality discussed below in the text, see Kerényi, *Eleusis*, pp. 27 ff.

228   *Mythographi Vaticani*, I, 47.

lowest and in a higher animal world, in the snake and in the bull, was also embodied in a more secret myth. The content of this myth was in turn framed in a mystic formula which may have been sung by the initiates in the corresponding mysteries and which served as a profession of faith and word of recognition (*symbolon*). In the form recorded in the Christian texts, through which it is known to us, it might be attributed either to the mysteries of Dionysos or to those of Sabazios. Even in the latter case, it may have been Cretan in origin and transmitted to the Greek mainland by way of Asia Minor. The formula diverges from the original Cretan Dionysos myth in introducing a cycle: the begetter alternately takes the forms of bull and snake. This, at least, was how the Christians who explained the *symbolon* and how the Latin translators understood it:

taurus draconem genuit et taurum draco.

The bull is father to the snake and the snake to the bull.[229]

In Greek the line runs:

ταῦρος δράκοντος καὶ πατὴρ ταύρου δράκων.

It also can be interpreted as in the Latin version, or tautologically, as follows: "The bull is the son of the snake and the snake is the father of the bull." Compared with myths in which snake and bull engender one another, or in which a snake merely engenders a bull, Pasiphaë's love affair with a bull, which produced the Minotaur—half man, half bull—is considerably "humanized." The Minotaur of the older myth was bull and star at the same time. If he lived in the labyrinth, he lived

229   A. Dieterich, *Eine Mithrasliturgie*, p. 215. For the Greek, see Firmicus Maternus, *De errore* XXVI 1; for the Latin, Arnobius, *Adversus nationes* V 21.

with the "mistress of the labyrinth," his mother, the queen of the underworld; he lived in the underworld, to be sure, but not in a place from which there was no issue.

In Minoan Crete the star whose early rising was celebrated in connection with honey, wine, and light was Sirius. Here a duality and parallelism may be observed. The star appeared in the sky; the light emerged from a cave. The festival of the light in the cave was a mystery rite. It has been possible to date this festival, but not the remaining elements. At Knossos the way to the "mistress of the labyrinth" and back again was danced publicly on a certain dance ground. The mistress was at the center of the true labyrinth, the underworld; she bore a mysterious son and conferred the hope of a return to the light. In antiquity the Cretan origin of the mysteries of Eleusis, Samothrace, and Thrace, that is, the Orphic mysteries, was deduced from the fact that in the Greek period everything that was kept secret in those mysteries was still open to the public at Knossos. In the known traditions of Eleusis the parallelism is apparent at two points: in the proclamation of the birth, to the queen of the underworld, of a mysterious child, and in the fact that the initiates in quest of supreme consecration were on their way to the mother of the child.[230] The parallel with the mysteries of the Great Mother at Samothrace has not yet been adequately studied, but in view of the foregoing there can be little doubt that the core of everything that was attributed to Orpheus, the mystical singer, was Minoan in origin.[231]

230   See Kerényi, *Eleusis*, pp. 92 ff.

231   M. P. Nilsson, *The Minoan-Mycenaean Religion*, p. 581, came very close to the truth when he observed: "Perhaps Crete was of greater importance with regard to Orphism, although the evidence has been swept away by time." The evidence is present, however, as soon as we realize that Nilsson starts from the false assumption that Orphism was ". . . a speculative religion created by a re-

The Zeus born on Crete and the Cretan Dionysos were not Greek gods. They were not distinguished from each other by such contours as defined "God,"[232] or a god, in his unique form for the Greeks—in fact, they were not separate at all. They may be aptly characterized by a name that Lewis Richard Farnell, the historian of Greek religion, devised for the divine being who in Olympia was known by the circumlocution "Sosipolis," "savior of the city," and who appeared in the form of a child and that of a snake: "the Zeus-Dionysos of Crete."[233] Zeus-Dionysos, the precursor of both Greek gods on Crete, changed his form as he passed through the three phases of his myth, which are comparable to the acts of a drama, and reproduced himself. The three phases and acts correspond to the three stages of *zoë*, or life, which in the Dionysos myth is masculine in its relation to women. The first act corresponds to the sperm, the second to the embryo, and the third to the male from infancy on. At the sperm stage the self-engendering god was a snake; at the embryo stage he was more animal than man; from infancy on he was the little and big Dionysos. As primal mother and source of *zoë*, his feminine counterpart was named "Rhea"; as mother and again as wife, she was named "Ariadne."

It was in the second act of the myth that the god was in the Minotaur stage, as a calf or a half-animal, premature child of the underworld, whereas Ariadne was at the stage of pure and wild animality,

---

ligious genius, at least in its most vital doctrines, and this man combined and reshaped the various elements with the independence and sovereignty of a genius." It is for *this* that no evidence is present. There is, however, an unbroken line of culture running through all the periods, as has been made clear in particular by the careful excavations of Professor Doro Levi in the region of Phaistos.

232 See Kerényi, *Griechische Grundbegriffe*, pp. 16 ff.

233 For "the Zeus-Dionysos of Crete," see Farnell, *The Cults of the Greek States*, II, 612. On Sosipolis, see note 222, above.

which accounts for her infidelity, her escape, and the manner of her death. Starting on this foundation, the hero mythology of the Athenians relates how in this case the queen of the underworld followed Theseus, the ravisher, who in another tale had tried unsuccessfully to ravish Persephone.[234] Here again he was ultimately unsuccessful, but a list of great women sinners[235] includes Ariadne as the murderer of her brother, the Minotaur! Thus essentially this is the story of a dark deed, based on the mythologem of a sacrificial rite. The stylistic laws of Minoan art did not allow a more explicit representation of these matters than what we have seen on the seals mentioned above.

The myth's final act, attested for both Crete and the island of Naxos, could not have taken place if *zoë* had been destroyed along with the sacrificial animal. The animal figure proved to be a transitional form, and this is indicated in the rite. As we learn from later witnesses, the male organ of the sacrificial animal was preserved as may well have been the case in the Minoan Age.[236] The god in the final phase of the myth appeared in human form, unmaimed and fully born, as though the preserved repository of *zoë* had been reawakened. A feminine task that had to be performed for the infant was that of wet nurse. The Naxos tradition concerning the nurses of Dionysos has come down to us in a late form which presupposes Semele as his mother.[237] One of the three nurses, however, was named "Koronis," a name which like "Ariadne" can stand for the same feminine figure.[238]

234 See Kerényi, *The Heroes of the Greeks*, p. 239.
235 Hyginus, *Fabulae* 26: "Quae impiae fuerunt."
236 Kerényi, *Der frühe Dionysos*, p. 48.
237 Diodorus Siculus V 52 2.
238 See above, p. 99. On the vase painting of Palermo (*Monumenti inediti*, II [1834–39], pl. 17, cited by Otto, *Dionysos*, p. 187), the name "Ariagne" seems to have been appended to one of the nurses by a later hand. But when we ask,

The nurses represented the mother, but she also could appear as one of them. It is highly probable that even before the historical period with which we are familiar, the Dionysian women began to impersonate the mythical nurses of Dionysos, a high, genuinely feminine dignity. The Minoan women's custom, which seems so strange to us, of totally baring their breasts on festive occasions is perfectly natural if they were playing the role of nurses of Dionysos.

The concluding event of the third act of the myth, the elevation of the divine pair Dionysos and Ariadne to the heavens, was based on the appearance of the goddess, in her full radiance, in the sky. Where the myth had reached this stage of humanization, as in the Theban story of the god's birth, Dionysos, fed by his nurses and grown strong, went down to the underworld and brought his mother back. Here there could be no question of a marriage. The marriage of Dionysos and Ariadne was a special one, an enhanced marriage that harkened back to an early stage, and in the Naxos myth was so interwoven with the ascent to heaven that we cannot tell which element came first. Even in the Cretan myth this marriage was placed in a definite setting: not the cave, but a small island, scarcely more than a rock in the sea. In the Greek text of the clay tablets, the island was given an eloquent name: "Dia." This is the name of a small island off the Cretan coast, facing Amnisos, one of the harbors of Knossos. The Naxians claimed that Naxos was originally called "Dia,"[239] so closely was this name identified with a marriage of the gods in which the bride played no less a role than the bridegroom. In this context "Dia" can scarcely be as-

---

Why this particular name?, we are compelled to assume that traces of it must have already been present.

239 Diodorus Siculus V 51 3.

sociated with the name "Zeus," but seems rather to be connected with the linguistically related names of goddesses: with the Latin "Dea" / "Dia" or with "Diana," all names signifying the light of the full moon.[240] The scene of this marriage was somewhere in the Aegean Sea. It is characteristic not only of the Minoan religion but also of the prehistoric religion of the entire island world. In the sixth century B.C., the Naxians began to build a magnificent temple on the rock facing the harbor of the city of Naxos.[241] Today the enormous marble frame of a gate —assuredly erected for Dionysos on the site of the sacred marriage— is still standing. According to another tradition, Dionysos took Ariadne to the small, round island of Donus or Donusia,[242] east of Naxos, which may thus also be taken into consideration as a marriage island. A very definite picture of the marriage island passed into ancient art, and the rock facing the harbor of Naxos is quite compatible with this picture. The harbor, from which a marriage procession could sail out in small boats to celebrate the union or reunion of the divine pair, is visible in the background.[243]

240   F. Altheim, *Griechische Götter im alten Rom*, pp. 55 ff.; G. Radke, *Die Götter Altitaliens*, pp. 104 f.

241   G. Welter, "Altionische Tempel I. Der Hekatompedos von Naxos," pp. 17–22. In view of its size, the temple must surely have been dedicated to the chief god of the island, who was Dionysos. Poseidon contested its ownership in vain; see Plutarch, *Quaestiones conviviales* IX 6 1.

242   See Stephen of Byzantium s.v. Δονουσία.

243   The scene appears in a mural painting in the house of Pammachius below the church of SS. Giovanni e Paolo in Rome, and on the front of a sarcophagus in the Vatican (Helbig, *Führer*, p. 4, col. 1, 176 ff.). An interpretation of the content and not of the geographical site, which is idealized in both of these representations, is provided in Kerényi, "Die Göttin mit der Schale," in *Niobe*, pp. 208–230. The youthful Dionysos pours wine into the bowl which the goddess Ariadne holds out expectantly. The smaller feminine figure beside her is the nurse Korkyne, whose tomb—a reinterpretation of a "tomb of Ariadne"—is shown on Naxos. (See also Plutarch, *Theseus* XX 5.) Her presence shows con-

The Naxians saw and celebrated Ariadne in two forms. According to their historians, a gloomy festival was devoted to a mortal Ariadne and a joyful one to another whom Dionysos took for his wife.[244] The god himself was also celebrated in two forms on Naxos. In one form he was called "Dionysos Meilichios," and his mask was carved of fig wood. In the other he was the ecstatic "Bakcheus," and his mask was carved from the wood of the vine.[245] In Dionysos Meilichios (the same epithet was applied to the subterranean Zeus,[246] who appears on Athenian votive reliefs in the form of an enormous snake) we may recognize the ancient seducer of the cave marriages; in Bakcheus, the young bridegroom of island marriages. The name "Bakcheus" is connected with the image of the Dionysian *thiasos*, the ecstatic band of bacchantes and agitated male nature gods in a state of heightened *zoë* which is not reflected in Minoan art. The description of the arrival of the bridegroom with such a retinue was reserved for later art and poetry. From the earliest times on, however, the core of the rite, the "higher marriage," had been associated with Naxos as well as Crete. On Naxos the site of the elevation to the heavens was also shown. It was Mt. Drios. According to the simple narrative of one historian, Dionysos appeared to Theseus in a dream, sent him away with threats, and that

---

clusively that the scene is Naxos, a point I was formerly unaware of. B. Andreae, in *Studien zur römischen Grabkunst*, agrees with my view up to a certain point but then interprets the scene as a view of the other world. The Erotes in the boats approaching the island (they are also represented in a lost painting from the Sepolcro Cornè, published by Andreae, pls. 78–79) are, however, most naturally interpreted in a this-worldly sense. They should be taken as idealized participants in the Naxian celebration around the marriage island.

244 Plutarch, *Theseus* XX 5.

245 Athenaios III 78 c, after the Naxian author Aglaosthenes (or Aglosthenes), fr. 4, in Jacoby, *FGrHist*.

246 A. B. Cook, *Zeus*, II, pp. 1108–10, figs. 944–46.

night led Ariadne up the mountain. There first he, then Ariadne, disappeared.[247] This was surely the scene not only of a disappearance, but also of an epiphany. One is reminded of the scene of Minoan visions.

Ariadne-Aridela, who had a cult period corresponding to each of her two names, was no doubt the Great Moon Goddess of the Aegean world, but her association with Dionysos shows how much more she was than the moon. The dimensions of the celestial phenomena cannot encompass such a goddess. Just as Dionysos is the archetypal reality of *zoë*, so Ariadne is the archetypal reality of the bestowal of soul, of what makes a living creature an individual. The soul is an essential element of *zoë*, which needs it to transcend the seminal stage. *Zoë* requires soul and every conception of life is a psychogony. At every conception a soul is born. The image of this event is the woman as conceiver, who bestows soul upon living creatures, and the reflection of this image is the moon, a mythological seat of the soul.[248] In image and reflection the feminine source of souls for Minoan Crete was the Great Goddess Rhea and Persephone, a duality only in appearance, fundamentally a unity.[249]

The image is an archetypal one expressing the same continuity and identity of mother and daughter as is expressed by Demeter and Persephone at Eleusis.[250] In the union of two archetypal images, the divine pair Dionysos and Ariadne represent the eternal passage of *zoë*

247 Diodorus Siculus V 51 4.

248 See Kerényi, "Seelenwanderungslehre bei Ennius," in *Pythagoras und Orpheus: Präludien*, pp. 77 ff.

249 According to the Pythagoreans, she was Rhea. See Kerényi, "Pythagoras und Orpheus," *Werke*, I, 49 f. According to Nikomachos: πηγὴ διανομῆς.

250 See Kerényi, *Eleusis*, pp. 32 ff.

into and through the genesis of living creatures. This occurs over and over again and is always, uninterruptedly, present. Not only in the Greek religion, but also in the earlier Minoan religion and mythology, *zoë* takes the masculine form, while the genesis of souls takes the feminine form.

Part Two The Greek Cult and Myth

IV. THE MYTHS OF ARRIVAL

From the History of Science

THE HISTORY of the sciences is a part of the history of thought, taken in the widest sense, but if we interpret "thought" very concretely as a broadening of man's field of vision, not every event in the history of science is *ipso facto* an event in the history of thought. The multiplication of knowledge with which only the learned can carry on further operations and which does not at the same time bring with it a broadening of our experience and our thinking is merely a potential event in the history of thought, whereas the advances of poets and philosophers into realms which were not previously sayable or thinkable, and for that very reason must be conquered for speech and thought, are themselves the history of thought in the making. Through classical studies and the contemplation of ancient works of art, men had gained a very considerable knowledge of Dionysos, his myth and cults, long before Nietzsche wrote *The Birth of Tragedy.* This knowledge made possible a coherent over-all picture. Yet it never achieved the position in the history of thought enjoyed by Nietzsche's ambitious work, though it deserved to do so.

Two older accounts of the Dionysian element in Greek culture are entitled to a place in a present-day reconstruction such as that attempted here. One earlier account, that of Karl Otfried Müller, has been taken up in Chapter I, above. The other is to be found in the "Introduction" to J. J. Bachofen's *Mother Right,* and quite apart from his general view of early world history and the prehistory of Greek culture[1] it can stand by itself as a characterization of Dionysos and the Greek Dionysian religion. "The magic power with which the phallic lord of exuberant natural life revolutionized the world of women is manifested in phenomena which surpass the limits of our experience and our imagination. Yet to relegate them to the realm of poetic invention would betoken little knowledge of the dark depths of human nature and failure to understand the power of a religion that satisfied sensual as well as transcendent needs. It would mean to ignore the emotional character of woman, which so indissolubly combines immanent and transcendent elements, as well as the overpowering magic of nature in the luxuriant south.

"Throughout its development the Dionysian cult preserved the character it had when it first entered into history. With its sensuality and emphasis on sexual love, it presented a marked affinity to the feminine nature, and its appeal was primarily to women; it was among women that it found its most loyal supporters, its most assiduous servants, and their enthusiasm was the foundation of its power. Dionysus is a woman's god in the fullest sense of the word, the source of all woman's sensual and transcendent hopes, the center of her whole existence. It was to women that he was first revealed in his glory, and it was women who propagated his cult and brought about its triumph."[2]

The abundance of observations combined in this picture reflects the wealth of the available material, in which there are, however, large gaps. Even without Bachofen such a picture is implicit in the material itself, but the more recent literature on Dionysos offers no account that is as complete or as human as his. Either the composition lacks co-

1   See Kerényi, "Johann Jakob Bachofens Porträt," p. 27.
2   J. J. Bachofen, "Introduction" to the section on "Mother Right," in *Myth, Religion, and Mother Right*, p. 101.

herence, or the color is wildly extreme and lacking in warmth. "Who is Dionysos?" Walter Otto asks. And in replying he remarks: "The god of ecstasy and terror, of wildness and of the most blessed deliverance —the mad god whose appearance sends mankind into madness—gives notice already, in his conception and birth, of his mysterious and paradoxical nature."[3] In Otto "the mad god" is not in quotes, because in his view the reality of Dionysos, his essence, is expressed in the word "mad." The words, however, were a quotation.

It is Homer who—in one of his rare mentions of the god—calls him *mainomenos Dionysos*, "mad Dionysos."[4] This Homer does quite obviously because of the god's effect on women, first on his mythical nurses, then on all women after them. With this as adjective the poet, who had mixed feelings about wine,[5] wished to designate a passing state of alienation, the intoxication which, along with its divinity, Plato imputes to wine—*mainomenos oinos*. Thus Plato cites Homer and is for us his best interpreter.[6] Women did not need wine when Dionysos intoxicated them: but their Dionysian intoxication seemed comparable to drunkenness.

Otto interpreted Homer's statement about Dionysos differently. "A god who is mad!" he writes. "A god, part of whose nature it is to be insane! What did they experience or see—these men on whom the horror of this concept must have forced itself?"[7] It was Otto's fundamental view

3 Otto, *Dionysos*, p. 65.   4 Iliad VI 132.
5 Iliad VI 264–65.
6 *Laws* VI 773 D: μαινόμενος μὲν οἶνος ἐγκεχομένος ζεῖ, κολαζόμενος δὲ ὑπὸ νήφοντος ἑτέρου θεοῦ . . . ("the mad wine boils, poured [into the mixing bowl] until chastened by the other, sober god (water) [it becomes a good drink]"). According to *Laws* II 672, wine was given to men "in order that we should go mad" (ἵνα μανῶμεν). In Euripides, *Bacchae* 130, μαινόμενοι Σάτυροι are the "drunken Satyrs"; and in Euripides, *Cyclops* 618, μαινόμενος Κύκλωψ is the "drunken Cyclops."
7 Otto, *Dionysos*, p. 136.

that men's visions of the gods came to them from outside, even when they rose up from the primordial depths of man himself. He held that Dionysos' divine being, his basic nature, was madness, a madness inherent in the world itself, not the passing or lasting derangement that comes to man as a disease, not a sickness, not a degenerative state, but the companion to his "most perfect health." In this context Nietzsche may be quoted to advantage: "Dionysos is the frenzy which circles round wherever there is conception and birth and which in its wildness is always ready to thrust forward into destruction and death. It is life." So it was for Otto, but life in only one particular state: "life which, when it overflows, grows mad and in its profoundest passion is intimately associated with death,"[8] not *zoë*, which is tested (though not affected in its innermost core) by its diametric opposite, *thanatos*.

It is highly characteristic that Otto differs from Bachofen at the very point where they come closest: "We should never forget that the Dionysiac world is, above all, a world of women. Women awaken Dionysos and bring him up. Women accompany him wherever he is. Women await him and are the first ones to be overcome by his madness. And this explains why the genuinely erotic is found only on the periphery of the passion and wantonness which make their appearance with such boldness on the well-known sculptures. Much more important than the sexual act are the act of birth and the feeding of the child. But more will be said about this later. The terrible trauma of childbirth, the wildness which belongs to motherliness in its primal form, a wildness which can break loose in an alarming way not only in animals—all these reveal the innermost nature of the Dionysiac madness: the churning up of the essence of life surrounded by the storms of death. Since such tumult lies waiting in the bottom-most depths and

8 Ibid., p. 141.

makes itself known, all of life's ecstasy is stirred up by Dionysiac madness and is ready to go beyond the bounds of rapture into a dangerous wildness. The Dionysiac condition is a primal phenomenon of life in which even man must participate in all of the moments of birth in his creative existence."[9]

But Dionysos was never a god of birth. In his myth there is no normal birth. He has very little to do with women's childbearing, but rather with their overflowing vitality, their milk and physical energy, their qualities as nurses and maenads. Otto evokes the experience of all peoples that "where life stirs, death too is near" to account for the combination of superabundant life and death-dealing power in Dionysos, and through it to explain Dionysian madness. Insofar as this experience relates to birth, it comes within the sphere not of Dionysos but of other gods. Eileithyia, Artemis, or a Great Goddess such as Hera, encompassing all the aspects of feminine existence, was invoked in connection with the wild experience of childbearing. The proximity of death in love does indeed come within the sphere of Dionysos, but the eroticism peculiar to Dionysian women, which excluded men from their ecstatic festivals and which Otto tried to explain by childbearing and nursing, is more likely connected—and this seems to be the crucial point—with their greater visionary capacities.

Otto also cites Schelling's *Die Weltalter*: "Ever since Aristotle it has become a commonplace to say that no one ever creates anything great without a dash of madness. We would rather say: without a constant solicitation to madness." And Otto adds: "He who begets something which is alive must dive down into the primeval depths in which the forces of life dwell. And when he rises to the surface, there is a gleam of madness in his eyes because in those depths death

9 Ibid., p. 142.

lives cheek by jowl with life."[10] It is obvious that Otto was concerned not with a medical definition of what the Greeks called *mania* and he and Schelling called "madness," but with a kind of visionary attempt to explain a state in which man's vital powers are enhanced to the utmost, in which consciousness and the unconscious merge as in a breakthrough. In such a state, he believed, men beheld a vision of Dionysos, or at least of the "Dionysian"—a word to which Otto prefers the name of the god, wherein precisely he goes beyond Nietzsche.

The adjective "Dionysian" was used by the Greeks themselves as a plural substantive to designate festivals at which they did or experienced the things that were most in keeping with the god celebrated. (The "Dionysian" was experienced in the "Dionysia.") The singular was employed for all the concrete particulars constituting the Dionysian element of the festival. The term is justified by the language and reality of the Greeks, but Nietzsche was first to introduce it into the history of ideas. Setting aside Bachofen's picture of Dionysos, Nietzsche prepared the way for Otto's vision. I shall cite here those words of his account that deviate most radically from the path taken by Müller and by Bachofen, which might have led to a true understanding of the origin of the Dionysian religion. "A tempest seizes everything that has outlived itself, everything that is decayed, broken, and withered, and, whirling, shrouds it in a cloud of red dust to carry it into the air like a vulture. Confused, our eyes look after what has disappeared; for what they see has been raised as from a depression into golden light, so full and green, so amply alive, immeasurable and full of yearning."[11]

Where Nietzsche remained closer to the ancient sources than to

10 Ibid., pp. 136–37.
11 Nietzsche, *The Birth of Tragedy*, §20, in *Basic Writings*, p. 123.

the "Dionysian enchantment" exemplified to his mind in Wagner's music, his account becomes a fairy tale: "Under the charm of the Dionysian not only is the union between man and man reaffirmed, but nature which has become alienated, hostile, or subjugated, celebrates once more her reconciliation with her lost son, man. Freely, earth proffers her gifts, and peacefully the beasts of prey of the rocks and desert approach. The chariot of Dionysus is covered with flowers and garlands; panthers and tigers walk under its yoke. Transform Beethoven's 'Hymn to Joy' into a painting; let your imagination conceive the multitudes bowing to the dust, awestruck—then you will approach the Dionysian. Now the slave is a free man; now all the rigid, hostile barriers that necessity, caprice, or 'impudent convention' have fixed between man and man are broken. Now, with the gospel of universal harmony, each one feels himself not only united, reconciled, and fused with his neighbor, but as one with him, as if the veil of *māyā* had been torn aside and were now merely fluttering in tatters before the mysterious primordial unity.

"In song and in dance man expresses himself as a member of a higher community; he has forgotten how to walk and speak and is on the way toward flying into the air, dancing. His very gestures express enchantment. Just as the animals now talk, and the earth yields milk and honey, supernatural sounds emanate from him, too: he feels himself a god, he himself now walks about enchanted, in ecstasy, like the gods he saw walking in his dreams. He is no longer an artist, he has become a work of art: in these paroxysms of intoxication the artistic power of all nature reveals itself to the highest gratification of the primordial unity."[12]

So Nietzsche painted and interpreted the "Dionysian Greek," now

12 Ibid., §1, p. 37.

borrowing from tradition, from the *Bacchae* of Euripides for example, and now drawing on his own imagination. He ignores the Dionysian woman, after the god the second person in the drama, in a manner that was almost as pathological as his later appalling preoccupation with Ariadne.[13] He was all the more determined to exclude the "Dionysian barbarian" with his "immoderate sexual frenzy" from this picture. The characterization cited above is preceded by a comparative study that made it more acceptable to scholars. "Either through the influence of the narcotic draught"—Nietzsche does not mention wine expressly because he wishes to claim *all* intoxication for Dionysos— "of which the songs of all primitive men and peoples speak, or with the potent coming of spring that penetrates all nature with joy, these Dionysian emotions awake, and as they grow in intensity everything subjective vanishes into complete self-forgetfulness. In the German Middle Ages, too, singing and dancing crowds, ever increasing in number whirled themselves from place to place under this same Dionysian impulse. In these dances of St. John and St. Vitus, we rediscover the Bacchic choruses of the Greeks, with their prehistory in Asia Minor, as far back as Babylon and the orgiastic Sacaea. There are some who, from obtuseness or lack of experience, turn away from such phenomena as from 'folk-diseases,' with contempt or pity born of the consciousness of their own 'healthy-mindedness.' But of course such poor wretches have no idea how corpselike and ghostly their so-called 'healthy-mindedness' looks when the glowing life of the Dionysian revelers roars past them."

This is Nietzsche's profession of faith in "intoxication," to his mind

13 See Kerényi, "Nietzsche et Ariadne," in *Bachofen und die Zukunft des Humanismus*, pp. 28–36. / For the Nietzsche passage that follows in the text, see his *Basic Writings*, pp. 36–37.

an equivalent to Schopenhauer's will (at that time Schopenhauer and Wagner were his mentors), a metaphysical principle that he identified with Dionysos. Nietzsche stressed the *eruptive character* of the Dionysian. The only element in all this that seemed acceptable to scientific thinking—the comparison with a religious epidemic—was rescued and consolidated by Nietzsche's friend, Erwin Rohde. Along with the eruptive, psychological factor, Rohde stressed an *irruptive*, supposedly historical, factor and assumed that the religion of Dionysos had originated somewhere outside of Greece. He believed that the irruption of the cult, which he like Nietzsche held to be exclusively a cult of intoxication, had taken place relatively late, "in the train of a religious agitation, we might almost say revolution." With it "something new and strange" entered into Greek life, something "of which Homer records, at most, only the first faint essays."[14] This provides roughly the same dating as did Wilamowitz, who put the incursion of Dionysos into Greece from the Lydian wine land "in the eighth century at the earliest"—a judgment refuted by the thirteenth-century tablets from Pylos.[15]

Rohde sought the source of the Dionysian religion in a country that was not among the oldest wine-growing regions of the Mediterranean, whose inhabitants, in the Greek view, never learned the proper use of wine and used it as an intoxicant even in warfare, to wit: Thrace.[16] His well-documented account of the way Thracian tribes swarmed round the god "later known to the Greeks as 'Dionysos,' "[17] his account

14   E. Rohde, *Psyche*, p. 256.
15   U. von Wilamowitz-Moellendorf, *Der Glaube der Hellenen*, I, 60. However, on the evidence to the contrary from Pylos, see above, in ch. III, the section on "Dionysian Names."
16   Pausanias IX 30 5.
17   Rohde, "Die Religion der Griechen," p. 332.

of ecstatic cult rituals in their wildest, most unrestrained forms, was taken as a model by subsequent scholars. Rohde provided Nietzsche's picture with historical underpinning and at the same time corrected it. The correction was that Rohde represented this manner of entering "into the ecstasies of divine universal life" as "an alien drop of blood in the Greek bloodstream," as a current which "roared down to Greece from the north." Never was any *proof* adduced that the Dionysian religion had come to Greece from the north and had not like viticulture spread from south to north, supported perhaps by secondary currents, which came to the north not only by the direct route from Crete but also by detours. The passage of elements of Minoan culture by way of the Aegean Sea to the immediate vicinity of Thrace is attested by the find of a rich Mycenaean tomb on Skopelos, the ancient Peparethos.[18] According to the tradition, Staphylos, the hero "grape," a companion figure to the wine god Dionysos, came from Greece to settle the small island in the Sporades.[19]

Nevertheless, in all modern accounts of the Dionysian, an explosive trait has remained dominant. This is Nietzsche's dubious contribution; it is reflected not only in Otto, but also in "sober-minded" scholars, who found the core of the Dionysian religion in orgiasm[20]—or more specifically, in accordance with the historical findings, in the orgiasm of women, for which the new term "maenadism" was coined.[21] This term is historically no more justified than that of "Orphism" and suggests the false notion that maenadism was a spontaneous phenomenon.

18 N. Platon, Ὁ τάφος τοῦ Σταφύλου, pp. 534 ff.

19 Diodorus Siculus V 79 2; [Scymnus], "Orbis descripto," in C. F. W. Müller, ed., *Geographi Graeci Minores*, I, 219, 580–82.

20 M. P. Nilsson, *Geschichte der griechischen Religion*, I, 569.

21 H. Jeanmaire, *Dionysos*, p. 157; E. R. Dodds, *The Greeks and the Irrational*, p. 270.

Actually this phenomenon, most aptly described by the medical term "collective hysteria," was marginal to the cult of Dionysos. It is quite erroneous to assert that the cult originated in "spontaneous attacks of mass hysteria," or to say with Aldous Huxley that "ritual dances provide a religious experience that seems more satisfying and convincing than any other. . . . It is with their muscles that they most easily obtain knowledge of the divine."[22] This conception is refuted by the traditions concerning the arrival of the god in Greece.

The Forms of Arrival

IN CERTAIN cult forms, Dionysos is represented as the god who arrives. Otto, who far more than all other students of the subject saw Dionysos as the "Coming One, the epiphanic god," adds that his "appearance is far more urgent, far more compelling than that of any other god."[23] Historical reconstruction makes possible a far more concrete statement. Here we shall attempt to define the types and forms of the epiphanies of Dionysos as accurately as possible. The epiphany of a god was known in Greece not only as *epiphaneia*, but also as *epidemia*,[24] "arrival in the land," among a particular people, or in a community such as the Attic *demoi*. A divine "epidemic"–whose kinship with "visitation by a disease" is undeniable at least insofar as it was always the incursion of something overpowering–is conceivable in three historical forms.

The unpredictable emergence of a new experience, on which a new religion could be based or by which an old one could be enriched,

22 Dodds, p. 271.   23 Otto, *Dionysos*, p. 79.
24 L. Weniger, "Theophanien, altgriechische Götteradvente," pp. 16 ff.

is the form to which, if it were reliably transmitted, a historian of religions would have to give priority. In connection with the mythological religions, however, reliable knowledge of this form is seldom available. Such an experience must rather be assumed to have occurred *before* the emergence of the traditional religion and mythology, "before" they began, and to constitute their foundation.[25] The second form would be the very concrete arrival of a missionary cult. The Dionysian religion shows so many indications of such an arrival that it has been termed a "missionary religion" and in this sense a precursor of Christianity.[26] But the Greeks often celebrated advents of gods, even when the presence of a god was revealed by the recurrence of a particular time of the year, day, or month. This third form of arrival is distinguished by the *call* that precedes it: this call provides the fundamental correlation through which the date or time of day becomes a divine event.[27]

Even an occurrence in the heavens can give rise to an overpowering divine "epidemic"; indeed, the *epidemia* can be repeated over and over again through the correlation between man and a perfectly natural cosmic phenomenon. "What a tremor passed through Apollo's laurel tree! The entire edifice trembled!" we read in Kallimachos' *Hymn to Apollo*, in which the poet combines the paean, the song in which the god is invoked, with a description of his epiphany, which is one with the sunrise of a feast day.[28] The experience of the Hebrew prophet Isaiah, who sees and hears seraphim, is the same: "And the posts of the door moved at the voice of him that cried."[29] Epiphanies of Diony-

25 See Kerényi, *Umgang mit Göttlichem*, p. 17.
26 J. Leipoldt, "Dionysos."
27 See Kerényi, "Hegel e gli Dei della Grecia," p. 2.
28 See Kerényi, "Apollon-Epiphanien," in *Niobe*, pp. 151–72.
29 Isaiah 6:4.

sos, even in the form determined by the call, were different from these, as we can infer with certainty from the famous paean of the women of Elis. The second, or historical, form of "arrival in the land," Dionysos' *epidemia* on shipboard, can also be reconstructed on the basis of its cultic repetitions, and this form merits priority. The third form, the god's answer to the call, has no exclusive foundation in a natural period such as the solar year. It could also occur in the course of a *trieteris*, or two-year period, which was current in many parts of Greece and must be understood on the basis of its inherent logic.

Arrivals in Attica

THANKS TO the Athenians' wealth of literary, epigraphic, and monumental traditions, we possess a more complete picture of the Dionysian festive year in Attica than in any other region of Greece, either on the mainland or in the islands. The first fact to be noted concerning this festive year is that it was actually a *year* and comprised all the festivals of Dionysos, which recur without exception at identical times. Nearby, in Boeotia, and further away, in particular at Delphi, which played so important a role in the religious life of Athens, the puzzling two-year period prevailed. This two-year period implied a manner of worshiping the god that differed somewhat from the annual cult. This is demonstrated by the fact that the Athenians thought it important to participate in it and sent some of their own female citizens to the college of women in Delphi who celebrated the special festivals of the two-year period there. This they actually did each year,[30] for the so-called *trieteris*

---

30 Pausanias X 4 3: παρὰ ἔτος ("each year"); see also *Tabulae Heracleenses* I 101.

comprised two such festivals which were not identical. These were definitely not innovations introduced at Delphi, for the two-year period had wide currency and is attested for Crete in connection with the rending of a whole bull, the almost incredible archaic form of a trieteric sacrifice. If the Delphic cult of Dionysos had been an innovation, the Athenians could have introduced it too. Evidently Dionysos came to them in a special way, at a time when the trieteric cult already existed elsewhere. But awareness of a link with precisely that older religion to which the two-year period pertained seems to have been preserved or revived after the cult of the god was established in Attica on the basis of the Dionysian year, and a difference in the manner of celebrating the two festivals had become apparent.

The Dionysian year is the year of the vineyards and wine cellars. Its events take place in the sky, on the surface of the earth, and in the wine containers which also stand for the subterranean sphere. The myths of the arrival of Dionysos offer reliable evidence that the grape —even the wild grape—was at one time unknown in Attica. They are among the myths of the culture bringers—in this case the bringer of the wine culture—which hark back to very early times and embody concrete historical memories. An example is the myth of Prometheus, the fire bringer, which, in association with one name or another, was widely distributed as early as the Neolithic era, varying from one region to another according to the sources of fire and the local experience of fusible metals.[31] Various wine-growing communities (*demoi*) of Attica preserved the memory of the fact that they had had to learn how to grow wine; they had learned not in a profane way, however,

---

31 See Kerényi, "Persephone und Prometheus: Vom Alter griechischer Mythen"; and *Prometheus: Archetypal Image of Human Existence*, p. 70.

but in very much the same way as they had acquired the mysteries which by their own resources they could have neither invented nor understood.

When historiography developed into a kind of world chronicle, it even established a relative chronology, according to which the Dionysos who came to Attica bringing wine culture was earlier than the Dionysos born in Thebes in the royal palace of Kadmos.[32] This attempt at a differentiation of chronology and cults is not entirely without value to the historian of culture and religion, who for more than one reason must begin his account of the Dionysos cult in Attica. One reason is the abundance of traditions; another is the fact that these traditions include a culture-bringer myth in several local variations.

An ancient clay tablet to be seen in the potters' quarter of Athens, dating probably from the sixth century, showed Amphiktyon, the pseudohistorical third king of Athens, feasting Dionysos along with other gods.[33] It probably portrayed the king receiving an entire divine procession, in which the wine god was hardly more recognizable than

32 In Hieronymus' version of Eusebios, *Chronicon* (in Helm, ed., p. 44), it is recorded for 1497 B.C. that "Dionysus verum non ille Semelae filius, cum in Atticam pervenisset, hospitio receptus a Semacho filiae eius capreae pellem largitus est"; and for 1387 B.C. it is recorded that "Dionysus, qui latine Liber pater, nascitur ex Semele" (in Helm, ed., p. 50). See also Eusebios, *Chronicorum Libri Duo* (in Schoene, ed., II, 28): Ἀμπελουργία ὑπὸ Διονύσου ἐγνωρίσθη, οὐχὶ τοῦ ἐκ Σεμέλης. See also p. 30: κατὰ Ἀμφικτύωνα τὸν Δευκαλίωνος υἱόν τινές φασι Διόνυσον εἰς τὴν Ἀττικὴν ἐλθόντα ξενωθῆναι Σημάχωι καὶ τῆι θυγατρὶ αὐτοῦ νεβρίδα δωρήσασθαι. ἕτερος δ᾽ ἦν οὗτος [ἢ ὁ ἐκ Σεμέλης] (the completion is mine). The distinction can surely be traced back to Kastor of Rhodes in the first century B.C., the date of arrival to the Atthidographes, the historians of Attica; see Jacoby, *FGrHist*, III, B, pp. 296 f. For another version of the arrival, see Stephen of Byzantium s.v. Σημαχίδαι: δῆμος Ἀττικῆς, ἀπὸ Σημάχου, ὧι καὶ ταῖς θυγατράσιν ἐπεξενώθη Διόνυσος, ἀφ᾽ ὧν αἱ ἱέρειαι αὐτοῦ.

33 Pausanias I 2 5.

on the krater of Klitias and Ergotimos, the so-called François Vase in Florence, where he is accompanied by the three Horai [37].[34] Dionysos was apparently thought to have been present in Athens even before Amphiktyon, though Dionysos' coming occurred in several phases. It was in the first phase that the third king learned from him to mix wine with water and dedicated to him an altar in the sacred precinct of the Horai. Here—probably in an inscription on the altar—he was designated as "Dionysos Orthos," the "Dionysos who stands upright." Thus, in all probability a phallus was set up for him in the temple as his cult image.[35]

The memory of Dionysos' arrival by sea was preserved by reminiscences of his ship. Vase paintings of the sixth century show how it was moved about on rollers at a festival, although it is hard to say what festival. It is unlikely that he came by way of the bay of Piraeus, which became the harbor of Athens at a relatively late date.[36] Such a possibility is suggested neither by the historical and mythological evidence, nor by the testimony that has been preserved concerning the cult, which was probably celebrated with particular magnificence in the seaport town.[37] In Phaleron, which at an early date was used more than the Piraeus as the seaport of Athens, Dionysos was celebrated in a rather complex way. This festival in which grape-laden vine branches were carried (its name "Oschophoria" means just that) down to Phaleron from Athens would ordinarily have been a perfectly simple affair.

34 Furtwängler and Reichhold, *Griechische Vasenmalerei*, Ser. I:1, pls. 1–3.

35 Athenaios II 38 CD (for the text itself, see below, note 92); also V 179 E.

36 See T. Lenschau, "Peiraios," col. 74.

37 Dionysia and a procession in the Piraeus are attested for the fourth and perhaps the fifth century and on; see P. Foucart, "Sur l'authenticité de la loi d'Evégoros," pp. 168 ff.

It occurred at the beginning of the month of Pyanopsion (roughly our October), the month of the wine harvest according to the Attic calendar.[38] The place in Phaleron to which the grapes were carried was named the "Oschophorion" and nothing would have been more natural if this had been a thanks offering to Dionysos for the wine harvest.

In this square, however, stood a temple of Athena,[39] and the thanks were addressed to Dionysos and Ariadne for releasing Theseus and not coming with him—addressed to the one as persecutor and avenger, to the other as the ravaged one. That with Athena's help the adventure had ended happily was the canonical view in Athens, represented by the vase painters on the basis of a painting that was to be seen in the sanctuary of Dionysos Eleuthereus.[40] According to this conception of the festival, Dionysos could not have landed in Phaleron where he received thanks for having remained absent. Moreover, this was a festival of the epheboi, which was particularly appropriate to Theseus and to the goddess who protected all youths. But—another contradiction—the two youths carrying grapes who led the procession were dressed as women[41] and women accompanied them with food to welcome the arrivals, that is (according to the Theseus myth prevailing in the historical period) the hero and the boys and girls who had been

38   See the calendar frieze of Hagios Eleutherios in Athens, in L. Deubner, *Attische Feste*, pl. XXXV 3.
39   See Hesychios s.v. Ὠσχοφόριον.
40   Pausanias I 20 3.
41   Proklos, *Chrestomathia*, in Photios, *Bibliotheca* 322 13 (ed. Bekker). The contention (repeated by Deubner, *Attische Feste*, p. 143) that the woman's garment in the background is the older Ionian men's costume, which was no longer recognized and falsely interpreted, is a pure absurdity. The Athenians would not have been surprised at the Ionian *chiton* and would have accepted it as such. If the tradition speaks of feminine dress, it is because this vestige of archaic times was regarded as an anomaly.

saved. At the end of the festival all the boys danced nude, which otherwise was done only in honor of Dionysos.[42] We can only infer that this festival of thanksgiving celebrated a very early arrival and reception of the god among the women.

The earliest serviceable harbors of Athens were situated on the east coast of Attica, and arrivals of Dionysos are reported in connection with wine-growing mountain villages first in the eastern coastal region and then in the west, near the Boeotian border. There is no indication that the arrival in the west was connected with political changes known in the historical period,[43] but it probably marked the beginning of the second phase of the god's presence in Athens. The potters and vase painters knew more details of all this than anyone else. That is why their wares are so important a source for the religion of Dionysos.

There is only a very brief literary account to tell us that Dionysos, who brought wine culture to Attica, was received as a guest by the founding hero of the *demos* of Semachidai, who bore the alien, non-Indo-European name "Semachos."[44] This arrival is concretized not so much by chronology—a late calculation places it in the year 1497 B.C.—as by geography. A sanctuary of Semachos (his *heroön*) was situated on the path that led "outside of Rhagon" to Laurion in a mining re-

42   Athenaios XIV 631 B.

43   A. Pickard-Cambridge, *Dramatic Festivals*, p. 58: "The action of Pegasos was probably an incident in the gradual spread of Dionysiac cults throughout Greece, which was unconnected with political motives." See further ch. IV, at note 95.

44   The derivation from a West-Semitic word is recommended by M. C. Astour, *Hellenosemitica*, p. 195. In this case the most likely possibility is the Hebrew *šimah*, "made to rejoice," a possible circumlocution for wine. / On the chronology, see above, note 32.

gion.[45] Nothing more can be ascertained than that this was in the vicinity of Sounion at the southeastern tip of Attica. Between Cape Sounion and the open beach of Marathon there were a number of favorable, indeed hidden, landing places. The people who brought the god and all the trappings of his cult could have landed in an inconspicuous harbor along this coast facing the Aegean Islands.

At the house of Semachos the god was received by women. The mythical account is appropriate to the circumstances, since women played the leading role in the Dionysos cult. It was expressly added that the priestesses of Dionysos were the successors of the daughters of Semachos. Another version mentions only one daughter, who received a deer skin (*nebris*) from the god as a present.[46] This was more than the gift of a special kind of garment. It also indicates the bestowal of a rite in consequence of which the deer skin could be worn: *nebrizein* also means the rending of an animal.[47] The cult action in which the sacrificial animal was dismembered, however, required at least two persons [38]. On a sixth-century vase in Orvieto, a man is leading Dionysos toward the host-hero, whose distinction is stressed by an eagle bearing a snake in its beak [39A/39B]. Two women making dance movements and two ithyphallic sileni are also present. In all likelihood the scene represents the god's arrival at the house of Semachos.

---

45   *IG* II² 1582 53–54; see also G. P. Oikonomos, "Eine neue Bergwerks-urkunde aus Athen," pp. 308 f.

46   For these details in the accounts of Stephen of Byzantium and Eusebius, see note 32, above.

47   Harpokration, *Lexicon* s.v. νεβρίζων: οἱ μὲν ὡς τοῦ τελοῦντος νεβρίδα ἐνημμένου ἢ καὶ τοὺς τελουμένους διαζωνόντος νεβρίσιν, οἱ δὲ ἐπὶ τοὺς νεβροὺς διασπᾶν κατά τινα ἄρρητον λόγον. See also Photios, *Lexicon* s.v. νεβρίζειν: ἢ νεβροῦ δέρμα φορεῖν ἢ διασπᾶν νέβρους· κατὰ μίμησιν τοῦ περὶ τὸν Διόνυσον πάθους. / On the cult action, see L. Curtius, *Pentheus*, p. 12.

An Attic amphora in Agrigento shows a couple receiving Dionysos [40].[48] In addition to the god with wine vessel and vine branch, the couple, and a silenus who is not ithyphallic, Hermes the guide is also present. With this companion the arrival can be only that of Dionysos. Another vase painting [41] of the same period represents the visiting wine god between a royal man and woman who are probably Ikarios, hero of the deme Ikarion,[49] and his daughter Erigone. She is mentioned as his only daughter in the myth recorded in a Hellenistic tale dealing with the arrival of Dionysos. When the tradition speaks of only one daughter of Semachos, it means that the myth of Semachos is assimilated to that of Ikarios.

We know exactly where Ikarion was situated. The village is still popularly known as "Sto Dionyso," "place of Dionysos." It is the only spot where the divine name has been preserved; everywhere else in Christian Greece it has been transformed into "St. Dionysios."[50] The ruins of a sanctuary of Dionysos with the vestiges of what may be two cult images have been excavated in Sto Dionyso. The village is situated in a high valley on the north side of the marble mountain of Pentelikon and is directly accessible from the coast only by way of the difficult Vrana ravine leading to the beach of Marathon. The detour around Pentelikon is more readily passable. Today it leads up through vineyards from Porto Raphti, the oldest good harbor of Athens. However the cult and culture of the vine may have come to Ikarion, this mountain village may well have been a center from which the Dionysian religion emanated in its first Athenian phase, insofar as the envy of the city dwellers and of the other demes presented no obstacle.

48   From the circle of the Edinburgh painter.
49   On the name of the deme, see D. M. Lewis, "The Deme Ikarion," p. 172.
50   J. C. Lawson, *Modern Greek Folklore and Ancient Greek Religion*, p. 43.

The claim of the Ikarians, and perhaps that of the competing Sema-chidai as well, that the first arrival in Attica occurred in their deme was preserved by Eratosthenes' elaboration of the myth in the Hellenistic period. If his elegy *Erigone* had been preserved, we should learn from it the story as it was then still told. Even the fragments that have come down to us tell us more than the meager tradition concerning the visit to Semachos.

One of the scattered lines quoted from the *Erigone* speaks of an arrival in Thorikos: perhaps it was Dionysos' ship, perhaps he himself, who arrived.[51] Situated between Sounion and Prasiai, the present-day Porto Raphti, Thorikos actually had two harbors. It had been inhabited since the Bronze Age and possessed a cult of Dionysos, at least in connection with its theater which was one of the oldest outside of Athens. According to the Homeric Hymn to Demeter, the goddess passed through Thorikos on her way from Crete to Eleusis.[52] This may also have been where Dionysos landed on his way to the house of Semachos, before visiting Ikarios, and it may have been for precisely this reason that Eratosthenes dealt with this tradition in his poem. It is not unlikely that the learned poet took account of it. As for Ikarion, if there was a tradition connecting the god's visit to Ikarios with one of these two old harbors, it would more likely have been Porto Raphti, where the ancient name of the deme of Prasiai was long preserved in the names "Prasas" and "Prasonisi."[53] This deme, whose name signifies a place distinguished by its striking gardenlike vegetation, may be linked with that other Prasiai on the Laconian coast not far from Nau-

51 In the tradition the beginning of the line is not clear. Meineke, in his edition of Stephen of Byzantium s.v. Ἄστυ, read ἡ δ' ὅτε. J. U. Powell, *Collectanea Alexandrina*, p. 64, has: Εἰσότε δὴ Θορικοῦ καλὸν ἵκανεν ἕδος.

52 The Homeric Hymn to Demeter 126.

53 See A. Milchhoefer, *Karten von Attika*, III–IV, 9.

plia. At that other Prasiai, a landing place of Dionysos in the Peloponnese, the plain was known as the "Garden of Dionysos."[54] The landing retained a special mythical form, as will be seen below.

The tradition tells us very little about the Athenian port of Prasiai, and nothing specifically connected with Dionysos. The fact that it was on the shortest route to Delos lent emphasis to the cult of Apollo, which by no means excludes a cult of Dionysos. Toward the end of antiquity and still later, two islands at the entrance to the sheltered bay bore, like pedestals, two colossal marble statues, probably the products of "a fancy for the monumental in the spirit of Hadrian or Herodes Atticus."[55] One of these still crowns a fair-sized pyramidal rocky island and suggests a figure in feminine dress, if not a Dionysos in woman's clothing then at least a divine woman, a priestess or a goddess,[56] perhaps Demeter or Kybele, both of whom were looked upon as great tutelary goddesses of the Dionysian religion. Another small island, very near the rocky promontory of the mainland, seems —like the cliff facing Naxos—made to order for a Dionysos cult.

I should not, however, have dwelt so long on this mere possibility if Porto Raphti were not still, in actual fact, the wine port of Attica. The maritime routes and the needs of simple life have not changed in thousands of years. Here we discern perspectives extending far beyond the texts and fragments that have been preserved by chance. At the time of the wine harvest we find the little port full of barks ready to carry the new wine northward to Macedonia and Thrace.[57] Turning

54   Pausanias III 24 3. On this transformation into "Brasiai" on the basis of a playful etymology, see below, note 167.

55   Milchhoefer, *Karten von Attika*, III–IV, 9.

56   See C. C. Vermeule, "The Colossus of Porto Raphti in Attica," pp. 75 f., according to whom the statue is a personification related to Demeter.

57   See Kerényi, *Die Herkunft der Dionysosreligion*, pp. 21 f.

southward, this is the shortest crossing not only to Delos but also to Naxos and Ikaros-Ikaria—the two islands deserving of mention in connection with Dionysos and Ikarios—which may well have derived their celebrated wine culture from Crete. In terms of cultural history this place must have been a station of the Dionysian religion in its spread from south to north.

A third landing place is so close to Porto Raphti—separated from it only by the promontory of Perati—that the same considerations can be applied to it. This is the mouth of the Erasinos River near Brauron and its sanctuary of Artemis. Indeed, with Prasiai this site may have formed a larger unit embracing several cults. Allusions to Dionysian goings-on in Brauron have been preserved, and the situation of the theater has also been observed.[58] The allusions occur in Aristophanes' *Peace* and in ancient commentaries on it that have come down to us in very much abbreviated form.[59] The poet merely hinted at the particular debauchery of these rites, but his audience understood him at once. The presence in the same place of both Dionysos and Artemis—the virgin huntress to whose sanctuary in Brauron Athenian maidens were sent to be educated—seems to have been possible in the light of early women's cults. The festivals of Dionysos were celebrated every fifth rather than every third year, a circumstance that argues in favor of a relatively late institution. To the Dionysian *pentaeteris* the Athenians sent a festive delegation,[60] or at least one having the appearance of a solemn *theoria* such as that which in Prasiai received the sacred fire from

58 This observation was made by the Greek archaeologist Ioannes Papadimitriou, who discussed it with me. His death prevented him from determining the topography of his discovery more closely and confirming it by excavations.

59 See Aristophanes, *Peace* 874 and 876 and the scholia on them (quoted in part in note 61, below).

60 *Suidae Lexicon* s.v. Βραυρών (I, 493).

Delos. The delegation probably went to Prasiai rather than Brauron for the sake of the hetairai, who were free game at the festival.[61] To judge by the style, this institution does not seem to have been much older than Aristophanes.

The myth of Ikarion, on the other hand, shows highly archaic features and it seems unlikely that it was Eratosthenes who first related it to the arrival of Dionysos as the bringer of wine culture. Originally "Ikarios" may have been the name of the culture bringer. The mountainous island of Ikaros or Ikaria in the "Ikarian Sea," as the part of the Aegean facing Karia in Asia Minor was called, was held to be a birthplace of Dionysos.[62] It possessed a clear relationship to the wine god: its chief city was named "Oinoë," "city of wine," and the main product of the island has always been wine. There was a tale to the effect that Dionysos, in the course of a sea voyage, was taken prisoner by Tyrrhenian pirates. Thus, the memory of his sea crossings was still alive at the time when the Homeric Hymns were composed. According to one version, Dionysos was on his way from Ikaros to Naxos when this happened,[63] an assertion of the priority of Ikaros over Naxos as the god's home island. It seems not unreasonable to infer that the bringer of wine culture came from Ikaros and founded Ikarion in Attica before the region was fully Hellenized.[64]

The phonetic instability of the names "Ikaros," "Ikarios," "Ikaria," and "Ikarion," argues in favor of a pre-Greek origin. The first vowel seems especially unstable; and the second, to have been pronounced

61 Scholium on Aristophanes, *Peace* 876: ἐν Βραυρῶνι δὲ δήμωι τῆς Ἀττικῆς πολλαὶ πόρναι . . . μεθύοντες δὲ πολλὰς πόρνας ἥρπαζον.

62 *Homeric Hymns* I 1.

63 Apollodoros, *Bibliotheca* III 5 3.

64 This was the opinion as far back as Arthur Evans; see his *Palace of Minos*, IV, 26.

both long and short. The name of the island was also written as "Eka-ros" and "Ekkaros,"[65] and in the inscriptions of the Ikarians in Attica the first vowel is sometimes omitted altogether: after Dionysos a certain "Karios," or "Kar," is named who received offerings for his cult.[66] In the fifth century B.C., the date of these inscriptions, this could only be understood as meaning a "Carian," but mentioned after Dionysos it assuredly did not mean "Zeus Karios," the "Carian Zeus." It was rather the hero of the deme who, along with the name "Ikarios" modeled on a Homeric name (that of Penelope's father), continued to be called at home by an older, more familiar name recalling his foreign origin.

In view of what has been said above about Sirius—in the section on "Iakar and Iakchos" in Chapter III—and the connection between Dionysos and the star Sirius, the same connection in the case of Ikarios cannot be regarded as a late invention, by a Hellenistic poet for example; it too must be very ancient. In the myth retold by Eratosthenes,[67] Sirius appears as the she-dog Maira—the "glittering one"—an appropriate name for this star.[68] The she-dog finds the corpse of Ikarios, or rather the place where his murderers had buried it.[69] Eratosthenes' story, tragic through and through, finds its solution in the transformation of master, daughter, and dog into stars. The daughter's name was

---

65 *RE*, IX, col. 978. The derivation from a West-Semitic root is possible. See Astour, *Hellenosemitica*, pp. 194 f., citing the Akkadian *ikkaru*, "farmer," "planter."

66 *IG* I² 186–87 (A 3, 6, 9, 19, 24). In the passage before last, probably KAP should be read.

67 See the texts in C. Robert, *Eratosthenis Catasterismorum reliquiae*, pp. 72 ff. E. Maass, *Analecta Eratosthenica*, pp. 57–138; G. A. Keller, *Eratosthenes und die alexandrinische Sterndichtung*, pp. 29–94.

68 From μαρμαίρω, a derivation from μαιρίην, τὸ κακῶς ἔχειν, according to Hesychios, a word of Tarentine dialect. See his *Lexicon* s.v. Μαίρα.

69 Apollodoros, *Bibliotheca* III 14 7.

"Erigone" and she played an important part in the story, which took a tragic turn while Ikarios was bestowing the gift of wine. In an ox cart he was carrying full wineskins about through the mountainous regions of Attica, then inhabited by wild shepherds.[70] The shepherds became drunk, thought they were poisoned (this is probably a late explanation; originally drunkenness would no doubt have sufficed), and murdered Ikarios. When they were sober again, they hid the corpse. In the late extracts they did this in various ways; in the original version they buried it. Accompanied by Maira, Erigone wandered about in search of her father. In form, the myth is a repetition of Isis' search for Osiris,[71] but it is not likely that this motif was first introduced by the Alexandrian poet. The early designation of Erigone as "Aletis," "she who wanders about," argues against this hypothesis. The searching, wandering woman and the she-dog have gone together since time immemorial.

In the original myth, wine culture began with this finding of a vine that had grown up into a tree, and in another archaic myth the she-dog Sirius actually gave birth to the vine.[72] According to the oldest myth of the Ikarians, they became acquainted with wine by killing a stranger who came to them unrecognized as the wine god. However, the murdered god, the prototype of the Dionysian sacrifice, only seemed to die. Erigone was his companion, the first Dionysian woman. The

70 See Hyginus, *Astronomica* II 4, which relates how Ikarios was transformed into the constellation of Boötes; see also the *boves Icarii* in Propertius III 33 24.

71 Maass, *Analecta Eratosthenica*, p. 136, note 120; continued by R. Merkelbach, "Die Erigone des Eratosthenes," pp. 489 ff.

72 On the tree version, see Hyginus' mention (in *Astronomica* II 4) of an *arbor, sub qua parens sepultus videbatur*. The *videbatur* shows that the "tree" was really Ikarios. For the myth about Sirius' giving birth to the vine, see the section on "Iakar and Iakchos," above, in ch. III.

first vine grew from his corpse and was at the same time a gift of the she-dog who helped to find it. The myth is inseparable from the rite—the one is an expression of the other, the story of the cult actions and the cult actions of the story—which the bringers of the vine and the wine, whoever they may have been and whatever their place of origin, communicated to the wine growers of the region. In the rite an animal (in Ikarion it was a he-goat) took the place of the god. This was the core of Athenian tragedy. But the tragic myth had a happy ending in the summer's green vineyards and in the winter's pious, merry drinkers.

There is nothing improbable about the assumption that the wine god introduced from outside underwent a split into two persons, god and hero, Dionysos and Ikarios. Every particular of the tradition finds its explanation in this reconstruction. She who fared the worst in the early literature, in the hands of explainers of myth even earlier than Eratosthenes, was the mythical companion of the god, Erigone, the Ariadne of Ikarion and Athens. To judge by her name, "she who was born at dawn," she must have been an aspect of the Great Goddess of Brauron who, under the name "Artemis," was the moon goddess. In her first phase she rose at dawn, nearly or wholly invisible but nevertheless welcomed with veneration. In the genealogy of the heroes who occupied the tragic stage, Erigone became the half-sister of Iphigeneia, a double of the same goddess, a daughter of Klytaimnestra by Aigisthos. In a late tragedy she was indeed, like the heroine honored by the girls of Brauron, chosen by Artemis to be her priestess.[73] It was the goddess of Brauron, who, in one of her aspects, accompanied Dionysos on his arrival. She was included in his myth which in joy and sorrow requires the role of a divine woman, the role of Ariadne. For this role the

73 Hyginus, *Fabulae* 122.

"Aletis" aspect was available, because in archaic myths the moon goddess was seen as "one who wanders about."

The wanderings of Erigone ended—according to the Dionysian feast period of the Athenians—on Choës Day with the Aiora, the "feast of the swings." That this festival signified the end of her wanderings can be inferred from the myth of the Ikarians in which Erigone—in line with a melancholy interpretation of the act of swinging by the explainers of her myth—put an end to her life by hanging herself from the tree that had grown from the corpse of Ikarios. In Athens the girls let themselves be swung in chairs hanging from trees, and the boys were permitted to imitate them, since on Choës Day, the "day of the wine pitchers," they imitated as far as possible everything that was done publicly at the great feast of Dionysos. It was and remained, however, a festival of the virgins.

Here a general observation seems to be in order: "Swinging as a simple bodily activity, as a means of expressing intense joy of life, is among the basic elements of human and (up to a certain point) animal nature—one need only think of the tireless swinging of the apes. It is the first game that is played with a newborn child, and it is played wherever there are happy days of childhood."[74] When people begin to swing, they are spontaneously inaugurating a feast. The feast is inherent in the act of swinging and not the other way round: the swinging is not an otherwise independent game appended to a feast with some mythical significance, but rather, the swinging and the feast enact the same myth. Swinging is also a natural magical action, for it artificially helps the swinger to attain an extraordinary state, hovering in mid-air in a kind of ecstasy. In this it is no "more magical" than

74   F. Boehm, "Das attische Schaukelfest," p. 290.

drinking wine.[75] Between the two there is a kinship, but swinging involves still another element: an approach to the sky, to the sun and moon. If this had really been a magical action in the vulgar sense, as is usually assumed in the scholarly literature,[76] one would indeed think most readily of sun or moon magic.[77] The gloomy interpretation of the swinging at the Attic feast of Aiora—an interpretation based on the legend that the Athenian maidens had been obliged to atone for the death of Erigone by an epidemic of self-hanging, and that swinging was a substitute for this punishment[78]—was an invention of the explainers, but it was not without basis. They could refer to both the character of the Anthesteria and the ambivalence of the moon goddess, who in her dark aspect was also regarded as the lady of the underworld. The terrifying conceptions of an Artemis Apanchomene ("hanged Artemis"), an Ariadne who hangs herself, or a hanged Helen are explained by this swinging or being swung in honor of the darkening Great Goddess.[79]

The most important monument to the swinging of the Athenian maidens, the vase painting by the Penelope painter [42A/42B],[80] stresses

75   See Kerényi, "Das Wesen des Mythos und seine Gegenwärtigkeit," p. 244.
76   See Frazer, *The Golden Bough*, III, 276 ff.
77   H. Wagenvoort, "Phaedra op de schommel," pp. 72 ff., 83 ff.
78   Hyginus, *Astronomica* II 4: "cum in finibus Athenensium multae virgines sine causa suspendio sibi mortem consciscerent, quod Erigone fuerat praecata, ut eodem leto filiae Athenensium adficerentur . . . ."
79   On Artemis Apanchomene, see above, ch. III, at note 195; for the corresponding cult legend of Artemis, see Pausanias VIII 23 6. On Helen, see Pausanias III 19 10; the swinging Helen was afterward called "Dendritis," "she of the tree."
80   Furtwängler and Reichhold, text volume to Ser. III (1932), text for pl. 125, pp. 28–32. See also Freud, *Three Essays on the Theory of Sexuality*, pp. 201–3. I am informed by medical men that the position of the neck induced by swinging arouses feelings of sexual pleasure. This should also be considered

both the erotic element and the modesty of the swung girl: the figure pushing her is a silenus. The strange fact that in the representations known to us a suspended chair is used proves that this was not an every-day game, for then a simpler and handier device would have been used. The day of swinging preceded the night of the queen's marriage to Dionysos. The swinging may be regarded as a chaste prelude to the marriage,[81] a prelude in which the virgins were permitted to participate in self-identification with Erigone. The Athenian maidens also sang the song of the wandering Erigone. The song was called "Aletis," and in Aristotle's time it was sung in the version of an erotic poet famous for his debauchery.[82] Among ancient writers only Ovid states that Erigone became the wife of Dionysos by merely eating a grape.[83] In Eratosthenes' poem we find the gloomy interpretation: Erigone hangs herself but is raised to the heavens as the constellation Virgo. It must have been different in an early tale. The tree that grew from the corpse

---

in connection with the corresponding head position of the dancing maenads, κρᾶτα σεῖσαι, in Euripides, *Bacchae* 185; *colla jactare*, in Ovid, *Metamorphoses* III 726; *iacere caput*, in Tacitus, *Annales* XI 31. See also Dodds, *The Greeks and the Irrational*, pp. 273 f., on the "carriage of the head in Dionysiac ecstasy." Beginning with Rohde (*Psyche*, p. 270, note 26), this "wild shaking and whirling-round of the head" was attributed "to ecstasy and frenzy," that is, to intoxication generally speaking.

81   This is corroborated by the representations of "Choës pitchers," the vessels characteristic of this festival.

82   Theodoros of Kolophon, in Athenaios XIV 618 EF.

83   *Metamorphoses* VI 125: Liber ut Erigonen falsa deceperat uva. Various versions of the theme occur in painting, but seem to have made their first appearance in the late Renaissance with Guido Reni and Poussin. See E. Panofsky, *A Mythological Painting by Poussin in the Nationalmuseum Stockholm*. It was probably the painters Jean-François de Troy (1679–1752) and Anne-Louis Girodet (1767–1824) who found their way back closest to the original myth (see Panofsky, figs. 18–19).

was full of grapes, a giant vine,[84] of which there were some examples. It was an epiphany of the slain bringer of the wine. That the love of the questing Erigone was fulfilled when she swung herself up to the grapes may have been the myth at the source of the swinging. Then came her ascent to the heavens.

The cultural-historical foundation which may be taken as a basis for this attempted reconstruction—though we raise no claim to certainty—reaches far back. Near the little palace of Hagia Triada a tomb almost resembling a cult sanctuary has been found, containing objects from various Minoan periods, among them a small representation of swinging which it has been possible to reconstruct with certainty [43].[85] The seated swinging feminine figure was hung up between columns on each of which sat a bird about to take flight. Here rigid interpretation of these birds as epiphanies of Minoan deities, who often appeared in this form, encounters difficulties; what these birds actually indicate is the state of swinging.[86] A seated feminine figurine also intended to be swung (dating from the middle of the third millennium B.C. and found in a sanctuary of the Babylonian goddess Ninhursag in the course of excavations in Mari on the Euphrates) and prehistoric figurines from Greece with holes for hanging up and perhaps for swinging have all been lumped together under the catchwords "déesse de la

84   See above, ch. III, note 23. L. A. Milani, *Museo Topografico dell'Etruria,* p. 145, no. 47, mentions *un ceppo di vite di eccezionale grossezza, trovato non lungi da Populonia,* now *nel Museo di Storia Naturale* [in Florence] *come oggetto di rarità,* but such things were no rarity in antiquity.

85   See R. Paribeni, "Ricerca nel sepolcreto di Haghia Triada presso Phaestos," p. 747 and figs. 42, 43; C. Picard, "Phèdre à la balançoire et le symbolisme des pendaisons," p. 50. Evans, *Palace of Minos,* IV, 24, note 4, suggests the resemblance to a cult sanctuary because of the varying ages of the things found with it (the last dating from roughly 1360 B.C.).

86   See M. P. Nilsson, *The Minoan-Mycenaean Religion,* p. 331, note 7.

fécondité" and "rite de la fécondité,"[87] as though the sport in which the apes also participate were inconceivable without fertility as an aim, as though life could not take an aimless pleasure in life.

The Arrival in Athens

THE FEAST of the swings is not the only consideration which makes it seem likely that Dionysos was brought to Athens by women. In its execution the joyful rite was exalted far above animal nature, and, as already indicated, it was connected with another, more secret cult action, the god's marriage to the highest ranking woman of the city, who under the democracy still bore the title of "queen." This action must have been of supreme importance for the city, but it is scarcely conceivable that it derived its importance from the men. The prelude—and it is as such that we must interpret the swinging—was based on the myth of the Dionysian heroine of Ikarion. The women of Athens—not only the swinging girls, but also the mature women, and especially those women who had achieved the fullness of life and hoped to preserve it in death—identified themselves with her. A large number of little oil pitchers from the sixth century B.C., black-figure lekythoi that have been found in tombs, repeat an otherwise incomprehensible image. The image is also present in larger and better executed form [44, 45],[88] but the scene, though varying in details [46], is always es-

87   C. Delvoyé, "Rites de Fécondité dans les religions préhelléniques," pp. 127 f. See also A. Parrot, "Les fouilles de Mari," pp. 18 f., pl. VIII.

88   On the other side of the krater shown in [44], a maenad stands between Dionysos and a nude man [45]. She appears to be leaving the bearded god—who is standing there in his wide garment, holding a cornucopia and looking after her—to follow the man. / One striking variation to be seen in [44] is the

sentially the same. A woman is mounting a chariot drawn by four horses; one foot is still on the ground and the other is in the chariot which, like the battle chariot of a hero, has two wheels. This is not an event in the life of women. The type is defined as the "goddess mounting her chariot." Sometimes a second woman is sitting in front of the team [46]:[89] an absurd and actually impossible situation unless this figure indicates that the heroic-divine ascension takes place in the community of women, whose smallest group consists of two persons —the two daughters of Semachos, for example. Dionysos is present in his gravest aspect, as a bearded god in his wide garment. The ascension takes place under his protection. This is the ascension of Erigone in a new, heroic stylization.[90]

To all indications the Athenian women were the actual bearers of the city's Dionysos cult. They had taken possession of the god, and through the queen's union with him the city participated in their pos-

---

he-goat with a man's head—a strange representative of the Dionysian afterlife— who is standing in front of Dionysos. The god himself wears his wide garment and holds a kantharos. I am indebted to Dr. Hans Peter Isler for parallels such as those in his *Acheloos*, p. 134, no. 62 (cf. pp. 113 ff.), and for [47] where there is a different distribution of roles as Dionysos mounts the chariot while a woman who is labeled "Semele" looks on. The vase painter has visualized a scene in the underworld: Dionysos, about to leave it, wishes to take his mother with him (interpreted by O. Höfer ["Semele," col. 676] as an introduction to Olympos). The motif is that of *ascensio*, here employed outside of the Attic myth but according to the Attic prototype whose heroine was not Semele. / Still another variation in details is to be seen in E. Haspels, *Attic Black-Figured Lekythoi*, pl. XXXVIII 2, where the lyre characterizes Dionysos as Melpomenos, whose cult had rather a private character (see Pausanias I 2 5).

89 Transcript of the painting on an Attic lekythos in O. M. von Stackelberg, *Die Gräber der Hellenen*, pl. XII 4.

90 The ascension is expressly called that of Erigone in Lucian, *Deorum concilium* 5.

session. A proof that this was the original situation is the fact that in Athens the women were the mistresses of the wine. They were active in the Lenaion—the sanctuary of Dionysos which also served as the public, sacred, and exemplary wine press—and thus identified themselves as those to whom, after the gods, the wine was owed. The myth according to which the queen received Dionysos as bringer of the wine culture, holding a kantharos and a vine branch laden with grapes, was preserved only pictorially. This is the third variation that occurs in the vase paintings showing the coming of Dionysos to Semachos and his two daughters or to Ikarios. Accompanied only by two ithyphallic sileni, the god is striding toward a royal woman; no one else is present [48].[91] A possibility of situating the Athenian arrival of Dionysos in the Athenian festive calendar would be to assume that this arrival took place in Phaleron and that the festival of thanksgiving in which it was commemorated, the Oschophoria, was later transformed into a feast day of the epheboi. The vestiges of the original festival would then have been the grape-laden vine branches carried and the feminine attire worn by the two youths who led the procession to the place where the god had once landed bearing the same gift. Now in thanksgiving the gift was again borne to that very place. In the revised festival, however, the main role would have been played by the two women and not by the queen, as shown by vase painters at the time when epheboi celebrated the Oschophoria with the Athenian women and took the leading part.

Dionysos, whether he came to Athens by way of Phaleron or became the god of the Athenian women in some unknown way, was a state deity even in the first phase of his cult. He did not possess a cult statue

91   By the Rycroff painter, in the Museo Faina, Orvieto.

but only a cult symbol, in the form of an erect phallus, in the sacred precinct of the Horai. That this, too, was secret may be inferred from the fact that the name "Orthos," under which he received his offerings, was interpreted to mean that thanks to his instruction men were able to mix their wine with water and hence walk erect.[92] He obtained a statue and a priest only after he had been publicly brought to Athens from Eleutherai, a mountain village on the Boeotian border. In this connection he was called "Eleuthereus," a name with a dual derivation. It stems from the village Eleutherai, named after the goddess Eleuthera, both of which come from the root "Eleuther." As Eleuthereus, Dionysos also bore the surname "Melanaigis," "he with the black goatskin." What little we know of the myth of Eleutherai is already familiar in style. The cult of Dionysos as Melanaigis was founded by the daughters of Eleuther, whose number is not indicated. Like Semachos and Ikarios, Eleuther was seen as the founding hero of a settlement and a double of the god. In this instance Dionysos comes to the daughters as an apparition, a *phasma*, dressed in a black goatskin. They do not want the god in that form: they revile him. Thereupon he makes them raving mad. In order to be cured, they are obliged to worship Melanaigis, that is, the dark Dionysos in league with the spirits of the dead.[93] It was in this quality that he was later, in Athens, to delight in tragedy.

The cult image was brought to Athens by Pegasos, a man whose name was preserved only in connection with this function. One might reflect on his name and ask whether it was not the self-chosen name of

92   Athenaios II 38 c: διὸ καὶ ὀρθοὺς γενέσθαι τοὺς ἀνθρώπους οὕτω πίνοντας, πρότερον ὑπὸ τοῦ ἀκράτου καμπτομένους.

93   *Suidae Lexicon* s.v. Μέλαν: . . . αἱ τοῦ Ἐλευθῆρος θυγατέρες θεασάμεναι φάσμα τοῦ Διονύσου ἔχον μελάνην αἰγίδα ἐμέμψαντο· ὁ δὲ ὀργισθεὶς ἐξέμηνεν αὐτάς. μετὰ ταῦτα ὁ Ἐλευθὴρ ἔλαβε χρησμὸν ἐπὶ παύσει τῆς μανίας τιμῆσαι Μελαναιγίδα Διόνυσον.

a missionary priest bearing the god with him. The man's existence cannot be doubted. His statue was situated in the same place as the representation of the gods receiving the hospitality of Amphiktyon.[94] Pausanias cites a response of the oracle of Delphi on the subject. The oracle was asked if the god might be brought to Athens. The answer was that Dionysos had already landed once in the days of Ikarios; consequently it was permissible to introduce him a second time. This demonstrates at least that there was an awareness of two phases of the Dionysos cult in Attica. It seems safe to look upon Pegasos as a missionary of this cult.[95] According to the tradition, it was this arrival that first led to the institution in Attica of the processions in which phalli were carried.[96] The men did not wish to accept the god in this form and consequently were punished—a repeated motif. Although the punishment did not affect the fertility of the country or fertility in general, it did affect the phalli of the men, who fell sick in this organ. Their ailment was not impotence, but satyriasis.[97] It may be assumed that the missionary brought to Athens not only the cult image of which we are told, a seated statue,[98] but also the prototype of the phalli that were carried about in public.

It was thus that the men acquired their role in the Dionysian religion. It is extremely unlikely that this occurred as late as the time of the tyrant Peisistratos, in the sixth century B.C. Pegasos, rather, followed in the footsteps of the seer Melampous, who according to He-

94 Pausanias I 2 5.
95 Pickard-Cambridge, *Dramatic Festivals*, p. 57.
96 Scholium on Aristophanes, *Acharnians* 243.
97 This is described in a scholium on Lucian, *Deorum concilium* 5 which supplements a scholium on Aristophanes, *Acharnians* 243 and originally formed part of the same explanatory text.
98 Philostratos, *Vitae sophistarum* II 1 3: τὸ τοῦ Διονύσου ἕδος.

rodotos was first to introduce the phalli to Greece and to make these cult implements understandable with his interpretation. It would be contrary to history to suppose that his interpretation was symbolical. It must have been mythical. Melampous was still one of the heroes; chronologically he dates from the Mycenaean era. The activity of Pegasos must be situated soon afterward. In the light of our present knowledge, Melampous, whose deeds were glorified by post-Homeric singers in a special epic, the *Melampodeia*, may therefore be regarded as no less a real person.[99] He came from Pylos where he spent his legendary youth.[100] The chief scene of his activity as soothsayer and expiatory priest was the Peloponnese. He allegedly cured the daughters of Proitos, king of Tiryns, of their madness, which overcame them because they opposed the worship of Dionysos.

The theme is the same as in the story of the daughters of Eleuther. At Pylos a text from the Mycenaean era bears witness to a cult, which can only have been that of Dionysos, under this name: *e-re-u-te-re di-wi-je-we*, "Eleuther, son of Zeus."[101] Melampous was connected with Pylos but acquired his cult as a hero in the small seaport town of Aigosthena, a hidden harbor in the Gulf of Corinth, the present-day Porto Germano. In Aigosthena there stood a sanctuary with a grave-relief of the hero, where in Pausanias' time offerings were still made to him and his annual feast day was celebrated.[102] From this port a road—for a time a military highway—led up to the mountain pass where Eleutherai is situated. In all likelihood this was the itinerary of the god who ultimately arrived in Athens as Eleuthereus.

99 Hesiod, *Carmina*, pp. 191 ff.; *Fragmenta Hesiodea*, pp. 133 ff.
100 Apollodoros, *Bibliotheca* I 9 11.
101 J. Puhvel, "Eleuther and Oinoatis: Dionysian Data from Mycenaean Greece," pp. 161 ff.
102 Pausanias I 44 5.

It should not be supposed that the inhabitants of Eleutherai were left without a cult statue because Pegasos moved the god, who had come to them by way of Aigosthena, to Athens. Pausanias tells of a copy which was shown him in Eleutherai, while the original was to be seen in a small temple on the southern slope of the Akropolis, the site of the plays. Thence on certain days of the year[103] it was borne to the *heroön* of Akademos (or Hekademos) in the precinct of the Akademeia, and then brought back to its own sanctuary for the performance of tragedies. This was assuredly done in memory of the statue's wanderings and first arrival in Athens. The cult statues of the Dionysian religion must have been more readily movable than most Greek statuary, because we have testimony to show that Dionysos was carried about, sometimes in a common cart.[104] His statues seem to have been cult implements no less than the masks which, with the god's wide garment attached to them, served as his cult images.

The statue of Eleuthereus was carried back and forth on a ship equipped with wheels. Representations on vase paintings show not only the cart in the form of a ship and the god wrapped in his wide garment enthroned on it, but also the little procession in which he made his entry. The ship places the arrival of the strange procession

103   Pausanias I 29 2.

104   On Delos this took place in the month corresponding to the Athenian Elaphebolion (A. Frickenhaus, "Der Schiffskarren des Dionysos in Athen," p. 68). "The car in which Dionysos was carried about" (see the excavation report in *BCH*, XXXIV [1910], 177) was kept in the treasure house of the Andrians (*BCH*, VI [1882], 125), an indication that a similar ceremony was performed on the island of Andros. Concerning the *periphora* of the statue as an important element of the Dionysia among the Phocians of Methymna, see *IG* XII:2 503 10; and in general, Athenaios X 428 E. All this is brought out by Frickenhaus.

in the perspective of the sea, which is no more than a day's journey for an animal-drawn vehicle from any point on the Greek mainland. The wheels show that the journey to Athens was made over land, but the ship took on a ritual significance which the vase painters easily raised to the level of myth. They were able to put life into the seated statue so convincingly that it became a god enthroned on a real ship [49, 50].[105] Exekias, the painter of the famous cup from Vulci, now in Munich, followed the poet of the Homeric Hymn to Dionysos: vines have grown up the mast and grapes hang down from them—a sign witnessed by the pirates who in the hymn had carried him off on their ship [51].[106]

The core of this ritual procession has its analogies in the religious and cultural history of Egypt, where gods in their chapels were borne by barks which the gods' servants carried on their backs.[107] What in Greece was an anomaly, limited to the cult of Dionysos, was held to be the most natural thing in the world in Egypt, where the Nile was the main avenue of communication. Threads of the tie with Egypt, which Herodotos assumed to exist in connection with Melampous, emerge with strange persistence in Greek style. The Dionysian element has become constitutive in this style. The ship car, which bore the goddess' new *peplos* like a sail in the procession of the Panathenaia, was introduced later, probably modeled on the Dionysian procession.[108]

105   See Frickenhaus, "Der Schiffskarren," pp. 76 f.; E. Buschor, *Griechische Vasen*, p. 128.

106   See *Homeric Hymns* VII 38–40.

107   The essential correspondence was noted by F. Dümmler, "Skenische Vasenbilder," p. 28, note 3. He refers to the picture in A. Erman, *Aegypten und aegyptisches Leben im Altertum* (1885 edn., p. 374), which cites K. R. Lepsius, *Denkmäler aus Ägypten und Äthiopien*, III, pl. XIV.

108   L. Ziehen, "Panathenaia," col. 462.

The Smyrniot rite attested for late antiquity may have been descended from the famous Athenian festivals with processions of ship cars.[109]

At the feast of Anthesteria, the Smyrniots, in memory of a naval victory, dragged a war trireme from the harbor to the agora; it was guided by a priest of Dionysos. A prow shown on Smyrniot coins of the Imperial Age may be an allusion to this ship.[110] Most probably the ceremony was an elaborate, late version of the above-mentioned festival of Dionysos, not without foundation in the myth—varied by the poets and painters—which every seaport town could claim for its own. After the Athenian potters, whose painted wares were in demand from the Tyrrhenian to the Black Sea, Attic comedy with its image of Dionysos as ship owner helped to elaborate this myth. In this reinterpretation he is evoked by Hermippos, the writer of comedies, as one who carried on maritime commerce in Athens but had not always done so.[111] The joke is an allusion not only to the importance of the Athenian trade in wine and wine jars, but also to the fact that with Athens as his base Dionysos achieved greater power than he had enjoyed since the Minoan and Mycenaean eras. It was this power that first led the sea to be taken as the scene of his epiphany, as shown in Attic art.

The question as to which Athenian feast of Dionysos was the first instance of the procession with ship cars cannot be answered on the basis of the later growth and increased magnificence of the cult in the

109 Philostratos, *Vitae sophistarum* I 25; Aristides, *Rhetorica*, in Dindorf, ed., I, 440.

110 From the second century A.D.; see H. Usener, *Die Sintflutsagen*, p. 116, note 2.

111 Hermippos, fr. 63A, line 2 (from the comedy *The Porters*): ἐξ οὗ ναυκληρεῖ Διόνυσος ἐπ᾽ οἴνοπα πόντον (in Edmonds, *The Fragments of Attic Comedy*, I, 304–305).

larger Mediterranean seaports. We are dependent on the vase paintings of the sixth century and the testimonies from Athens. Greek vase paintings, like myths, vary their theme, and this phenomenon may be observed in the representations of Dionysos' ship car. The actual theme is not the procession as it was seen in Athens, but the god's arrival, repeated and ritually represented in the *pompe*, the procession. To what extent any particular variant goes beyond what was actually shown at the festival we can never be quite sure. A vase painting was an autonomous work of art, in this case a representation of the arrival as the vase painter chose to see it.

The painter of a black-figure cup now in Berlin combined the arrival on shipboard with the arrival on a mule. The circular picture inside the cup shows the bearded god with a rhyton in his ship, the prow of which is shaped like the head of a mule [52A].[112] The role of the mule in the entry that the painter had in mind is further emphasized by the fact that the seated Dionysos is shown on both sides of the outside of the cup, each time flanked by two women riding on mules [52B].[113] What entry did the painter have in mind? One connected with one of the known Attic festivals? If so, we think most readily of Dionysos' marriage to the queen on the night after Choës Day. The mule was a favorite animal of Dionysos. Here there can be no thought of fertility, although there are mules of both sexes. An Attic amphora in the Museo di Villa Giulia in Rome shows Dionysos on a mule on whose phallus a kantharos is hanging. An ithyphallic silenus leads; another follows [54A].[114] On a fragment of an amphora by the Amasis

112   See Nilsson, "Dionysos im Schiff," p. 21.

113   A similar scene has been transcribed from a lekythos in Athens [53] by Stackelberg, *Die Gräber der Hellenen*, pl. XIV 5.

114   Museo Nazionale di Villa Giulia, no. 3550 (*CVA*, pl. VIII 5). A very similar scene is depicted on an Attic stamnos in the museum of Cerveteri.

painter an ithyphallic mule is dancing among drunken companions of Dionysos [54B].[115] On one of the wine pitchers characteristic of the Choës festival, love play between mules is represented [55].[116] The Greeks who had, and still have, ample opportunity to observe such love play still find ground for meditative amusement at the invincible power of the sexual drive, even when it leads to nothing.[117] Here again, just as in the swinging that was one of the amusements of the same festival, we have an expression of the aimless joy of life. In the present case the painter's abbreviation, in which ship and mule are combined into a single Dionysian vehicle, must be resolved as follows. The god crosses the sea on shipboard, but in the harbor—perhaps in Phaleron, where he was received by two women who were later replaced by two youths dressed as women—he was made to mount a mule and led to the queen. There is nothing to indicate that he came to her on a ship equipped with wheels. No chous (pitcher) shows a ship as a marriage symbol, and only one shows a car, probably drawn by mules. On the strength of these representations alone we can exclude the possibility of a procession of ship cars at the feast of the Anthesteria with its climax on Choës Day.

At what feast, then, was the ship car that had been held in readiness in some storeroom paraded with the enthroned statue of the god? We are more likely to find an indication in the vase paintings where the ship car appears, though it should not be forgotten that the vase painters were never interested in rendering a historical procession. The painter's interest was solely in evoking the arrival itself, the *epidemia*

115 Semni Karouzou, *The Amasis Painter*, pl. XXX 2.

116 Frickenhaus saw the connection; see Deubner, *Attische Feste*, p. 102. Also see below, ch. VI, note 48.

117 See Kerényi, *Werke*, II, 48, 49; and on the carrying of wine on mule back, p. 24.

of the god seen as a divine event that was the common source of feast and painting. In two of the three such representations that have been preserved, the god is so lifelike as to suggest that on this occasion a man played the part of Dionysos.[118] This was not fundamentally impossible, but we do know from witnesses that the seated statue was carried about. A more likely supposition is that the sileni who play flutes before and behind the god on the ship and those who draw the ship car on the skyphos of Bologna are masked men [56A/56B].[119] As for the fragmentary skyphos in Athens, too little of it has been preserved [57].[120] The ivy-wreathed, bearded Dionysos holds the vine branches with hanging grapes, but this tells us nothing about the season because in the suprahistorical sphere of myth in which the vase painter envisioned the *epidemia,* the power of the god could ripen them. This is also the case with the other skyphoi [58] offering pictures of the procession—or we might well say a primordial image, representations of the primordial procession.

On the London skyphos [59A/59B] as on the skyphos in Bologna, the same animal head (but not the head of a mule) is affixed to the prow. This does not seem to be an invention of the vase painter, for the sculptor of the so-called Bema of Phaidros in the Athens theater employs this same head for the she-dog Maira in his representation of Dionysos' visit to Ikarios [60].[121] This leads us to suppose that the ship car itself was constructed as a kind of abbreviation, unless the she-dog also played a role outside the myth of the arrival in Ikarion. She was not invented by a Hellenistic poet—this can be taken as dem-

118 Deubner, *Attische Feste,* pp. 107 f.
119 See Frickenhaus, "Der Schiffskarren," p. 72.
120 After Graef and Langlotz, *Die antiken Vasen von der Akropolis,* I : iv, pl. 74 (no. 1281A/B).
121 See Picard, *L'Acropole,* p. 76.

onstrated—but had her place from time immemorial in the Attic myths of arrival, as had Sirius in the year of the wine god. A survey designed to show which of the Athenian Dionysian feasts could *not* have featured a ship car pointed exclusively to the arrival in Ikarion.[122] The ship could have been brought indirectly from Prasiai or Brauron, but in Athens itself there was no festival offering room for this rite. An allusion to the myth of Ikarion in the form of an abbreviation, a combination of ship and she-dog, was just as possible as the allusion to the use of mules.

Although the procession of the Great Dionysia is the only one for which we have express testimony that a statue of the god was carried, it was thought necessary on general principles to exclude it as a possibility for the ship car procession: it seemed impossible to conceive of Eleuthereus on shipboard. Yet this was the solution to the riddle, confirmed by all the particulars that enable us to determine the god's sea route to Eleutherai.[123] The decision between the two itineraries— by way of the sea and Ikarion or by way of the sea and Eleutherai to the Great Dionysia—is provided by the composition of the procession in which the vase painters represent the ship car, for it contains nothing characteristic of Ikarion and everything that is characteristic of Athens.

The small procession depicted on the skyphoi appears to be a scanty excerpt of the great festive procession, richly laden with wine and bread and costly vessels, which passed through the crowded theater at the height of Athenian power.[124] But the painters intended it as the

---

122   E. Pfuhl, *De Atheniensium pompis sacris*, p. 73.

123   See Frickenhaus, "Der Schiffskarren," pp. 61–79.

124   See E. Bethe, "Programm und Festzug der grossen Dionysien," pp. 459–64, especially p. 463.

core and prototype of the great procession. The *kanephoros*, the virgin bearing on her head the basket of accessories for the sacrificial ceremony, was chosen for the City Dionysia by the archon of the year, from whom the year took its name.[125] A youth carried the fire in a *thymaterion*, or censer. Among the men accompanying him it is not possible to distinguish the most necessary person at the sacrifice, the priest who will kill the bull. He does not occupy a prominent position and wishes to be nothing more than a necessary instrument in the ambivalent act of slaughtering. Among the Athenians—and others—even the instrument earned punishment for such an act. The protagonist is the bull himself. In a representation without the ship car, on a sixth-century lekythos, the bull is motley [61A].[126] A great many bulls were sacrificed on this occasion,[127] but *one* bull is singled out with the words otherwise used to invoke Dionysos: *axios tauros*, "worthy bull." This was the animal that the epheboi sacrificed at the great feast after they had, on the previous evening, brought the statue of the god back from the *heroön* of the Akadameia to his sanctuary in the city.[128]

The small ideal procession—like the magnificent one of the great historical period—is accompanied by flute players and (on the same lekythos with the motley bull) is led by an instrument that commands our attention [61B]. This is the *salpinx*. In this instance it resembles

---

125   K. Mittelhaus, "Kanephoroi," col. 1856.

126   See Stackelberg, *Die Gräber der Hellenen*, pl. XVI; Frickenhaus, loc. cit.

127   This is proved by the accounts concerning the hides of the sacrificial bulls for the years 334/333 B.C. and 331/330 B.C. in *IG*, II, 741.

128   *IG* II-III: I² 1006 (concerning the period from 123/122 B.C. to 122/121 B.C.), lines 12–13: εἰσήγαγον δὲ καὶ τὸν Διόνυσον ἀπὸ τῆς ἐσχάρας εἰς τὸ θέατρον μετὰ φωτὸς καὶ ἔπεμψαν τοῖς Διονυσίοις ταῦρον ἄξιον τοῦ θεοῦ, ὃν καὶ ἔθυσαν ἐν τῶι ἱερῶι τῆι πομπῆι. ("They also led Dionysos from the hearth to the theater by torchlight and sent for the Dionysia a bull worthy of the god, which they sacrificed in the holy precinct when the procession entered it.")

the long *tuba* of the Romans which was later to be blown by the angels of Christianity to awaken the dead. The instrument thus had a long history in the Etruscan-Roman cultural sphere,[129] of which it was more characteristic than it was for the Greeks. Homer's heroes did not make use of it, and he mentions it only in metaphors as something foreign which had, however, been introduced into Greece.[130] In Greece it was used chiefly in war. Its use in processions and sacrificial ceremonies, it has been remarked, is peculiar to the Egyptians, Argives, Etruscans, and Romans.[131] In Argos it is mentioned in connection with the very archaic Dionysos cult of Lerna.

How long this archaic element of the procession was retained in Athens we do not know. Time and again the tragic poets term the *salpinx* "Tyrrhenian," that is, Etruscan,[132] thus stressing its foreign character. The use of this adjective would be odd if in a festive procession in Athens, especially that which inaugurated the tragedy, the *salpinx* had been used solely for practical purposes, such as to clear the crowd from the path of the procession.[133] In the cult it was also employed on Choës Day. The unique representation on this small sixth-century lekythos is an important testimony to the past, when the cult

129 In the book *De saeculis* of his *Antiquitates rerum humanarum*, Varro —evidently at the end of one *saeculum* and the beginning of another—mentions *auditum sonum tubae de caelo*, "the sound of a *salpinx* heard from heaven" (Servius' commentary on *Aeneid* VIII 526).

130 Iliad XVIII 219; XXI 388. See also K. O. Müller and W. Deecke, *Die Etrusker*, II, 207; H. L. Lorimer, *Homer and the Monuments*, p. 490. Athena Salpinx, who according to the founding legend possessed a temple in Argos (Pausanias II 21 3), was undoubtedly of Lydian, that is, Etruscan-related, origin.

131 Pollux IV 86: ἔστι δέ τι καὶ πομπικὸν ἐπὶ πομπαῖς, καὶ ἱερουργικὸν ἐπὶ θυσίαις, Αἰγυπτίοις τε καὶ Ἀργείοις καὶ Τυρρηνοῖς καὶ Ῥωμαίοις.

132 Aischylos, *Eumenides* 567; Sophokles, *Ajax* 17; Euripides, *Phoenissae* 1377, *Heraclidae* 830, *Rhesus* 988.

133 Frickenhaus, "Der Schiffskarren," p. 66.

of Eleutherai made its entrance into the city. It would be still more individual and unrelated to Athenian existence as reflected in the monuments if it were not connected with the history of the Dionysian religion. In this history, not only the islands of the Aegean Sea but also the cult sites of the Peloponnese seem to have played an intermediate role.

Myth of Arrival and Ancient Rite outside of Attica: Thebes and Delphi

THE ARRIVAL of Dionysos in Attica and Athens can be traced back to the missionlike introduction of wine culture and the cult of the god, events in the prehistory and early history of Greece, the last event of which, though impossible to date, was the bringing of the statue of Eleuthereus. Probably he had long been worshiped in the place from which his statue was repeatedly brought, in the Akadameia, before his temple was built in the sixth century B.C. A myth of arrival whose main themes were resistance to the new cult, which the people did not understand, and persecution of the god and the women who worshiped him, was current in various regions on the mainland. It represented itself as a reflection of a historical event. This puts it in the class not of primary myths but of edifying tales, in which the enemies and persecutors play an almost greater role than the god himself. Nevertheless, as Erwin Rohde said, such tales have a "substratum of historical fact."[134] Such a truth is the arrival itself, the foun-

134   Rohde, *Psyche*, p. 283.

dation of all these tales—but not an arrival from the north! In essence, the story of the persecution of the Dionysian women by the king of Thrace is identical with the story of how they were combated by Perseus in Argos.[135] Both in the southern and in the northern mainland the cult of Dionysos was an intruder.

Lykourgos, son of Dryas, is identified as a Thracian by his genealogy. To Homer he was the exemplar of an enemy of the god who was punished for his sacrilege with blindness.[136] There was a pre-Homeric tale about him, which Glaukos briefly repeats in the Iliad. His words there are based on the tale, which can be reconstructed through them. A site for the cult of Dionysos—a *nyseïon*[137]—had already been chosen in the region ruled over by Lykourgos, and the god's nurses were already engaged in carrying out a sacrificial rite for him. It is here that Homer calls him *mainomenos*, "mad." The word, as defined at the beginning of this chapter, designates the state induced by wine, into which the women who worshiped Dionysos could enter even without wine. In this state each one of them was a *mainas*, a "raving woman."[138] Their rage was of a particular kind, which we shall later try to define more closely than can be done with either this word or the word "madness." "Madness" would apply to the condition of Lykourgos,[139] who flung himself on the women engaged in sacrifice and seized the "ox club" (*bouplex*). This can only refer to the traditional double ax used

135   Rohde (ibid., pp. 282; 305, note 3) separates them—for the sake of his thesis that Dionysos was of Thracian origin. He gives no reason for doing so.

136   Iliad VI 130–40.

137   See Kerényi, *Eleusis*, p. 34.

138   Iliad XXII 460, in a metaphor. See Otto, *Dionysos*, pp. 54–55; Dodds, *The Greeks and the Irrational*, p. 271.

139   This was the Greek conception, attested by Apollodoros, *Bibliotheca* III 51.

for the sacrifice.[140] With it Lykourgos created a blood bath among the nurses as they dropped the *thystla*, the other sacrificial accessories.

Homer's commentators tried to attenuate the horror by interpreting the *bouplex* as a whip or goad for driving cows,[141] but merely to have scattered the maenads would not have been the great sacrilege that made Lykourgos an exemplar for Homer. He makes himself very clear:

ὑπ' ἀνδροφόνοιο Λυκούργου / θεινόμεναι βουπλῆγι·

struck by Lykourgos, / murderer of human beings . . .[142]

This bloody deed and the unattenuated archaic form of the tale correspond exactly to a story dealing with Perseus and the region over which he ruled. In Argos visitors were shown not only the tomb of the maenad Choreia ("choral dance"), who was killed by Perseus, but also, near the temple of Hera Antheia, the tomb of the Haliai (the "sea women"), who fell in battle with Perseus—a mass grave[143] presupposing a blood bath. A roving legend, such as this one must be, would appear to show more substantial ties with definite monuments than with a *nyseïon* in Thrace whose geographical situation cannot be determined, and the immoderate bloody deed seems more appropriate to a king of that wild country than to a Mycenaean hero. It is more likely that the story was transferred from Perseus to Lykourgos than the other way round. Even the "wolf against bull" motif—"wolf" is present in the name "Lykourgos"—may be of Argive origin. According

140   Ovid, *Metamorphoses* IV 22, *Tristia* V 3 39.

141   Scholium on Iliad VI 135: βουπλῆγι· μάστιγι ἤ πελέκει. The second meaning was the universally accepted one; see B. Schweitzer, *Herakles*, p. 46.

142   Iliad VI 134–35. In a previous line (130) Lykourgos' only epithet was κρατερός ("strong").

143   See Pausanias II 20 4, and 22 1.

to the legend, it was the victory of an attacking wolf over a bull, as announced in an oracle, that gave Danaos power over Argos.[144]

More important than all these indications of Argive origin is the story's connection, in a point essential for religion, with a highly archaic Dionysos cult in Argos, that of Lerna, to which we have referred above. The essential point is the fate of the god. After the sacrificial rite of Dionysos' nurses had been broken up by Lykourgos and they themselves had been killed like sacrificial animals, the god, who is described by Homer as a child needful of nurses, took fright and dived under the sea. There he was adopted by Thetis,[145] who in the Homeric view of the world was best suited to this function. Here only the mode of mythological expression is Homeric. In Plutarch we find another name for the same function at the end of the sacrificial rite performed in the course of the Agrionia, a somber biennial[146] Dionysian festival in Boeotia. The women search for the god as though he had fled and finally say he has taken refuge with the Muses, who have hidden him. The priest of Dionysos pursues the women with his sword and is permitted to sacrifice the one he catches, but if he does so, it is a catastrophe for the country. The gods punish this cruelty in the performance of what was meant to be mere ritual.[147]

144 Pausanias II 19 3–4.

145 Iliad VI 135–36: Διώνυσος δὲ φοβηθεὶς / δύσεθ' ἁλὸς κατὰ κῦμα, Θέτις δ' ὑπεδέξατο κόλπωι . . . . The last word refers both to the "bosom" of the goddess and to the broad-bosomed sea (Iliad XXI 125).

146 Plutarch, *Quaestiones Graecae* 299 F: παρ' ἐνιαυτὸν. The meaning is "in alternating years," when, as in the case of a *trieteris*, there is a possibility of alternation; once this way (with persecution) and once that way (without persecution). *Quaestiones conviviales* VIII *Praefatio*: οὐ φαύλως οὖν καὶ παρ' ἡμῖν ἐν τοῖς Ἀγριωνίοις τὸν Διόνυσον αἱ γυναῖκες ὡς ἀποδεδρακότα ζητοῦσιν· εἶτα παύονται καὶ λέγουσιν, ὅτι πρὸς τὰς Μούσας καταπέφευγε καὶ κέκρυπται παρ' ἐκείναις.

147 Plutarch tells us of the priest Zoïlos, a contemporary of his, who performed the rite literally: *Quaestiones Graecae* 299 F.

It is especially clear in Boeotia, Plutarch's place of origin,[148] that the ambivalent ceremony of the nurses—for the Dionysian women functioned both as nurses and as slaughterers—was the basis of an arrival and resistance myth. The daughters of Minyas, the founding hero of Orchomenos, resisted when Dionysos summoned the women to a secret celebration in the mountains.[149] As punishment they became not only *mainades*, which as married women they could not reconcile with love of their husbands,[150] but madwomen. They chose the child of one of their number by lot and tore it to pieces, while those in the mountains did the same with a young animal. Therein consisted the ambivalent ceremony: in the sacrificing of the god whose nurses they had been appointed.

The evidence is clear and leaves no room for doubt as to the core of the Dionysian religion, the essence that endured for thousands of years and formed the very basis of its existence. In the form of an animal the god suffered the extreme reduction, a cruel death, but he, indestructible *zoë*, escaped—to Thetis, to the Muses, or however this was expressed mythologically. According to the Argive tradition as expressed in the dry language of a scholiast of Homer, Perseus killed Dionysos the intruder and threw him into the deep lake of Lerna.[151]

148 It is probable that Plutarch always means Orchomenos even when, as above in *Quaestiones conviviales* VIII, he only says "in our region," for his native city of Chaironeia is very near Orchomenos.

149 Antoninus Liberalis X; Ovid, *Metamorphoses* IV 1–2 and 389 ff. The situation of Orchomenos near Thebes made it impossible to describe an arrival from afar. The daughters of Minyas were to join in the cult which the Thebans celebrated on Mt. Kithairon.

150 See Aelian, *Varia historia* III 42, who speaks very clearly in other respects as well: ἐνταῦθά τοι καὶ πάθος εἰργάσατο, ἔξω τοῦ Κιθαιρῶνος, οὐ μεῖον τοῦ ἐν Κιθαιρῶνι ("suffering was inflicted outside of Kithairon, no less than that inflicted upon Kithairon").

151 Scholium on Iliad XIV 319: Διόνυσον ἀνεῖλεν εἰς τὴν Λερναίαν ἐμβαλὼν λίμνην.

The sequel to this version of an evasion, which seemed to be death but was not the end, is supplied by the historian Sokrates of Argos who tells us that the god known to the Argives as Dionysos Bougenes (the "cow's son") was called back from the water by the sound of *salpinges*. Before resounding, these *salpinges* had been hidden in the *thyrsoi*, the long, fillet-adorned staffs of the worshipers of Dionysos.[152]

Previously a ram had been thrown into the water as a sacrifice to Pylaochos (the "guardian of the gate)." The lake of Lerna, situated between the limestone mountain of Lerna, whose flanks had been inhabited since Neolithic times, and the sea, was fed by inexhaustible springs, which characterized it as belonging to the underworld. The "guardian of the gate" is known to us as the Hydra, the female water serpent whose heads were struck off by Herakles.[153] Dionysos disappeared for a time into the underworld, and ever since his cult had come to this coast, his disappearance had been enacted in a ceremony in which a young bull was sacrificed. The region is that of the mouth of the Inachos River, one of the three known places of the god's arrival in the Peloponnese. In the city of Argos, Dionysos Kresios (the "Cretan Dionysos")—after his reconciliation with Perseus, so it was said—possessed a temple in which there was also a tomb of Ariadne.[154] His epithet shows clearly where he came from.

When the Theban myth attained universal currency, the birth of

152 For the account by Sokrates the historian, see Jacoby, *FGrHist*, 310, fr. 2 (III, B, p. 15). Plutarch quotes this account in *De Iside et Osiride* 364 F: Ἀργείοις δὲ βουγενὴς Διόνυσος ἐπίκλην ἐστίν· ἀνακαλοῦνται δ' αὐτὸν ὑπὸ σαλπίγγων ἐξ ὕδατος, ἐμβάλλοντες εἰς τὴν ἄβυσσον ἄρνα τῶι Πυλαόχωι· τὰς δὲ σάλπιγγας ἐν θύρσοις ἀποκρύπτουσιν. ("Dionysos is known to the Argives as 'Cow's Son': they call him out of the water with *salpinges*, while hurling a ram into the lake to the 'guardian of the gate': they hide the *salpinges* in the *thyrsoi*.")
153 See Kerényi, *The Heroes of the Greeks*, p. 143.
154 Pausanias II 23 7–8.

Dionysos by Semele under the protection of the nymphs of Inachos was even transferred to Argos,[155] and the god's descent into and return from the waters of Lerna was interpreted as a journey to bring back his mother from the realm of the dead.[156] In connection with this interpretation, there is a strange tale to the effect that Dionysos paid a high price for his journey to Hades in the lake of Lerna—total effeminization—and that after his return from the underworld he set up a phallus as a cult symbol.[157] Here we have unique indications of the core of the Dionysian religion, though they have been preserved in a stylized form in keeping with the taste of a late period.

At still another spot in the Peloponnese, the mouth of the Alpheios River, the birth of the god, an event of the authentic primary myth and hence of the festive calendar, takes the place of a record of his arrival. He seems to have arrived there very early, as may be inferred from a fragment of a Homeric hymn in which it is denied that Semele gave birth to the god on the Alpheios, and from the statement of the historian Theopompos that the first vine in Olympia was found near the Alpheios.[158] From the corresponding early cult a song of the Sixteen Women of Elis has been preserved. This was a college of women who served not only Dionysos but also Hera, goddess of the oldest temple in Olympia.[159] Plutarch cites the text of the song, which mentions a

155 On this tradition is based a tragedy of Aischylos, *Semele* or *The Water Carriers*, in H. J. Mette, ed., *Die Fragmente der Tragödien des Aischylos*, frs. 355–62.

156 Pausanias II 37 5; see also the scholium on Lykophron, *Alexandra* 211 ff.

157 Made of fig wood; see Clement of Alexandria, *Protrepticus* II 34 3–4.

158 *Homeric Hymns* I 3–4; Theopompos quoted in Athenaios I 34 A.

159 Pausanias V 16 2–8. See L. Weniger, *Das Kollegium der Sechzehn Frauen und der Dionysosdienst in Elis*, where, however, the localization given in the transmitted text, "by the sea," is not taken into account.

"temple by the sea" (ἅλιον ἐς ναόν).[160] The temple has not yet been found but was presumably situated both on the Alpheios and on the sea—on the water that contained the underworld. Dionysos was addressed by the title of "hero,"[161] as befitted the dwellers in the underworld:

> *Come, Hero Dionysos*
> *to the temple by the sea*
> *with the Graces to the pure temple*
> *raving with the bull's foot.*[162]

The verb *thyein* is employed for "to rave." In conclusion the women sing "worthy bull, worthy bull!" (*axie taure*), for here as in Athens the sacrificial animal could be nothing else.

Dionysos is bidden to come with the Graces, the Charites, because without the soothing power of these goddesses what the women ex-

160 Plutarch, *Quaestiones Graecae* 299 AB (for the text, see below, note 162). In almost all new editions, ἅλιον is changed (with Bergk) to Ἀλείων, but not in W. R. Halliday, *The Greek Questions of Plutarch*, p. 29. In *opposition* to this change, see Kerényi, "Dionysos am Alpheios."

161 See Kerényi, *The Heroes of the Greeks*, pp. 14 f. Because Dionysos was a hero in this sense, Eleuthereus was placed in the *heroön* of Akademos near a "hearth," *eschara*, an altar for a hero.

162 The text of the song given by Plutarch (*Quaestiones Graecae* 299 AB):

> Ἐλθεῖν, ἥρω Διόνυσε,
> ἅλιον ἐς ναόν,
> ἁγνὸν σὺν χαρίτεσσι ἐς ναόν,
> τῶι βοέωι ποδὶ θύων.

This is as it was probably written by Sokrates of Argos. If the song, which was undoubtedly sung in the college of women, from which men were excluded, had not been published before Plutarch, it is unlikely that he would have taken the initiative in doing so.

pected of him would have been a rape.[163] What they wished was probably the raving of the "bull's foot"—which the god brought back with him after his absence in the realm of the dead—but this was a different kind of raving from that of the *mainomenos*. This was the time of the reappearance of what Dionysos, after his re-ascent, in Lerna, set up as a cult symbol. It is possible that, thanks to a visionary capacity which we may presume to have existed in early times, the women saw the god wholly as an aroused bull. According to Plutarch, however, a "large foot" was also called a "bull's foot,"[164] and this was probably a euphemism whose meaning was generally understood. The raving that the god now transferred to the women is expressed by *thyein* and "Thyia," which was probably the name of the Dionysian festival that was publicly celebrated near the city of Elis by priests who performed a wine miracle.[165] In view of the song cited above, the *thyein* can be taken only as erotic ecstasy,[166] the experience of *zoë* at one of its peaks. Thus, the somber sacrificial ceremony found its counterpart in the joyful feast of Dionysos, at which the god, in response to the call, reawakened and rose up out of the underworld.

A further place of arrival in the Peloponnese was Prasiai, which Pausanias, because of this very tale, calls "Brasiai." It lay south of Lerna on the Laconian coast, probably on the large bay near Leonidi.[167] This was a very strange arrival: it was related that the god, in dire

163   See Pindar, *Pythia* II 42; thanks to the Charites the epiphany could take place in a pure temple.

164   *Quaestiones Graecae* 299 B.

165   K. Preisendanz, "Zum Thyiafest," pp. 231 f.; see also note 169, below.

166   H. von Prott, "MHTHP," p. 88: "originally θύειν was always sexual ecstasy."

167   Pausanias III 24 3–4; "Brasiai" comes from ἐκβράσσειν, "to throw out." See also Frazer's commentary in Pausanias, *Description of Greece*, III, pp. 391 f.

plight because he had not yet found a nurse, was washed ashore at Prasiai in a chest (*larnax*) with his dead mother Semele. This highly archaic
motif, influenced by the Theban myth, may have been taken from the
Perseus myth[168] and later connected with Thebes as the starting point
of a sea journey, perhaps by way of Anthedon. The chest and floating
god, however, seem to point more clearly to the Nile Delta, which is
also connected with the mouth of the Inachos in the story of Danaos
and his daughters, as well as by the trading of the Mycenaean Greeks
with Minoan Crete.

We possess more concrete information about the reception of the
Dionysos cult in the domain of Hera, the Great Goddess of Argos. The
college of the Sixteen Women also served the cult of Hera in Olympia
and, so it would seem, enabled the god, starting at the mouth of the
Alpheios River, to take possession of the whole country. The Eleans
were regarded as special devotees of Dionysos.[169] Soon after its arrival
at the mouth of the Alpheios, the Dionysos cult attached itself to a
Great Moon Goddess, Hera, just as on the east coast of Attica it had
attached itself to Artemis. The same thing happened in Argos. Evidence of this is another story of resistance—not the tale in which Perseus combats the arriving god, but in all likelihood another roving tale.
Again it is the women who resist in this story which is about the daughters of Proitos and largely coincides with that of the daughters of
Minyas.

168 See Kerényi, "Sonnenkinder-Götterkinder," *Werke*, II.
169 Pausanias VI 26 1. In Pausanias' day, each of the eight *phylai* of the
Eleans sent two women to the college; see V 16 7. They undoubtedly also presided over other Dionysos cults in the country, including the cult in the temple
where—eight stadia from the city of Elis (founded 471 B.C.)—the wine miracle
was publicly repeated amid ceremonies in a very late style. This, as Pausanias
noted (VI 26 1), occurred on the feast day named "Thyia" after them.

It is quite possible that the story's wanderings started in Boeotia. It was thence that Semele as a figure inseparable from Dionysos came to the Peloponnese. But it is also possible that the opposite occurred, that here again something which was already present in Argos was later adapted to Boeotian conditions. It is probable that Megapenthes, son of Proitos, king of Argos, also figured originally in this story of resistance. According to his name, he was a "man of great sufferings" like Pentheus, the "man of suffering" who persecuted Dionysos in Thebes. In the few references we have to him Megapenthes is a decidedly evil figure, but in our sources the story of resistance relates exclusively to the sufferings of his sisters.[170]

The sisters' names have come down to us in various forms,[171] a sure sign that originally only their number was given. They may have been only two and have become three by adaptation to the Minyades and to the daughters of Kadmos who resisted Dionysos in Thebes. All the versions have essentially the same foundation in cult: the ritual persecution of the women celebrants after the somber sacrificial ceremony of the feast that was called "Agrionia" in Boeotia, and "Agrania" or "Agriania" in Argos. One of Proitos' daughters was said to have been killed in the course of this persecution.[172] This too may have been the product of an adaptation or compensation within the traditions of the

170   On the genealogy of Megapenthes, see Apollodoros, *Bibliotheca* II 2 2; on his being evil, see Hyginus, *Fabulae* 244; and *Anthologia Palatina* III 15.

171   "Lysippe" and "Iphianassa" according to Pherekydes, fr. 114, in Jacoby, *FGrHist*; "Elege" and "Kelaine" according to Aelian, *Varia historia* III 42; "Lysippe," "Iphinoë," and "Iphianassa" according to Apollodoros, *Bibliotheca* II 2 2; "Lysippe," "Hipponoë," and "Kyrianassa" according to Servius' commentary on Virgil's *Eclogues* VI 48.

172   The eldest, Iphinoë, according to Apollodoros, *Bibliotheca* II 2 2; see also Hesychios s.v. Ἀγριάνια.

Dionysian religion as determined by the Theban myth. Two deviations are characteristic of Argos and the domain of Hera.

One concerns the punishment, which differed from that of the daughters of Minyas. In this type of edifying tale, punishment always presupposes a definite transgression: it is the wicked, irreligious form of what the sinners do not wish to do in the right, religious form. The daughters of Proitos wandered about Argos, Arcadia, and the wild regions of the Peloponnese in a state of extreme and indecent nymphomania. Thus, it was possible to explain their madness by saying that they had been punished by Aphrodite.[173] An archaic expression of their fate was that they lost the hair from their heads and that white spots appeared all over their bodies; in other words, they began to turn into cows, animals in heat calling for the bull.[174] Their transgression was to have refused to participate in ceremonies that would have enabled them to experience a similar state—the *thyein*—in a good and religious way. In the old version, however, it was not Aphrodite but Hera, the Great Goddess of women, who punished them for their refusal. This was the second characteristic deviation of the tale in Argos that distinguished it from all other stories of arrival and resistance.

It seems likely that in all versions of the tale the anger of Dionysos was mentioned only in passing; it was self-evident.[175] In a later day the understanding of Hera's anger was lost, and people thought up

173 Apollodoros, *Bibliotheca* II 2 2: ἐμάνησαν . . . γενόμεναι δὲ ἐμμανεῖς . . . μετ' ἀκοσμίας ἀπάσης διὰ τῆς ἐρμίας ἐτρόχαζον. Aelian, *Varia historia* III 42: μάχλους δὲ αὐτὰς ἡ τῆς Κύπρου βασιλὶς εἰργάσατο (an expression that leaves no doubt as to their nymphomania; moreover, their nakedness is stressed in the text).

174 See Hesiod, in *Rzach*, ed., frs. 28–29. The punishment is interpreted in this sense by Virgil, *Eclogues* VI 48: "Proitides implerunt falsis mugitibus agros"; see also the commentary of Probus: "quae crederent se boves factas."

175 In Hesiod, according to Apollodoros, *Bibliotheca*, II 2 2; and in Diodorus Siculus IV 68 4.

the most naïve explanations for the punishment of which she was the source.[176] Hera after all was the Great Goddess of marriage; in the anthropomorphic characterization prevalent in Greek mythology after Homer, she was imbued with jealousy and hatred of everything that interfered with the order of marriage. This hostile attitude was extended to Dionysos, however, only in exceptional cases, as in Athens, where it had to do with the complex relationship between Hera and the Eleusinian gods.[177] Not even the prohibition of ivy in a temple of Hera[178] was universal. The votive offerings in the "old temple" of Hera on Samos included vine and ivy leaves.[179] The two great archaic poets of Lesbos, Sappho and Alkaios, celebrated the divine triad: Zeus, Hera, and Dionysos.[180] The Dionysos cult entered into contact with the Hera cult in Argos during the Mycenaean—perhaps the early Mycenaean—era. The port for this early arrival may have been Asine at the southern edge of the domain of Hera.[181] The fact is that throughout antiquity the life cult of the Dionysian women remained compatible with married life, which it complemented.

The story of the daughters of Proitos was also connected with the activity of Melampous, the missionary of the Dionysian religion, pro-

---

176   According to Akousilaos (Apollodoros II 2 2), the Proitides despised the ancient cult image of Hera. According to Bakchylides X 47, they said their father was richer than the goddess—surely inadequate grounds for so extraordinary a punishment!

177   Allegedly the priestesses of Hera and of Dionysos were not permitted to speak to each other: Eusebios, *Praeparatio Evangelica* III 1 2, after a lost text of Plutarch. See also Kerényi, *Eleusis*, p. 213, note 160.

178   The prohibition prevailed in Athens according to Plutarch, *Quaestiones Romanae* 291 A.

179   Displayed in the museum of Vathy on Samos.

180   Lobel and Page, eds., *Poetarum Lesbiorum Fragmenta*, frs. 17, 129.

181   For my first intimation of this, see the comment in *Werke*, II, 54; see further ibid., III, April 15 and 25, 1956.

ducing a pseudomyth to which Herodotos gave a universal form. The women of Argos, so the story goes, were seized with *mania*, whereupon the Argives sent to Pylos for the seer, who cured the women for a high price which he doubled when the Argives declined to pay him.[182] Herodotos speaks not of a punishment but of an epidemic which broke out anew when the Argives declined. This is assuredly not the early form of the tale, which mentions at most three madwomen, but the latest. Not only in Herodotos were the characteristic features of the original tale effaced.[183] The details of the cure, which even included a persecution, are of less importance to the over-all picture of the spread of the Dionysos cult in Greece than the *arrival of the god*. Two particular sites, Thebes and Delphi, call for a special investigation, while Athens will require several.

182   Herodotos IX 34. The motif of the raising of the price occurs in a different form in the well-known story of the Sybil and Tarquinius Priscus (G. Wissowa, *Religion und Kultus der Römer*, p. 536, note 5); here it revolves around the division of the kingdom of Proitos.

183   In this connection, for example, the killing of their own children is mentioned by Apollodoros (*Bibliotheca* II 2 2), who does not know the story of the Minyades, to which the Proitides story belongs. His version is influenced by that of Herodotos, in which madness also infects the other women.

V. DIONYSOS TRIETERIKOS
GOD OF THE TWO-YEAR PERIOD

Age and Continuity of the Trieteric Cult

A FIRMLY ESTABLISHED schema of the Dionysian religion outside of Attica, possessing an inner logic of its own that relates even the dispersed elements of the over-all rite, can be gained from the tales of arrival and resistance. The women celebrated two secret feasts which to a certain extent explain the resistance of the uninitiated "good wives" and especially that of the men who were concerned with maintaining their hegemony and the order of the state. Terrible suffering was inflicted on a living creature during one of these feasts. The relationship of the women to this being is made evident by the punishment. This was nothing other than an intensified, wicked form of the cult action which the sinners refused to perform for the god: they tore to pieces the child of one of their number, for whom they were supposed to care in common.[1] Their victim was as close to them as a foster child to its nurse. What occurred was contrary to the substance and intention of law and custom.

This deed, to be performed in a maenadic state of mind—the state of a *mainomenos*, which the god himself had experienced for a time—was the punishment of the recalcitrants. The other secret feast, which according to the inner logic inevitably followed the first, was celebrated by the women in another state of mind which may be called "thyiadic" from the verb *thyein*. We are assured that Dionysos was

1 Aelian, *Varia historia* III 42; see above, ch. IV, note 150.

accustomed to attend (*epiphoitan*) the feast of Thyia in connection with his temple situated near the city of Elis.² In accordance with an unwritten law of *zoë*, a punishment connected with the somber maenadic feast was also assigned to those who piously enacted the cruel deed. This was regarded in Athens, even outside the Dionysian religion, as a way of making amends to the sacrificed bull.³ This may be a feature inherited from the Minoan culture, and hence an emanation of the Dionysos cult that reached Attica before the arrival of the god himself.

The details of the rite performed on the island of Tenedos, in which a bull calf played the role of the suffering god and the sacrificer was punished, have come down to us. Because of the highly archaic character of the whole ceremony, there can be little doubt as to its great age or its connection with the trieteric bull sacrifice of the Cretans. On this small island off Troy, a gravid cow was dedicated to "Dionysos, crusher of men"⁴—Dionysos as god of the underworld. The cow was specially fed and when she calved was treated like a woman in childbirth. Hunting boots befitting a little Zagreus were put on the newborn calf. Thus attired, the calf was sacrificed to the god. The man who struck it with the double ax was publicly stoned—but only

2 See above, ch. IV, note 169. The presence of the god was demonstrated by the priests with a wine miracle, while the Sixteen Women celebrated the arrival among themselves in the "temple by the sea."

3 See W. F. Otto, "Ein griechischer Kultmythos vom Ursprung der Pflugkultur," *Das Wort der Antike*, pp. 140 ff.

4 The translation of τῶι ἀνθρωπορραίστηι Διονύσωι (Aelian, *De natura animalium* XII 34) as "render of men" (Otto, *Dionysos*, p. 105) is wrong both linguistically and objectively. The rending of a human being, if it occurred, was a crass brutalization of the rite, contrary to its original meaning. The *bios* or *aion*, the individual lifetime, is crushed in death with the bones themselves: see Bowra, *Pindari Carmina*, fr. 100, line 5, αἰὼν δὲ δι' ὀστέων ἐραίσθη.

symbolically, for he was permitted to escape. If he reached the sea, the punishment was regarded as fulfilled. In the Classical age the coins of Tenedos, whose wine culture outlived the Turkish period,[5] show a double ax and a grape, which Friedrich Gottlieb Welcker writing in the mid-nineteenth century already associated with this sacrifice.[6] At the time when the ceremony was recorded, the bull calf was killed by a man,[7] but undoubtedly the task of caring for the cow and calf as if they had been human still fell to the women.

Excavations on the island of Keos show that in a sanctuary where wine vessels—assuredly not empty—were offered up to Dionysos in the sixth and early fifth centuries, the cult went back to the early Mycenaean Age. The same excavations brought to light a number of terracotta statuettes in the Minoan style of feminine figures nude from the waist up.[8] A college of women, similar to that of Elis in a later day, may have existed on Keos in the Minoan palatial period. For the present this must remain a matter of conjecture, but not so the continuity of the cult in the last phase of which Dionysos was mentioned by name. We have indications that a sacrifice similar to that offered on Tenedos was performed on Keos in Simonides' day, the sixth and fifth cen-

5   Described by L. Lacroix, *Iles de la Grèce*, pp. 33 f.; C. T. Newton, *Travels and Discoveries in the Levant*, pp. 271 f.

6   Welcker, *Griechische Götterlehre*, I, 444. The numismatist Warwick Wroth (*Catalogue of the Greek Coins of Troas, Aeolis, and Lesbos*, p. xlvii) writes: "The coins themselves lend some support to the view that the Tenedian double-axe is connected with Dionysos, for all the silver pieces from *circa* 420 B.C. onward show, in addition to the double-axe on the reverse, a bunch of grapes as a constant symbol." Wroth was apparently unfamiliar with Aelian's account and Welcker's view, since he cites only the two travel accounts (as in note 5, above).

7   Aelian, *De natura animalium* XII 34: ὅ γε μὴν πατάξας·

8   J. L. Caskey, "Investigations in Keos, 1963," p. 33. An Attic skyphos (pl. 64A/B) bears the graffito: εὐξάμενος Ἄνθιππος Διονύσωι ἀνέθηκεν τὴν κύλικα τήνδε. See also his "Excavations in Keos, 1964–65," pp. 369–71, pls. 87–89.

turies.[9] The double ax had to be new, direct from the smithy, and to be wielded by a youth. In a poem Simonides calls the murderous implement the "bull-slaying servant of Dionysos,"[10] a servant who acted in accordance with its master's wishes. One could go still further, however, and call the god himself "double ax," "Dionysos Pelekys," as was done in the Thessalian seaport town of Pagasai.[11] By a strange contradiction, the slaying was done for the benefit of the god, who died —as the evolution of the two-year period showed—yet did not die. A two-year period may also be inferred from the two feasts of Ariadne on Naxos, one somber with a fig-wood mask of the underworld Dionysos, the other joyous with a vine-wood mask of the Bacchic Dionysos.

On the mainland we are not reduced to mere inferences. Where the two-year period prevails, arrival is replaced by continuity. This is the case in Boeotia in particular. Even in the story of the daughters of Minyas who turned away Dionysos in Orchomenos, there was no suggestion of an arrival from afar. The daughters of Minyas were expected to join in the secret cult which the hunt-crazed women of Thebes celebrated on Mt. Kithairon.[12] Thebes itself possessed a myth of resistance which Euripides chose as the theme of his *Bacchae* because the core of the tragedy was already implicit in the story. He

9 Athenaios X 456 E.

10 Simonides, in Diehl, *Anth. lyr.*, fr. 69.

11 Theopompos, fr. 352, in Jacoby, *FGrHist*, 115 (II, B, p. 609). In another text of the scholia on Iliad XXIV 428, we find ὃς ἐκαλεῖτο Πέλεκος as opposed to the Πελάγιος of the Towleianus. Πέλεκος is a *difficilior lectio*, whose correctness was recognized by the numismatists: W. Wroth, *Greek Coins of Troas, Aeolis, and Lesbos*, p. xlvii; B. V. Head, *Historia Numorum*, pp. 308 and 551. In the story told by Theopompos, Dionysos appears to a fisherman and tells him what is in the depths of the sea. The double ax was also lowered into the sea.

12 For the character of the somber feast on Mt. Kithairon, Euripides is our main source.

amplified it with the motif of the god's departure and return, which also stems from the cult, and so adapted it to the stories of arrival. Originally there was no arrival in the Theban myth. The punishment which followed the sacrifice as a complementary rite had spontaneously given birth to the persecutor who resisted and thus earned suffering: Pentheus.

It is certain that if Pentheus, a transparent and unequivocal name with the somber meaning "man of suffering," could become a man's name at Knossos it was only because the names of gods—"Zagreus" as well as "Pentheus"—were also given to persons and because in the festive calendar the god's somber aspect prepared the way for the opposite aspect. In Thebes there were deeper reasons for the same name. The inherent dialectic of the cult, whose sacrificial offering the god himself voluntarily became, made "Pentheus" into the name of a punished enemy of god, who nevertheless in his suffering remained so close to the god as to represent him. The contradictory nature of the tragic fate of a god who suffers and lets himself be killed—a god whose servant, indeed he himself, was the sacrificial ax—was embodied in a man who destroyed himself, a frequent character in later Attic tragedy. This lent new depth to the Greek religion of Dionysos which took its departure from its Minoan-Mycenaean heritage and bore its enduring fruits in Athens. In Thebes the Minoan-Mycenaean element was very concretely present and bore witness to the continuity in which the new, most humane sublimation of the religion of life was enacted.

The Theban cult site of the Dionysian religion was situated in a palace complex which, on the strength of an Oriental cylindrical seal, can be assigned to the fourteenth or thirteenth century B.C.[13] Exact

---

13　E. Touloupa, "Bericht über die neuen Ausgrabungen in Theben," pp. 25–27; W. G. Lambert, "The Reading of a Seal Inscription from Thebes," pp. 182 f.

topographic orientation within the Kadmeia, the ancient palace of Thebes, is not yet possible because the present-day city has been built over it; but some investigations have been made possible by the demolition of modern houses. At one point the excavators, to their surprise, penetrated directly to foundations from the Mycenaean era, encountering no intervening layers from later antiquity.[14] When Pausanias visited Thebes in the second century A.D., only the Kadmeia, the city's akropolis, was inhabited, and it alone bore the name "Thebai."[15] Here visitors were shown the *thalamos* of Semele, the bridal chamber where Zeus visited her, begot Dionysos upon her, and finally burned her with his lightning. The palace itself was preserved as a sanctuary of Demeter Thesmophoros, a goddess exclusively of women. Her statue, from the waist up, protruded from the earth.[16] The *thalamos* can have been nothing other than the *sekos*, an enclosure never to be entered, an *abaton* in the temple, which was known to Euripides and which is also mentioned in an inscription in the treasure house of the Thebans at Delphi.[17] In Euripides' *Bacchae*, Dionysos finds the tomb of his mother in this place, in the palace of Kadmos, before the fire was wholly extinguished. This was a tomb in the same sense as the tombs of Ariadne, in reality altars at which an underworld goddess was worshiped.

The god made the leaves of a vine grow around his mother's *sekos*. This may be Euripides' poetic addition,[18] but everything else can be

---

14   A. D. Keramopoullos, Ἡ οἰκία τοῦ Κάδμου, p. 111. Over the recently discovered complex there were a Roman bath and a Byzantine bath. It was the Byzantine structure in the twelfth century A.D. which first wholly eliminated a part of the Mycenaean palace. See Touloupa, pp. 25 f.

15   Pausanias VIII 33 2, IX 7 4; *IG* XII:3 1089 (from Melos).

16   Pausanias IX 12 3. On Demeter, see IX 6 5.

17   É. Bourguet, "Inscriptions de l'entrée du Sanctuaire au Trésor des Athéniens," p. 195, no. 351.

18   Euripides, *Bacchae* 6–12.

taken as part of the tradition relating to the cult site. There Pausanias
saw a wooden cult statue set in bronze, said to have fallen from the
heavens at the same time as Zeus' thunderbolt and to have been given
its bronze setting by Polydoros, the son of Kadmos.[19] Beside it Pausanias saw an all-bronze statue of Dionysos by the otherwise unknown
sculptor Onasimedes and a fourth-century altar of Dionysos by Praxi-
teles' sons Kephisodotos and Timarchos. The protective bronze setting
of the first statue argues in favor of its great age. Pausanias has a special name for the wooden image of the god. In the manuscripts we
read "Dionysos Kadmos" or "Dionysos Kadmios." A third-century Delphic inscription calls him "Dionysos Kadmeios." To judge by an attested pre-Hellenic meaning of the word "Kadmos"–"Hermes"[20]–the
wooden statue was looked upon as a phallus idol, a "Dionysos Hermes,"
which it assuredly was. But the later view, expressed in the transformation of "Kadmos" into the adjective "Kadmeios" (wrongly written "Kadmios"), is also perfectly understandable. The fact was the
connection between *sekos* and statue on the one hand and a building
of the Mycenaean Age on the other, and this building was held to be
the palace of Kadmos, founder of the city.

It can scarcely have been pure chance that a wooden column
among the ruins of the palace was taken for a cult statue because it
happened, by a very natural accident, to have been entwined with

19   Pausanias IX 12 4.

20   *Etymologicum Gudianum* (ed. Sturz): Κάδμος, λέγεται ὁ Ἑρμῆς παρὰ τοῖς
Τυρσινίοις, supported by the diminutive form in the scholium on Lykophron,
Alexandra 219 ff.: Καδμίλος δὲ ὁ Ἑρμῆς and by the Boeotian historian Dionysodoros, in Jacoby, *FGrHist*, 68 (II, A, p. 35): Κάσμιλος ὁ Ἑρμῆς ἐστιν, which probably
means the *pais* of the Theban mysteries of the Kabeiroi, a young Hermes (see
Kerényi, *Griechische Grundbegriffe*, p. 30). The reading "Kadmos" in Pausanias
is rendered probable by his explanation of the name by the etymological play
ἐπι-κοσμεῖν.

ivy.[21] Only a late oracular verse, probably written by Jews or Christians in mockery of paganism, says that "to the Thebans a column was the joyous Dionysos."[22] The attested Theban designation of the god as "Dionysos Perikionis"[23] is very clear: it means the "Dionysos who twines himself around the column." In Attica he was not the column but the ivy, "Dionysos Kissos," "Dionysos the ivy," and in the palace of Kadmos as well, he took this form in addition to that of the old idol. This is said in the Orphic Hymn to Perikionios.[24] The wooden statue was certainly not one of the architectonic elements of the palace, or else the legend that it fell from heaven could not have arisen. It is probable that the ruins of the palace were preserved only because it was originally the site of a cult, perhaps of several cults, one of which was the cult of Dionysos and Semele.[25]

21   A. D. Keramopoullos, "Θηβαϊκά," pp. 341 f.; and after him Nilsson, *Geschichte*, I, 572, note 5.

22   Clement of Alexandria, *Stromateis* I 24: στῦλος Θηβαίοισι Διώνυσος πολυγηθής. The lines of the *Antiope* of Euripides cited by Clement should probably be read as follows:

εἶδον δὲ θαλάμοις βουκόλων
κομῶντα κισσῶι στῦλον Εὐίου θεοῦ.

In the house of the cowherd
I beheld a column overgrown with the ivy of Dionysos.

The god was present in the ivy. The scene is Eleutherai, which from the standpoint of the cult of Dionysos, should be assigned to Attica rather than Boeotia. The column had its function in the Attic cult; see below, in ch. VI, the text preceding note 28.

23   Mnaseas in the scholia on Euripides, *Phoenissae* 651.

24   In Attica, Pausanias I 31 6; in the palace of Kadmos, Quandt, *Orphei hymni* XLVII. According to Mnaseas, the ivy grew around several columns; see note 23, above. According to Euripides (*Phoenissae* 650–54), the god was covered with ivy after his premature birth, but this intercalation of an otherwise unknown phase of the birth myth between the bearing of the god by Semele and his entrance into the thigh of Zeus may be pure poetic invention.

25   Still another possibility is Harmonia (Pausanias IX 12 3), an Aphro-

The Delphic inscription shows that the Dionysos of the palace of Kadmos was connected with the trieteric cult.[26] The inscription does not mention the secret feast days of the Theban women, which formed the basis of the story of resistance, but only public festive gatherings ("Panegyreis") with dramatic performances. When Diodorus Siculus speaks of the trieteric rites, however, he mentions the Boeotians before the "other Greeks and Thracians" and speaks of the "Bacchic celebrations" ("Bakcheia") of the women.[27] He was referring to the "maenadic" as well as the "thyiadic" secret festivals. In the Delphic inscription it is not clear to which of these the Panegyreis corresponded but it was probably to the somber festival of the maenads, the feast in which the two-year period found its culmination and end. That is the main reason why it is called "trieteric." The relation between the public and the secret feasts must have been the same as that between the festive gathering at the temple of Dionysos near the city of Elis and the celebration of the Sixteen Women who called out to the god by the sea and welcomed him.

The mystery character of the women's ceremonies, the true trieteric rites, is shown by the fact that the public was offered dramas in Thebes and wine miracles in Elis. This was not so at the start, however; the need for dramas and miracles arose in a later day. The inner logic of the two-year period, a living dialectic corresponding to the building, destruction, and rebuilding of life, operated in secret. Its continuous realization in the trieteric cult may be taken as demonstrated from

---

dite figure along with Semele, just as in Argos the cults of Ariadne and Aphrodite Urania were carried on side by side (Pausanias II 23 8).

26   Bourguet, "Inscriptions de l'entrée," p. 198.
27   Diodorus Siculus IV 3 2.

the Mycenaean, indeed from the Minoan, period on. Despite the secrecy, its meaning is made clear by precise indications.

The Dialectic of the Two-Year Period

IN THE SECOND year of a *trieteris* the opposite happened of what had happened the first year, and it was not until the third year that repetition set in: hence the name *trieteris* for a two-year period. The god who was celebrated in both years was "Trieterikos" in relation to his festivals, which recurred only beginning in the third year, but he was also termed "Amphietes," "he of both years."[28] For it was only the two taken together that fully corresponded to the god who combined them both, with their oppositions, in himself. The Orphic Hymn Book was a compendium of the world of the Greek gods from the standpoint of a worshiper in the early Christian era; the author's central, personal religion was the cult of Dionysos. He describes Amphietes as he who "beds down" the seasons "and sets them in motion."[29] By "seasons" he means the years which alternately form a *trieteris*.

The exact period of Dionysos' absence is indicated in a passage from a *dithyrambos*, a Dionysian song of triumph:

ἀναβόασον αὐτῶι
Διόνυσον ἀείσομεν
ἱεραῖς ἐν ἡμέραις
δώδεκα μῆνας ἀπόντα
πάρα δ᾽ ὥρα, πάρα δ᾽ ἄνθη·

28 "Trieterikos," in Quandt, *Orphei hymni* XLV and LII; *Homeric Hymns* I 10–11 says this in the Homeric style. For "Amphietes," see *Orphei hymni* LIII.
29 According to Quandt's reading, *Orphei hymni* LIII 7: εὐνάζων κινῶν τε χρόνους ἐνὶ κυκλάσιν ὥραις.

> *Cry out to him:*
> *We shall sing Dionysos*
> *On the holy days,*
> *Him who was twelve months absent.*
> *Now the time has come, now the flowers are here.*[30]

A twelve months' absence of the god is conceivable only in a festive period of two years, in which absence and presence keep balance. In Athens, a two-year period is neither attested nor conceivable. Here at least three festivals in every year presuppose the presence of Dionysos: the Lenaia, the Anthesteria, and the Great Dionysia. The verses cited above are taken from a theoretical work, dealing with the Athenian dithyrambic poetry of the fifth and fourth centuries, which has come down to us in extremely fragmentary form on two papyrus rolls. The theoretician obviously took his examples not only from dithyrambs written for Athenian use but also from others composed for trieteric use all over the Greek world.

The *trieteris* began with a year of the god's absence. The Hymn to Amphietes tells us that Dionysos lays the trieteric period to sleep and that he himself passes this period of sleep in the holy palace of Persephone.[31] Thus, the god closed one *trieteris* and began a new one. In the first year, he is the Chthonios, the "subterranean," Dionysos, but precisely in this interval he is not worshiped as a god of the dead who enacts the state of death. According to the hymn, he is the god who wakes with the nymphs—the prototypes of those Dionysian women who awaken the god—as well as the god who reawakens the trieteric

---

30   According to H. Oellacher, in *Mitteilungen aus der Papyrussammlung Rainer*, pp. 136 ff.; see also J. U. Powell, *New Chapters in the History of Greek Literature*, pp. 209 f.

31   Quandt, *Orphei hymni* LIII 3: ὃς παρὰ Περσεφόνης ἱεροῖσι δόμοισιν ἰαύων κοιμίζει τριετῆρα χρόνον, Βακχήιον, ἁγνόν.

cycle.[32] This occurs during the year of his absence: the life aspect of the subterranean Dionysos is cultivated up to the time of his epiphany, in which *zoë* is fully revealed. According to Diodorus Siculus, in those places where the trieteric festive period is observed, virgins too are permitted to wear the *thyrsos* and to participate, rejoicing and worshiping, in *enthousiasmos*, the state and act of being filled with god. The women worship the god in separate groups—that is their *Bakcheia*— and celebrate the presence of Dionysos with hymns.[33] That was the feast which concluded the year of absence and lasted for more than one day, for it was termed a festival of "holy days." Thus twelve months passed.

If it were not for the god's long preceding absence, the flowers (ἄνθη) that were now present, the pre-spring flowers that sometimes appear in Attica in the February snow, might point to the spring festival of Dionysos in Attica, the Anthesteria; but in the *trieteris* the periodicity of nature is broken. Nevertheless, within the space of a year the paradoxical union of life and death, dominated by life, is realized. It is not the life of nature that should be aroused from the seeming death of winter! The flowers have already sprung up; they spring up each year and not just every second year as the god does. What occurred, not in conscious thought but in an unconscious process expressed in myth and rite, was an orientation toward a pure dialectic: life out of death and death out of life in an endless repetition encompassing the indestructibility of life, though it would be more correct to say that the indestructibility encompassed the repetition. When introduced into the observation of the periodicities of nature, this sim-

---

32 *Orphei hymni* LIII 2: ἐγρόμενον Κούραις ἅμα νύμφαις εὐπλοκάμοισιν. LIII 5: . . . ἡνίκα τὸν τριετῆ πάλι κῶμον ἐγείρηις.

33 Diodorus Siculus IV 3 3: τὴν παρουσίαν ὑμνεῖν τοῦ Διονύσου.

plifying vision, whose truth was not questioned in myth, provided unique depth and concentration. This is what happened in Attica, where the *trieteris* did not gain acceptance but its dialectical content presumably did, even—as may easily be understood—at the Anthesteria.

One element of the trieteric rites that did perhaps gain acceptance in Athens by way of Eleutherai, only to be discarded later, was a call for the god before the epiphany—the achieved goal of the first year— louder than the song of the women: the call of the *salpinges*. Such a call, worthy of what was to be attained, resounded in Lerna. The *salpinges* were kept hidden behind the *thyrsoi* and when they were brought out and blown, the turning point had already occurred: the realm of the dead had opened, discharging Dionysos, that most living of all beings for whom the aroused thyiadic women yearned. This artificial call of the *salpinges* was extremely archaic. The instrument used changed later on, but remained a musical indication of the survival and spread of the *trieteris*. An inscription found on Rhodes mentions the payment of a water organist who "awakened the god," of men who sang hymns to him, of an individual who was probably a priestess, and of women who had their functions at the "god's two arrivals," assuredly a reference to his arrival above and—at the end of the *trieteris*—below.[34] An inscription from the first century B.C. in Priene mentions the engagement of a singer, of a flute player to accompany the choral singing, and of a lute player, for two days at the end of a year which did not include trieteric ceremonies, that is, in which the

34 The inscription was published, after a copy of an apparently lost stone, by S. Saridakis, "Inschriften," pp. 92–94. Lines 24–25: τῶι ὑδραύληι τῶι ἐπεγείροντι τὸν θεόν. Line 26: ταῖς τοῦ θεοῦ δὲ καθόδοις δυσὶ τὸν. . . . The *trieteris* is also attested for Rhodes; see *IG* XII:1 155a II, lines 50–51. / On the *salpinx*, see above, in ch. IV, the end of the section on "The Arrival in Athens."

somber rites were not performed.[35] The function of the singers and musicians was certainly the calling and awakening, which the *salpinges* did less gently.

The second year of the *trieteris* was a contrast to the first. Now Dionysos was no longer the subterranean, the absent one, called publicly by loud instruments and by the women among themselves. They awakened him by being awakened by him. The god was now present. Whatever form his presence assumed, it was a *parousia* of *zoë*. Men were not wholly excluded from the *parousia*. On the contrary, if the attested visionary power of the bacchantes[36] did not suffice to make them see the god himself physically embodied in their midst or at the head of their throng, someone could take his place, either at the moment of the epiphany provoked by the exertions of the first year, or more likely in the maenadic frenzy that sometimes led to abnormal acts, including human sacrifice.[37] Not only a sacrificial animal but also a man could be equated with Dionysos in this state, in which the

35 For the Priene inscription, see F. Hiller von Gaertringen, ed., *Inschriften von Priene*, no. 113, lines 78–80. Somber rites are connected with "Trieterikos" in *Orphei Hymni* XLV and LII 7 (ὠμάδιε). See the inscription with regulations for the Dionysos cult in Miletos, which speaks of a "sacrificial animal to be eaten raw" (ὠμοφάγιον) and of the *trieteris*, in F. Sokolowski, *Lois sacrées de l'Asie Mineure*, no. 48.

36 Philo, *De vita contemplativa* II 2, cited by Rohde in connection with the "excessive stimulation of the senses, going even as far as hallucination," in *Psyche*, pp. 258; 270, note 25.

37 Thus it was in Boeotian Potniai, where the sacrifice of a priest is explained by the drunkenness of the sacrificers, and that of a beautiful boy by an oracle. Ordinarily a goat was sacrificed: Pausanias IX 8 2. The reference to Lesbos by Clement of Alexandria (*Protrepticus* III 42) and to Chios by Porphyry (*De abstinentia* II 55) probably apply to isolated cases. The reference to Tenedos by Porphyry (II 55) is a false inference from the epithet "Anthroporraistes"; see note 4, above. An extraordinary isolated instance was the sacrifice of Persian youths related in Plutarch, *Themistocles* XIII.

bacchantes became *mainades* just as their god was *mainomenos*. A frank admission of this occurs in the *Bacchae* of Euripides:

Βρόμιος ὅστις ἄγηι θιάσους·

He who leads the throngs becomes Dionysos.[38]

Here the chorus speaks of a phenomenon of the Dionysos cult in general and does not distinguish between illusion and reality. Thus, Euripides proves to be an objective observer. His account also shows the dangers of equating truth and illusion, not only in the example of Pentheus, but also in a more general sense when he hints at the hunting-dog character of the maenads. The god who goads them on is the opposite of what he was in the first year, the opposite of him who roused beings to life, of the lord of the dead who wants to be awakened. Now he is the lord of all living creatures who drives them to kill and in the death of the slain is so reduced that he is in need of awakening. Dionysos is the quarry of the hunt and the sacrificial animal, both of which are eaten raw (Tauros[39] and Eriphos, "bull" and "kid"). He is also Omadios and Omestes ("he who is fed with raw meat") to whom such a sacrificial meal is offered, a mystery meal of the Cretans who once in each *trieteris* rent a living bull with their teeth. This conclusion of the two-year period would surely have been a feast more worthy of the underworld and its lord; indeed in Argos it was a feast of the dead.[40] It could scarcely have formed the *end* of

38 Line 115: "Bacchus fit, quicunque ducit thiasos," according to the interpretation of Gilbert Murray in his edition of Euripides. Cf. 141: ὁ δ' ἔξαρχος Βρόμιος ("The leader is Bromios"—the "noisy god").

39 On five votive inscriptions from Boeotian Thespiai: θεὸς ταῦρος (see Nilsson, *Geschichte*, I, 571).

40 Hesychios s.v. Ἀγριάνια: νεκύσια παρὰ Ἀργείοις. / On the Cretan rite of tearing apart a live bull, see above, ch. III, at notes 113 ff.

the two-year period without the dialectic which in every moment of the
trieteris combines life and death.

Dionysos in Delphi

THE INNER logic of the Dionysian two-year period is so exclusively
the logic of *zoë* and of its opposite death that it could stand by itself without support from the periodic events of nature. There must be a reason
for its formal similarity to Hegel's dialectic, because the word "dialectic" in the Hegelian sense is applicable to it. Hegel's dialectic would
seem to be a reflection in conscious, conceptual thought of this primordial dialectic. The natural, primordial dialectic may be explained by
the assumption that in every living being there are two innate tendencies: a tendency to build and a tendency to destroy, on the one hand
a life drive and on the other a death drive. Thus, death and the destruction of life would be a part of life itself.[41] Hegel did not think in
terms of "drives," but he pointed to the basis of the primordial dialectic
when he said: "It is the nature of the finite to have within its essence
the seeds of extinction; the hour of its birth is the hour of its death."[42]
Zoë is the presupposition of the death drive; death exists only in rela-

41 I formulated this view in my book *Die antike Religion*, taking account
of Freud, *Beyond the Pleasure Principle*. On this occasion, however, I observed:
"Though in the following I invoke well-known findings of psychological research,
I identify myself with no exclusively psychological or biological trend" (*Die
antike Religion*, 1940 edn., p. 273, note 36). In the case of Dionysos, a biological
interpretation seems most relevant and remains indispensable as a working
hypothesis.

42 Cited from Hegel's *Logik* (*Sämtliche Werke*, IV, 147 f.) by Otto, *Dionysos*,
p. 135, who finds the cause of Dionysian madness in this unity of life and death.

tion to *zoë*. It is a product of life in accordance with a dialectic that is a process not of thought, but of life itself, of the *zoë* in each individual *bios*.

A two-year period embracing both tendencies, based on human nature—and not on animal nature whose reproductive periods are conditioned by the seasons—can begin at the outset of every conceivable kind of year, even the Sirius year. This seems to have been the case at Delphi where we encounter the most impressive form of festivals based on the primary expression of that dialectic, namely, the Dionysos myth. The Delphic calendar was based on the Sirius year. This is made evident not only by an enumeration of the months, showing that the year began in high summer, but also by the myth of Apollo's annual visit in the first month, *his* month, Apellaios, which began in our July. The Apollo myth points to an even earlier state of affairs, prehistoric from the standpoint of what we now know about Delphi, in which the visit took place only in the second year after the birth of the god. Paradoxically, he inaugurated his calendary *epidemiai* at Delphi with a year of absence. The explanation of why such odd behavior could be imputed to Apollo[43] is surely to be sought in the *trieteris* that prevailed at Delphi in an earlier period and remained in force in connection with Dionysos. Since the same system of intercalary years was employed both in Athens and at Delphi, it may be assumed that the older Delphic calendar was adapted to the one-year calendar

---

43 See Alkaios' *Hymn to Apollo* (fr. A 1, in Lobel and Page, *Poetarum Lesbiorum Fragmenta*) in the prose translation of Himerios, *Orationes* XIV 10–11. Only a calendary explanation, that is, a tradition based on a calendar older than that of Alkaios' time, can account for the inconsistency of Apollo's being sent by Zeus to Delphi but driving his swan chariot to the land of the Hyperboreans and spending a whole year there.

of the Athenians.[44] From then on Apollo's visit to Delphi was celebrated annually.

The festival of his arrival fell in the ambivalent period of the early rising of Sirius, in which summer's gifts ripen but, "hidden as it were behind the twittering of birds, the all-killing heat attains its climax on the mountain ridges transfigured in incandescence."[45] The life-and-death aspect of nature corresponded to the summers of the two-year period. This season cannot be confused with the pre-spring month of Bysios, on the seventh day of which, Apollo's birthday, the Pythia began to deliver her oracles.[46] Here we confront the rather baffling situation that a god's birth and his arrival among his worshipers did not coincide. Moreover, Apollo arrived from the land of the Hyperboreans in midsummer, long after the spring month of Theoxenios when gods were ordinarily received among mortals. The calendar as we know it is clearly not the same as that corresponding to the original myth of Delphi. Its conversion to a single year corresponding to the course of the sun and the seasons (particularly pronounced in the mountainous region of Delphi) was undoubtedly determined by the reign of Apollo, who more than any of the other great gods was identified with the sun.[47] At Delphi, however, the new reckoning encountered a two-year calendar, based on the Dionysos myth, to which it adapted itself for a time. This may be inferred with certainty from the myth of Apollo's arrival in the second year.

Equally significant is the fact that no story of the arrival of Diony-

---

44 See E. Bischoff, "Kalender," col. 1570.

45 Kerényi, *Apollon*, p. 42; also see above, in ch. III, the section on "Iakar and Iakchos."

46 See Plutarch, *Quaestiones Graecae* 292 EF. Confusion has, however, occurred: see H. Pomtow, "Delphoi," col. 2528.

47 See W. F. Otto, "Apollon," *Das Wort der Antike*, pp. 54 ff., 68 ff.

sos or of resistance to him has come to us from Delphi; nor is there a story of his birth that might have stood for his arrival, nor one that connected him with the Mycenaean palace, as at Thebes. Here the arriving god is Apollo. According to the myth, he comes as a conqueror and takes possession of the oracle which formerly belonged to a Great Goddess—in the simplest form of the tradition she was Ga, Earth— and was guarded by a female serpent.[48] On the strength of the tradition and of archaeological findings, the existence of a pre-Apollonian earth oracle at Delphi may be taken for certain. Equally certain is the archaeological observation that at the height of the Bronze Age the people of Delphi were still living under Neolithic conditions and that the place was already a holy site, although the sanctuaries were situated otherwise than they were later.[49] The famous stone navel, the *omphalos* of Delphi, bears witness to a belief in a passage between upper and lower worlds, not through water as at Lerna, but through the rocky ground.[50] Yet there was no lack of springs at Delphi; one need only recall the abundantly flowing Kastalia. In general we may speak of a similarity in the position of the two cults in the history of religion, but important differences must be taken into consideration.

Among these was the function of the oracle which tradition traced back to its original goddess. As we have seen, the priority of the earth oracle is a definite element in the Delphic tradition, and it does not seem unduly adventurous to trace this oracle back to Neolithic times. That prophetic dreams could be expected from mere contact with the

48   Aischylos, *Eumenides* 2; Pausanias X 6 6; this serpent had been regarded feminine since the Homeric Hymn to Apollo, line 300.

49   L. Lerat, "Fouilles de Delphes (1934–35);" p. 205. P. Amandry, *La mantique apollinienne à Delphes*, pp. 204 ff.

50   The conception and use of a cult stone as a "navel" (*omphalos*) stems from the ancient Orient; see Kerényi, *Eleusis*, p. 80.

earth—and not just from contact with the vapors rising from it[51]—is demonstrated by the Homeric epithets for the Selloi, the inspired inhabitants (*hypophetai*) of Dodona: *aniptopodes* and *chamaieunai*, signifying that they always went barefoot with unwashed feet and slept on the bare ground.[52] The connection between such experience and certain sites may be taken as a historical—or prehistorical in the case of Dodona and Delphi—fact. At Delphi moreover it seems likely that linguistic changes occurred in prehistoric times.

The Greek name "Delphoi" corresponds exactly to "Pytho," the earlier name of the place, for which Greek origin could be claimed only by means of a false etymology,[53] but which in a West-Semitic language applies to the topography of the Delphic countryside. *Puth* signifies "to gape" (*a se invicem distare*), while its derivative *poth* signifies "fissure" (*fente, vas feminale*), in Greek *delphys*.[54] The Semitic derivation of "Pytho" has been rendered all the more plausible by our increasing certainty that the Minoans possessed a Semitic language before their Mycenaean Greek language, but it does not absolutely require this corroboration. The name "Parnassos" may also be of Near Eastern origin, a possibility supported by the fact that Apollo came from Asia Minor.[55] The priority of his cult on Delos and his birth on

51 Vapors were and still are a possibility at Delphi. See S. Marinatos, Τὸ δελφικὸν χάσμα καὶ τὸ "πνεῦμα" τῆς Πυθίας. The importance of vapors in the history of religion, however, is much less than Marinatos and others suppose. Vapors may have been the outward but never the inner occasion of the oracle, whose functioning required the liberation of great human energies.

52 Iliad XVI 235.

53 The Homeric Hymn to Apollo 363–74, as though Πυθώ derived from πύθειν, "to cause to rot."

54 L. Bayard, "Pytho-Delphes et la légende du serpent," pp. 25–27. See also Kerényi, *Werke*, I, 97 ff.; Jung and Kerényi, *Essays on a Science of Mythology*, pp. 68 f. (Princeton/Bollingen Paperback, pp. 50 f.).

55 "Parnassos" occurs as the name of a city in Asia Minor; see L. R.

that island were recognized at Delphi. At one time the Delian cult had close ties with the Lycian Patara: thither the god went from Delphi during the winter months to deliver oracles in his temple,[56] just as from Delphi he went to the Hyperboreans.

A distinction must be made, however, between his historical and his mythical *apodemiai* and *epidemiai*, departures and arrivals. The *epidemiai* of Apollo's matriarchal family, his mother Leto and his sister Artemis, from Asia Minor to Greece was a constitutive event in the history of Greek religion, which is inconceivable without the presence of these three deities. The Greek reaction to the arrival of Apollo as a divine being who conferred and withdrew the sunlight[57] was the rise of a religion of sensuous and spiritual light, which at its summit became the Greek spiritual religion with its insistence on clarity and purity, order and harmony. This was a crucial element in the history of Greek culture, far exceeding any importance ever attained by the Delphic oracle. The mythical line of arrival from and return to the north —in contradistinction to the historical east-west line—corresponded to Apollo as the god not of the day but of the year. In the mythical dimension it reflected the itinerary by which as the nights grew longer the god of light vanished in the direction of the longest winter nights and ultimately attained his own realm among the Hyperboreans. As god of

---

Palmer, *Mycenaeans and Minoans*, p. 343, and map fig. 46. In the language of the Luvians, the word *parn-assos* has the primary meaning "(mountain) of the house"; "(mountain) of the temple" is only a secondary meaning.

56 Servius' commentary on *Aeneid* IV 143: Constat Apollinem sex mensibus hiemalibus apud Pataram Lyciae civitatem dare responsa . . . et sex mensibus aestivis apud Delum.

57 Here I formulate Apollo's original nature, which includes not only a positive relation to the sun and the light, but also an equally positive relation to darkness; see Kerényi, *Apollon*, pp. 33 ff.

the solar year, Apollo inevitably transformed the trieteric calendar wherever he encountered it.

Our two oldest sources for the *diadoche*, the sequence of rulers over the Delphic oracle, are Aischylos and Euripides. In the *Eumenides*, Aischylos lists the owners in chronological order and Apollo appears only in fourth place. First came the Earth Goddess, followed by two of her daughters: Themis, her mother's double who was elevated to the rank of guardian over natural right, and Phoebe, the mother of Leto. To her grandson Phoibos Apollon, Phoebe left her name and the site as well. Apollo was to deliver oracles that came from Zeus. This was assuredly the classical doctrine of the Delphics concerning the inner history of their oracle. Dionysos is very emphatically associated with an adjoining territory, namely, the whole of Parnassos including the *Korykion antron*, whose nymphs are named in a list including all the great gods. Moreover, the hunt for Pentheus is also mentioned, so that the entire mountainous region between Delphi and Thebes becomes one great hunting ground.[58]

In *Iphigenia in Tauris*, Euripides mentions the goddesses Gaia and Themis, mother and daughter, as possessors of the oracle before Apollo and tells of the killing of Python.[59] In Aischylos the Pythia had no reason to go into this, while for the author of the Homeric Hymn to Apollo this alone was worth mentioning and not the right of the older goddesses to the oracle.[60] Euripides had them defend their privilege. Earth, the "nocturnal one," sent oracular dreams with which the child Apollo could not compete, until finally his father Zeus set him upon the Delphic throne. But Dionysos is not forgotten. Parnassos,

58 For the *diadoche*, see Aischylos, *Eumenides* 1–8; on Pentheus, 24–26.
59 *Iphigenia in Tauris* 1244–82.
60 The Homeric Hymn to Apollo 300–304.

whither Leto bears her little son in her arms—it was in her arms that he shot the snake—was already the scene of Bacchic rites in honor of Dionysos.[61] The "throne" of Delphi was the *tripous*, a tripod supporting the kettle on which the Pythia sat in the historic period. According to one of our learned sources, however, it was Dionysos who first sat on the tripod, performing the role of the oracle-giving Themis.[62] The calendar is not the only indication that the cult of Dionysos preceded the religion of Apollo at Delphi.

It is probable that before the arrival of Apollo, Delphi already possessed the cult with the mythologem of the "leather sack," a story that came to Parnassos from the Orient at an early date.[63] Its hero and victim, the Greek Dionysos, entered into the chthonian-subterranean and nocturnal sphere of the oracle. As the third possessor of the oracle, after the goddesses Night and Themis, the learned scholiast mentions not Apollo but Python, the serpent with the name formed from a Semitic root. At the same time this source refers to Dionysos as the first occupant of the *tripous*.[64] The serpent's Greek name was "Delphyne," and according to a myth, common to both the Greeks and the Hittites,

61   *Iphigenia in Tauris* 1239–44.

62   Scholium on Pindar *Pythia*, ὑπόθεσις (in A. B. Drachmann, ed., *Scholia Vetera*, p. 2): πρώτη Νὺξ ἐχρησμῴδησεν, εἶτα Θέμις. Πύθωνος δὲ τότε κυριεύσαντος τοῦ προφητικοῦ τρίποδος, ἐν ὧι πρῶτος Διόνυσος ἐθεμίστευσε . . . ("the first to give oracles was the goddess Night, then Themis. But when Python gained power over the prophetic tripod on which Dionysos was first to perform the function of the [prophetic] Themis . . ."). Themis evidently gave oracles without a tripod, that is, she sent dreams as in Euripides, *Iphigenia in Tauris* 1261–65, where earth and night are one, *nychia Chthon*.

63   J. Fontenrose, *Python*, provides information about the spreading of the cult, but strays too far from the main point, the connection between the Delphic and the Cilician myths—already indicated in 1951 in Kerényi, *The Gods of the Greeks*, p. 26. See also "Mythology of the Leather Sack," above, in ch. II.

64   See note 62, above.

the snakelike monster is for a time victorious and is defeated only when its dismembered adversary and prisoner recovers the limbs that had been taken from him and preserved in a leather sack. At Delphi this could apply only to the dismembered Dionysos. The last victor and slayer of the serpent was Apollo, who was also called—the name has been preserved in the mystical literature—"Dionysodotes," "giver of Dionysos."[65]

This completes the mythical history of the oracle's possessors from the Earth Goddess to Apollo. Originally the cult did not require this completion. The Thyiades, as the Dionysian women were called at Delphi, awakened the god who for the first half of the two-year period vanished into the dark depths of the Delphic mountain country around Parnassos. Apollo and his priests helped the Thyiades in a manner taken over from Crete, as the Homeric Hymn to Apollo records, with the paean. Stressing the masculine element in the oracle, the hymn relates that some Cretan merchants once sailed from "Minoan Knossos" to Pylos. First in the form of a dolphin, then in that of a star more luminous than the day, Apollo enjoined them to settle at Delphi as priests of his temple, because no one could sing and dance the paean like the Cretans.[66] The god "Paian," in Homer "Paieon," physician of the gods, was worshiped at Minoan Knossos as "Paiawon."[67] He was not yet Apollo in all the fullness of his being, but only in one of his aspects: the god of light as healer,[68] precisely the one to heal a god

65 Olympiodoros, *In Platonis Phaedonem commentarii*, p. 111: ὁ δὲ Ἀπόλλων συναγείρει τε αὐτὸν καὶ ἀνάγει καθαρτικὸς ὢν θεὸς καὶ τοῦ Διονύσου σωτὴρ ὡς ἀληθῶς, καὶ διὰ τοῦτο Διονυσοδότης ἀνυμεῖται. ("But Apollo gathers him up and leads him aloft, for he is truly the purifying god and the savior of Dionysos, for which reason he is called 'Dionysodotes' in the songs to his praise.")
66 The Homeric Hymn to Apollo 389 ff., 516–19.
67 Iliad V 401–2 and 899–900; Knossos tablet V 52.2, *pa-ja-wo*.
68 See Kerényi, *Asklepios*, pp. 81 f.

who was suffering, dismembered, and dead, or one who was temporarily mad, and enable him to become alive and whole again.

Dionysos, the Trieterikos and Amphietes, had his great cult, occupying both years, at Delphi. The Athenians did not allow such a cult to arise in their midst, nor did they permit their Pythion, the Athenian sanctuary of Apollon Pythios, to become an oracle site. For them Delphi was a superior holy site in more than one respect, definitely in respect to the Pythian cult of Apollo, but also in respect to the Dionysos cult which was firmly correlated with the Apollo cult at Delphi. Athens was connected with Delphi by a ritual path over which traveled the Pythais, a procession in which sacrificial bulls were sent to Delphi accompanied by ax bearers.[69] As a return gift they brought a tripod back with them to Athens.[70] Athenian women took the same path to participate in the rites of the Delphic Thyiades. In this way Athens participated in the trieteric cult that was the universal form of the Dionysian religion from the Boeotian border on.

The path led over the pass to Daphni, where Apollon Pythios possessed a small sanctuary; passed near Eleusis; led through Oinioe, the "wine village" that bordered on both Eleutherai and Boeotia; and touched Thebes as well.[71] Between Thebes and Delphi it entered into the region of Parnassos below Panopeus. This dismal mountain city

69   The bearers are mentioned in relation to Athens in a scholium on Aischylos, *Eumenides* 4, with an explanation invented at a late date. The corresponding procession of the Ainians is described in detail by Heliodoros, *Aethiopica* III 1 3–5; according to him the hecatomb consisted entirely of black oxen.

70   See A. Boëthius, *Die Pythaïs*, who failed to note the reciprocity between the Athenian and the Delphic gifts and consequently missed the meaning of the procession. An imitation of the theft of the tripod committed by Herakles (Boëthius, p. 73) is out of the question: the inscriptions cited by Boëthius himself argue against such an idea.

71   Ibid., pp. 47 ff.

was known to Homer because of the crime of Tityos, the giant son of Mother Earth who attacked Leto and tried to drag her away, and because of the fine dancing ground situated on the Great Goddess' path to Delphi.[72] It may be assumed that a pre-Homeric tradition numbered Apollo's mother[73] herself among the Dionysian women—all of whom were divine in the primordial mythical past—who celebrated the thyiadic festivals on Parnassos. Pausanias came to understand the Homeric epithet for Panopeus, the city "with the fine dancing ground," only when the Attic Thyiades told him of the dancing grounds they had, not only near Panopeus but also in other places on the way from Athens to Delphi.[74] Pausanias' belief that this was already the case in Homer's day is by no means implausible. Over a period of more than a thousand years, women selected for the purpose went from Attica—and surely from other surrounding regions as well—to Delphi for the Dionysian festivals that were cloaked in particular secrecy, and danced at certain stations along the sacred road. It was forbidden to record this pilgrimage in art or poetry.

From Pausanias we learn that this pilgrimage occurred annually, though there is no doubt that the principal phases of the festive period, and hence the period itself, were trieteric.[75] In the solar year the shifting trieteric phases always occupied roughly the same winter period. That is why, as Plutarch tells us, they sang "the paean at their sacri-

---

72 Odyssey XI 580–81:

> Λητὼ γὰρ ἥλκησε, Διὸς κυδρὴν παράκοιτιν,
> Πυθώδ' ἐρχομένην διὰ καλλιχόρου Πανοπῆος.

73 See Kerényi, *The Gods of the Greeks*, p. 135 (Pelican edn., pp. 119 f.).

74 Pausanias X 4 3.

75 Pausanias X 4 3: παρὰ ἔτος. Aristonous Corinthius in his *Paean* 37 (in Powell, *Collectanea Alexandrina*, p. 163) speaks of τριετέσιν φαναῖς. In Euripides, *Ion* 550 and 716–17, dances illumined by torches, ἐς φανάς γε Βακχίου, are mentioned.

fices for a large part of the year; but at the beginning of winter they awake the dithyramb and, laying to rest the paean, they use the dithyramb"—and for three months invoked Dionysos instead of Apollo who was also called "Paian." Plutarch characterizes these dithyrambs as "full of passion and change, of confusion and swaying," and the paean as "orderly, measured song."[76] This difference between the tones of the two different periods of the year was bound to strike the attention of all (hence Plutarch speaks of it openly) even if the Dionysian period possessed a changing character for the initiate. The period began—roughly on the 8th of November[77]—with the first winter month, Dadophorios, the "torchbearing month," although we know that this particular month deserved its name only every second year. The torchlight feast is explicitly termed trieteric.[78] Likewise Plutarch's summary of the events in the dithyrambic periods—"death and disappearance; revival and rebirth"—cannot refer to the winter months of the same year.[79]

The *trieteris* was replaced by two solar years which only seemingly and only partially had the same cultic content. At most the same con-

76 *De E apud Delphos* 389 c. 389 A: παθῶν μεστὰ καὶ μεταβολῆς πλάνην τινὰ καὶ διαφόρησιν ἐχούσης. 389 B: τεταγμένην καὶ σώφρονα μοῦσαν.

77 "November 8th marks the early rising of the Pleiades and consequently according to a widespread popular calendar is the beginning of winter." This remark by F. Boll ("Zu Holls Abhandlung über den Ursprung des Epiphanienfestes," p. 190) is cited in reference to the Delphic calendar by E. Norden, *Die Geburt des Kindes*, p. 36. But Norden is mistaken in also placing the awakening of Liknites at the beginning of winter; see below, p. 222. According to this calculation, the wild hunter set in the sky at the end of the year; see Boll, *Griechische Kalender*, III, p. 11.

78 On the torches, see note 75, above.

79 Plutarch, *De E apud Delphos* 389 A: φθοράς τινας καὶ ἀφανισμοὺς εἶτα δ' ἀναβιώσεις καὶ παλιγγενεσίας. The older calendary investigations on Delphi already showed that these were the occasions of the festival: "Every two years, the birth of Dionysos—every two years, the death of Dionysos"; see Pomtow, "Delphoi," col. 1532.

tent can be attributed to the first nine months beginning in the spring with Apollo's supposed birthday on the seventh day of Bysios, when the oracle began to give answers. In the earliest times, as was later asserted, it gave answers only on this day.[80] In its historical golden age the oracle functioned in principle at all times except for certain *apophrades hemerai*, "unlucky days,"[81] which are more readily explained by the myth of Dionysos than by that of Apollo. There was even a proverb to the effect that an answer was false because it had been given in the absence of the god.[82] Apollo was absent from Delphi at the time of his *apodemia*; but the oracle functioned then too. Plutarch gives the reason when he says that Delphi belonged to Dionysos no less than to Apollo.[83] Such was the reserve with which this initiate into the secrets of Delphi expressed himself when, as so often, he knew more than he was permitted to utter.

Not only were dithyrambs sung to Dionysos at Delphi; paeans were also addressed to him, and not just implicitly (because he was in need of healing and awakening), but sometimes quite explicitly as in the Dionysian paean of Philodamos, whose beginning is similar to that of the dithyramb by an unknown Athenian poet cited earlier. The words of Philodamos are:

[Δεῦρ' ἄνα Δ]ιθύραμβε Βάκχ'

.   .   .   .   .   .

. . . Βρόμι', ἠρινα[ῖς ἵκου]
[ταῖσδ'] ἱεραῖς ἐν ὥραις·

80   Plutarch, *Quaestiones Graecae* 292 E.
81   Plutarch, *Alexander* XIV 4.
82   Scholium on Pindar, *Pythia* IV 4; scholium on Kallimachos, *Hymn to Apollo* 1.
83   *De E apud Delphos* 388 E.

> *Come hither, Lord Dithyrambos, Bakchos*
>
> .   .   .   .
>
> ... *Bromios now in the*
> *spring's holy period.*[84]

At the latest Dionysos could be invoked with such words in Theoxenios (March), the "month of hospitality to the gods," or in Bysios—in common Greek, "Physios," the "month of growth."[85] This was possible either in the year of his awakening or in that of his dismemberment, whereas Apollo, according to his own myth, did not come to Delphi from the land of the Hyperboreans until midsummer.

To the three Delphic winter months—beginning with Dadophorios, whose wholly or partly secret feasts had the Dionysos myth as their content—the distinction between thyiadic and maenadic character is surely applicable, especially since the tradition relating to Delphi speaks only of Thyiades and mentions only what contrasts with the somber maenadic activities. "Thyiadic" applies with precision only to one half of what happened in a *trieteris*; Aischylos alludes to the other half, when he relegates the hunt for Pentheus to Parnassos, and Plutarch speaks of it.[86] At Delphi there is never any mention of an exclusive college of Dionysian women, such as the Sixteen Women of Elis or the fourteen Gerairai in Athens. We hear only of a square or locality named "Thyiai," not far from the temple of Apollo but a little outside the inhabited section of the holy place, probably on the present plateau of the threshing floors.[87] This was the gathering place of the selected

---

84   After Powell, *Collectanea Alexandrina*, pp. 165–66, but with sure additions.

85   Plutarch, *Quaestiones Graecae* 292 E.

86   Aischylos, *Eumenides* 11, 26; Plutarch, *De E apud Delphos* 389 AB.

87   The ἀλώνια; see É. Bourguet, "ΘΥΙΑΙ-ΘΥΣΤΙΟΝ," p. 27; for the inscriptions,

women who came not only from Delphi and the surrounding region but also from as far away as Athens and who were known by the milder name for their consecrated character, to wit, as Thyiades.

These women were a part of the picture of the winter months at Delphi, though it is hardly likely that they could be viewed close at hand when they climbed Parnassos, which they apparently did repeatedly. In *one* year of the *trieteris* this occurred by torchlight between the time when, according to Plutarch, Dithyrambos was awakened and the awakening of Liknites, the "being in the winnow" (*liknon*), who was in need of revival. It is doubtful whether the *hunt* at the onset of winter in the second year also began by torchlight. In the first period the Thyiades ascended (repeatedly, so it would seem) Parnassos, running impetuously in a manner that made them resemble the *thyellai*, or storm-winds.[88] This was no mean accomplishment, especially in winter. Not even the daughters of the rugged mountains would have been capable of it without special training. We hear that Dionysos danced down from Parnassos with *thyrsos* and deerskin, accompanied by Delphic virgins, and we know that even as young girls the Dionysian women in Boeotia practiced not only the closed rites but also the bearing of the *thyrsos* and the Bacchic dances.[89] At Delphi this enormous exertion of the women, spontaneous despite long practice, was dedicated both consciously and unconsciously to the service of *zoë*; psychosomatic ener-

---

see p. 25. With Wilamowitz (*Sappho und Simonides*, p. 209, note) we read Θυίηις in Herodotos VII 178.

88   That is why the Delphians erected an altar to the winds at the place called "Thyiai" or "Thyia"; see Herodotos VII 178 and note 87, above.

89   Euripides, *Hypsipyle* in Nauck, *TGF*, fr. 752; see also above, ch. IV, at notes 146 ff.

gies were summoned up from the depths and discharged in a physical cult of life.

The Thyiades from Athens began their dancing on the way. It must have been in a trancelike state that these women kept a sure footing as they danced over mountain paths by night. Sometimes they knew and sometimes they did not know how far they had come. The inner experiences of the Thyiades were not permitted to be made public; they did not enter into literature. After the Lykourgos tetralogy of Aischylos the Thracian bacchantes appeared in their stead, and the Pangaion or Rhodope mountains took the place of Parnassos. In Greek-inspired Roman poetry the experience of the Thyiades is associated with Thrace. In Horace Euhias, "she who calls Dionysos," is *astonished* when the snow-covered landscape opens before her eyes after she has danced through the night:

> *exsomnis stupet Euhias*
> *Hebrum prospiciens et nive candidam*
> *Thracen . . .*[90]

The Hebrus which lies wintry-white at her feet is a river in Thrace. Lucan imputes the experience of the Thracian bacchantes to a Roman matron endowed with the gift of prophecy. He knows that in the prophetic realm Apollo and Dionysos are scarcely distinguishable. Possessed by Apollo, the matron flies across the sea to Thrace. These are her words:

> *Quo feror, o Paean? Qua me super aequora raptam*
> *Constituis terra? Video Pangaea novosis*
> *Cana iugis . . .*

90 Horace, *Carmina* III 25 9–11.

Whither am I borne, O Paean, in haste across the sky?
In what land do you set my feet? I see Pangaeus white
with snow-clad ridges . . .[91]

The landscape is the same, and again it is wintry.

Concerning the outward experience of the Thyiades on Parnassos we possess very concrete details. Once during a war in the middle of the third century B.C., the entranced Thyiades lost their way and arrived in Amphissa, a city near Delphi. There they sank down exhausted in the market place and were overpowered by a deep sleep. The women of Amphissa formed a protective ring around them and when they awoke arranged for them to return home unmolested.[92] On another occasion—this probably occurred in Plutarch's time, toward the end of the first or beginning of the second century A.D.—the Thyiades were snowed in on Parnassos and it was necessary to send a rescue party. The clothing of the men who took part in the rescue froze solid.[93] It is unlikely that the Thyiades, even if they wore deerskins over their shoulders, were ever dressed more warmly than the men. The background of their *thyein*, a leaping run so impetuous as to verge on flight, was the high, wintry mountain in all its concreteness, and from this background they are inseparable.

In the southern winter, nature does not give the impression of dying away, and this is generally true of Greece. The vegetation never looks wholly dead. Nevertheless the reality of winter on 8,060-foot Parnassos must be taken very seriously. The rigidity of its stony na-

---

91 Lucan, *De bello civili* I 678–80; see also Kerényi, "De teletis mercurialibus observationes, II," pp. 150 ff.
92 Plutarch, *Mulierum virtutes* 249 EF.
93 Plutarch, *De primo frigido* 953 D.

ture is enhanced by the freezing of the watercourses. To a southerner the snow in the mountains is in itself horror-inspiring. Horses and mules take fright; and in antiquity this cannot have been very different from today. The fir woods on Parnassos seem harsh and unfriendly with their jagged contours and somber color. The innermost essence of this mountain nature is, however, stone. Here stone in all its deadliness becomes the sole ruler. One would expect the movement of the Dionysian women to have contrasted sharply with this stone world, but this was not entirely the case. The impetuous movement of the bacchantes had something rigid about it, exemplified, as the representations show, in the gaze and in the attitude of body and head. The rigidity of nature and the frenzy of the Dionysian women—a frenzy revealing almost unlimited power—converge and complement one another. Where Dionysos rules, life manifests itself as boundless and irreducible. Irreductibility is present in stone. Here it would seem as though the Dionysian women, their frenzy enhanced by the wintry stone, had become embodiments of both extreme rigidity and extreme movement. With their living fire they became, as it were, a counterweight to the ice-cold hardness of the stone world, where without this contrast life would have been forgotten and only the rigidity of death reflected.

The agitated bacchantes' rigid attitude of head and body was not unerotic. *This* in itself was the source of erotic desire, and this too called for discharge. It is certain that the Thyiades did not derive the strength for their feat from wine. Wine would rather have rendered them incapable of it just as one would expect the wintry cold to have made them incapable of love. Yet those familiar with the popular customs of the Austrian Alps tell of young people engaging in repeated acts of love while running up the mountains (on the occasion of certain church festivals).[94] There is a classical account of a young man's being taken along on the torchlight festival at Delphi, although he was in a state of drunkenness, which was not necessarily true of the bacchantes who were with him. Euripides treats this episode as a possibility and relegates it to the heroic age: his hero Ion believes that he was begotten on such an occasion. This was held to be a marginal manifestation of the cult, occurring perhaps not among the true Thyiades but among the younger bacchantes who went along, virgins and not mature women.[95] On the other hand, Plutarch speaks of *aschrologia*, indecent language, in the holy rites themselves, accompanied by screams and heads flung backward.[96] All this calls for a distinction between preparatory dances and the cult action proper.

The cult of the three winter months, which may be termed "thyiadic" in the strict sense, attained its climax and goal in the first year of the *trieteris* with the secret act of awakening, which—if everything that happened during this period on Parnassos was not to be utterly meaningless—had to take place soon after the completion of this festive period, perhaps in or just before the month of Bysios. All that has come down to us is a clear characterization of the action (an awakening), the nature of the small container in which the one to be awakened lay (a winnow, *liknon*, hence the name Liknites),[97] and the fact that it took place simultaneously with another sacred action. Plutarch was permitted to say just this much to his friend Klea, who was at that time both the leader of the Thyiades at Delphi and an initiate

94 I owe this information (from Carinthia) to the archaeologist Rudolf Egger.

95 Euripides, *Ion* 551–52.

96 Plutarch, *De defectu oraculorum* 417 c. / On the rigid head position, see also above, ch. IV, note 80.

97 ὅταν αἱ Θυίαδες ἐγείρωσιν τὸν Λικνίτην; see note 99, below.

in the mysteries of Osiris.[98] He tells her in order to draw her attention to the consonance between the *two* mysteries: in both cases a reawakening was preceded by a state of lying in the tomb. The simultaneous actions were performed secretly in the temple of Apollo by the Hosioi, the specially consecrated bearers of the Delphic traditions, and in the exact place, so it was said, where the remains of the dismembered Dionysos were kept.[99] Elsewhere Plutarch alludes to this rite as "that with the tripod"![100] *This* is what the twofold action, in the temple and in the place where the awakening from the *liknon* occurred, was about.

The Thyiades did not celebrate the awakening in the temple of Apollo; they had no access to the part of it where sacred actions were performed. From the Mycenaean period on, there was at Delphi a Dionysion—a small sanctuary—in a section densely occupied by dwellings, to the east outside of the great holy precinct. Vestiges of the name "Dionysos" have been found there.[101] It is very doubtful, however, that the bands—the *thyiasoi*—of Dionysian women gathered on the Thyia plateau were led here; they would not have found room enough to move freely. But the whole of Parnassos was available, as was the great stalactite cave, the *Korykion antron*, where in times of war the male

98   Plutarch, *De Iside et Osiride* 364 E.

99   Plutarch, *De Iside et Osiride* 365 A: Δελφοὶ τὰ τοῦ Διονύσου λείψανα παρ' αὐτοῖς παρὰ τὸ χρηστήριον ἀποκεῖσθαι νομίζουσι· καὶ θύουσιν οἱ Ὅσιοι θυσίαν ἀπόρρητον ἐν τῶι ἱερῶι τοῦ Ἀπόλλωνος, ὅταν αἱ Θυίαδες ἐγείρωσιν τὸν Λικνίτην. ("The Delphians believe that the remains of Dionysos rest with them, within the place of prophecy: and the Holy Ones offer a secret sacrifice in the temple of Apollon, whenever the Thyiads wake the One in the Winnowing Fan." English translation by L. B. Holland in "The Mantic Mechanism at Delphi," p. 204.)

100   *De E apud Delphos* 385 D: τὸ τοῦ τρίποδος.

101   "Chronique des Fouilles en 1950" and ". . . en 1951," *BCH*, LXXV (1951), 138, and LXXVI (1952), 249 f.; see also my note in *Werke*, II, 49.

population could take refuge.[102] Pausanias describes the way to the cave and beyond in connection with the feat of the Thyiades: "The climb to the Korykian Cave is relatively easy for a sturdy man or for mules. . . . From the Korykian Cave on it is hard, even for a sturdy man, to attain the peaks of Parnassos: for these peaks are higher than the clouds and over them the Thyiades swarm in a trance for Dionysos and Apollo. . . ."[103] The rocks of the cave shone golden in the torch-light. A Greek inscription to the right of the entrance celebrates Pan and the nymphs, who were said to be the possessors of caves everywhere, especially stalactite caves. In relation to this cave, Sophokles calls them "Bacchic nymphs."[104] To judge by the linguistic form, the incised letters which also name the Thyiades are probably a forgery.[105] A hoax of this kind was possible because of the general and enduring belief that the scene of the secret thyiadic ceremony, the awakening of Liknites, could only have been this cave. The fact that Pausanias skips over the secret action but then refers to both gods, Dionysos and Apollo, reveals his thinking. Like Plutarch he was thinking of the connection between the festivals on Parnassos and the oracle and was referring implicitly to the oracle.

From the lighting of the first torch,[106] the rites enacted on Parnassos and concluded in the *Korykion antron* were mysteries. Apart from the

102 In the Persian Wars (Herodotos VIII 36) and most recently in the resistance of 1941–44.

103 Pausanias X 32 2 and 7.

104 *Antigone* 1128–29: ἔνθα Κωρύκιαι στείχουσι νύμφαι Βακχίδες.

105 ΘΥΑΔΑΝ in H. Collitz and F. Bechtel, *Sammlung der griechischen Dialekt-inschriften*, II, no. 1536 b, where it is rightly observed: "according to our present knowledge, not Greek," that is, probably an awkward archaizing invention.

106 Scholium on Lykophron, *Alexandra* 212: μετὰ φωτὸς καὶ λαμπάδος ἐπιτελεῖσθαι αὐτοῦ τὰ μυστήρια.

torchlight that could be seen from afar, their "how" has *remained* a secret: no source tells us what happened in the ceremony devoted to the *liknon* and its contents. It seems likely that an older rite with the same content took place in the cave. Originally, in an early age, the god, who was but indestructible life, began to move in the *korykos*, the leather sack containing honey and water. He who lay in the *liknon*, which succeeded the leather sack in a later period of cultural history, was treated by the women as an awakening child. He was *spoken* of in such a way that inevitably everyone thought of a child, a Divine Child cared for by his divine nurses. That was the mythological tale and where the cult name "Liknites" was used, one thought not of Zeus but *only* of Dionysos.[107] Here again, however, as in all the original mysteries of antiquity the "what" was a "holy open secret."[108] Long before there were representations of the winnow with phallus, the phallus was placed in the winnow. As the indestructible god's severed member it had lain in the winnow ever since the unrevealed symbolic actions by which the god was revived ceased to be leather-sack rites and became *liknon* ceremonies. The awakening was "successful": that was the meaning of the Thyiades' physical feat. It was successful because they had begun it with their incredible exertions of the three winter months.

107   See Quandt, *Orphei hymni* XLVI 1, LII 3. / See also in ch. II, above, the section on "Mythology of the Leather Sack."

108   This Goethe quotation from the "Epirrhema" to the elegy in "Die Metamorphose der Pflanzen" is here employed in the same sense as in Kerényi, "The Mysteries of the Kabeiroi," p. 37: "What was concealed in the Greek cult must certainly have been known to all those who lived in the vicinity of the cult sites, but it was unutterable. It possessed this character—the character of the *arreton*—independently of the will of those who participated in the cult. For in the profoundest sense it was ineffable: a true mystery. Only subsequently did express prohibitions make the *arreton* into an *aporreton*. Such 'holy open secrets' were always more frequent than genuine *arreta*."

The "that with the tripod"[109] at Delphi was a "holy open secret"—
if not an *arrheton* like the experience of the women who awakened
Dionysos, then at least an *aporrheton*, of which people knew though
they did not speak of it. It required that, simultaneously with the awakening of the Liknites, the "consecrated men" should perform a secret
action in the temple of Apollo, or in the words of Plutarch, that they
should perform a "secret sacrifice."[110] Throughout his *Delphic Dialogues*, which were not addressed to the Archythyias Klea, Plutarch assumes a more or less general knowledge of the reasons for these *apor-
rheta* and for their simultaneity. Apparently it was only of the mysteries
of Osiris (into which Klea had been initiated by her family) that she
knew more than the local participants in the cults of Delphi. Before
speaking of "that with the tripod," Plutarch, in one breath with her,
tells us that women were forbidden to approach this main utensil surrounded by open secrets.[111] Altogether, as can be seen from the *Ion*
of Euripides, it was no easy matter for the "white feet of women" to
enter the temple of Apollo.[112] Ultimately, perhaps only from the Classical period on, women under certain conditions were admitted as far
as a spot from which the tripod could be *seen*.[113] It was forbidden, as
contrary to *themis*, religious law, for any woman except the Pythia to
approach the tripod, not to speak of touching it.

It is nowhere stated or even hinted at that a Pythia, at least during
the period in which she performed *her* feat, took part in the activity of

109 Τὸ τοῦ τρίποδος, in Plutarch, *De E apud Delphos* 385 D.

110 See note 99, above.

111 *De E apud Delphos* 385 CD: τὸ μηδεμίαι γυναικὶ πρὸς τὸ χρηστήριον εἶναι
προσελθεῖν. The women, however, were not forbidden to consult the oracle; see
Amandry, *La Mantique*, p. 111, note 4.

112 Euripides, *Ion* 222–32.

113 Ibid., 232: πάντα θεᾶσθ᾽, ὅ τι καὶ θέμις, ὄμμασιν.

the Thyiades. This feat, which was no less than that of the Thyiades
and Mainades, was that of one endowed with the powers of a medium
—that is the modern term for the phenomenon[114]—and she had to be
selected from the feminine population.[115] In early times the requisite
physical and psychic gifts were abundant and large numbers of mediums were available.[116] Later on they became fewer and fewer. The universally human typology of the phenomenon has hardly changed to
our own day.[117] It implies an ability to deal not with life in its material
forms, but with a stratum of the mind that knows or believes itself to
be outside the body, a distinction that does not alter the nature of the
phenomenon. The Pythia was not one of the awakeners or dismember-
ers of Dionysos. She was capable of communicating with that apparently extraphysical realm where Dionysos held sway during the

114 Amandry, *La Mantique*, p. 116, speaks of *"jouer le rôle de médium,"* but
does not treat in depth the question of the Pythia's medial nature. E. R. Dodds, *The
Greeks and the Irrational*, p. 73, also assumes that the Pythia acted as a medium,
though he does not enter into the question more closely: "I take it as fairly
certain that the Pythia's trance was auto-suggestively induced, like mediumistic
trance to-day." I have attempted a more precise treatment of the phenomena on
the basis of the known typology of medial activity; see Kerényi, "Gedanken
über die Pythia," *Werke*, I, 357 ff.

115 When in Euripides' *Ion* 1353 the Pythia speaks of herself as πασῶν
Δελφίδων ἐξαίρετος ("chosen among all the women of Delphi"), this is not at all
an "expression vague"—as Amandry (*La Mantique*, p. 115) suggests—but implies careful and necessary selection.

116 During the golden age of the oracle, two Pythias were in use and a
third in readiness; see Plutarch, *De defectu oraculorum* 414 B. In this case it
must be assumed that there were several successive oracle days.

117 See E. Bozzano, *Übersinnliche Erscheinungen bei Naturvölkern*, citing
Louis Jacolliot, *Occult Science in India* and chiefly dealing with telekinesis:
"The fakir stretched out both legs in the direction of a bronze vessel filled with
water. After five minutes the vessel began to shake and finally to slide smoothly
toward the fakir. As the distance decreased, more and more frequent and loud
blows resounded on the bronze vessel, as though it were being struck with a
rod. . . ."

time of his absence, and this required an exertion (bodily as well as psychic) which was greater still than that of the Thyiades.

The famous *tripous* at Delphi was the utensil employed in this extraordinary feat. A bronze kettle stood on three metal legs.[118] Its traces and that of a prop in the middle were found on a stone block fashioned for the purpose, a remnant of the floor of the *adyton*, or holy of holies, of the temple of Apollo [62].[119] According to the most reliable representations, the *omphalos* was situated in front of the traces of the *tripous*.[120] The Pythia was the only mortal woman permitted to penetrate to this place; at most others were permitted to come within view of it. According to matter-of-fact ancient accounts, the kettle contained "soothsaying lots that began to jump when a question was asked of the oracle, whereupon the Pythia, carried away or filled with the god, said what Apollo revealed."[121] The lots jumped upward toward the hand of the Pythia who then demonstrated the telekinetic power typical of mediums: she was immediately able to read the lots, to interpret them in terms of speech.

Plutarch describes how the Pythia was tested before her activity. On the sixth day of the month—the questioning of the oracle took place on the seventh—she was led to the *prytaneion*, gathering place

118 Both gold and bronze are mentioned in the tradition; see F. Willemsen, "Der delphische Dreifuss," pp. 80 f.

119 Ibid., p. 92.

120 See F. Courby, "La Terrasse du Temple," p. 67; Holland, "The Mantic Mechanism," p. 207.

121 *Suidae Lexion* s.v. Πυθώ (in Adler, ed., IV, 268–69): . . . ἐν ὧι χαλκοῦς τρίπους ἵδρυτο καὶ ὕπερθεν φιάλη, ἣ τὰς μαντικὰς εἶχε ψήφους, αἵτινες ἐρομένων τῶν μαντευομένων ἥλλοντο, καὶ ἡ Πυθία ἐμφορουμένη, ἤτοι ἐνθουσιῶσα, ἔλεγεν ἃ ἐξέφερεν ὁ Ἀπόλλων. This clear and decisive text, which is represented in Eudocia, *Violarium* (in Amandry, p. 259), was overlooked at an important point by W. Fauth, "Pythia," col. 528, lines 42 f.

of the overseers of the holy site. In addition to the Hosioi, at least one
prophetes, or priest, the Pythia's examiner and guide, was present.
She was obliged to try her hand at the lots: if her lots completed those
of the men to make five, she had withstood the test.[122] It must be assumed that she spent the night from the sixth to the seventh in the holy
of holies, on the kettle in a state of sleep or half-sleep. This was the
time of her physical contact with the mysterious source of her trance,
a state that endured by daylight under the sign of Apollo.[123] A special
concave *epithema*, or lid, was put on the kettle in order that she might
sit on it.[124] The water of the spring of Kassotis flowed through the
adyton.[125] She drank of it early in the morning and when she trembled
in her cold ecstasy she clung to a laurel tree which trembled with her.[126]
She seems to have taken various positions after becoming one with her
god Apollo.[127] The corresponding Greek word—*aneile*—refers strictly
speaking to the activity of the god.[128] As Pythios he drew his prophecy
from the kettle and passed it on through the Pythia. The answers came
out of the *tripous* through her.

122   Plutarch, *De E apud Delphos* 391 D. This text is corrupt in certain
places but reliable in the main point I have cited.
123   A cruder explanation of the trance was that the Pythia with spread
legs received the dangerous vapor from below; see the scholium on Aristophanes,
Plutus 39.
124   According to Pollux X 81, the *epithema* "where the prophetess sits" is
called *holmos*. The spending of the night in the *holmos* follows from the proverb
ἐν ὅλμωι εὐνάσω, meaning roughly "I become prophetic," and from other passages
collected by Amandry, *La Mantique*, p. 40, note 2, though he did not draw from
them this concrete inference for the procedure at Delphi.
125   Pausanias X 24 7; Holland, p. 210.
126   See Aristophanes, *Plutus* 213 and the scholium.
127   See F. Hauser, "Ein neues Fragment des Mediceischen Kraters," p.
43.
128   The usual expression is ἀνεῖλεν ὁ θεός (see Amandry, p. 25).

Knowledge of the connection between the *tripous* and the subterranean, nocturnal sphere, the chthonian aspect of Delphi, was expressed in various ways, for it was actually *spoken* of. In the fourth-century temple whose ruins have been investigated, the tripod was not placed over the cleft in the earth, for which, according to a later tale, this *mechane*, or mechanism, of the oracle was originally constructed. The use of a kettle at an oracle site that claimed to be connected with the realm of spirits is attested by the phrase the "resounding Thesprotian kettle," and the Thesprotian oracle of the dead, Ephyra in Epirus, has been excavated.[129] A similar connection between the underworld and the Delphic *tripous* was expressed both in the myth of the dragon Python and in that of Dionysos.

The story of Apollo's victory over Python may be read in a mythological handbook of the Augustan Age. It ends as follows: the god, called Pythios after this event, threw the dragon's bones into a kettle, set it up in his temple, and arranged funeral games, the Pythian *agone*, for the slain dragon.[130] At the time this story may have been told at Delphi itself, probably in the vicinity of the tripod, to explain the origin of the *mechane*. The bones and teeth, even the skin, the *corium*, of the giant serpent (after which the kettle was called *cortina* in Latin) were taken up by the Roman commentaries on the poets, suggesting

129 By Sotiris J. Dakaris. See the expression ἠχῶν λέβης Θεσπρώτειος in M. Psellos, *Graecorum opiniones de daemonibus*, p. 39; and the finds reported in "Chronique des Fouilles en 1964," *BCH*, LXXXIX (1965), esp. fig. 11. Dodona also had its tripods with bronze kettles, probably around the sacred oak; see Dakaris, "Neue Ausgrabungen in Griechenland," pp. 38 ff., fig. 5.

130 Hyginus, *Fabulae* 140: "Pythonem sagittis interfecit (inde Pythius est dictus), ossaque eius in cortinam coniecit et in templo suo posuit, ludosque funebres ei fecit, qui ludi Pythia dicuntur." This was done on the fourth day after the birth of Apollo; so the author explains why the Pythian Agones were repeated every four years.

allusions to the lots and to a covering that was thrown over the kettle when no oracles were being drawn from it.[131] Another etymology of *cortina*—"because it contains the heart" (*quod cor teneat*)[132]—shows that these plays on the remains of the dragon were not based on mere superficial invention.

After Onomakritos put forward—in the sixth century B.C.—a new interpretation of the somber sacrifice, the Titans were regarded as the murderers and renders of Dionysos. Their deeds were looked upon as the models for the ceremonies of the second year of the *trieteris*. Thus, in connection with the somber rites of the Thyiades in the "maenadic" year, Plutarch refers to Dionysos not only as "Zagreus," "Nyktelios" ("the nocturnal"), and "Isodaites" ("the exact divider of the sacrificial meat"), but also as "titanic and nocturnal."[133] He had in mind the dismembering of Dionysos. Concerning the fate of the dismembered god there were two Orphic traditions. According to one, which became a widespread Orphic doctrine, the Titans devoured all the pieces but one which, for the uninitiated, was the heart. According to the other tradition, adapted to the situation at Delphi, Apollo took possession of the pieces after the Titans had thrown them into a kettle standing on a tripod and cooked them. Apollo then buried them on Mt. Parnassos.[134] For the place of burial a vague expression was chosen: "somewhere

131   See Servius' commentary on *Aeneid* III 92 and 360. / The very plausible idea of the lots was stated by A. B. Cook, *Zeus*, II, 221: "Perhaps the pebbles, which for purposes of divination were really kept in the bowl of the tripod, had been explained as the relics of Python. . . ." A snakeskinlike covering of the *holmos* is described by Dionysios Periegetes, "Orbis descriptio," in C. Müller, ed., *Geographi Graeci Minores*, II, 130, lines 443–44.

132   See Servius' commentary on *Aeneid* VI 347.

133   See *De E apud Delphos* 389 A and *De Iside et Osiride* 364 F.

134   Kern, ed., *Orphicorum fragmenta*, fr. 35.

on the Delphic tripod.”[135] In the holy of holies, however, the tomb of Dionysos was shown. It is described by Philochoros, an Athenian historian of the third and second century B.C., and is represented in an Attic votive relief of the late fifth century.

According to Philochoros the tomb looked like a *bathron*, a kind of stairway.[136] The Attic votive relief represents a tripod on which Apollo sits, his feet resting on a *bathron* consisting of two steps [63].[137] In all representations the Delphic *tripous* is so high that steps were necessary if the Pythia wished to sit down on the concave *epithema*, the *holmos*. Sitting in her place, touching the *bathron* with both feet, Apollo reveals the idea and implication of the oracle, its connection with the upper and lower worlds. What lay below was the sphere of the subterranean Dionysos, from which Apollo derived his revelations. It was called a tomb, but there was no actual tomb; rather, the steps were said to be the tomb of Dionysos, and it was hinted that perhaps he made his way to the underworld through the kettle. The report of an inscription saying, “Here since his death lies Dionysos, son of Semele,” is an invention,[138] unless such an inscription was added at a late date. Even with-

135 This is the wording of Kallimachos, fr. 643. See also *Etymologicum Magnum*, p. 255, lines 14–16: παρὰ τῶι τρίποδι ἀπέθετο παρὰ τῶι ἀδελφῶι.

136 Philochoros, fr. 7, in Jacoby, *FGrHist*, 328 (III, B, p. 100): βάθρον δέ τι εἶναι ὑπονοεῖται ἡ σορός. . . .

137 After Svoronos, *Das Athener Nationalmuseum*, pl. LIV. The link with the indication given by Philochoros was pointed out by Cook, *Zeus*, II, 221: “we should regard the stepped base . . . as a representation of Dionysos’ tomb.” The traces that have been found of the tripod and *omphalos* do not preclude the possibility that the *bathron* was situated before the tripod on the opposite side from the *omphalos*.

138 Philochoros, fr. 7 (continuation of the quotation in note 136, above): ἐν ὧι γράφεται· Ἐνθάδε κεῖται θανὼν Διόνυσος ἐκ Σεμέλης. The invention follows familiar models which go back to the romance of Euhemeros; see Cook, *Zeus*, II, 220. The last of such romanced variations was that of Porphyry, *Vita Pythagorae*

out it the connection between Apollo and Dionysos was known. It was stated by the tragic poets of Athens, by Aischylos as well as by Euripides in whose lifetime the relief may have been cut.[139]

In the Lykourgos tetralogy of Aischylos, the cry "Ivy-Apollo, Bakchios, the soothsayer,"[140] rings out, probably when the Thracian bacchantes, the Bassarai, attack Orpheus, the worshiper of Apollo and the sun. The cry suggests a higher knowledge of the connection between Apollo and Dionysos, the dark god, whom Orpheus seemed to deny in favor of the luminous god—Apollo and the sun as one person. In the *Lykymnios* of Euripides the same connection is attested by the cry, "Lord, laurel-loving Bakchios, Paean Apollo, player of the lyre."[141] Another indication of the connection is the fact that at Delphi paeans were addressed not only to Apollo but to Dionysos as well. But the simplest, most unmistakable evidence of this relationship, without which the oracle could not have functioned, is the sacrifice of a goat: a Dionysian act preceding the Apollonian rite. In the story that traces the origin of the oracle to vapors rising from a cleft in the earth, it is the goats who are thrown into a state of ecstasy by the vapors and who thus discover the special nature of the site.[142] We know little about the great sacrifice that inaugurated the official questioning of the oracle on the seventh day of Bysios, the month of renewed growth[143] cor-

---

XVI, according to which Apollo, son of the silenus—hence a second Dionysos—was buried in the tripod. This invention also goes back to the chthonian character of the tripod.

139 Willemsen, "Der delphische Dreifuss," p. 85.

140 Mette, *Die Fragmente*, fr. 86: ὁ κισσεὸς Ἀπόλλων ὁ Βάκχιος ὁ μάντις.

141 Nauck, *TGF*, fr. 480: δέσποτα φιλόδαφνε Βάκχιε, Παιὰν Ἀπόλλων εὔλυρε
. . . . Both passages are quoted in Macrobius, *Saturnalia* I 18 6.

142 Diodorus Siculus XVI 26 2–3.

143 Plutarch, *Quaestiones Graecae* 292 E.

responding to the Attic Anthesterion. This season seems to have been a great time of *patet mundus*, when the subterranean sphere lay open and sent up its gifts, as well as a time of answers and injunctions to men. Questioners were admitted in an order determined by lot,[144] but when an individual came to question the oracle for some special reason, it was a particular animal, usually a goat, who decided whether he was to be admitted.[145]

In other sacrifices and chthonian rites, Plutarch tells us, it sufficed for the animal, after having been sprinkled with water in the first phase of the ceremony, to shake its head. But in the case of the sacrifice inaugurating the official questioning, the entire sacrificial animal was expected to shudder, to tremble in every limb and emit quaking sounds.[146] The sacrificial victim, standing for the sacrificer and the god who descended to the subterranean sphere and opened it to questions and answers, consented as it were with his whole body.[147] Once in Plutarch's time the reaction required of the animal was obtained by force, and the Pythia suffered in consequence. She was assailed by terrible pains, ran out of the holy of holies with inarticulate screams, and collapsed. Plutarch does not state expressly that this was the cause of her death.[148]

There was a connection between the "voluntary" death of the sacri-

---

144   Aischylos, *Eumenides* 31–33.

145   The significance of the goat is stressed also by Amandry, *La Mantique*, p. 104. The question whether it must not have been a he-goat is justified. But even if the he-goat had a special significance in the rite (see ch. VI), we cannot expect this to be stated. Most often Plutarch speaks merely of a "sacrificial animal": ἱερεῖον.

146   *De defectu oraculorum* 435 C.

147   This interpretation is that of Plutarch himself: *Quaestiones conviviales* 729 F.

148   *De defectu oraculorum* 438 AB.

ficial animal and the functioning of the kettle on the tripod. The very existence of the oracle demanded a cruel death, a repetition of the rending of Dionysos; such a death was re-enacted, probably in a very much abbreviated and simplified form, in each sacrifice of a goat preceding the questioning. Now we understand why no woman was permitted to come too close to the *tripous*. The maenadic women on Parnassos had been guilty of the murder indispensable to the oracle: they had torn the god to pieces, perhaps with their own teeth. The tradition does not reveal how the women performed their sacrifice every second winter at the approach of spring, at a time when young animals were already available. It permits only a general reconstruction which must take account not just of the rending but also of a more methodical dismemberment.

At Delphi, if the oracle were not to function only every second year, another ceremony was necessary. The secret rite which the Dionysian women performed on Parnassos and which filled the kettle and the underworld with the divine presence sufficed for Bysios of the first year of the *trieteris*, but when the Hosioi awakened Liknites and claimed him for themselves, they had to perform in the temple of Apollo another ceremony the details of which might not be divulged.[149] The Hosioi were five in number and were present at all important cult actions at Delphi. They came of an ancient family, which traced its descent to Deukalion, the primordial man whose ship landed on Mt. Parnassos after the flood.[150] This genealogical legend offered a guarantee that they maintained the oldest tradition. It was they who knew most about the secrets of Delphi.

149   See above, note 99.
150   Plutarch, *Quaestiones Graecae* 292 D; H. Usener, *Die Sintflutsagen*, p. 40.

Their quality as Hosioi, however, was not inherited but acquired. It implied freedom from every sin of the kind that the Dionysian women incurred every second year as murderesses of the god. *Hosiotes* was acquired by the sacrifice of an animal, the *hosioter*.[151] This was obviously a substitutive sacrifice presupposing the identity of god, man, and animal—a sacrifice characteristic of the Dionysian religion. The processions of Pythaists have shown us that at Delphi the bull may well have been the representative sacrificial animal. Through their identification with the sacrificed one, the Hosioi enjoyed perfect freedom in the sphere ruled by the subterranean Dionysos. In a work by the Alexandrian poet Lykophron telling of a secret sacrifice performed by Agamemnon at Delphi, the oracle refers to Dionysos as Tauros, "bull."[152] An inscription relating to this legendary sacrifice has made it possible to situate approximately the Delphic Dionysion, the small sanctuary outside the great sacred precinct.[153] It may be presumed that the Thyiades did not gather in the Dionysion, but that quite possibly the "consecrated men" officiated there.

It seems likely that this was the function of the Dionysian corner outside the temple of Apollo, but this is no more than a presumption. Parnassos formed a far larger precinct for the mysteries of Dionysos

---

151 See Kerényi, *Die antike Religion*, 1952 edn., p. 87. See also *The Religion of the Greeks and Romans*, p. 111: "A characteristic of Greek religion is the *remoteness* of the underworld domain, and this remoteness, though it varies at different times, also keeps the idea of the 'sanction' more in the background. It is part of *hosiotes* that the underworld domain is known to be in the background and at the same time kept at a distance. It is the quality of *hosiotes*, preserved in all situations, which keeps the menace of the subterranean beings at a distance." On the *hosioter*, see Plutarch, *Quaestiones Graecae* 292 D.

152 Lykophron, *Alexandra* 209–10.

153 G. Daux and J. Bousquet, "Agamemnon, Télèphe, Dionysos Sphaleôtas et les Attalides," pp. 119 ff.; also note 101, above.

than did Delphi with its Apollo cult, and the mysteries of Dionysos outlived the public cult. The price of this survival was no doubt the simplification and vulgarization of the rites, a development to which the
secret Dionysian orgies were always prone. About 400 A.D. the Roman
Macrobius reported a male *thiasos*—a *coetus* of men who disguised as
satyrs took part in the rites of the Thyiades. "On this Mt. Parnassos," he
writes, "trieteric Dionysian festivals are celebrated; here a company of
satyrs (so it is alleged) is often seen and their voices frequently heard.
Often the sound of cymbals is also heard."[154] The memory of the
Thyiades and of their cymbals (*tympana*), which people thought they
heard, was still alive in the vicinity of Mt. Parnassos at the beginning
of this century. For the peasants the Thyiades had become Neraides,
ghost women, of whom folk stood in awe believing that they possessed
a power which made the tops of the firs touch the ground.[155] With
just such power Dionysos himself, in the *Bacchae* of Euripides, bends
a fir tree, and in unison the bacchantes imitate him.[156] Perhaps this
motif, the bending of a fir, has been from time immemorial an expression of the superabundant force that filled the Thyiades.

154   Macrobius, *Saturnalia* I 18 6: "In hoc monte Parnaso Bacchanalia
alternis annis aguntur; ubi et Satyrorum, ut affirmant, frequens cernitur coetus,
plerumque voces propriae exaudiuntur: itemque cymbalorum crepitus ad aures
hominum saepe perveniunt."

155   A. E. Kondoleon, Ὁδηγὸς τοῦ Κωρυκίου Ἄντρου, pp. 15–18; ὥστε αἱ κορυφαὶ
τῶν ἐλατῶν καμπτόμεναι ἐγγίζουσι τὴν γῆν.

156   *Bacchae* 1064–69, 1109–10.

The Mystical Sacrificial Rite

A N A C C O U N T of a great living cult of antiquity, especially of one so rich and varied as the Delphic cult, is bound to show large gaps and to lean heavily on hypothesis. (This was the case at the end of the preceding section.) Throughout the loud festivities of the winter months and the secret ceremonies on Parnassos and in the temple of the oracle, Dionysos remained in the background. His cult at Delphi was the nurturing soil from which the illuminations of the religion of Apollo grew. The Apollonian religion, however, concerned chiefly the larger communities, the states. The god of *zoë* was confined to his *trieteris*, and found his way to man through smaller communities and, paradoxically, through books.

In Greece a living cult needed no books. The content and design of cult actions were provided by myth. These actions *were* myth, just as myth *was* the reality expressed. The myth of Dionysos expressed the reality of *zoë*, its indestructibility, and its peculiar dialectical bond with death. The cult had set rites that were performed for centuries according to the same patterns. All those entitled to witness and take part in them did so. Innovations required literary expression, and the *Teletai* ("Initiations") of Onomakritos provided such an expression. The author, a definitely historical theologian of the sixth century B.C.,[157] also wrote oracles and was accused of forgery; he was not numbered among the sages of Greece or, later, included in the history of philosophy. In addition to oracles, Onomakritos had available to him another type of religious writing, and he chose to write in this genre.

157 Herodotos VII 6; see also Kerényi, "Die Münzen des Onomakritos."

There was among the Greeks a variety of myth that had no connection with cult but was literary from the first. Its concern was not
with life, but with its continuation in fantasy, with a permanence attributed to life but distinct from it. Homer attempted this genre in his
own way in the eleventh book of the Odyssey, Odysseus' journey to
the underworld. The myth of Orpheus also included a journey to the
underworld. In contrast to the Dionysian religion—both the myth and
the cult—this myth was characteristically connected with literature,
a form of permanence. The Dionysian religion possessed its own inherent and immanent "philosophy"—its "dialectic"—differing from that
of the Orphic literature based on Orpheus' journey to the underworld.
In the journeys of mortal men (not of gods like Dionysos) to the underworld, at least the beginnings of a psychology and ethical philosophy are inherent: a doctrine of the immortality of the soul and of
the punishment of sinners. This is no longer a mere "immanent philosophy" as in the dialectic of the Dionysian religion, but rather a prephilosophical view of the world.

There can be no doubt that when Melampous in introducing the
religion of Dionysos "interpreted" the *phallophoria*, the procession in
which phalli were carried about, and the *phallagogia*, the most conspicuous action of the cult, his interpretation consisted merely in a
telling of the underlying myth. There is no reason to suppose that his
explanation was "symbolic"—in the sense employed by later sym-
bolists—or philosophical. But when in the sixth century B.C. the philosopher Herakleitos of Ephesos encountered the *phallophoriai*, he hit
on the philosophical significance of the seemingly offensive action
with the words: "If they did not order the procession in honor of the
god and address the phallus song to him, this would be the most shame-
less behavior. But Hades is the same as Dionysos, for whom they rave

and act like bacchantes."[158] For Herakleitos this identity was a crucial fact, which he could invoke because it was known to all. He used it in support of his own philosophy of the identity of opposites, and because of his philosophy he was able to recognize and express, as could no one else, the *importance* of the unity of the god Dionysos and Hades.

Although the Orphic books never attained this height, Onomakritos, appearing in the role of Orpheus—that is, as an Orphic writer—brought about a reform of the Dionysian religion and gave it a new mission. We have already seen a man, allegedly its first missionary in Greece, Melampous of Pylos, prepare the way for the cult, but the most secret ceremonies were enacted by women for the benefit of the whole community of men and women. The women's rites were concerned with the life of all. Still, they were women's actions, exclusive women's mysteries; women seemed to be in exclusive possession of the god, although in this possession they necessarily became sinners. The Athenian Onomakritos dissolved this archaic bond between the mystic actions and women, and permitted the men, but only men of the primordial age, to sin for all future mankind, in order that all men, through the same mystic rites that now ceased to be a secret women's cult, might identify themselves with the god and partake of his indestructibility.

Onomakritos is said to have taken the "name of the Titans" from Homer[159] and to have "composed" (*synetheken*) "orgies" (mystery ac-

---

158 Herakleitos, in H. Diels, ed., *Die Fragmente der Vorsokratiker*, 22 [12] B 15 (I, 154 f.): εἰ μὴ γὰρ Διονύσωι πομπὴν ἐποιοῦντο καὶ ὕμνεον αἶσμα αἰδοίοισιν, ἀναιδέστατα εἴργαστ' ἄν· ὡυτὸς δὲ Ἀίδης καὶ Διόνυσος, ὅτεωι μαίνονται καὶ ληναΐζουσιν. In opposition to the false interpretation of these lines given by A. Lesky in "Dionysos und Hades," see G. A. Privitera, "I rapporti di Dioniso con Posidone in età micenea," p. 203.

159 Iliad XIV 279.

tions) of Dionysos. He invented (*epoiesa*) the story that the Titans were responsible for the death of Dionysos.[160] This is known to us through the pious Pausanias, who was well versed in the religious books still available in his day, during the reign of Hadrian. One such work may have been the *Teletai* of Onomakritos, a work that probably dealt both with cult actions and with their mythical prehistory.[161] The new mysteries of Dionysos that Onomakritos composed from the old required a mythical foundation, which now had to be set forth in writing. Through Onomakritos and his interpretation, the mystic sacrifice, which the Dionysian women performed in secret, was taken into the literature of the Neoplatonists; thus it can be reconstructed. The texts we must analyze to this end are far removed from the Delphic cult in place and time. They belong to the last centuries of antiquity and have as their sources works which, by the mere fact that they were written down, can have sprung from the old religion of Dionysos only in a paradoxical way. Still, they enable us to reconstruct historical particulars that may well reach back to the early, or even the earliest, days of the god's presence in Greece.

After Onomakritos there was an Orphic doctrine that, although never so stated, might have been expressed in the following words. Not only in the Dionysian women, the handmaidens of Dionysos, but in all human beings there lurks at all times an enemy of the god, ready to erupt and to murder him. All men resemble the first enemies of the god, because all are of the same substance; but all have within them something of the selfsame god, to wit, divine indestructible life. Ono-

---

160   Pausanias VIII 37 5: παρὰ δὲ Ὁμήρου Ὀνομάκριτος παραλαβὼν τῶν Τιτάνων τὸ ὄνομα Διονύσωι τε συνέθηκεν ὄργια καὶ εἶναι τοὺς Τιτᾶνας τῶι Διονύσωι τῶν παθημάτων ἐποίησεν αὐτουργούς.

161   See *Suidae Lexicon* s.v. Ὀρφεύς; A. Krueger, "Quaestiones Orphicae"; also K. Ziegler's criticism in "Orphische Dichtung," col. 1414.

makritos gave expression to this thought by taking over the name of the Titans from Homer. From the Titans men were descended, and in a very special way that is described with precision by Olympiodoros, a Neoplatonic philosopher, in his commentary on Plato's *Phaedo*. According to Olympiodoros, after Ouranos, Kronos, and Zeus, Dionysos became the fourth ruler of the world, but at Hera's instigation the Titans around him tore him to pieces and ate of his flesh. Zeus flew into a rage and slew the Titans with his lightning. From the vapor they gave off, soot formed, and from the soot, a stuff. Of this stuff men were made.[162]

Thus, it is not simply stated as a "central dogma of Orphic theology,"[163] that the human race arose from the ashes of the Titans. If such a summary interpretation of the doctrine were correct, it would have been superfluous to note the details of the burning. "Our body is Dionysian," Olympiodoros added; "we are a part of him, since we sprang from the soot of the Titans who ate of his flesh." Soot and ashes are not identical. In the alchemy of late antiquity the word employed for soot, *aithale*, means "sublimated vapor."[164] If this story had been a free invention, not rooted in myth and cult, it would have sufficed to say that the Titans sprang from ashes, in Greek, *spodos*. Both components, the titanic as well as Dionysian, might have been contained in ashes. The detour of vapor and its concretion into a stuff, the "soot of the Titans," reveals the work of a thinker aiming at a synthesis in which he wished to embrace all the elements at his disposal, and this thinker can only have been Onomakritos.

162 Olympiodoros, *In Platonis Phaedonem commentarii* 61 c, in W. Norvin, ed., p. 2, 21; in O. Kern, ed., *Orphicorum fragmenta*, fr. 220.

163 Kern, *Orpheus*, p. 43; "Orphiker auf Kreta," p. 554.

164 M. Berthelot, *Collection des anciens alchimistes grecs*, III, 250.

He adopted the name of Titans for the beings who originally undertook the somber Dionysian sacrifice, the murder of the god. But this did not prevent the Titans from remaining concrete figures of Greek mythology. Their fate was known: Zeus had defeated them in the Titanomachia and hurled them into Tartaros. The belief, held by popular philosophers of the Roman period,[165] that men had sprung from the blood of the Titans, appears to have been a secularization of Onomakritos' new myth (which became a dogma of the Orphic mysteries) rather than the survival of an older myth. In the Orphic Hymn Book, dating from the post-Christian period,[166] there is a prayer to the Titans, invoking them as "our fathers' ancestors," "origin and source of all care-worn mortals." This they had been since Onomakritos.[167] Moreover, they are called upon for help when a house is molested by an ancestral spirit.[168] The Titans have the power to dismiss disgruntled spirits because they themselves have become such ancestral spirits and ghosts. The hymn (XXXVII) follows the generally accepted tradition in assigning them to the deepest subterranean realm into which Zeus had hurled them.

When the Titans came to kill the child Dionysos, they came like ghosts from the underworld and were hurled back into their eternal

165 Dion Chrysostomos, *Orationes* XXX 10 (in Cohoon, ed., II, 428); Ovid, *Metamorphoses* I 156–62. See also Krueger, "Quaestiones Orphicae," p. 46.

166 See above, p. 198; Ziegler, "Orphische Dichtung," col. 1332.

167 Quandt, *Orphei hymni* XXXVII 2: ἡμετέρων πρόγονοι πατέρων, and 4: ἀρχαὶ καὶ πηγαὶ πάντων θνητῶν πολυμόχθων. The following two verses in which all living creatures are viewed as the progeny of the Titans embody the doctrine of the transmigration of souls. In Greece this doctrine probably goes back to the Orpheus myth and the orgiastic experiences of the Dionysos cult as known to us through Euripides' *Cretan Men*. See Kerényi, "Pythagoras und Orpheus," *Werke*, I, p. 43; and above, ch. III, at notes 113 ff.

168 Quandt, *Orphei hymni* XXXVII 7–8.

abode by Zeus' lightning. Accordingly, Onomakritos explains, they gave off a smokelike vapor caused by the heat of the lightning. They themselves vanished into Tartaros; the vapor became soot; and the soot became the stuff of mankind. Thus, two elements were combined: the old myth of the Titans and another cultic element, a stuff that was the residue of a fire. This stuff, says Onomakritos, contained not only the earthly remains of the Titans, but Dionysos as well. The soot concealed within it the Dionysian substance that is inherited by man from generation to generation. In this way Onomakritos endowed the god with a material substantiality such as we find nowhere else in Greek religion and certainly not in the Dionysian religion, but at most in the "physiological" explanations of the gods.

Here the most concrete consequences were drawn from the myth of Dionysos as embodied in cult. In Onomakritos' synthesis the myth of the reappearance of the Titans, combined with an older myth of the Divine Child, became the first act of a drama; its second act was the myth of the fire in which the little Dionysos perished. These myths were the content of two mystic ceremonies that Onomakritos transformed and reinterpreted by introducing the Titans. The concluding section of Chapter V is devoted to the first act, the enthronement. The second act was based on the mystic sacrificial ceremony of the Dionysian women, for a meal provided the tragic climax of the entire drama, the *katastrophe* redounding to the benefit of mankind.

The Orphic history of the world[169] culminates in the Dionysian era, which succeeded the reign of Zeus. The Dionysian era—the period of the Orphics themselves—takes in the thousand years from Onoma-

169 The Orphic history in its latest form is "The Holy Tales in Twenty-Four Cantos" ('Ἱεροὶ λόγοι ἐν ῥαψωιδίαις κδ'); see Kern, *Orphicorum fragmenta*, frs. 60–235.

kritos to Nonnos, whose Dionysian epic is the last great record of the Orphic Dionysian religion. Onomakritos had related that the Titans took the Divine Child Dionysos by surprise, killed him, and prepared to eat him. In the generally known version of the story, the child was slain by being torn to pieces. This was the *sparagmos*, the ecstatic action known to us from Crete. Nonnos, however, also mentions the "infernal knife" of the Titans, the *Tartarie machaire*, the instrument of the titanic sin. It had its part in the ceremony, but in another rite that was more complicated than the *sparagmos*. Where the slain being was cut into seven parts and one particular organ retained, the participants must have used a knife. The preparation of the meal is described as follows: The Titans' victim was cut into seven parts and thrown into a kettle standing on a tripod. In it the seven parts were boiled. Afterwards the pieces of meat were removed from the kettle, put on spits and placed over the fire.[170] The meal, however, was not eaten. Enticed by the aroma, Zeus appeared and with his lightning prevented the Titans from completing their cannibalistic repast. The meal was cannibalistic because divine beings were preparing to eat divine beings. The rites in which men imitated this event were not cannibalistic because a sacrificial animal was substituted for the Divine Child. That is why Nonnos calls the child Dionysos *keroen brephos*, the "horned infant."

Dionysos himself was called "Eriphos," "kid," the animal form he most often assumed in mythology.[171] The boiling motif also occurs in

170 *Orphicorum fragmenta*, frs. 34, 35, 210, and 214.

171 Hesychios s.v. Ἔριφος, ὁ Διόνυσος. This is the correct reading. The *Eriphi-os* in Stephen of Byzantium s.v. Ἀκρώρεια is probably Pan. See also Antoninus Liberalis XXVIII; Ovid, *Metamorphoses* V 329; *Mythographi Vaticani* I 86 (in Bode, ed., p. 24).

a late myth.[172] After the birth of Dionysos, Zeus entrusted the infant to Hermes. Hermes brought him to Ino who is also known as the nurse of Dionysos. She and her husband Athamas were to bring up Dionysos as a girl along with their two sons. The jealous Hera made Ino and Athamas mad. Athamas in his madness hunted Learchos, their elder son, as a stag and killed him. Ino threw Melikertes, their younger son, into a kettle full of boiling water and then flung herself into the sea with him. Zeus saved his son Dionysos from Hera's fury by turning him into a kid and sending him with Hermes to the nymphs of Nysa.

This tale is replete with Dionysian motifs: the young god dressed in a manner suggesting effeminacy, madness, the hunt for a supposed stag, the boiling of the Divine Child in a kettle, the transformation into a kid. Undoubtedly the cultic background of the mythologem was the Dionysian sacrifice in which a kid was slaughtered and boiled in a kettle. The Titans had not yet been introduced, and the mythologem shows that the rite could be performed without them, by a woman or women. This was indeed the case in the Dionysian cult. Ino was a primordial Dionysian woman, nurse to the god and a divine maenad. She takes the place of the nurses who became the murderesses of their charge whom they worshiped and—as we may safely say on the strength of the Delphic cult—whom they had awakened.

In the Titans' preparation of the meal, however, not only the dismemberment and boiling were important, but also the roasting that followed the boiling and the order in which these things were done. We have express testimony that the whole procedure was a mystery rite. In Aristotle's *Anecdota problemata*, so-called because they long remained unpublished, it is asked: "Why is it forbidden to roast what

172 Apollodoros, *Bibliotheca* III 4 3; Kerényi, *The Gods of the Greeks*, p. 264 (Pelican edn., p. 232 f.).

has been boiled, but customary to boil what has been roasted?"[173] Was it because of what was said in the mysteries? It was related in the mysteries—first, no doubt, in the *Teletai* of Onomakritos—that the infant Dionysos, like the sacrificed kid, was first boiled and then roasted. This sequence ended in disaster: Zeus burned roast and roasters with his lightning. The mystic sacrifice underlying the tale ended with the burning of the meal, with the charred, smoking flesh that turned to soot, the stuff to which Onomakritos attached so much importance.

We now have a good general idea of the ceremony from the dismembering of the sacrificial animal to the burning of the remains (except for the one piece which was kept). All the questions have not, however, been answered. What part of this ceremony was secret if not unutterable: *aporrheton* or *arrheton*?[174] What are the details of Dionysos' connection with the ceremony? This connection is now clear only in the very general sense that we know of somber sacrifices to Dionysos performed only at certain times and embodying his dark aspect. The *sparagmos* of young animals, in which the maenads engaged, was such a sacrifice: a murderous act performed without a knife. This was public enough and was also described and represented. It seems likely that at Delphi it was enacted only on the periphery of the mystic ceremony as an introduction to the *arrheton* in which the knife was used.

The cutting into parts—not the rending and devouring—calls for comparison with the myth of Osiris. Isis found the parts of her husband's body and put them together. She reawakened him by setting the male organ in place and uniting herself with him in love.[175] The Greek

173 Aristotle, *Anecdota problemata* III 43; see also S. Reinach, *Cultes, mythes et religions*, V, 61 ff.

174 See Kerényi, *Eleusis*, pp. 24 f.; and above, ch. V, at notes 109 ff.

175 After an old Egyptian text in E. Otto, *Osiris und Amun*, p. 27: "To you [Osiris] comes your sister Isis, rejoicing for love of you. You have placed her

myth as reflected in literature deviates from this story. According to the Greek version, Rhea, mother of the gods, put Dionysos' pieces together and brought him back to life.[176] Her role corresponded to the genealogy that made Dionysos the son not of Semele but of Persephone, here the daughter of Rhea rather than of Demeter. According to Diodorus Siculus, this genealogy originated with the Cretans. The motif of the search for the parts of Dionysos' body also occurs in variants of the Dionysian myth. It has its place in the story of Antinoë, a sister of Semele, and Antinoë's son, Aktaion, the hunter, a double of Learchos, son of Ino, another sister in the same family. Antinoë had to search for the pieces of Aktaion, who had been hunted like a stag and torn to pieces by his dogs.[177]

If the cutting into pieces in the mystic sacrificial ceremony was based on such a mythical cutting into pieces—prerequisite to the reconstitution and reawakening of the god—the sacrificial flesh was certainly not meant to be eaten. Diodorus makes no mention of Rhea in his story of the dismembered Dionysos, whom he calls the son of

---

on your phallus. Your seed flows into her . . . flows out of you as Horus." Otto adds: "In later representations she, in the form of a sparrow hawk, . . . alights on the body of her dead husband and receives a son from him." See *Osiris und Amun*, p. 56; figs. 5, 16–19. Further documentation (pictures and text) in T. Hopfner, *Plutarch über Isis und Osiris*, pp. 82 ff. According to Plutarch, *De Iside et Osiride* 358 B, Isis did not find the phallus because it had been devoured by certain fishes. Consequently she set up a replica and so sanctified the phallus: ἀντ᾽ ἐκείνου μίμημα ποιησαμένην καθιερῶσαι τὸν φαλλόν, ὧι καὶ νῦν ἑορτάζειν τοὺς Αἰγυπτίους. The addition, "whom the Egyptians still celebrate today," makes it certain that the legend explains the use of an artificial phallus in certain rites. Here Plutarch confined himself to the Egyptian rites, since he was permitted to speak openly only of these and not of Greek rites.

176 Philodemos, *De pietate* 44 (Gomperz, ed., p. 16); Euphorion, in Powell, *Collectanea Alexandrina*, fr. 36; Kern, *Orphicorum fragmenta*, fr. 36.

177 Kerényi, *The Gods of the Greeks*, p. 146 (Pelican edn., p. 129).

Demeter—which was compatible with the mythology of the Orphics as well as the Cretans. He relates how Demeter gathered the parts of her son Dionysos' body, and he offers the explanation of the "physiologists": when the vine has been heavily pruned after the wine harvest, the earth restores it in order that it may bear fruit again in due season. "This is consonant with what is said in the Orphic poems and presented in the mysteries."[178] This second explicit mention of the mysteries, which can only be those of Dionysos, refers to the same actions, from the slaying and cutting into parts to the burning.

According to the great Orphic didactic poem, the last gift of Dionysos was wine, and the author of the poem calls the god himself "Oinos," "wine."[179] The sacred action is transposed from the vineyards to the books and mysteries of the Orphics through a reinterpretation of the secret sacrifice with which the *trieteris* was concluded. A simplified form of the great rite was preserved in the vineyards. Throughout Greek and Roman antiquity the custom of sacrificing a goat to the vine remained in force. The sacrifice was explained by a kind of law of *talion*, for when goats were admitted to a vineyard they sinned against the vines. "So it came about," says Marcus Terentius Varro, "that the he-goats were sacrificed to Dionysos, discoverer of the vine, as though to make atonement, a head for a head." This explanation presupposes the idea of substitution—goat for vine. In an epigram by Leonidas of Tarentum, a voice rises from the earth where the dismembered Dionysos lies and threatens the goat: "Very well, eat my fruit-bearing vines: the root will still bear enough wine to pour on you when you are sacrificed."[180]

178   Diodorus Siculus III 62 7–8, τὰ παρεισαγόμενα κατὰ τὰς τελετάς.
179   Kern, *Orphicorum fragmenta*, fr. 216.
180   Varro, *De re rustica* I 2 19. See also Leonidas in *Anthologia Palatina* IX 99, and Euenos, *Anthologia Palatina* IX 75.

A still more extensive substitution was expressed in the boiling of the sacrificial animal. This was also customary in the sacrifices to the Horai, the goddesses of ripening, who first sheltered Dionysos in Athens. In his *On Sacrifices*, Philochoros, a third century B.C. practitioner and theoretician of cult actions, wrote: "When the Athenians sacrifice to the Horai, they do not roast the meat, but boil it. They petition the goddesses to avert lasting heat and drought and pray to them to ripen everything that grows by favorable warmth and timely rain. Roasting is indeed less useful; boiling not only takes away the rawness but also softens the hard parts and makes the rest edible."[181] For "to make edible" Philochoros used the word *pepainein*, which also means "to make ripe."

Thus far the meaning of the ceremony is patent, for thus far we find no discernible reason for keeping it secret. A kid had to die in order that the vine should grow again from the earth. The flesh of the sacrificial animal was boiled, and by a similar process the grapes on the vine would become ripe and edible. Then the flesh of the sacrifice was held over the fire and burned. In Greek it was possible in this context to say *holokarpoun*, "to make entirely into fruit," for "to burn entirely."[182] The mixing of burnt flesh with earth is stressed in an inscription from Perinthos, a city on the Hellespont. This oracular utterance of the sibyl presents a rather mysterious summary of the act of sacrificing a he-goat. The Dionysian community of Perinthos was probably founded by an oracle, which enjoined the sacrifice as a foundation ceremony:

181 Philochoros is quoted in Athenaios XIV 656 A; cited by Reinach, *Cultes, mythes et religions*, V, 61 ff., in connection with the passage here quoted from Aristotle, *Anecdota problemata* III 43.

182 See Wilamowitz-Moellendorf, *Der Glaube der Hellenen*, I, 288.

ἐπὰν δ' ὁ Βάκχος εὐάσας πληγήσεται

τότε αἷμα καὶ πῦρ καὶ κόνις μιγήσεται ·

After Bakchos, who cried "euoi," is struck,

Blood and fire and dust will mix.[183]

This mixture includes fire instead of soot. The reserve with which the sacrifice is alluded to not only here, but still more in other sources, indicates that this was a highly ambivalent action of which people did not like to speak. Here we have a hint of a reason for secrecy. The oracle alone could permit itself to reveal more than any author until Himerios—a late pagan orator living at a time when such secrets were less closely guarded.

It is plain that the lines of the oracle referred to the killing of Dionysos, which was to be repeated in Perinthos in the form of a sacrifice. The Bakchos who cried "Euoi!" was the young god whom the goat represented. Himerios mentions the blow: "Dionysos lay there struck down, still moaning under the blow."[184] Then in his account of the sacrifice the orator goes on to speak of the grief of the vine, wine, and grape: "The vine hung down, the wine was disconsolate, the grape as though bathed in tears." This sympathy strikes one as rhetorical sentimentality, but basically it is not a sentimental invention any more than is the lament in Homer's description of the wine harvest. The sympathetic relation between the victim and the vine was essential to the Dionysian sacrifice. The god was manifested no less in the vine than in the sacrificial animal.

The continuity and indestructibility of *zoë* were not taught, but

183 After Albrecht Dieterich who supplied πληγήσεται in the poor copy; see his "De hymnis orphicis," pp. 72 ff.

184 Himerios, *Orationes* XLV 4; Kern, *Orphicorum fragmenta*, fr. 214.

were set forth as self-evident in a small, concrete sector of an equally concrete over-all life. To the Greeks Dionysos was a god over goat and vine. Goat and vine belonged to his myth, through which the common element in them—but not in them alone—was expressed. The common element was overflowing life. The self-evident assumption that it passed from one to the other and continued was an allusion to the god who was enclosed in no single being. Further reference to the great myth contained in the great ceremony surpassed the limits of a wine grower's religion which was not originally an exclusively Greek religion but which in Greece took on its spiritual character, its clear "dialectic." Those elements in the ceremony that were kept most secret are hints at the archaic core of the myth, which for the Greeks remained unutterable.

None of the historic sources tell us what the liquid was in which the dismembered kid had to be boiled. Tombs of the fourth to second centuries in Crete, in Lipari, and near Sybaris in southern Italy, have, however, disclosed gold leaves that were to accompany the initiates in the Orphic mysteries to the other world. Near Sybaris, at the site of the Greek city of Thourioi, two such gold leaves were found. The first bears the words:

ἔριφος ἐς γάλ' ἔπετον ·

A kid, I fell into milk.

The second reads:

χαῖρε παθὼν τὸ πάθημα τὸ δ' οὔπω προσθ' ἐπεπόνθεις
θεὸς ἐγένου ἐξ ἀνθρώπου· ἔριφος ἐς γάλα ἔπετες ·

Welcome, thou who hast suffered such suffering as thou hadst never before suffered.

> *From man thou hast become a god; a kid, thou hast fallen into*
> *milk!*[185]

On one leaf an initiate speaks thus of himself and awaits a favorable reception among the gods of the underworld. On the other he expects them to speak thus to him. He equates himself with the kid that fell into milk (that the kid was in pieces is not said) and so demonstrates his divine rank. The words "thou who hast suffered such suffering as thou hadst never before suffered" allude to the dismemberment and clearly state the outcome, the apotheosis: "From man thou hast become a god." The allusion to an initiation through the mystic sacrifice is unmistakable. Thus, we learn that the sacrificed kid was boiled in milk but was nevertheless to prove its divine indestructibility. The identification of a man with the animal and the god was an addition to the original sacred action, which the Orphics not only reinterpreted but also employed for purposes of private apotheosis. This could be done through words spoken by the initiate, words such as those a Christian author put into the mouth of the sun god: "in olla decoquunt . . . septem veribus corporis mei membra lacerata subfigunt" ("they boil me in a kettle, they spit the torn-off parts of my body on seven spits . . .").[186]

No Roman or Greek author spoke more clearly of boiling in milk at the mystic sacrificial ceremony than did the brief Orphic texts on the gold leaves. It was customary for the Romans to boil kid and lamb in milk or to pour milk over them after roasting.[187] (The forbidden order did not actually occur.) A neo-Attic work of art merits scrutiny in this

185   Kern, fr. 32.
186   See Firmicus Maternus, *De errore profanarum religionum* VIII 2: "aut in olla decoquunt, aut septem veribus, etc." Firmicus probably did not know the rite; he took the words from a Greek source and combined them erroneously with *aut*.
187   Caelius Apicius, *De re coquinaria* VIII 6 6–7 and 11.

connection. The reliefs on a marble pedestal in the Vatican, probably
after a model made in the second century B.C., seem to represent preparations for a more secret Dionysian sacrificial rite.[188] It was customary
in ancient art to represent preparations for other mystery actions, but
not these. One side of the pedestal shows an often repeated picture:
the aged Dionysos, heavy with wine, visiting a Dionysian artist [64A].[189]
The other side depicts a highly suggestive scene: weeping, two Erotes
are burning a butterfly, "Psyche," their victim and beloved [64B]. (In
Greek, "Psyche" means "butterfly," "soul," and "the mythical companion
of the Erotes.")[190] They do what the Dionysian women did to their victim, the kid, which in a way remains indestructible. A centaur bearing
a lyre-playing young satyr and a centauress bearing a maenad extend
the scene to the Dionysian hereafter, whither centaurs carry the
blessed.[191] On both ends of the same pedestal we see scenes which take
on their true perspective only when we have understood that they are
preparations for a Dionysian sacrifice. On one end a fawn is taken
away from its mother who is suckling it [64c]. This is done by a half-
naked woman, probably a maenad who will perform the *sparagmos*
on the young animal. The shepherd who has raised the family of deer,
surely for this purpose, looks on. On the other end of the pedestal, an
elderly man is milking a goat whose head a woman is holding [64D].

188 See B. Nogara, "Una base istoriata di marmo nuovamente esposta nel
Museo Vaticano," pp. 261–78; W. Fuchs, *Die Vorbilder der neuattischen Reliefs*, p. 157.

189 See C. Picard, "Observations sur la date et l'origine des reliefs dits de
la 'Visite chez Ikarios,'" pp. 137 ff.; C. Watzinger, "Theoxenia des Dionysos,"
pp. 76–87; H. von Rohden and H. Winnefeld, *Architektonische römische Tonreliefs der Kaiserzeit*, pl. XXX.

190 See W. Helbig, *Führer*, I, 138 f.; also Kerényi, "Die Göttin mit der
Schale," *Niobe*, pp. 220 ff.

191 See K. Meuli, "Nachwort," in Bachofen, *Gesammelte Werke*, VII,
500 f.

She is waiting for the milk, which in this series of representations can be assumed to serve a ritual purpose.

The cooking of a kid in its mother's milk is not attested for Greece, but in nearby Semitic territory. The testimony, which is indirect but all the more compelling, is the often-repeated prohibition: "Thou shalt not seethe a kid in its mother's milk."[192] The Israelites were forbidden to do something to which the neighboring Canaanites evidently attached great importance. The occasion on which they boiled a kid in milk seems to have been a rite of the wine growers, whose cultivation of the vine is described in lines that had to be repeated seven times.[193] We find these lines in a text from Ras Shamra, the region of the Cilician-Hittite dragon myth which, when transported to Delphi, moved from one *Korykion antron* to another. The language is the West Semitic language spoken in Ugarit by the Phoenicians and in Palestine by the Canaanites. We cite the lines in the literal translation of Theodor H. Gaster:

> *Over fire seven times . . . young men*
> *coo[k a k]id in milk, a . . . in curd*
> *and over a basin seven times. . . .*[194]

192 Exodus 23:19, 34:26; Deuteronomy 14:21. The explanation that this prohibition was directed against a usage of the heathen Canaanites occurs in the Jewish philosopher and commentator Maimonides' *A Guide to the Perplexed* III 48 (cited by T. Gaster, *Thespis*, 1961 edn., p. 423). The historians of religions have come around only very slowly to this correct view. See W. M. Ramsay, "Phrygians," in Hastings, *Encyclopaedia of Religion and Ethics*; S. Reinach, "Une formule orphique," in *Cultes, mythes et religions*, II, 133; M. Radin, "The Kid and Its Mother's Milk," pp. 209–18; S. H. Hooke, "Traces of the Myth and Ritual Pattern in Canaan," in *Myth and Ritual*, pp. 71 ff.

193 T. H. Gaster, *Thespis*, 1961 edn., pp. 420 f. The title of the song should be "Song of Vintage," not "Song of Vintage and Harvest." The titles are supplied by Gaster.

194 *Thespis*, 1950 edn., p. 243.

In the Greek ceremony seven pieces after having been boiled were roasted on spits. If they were boiled in the milk of the mother goat, the rite cannot have been without mystic content. It evoked the image of infantile bliss with the mother. The kid become god was reunited with her, as in the myth Dionysos was reunited with his divine mother when he went down to her in the underworld. In the version of the myth from which we know the story of the god's journey to the underworld, his mother is called "Semele"; for the Orphics she was Persephone, daughter of Rhea. The Argonauts regarded a giant vine[195] as the most worthy wood of which to fashion a cult statue of Rhea, who, as we know, put the dismembered child Dionysos together again. This occurred in Asia Minor on Mt. Dindymon, the mountain of the Great Goddess. In the Greek poetic language the vine or grape is called the mother of the wine,[196] and in the Orient we also encounter a divine "mother of the grape."

One may speak of a Dionysian religion of the West Semites, which was not introduced to that region from the Graeco-Roman world but did take over certain late Graeco-Roman art forms. Franz Cumont found such monuments on his travels in northern Syria. He was also struck by the vineyards on Dolukbaba, the sacred mountain of Jupiter Dolichenus. He suggests that the great Hittite god with the grapes[197] may have been the predecessor of the sky god of Doliche since the latter was also a wine god.[198] Cumont also speaks of Dusares, "the Arabian

---

195 Apollonius Rhodius, *Argonautica* I 1117–19.
196 Aischylos, *Persians* 614; Euripides, *Alcestis* 757.
197 F. Cumont, *Études syriennes*, p. 185.
198 Rock relief in Ivriz, a region possible for the "myth of the leather sack." See the new reproduction in E. Akurgal, *Die Kunst der Hethiter*, pl. XXIV. The god holds grapes in his right hand; in his left hand, ears of grain. Hence he

Bacchus," whom Herodotos knew as Dionysos.[199] The Sumerians had a goddess whom they called "heavenly vine."[200] As late as 1203/1204 A.D. an Arabic source speaks of a vineyard, wine, and grape cult so deeply based as to have given rise to a curative magic—originally a *piaculum*, an act of appeasement following the wine harvest.[201] To cure a disease of the throat the following words were spoken: "A Djinn woman [Umm Unkud, 'mother of the grape'] has lost her son, and all who have neglected to mourn his death are afflicted with this ailment. Death can be avoided if we gather, beat our faces, and loudly raise the lament: 'O, mother of the grape, forgive us! The grape is dead! We did not know!'" The basis of this plea for forgiveness is the tradition that in the Near East, as in Homer, the grape was entitled to a dirge at the time of the grape harvest.

The existence of a massive non-Greek religion of Dionysos between the lake of Genesareth and the Phoenician coast was attested by the founder of Christianity, who journeyed through that region as far as Tyre. He took many of his metaphors from the life of the wine growers, as did the poets and prophets of the Old Testament before him.[202] Of himself he said: "I am the true vine."[203] When Jeremiah spoke of the originally noble but later bastard vine of Israel—the closest Old Testa-

---

is called a "peasant-god" (J. Garstang, *The Hittite Empire*, p. 165) or a "vegetation god" (E. Akurgal, *Späthethitische Bildkunst*, p. 106). But a "god vine" occurs in hieroglyphic Hittite as a "ruler," *taparas* (information provided by L. R. Palmer). This is probably the same god.

199   Cumont, *Études syriennes*, p. 260; Herodotos III 8 1.

200   A. Moortgat, *Tammuz*, p. 30.

201   See W. R. Smith, *Lectures on the Religion of the Semites*, p. 417, citing the Arab historian Ibn al-Athir.

202   Mark 7:24; Psalm 80:9; Jeremiah 2:21.

203   John 15:1: ἐγώ εἰμι ἡ ἄμπελος ἡ ἀληθινή.

ment parallel to these words of Jesus, and perhaps their model—[204] he remained within the sphere of metaphor; not so Jesus, who took the direction of a mystic identity. In the parable containing these words, the wine grower stands for the father and the vines for the disciples. In the gospel of St. John, this parable replaces and at the same time explains Jesus' words about the wine at the Last Supper: "This is my blood." When the fourth Evangelist was writing, the Last Supper had already become the great mystery action of the Christians. The Evangelist thought the story of its founding and first occurrence too sacred to be narrated in a book intended for the public. *In place of it* he wrote that Jesus equated himself with the vine. The consequence of this equation was that Jesus spoke of the wine as his blood; and its extension was that he spoke of the bread as his body. By emphasizing that he is the *true* vine, he dissociates himself from the vineyard, its vines and events, with which he had identified himself too closely. It was necessary to dissociate himself from the "false" vine, the vine that led people astray, because it concealed within itself a false god and a false religion.

The Mediterranean wine culture was the common concrete background of two very divergent realities, the founding of Christianity on the one hand and everything that can be subsumed under the comprehensive term "Dionysian religion" on the other. Thus far an essential component of the Greek Dionysian religion, the great sacrificial rite of the women and the Orphics, has been only partially laid bare. One particular of this cult has not yet been decoded, and it is that particular which contrasts most drastically with Christianity. When

---

204 See the Septuagint translation: ἐγὼ δὲ ἐφύτευσά σε ἄμπελον καρποφόρον πᾶσαν ἀληθινήν ("God to the people of Israel: 'Yet I planted thee a chosen vineyard'").

the sacrificial animal was dismembered, something was set aside and kept. Concerning this piece the greatest secrecy was observed. In the Greek context it is not easy to understand why. The secrecy proves the importance of the thing in question and also proves that it was charged with an irrational content which was of special concern to the participants. Magic actions are rational in their structure. They are rendered irrational by the mistaken idea and act of will by which the agent tries to attain something that is impossible. In the Dionysian sacrificial rite the irrational factor was not confined to the intention of the women, who were pursuing not an idea of their own but a traditional custom; it was more far-reaching.

In dismembering the sacrifice, the sacrificers—the Titans according to Onomakritos' version of the scene—set the heart aside. In the last, philosophical formulation of the Orphic books we read:

μούνην γὰρ κραδίην νοερὴν ἱ ὑπον ·

for they left only the knowing heart.[205]

The heart is indeed a tough, none too edible morsel. It seems perfectly reasonable to have set it aside. This heart, however, was an essential feature of the literary mythology of Dionysos that was constructed with the help of Orphism. Pallas Athena picked it up and brought it to Father Zeus,[206] who from it prepared a potion that he gave Semele to drink. It is thus that Dionysos was born a second time. In the Euhemeristic version that makes Zeus a Cretan king, his daughter

---

205   Kern, *Orphicorum fragmenta*, fr. 210.

206   Most clearly stated by Proklos, *Hymn to Minerva* 13: πόρες δὲ ἑ πατρὶ φέρουσα, cited by Kern in connection with fr. 210. On the second birth, see Hyginus, *Fabulae* 167.

Athena hid her brother's heart in a basket, and this basket—a true *cista mystica*—was carried about with Dionysian utensils.[207]

What was carried about—whether in a *cista mystica* or in a *liknon* —could not, however, be kept entirely secret. It was not a heart but a phallus. This is evident from the Orphic books themselves. In a text about which we shall have more to say later, the object that the goddess Hipta took from Zeus and carried on her head in a *liknon* was called the "Kradiaios Dionysos."[208] "Kradiaios" can have two meanings, and this is the key to the secret. It can be derived either from *kradia* ("heart") or from *krade* ("fig tree"); in the latter case, it means an object made from a fig branch or fig wood. According to one myth, Dionysos himself fashioned a phallus from fig wood for use in a mystic rite connected with his return from the underworld. The soft wood was suitable for the Dionysian utensil, which was referred to by the euphemism "heart." According to the sources the object that was pre-served by Pallas Athena was the sacrificed he-goat's male organ, which was neither boiled nor roasted and burned, but set aside and hidden. The action was symbolic, and it is very likely that in place of the dried member, or along with it, a phallus of fig wood was used the following year in the ceremony serving to "awaken" Liknites, the god lying in the *liknon*, the basket serving as a winnow.

In the sacrificial rite, the animal member played the mystic role in which it might not be mentioned. But it would not have been charged with irrational content if it had not also signified the virility that the wooden utensils carried about in the *phallophoriai* repre-sented. The relation of the women to this *pars pro toto* of indestructible

207 Firmicus Maternus, *De errore profanarum religionum* VI, cited by Kern, *Orphicorum fragmenta*, in connection with fr. 214.

208 Proklos, *In Platonis Timaeum* 30 B, in Kern, *Orphicorum fragmenta*, fr. 199.

life, to this concrete part of the concrete whole of *zoë*, was unutterable, an *arrheton*. They took upon themselves both the part and the whole by seemingly making themselves guilty of devouring and extinguishing the male sex of their species. They killed the indestructible, the god, but only seemingly, for they preserved and reawakened him periodically, in every second year. This was the content of their great mysteries.

The Delphic tradition to the effect that Apollo buried the parts or even the heart of his dismembered brother in or near the *tripous*[209] probably arose under the influence of Orphism but not within it. According to the Orphics, the parts of the body were burned and scattered, whereas the heart went to Zeus. Originally there was merely a parallel between the rites of the women in the *Korykion antron* and those of the Hosioi in the temple, for the parts of the sacrificial animal's body were not taken into the sanctuary. The ancient philosophical explainers of myth were, however, struck by the fact that the number seven, which plays so important a role in the mystic sacrificial rite, is the sacred number of Apollo.[210] This must indeed be regarded as a sign of a tie with the Orient. We have encountered the number seven in the ceremony of Ugarit, a region from which Delphi derived still other elements that can be traced back to the Hittite and Semitic Near East via Minoan Crete. Not the least of these other Oriental elements is the *Korykion antron*.[211] The Dionysian sacrificial rite with its complex structure and strict inner logic was one of the basic facts of Greek religious history. This had far-reaching developments, including Orphism in the form given it by Onomakritos.

209   For the burial on the *tripous*, see above, note 135. See also the scholium on Lykophron, *Alexandra* 208; Servius' commentary on *Aeneid* VI 347.
210   Proklos, *In Platonis Timaeum* 35 B, in Kern, fr. 210.
211   Nilsson, *Geschichte*, I (1941 edn.), 329.

The Enthronement

ORPHISM has been termed "a religious-philosophical-literary move-ment that cannot be defined with precision,"[212] but within its own setting, the Dionysian religion, it can be summed up and characterized. It was a masculine, speculative tendency within a religion having women's cults as its core. Onomakritos embodied this tendency. In the light of its initiations, through which individuals made atonement and strove for apotheosis, Orphism may be characterized as a kind of private re-ligious exercise. The mythical prototype expressive of this tendency was the figure of Orpheus, who was not only a solitary strolling singer but also an initiator of men and youths.[213] Another feature of Orphism was its predilection for archaic elements of myth and cult, which it sought to preserve in writing. The Orphics wrote sacred books, linked myths together, and created a mythology of Dionysos.

They did not divulge the women's cult secrets. Rather, they covered them with a cloak that was transparent enough to those in the know, and they constructed their mythical history of the world in such a way that everything on which the Dionysian religion was based had already happened before either the women's cults or the Orphics' cults made their appearance. In so doing they observed the spirit of the living myth, whose function was precisely this,[214] and largely followed the history and Minoan prehistory of the Dionysian religion. From the

212   W. Fauth in his compendious article of 1967 on "Zagreus," col. 2222.
213   See Kerényi, "Die orphische Kosmogonie und der Ursprung der Orphik," *Werke*, I, 323–39.
214   See my remarks in Jung and Kerényi, *Essays on a Science of Mythol-ogy*, pp. 5–9.

Cretan tradition they took the doubly archaic myth of the god's birth whereby his father in the form of a snake begot him incestuously upon his own daughter. Also of Cretan origin was the act in Onomakritos' dramatic composition that preceded the slaying and dismembering of the scarcely born Divine Child. In this act, according to the Orphic conception, Dionysos appeared whole for the last time as the ruler of our age of the world.

At the heart of this act is a scene corresponding to a rite of initiation known to us in other contexts: the *thronosis* or *thronismos*, the enthronement. In late antiquity Crete was still said to be *threskeuousa thronosin*, practicing the rite of enthronement as a cult.[215] Homer *characterizes* Minos, in his function of judge of the dead, as *seated* and holding his scepter in his hand while the others most uncharacteristically sit or stand.[216] The throne itself is not of particular importance to the Greek poet, but in the centuries that had passed since the Minoan culture no one had forgotten the motif of the king sitting on his throne. The prominent part in the throne room where the ceremonial sitting occurred is known to us from the palaces of Knossos and Pylos.[217] The worship of gods in the cult of *thronosis* meant more than the offering of a chair or throne, which often occurred in Greek temples as a sign of hospitality to the god.[218] The *thronosis* was a special festive act in which the god or his representative was placed on a chair standing by itself. If one looks closely at the painting on a calyx krater of the Classical period [98], one sees that precisely this is being done with a

215   *Oracula Sibyllina* VIII 49; T. Klauser, *Die Cathedra im Totenkult der heidnischen und christlichen Antike*, p. 44.

216   Odyssey XI 568–71.

217   For Knossos, see Evans, *The Palace of Minos*, IV, 915–20; for Pylos, see Blegen and Rawson, *The Palace of Nestor in Western Messenia*, I, 87–88.

218   See A. Furtwängler, *Meisterwerke der griechischen Plastik*, pp. 188 ff.

frail human figure in the role of Dionysos. The *thronosis* is explicitly said to be the first act of what happened to the *myoumenoi*, the participants in an initiation.[219] The most likely meaning of the word *mu-jo-me-no* on a tablet at Pylos was found to be "on the occasion of the initiation of the king."[220]

How the ceremony was to be performed is related in a didactic poem, *Thronismoi metroioi kai Bakchika*, attributed to Orpheus but believed to have been written by a certain Nikias of Elea.[221] Such didactic poems made it possible to perform initiations in private cults or in small religious communities like the Orphic societies. The title indicates the Dionysian character of the rites, and also shows that the Mother Goddess Rhea or Kybele presided over them, as she may already have done over the enthronement of the Minoan kings. Her name covers not only the period extending from the Minoan era to late antiquity but also the whole territory from Crete via Asia Minor to northern Greece and Samothrace. Her sons and servants who danced around the enthroned one and carried out the initiation were called "Kouretes" in Crete, but more often "Korybantes." In Samothrace they probably danced on an archaic round platform and later in the Arsinoeion erected over it.[222] Sokrates describes the rite in Plato's *Euthydemus*, in which he likens the courting of a young man by two Sophists to this rite as it was performed in the Classical period. It seems unlikely that the choreography of this rite—an ecstatic dance around the enthroned one—had changed since earlier times. "They are doing the same as the Korybantes do in their initiations, when the one to be initiated is being

219 Hesychios s.v. Θρόνωσις: καταρχὴ περὶ τοὺς μυουμένους.
220 Ventris and Chadwick, *Documents in Mycenaean Greek*, p. 221.
221 See Kern, *Orphicorum fragmenta*, p. 64.
222 See K. Lehmann, *Samothrace*, pp. 49–52; with my interpretation, "Unwillkürliche Kunstreisen," in *Werke*, II, 148.

enthroned. There is dancing and play there also, as you know if you have been initiated; and now these are only dancing round you in play, meaning to initiate you afterward."[223]

According to the Orphic history of the world, Dionysos was no sooner born to Persephone daughter of Rhea than he was enthroned king of the world—ruler of our era—in the birth cave itself. On an ivory pyxis in Bologna, the birth and enthronement of Dionysos are shown as two successive scenes in a series of four. This pyxis was fashioned not before the fifth century A.D.,[224] but it sums up most impressively the Orphic myth, which was then still known and available in written form. A nurse takes the child from his mother, who has given birth in bed and—unlike the dying Semele depicted elsewhere [65A/ 65B][225]—is sitting upright [66A/ 66B]. A second nurse is standing by and a third holds up a mirror to the child who is already seated on the throne. Behind him the wall of the cave is clearly discernible. The nude boy raises both hands, as though saying delightedly, "Here I am!" Beside him two armed Kouretes are seen. One is performing a knife dance; the other, drawing his knife, is about to take part. The child will be stabbed while looking at himself in the mirror. Nonnos provides the text to the pictures.[226] The mirror, which catches the soul along with the image, gives promise that the murdered god will not pass away entirely.[227]

The other scenes in the series on the Bologna pyxis show first the boy riding away on a he-goat [66c], then the youth driving a team of

223 *Euthydemus* 277 D (in *Plato: Collected Dialogues*, p. 391).

224 See H. Graeven, *Antike Schnitzereien*, p. 5.

225 For the dying Semele represented on the silver vessel, see also A. Maiuri, *La Casa del Menandro*, pl. XXXVIII, and fig. 130.

226 Nonnos VI 172–73.

227 See Kerényi, "Der spiegelnde Spiegel," pp. 285–91.

panthers to his marriage with Ariadne [66D]. In both representations he has a complete Dionysian retinue. Neither Seilenos, nor Pan, nor the maenads, nor a shepherd with a shepherd's crook is lacking [66E]. The murder is supposed to have taken place *before* these scenes. The murderers were armed youths, the Kouretes, although in the Cretan myth of Zeus they played a very different role. On Crete the child Zeus was also threatened with destruction, but—according to the generally accepted myth[228]—Rhea bade the Kouretes make a great deal of noise with their war dance in order that Father Kronos who wished to devour his son would not hear the child's cry at birth. A Cretan hymn—incised in the third century A.D. but composed at least five centuries earlier—invokes the Divine Child, the "greatest *Kouros*," and bids him "jump."[229] The invocation signifies that the Kouretes were called *kouroi* for short. This is in keeping with a relationship already known to us from the mythology of Rhea: the dancers are just as much her sons as the smallest who is also the greatest.[230] In the Cretan hymn the sacred cave of Dikte is named as the place of birth. If the dancers had not previously danced around the child Dionysos in order, seemingly, to kill him, it would be impossible to understand how they could cease to be the child's saviors, as they were elsewhere in Greek mythology, and become his murderers. The development is from less humane to more humane gods, not the reverse. Ceasing to be murderers, they become saviors, while the Minoan caves of Dionysos became Greek caves of Zeus. In late antiquity it was still known that the Idaean Cave contained a *throne* for Zeus, which was prepared each year for him to sit upon.[231]

228 Kerényi, *The Gods of the Greeks*, p. 94 (Pelican edn., pp. 81 f.).
229 See J. E. Harrison, *Themis*, p. 8.
230 Kerényi, *The Gods of the Greeks*, p. 87 (Pelican edn., p. 76).
231 Porphyry, *Vita Pythagorae* XVII.

Stories about a mythical murder that did not however end with the total destruction of the slain child—a murder that was hinted at (how we can only conjecture) in the rite of initiation[232]—have been preserved from the sphere of the Samothracian mysteries. The story told by Clement of Alexandria of the three Korybantes of Thessalonike, the two elder of whom killed the youngest, is an example.[233] The murderers wrapped the severed head in a purple garment, put a wreath on it, and bore it on a bronze shield to the foot of Mt. Olympos—perhaps because this was the birthplace of Orpheus, who, with the exception of his head which went on singing, was torn to pieces by women like a second Dionysos.[234] According to our Christian source, the same two brothers carried the pagan secrets unveiled, the phallus and with it the Dionysian religion, in a basket to the Etruscans. These two stories —the one speaking openly of a phallus, the other employing the cover word "head"—are variations on the same theme.[235] The murder of the Divine Child was his reduction to an organ from which—or as which— he could be reawakened. The murder was prerequisite to the reawakening.

"He did not long occupy the throne of Zeus," writes Nonnos of Persephone's just-born child, whom he calls "Zagreus." "Hera in her anger moved the Titans, their faces whitened with plaster, to kill him with infernal knives while he was looking at his reflection in the mirror."[236] Nonnos holds to the tradition that the murderers were two in

232   By blows with straps; see below, ch. VI, at note 304.
233   Clement of Alexandria, *Protrepticus* II 19 1.
234   Kerényi, *The Heroes of the Greeks*, p. 286.
235   Along with κεφαλή ("head"), there is also the word κέφαλος (a "large-headed sea-fish"), evidently an ambiguous word in Greek too. The Italian cognate *cefalo* is also used for "phallus"—as, for example, in a pun by Cardinal Azzolino to Queen Christina of Sweden, cited by S. Stolpe, *Från stoicism till mystik*, p. 212.
236   Nonnos VI 165–73.

number.[237] The meaning of the faces daubed with plaster is made evident by the Orphic Hymn to the Titans which invokes them as ancestral spirits and ghosts, and by a line in which the poet Euphorion speaks of the "deathlike white face" of a mythological or ritual person.[238] In archaic times, we are told, the Phokians painted their faces with plaster and fell on their enemies by night—under a full moon, according to certain sources.[239] Their enemies took them for an army of the dead and were defeated in their first fright. The similarity of this warlike ruse to the procedure of the Titans is evident.[240] It seems likely that the Phokians derived the idea of their ruse from an archaic initiation ritual, in which the initiators appeared as ancestral spirits to the boy initiand and seemingly killed him. References to the use of plaster in initiations and a pun on *titanos* (lime) and *titan* (Titan) have come down to us.[241]

There are numerous ethnological parallels to the role of the Titans as initiators.[242] Onomakritos' innovation, the introduction of the Titans into the Dionysian religion as substitutes for the Dionysian women, was not drawn out of the air. The idea had a basis in the initiations of boys into archaic men's societies, which may be assumed to have existed in Greece as elsewhere.[243] Moreover, there was a particular ecstatic

237 Ibid., XLVIII 28.

238 For the Hymn to the Titans, see Quandt, *Orphei hymni* XXXVI, and above, note 167. See also Euphorion, in Powell, *Collectanea Alexandrina*, fr. 88: Πάντα δὲ οἱ νεκυηδὸν ἐλευκαίνοντο πρόσωπα.

239 Herodotos VIII 27; Polyainos, *Strategemata* VI 18; Pausanias X 1 11; L. Weniger, "Feralis exercitus," pp. 223–30.

240 See K. O. Müller, *Prolegomena zu einer wissenschaftlichen Mythologie*, pp. 390 ff.

241 C. A. Lobeck, *Aglaophamus*, p. 654; L. Weniger, "Feralis exercitus," pp. 242 f.; A. Dieterich, "De hymnis orphicis," pp. 120 ff.

242 Harrison, *Themis*, pp. 17 ff.

243 See Kerényi, "Man and Mask," pp. 162 ff.; "Il dio cacciatore," pp. 7 f.

type of boys' rite which was preserved as the first act of the mysteries of the Great Mother and her sons—the Kouretes, Korybantes, or, as they and their father were called on Samothrace and in the vicinity of Thebes, "Kabeiroi." This rite may well have harked back to the Minoan and Mycenaean epochs and originated in the enthronement of future kings and rulers.

The master of the Bologna pyxis, who probably drew on the work of earlier masters, recorded only the essentials of the mystic career in which Dionysos preceded the initiates into his mysteries. He omits not only the use of the knife in carrying out the initiation, which as actually performed consisted in the sacrifice of a substitute animal, but also a particular of the rites: the boy's games the purpose of which was to divert him from the murderous intentions of his enemies by lulling him into the blissful existence of a true Divine Child. His enemies were his elder brothers, sons like himself of the Great Mother. Here we discern the influence of a wholly anthropomorphic myth. The toys, cited from a didactic Orphic poem on initiation, perhaps the *Teletai* of Onomakritos, are: tops, a bull-roarer, jointed dolls, golden apples, and others.[244] These are not mystic symbols but real toys worthy of a Divine Child. Women executed the Korybantic dance around a sick child in order to lull it to sleep and make it well again.[245]

The mirror seems to have been the last addition to the accessories. The enthroned boy was supposed to fall blissfully asleep over his toys. This prepared him for the rite that was originally confined to human beings. The sacrifice of an animal can have been substituted only at a relatively late date. In early times, where human children were concerned, it seems likely that the rite consisted in a mutilation

244   See Kern, *Orphicorum fragmenta*, fr. 34.
245   Plato, *Laws* VII 790 DE.

of the genitals, such as circumcision, which, though not customary among the Greeks, was practiced by the Egyptians, Semites, and many other primitive peoples.[246] It is attested by Herodotos among the Colchians, a people of Asia Minor.[247] The human sacrifice could, however, be totally excluded when the representative animal made its appearance. It was perhaps a calf like the one on Tenedos that was sacrificed in hunting boots. In Greek territory the usual substitute animal was a he-goat. In a later day, when the strict forms of ancient art were relaxing, a hybrid figure appears. The Bologna pyxis still shows three Dionysian women as the child's nurses—persons already eliminated in the Orphic version—but the horns of the enthroned boy are visible [66A]: he is a hybrid like Zagreus in Nonnos, a "horned infant."[248]

In the following scene on the pyxis Dionysos is shown as a little naked boy riding off on a he-goat [66C]. This means that the knife had no power to harm them: they were preserved—the goat assuredly in the form of a vine to which he gave his blood. The name "Oinos" was given to Dionysos by the Orphics, who also taught that the wine was his last gift to man.[249] Here we have an intimation that, after having been enthroned as Zeus's successor and seemingly murdered, the god was given the vineyards for his dwelling place, his Olympos. True, he ascended to heaven with Ariadne, but it was not out of keeping with the spirit of the Orphic history that the "physiologists" attributed his third birth to the vine.[250] This world history culminated in the Diony-

246 See A. E. Jensen, "Beschneidung und Reifezeremonie bei Naturvölkern."

247 Herodotos II 104.

248 See Nonnos VI 165. For the sacrifice of a calf in hunting boots on Tenedos, see above, ch. V, at notes 4 ff.

249 Kern, *Orphicorum fragmenta*, fr. 216.

250 Diodorus Siculus III 62 6.

sian life, which was full of feasts and *zoë*. Though it lacked the sever-
ity of the great archaic rites, the enthronement and the mystic sacrifice, the Dionysian life preserved an unbroken continuity with them.
Orphism helped by raising the continuity to greater awareness and
by preserving the meaning of the various elements. Orphism was never
the sole bearer of the Dionysian religion, but only its interpreter for
many.

A whole series of terra-cotta friezes adorning Roman buildings of
the late Republican or early Imperial period reflect this situation exactly. In these often exceedingly fine works, we encounter the Divine
Child growing out of the roots of the vine, which in Greek is also called
oine [67].[251] Vines and grapes grow from the same roots; two crude
satyrs, treaders of grapes at the wine harvest, welcome the little god
with Dionysian instruments. He will be the god Oinos if he is not already. The treaders take over the role of the former male and female
renders, not that of the Titans who dismembered and devoured the
child. The wiry satyrs who appear as dancers and companions of
lovely maenads are neither titanic beings nor representatives of the
Titans [68].[252] The mirror in the hands of the two satyrs relates no
doubt to the murderous deed of the Kouretes, but far more to the
happy outcome. For the god is present in the state of the celebrants.
The rigid posture of the dancing men and women—their upturned
faces [69]—reveals an erotic agitation enhanced by flute playing. The
panther [70] and the half-naked girl flute player bear witness that the

251   See Rohden and Winnefeld, *Architektonische römische Tonreliefs der
Kaiserzeit*, pl. XXIV 2; and E. Simon, "Zagreus," p. 1424 (her mention of the
Titans is a mistake).

252   See Rohden and Winnefeld, pl. XVI; and Simon, pp. 1419 ff.

supreme limit will soon be attained. A satyr and a maenad dance wildly and swing the *liknon* with the child [71],[253] who is awake. They swing the *liknon* not in order to tear the child to pieces but in order to celebrate the awakened Liknites.

253 Rohden and Winnefeld, pl. XCIX; misinterpreted by Simon, p. 1426.

VI. THE DIONYSOS OF THE ATHENIANS
AND OF HIS WORSHIPERS
IN THE GREEK MYSTERIES

The Thigh Birth and the Idol with the Mask

THE QUESTION as to the form in which *zoë* was concealed in the *liknon* and reawakened has now ceased to be anything more than rhetorical. It remains, however, to elucidate the reasons for a secrecy that was not confined to one object and for the perpetuation of the ambiguity that presented Liknites as an infant and the women who awakened him as his nurses. In the Greek world the phallus as such gave no grounds for secrecy. A separate scene is devoted to the uncovering of the phallus in the series of terra-cotta reliefs whose manufacture was Roman but whose subject matter was Greek [72]. The phallus stands upright in the *liknon* and a kneeling woman uncovers it; a virginal, winged goddess is repelled but an ithyphallic man is drawn to it.[1] Thus, it was permissible to represent the phallus removed from the context of a cult scene.[2]

Aretaios of Cappadocia, a physician of the first century A.D., tells us that reference to the ithyphallic state could, however, have a very

---

1 See Rohden and Winnefeld on pl. CXXIII. Concerning a variant, they remark (p. 53): "What arouses the horror of the winged figure" is "not only the phallus in the basket and on the satyr, but also the unmistakable order of the garments on the kneeling girl's belly." See also *A Description of the Collection of Ancient Terracottas in the British Museum*, pl. XVI 27 (no longer extant: "perhaps removed because of its indecency").

2 Representation of the phallus was permissible also in a preparatory context; see below, in ch. VI, the text following note 46.

special extramedical significance. He speaks of the agitation of the satyrs, the "sacred" companions of Dionysos in many representations, and says expressly that this is a *"symbolon* of the *theion pregma."*[3] Writing in the same Ionic dialect as the physician, Herodotos says that in connection with a *pregma* such as mourning and the tomb he would not wish to mention a certain god by name.[4] Thus, we can be sure that Aretaios' "divine *pregma"* was not a thing but a fact, a reality that stood in the same relation to Dionysos as mourning and the tomb to Osiris. The name of Osiris would have divulged the mystery. The reason for secrecy in connection with the *theion pregma* is to be sought not only in the thing that lay hidden in the *liknon* and was visible on the satyrs, but also in a mystery, as is expressly stated: "The phallus was uprighted for Dionysos in accordance with a mystery."[5] The phallus itself was not the *mysterion* and divine *pregma* but had to do with it. Indeed, though not intended as such, the phallus could be interpreted as its *symbolon—*suggestion and abbreviation.[6]

The Orphic source that speaks of the Kradiaios Dionysos, the "fig-wood Dionysos," tells how he was given to the goddess Hipta, who carried him on her head in a *liknon* around which she allowed a snake to entwine itself.[7] This particular and the name of the goddess—who, we learn in the same source, "assisted the child-bearing Zeus" at the

3 Aretaios, "De acutis morbis," in *Corpus medicorum graecorum*, Hudé, ed., II, 12: οἱ σάτυροι τοῦ Διονύσου ἱεροὶ ἐν τῇσι γραφῇσι καὶ τοῖσι ἀγάλμασι ὄρθια ἴσχουσι τὰ αἰδοῖα, ξύμβολον τοῦ θείου πρήγματος ("The satyrs belonging to Dionysos are represented as ithyphallic in the paintings and sculptures, a symbol of the divine thing [*pregma*]").
4 Herodotos II 132 170.
5 Scholium on Aristophanes, *Acharnians* 243: ἵστατο ὁ φάλλος τῶι Διονύσωι κατά τι μυστήριον.
6 See Kerényi, "Symbolismus in der antiken Religion," *Werke*, II, 213–20.
7 Kern, *Orphicorum fragmenta*, fr. 199.

birth of Dionysos—are of Near Eastern origin, as presumably was the author of the Orphic book *On Hipta*.[8] According to the Orphic Hymn Book, Hipta's home was in the Tmolos mountains of Lydia and on Mt. Ida in Phrygia.[9] Originally she was the Great Mother, who was also called Rhea. The Hymn Book also has a Phrygian name for the god she assisted: "Sabazios," who could be either Zeus or Dionysos in the Greek interpretation.[10] When in the fifth century B.C. his cult was accepted by the city of Athens—though not by the state—it was as though the Dionysos cult had been reintroduced in an archaic form. We are told expressly that the content of the religion of Sabazios was the same as that of the mysteries of Dionysos.[11] In this hymn addressed to him, Sabazios is invoked as the son of Kronos; hence he is equated with Zeus. It was he, according to the hymn, who sewed Dionysos, the *Eiraphiotes*, into his thigh, in order that when "he who had been sewed in" was "ripe" he might be brought to the goddess Hipta on Tmolos. Here it is not said that Hipta carried him on her head, but only that she received him after his birth. And it was known that he was reared by Rhea.[12]

For one region, at least, it is easy to answer the question as to whether this child was really borne by his father or whether the father merely mutilated and emasculated himself. In Asia Minor the Great Mother's priests and her lover Attis sacrificed their manhood to her,[13]

8   See Kern, "Die Herkunft des orphischen Hymnenbuchs," pp. 90 ff.

9   Quandt, *Orphei Hymni* XLVIII 4, XLIX 5.

10   *Orphei Hymni* XLVIII 1. On Zeus, chiefly in Phrygia, see T. Eisele, "Sabazios," col. 236 (even in a city that was called "Dionysopolis"). On Dionysos, see J. Schaefer, "Sabazios," col. 1542.

11   Strabo X 3 15: παράδους τά τοῦ Διονύσου καὶ αὐτός.

12   Scholium on Iliad VI 131.

13   See H. Hepding, "Attis, seine Mythen und sein Kult," pp. 121, 160 ff.

and from her Phrygian mysteries the story has come down to us that after committing incest with her, his mother, Zeus seemingly emasculated himself. In reality he threw a ram's testicles into the goddess' womb.[14] The inner logic of this myth and of a corresponding rite performed in Asia Minor is clear. Nothing is said of a dismemberment of the god or of a substituted sacrificial animal. Whether it was a bull, a ram, or some other male animal, its severed manhood had to return to the Great Mother in order that the endless cycle of births might continue. In the mother religion of Asia Minor this concept of womanhood was dominant. In Greece the women preserved and cared for manhood as the *zoë* entrusted to them. Just as Hipta herself became the "nurse of Bakchos" among the Orphics,[15] so in Greece, and perhaps even in Crete, Dionysian colleges of women replaced the Mother Goddess and represented themselves *only* as the god's nurses.

The logic of the Greek version of the myth—and this version had its impact on the Phrygian Sabazios—is marred only by the substitution of the thigh birth for the god's self-emasculation, a terrible but not meaningless act. The invention of a birth from the thigh of Zeus had its function in Greece: to cover over the god's lavish gift at the expense of his own body. The myth cruelly emphasized the eternally necessary self-sacrifice of male vitality to the feminine sex, and hence to the human race as a whole. One account of the concrete mission of the Dionysian religion—in its more masculine form, the mysteries of the Kabeiroi—tells us that the murderers of the god brought his male organ in a basket from northern Greece to Italy. "For this reason," Clement of Alexandria, our Christian source, concludes, "certain per-

14 Clement of Alexandria, *Protrepticus* II 15 2; Arnobius, *Adversus nationes* V 21.
15 Quandt, *Orphei Hymni* XLIX 1.

sons, not inappropriately, equate Dionysos with Attis, because he too was separated from his reproductive organ."[16]

Eunuchism was as characteristic of Dionysos as of Attis. It was one of the secret components of the Dionysian religion, but to the connoisseurs of the Dionysos cult cited by Clement it was an open secret. This probably accounts for a strange cult usage encountered in Asia Minor. On Cyprus the person who imitated a woman in labor, so recalling the labor pains of Ariadne dying in childbirth, was not a Zeus-like man but a youth.[17] In all likelihood his pains were only symbolic, but they were the symbolic pains of an Attis, veiled—just as the miscarriage and death of Ariadne veiled the birth of Dionysos by the mistress of the underworld.

His birth from his father's thigh linked Dionysos with the epithet "Eiraphiotes," and not Dionysos himself but Father Zeus was made into the sufferer. "Eiraphiotes" means "he who has been sewed in."[18] The god of *zoë* had been sewed into a skin at a time when skins contained not wine but fermenting honey water, at the time of the myth of the leather sack. The epithet "Eiraphiota" was preserved in poetry[19] and cult. It was revived at a relatively late date by way of Hellenizing an archaic myth of non-Greek style. In the Orphic Hymn Book Dionysos is "Trigonos," "thrice born," but only "Dimetor," "he with two mothers."[20] The Hymn Book also includes a hymn to Semele, the Theban mother of Dionysos, but the main book of Orphic literature says noth-

---

16   *Protrepticus* II 19 4: δι' ἣν αἰτίαν οὐκ ἀπεικότως τὸν Διόνυσόν τινες Ἄττιν προσαγορεύεσθαι θέλουσιν, αἰδοίων ἐστερημένον.

17   Plutarch, *Theseus* XX 4, after the historian Paion of Amathus.

18   Εἰραφιώτης comes from ἐνραφιώτης by way of ἐρραφιώτης.

19   See *Homeric Hymns* I 2, 17, 20.

20   Quandt, *Orphei Hymni* XXX 2; L 1; LII 9.

ing of her or of the thigh birth. The Orphics were not responsible for the palliating invention of the thigh birth.

Its ready acceptance in Athens suggests that the thigh birth was an Athenian invention modeled on the famous "head birth," the springing of Pallas Athena from the head of Zeus. It presumably stems from the period when the Attic religion of Dionysos fused with the Theban myth and cult. This fusion, going hand in hand with a radical simplification, resulted in the Athenian mythology of Dionysos, which also took into account the content of the Mysteries of Eleusis—to wit, the proclamation of the birth of a Divine Child in the underworld and the epiphany of his mother Persephone seven months after the subterranean marriage.[21] The Athenians did away with the two-year period. They found room for their Dionysian festivals and for their mysteries, the Lesser Mysteries of Agrai and the Great Mysteries of Eleusis, in a single year, which was at the same time the year of the vineyards. The calendar they created—assuredly before Onomakritos and independently of the Orphics—was a discreet compromise, respecting both the phases of wine-making and the *parousia* of *zoë* in women and men. Since the lunar periods retained their validity, the result could only be an approximation, a product of the human imagination rather than mathematical precision.

21 In my book *Eleusis* I assumed no connections which were kept secret but had existed from time immemorial between the Eleusinian religion and the Dionysian religion; see *Eleusis*, p. 241, the index s.v. Dionysos. The Eleusinian religion believed that Hades-Plouton-Dionysos *was* in command of his virility during the period of the Lesser Mysteries, following the Anthesteria. Orphic influence can be inferred from an Eleusinian inscription Διονύσωι παραπαίζοντι of the third century; see K. Kourouniotes, Ἐλευσινιακά, pp. 171 ff. A thymiaterion was dedicated to the playing Divine Child with this inscription: "To Dionysos, he who plays alongside." On the subterranean birth, see further the section on "Ariadne," in ch. III, above.

The annual birthday of Dionysos depended not only on the position of the sun at the solstice, but also on the state of the wine, whose clearing coincided with the first intense winter cold.[22] At this time, at the festival of the Lenaia, the Dadouchos, the second priest of Eleusis, summoned the Athenians to call the god.[23] By then he had long been "sewed in," that is, the wine had been poured into earthenware vessels and was almost ready. The people cried out: "Son of Semele, Iakchos, bestower of wealth!" This cry presupposes a unification. The birth celebrated in the autumn at the Great Mysteries—the birth of the subterranean Persephone's child—was a provisional birth. In the winter he was born definitively as the son of Semele and Zeus. Dionysos' two mothers, Semele and Persephone, were originally two names for the same goddess. Now they were equated by the Athenians. Likewise equated were the young Cretan Dionysos, god of the light that ripens, who participated as Iakchos in the Eleusinian festival, and the mature son of Zeus to whom Zeus himself gave birth. The representations of the thigh birth reflect this state of the mythology of Dionysos in Athens.

The oldest in the series of thigh birth representations shows the son already standing on Zeus's lap [73]. Turned outward with two torches, he announces his completion to Hera, at the risk of sending her into a rage. According to the inscription he is ΔΙΟΣ ΦΩΣ, "the light of Zeus." This is a dignified representation from the late sixth century B.C., by the artist now known as the Diosphos painter. Recording not the realistic process of birth but the outcome, this representation corresponds to the cover myth in which Zeus played the role of a childbearing god rather than that of one who emasculated himself. Yet, de-

22 See Kerényi, "Parva realia," p. 9.
23 Scholium on Aristophanes, *Frogs* 479; L. Deubner, *Attische Feste*, p. 125.

spite the seriousness with which this version of the myth was represented, it struck later generations as unintentionally comic. On a Tarentine vase of the late fifth or early fourth century the realistic scene of the thigh birth gives the impression of a common happening in the life of the gods, an event without deeper meaning [74].[24] When in the third century B.C. a pupil of Apelles painted Zeus in labor and wearing headbands (*mitratus*)—which in the Dionysos cult, as the ornament of Dionysos Mitrephoros, assuredly had a seriously justified significance—his work was regarded as an impertinence.[25] It is very different when in a vase painting by the Altamura painter, circa 465 B.C., a Zeus-like Dionysos, identified by *thyrsos* and panther skin, is shown sitting (like the Zeus of the Diosphos painter), confronting his youthful alter ego [75].[26] The alter ego appears as a nude boy with a kantharos, a large plant, and an ivy wreath, who is standing on the god's knees and is admired by a Dionysian woman or nurse. This rigid standing on the lap or knees, in contrast to more flexible postures,[27] indicates the closest relationship—between Zeus and Iakchos in the work of the Diosphos painter, and between Dionysos and his alter ego or mystic son in that of the Altamura painter. A comparison of these two representations shows that they embody a deeper meaning, which is to be sought not in the myth of Zeus but in that of Dionysos.

24　See A. D. Trendall, "A Volute Krater at Taranto," pp. 175–79, pls. VIII–IX.

25　C. Picard, "Διόνυσος Μιτρηφόρος," pp. 709–21, does not analyze the scenes in the vase painting in which Dionysos or men who are celebrating him wear the *mitra*. As to the impertinence, see Pliny, *Natural History* XXXV 140: *petulanti pictura*.

26　See Alfieri, Arias, and Hirmer, *Spina*, pls. 10–11, with the misinterpretation of the boy on p. 31.

27　See the volute krater in Ferrara and the bell krater of Compiègne, in H. Fuhrmann, "Athamas," p. 117, fig. 4; and p. 119, fig. 8. Here other interpretations are admissible, but only here.

Two characteristic Dionysian idols, both easily fashioned, were in use in the Archaic period. They complemented one another and bore witness to a myth of Dionysos that never became as public as that of the thigh birth. One of these idols was unphallic. The paradoxical term is unavoidable: the unphallic character is *stressed.* Not only in comparison with the pronouncedly phallic beings who appear as the god's companions and worshipers, but also taken in itself, this idol lacks all phallic suggestion. Over a column in the sanctuary a mask was hung and below the mask a long garment—sometimes two, an overgarment and an undergarment—which also embraced the column. A column with a capital is a recurrent component of this rigid composition, which can also include plant life; branches can grow from it. The column can also be without a capital, that is, it can be a post, but —and again this is stressed—this post does not resemble an authentic herm. Sometimes, even when the idol is standing out of doors, it bears a capital, which seems to have been added for the sole purpose of avoiding all resemblance to a herm and stressing the column character. An Attic skyphos with black figures on a white ground discloses a rare rural scene: before the idol an ithyphallic satyr is pursuing a maenad, while two men approach the idol, leading a half-naked hetaira and a he-goat to be sacrificed [76A–76C].[28] It seems unlikely that the idol is the abbreviation of a cult statue with similar face and dress. More probably it is an abbreviation of a small sanctuary that was constructed for this cult statue. From the idol there developed the "bearded Dionysos with long garment" type of representation which so many cult statues show in movement [39A, 40, 41] and which appears so impressively on the "visit of Dionysos relief" [64A]. This is discernibly

28   See A. Frickenhaus, *Lenäenvasen,* no. 2, with the erroneous remark that only the representation on one side is "interesting."

an emasculated Dionysos. A number of representations exemplify the transition [77, 78].[29]

This type of idol also occurs in the cult of Osiris and a myth recorded by Plutarch relates it closely to the dead god.[30] Osiris' coffin, according to this myth, was borne by the sea to Byblos where it was washed ashore at the foot of a heath tree. The tree grew around it, so that it became part of the tree. From the tree a pillar of the royal palace was made. There Isis, searching for her husband, found him in the pillar. She took the dead Osiris with her, but she wrapped the heath column in a garment, anointed it with oil, and left it with the kings of Byblos to be worshiped in her own temple.

Quite apart from the mask, which belongs specifically to the Greek god, the exact correspondence between this tale and representations of Dionysos points clearly to the meaning of the construction. The mask confirms this meaning. The correspondence not only indicates the "primitive" character of these cult statues but also demonstrates that such an idol could be regarded as the tomb of a dead god. The construction was retained not as a vestige of a former day but as a meaningful symbol appropriate to the god during his absence beneath the earth. Its characterization as "markedly unphallic" fits in with the reduced existence befitting the god—Osiris as well as Dionysos—in his underground state.

The temple of Dionysos in Ikarion possessed this type of cult statue in a renovated form. The mask, which was originally carved from wood —probably fig wood—was copied in marble about 530 B.C. and retained its character as a mask except for the highly impressive eyes given

29 On [77], see Frickenhaus, *Lenäenvasen*, pp. 6–7. On [78], see Frickenhaus, p. 12, no. 26; cf. nos. 27, 29A.

30 *De Iside et Osiride* 357.

it by the sculptor [79].[31] They gaze at us like the eyes of a bull. This may or may not have been the artist's intention, but it fits in with the god's re-emergence from the underworld in the form of a bull, as expected by the women of Elis. The garment that hung below the mask was of heavy material and was renewed from time to time. Whether mask and garment were attached to a column with a capital or to a pillar cannot be determined. But along with its mask and garment idol, the temple in Ikarion had another cult statue, a statue of Dionysos seated on a throne and holding a kantharos in his right hand [81, 80].[32] Enthroned, Dionysos was wholly himself; the mask and garment hung on the pillar or column were only a part of him. In the event that the *trieteris* was observed in Ikarion in earlier times, it is not hard to guess that mask and garment represented Dionysos in the year of his absence. If among his idols in the Attic countryside there were double masks [82A/ 82B, 83A–83C],[33] these meant, after the two-year period was done away with, that in both his aspects Dionysos was ruler over the whole year. *One* mask was never the *whole god*, for only in half his being was Dionysos the "mask god" or the bearded Dionysos in the long garment who developed from this idol.

In Athens the "mask god" was the cult statue of the Lenaion, the temple in which Dionysos' birthday was celebrated. A series of magnificent vases—rightly called "Lenäenvasen" after the feast, the Lenaia[34]—give us a view of the temple. We see dignified women, probably

31 See W. Wrede, "Der Maskengott," pp. 57–70; Kerényi, "Man and Mask," p. 157. / On the bull envisioned by the women of Elis, see above, ch. IV, at notes 159 ff.

32 According to H. Luschey (see Kerényi, *Werke*, III, 159), the seated statue is at the most fifty years more recent than the marble mask, which is dated to about 530 B.C.

33 Frickenhaus, *Lenäenvasen*, nos. 5 and 7.

34 By Frickenhaus, whose original twenty-nine Lenäenvasen have been

the Gerairai, in the role of nurses attending the birth of the wine. Before an idol of the god, consisting of a mask, a garment, and ivy branches [84, 85],[35] they are ladling wine very carefully, thus confirming its completed birth to the people outside who—from the introduction into Athens of the Theban myth—would be shouting "son of Semele." In one vase painting[36] a woman celebrant has at her breast a child who is holding out his hands [86A/86B]. Why does he appear before the idol whom the women are worshiping at the same time? Here again we find an analogy with the religion of Osiris. The birth of Harpokrates, son of Isis and Osiris, was celebrated at a time when Osiris was simultaneously mourned as dead and greeted as king of the underworld, as though he had come to life again.[37] In Athens the mask and long garment suggested the god whose role Zeus took over with the thigh birth and who now stood there, distinct from the child Dionysos and at the same time celebrated as ruler of the underworld. As he gave himself to the people, the long garment concealed his condition—that he was only a part of himself, an earnest dignified god of the Athenians, comparable in his uniqueness to no foreign god. The mask belongs only to him, not to Osiris. It is only seemingly empty. Behind it dwells a world of spirits, which sends its inhabitants out onto the Dionysian stage.

---

supplemented by the examples given in A. Pickard-Cambridge, *Dramatic Festivals*, pp. 30 ff. In opposition to Nilsson's criticism, see Deubner, *Attische Feste*, p. 130, and my remarks now in the present work.

35 For [84], see Frickenhaus, *Lanäenvasen*, no. 19 (in Beazley, *Attic Red-Figure*, p. 621, no. 33). For [85]: Frickenhaus, no. 29; Beazley, pp. 1151–52, no. 2.

36 Once in Paris. See J. J. Witte, *Description des Collections d'antiquités conservées à l'Hôtel Lambert*, p. 48, pls. XI and XII.

37 See T. Hopfner, *Plutarch über Isis und Osiris*, I, 77.

The second type of idol characteristic of Dionysos was simpler: it represented a phallus. Dionysos separated and yet did not separate from this part of himself. His contradictory condition—the consequence of a contradictory identity—is evident even to a superficial observer. To quote a succinct account: "The phallus is the constant companion of Dionysos." It seems to have been absent from scarcely any Dionysian procession; the participants tied it to themselves, so that it became an accessory of comic actors and was also set up as a choragic monument. The god never wears it, but his companions, the sileni and satyrs, are ithyphallic. Phallus processions and merry Dionysian festivals were held throughout the Greek countryside. As Plutarch describes them, "in the lead an amphora of wine and a vine branch were carried about; then came a man drawing behind him the sacrificial animal, a he-goat; another followed him with a basket of figs, and last a phallus was carried."[38] Examples can easily be multiplied, lending some support to the contention—though this explanation could not account for all the facts, let alone the contradictory character of the god—that "Dionysos was, among other things, a god of fertility."[39]

The myth solves the contradiction of identity and non-identity by drawing a distinction between the god and his gifts, corresponding to the similar relationship between *zoë* and its embodiments. The myth does not, however, speak even indirectly of fertility, as it might, for example, by saying that Dionysos had afflicted his enemies with barrenness. In introducing the *phallophoriai*, Melampous had explained them probably with the myth of the god's dismemberment and emasculation, and had called on the faithful to worship the part for the whole. The oldest idol of Dionysos known to Athenian tradition was a phallus

38 Plutarch, *De cupiditate divitiarum* 527 D; Nilsson, *Geschichte*, pp. 590 f.
39 Nilsson, p. 593.

set up in the temple of the Horai, but the identity disclosed in the epithet "Orthos," "he who stands erect," was intentionally veiled by the explanation that the right mixture of wine and water enabled men to stand upright. On Samos and Lesbos the epithet "Enorches," "he who is in possession of his testicles,"[40] points clearly to emasculation. When set up as a phallus, Dionysos was Enorches, in contrast to the "mask god" who was no longer in possession of his testicles. In a later day the outspoken archaic epithet seemed so offensive that it was transferred, with a different explanation, to another mythical being.

The Dionysos myth with its inner logic resolved the contradictions of the living cult and of cult life, but not the contradictions and ambivalences inherent in the sexual sphere which was drawn into the cult of *zoë*. An essential quality of this myth is that it was applicable to the universal, in this case very concretely to that which is characteristic of all men; hence it was capable of cutting through such ambivalences. Comparison of a phallic poem by Walt Whitman with a song of the Greek *phallophoriai* clearly brings out the impact that the rule of Dionysos had in this sphere. What sets the *phallophoriai* in motion is phallic pride, which is also evident in Whitman's poem "From Pent-up Aching Rivers":

> *From pent-up aching rivers*
> *From that of myself without which I were nothing,*
> *From what I am determined to make illustrious, even*
> *if I stand sole among men,*
> *From my voice resonant, singing the phallus,*
> *Singing the song of procreation,*

40 Hesychios s.v. Ἐνόρχης. See also J. Tzetzes' scholium on Lykophron, *Alexandra* 212.

> *Singing the need of superb children and therein*
> *superb grown people,*
> *Singing the muscular urge and the blending,*
> *Singing the bedfellow's song.*[41]

The American poet is proud of his phallic pride, proud of his daring to express it, proud of the superb progeny as though it were the infallible consequence of his virility, assured throughout the generations. The poem is sustained by a highly self-conscious observation of, and reflection on, a condition which is normally characterized by self-forgetfulness. The Delian poet Semos' song of the *phallophoriai* is wholly faithful to the condition that Whitman describes and Rilke tried to describe.[42] Semos calls upon the people who fill the theater:

> ἀνάγετ᾽ εὐρυχωρίαν
> εἶτε τῶι θεῶι· ἐθέλει γὰρ
> [ὁ θεὸς] ὀρθὸς ἐσφυδομένος
> διὰ μέσου βαδίζειν.

> *Give way, make room*
> *For the god! For it is his will*
> *To stride exuberantly*
> *Erect through the middle.*

The phallic pride is transferred to the god: "It is his will." One must give way to him, make room for him. This god is Dionysos, who from time to time strides proudly through the countryside in this form. His right to be proud is consecrated, for example, by a choragic monu-

---

41 Walt Whitman, *Leaves of Grass*, p. 79.
42 Semos in Athenaios XIV 622 B. Rainer Maria Rilke, *Sämtliche Werke*, p. 473: "Dies ist das schweigende Steigen der Phallen."

ment in the form of a marble phallus set up in the theater to celebrate the victory of a male chorus.[43] He is at the root of masculine achievement in his own realm, the realm of *zoë*, though this gift of the gods is not always easy for men to bear and it ultimately consumes them. Two representations on a black-figure cup show in comic exaggeration the relationship between mortal men and the divine phallus [87A/87B],[44] for the realm of Dionysos takes in the entire province of comedy and with it the counterpart of phallic pride, the laughter to which it can give rise. The bearing of the phallus is made more difficult for the scrawny ithyphallic men shown in the picture by the fact that along with it, on the same tray, they are obliged to carry huge Dionysian figures. Here the *phallophoria* becomes a satiric drama or a comedy.

It may seem strange to us but it is only natural that the women should have adhered so tenaciously to the concealing fiction that the Dionysian women served as nurses in awakening and caring for the Liknites. In contrast to the *phallophoriai*, which were essentially public—though we find them represented only in the vase painting mentioned above—during the Classical period the contents of the Dionysian women's *liknon* was kept no less secret in Athens than at Delphi. In about 440-430 B.C., a well-known vase painter devoted a picture on a magnificent krater to the mysteries of Sabazios and the Great Goddess of Asia Minor, which had been introduced as an archaic Dionysos cult. Snakes figure in the prologue, the ecstatic dance of the women and girls who are to be initiated [88B–88D].[45] Sabazios, a Pluto figure

43 See "Fouilles de Délos," *BCH*, XXXI (1907), pp. 504–11; E. Buschor, "Ein choregisches Denkmal," pp. 96–98.

44 See Pickard-Cambridge, *Dithyramb*, p. 303, no. 15.

45 The identification by E. Simon (*Opfernde Götter*, pp. 79 ff.) of the Sabazios cult, whose earliest monument in Athens is this vase, is confirmed in this context. See also S. Patitucci, "Osservazioni sul cratere polignoteo," pp.

without the impressive features of the subterranean Dionysos as shown in his mask, also has snakes in his headband [88A]. The priestess who is to initiate the women steps before the divine pair bearing the *liknon* on her head, but the *liknon* is wholly covered by a cloth.

On a chous of the same period, the *liknon*, which is entwined in ivy, lies on a ceremonial table; in the *liknon* is the ivy-crowned mask of Dionysos [89].[46] Two women officiate at this wine ceremony: one holds the kantharos; the other, a bowl containing sacrificial cakes. The second woman is followed by a smaller figure, evidently a maidservant. Beside the first woman, a krater has been prepared. Because the mask lies on a cloth in the *liknon*, the actual content is concealed, and only an introductory rite is performed. This prelude however makes it clear whom the women are worshiping and to whom the secret action that is not represented is addressed, namely, the subterranean Dionysos, who in addition to wine bestowed still another gift on man: a gift in which he, as the perpetually increasing and decreasing abundance of *zoë*–comparable to the son of Poros and Penia in Plato's *Symposium*[47]–remained present. The gift was his manhood, distributed among men.

The secret action performed by itself may have been unutterably lustful, but no such action can be performed by women without an unreflecting, irrational, and unconscious implication, rooted in woman's innermost nature, of the child. Thus, there was a profound truth in the concealing fiction of the Dionysian women's nursehood. From the

---

146 ff. The new (and yet age-old) gods are greeted in the inscriptions over the divine pair as καλός ("the beautiful one," masc.) and καλή ("the beautiful one," fem.). Further hypotheses, including my own, are now superfluous.

46   See G. van Hoorn, *Choes and Anthesteria*, p. 24.

47   *Symposium* 203 BC.

standpoint of animal fertility this action could only be sterile. This was hinted at by the pairing of sterile animals, two mules, on another Attic chous [55].[48] In the ceremony whose prelude rite [89] we have witnessed, Dionysos arose revived as a child and youth, a repetition of himself. One person, the queen, had celebrated the *mysterion* on behalf of the women of Athens, but long before she entered the sacred room of which we shall speak in the next section she had derived strength from the vision of all Athenian women. The significance of the Altamura painter's work [75] representing a silent dialogue between the enthroned Dionysos and the mysterious young Dionysos, nowhere else depicted in this way, is that the Athenian religion of Dionysos knew him as a divided and double god.

The Dionysian Festivals of the Athenians

IN ATHENS as at Delphi the winter months belonged to Dionysos. Though nowhere explicitly stated, this can be reliably inferred from the Attic calendar and from the traditions of the cult, provided concrete natural realities are given priority over learned speculation.[49] At

48 This was not recognized by the archaeologists. At least one of the animals was regarded as an ass. A. Rumpf took them both for asses; see his "Attische Feste—Attische Vasen," pp. 209 f. He failed to notice that the animals are painted, and not only with broad stripes on the shoulders but also with dots. It is possible that these animals were harnessed to the car in which the queen, accompanied by a man disguised as Dionysos, rode to the Boukoleion; see below, p. 308. The mule on an Attic vase in New York is also painted; see the *Bulletin of the Metropolitan Museum of Art*, XX (1925), 130, fig. 5. Concerning mules, see here ch. IV at notes 112 ff., and Bachofen's remarks on the "sterile passion of the mule" in "Die Unsterblichkeitslehre der orphischen Theologie," *Gesammelte Werke*, VII, 102.

49 Pickard-Cambridge, *Dramatic Festivals*, presents a learned discussion that is more copious than fruitful.

approximately the time of the beginning of the Dionysian winter period at Delphi,[50] a very natural festive action was performed in Athens.
Since this action depended on the state of the wine and was not attached to any particular day, it was not indicated in any festive calendar, but it was described by Phanodemos, an Athenian historian, and
his account has come down to us.[51]

Near the temple of Dionysos worshiped "in the swamps"—*en limnais*—the Athenians mixed wine and offered it to the god. At their
homes they drew the still sweet new wine—*gleukos*—from large clay
vessels—*pithoi*—and brought it to the scene of the festival where they
themselves drank it. Phanokles, an author of the post-Classical period
in which the Dionysian religion had grown tame, was interested chiefly
in the civilized mixing of the wine. Consequently it is he who stresses
the presence of springs near the temple of Dionysos Limnaios, springs
whose nymphs, in his opinion, were known as the nurses of Dionysos
because water made the vine grow. He goes on to describe the activities of the Athenians on this occasion. They sang songs to Dionysos,
danced, and invoked him as "Euanthes," "Dithyrambos," "Bakcheutas,"
and "Bromios." He does not speak of a date fixed by the calendar for

50   Roughly November 8th; see above, ch. V, note 77.
51   Phanodemos' account is preserved by Athenaios, who quotes it in *The
Deipnosophists* 465 A (in Gulick, ed., V, 26–28). The passage is also recorded
by Jacoby, *FGrHist*, 325, fr. 12 (III, B, p. 82; for the different readings of particular words, see Jacoby's critical apparatus, p. 82). The account given by
Athenaios is as follows: Φανόδημος δὲ πρὸς τῶι ἱερῶι φησι τοῦ ἐν Λίμναις Διονύσου τὸ
γλεῦκος φέροντας τοὺς Ἀθηναίους ἐκ τῶν πίθων τῶι θεῶι κιρνάναι, εἶτ' [αὐτοῖς] προσφέρεσθαι·
[αὐτοῖς is the correct reading, not αὐτοῖς.] ὅθεν καὶ Λιμναῖον κληθῆναι τὸν Διόνυσον, ὅτι
μιχθὲν τὸ γλεῦκος τῶι ὕδατι τότε πρῶτον ἐπόθη κεκραμένον. διόπερ ὀνομασθῆναι τὰς [πηγὰς]
Νύμφας καὶ τιθήνας τοῦ Διονύσου, ὅτι τὸν οἶνον αὐξάνει τὸ ὕδωρ κιρνάμενον. ἡσθέντες οὖν τῆι
κράσει ἐν ὠιδαῖς ἔμελπον τὸν Διόνυσον, χορεύοντες καὶ ἀνακαλοῦντες Εὐανθῆ καὶ Διθύραμβον
καὶ Βακχευτὰν καὶ Βρόμιον.
Everything happens πρὸς τῶι ἱερῶι ("at the sanctuary"); this meaning of πρὸς
τῶι is confirmed by other examples.

the festival or for the opening of the temple. All we know is that people came to the sanctuary with the *gleukos*, mixed it with water for the god, and drank to him for the first time in the new wine year.

According to Thukydides, the temple of Dionysos Limnaios was situated to the south of the Akropolis and was one of the city's oldest sanctuaries.[52] The nature of the "swamps" is indicated by representations on certain choës showing a rock[53] and by Phanodemos' statement that the wine was there mixed with spring water. The place must have been a geological formation characteristic of Greece, the best known example of which is the swamp of Lerna: water pours abundantly from under the rocks, yet despite its purity it forms a "swamp." Dionysos entered into the underworld and returned from it near Lerna; it was a gateway to Hades. The *limnai* of Dionysos must have had the same significance for the Athenians. That is why in Aristophanes the song of the frogs of this swamp accompanied Dionysos on his journey to the underworld, and why at the end of the all-souls-feast of the Anthesteria the people returned once again to this sanctuary of Dionysos.[54]

In time the springs dried up. According to Strabo—at the time of Christ's birth—the sanctuary stood on dry land.[55] The connection with the Anthesteria, the "old" Athenian festival of Dionysos set by the calendar,[56] remained unchanged. Only on the principal day (Choës Day) of this festival was the sanctuary opened to the people and then for a rather brief visit.[57] Beside the altar of the temple stood a stele

52 Thukydides II 15 3–4.
53 See Van Hoorn, *Choes and Anthesteria*, p. 29.
54 See Aristophanes, *Frogs* 215–16, 217–19.
55 Strabo VIII 5 1.   56 Thukydides II 15 4.
57 Pseudo-Demosthenes LIX (*In Neaeram*), 76.

bearing the law regarding the queen—after the introduction of democracy, the wife of the *archon basileus*. She had to be an Athenian and a virgin at the time of her marriage, because it was her duty to perform the "ineffable sacred rites"—*arrheta hiera*—for the city and to be given to Dionysos as his wife.[58] She had to swear in the fourteen "venerable women"—the Gerairai—who devoted themselves to the Athenian cult of Dionysos at fourteen altars.[59] It may be inferred that an archaic college of women functioned in the Dionysos cult of Athens as in that of Elis. Strange to say, the difference in the numbers—fourteen in Athens, sixteen at Elis—also appears in the religion of Osiris, where the number of the god's members, who must be gathered together, is sometimes set at fourteen and sometimes at sixteen.[60] The sanctuary in the swamps was regarded in Athens not only as the oldest but also as the most sacred temple of Dionysos.[61] Where the fourteen altars were located we do not know; in connection with the temple *en limnais* only *the* altar is mentioned. But a connection with the old Dionysos cults of the Peloponnese—of Lerna and Elis—is as good as manifest.

Near this temple associated with the secrets of the Dionysian women, the wine was mixed with water not on Choës Day, the one day when the temple was open, but considerably earlier and, as we have already seen, not on any fixed date. The date of this festival, at which the *gleukos*, the first wine of the year, not yet fully fermented but nevertheless intoxicating,[62] was brought to the temple for tasting depended on the date of the harvest. According to an interpretation of

58 Ibid., 73, 75.

59 Ibid., 78; Pollux VIII 108. On the Gerairai, see note 88, below.

60 See H. Brugsch, "Das Osiris-Mysterium von Tentyra," pp. 88 ff. / On the Sixteen Women of Elis, see above, ch. IV, at notes 159 ff.

61 Pseudo-Demosthenes, 76.

62 "Suser im Stadium," in Swiss dialect; see Kerényi, "Parva realia," p. 9.

the Codex Theodosianus, relating to Spain, wine was harvested between August 23rd and October 15th.[63] The conventional period for the first fermentation was forty days. Thus, the *gleukos* was usually ready in November, or at the latest in December, roughly the period corresponding to the Delphic Dadophoriai. November 3rd and St. Martin's Day on November 11th are dates frequently mentioned in Italy and Greece, and they are also mentioned in the more recent literature.[64] At this time Dionysos was "called" in the swamps of Athens and—as is usual when the gods were called in this way[65]—he was already present. The names used in calling him anticipated the festivals that were to follow and whose advent now began: "Euanthes" and "Dithyrambos" anticipated the Anthesteria; "Bakcheutas" and "Bromios," the time of Dionysian swarming in Athens.

In the artfully constructed Attic calendar the myth of *zoë* approached its fulfillment on different levels. These were first the wine; then the generation, that is, the embryonic state (premature birth), and the birth of the child; and finally the re-established wholeness of a dismembered god who had dwelt for twelve months with the dead. For all this, room had to be found in the solar year which encompassed the content of a *trieteris*. The motif of premature birth was so important an element in the Dionysian religion that on the basis of the early bond between the two religions it was taken into the myth of Osiris, probably into its latest stratum. Horus, the son of the dead Osiris, was said to have been born at the end of eighty-one or eighty-seven days.[66]

---

63 Codex Theodosianus II 8 19; see H. Usener, "Der Heilige Tychon," p. 44, note 2.

64 See Kerényi, "Parva realia," pp. 8 f.

65 See Kerényi, "Ankunft des Dionysos," *Werke*, II, 271.

66 Plutarch, *De Iside et Osiride* 358 E, 377 BC; Hopfner, I, 79 f. According to the older Egyptian sources he was born after nine months and a few days.

A more human measure is observed in the myth of Dionysos, who spent seven months in the womb. This seven-month period not only is recorded in the literature, but also entered into a tradition that modern Greek folklore has preserved in a Thracian Shrovetide play.[67] The connection between Dionysos and the embryonic state was reflected in concrete observances. A law of the temple of Dionysos in Smyrna in the second century A.D. barred from the sanctuary not only those women who had exposed a child but more particularly those in whom a pregnancy had been violently interrupted.[68] Dionysos was the protector of life especially in those phases where it was *little else than zoë.*

The Attic calendar provided, as we have seen, for an interval of seven months between the Lesser Mysteries of Agrai, which followed the Anthesteria,[69] and the Great Mysteries of Eleusis. In the Athenian interpretation, the Divine Child whose birth in the underworld was proclaimed to the initiates in Eleusis was the child of Semele, born after seven months. A full period of pregnancy—ten lunar months in the ancient reckoning[70]—and hence the additional pregnancy of Zeus according to the Athenian myth, was not yet complete at the first half of November when the Athenian month of Maimakterion began. Nor was the fermentation of the new wine complete. With regard both to the pure, finished wine and to the Divine Child, there began a period of advent, which, exceeding the limits of human pregnancy, extended over the ensuing months. Beyond the birth and marriage of the god—

67 On the seven-month period, see above, ch. III, note 197.

68 See J. Keil, "Inschriften aus Smyrna," p. 17. Probably the parallel to this, a monument of Greek religion in Egypt (G. Plaumann, "Ptolemais in Oberägypten," p. 55, place of find not given), also comes from a Dionysian sanctuary. Its significance was not understood by Nilsson, *Dionysiac Mysteries*, pp. 134 f.

69 This is attested by the chous in the hand of Herakles in Agrai; see Kerényi, *Eleusis*, pp. 51–52 and fig. 10.

70 See Virgil, *Eclogae* IV 61; E. Norden, *Die Geburt des Kindes*, p. 61, note 1, and p. 116.

in Gamelion and Anthesterion, our January and February—the Dionysian period was extended to Elaphebolion, our March, the month of the Great Dionysia.

The month of Poseideon, our December,[71] was filled with the Dionysian activities of the Attic peasants. These rites were known as the "rural Dionysia," as opposed to the "city," or "Great Dionysia."[72] This distinction was possible only after the institution of the great Dionysian procession and the dramatic plays for Dionysos Eleuthereus in Elaphebolion, which was an elaborate festive period, a sumptuous state display. In it the rural communities, especially Ikarion, played an important part. On the other hand, from the Classical period on, the Great Dionysia exerted an important influence on the rural communities and led to the building of theaters in small towns. A differentiation between what occurred in the country and what occurred in the city in the *winter months* of Maimakterion, Poseideon, and Gamelion is probably unjustified. The rural Dionysia probably continued in Poseideon what had begun in the city at the sanctuary in the swamps with the tasting of the first mixture of the wine. This rural festival was the "Lenaia" of the countryfolk, a festival that the city dwellers celebrated in a concentrated fashion later, in Gamelion. According to one testimony, the rural Dionysia was even called "Lenaia."[73] It was a prolonged anticipatory celebration of the birth of Dionysos.

The character of this country festivity excludes the possibility that the Dionysian women who were called "Lenai" gave their name to the festival of the Lenaia in the historical period. For this was the time

71 Our months correspond only approximately to the movable Attic lunar months. I equate the first half of the month with the modern month.

72 Pickard-Cambridge, *Dramatic Festivals*, pp. 42 ff., 57.

73 Scholium on Aristophanes, *Acharnians* 202.

of the *phallophoriai*. Men were now the bearers of the god—if not of the whole god, then of as much of him as could be gathered from the not yet fully fermented wine. Not only the birth of Dionysos but also the impending birth of comedy was in the offing.

A magnificent representation on a large calyx krater shows the god Poseidon, to whom the month of Poseideon was dedicated, in his relation to Dionysos [90].[74] He is one of three brothers, the supreme gods. Identified by his trident, the ruler of the sea lies on a raised couch, but bottommost among the gods of Attica. It is certain that the artist —known as the Kekrops painter, from the main figure of the painting— did not wish to represent him as the ruler of a single month. In the composition Poseidon looks across to an enthroned god distinguished by a long scepter, situated in the same low region, and to him also point the three serving figures in front of him: an Eros and two nobly dressed Dionysian women standing on either side of a large krater, with one woman holding a wine pitcher that is probably empty. This other god is not without resemblance to Poseidon, nor is he lower in rank; evidently he is the ruler of the underworld, Hades and Dionysos in one, Poseidon's brother. He is awaited in order that Eros may proffer not only a grape but also wine to Poseidon. For while holding out the grape Eros points his finger at the enthroned figure—a composition which shows as clearly as possible the situation I have designated by the word "advent." In his month Poseidon himself, like the women of Athens, is filled with Dionysian expectation.

The next month, which might be called the Attic Christmas and Epiphany month, was called in Athens "Gamelion," the "wedding

74 *CVA*: Deutschland, *Schloss Fasanerie* (*Adolphseck*), pl. 46. The enthroned deity and the situation were not understood by the volume's editor, Frank Brommer.

month"; on Ionian territory, "Lenaion"; and on the island of Amorgos, probably "Eiraphion," month of Eiraphiotes, the "sewed in" Dionysos,[75] who was now to appear. The name "Lenaion" came from Lenaia, the name of the festival, but the Lenaia were not always and everywhere a festival of the Lenai, as the bacchantes were called in Ionian territory and elsewhere.[76] In Athens the women who celebrated the Dionysos cult in its highest form in the city were called Gerairai, the "venerables"; and those who went to Delphi each year, "Thyiades."

The festival name "Lenaia" is derived from *lenos*, "pressing vat," and *lenaion*, "the place where the wine was pressed and preserved until fermentation was complete." The nature of such a place is indicated by an early nineteenth-century report from Cyprus, where the word for wine cellar is still *linos*. "The grapes, which have previously been shoveled into a pile, are brought to the *linos*, where they are crushed and then placed under the press. The juice is poured into large earthenware jars which are half buried in the ground. Here the wine ferments and is not moved until it is poured into skins and taken to the markets."[77]

The conflicting reports concerning the Lenaion of the Athenians—

75 See J. Delamarre, "Location du domaine de Zeus Temenites," pp. 180 f.

76 See Hesychios s.v. Ληναὶ: Βάκχαι, Ἀρκάδες. It was believed that the Ionian name of the bacchantes, Λῆναι, must be distinguished from ληνός, "wine press," since it pointed to an old η among the Arcadians, where the word for "wine press" would have to be λανός. This is contradicted by the fact that on Cyprus, where the Arcadian dialect was spoken, the place where wine is made and stored is called *linos* (ληνός). Λῆναι means the "wine-press women" who assisted at the birth of Dionysos.

77 See A. Mommsen, *Heortologie*, footnote on p. 341, citing A. Jullien, *Topographie der Weinberge*, II, 139. This indication is lacking, however, in the French original (Paris, 1822, pp. 469 f.); it was taken into the German translation from another source.

in the city and in the country[78]—indicate that there were at least two such sanctuaries of Dionysos, which were also wine cellars resembling the one described on Cyprus. These sanctuaries were exemplary wine presses where the religious rites connected with wine-making were performed on behalf of the numerous productive *lenoi* throughout the city. The city Lenaion was near the Agora. Here the birth of the wine and the Divine Child was celebrated before the idol of the subterranean Dionysos, while the people filled the square outside the temple. Perhaps the large crowds were the reason why, in time, a second Lenaion was built outside the city.

In Greece the month of the Lenaia is the coldest of the year. Wine needed cold weather for its final clearing;[79] this is one reason why the gestation of the god was extended, beyond that of humans, to our January. Another reason was the winter solstice which was also to determine the dates of the Christian Christmas and Epiphany. In Egypt the night of January 5th had since 1996 B.C. been a festive date, marking the birth of light.[80] On the island of Andros, after the introduction of the Julian calendar, the same date was set for a Dionysian miracle, the transformation of the water from a certain spring into wine—a form of the god's birth.[81] Such precision was not possible with the Attic calendar.

It seems strange, however—and was already thought strange in antiquity—that the Athenians should have chosen so cold a month as their Gamelion for marriages. Surely they did not, as Aristotle sup-

78 Pickard-Cambridge, *Dramatic Festivals*, p. 37.
79 See Kerényi, "Parva realia," p. 9.
80 Norden, *Die Geburt des Kindes*, p. 38.
81 Pliny, *Natural History* II 231, XXXI 16. Also see Kerényi, "Die andriotische Säule," *Werke*, III, 408–9.

posed, do so for reasons of health.[82] Each year a general marriage celebration followed the festival of the marriage of Zeus and Hera.[83] The
month took its name from this festival which in late antiquity is mentioned as *Theogamia* and among the Athenians was called *Hieros
gamos*, "sacred marriage."[84] The celebration on the night of Choës Day
is never called by this name and, as we shall see, Aristotle distinguishes
between this celebration and the *gamos*, or marriage, in which earthly
couples followed the example of the divine pair. The marriage performed between the two festivals of Dionysos, the Lenaia and the
Anthesteria,[85] permitted the young wives to participate in the second
festival in a different way from the virgins. In that night Dionysos
appeared as the woman's higher husband, the embodiment of indestructible *zoë*, and for this their marriage was a preparatory phase.

The winter drew to an end, and the first flowers sprang from the
ground, sometimes through the snow; hence—from the verb *anthein*,
"to flower"—come the names of the festival and the month, "Anthesteria" and "Anthesterion." There now began a time for which the Romans
coined the expression *mundus patet*:[86] for some days the lower world

82 *Politics* VII 1335a.

83 See A. Brueckner, "Athenische Hochzeitsgeschenke," pp. 114 f.; and
Kerényi, "Zeus und Hera," p. 248.

84 Photios, *Lexicon* s.v. ἱερὸς γάμος. See also Kerényi, Ἱερὸς γάμος. Concerning the *Theogamia*, see Deubner, *Attische Feste*, pp. 177 f. The supposition that
this festival was a Neoplatonic invention is quite arbitrary.

85 This can also be inferred from the scholium on Hesiod, *Works and Days*
780, according to which the marriage feast of young couples took place on one
of the days before the new moon. According to Menander, fr. 320, line 4 (in
Edmonds, III, B, pp. 678–79), the feast of the *Hieros gamos* was held on the
24th of the month, and this is not subject to doubt. The Lenaia were held at the
time of the full moon, "most probably" on the 12th; Deubner, *Attische Feste*,
p. 123.

86 See W. W. Fowler, "Mundus Patet," p. 25.

was open. The god who had been called since November now made his entrance—which was his emergence from the underworld—among the women of Athens. Of the names by which he was called at the temple in the swamps, "Euanthes" and "Dithyrambos" referred to the Anthesteria. One of the dithyrambs mentioned earlier has the line: "Now the time has come, now the flowers are here." A dithyramb by another unknown poet describes the time of flowers that has just begun:

> Ἔνθα δὴ ποικίλων ἀνθέων ἄμβροτοι λείμακες
> βαθύσκιον παρ' ἄλσος ἀβροπαρθένους
> εὐιώτας χοροὺς ἀγκάλαις δέχονται.

> *When the divine fields of motley flowers*
> *In the shady grove receive with open arms*
> *The Bacchic dances performed by tender virgins.*[87]

These verses are of the post-Classical period and the scene, like that of the other dithyramb, is not Athens, but rather the fantastic shores of Okeanos where Persephone was picking flowers when she was carried away by the king of the underworld. From Athens we hear only of the swinging of the virgins on the second day of the Anthesteria. Moreover, the women were represented vis-à-vis the god by one person, the wife of the *archon basileus*, who for that reason retained the dignity of a queen of former times. Apart from her, the fourteen "venerable women" whom she swore in joined in evoking the god at fourteen altars with the help of the contents of fourteen mystery bas-

---

87 Powell, *Collectanea Alexandrina*, p. 192, fr. 22. For the dithyramb containing the line, ". . . now the flowers are here," see the quotation above, in ch. V, at note 30.

kets.[88] The central action was performed in the deepest secrecy within the narrowest limits of strict women's mysteries which no man could approach. The vase paintings, however, show that the whole city was very much concerned with the secret action of these days. The restriction of its efficacy to the feminine sex seems to have relaxed in the course of time and may never have existed in the uplands between Athens and Mt. Kithairon.

The cult actions of the Anthesteria were performed in and near the temple of Dionysos Limnaios. Thukydides states expressly that this occurred on the second day of the festival, the only day of the year on which the temple was open. The three feast days fell on the eleventh, twelfth, and thirteenth of the month. The first was called "Pithoigia," "day of the opening of the pithoi." The large earthenware jars, which were usually half buried, were certainly not dragged to the "swamps" any more than they had been in November when wine was drawn from them for the first mixing and tasting. At the time of fermentation the jars had to be left open; afterwards they were covered—otherwise all sorts of things, even a child, might have fallen in. If the lid was removed on this day, it was for a religious reason. In Plutarch's time and in his social circle this reason was no longer understood.[89] The

88 See Deubner, *Attische Feste*, p. 100, note 5. On the fourteen altars, see *Etymologicum Magnum* s.v. γεραιραί. On the basket, see Pseudo-Demosthenes LIX (*In Neaeram*), 78.

89 See Plutarch, *Quaestiones conviviales* 655 A, where an obviously false explanation is given for the Athenian Pithoigia, as though this festival occurred at a time when a fermentation was still possible. The wine is said to be an ambivalent medicine (*pharmakon*), a notion connected with an earlier stage of fermentation. The Romans celebrated the wine festival of the Meditrinalia on October 11th, on which occasion they said, "Novum vetus vinum bibo, novo veteri morbo medeor" ("I drink new old wine, I heal new an old sickness"); see G. Wissowa, *Religion und Kultus der Römer*, p. 115.

explanation has been found in the Mycenaean texts of the Pylos clay tablets. Here the souls of the dead are called *dipsioi*, the "thirsty ones."[90] They were thirsty not for water but, in the year when Dionysos dwelt emasculated among them, for wine. A painting on an Attic lekythos of the fifth century shows winged souls under the supervision of Hermes, guide of souls, swarming around a half-buried pithos on the day of the Pithoigia, when the underworld was open for the ascent of Dionysos [91].[91] One is seen rushing up to drink while three others are flying away satisfied.

Attracted by the smell of the wine that rose from the opened pithoi and spread throughout the city, the souls emerged from the underworld. No one, not even slaves, was prevented from drinking wine on this day, even though it was only a day of opening, not just of the wine jars to lure the souls, but also of the festival, the main day of which, on the twelfth, took its name of "Choës" from the wine pitchers.[92] With their *mundus patet* the Romans meant something very simple: "When the world is open, it is as though the gates of the sad subterranean gods were open."[93] It would be a mistake to apply this literally to the festival of the Athenians. Choës Day was marked by an erotic atmosphere and the presence of ghosts, an unusual phenomenon but

90   See L. R. Palmer, *The Interpretation of Mycenaean Greek Texts*, pp. 244 f. Palmer (p. 252) connected *di-pi-si-jo-i* (Pylos Fr 1231) with the Anthesteria.

91   This representation has been connected with the Anthesteria by J. E. Harrison, "Pandora's Box," pp. 101 ff., and *Prolegomena to the Study of Greek Religion*, pp. 43 f. In her view the pithos itself was the entrance to the underworld: a gratuitous assumption which provided sterile discussion.

92   See the scholium on Hesiod, *Works and Days* 360; and the scholium on Aristophanes, *Acharnians* 961.

93   Varro, in Macrobius, *Saturnalia* I 16 8: "Mundus cum patet, deorum tristium atque inferum quasi inanua patet."

not humanly impossible.[94] Even if we had no other example of it, the documents show that this was here the case.

There can be no doubt of the Athenian belief that the city was full of ghosts on Choës Day, for the next day, the "Day of the Pots"—the 13th of Anthesterion, which was dedicated to Hermes as well as Dionysos[95]—was wholly devoted to driving out and appeasing the spirits. The god who had led them up from the underworld was supposed to lead them back down again. A sentence called out to them became proverbial: "Out, you Keres, it is no longer Anthesteria!"[96] The pots, after which the day was named "Chytroi," contained food for the journey of the Keres: cooked vegetables and seeds, a sacrifice to Hermes Chthonios and in Greece from time immemorial to the present, the food of the spirits of the dead.[97] Their heads heavy with wine, the ghosts returned to the "swamps," whither the Athenians escorted them.[98] According to the trieteric order, Dionysos would now have remained on earth for the next twelve months. According to the Athenian order, he was divided again after a brief period and became double, simultaneously above and below.

It was the superstitious fear in a later period that made the Atheni-

---

94　See M. Buber, ed., *Chinesische Geister- und Liebesgeschichten.*

95　Rightly included in the scholium on Aristophanes, *Acharnians* 1076.

96　Θύραζε, κῆρες, οὐκετ' [or: οὐκ ἔνι] Ἀνθεστήρια; see *Suidae Lexicon* s.v. Θύραζε. The explanation to the effect that the Keres are not spirits of the dead but *Kares,* "Carian slaves," is far removed from the archaic and classical content of the feast day. See Deubner, *Attische Feste,* p. 113.

97　See E. Gjerstad, "Tod und Leben," pp. 152–86.

98　Aristophanes, *Frogs* 213–19 (Rogers, ed., II, 317):

The song we used to love in the marshland up above,
In praise of Dionysos to produce, of Nysaean Dionysos, son of Zeus.
When the revel-tipsy throng, all crapulous and gay,
To our precinct reeled along on the holy Pitcher day.

ans chew rhamnus leaves all day on the 12th of Anthesterion and
smear their doors with pitch.[99] The singers of dithyrambs who appeared that day at the Altar of the Twelve Gods on the Agora must also
have been chewing leaves! For the first time we glimpse such a chorus
on an Attic krater of the fifth century [92A/92B].[100] This vase painting
represents four men whose names are indicated, all wearing long garments. The poet Phrynichos[101] and a flute player are in the middle.
They are all characterized by branches or wreaths of ivy, and since
they do not wear masks or theatrical costumes it seems probable that
they are singing no other Dionysian song than the dithyramb. The
strange structure consisting of a long pole and a crossbeam around
which they are grouped is also carried on an Attic chous by children
acting out the marriage procession of Dionysos [93]. This same structure appears again much later in representations of the myth of Dionysos' childhood. This object can only be explained as a vestige of the
Dionysian idol,[102] which after the thigh birth was replaced by the god
in mobile, dynamic forms.

In the dithyramb the god is sung to as one who has just been born
after a long childbirth. "Dithyrambos" was one of the names of Dionysos himself, and this name was given to the type of choral song
whose original, though not exclusive, theme was the birth of the god.
Archilochos, the earliest known composer of dithyrambs, confessed
that he knew how to sing the dithyramb as soon as the wine shook his

99   Photios, *Lexicon* s.v. μιαρὰ ἡμέρα and ῥάμνος. The rhamnus is probably
the *spina alba* of the Romans; see E. Rohde, *Psyche*, p. 198, note 95.

100   See K. F. Johansen, *Eine Dithyrambosaufführung*, pp. 3 ff.

101   Probably the Phrynichos who also wrote comedies. See Johansen, p. 10.

102   The Swedish maypole as parallel in Johansen, p. 31, seems to have
been invoked as a last resort.

mind with its lightning,[103] a clear allusion to the lightning that struck Semele and ushered in the birth of her son. Timotheos, a younger poet, was the author of a dithyramb entitled "Semele's Labor" (*Odis Semeles*) in which the mother's cries could be heard.[104] In Euripides, Zeus calls out to the prematurely born child: "Come, Dithyrambos, into my virile womb."[105] The basis of Pindar's pun, "Lythirambos" for "Dithyrambos," is the story that when delivering the child the king of the gods cried out: *Lythi, rhamma, lythi rhamma*—"Seam, undo yourself, seam undo yourself!"[106] Dionysos had all this behind him on this feast day, on the eve of which his full presence was expected.

The throng sent ahead of him was formed by the children of the city, who took no notice of the spirits flitting about them and feared no harm from them. This throng consisted chiefly, and at first entirely, of boys beginning at the age when they were able to crawl, often represented on the pitchers given to them as though they were the child Dionysos himself.[107] The three-year-olds, who in the same year were inscribed in their *phratria* or clan, were especially heaped with presents. As representatives of the male sex in its first childlike form, they received among other things a chous, a somewhat smaller version of the customary vessel with which on the same day the men poured their wine in their drinking bouts.[108] The paintings on the pitchers show that on this day of joyous *mundus patet*, the children took part in everything

---

103 Archilochos, fr. 77, in Diehl, *Anth. lyr.*:

ὡς Διωνύσοι᾽ ἄνακτος καλὸν ἐξάρξαι μέλος
οἶδα διθύραμβον οἴνωι συγκεραυνωθεὶς φρένας.

104 Athenaios VIII 362 A.
105 *Bacchae* 523–24: ἴθι, Διθύραμβ᾽ ἐμὰν ἄρσενα τάνδε νηδύν.
106 See Bowra, *Pindari Carmina*, fr. 75.
107 See Van Hoorn, *Choes and Anthesteria*, p. 26.
108 Deubner, *Attische Feste*, pp. 96 ff., 116.

and imitated everything that was permitted to be seen of the festive happening. By their drinking contest—their share in Dionysos—the men were diverted from the mystery action of the women.

Amid this erotic, ghostlike atmosphere of the Aiora, the virgins did their swinging in the houses and in the courtyards where the pithoi stood open [94, 95].[109] The swing moved in the world that had opened between the upper and lower regions, in imitation of the exalted and spectral Erigone, the Ariadne of Ikarion, who belonged to both realms. A skyphos, a form of drinking cup that was probably customary on Choës Day, shows on one side a girl on a swing being pushed by a silenus and on the other a dignified lady accompanied by a silenus holding over her head an otherwise unknown three-cornered umbrella [42A/42B].[110] It was in all likelihood thus that the fourteen Gerairai were escorted by their servants to the sanctuary where they performed their mystic actions. Most respectable in appearance, they were surrounded by a Dionysian atmosphere. A possible scene of their actions, in addition to the temple in the swamps, was the so-called Boukoleion. Among the cult objects depicted on the pitchers, a conspicuous role is played by ithyphallic herms, one with the head of the young Dionysos.[111] It seems probable that on Choës Day these figures indicate Dionysos and not Hermes Chthonios as a god distinct from him. These are two names for the same divine person, whose condition points to the mysteries for which the "venerable women" performed preparatory services.

As for the queen's preparations,[112] we can merely guess that she is the distinguished woman whom the Meidias painter represented on

---

109 The boy is also allowed to swing. On this and the Aiora (the "feast of the swings"), see above, p. 156.

110 See also E. Simon, "Ein Anthesterien-Skyphos des Polygnotos," pp. 8 f.

111 Van Hoorn, fig. 5, and pp. 26 f.

112 See Buschor, "Ein choregisches Denkmal," p. 100, note 2.

a notably sumptuous chous [96]. Her heavy festive garments, lying on a swing, are being perfumed with incense. A wreathed boy representing the common people is looking on as a woman pours aromatic oil on the fire. A magnificent chair on which garments have been set out is waiting for the queen. Perhaps she will soon be led to a building that will be opened for her alone. In her fragrant dress she will enter a musty place, the Boukoleion, or "bull's stable," situated on the official estate of her husband, the *archon basileus*.[113] The name "bull's stable" is evidently a vestige of the old stratum of the Dionysian religion, to which belong the Sixteen Women of Elis and their call for the god with the "bull's foot."

We learn something about the queen's privileges and duties from a court oration of the middle third century B.C.[114] She was privileged—while executing the mystic ceremonies—to see something that no non-Athenian woman might look upon. This must have been an archaic cult statue, an *agalma*. The Gerairai, "venerable women," may have been permitted to glimpse it, but the queen alone was allowed to enter the place where it was kept. This place was the Boukoleion or perhaps its innermost room. The queen was escorted to the threshold. Was she brought there in a kind of marriage procession? This seems to follow from the painting in which the children act out such a procession [93]. A boy disguised as the bearded Dionysos is sitting under a canopy on a wagon drawn by mules, to judge by their visible hind parts. Another boy, dressed as a bride, is about to take his place beside the bridegroom, and behind the wagon the mysterious pole and crossbeam

113　The *archon basileus* lived next to the Boukoleion—see *Suidae Lexicon*, s.v. Ἄρχοντες, and Bekker, *Anecdota Graeca*, I, 449, line 20—but it was within his sphere of power, according to Aristotle, *Atheniensium Respublica* III 5, in Ross, ed., vol. X.

114　Pseudo-Demosthenes, LIX (*In Neaeram*), 73.

structure is carried. A man could represent the god in every *pompe* or procession, as on the ship in the Great Dionysia,[115] but afterwards he had to disappear, for a marriage procession to introduce the events awaiting the queen could only be a game and masquerade. The dignified persons who escorted her to the threshold were probably the fourteen Gerairai.

In order to fulfill her duties the queen had not only to be an Athenian, but also to have been a virgin at the time of her marriage to the *archon basileus*.[116] Her pure, unmarred womanhood was required for the fulfillment of her duties; for it was as her husband's wife that she was given in marriage to Dionysos and performed the ineffable sacred ceremonies connected with this event in accordance with the ancient tradition.[117] The two duties were inseparable and yet there was an important difference between them. It was permissible to speak of the queen's marriage to Dionysos, but not of the "ineffable sacred ceremonies." They were the "divine *pregma*" hinted at by the physician Aretaios, the *mysterion*. No one doubted that she could become the wife of Dionysos only through a *mysterion*. It was a *theion pregma* that joined her to the god, but here we have come to the threshold of secrecy.

Aristotle did not break this secrecy when he spoke of the marriage in the Boukoleion in well-balanced words that were understood in his time and would also have been understood in the Classical period. The words are *symmeixis* and *gamos*.[118] The second word stands for a

115 See above, ch. IV, at notes 104 ff.
116 Pseudo-Demosthenes, LIX 75.
117 Ibid., 73: ἐξεδόθη τῶι Διονύσωι γυνή. c. 75: ἵνα κατὰ τὰ πάτρια θύηται τὰ ἄρρητα ἱερὰ ὑπὲρ τῆς πόλεως. / For Aretaios, see above, note 3.
118 Aristotle, *Atheniensium Respublica* III 5: τῆς τοῦ βασιλέως γυναικὸς σύμμειξις ἐνταῦθα γίνεται τῶι Διονύσωι καὶ ὁ γάμος.

bodily union, a *consummatio matrimonii*, between the god and the queen. It would be wrong, however, to interpret the word *symmeixis* as a crude concretization of the physical union; on the contrary, it shifts the accent to the non-physical union. The copulation of animals could be termed *meixis*, "mixing," but not *symmeixis*.[119] In a model wedding oration from the first century B.C., we read that in contrast to the *meixis* of animals human marriage was *meixis* and *koinonia*, "companionship."[120] Still more plainly, it was *symmeixis* and *koinonia*. The introduction of the word *symmeixis* in place of *meixis* is a raising of the plane. *Symmeixis* and *gamos* signify a higher marriage than *gamos* alone. According to Aristotle, the wife of the *archon basileus*[121] entered into a higher marriage with Dionysos, made higher no doubt by the ineffable sacred ceremonies whereby she restored the god's wholeness and created his full *parousia*. It was her duty to do this each year.

Despite the plural form, *arrheta hiera*, "ineffable sacred ceremonies" need not refer to more than one action. The rite may have consisted of a single *pregma*, a single *mysterion*. Three analogies come to mind that make this seem possible. One is the secret awakening of Liknites, which in the trieteric order was enacted every second year on the same date as the queen's *mysterion* in the Athenian Bouko-leion. Another is the union of Isis with the reassembled Osiris, who

119 See the fundamental observations of A. Wilhelm in "Symmeixis," pp. 39–57.

120 Dionysius of Halicarnassus, *Ars rhetorica* II 3; Wilhelm, "Symmeixis," p. 49.

121 It was probably she who had borne the title βασίλιννα, "queen," from time immemorial, and it was probably because of her that the ἄρχων βασιλεύς retained the title "king." G. M. Macurdy comes to an erroneous conclusion in "Basilinna and Basilissa, the Alleged Title of the 'Queen Archon' in Athens," pp. 276–82.

was thereby reawakened. The third is the myth that explained why in a place by the bottomless Alkyonic Sea—near Lerna where Dionysos found his way to Hades and back[122]—a phallus stood on a tumulus. The description of the place is instructive enough in itself. Phalli as mortuary monuments are known to us from antiquity.[123] They are explained by the myth of the subterranean Dionysos. The local myth, however, relates not to mortuary phalli, but to the usual fig-wood phalli. Dionysos set up such a phallus out of gratitude to Prosymnos or Polymnos—both names signify the cult phallus celebrated with songs—who had shown him the way to the underworld and in return demanded that Dionysos serve him as a woman. Prosymnos died, however, before the god's return. Dionysos performed his act of subservience by sitting down on the phallus.[124]

Through these archaic analogies we can reconstruct an archaic *core*, a strange act of *zoë* that was presumably retained even in later times in the women's mysteries outside of Attica. At a time when Athens was far removed from the archaic period, the most likely hypothesis seems to be a physical contact of the queen with an archaic *agalma*, the primitive sign for the phallic quality of indestructible life. It also seems likely that in the solitude of the Boukoleion the queen engaged in a *conversazione sacra* with the divine image that had been worshiped for centuries—a highly erotic conversation, but the metaphors employed even by Christian nuns in their mystic conversations can also be highly erotic. Such a conversation took place no doubt in the plane of *symmeixis*. *Along with* it, Aristotle retained the word *gamos* to express the complete event. For all Athens knew that the

122 See Pausanias II 37 5; Arnobius, *Adversus nationes* V 28.
123 See H. Herter, "Phallos," cols. 1728–33.
124 Clement of Alexandria, *Protrepticus* II 34 5: κλάδον οὖν συκῆς, ὡς ἔτυχεν, ἐκτεμὼν ἀνδρείου μορίου σκευάζεται τρόπον ἐφέζεταί τε τῶι κλάδωι . . . .

queen was given the god to wife in the manner customary in earthly marriages—even if, paradoxically, a heavenly marriage was earthly or an earthly marriage heavenly.

Athens had prepared all day for the queen's divine marriage. The girls, and probably the women as well, did so by swinging. It does not seem humanly possible that alone in their homes they did not also expect the god. As we have seen, the attention of the men was diverted from them. The *archon basileus* was also away from home, presiding over the great festive event of the day in the Thesmothetion, the palace of the *archontes*.[125] This event was the drinking contest, the winner of which was the man who could empty a drinking cup of a certain size the most quickly; the *archon basileus* was the supreme judge, and it was he who conferred the first prize, a wineskin.[126] The drinking was done in silence, but each round was opened by a blast of the *salpinx*. The *salpinx*, as we know, was also the instrument employed to call Dionysos and introduce him at the Great Dionysia. At the end of the contest the wreaths worn by the men were carried down to the sanctuary in the swamps.[127] All this was done strictly in the service of the wine god, the *other* aspect of Dionysos, not his aspect as the god of women. The men, however, do not seem to have returned home to their wives after the officially scheduled festivities. *Askoliasmos*, jumping on wineskins, is mentioned as an additional entertainment, and Aristophanes also speaks of hetairai and dancing girls who joined the men in their drinking.[128] Would the women have languished alone at home on the feast day of their god? Might they not have received a

125 See Deubner, *Attische Feste*, p. 96.

126 See Aristophanes, *Acharnians* 1224 and the scholium on it. For the *salpinx*, see line 1001: πίνειν ὑπὸ τῆς σάλπιγγος, and see also above, in ch. IV, the text at notes 129 ff., and in ch. V, the text preceding note 34.

127 Athenaios X 437 D.

128 Aristophanes, *Acharnians* 1091, 1092; see also the scholium on 1000.

Dionysian visit in their homes or a Dionysian call from outside? Was the presence of the god not actualized outside the Boukoleion and the drinking contest?

Except for what was scheduled and supervised by the Athenian state, we have no written evidence as to what happened in the night between Choës and Chytroi, but the vase paintings relating to the period record nocturnal doings. A skyphos of high artistic quality shows, on one side, a young woman answering the "call" [97A]. Her facial expression, dress, and head covering are not those of a bacchante. With wide-open eyes she strides forth to an unknown adventure.[129] This adventure is probably similar to that of the less distinguished couple on the other side of the skyphos [97B], where both man and woman are characterized by a thyrsus—the man also by a silenus face and pointed ears—as participants in a Dionysian *thiasos*. He is leading her by the hand as a bridegroom leads his bride. The woman with the wide-open eyes is not led in this way. The man walking ahead of her is also disguised as a silenus, but he is more elegant than the man on the other side and wears hunting boots. He is carrying two torches. The woman is probably being led to a nocturnal *thiasos* in the mountains, but she is not led by the hand like a bride. She is being brought to a higher husband. The escort with the two torches is not—at least not in this painting—the one to whom she is hastening. On her own, apart from the state order, this woman is on her way to an action parallel to that of the queen in the Boukoleion.

A corresponding figure is a man on the back of the fifth-century krater [92B] showing the dithyrambic chorus; in all likelihood it relates to the same festival. The man has the beard and blunt nose of

129   The skyphos has been published by E. Simon, *Opfernde Götter*, who interprets the young woman as the queen herself on her way to the Boukoleion. There is nothing in the scene to indicate this.

a silenus, but is wrapped in his cloak as sileni never are. Two women with *thyrsoi* are abducting him, but he is offering no resistance. "Perhaps," writes the publisher of the vase, "the painter is alluding to the festivities in the streets of Athens on the night of Choës Day."[130] Here again the silenus was probably a masked Athenian. It was easy and customary to mask oneself as Dionysos. We have seen a small man, probably a youth, being dressed and enthroned as Dionysos [98],[131] but this was not even necessary: the headbands of Dionysos Mitrephoros sufficed to indicate festive worship of the god and hence self-identification with him.

A representation on an Attic chous shows a man wearing such headbands. He is probably a drunken Athenian in the role of Dionysos [99]. We see him storming through the door of a house at night. The lady of the house, bearing a little lamp, receives him with a gesture of secrecy.[132] In a mythological scene Dionysos, wearing the same headbands, is announced by a real silenus and accompanied by a boy satyr [100].[133] A heroine, the no longer young Althaia, is awaiting him in the house of her absent husband, King Oineus. In the Boukoleion no man represented the god with the queen. But the same night, the

130   Johansen, *Eine Dithyrambosaufführung*, p. 42.

131   Not recognized by N. Himmelmann-Wildschütz, *Zur Eigenart des klassischen Götterbildes*, pp. 27 f.

132   The homecoming master of the house would not approach so impetuously, nor would he be received with such an air of mystery. This is a visit of the god even if the husband represents him.

133   The main figures in this painting have been mistakenly interpreted as Dionysos and the Basilinna by L. Curtius, "Zur Aldobrandinischen Hochzeit." / The text that explains the scene is in Hyginus, *Fabulae* 129. Euripides alludes to the scene, perhaps a scene in a satyr play, in *Cyclops* 38–40:

> . . . ὅτε Βακχίωι
> κῶμοι συνασπίζοντες ᾽Αλθαίας δόμους
> προσῆιτ᾽ ἀοιδαῖς βαρβίτων σαυλούμενοι.

second night of *mundus patet*, according to the Greek reckoning the night of Chytroi ("pots for the food of the dead"), offered the possibility of Dionysian mysteries of which the written sources say nothing, but which are attested in vase paintings from many regions.

The Beginnings of Tragedy in Attica

> If we are truthful, we shall admit that we do not understand it. Philology has not yet sufficiently prepared us to attend a Greek tragedy. Perhaps no product of artistic creation is so shot through with purely historical motives. It must not be forgotten that in Athens the tragedy was a religious ceremony, enacted not so much on the boards as in the souls of the spectators. Stage and audience were enveloped in an extrapoetic atmosphere: religion. What has come down to us resembles the libretto of an opera of which we have never heard the music—the reverse of a carpet, ends of multicolored thread that come through from a surface woven by faith. Greek scholars are baffled by the faith of the Athenians; they are unable to reconstruct it. Until they have done so, Greek tragedy will be a page written in a language to which we possess no dictionary.
>
> —ORTEGA Y GASSET, *Meditaciones del Quijote*[134]

DITHYRAMB and Boukoleion connected the feast of the Anthesteria with one ancient stratum of the Dionysos religion. The dithyramb was the accompaniment for the sacrifice of a bull, and correspondingly a bull was the prize given to the leader of a victorious dithyrambic

134 José Ortega y Gasset, *Meditaciones del Quijote* (Meditación Primera: 17, La tragedia), pp. 191–92: "Si somos sinceros, declararemos que no la entende-

chorus.[135] The bull was the representative sacrificial animal offered up as the ship procession entered the city for the Great Dionysia. With this feast the Dionysian festive period in Athens, which opened with the beginning of winter, reached over into Elaphebolion, our March. Thus, it exceeded in scope not only the Dionysos cult of Delphi, which remained essentially a women's cult, but all other Dionysos cults of the same style. The Anthesteria, the oldest Athenian festival of Dionysos, preserved the old style; it was rooted in a broad stratum of Greek culture reaching back to the Mycenaean era.[136] The Great Dionysia were a creation of the Athenians themselves, in which the *mundus patet* of the Anthesteria became the occasion for an extraordinary artistic activity, a particular type of dramatic art, distinguished from another type which originated in the Lenaia and of which we shall speak in the next section.

The motivation for this first type of drama was present wherever

---

mos bien. Aún la filología no nos ha adaptado suficientemente el órgano para asistir a una tragedia griega. Acaso no haya producción más entreverada de motivos puramente históricos, transitorios. No se olvide que era en Atenas un oficio religioso. De modo que la obra se verifica más aún que sobre las planchas del teatro, dentro del ánimo de los espectadores. Envolviendo la escena y el público está una atmósfera extrapoética—la religión. Y lo que ha llegado a nosotros es como el libreto de una ópera cuya música no hemos oído nunca—el revés de un tapiz, cabos de hilos multicolores que llegan de un envés tejido por la fe. Ahora bien, los helenistas se encuentran detenidos ante la fe de los atenienses, no aciertan a reconstruirla. Mientres no lo logren, las tragedia griega será una página escrita en un idioma de que no poseemos diccionario."

135 See Pindar, *Olympia* XIII 19, where Dithyrambos is called βοηλάτης ("bull driver"). The answer to the riddle of Simonides—in Athenaios X 456 CD —to the effect that the "bull-killing servant of Dionysos" is the dithyramb, points in the same direction. Another solution to the riddle would be the double ax; see ch. IV at note 140. Simonides won the "bull and tripod" 56 times; *Anthologia Palatina* VI 213.

136 The Ionians are mentioned in Thukydides II 15 4.

the *parousia* of the subterranean Dionysos was celebrated and the dithyramb sung. Later, when Attic art had long since triumphed, people came to believe that the "tragic choruses" (*tragikoi choroi*) and the "tragic genre" (*tragikos tropos*) had also existed elsewhere.[137] The view that the Great Dionysia with their art were an appendage to the Anthesteria derives from the Athenian festive calendar, but this art soon made its appearance at the Lenaia as well. It prolonged the *mundus patet* and, insofar as it was not related to Dionysos himself, derived its justification from the festival that opened the world toward the past, toward what had been. The opening at the Anthesteria was too brief. *Zoë* wanted to leave the dead behind it. But the somber aspect of Dionysos, in which death and the destruction of life were connected with life itself, was manifested most impressively after the god was brought to Athens from Eleutherai. Apart from being a festival of souls, the Anthesteria were chiefly a festival of children and of women's mysteries. The Great Dionysia became a true festival of the men. Though plenty of wine was consumed, the men participated in other ways than by getting drunk. The drinking began early in the morning before the play.[138] Men alone wore masks and were the spirits who appeared.

The dithyrambic poet with his Dionysian theme entered into the

137 Herodotos V 67; *Suidae Lexicon* s.v. Ἀρίων. Solon gave Arion precedence over Thespis, to whom he was not well disposed. Considerations of elegiac style make it highly improbable that he should have used the word *tragodia* in the poem.

138 Philochoros, fr. 171, Jacoby, *FGrHist*, 328 (III, B, p. 148): Ἀθηναῖοι τοῖς Διονυσιακοῖς ἀγῶσι τὸ μὲν πρῶτον ἠριστηκότες καὶ πεπωκότες ἐβάδιζον ἐπὶ τὴν θέαν καὶ ἐστεφανωμένοι ἐθεώρουν, παρὰ δὲ τὸν ἀγῶνα πάντα οἶνος αὐτοῖς ᾠνοχοεῖτο. ("At the time of the Dionysian contests the Athenians went to the theater after breakfasting and drinking; during the play they wore wreaths and wine was poured for them during the entire contest.")

"opening" and, just as the bull sacrifice was not confined to a single festival or god, the poet did not confine himself to any particular season or theme. An authentic dithyramb could deal with the recollections of heroes or with Herakles' journey to Hades.[139] Aristotle's statement that tragedy "began with those who struck up the dithyramb"[140] is perfectly correct and in keeping with the history of Greek literature and religion. But the name of the new genre—*tragodia*, to which belongs the adjective *tragodikos* or more frequently *tragikos*—points to an element of the cult with which the innovation was connected: another sacrificial animal, no longer the bull. From this alone one could infer a synthesis that occurred within the framework of the Great Dionysia. The word *tragodia* may be rendered as "song on the occasion of a he-goat." A parallel to the word *tragodos*—singer of a *tragodia*[141]—has come down to us. The word *arnodos* is formed in exactly the same way and is explained by the fact that a sheep (*aren*) was the prize for the song,[142] its occasion, one might say, just as a he-goat was the occasion for a *tragodia*.

The bull is not wholly absent on the pitchers at the Choës, but it is not drawn into the children's games.[143] A bull was sacrificed when the dithyramb was sung. The he-goat is represented more frequently, not however as the sacrificial animal, but as the children's playfellow. Yet this is not the same kind of comradeship as that between child and dog, which is often shown.[144] On one pitcher we see a wreathed

139   See Bowra, *Pindari Carmina*, fr. 61.

140   *De poetica* IV 1449a: γενομένη . . . ἀπὸ τῶν ἐξαρχόντων τὸν διθύραμβον.

141   See W. Burkert, "Greek Tragedy and Sacrificial Ritual," pp. 92 f., with reference to the parallels.

142   So says Dionysios of Argos, fr. 2, in Jacoby, *FGrHist*, 308 (III, B, p. 14): τοῦ δὲ ἄθλου τοῖς νικῶσιν ἀρνὸς ἀποδεδειγμένου προσαγορευθῆναι . . . ἀρνωιδούς.

143   Van Hoorn, *Choes and Anthesteria*, fig. 296.

144   Ibid., pp. 46, 47.

boy riding on a he-goat; another boy is holding out a cluster of grapes to him [101].[145] The scene raises play to the level of myth and makes the riding boy into a little Dionysos. The same occurs in a representation of a child playing with what seems to be a fawn [102].[146] Pitchers with such scenes were originally intended to be placed in the tombs of children; they are the precursors of the children's sarcophagi with reliefs showing the Dionysian *thiasos* of dead boys. He-goat and child are Dionysian partners.

The he-goat became the sacrificial animal in the month of Elaphebolion. In the calendar frieze which was built into the Small Mitropolis in Athens and has been preserved, the month is symbolized by a bigger-than-life size woman and by a small he-goat that is being led away to sacrifice [103]. A bearded man is drawing the kid along with him. The sacrifice the artist had in mind will take place out in the country: consequently the man is wearing the costume worn by peasants in the New Comedy.[147] Concerning what must have taken place in the city in the sacred precinct of Dionysos Eleuthereus, a sacrifice of black goats to the god with the epithet "Melanaigis," we possess no representation or even so much as a hint. It is, however, highly probable that this sacrifice was performed on the sacrificial table, known as *thymele*, situated in the sacred precinct of the theater.[148] The table was also called *eleós*, a word which its accent distinguished only seemingly from *éleos*, "pity," and which played an important role in the early phase of the *tragodia*.[149] We must assume

145 See also ibid., fig. 306.   146 Ibid., p. 46.

147 See Deubner, *Attische Feste*, p. 252.

148 See *Etymologicum Magnum* s.v. Θυμέλη; and Pickard-Cambridge, *The Theatre of Dionysus in Athens*, in the index s.v. Altar in Orchestra.

149 See Pollux IV 123: ἐλεὸς ἦν τράπεζα ἀρχαία, ἐφ' ἣν πρὸ Θέσπιδος εἷς τις ἀναβὰς τοῖς χορευταῖς ἀπεκρίνατο. Hesiod, *Works and Days* 205: ἣ δ' ἐλεόν ("lui, pitoyable-

that the sacrificial rite was not public, but was performed before the dramatic play, presumably at night after the statue of Eleuthereus was brought from the Akademeia. It was not connected with the bull sacrifice of the epheboi and seems rather to have been a mystic sacrifice performed not by Dionysian women but by priests of Dionysos.[150] Only in the case of Thespis is a he-goat named as the victor's prize in the dramatic contest.[151] Later on the prize was a tripod, a highly solemn object with an important role in the mystic ceremony at Delphi.

The significance of a goat sacrifice in the country and in this month is known to us. In March the vines are still bare leafless stalks. They will now be given to drink the blood of their enemy the he-goat, a Dionysian relative almost consubstantial with them. The anticipated punishment will strike a sinner who knows nothing of his sin, who indeed has not yet committed it. In a prescribed ceremony he becomes the victim of the cruel game that life plays with its creatures, so sharing in the fate that will come to be known as "tragic"—from *tragos*, the he-goat. This ambivalence—the intentional killing of the animal accompanied by compassion for it—would not in itself have given rise to an art form, any more than did the bull sacrifice, at which the women cried out with terror and pity.[152] *Tragodia*, the art form "on the occasion of a he-goat," had two other constitutive ele-

---

ment"—Mazon). See also Kerényi, "Geburt und Wiedergeburt der Tragödie," pp. 46 and 58.

150 The hypothesis that a he-goat was sacrificed at the *thymele* is also put forward by Burkert, "Greek Tragedy and Sacrificial Ritual," pp. 101 f.

151 *Marmor Parium* 43. / On the sacrificial rite alluded to as "that with the tripod," see above, ch. V, at notes 109 ff.

152 See Kerényi, *The Religion of the Greeks and Romans*, p. 181.

ments: a myth and an attempt to explain it. The myth was that the killing of the animal at the god's behest gave the god pleasure and that he himself suffered this death. The other element was a rationalization of the simple sacrificial rite, according to which the goat sacrifice was punishment for the goat's sin. But this attempt at an explanation involved a difficulty. How can one account for the punishment of a being that knew nothing of its sin? The only possibility was to take an anthropomorphic view of the sinner, and this seems to have been easier in the case of the he-goat, with whom the shepherds lived on terms verging on friendship, than in the case of the bull, which was more a theomorphic animal of the primordial period. Thus, the foundations of tragedy—both its name and its inner form—were laid in the country and not in the city where the bull sacrifice predominated. The Dionysian hero, who was at the same time the god's persecutor—Dionysos and Anti-Dionysos in one—made his appearance in the literary phase. It had been preceded by a phase of improvisation.

Aristotle's point of view in his *Poetics* was literary. He contented himself with saying that tragedy began with the improvisation of dithyrambs, but in this he is very explicit: *ap' arches autoschediastike.*[153] The dithyrambs were improvised songs in celebration of Dionysos, who was now recognized not as the mover of children, women, and drunkards, but as the lord of all who participate in *zoë*. Unlike the choral or solo songs of the Anthesteria, the dithyrambs, if tragedy was to be born of them, must have at least included dances and elements of mimicry. Singing and dancing choruses had been current since the rural Dionysia which gave, not to the jokes, of which we shall speak in the next section, but to the improvisations and choruses of the dithy-

153   *De poetica* IV 1449a 9.

rambic poets, an impetus that was not forgotten. An incursion of countryfolk from Ikarion would seem probable even if it had not been recorded in the tradition. A community of winegrowers and shepherds offers the sociological foundation of what I have called the inner form of tragedy. Despite the unchanging dialectic of the myth of *zoë*, the mystic sacrifice of a kid—of a young he-goat as a representative of Dionysos—lacked the social motif: the idea of punishment. This was what made the sacrificial ceremony stageworthy, whereas the sacrifice itself, without this idea of punishing a sinner, provided the general foundation for the drama.

Virgil, who was thoroughly familiar with the centuries-old realities of a winegrowing country, lends support to this derivation of the literary *tragodia* of the Athenians from the improvised *tragodia* of the Ikarians. No mean witness![154] As we have seen, the necessary religious conditions were present in Ikarion. We have spoken of two cult images in the temple. Toward the end of the sixth and at the beginning of the fifth century, these were replaced by works in marble, a sign of the temple's increasing importance. The mask was replaced after the victory of Thespis with his tragic chorus at the Great Dionysia in Athens

---

154 In *Georgics* II 380 ff., Virgil speaks of the damage done to the vineyards by the herds:

> *non aliam ob culpam Baccho caper omnibus aris*
> *caeditur et veteres ineunt proscaenia ludi,*
> *praemiaque ingeniis pagos et compita circum*
> *Thesidae posuere, atque inter pocula laeti*
> *mollibus in pratis unctos saluere per utres.*

("For no other crime is it that a goat is slain to Bacchus at every altar, and the olden plays enter on the stage; for this the sons of Theseus set up prizes for wit in their villages and at the crossings, and gayly danced in the soft meadows on oiled goat skins.")

(536–532 B.C.).[155] The enthroned Dionysos, the god who arrived in Athens in this seated form, was the lord of all living creatures. According to the trieteric order the two statues stood for festivals of two kinds: one centering on the apparent slaying and mutilation of the god and the real slaying of his representative, the kid; the other expressing joy at the happy end of the somber action that had been performed a year before. When the *trieteris* was replaced by the one-year period—a process probably completed in the sixth century[156]—the sad and joyful elements were combined in a complex game. The Ikarians had a tragic myth, that of Ikarios and his daughter Erigone. It was not tragic enough for the purposes of the *tragodia* that was emerging in this century. Ikarios was given wine by Dionysos; it was he who brought the unknown drink to his compatriots and was killed by the intoxicated shepherds—as the god's representative no doubt, but not as a sinner against him.

It was in Ikarion, so we learn from the *Erigone* of Eratosthenes, that people "first danced around a he-goat."[157] Eratosthenes, to be sure, was an Alexandrian, but his line presupposes an established tradition and its authority is not open to doubt. At the most we hesitate between two possible meanings, but they do not conflict. *Peri tragon* ("around" or "for a he-goat") could mean that the he-goat was the prize of victory, but also that the game in which victory was possible was a dance around the he-goat. As a sinner against Dionysos, the goat had to die after having been his representative. At the end the tri-

155 *Marmor Parium* 43. On the two cult images in Ikarion, see above, ch. VI, at notes 31, 32.

156 In an epigram of Dioskorides (*Anthologia Palatina* VII 413 3) τριέτη was conjectured. More likely is τρυγικόν.

157 Ἰκαριοῖ, τόθι πρῶτα περὶ τράγον ὠρχήσαντο. This is the correct reading, as in Powell, *Collectanea Alexandrina*, p. 64.

umph over the sinner was enacted in a special way: this was the significance of the *askoliasmos*, a game also played in Athens at the Anthesteria.[158] After the animal was sacrificed this other Dionysian use was often made of its skin. A wineskin was made of it. Before it was filled with wine, it was blown up and men jumped on it. It was even made slippery with oil. The contestant who could keep his place on it the longest was the winner. In this way the enemy was trampled amid general laughter: a gay conclusion to the sacrifice of the he-goat.

Nietzsche believed that in line with an unassailable tradition the oldest forms of Greek tragedy dealt exclusively with the sufferings of Dionysos and that for a long time the sole hero of tragedy was Dionysos.[159] This is false, for there was no such direct tradition. Such a view is also a misunderstanding of the tragic form which implied the fundamentally contradictory character of *zoë*, the basis of its dialectic. The oldest stage hero was an enemy of Dionysos. In order that the god himself might be embodied in his enemy as in a representative sacrificial animal, his representative had *to die* and before dying try *to kill* the god himself. For this he had to atone. The *tragodia* of the Ikarians went still further. The jumping on the skin of the enemy—not of the one slain enemy but of any representative of the enemy species—constituted a happy ending. In Athens, by way of fulfilling the same function, Pratinas of Phleious, a Dionysian tragic poet of the first generation after Thespis, introduced the satyr play[160] from Doric territory: after

158 Hyginus, *Astronomica* II 4. The excerpt combines the two parts of the game—the dance around the he-goat and the *askoliasmos*—but they are easily distinguished. The Eratosthenes quotation given above in note 157 pertains to the first part. On the *askoliasmos*, see also above, ch. VI, at note 128.

159 In §10 of *The Birth of Tragedy* (in *Basic Writings*, pp. 73–74), Nietzsche draws this inference from the proverb *Ouden pros ton Dionyson*. See further pp. 329–30, below.

160 *Suidae Lexicon* s.v. Πρατίνας. See also Athenaios XIV 617, where the

the tragedies a ridiculous piece was played. It seems most unlikely that such an element was lacking in the improvisations that preceded tragedy, but for a long time there were probably no rules governing its use. Choruses of satyrs could exist without being used in a dramatic context, and certain vase paintings show that they played a minor role in the Anthesteria.[161] Such choruses did not represent the enemies of Dionysos. On the contrary, there is good reason to assume that "Dionysian brotherhoods" existed in Athens and elsewhere in Attica.[162] These were groups of men who, half-disguised as animals, played the roles of the god's mythical companions, the bearers of his phallic quality. In Attica the elements of their disguise were taken not from the he-goat but from the stallion.

The one piece of information we possess about the nature of a dramatic play at the Great Dionysia before the appearance of Thespis suggests that such beings played an important role. Before Thespis someone climbed on the table, the *eleós*, on which the sacrificial animal was dismembered, and responded to a chorus.[163] A dialogue developed. Was it the supporters of the god who questioned the performer of the sacrifice, in this capacity a seeming enemy of Dionysos? This appears to be the most likely interpretation because in this early phase the sacrificial animal was not yet represented as the enemy. With the killing of the enemy, the play became serious. Aristotle regarded the development of tragedy from the early improvisations as a "growing serious." It began, so he tells us, with a *satyrikon* based on lesser myths

---

song and dance with which the new chorus of satyrs burst into the Athenian theater are mentioned.

161 See [87A / 87B]. Macrobius speaks of certain male groups which still existed in late antiquity; see above, ch. V, note 154.

162 See H. Herter, "Vom dionysischen Tanz zum komischen Spiel," p. 16.

163 Pollux IV 123; see also note 149, above.

(*mikroi mythoi*).[164] The myth in which a mythical enemy of the god appeared was a great myth.

Thespis is not mentioned in the *Poetics*, but in a lost work Aristotle assigned him first place in the development of the tragedy.[165] For the Athenians Thespis was an "Athenaios," so designated in a monument; in the history of literature he was an Ikarian.[166] We are free to regard him either as the earliest known Dionysian artist, actor, and stage director, who learned from the Ikarians and brought their dramatic accomplishments to the city, or as an Ikarian who enriched the Great Dionysia with the art of his native place and replaced the flights of the dithyrambic poets with very earthly dramatic action. The date assigned to his first victory—roughly a quarter of a century after Onomakritos had completed his very different work—is a significant date in the cultural history of Athens. In the Athenian democracy the Dionysian religion was to take not an Orphic form but a poetic and artistic one. The name Thespis cannot serve as a title for any chapter dealing exclusively with the history of religion.

Concerning Thespis there were innumerable ancient traditions rich in concrete detail. A historian can dismiss none of them. The ancients knew of the "cart of Thespis," on which he carried the properties for his plays, and they told an anecdote about the effect of a play on the aged Solon. The old man reproached Thespis for what we should call the core of the dramatic art, its *hypokrisis*, then still signifying the power of evocation, which the productions of the dithyrambic choruses

164 *De poetica* IV 1449a: ἐκ μικρῶν μύθων καὶ λέξεως γελοίας διὰ τὸ ἐκ σατυρικοῦ μεταβαλεῖν ὀψὲ ἀπεσεμνύνθη.

165 See Themistios, *Orationes* XXVI 316 D; A. Lesky, *Die tragische Dichtung der Hellenen*, pp. 40 f.

166 On the designation of Thespis as an Athenian, see Lesky, p. 39; as an Ikarian, *Suidae Lexicon* s.v. Θέσπις.

did not possess.[167] For Solon this amounted to a monstrous lie,[168] perhaps among other reasons because it brought the dead forth from the underworld. There was also a tradition concerning the experiments of Thespis with the masking of his actors.[169] At the Lenaia, lees of the wine were still available, an excellent substance for painting faces. Thespis also made use of white chalk, well suited to the spirits of the dead, and in the end used canvas masks which perhaps made the heroes look more dignified. For their wreaths he used fronds of a not un-Dionysian plant, *andrachne*, the wild strawberry tree, which in Greece is also called *komaros* and whose fruits are used for fortifying wine.[170] According to a Boeotian tradition Hermes, who as the guide of souls tacitly participated in this evocation of heroes, grew up under such a tree.[171]

Like the dithyrambic poets, Thespis entered into the Dionysian "opening" of the world. His *tragodia* was still a drama with one actor, a masked person who took the place of the animal enemy. It does not seem too venturesome to speak of this as the "primordial tragedy." There was, one might say, a point of intersection between the religion of Dionysos and the worship of heroes. An awareness of this is expressed by the "hero Dionysos," who was "called" by the women of Elis and who on Spartan tombstones is represented as an enthroned god, holding the kantharos[172] and closely resembling the seated cult

167   Horace, *Epistolae* II 3 275–77; Plutarch, *Solon* XXIX. See also Kerényi, "Geburt und Wiedergeburt der Tragödie," pp. 42 ff.

168   τηλικαῦτα ψευδόμενος.

169   See *Suidae Lexicon* s.v. Θέσπις.

170   According to my own inquiry this is done in Greece, especially on Andros.

171   Pausanias IX 22 2.

172   See Tod and Wace, *A Catalogue of the Sparta Museum*, p. 102, and figs. 1–3, 10; also Kerényi, *The Heroes of the Greeks*, pp. 16 f.

statue at Ikarion. This awareness lived in Thespis and was reflected in Aischylos when he derived the costumes for his heroes from the magnificent dress of Dionysos, so that—to quote the archaeologist who made this observation after thorough study—they corresponded in all significant details "to the Athenian conception of the god."[173]

At the time of Aristophanes, at the end of the fifth and beginning of the fourth century, there were still old men who at night, drunk and inspired by the playing of a flute, danced out the plays in which Thespis had appeared before the Athenians.[174] In Horace's day the plays were still available along with those of Aischylos and Sophokles.[175] Four quotations and the titles of four plays have come down to us; one of the quotations is from the *Pentheus*.[176] Meager as they are and perhaps falsified in the light of a general idea, these fragments provide an over-all picture which no forger could have invented and which agrees with what has been said here about the poet and his relation to the Dionysian religion. Of the four dramas, the *Athla Peliou* or *Phorbas* dealt with an otherwise unknown incident that occurred at the funeral games of the Thessalian king Pelias. The subject is the destiny of a hero, Phorbas, an arrogant boxer and enemy of Apollo, who was struck down by the god. This much can be inferred from other mentions of Phorbas. We have no quotation from *Hiereis* (*The Priests*), but something from *Eitheoi* (*The Youths*), and more from the *Pentheus*. It would have been surprising if there had been no tradition

---

173 M. Bieber, "Die Herkunft des tragischen Kostüms," pp. 15–48; the phrase cited is at the end.

174 Aristophanes, *Wasps* 1476–78.

175 See Horace, *Epistolae* II 1 161–63.

176 *Suidae Lexicon* s.v. Θέσπις; Nauck, *TGF*, pp. 832 f. / On the hero Phorbas, mentioned below, see the scholium on Iliad XXIII 660.

concerning a *Pentheus* of Thespis, or if such a tragedy had not at least been attributed to him.

Not Dionysos pure and simple, as Nietzsche believed, but Pentheus was the subject and hero of the primordial tragedy. The suffering Dionysos was at one time called "Pentheus," the "man of suffering." As a hero, only an enemy and victim of the god could bear this name. This Pentheus was in the Theban myth. He was hunted like a hare and the Dionysian women—among them his own mother—tore him to pieces as if he had been a lion. The primordial tragic theme was treated in this way in the *Bacchae* of Euripides, which by chance was the last work of the last of the great Greek tragic poets. Before him Aischylos had twice taken up the theme: once in his *Pentheus* and once in his tetralogy, the *Lykourgeia*,[177] in which not only the Thracian king Lykourgos, another enemy of Dionysos, but also Orpheus, a seeming enemy of the god, is punished. In the second play of the tetralogy, *Neaniskoi (The Youths)*, he is torn to pieces by the Thracian maenads.[178] Thespis, in his *Eitheoi*, may have dealt for the first time with the same material, or perhaps it was merely thought appropriate to the traditional image of Thespis to attribute an *Orpheus* to him in addition to his *Pentheus*.

Tragedy presupposed an awareness of the intersection of the Dionysian and heroic spheres, based on the myth of the subterranean Dionysos. Such an awareness was lost when a judgment of the Athenians, which had become proverbial, was no longer understood. When a tragedy displeased the Athenians, they said: *Ouden pros ton Dionyson* —"It has nothing to do with Dionysos." If this judgment had originally

177   Mette, *Die Fragmente*, pp. 25–34, 137.
178   See Kerényi, Preface to *Orpheus und Eurydike*, pp. 12 f.

referred to the subject matter, very few tragedies would have had anything to do with Dionysos. It was not a thematic judgment but a judgment on the superficiality of a play, its irrelevancy to the god in whose sacred precinct it was performed. The perception of the immanent relationship demonstrated by the possibility of such an immaterial judgment was not something that could be handed on to all those who acquired Athenian culture. Plutarch was one of those who could no longer learn it. In Phrynichos and Aischylos, we read in Plutarch, tragedy had already digressed into *mythoi* and *pathe*, "stories" and "passions," both of course un-Dionysian.[179] Chamaileon, a pupil of Aristotle, seems to have accused even Thespis of digression into fields unrelated to Dionysos. In this view only the satyr plays would still have been worthy of Dionysos.

The Birth and Transformation of Comedy in Athens

> Think of something compared to which Mozart's music for *Figaro* or a bacchanalian scene from the brush of Rubens seems awkward. Think of a dance, a real dance, devised after a delightfully clever plan—in which all that in your language is called theater ceases to be anything other than the motifs and figures of a dance; the whole world put into masks and dancing with the most exuberant, unrestrained gestures—the whole burden of life transformed not into dark-glittering dreams as in Shakespeare but into whirling movement; even the most insolent insolence ennobled by

179 Plutarch, *Quaestiones conviviales* 615 A. / For Chamaileon, see *Suidae Lexicon* s.v. Οὐδὲν πρὸς τὸν Διόνυσον.

a nameless rhythm. Think of all this and on it shimmering
the dew of early times, the wind of the Greek sea blowing
through it, the breath of saffron and crocus and the pollen
of the bees of Hymettos. All this mortal, but born from
what a world! Think of that world, the bloody lances of the
Peloponnesian War, Socrates' cup of poison, the informers
lurking in the darkness, the Council of Ten Thousand, the
hetairai of Alkibiades, as colorful and winged as birds, and
over it all the golden shield of Athene. Think of this all-in-
all: in the whirl of this world this comedy dancing like a
top lashed by wild children.

—HUGO VON HOFMANNSTHAL, Prologue to
Aristophanes' *Lysistrata*[180]

THE OPINION expressed by Ortega y Gasset in 1914 to the effect that
we were inadequately equipped for an understanding of Greek tragedy
was valid so long as the great presence of the subterranean Dionysos,
the reverse side of life itself, was not discerned in the background of
tragedy. Up to now this has been largely the case. For this posterity
cannot be blamed. Even contemporaries, their perceptions deadened
by the baffling involvements of earthly affairs, which beginning with
Euripides became the exclusive concern of tragedy, began to forget
the archaic god. The way in which the Athenian people received and
assimilated tragedy and its immanent connection with the dark god
is the greatest miracle in all cultural history. The magnitude of the
miracle can be measured by the richness and complexity of the language of the plays, especially the choruses, which the audience was
expected to follow (and as a rule did follow) through all their subtleties.
This assimilation of the drama also meant the greatest deepening of

180   Hugo von Hofmannsthal, "Prolog geschrieben für die erste Aufführung
der *Lysistrata* des Aristophanes im deutschen Theater," p. 78.

religion—though not in the sense of the Christian or any other spiritu-
alist-mystic religion—ever achieved by any people. This *deepening* was
balanced by the *broadening* that distinguished the dramatic counterpart of tragedy: to the Dionysian systole, or concentration, of tragedy
corresponded the Dionysian diastole, or expansion, of comedy.

Aristotle says in his *Poetics*: "Though the successive changes in
Tragedy and their authors are not unknown, we cannot say the same
of Comedy; its early stages passed unnoticed, because it was not as
yet taken up in a serious way. It was only at a late point in its progress
that a chorus of comedians was officially granted by the archon; they
used to be mere volunteers. It had also already certain definite forms
at the time when the record of those termed comic poets begins. Who
it was who supplied it with masks, or prologues, or a plurality of
actors and the like, has remained unknown. The invented Fable, or
Plot, however, originated in Sicily, with Epicharmos and Phormis;
of Athenian poets Krates was the first to drop the Comedy of invective
[mockery] and frame stories of a general and non-personal nature, in
other words, Fables or Plots."[181] The archon to whom Aristotle refers
was the *archon basileus*, the highest religious official of the state. The
fact that he presided over performances of comedies is sufficient proof
that not only systole but diastole as well was a sacred affair. Earlier
in the *Poetics*[182] Aristotle points out that, just as tragedy stemmed from
the improvisations of the dithyrambic poets, so comedy originated in
phallic dances and songs. Here he makes it clear that before undergoing the influence of the mimetic farces of the Dorians of Sicily,
comedy was without dramatic action. The introduction of masks was
a crucial event in the history of the Attic comedy.

181   Aristotle, *De poetica* V 1449a 37–b 9, in Ross, ed., vol. XI.
182   Ibid., IV 1449a 11–13.

Here again, as in tragedy, language serves as a guide. The word "tragedy" is a lasting reminder of a strict and somber Dionysian rite. *Tragodia* meant "song on the occasion of a he-goat," the sacrificial animal condemned to death both as the god's representative and as his enemy. The word "comedy" embodies a similar memory. It points to *komos*. *Komodia* is a "song on the occasion of a *komos*." Since time immemorial, *komos* or *komazein* had referred to the swarming bands of men who went about honoring the wine god with dancing and singing, but following no strict, let alone somber, rite.[183] In these non-dramatic rejoicings, Dionysos was no less present than in the dithyramb, though in a different way: not in dithyrambic tension, but free and unrestrained, a true diastole.

This diastole requires special attention, for it is a specific Dionysian state rooted in the myth of the god as it affected men. It is a male intoxication. This intoxication there is good reason to distinguish from mere drunkenness, for in this state men executed intricate dances with a light step and spoke difficult lines full of ingenious wit. The salient characteristic of this intoxication was the falling away of inhibitions, including those of the mind. Laughter swept away the last barriers. The atmosphere of comedy can be said to have originated in the *ecstasy of the komos*.

The intoxication of the men in the *komos* developed into a unique artistic game, exemplified by the works of Aristophanes, full of Dionysos but also full of *phoberai Charites*, "terrible Graces."[184] Aristotle also noted that comedy abandoned its character of mockery only when the singers and dancers formed a chorus that appeared on the stage.

183 This follows from the texts cited in Pickard-Cambridge, *Dramatic Festivals*, p. 102.

184 *Anthologia Graeca* IX 186 3–4 (Paton, ed., III, 96).

Actually, comedy never renounced this character entirely, but only attenuated it. An ancient explanation connected this mockery with *kome*, "village," by a false etymology of the word *komodia*. But this explanation also takes account of the older manner of masking the members of the chorus, a masking without masks. Supposedly the *komos* consisted originally of poor peasants who entered the city at night, went to the houses of rich people from whom they had suffered injustice, and avenged themselves with songs of mockery. In thus playing the part of avenging spirits, they supposedly were obliged to smear their faces to avoid being recognized in the theater where they were allowed to make their public appearances.[185] The expression of private vengeance was turned into a harmless and indeed educational institution. Even this explanation which was adjusted to pedagogical designs cannot conceal an archaic world in which "openings" for spirits were still possible. The "spirits" were smeared with lees of wine, in Greek *tryx* or *trygia*. Writers of comedies jokingly called their genre *trygodia*,[186] "song on the occasion of lees," thus associating it with *tragodia*. From the first this parodistic association with the other, strict and somber, Dionysian genre played a role in the genesis of comedy. Comedy was both younger and older than tragedy, older in its formless beginnings, younger as a set form. And it occupied an earlier position in the calendar.

None of the elements of the ecstasy of the *komos* thus far mentioned could be said to "have nothing to do with Dionysos": neither the aggressive unrestraint—of men who had made themselves unrecognizable—nor the occasion for such disguise. The great moment for smearing oneself with lees was the festival that was always most

185 See the scholia on Dionysios Thrax 18, lines 27–31.
186 Aristophanes, *Acharnians* 499–500.

closely bound up with comedy, the Lenaia. Comedy and contest—an *agon* presided over by the *archon basileus*—were included in the festive order of the Lenaia, although comic contests were not excluded from the Great Dionysia any more than tragedy was from the Lenaia.

New comedies were an essential feature of the Lenaia. Each year comedies that had never been seen or heard were performed, just as at the sacrifices—the comparison is relevant[187]—new, flawless young animals had to be offered up to the gods. In the golden age of comedy (for the Old Comedy, up to roughly 400 B.C.; for the so-called "New Comedy," after 320 B.C.), it was very rare for a play to be performed more than once. Thus, the comedy preserved its character of festive surprise. This was especially true at the Lenaia, since at the Great Dionysia the emphasis was on the works of the tragic poets. At the Lenaia the sufferings of the hard winter days, the days which, as Hesiod said, "flay the oxen,"[188] were forgotten amid pleasures and customary amusements that were not always regulated by strict ceremony. Such customary amusements contributed to the fullness and greatness of Athenian life: the *komos* was one of them.

In the country the *komoi* went about from the beginning of winter on, throughout the Dionysian period of the year. Every occasion for a *komos* was seized upon, both the *phallophoria* and the dressing of the men as women.[189] The peasants celebrated the rural Dionysia in December; these were their Lenaia.[190] The peasants did not perform

---

187 See O. Weinreich, *Einleitung*, p. xxxi.

188 *Works and Days* 504.

189 The doubts as to whether *komoi* were permitted at the Lenaia (Pickard-Cambridge, *Dramatic Festivals*, p. 36) are unfounded. See also Deubner, *Attische Feste*, p. 133.

190 On the rural Dionysia, see above, ch. IV; and Pickard-Cambridge, *Dithyramb*, pp. 144 ff.

comedies, but there were contests between the *komoi* of the different villages,[191] and on all these festive occasions new wine was drawn. In Athens this was done officially and with the solemnity of an important rite in the Lenaion. The Gerairai drew new wine from large jars before the idol with the mask. They drew it carefully, with ladles, in order that the lees should remain behind when the wine was transferred to another vessel: first drink, then theatrical makeup.[192]

Lees for the concealment of faces were provided ritually in the temple and in all the wine presses of the countryside as the self-evident gift of the god who was born. While the childbirth proceeded in the sanctuary, the people outside—who called out from time to time for the Divine Child[193]—were entertained with dramatic contests, or in earlier times with a contest of undramatic *komoi*. Even at performances of comedy it remained customary for the poet's servants to throw nuts among the spectators.[194] Aristophanes, however, thought it unworthy of himself to heighten their pleasure in this way. His plays were themselves gifts for the day of Dionysos' birth, and that was true of all comedies. Comedy was born with Dionysos in the increasing light, an occasion for, and product of, the greatest masculine unrestraint.

The phallic element was only at the root of this unrestraint. A scene in the *Acharnians*, an early play by Aristophanes, shows that a phallic procession in itself implied no particular unrestraint. The higher unrestraint of the Old Comedy, which developed from that of

191   Deubner, *Attische Feste*, pp. 136 f.
192   See Kerényi, "Parva realia," pp. 9 ff.
193   Scholium on Aristophanes, *Frogs* 497: καλεῖτε θεόν, καὶ οἱ ὑπακούοντες βοῶσι.
194   Aristophanes, *Wasps* 58–59 with the scholium.

the *komos*, went far beyond the merely phallic. The unrestraint sprang from a thought winged by desire and breaking through all barriers. How would it be—this is the sublime thought of the *Acharnians*—if in the midst of the hopeless and horrible Peloponnesian War a highly respectable citizen of Athens, a just state, should decide to make his own peace with the Spartans and actually succeed?

The citizen is Dikaiopolis, the play's protagonist. His eloquent name signifies his natural appurtenance to a just state. At the very start of the comedy, he succeeds in making his private peace. We look on as with his household he prepares for the first peaceful cult rite on his country estate. He cries out *"Euphemeite, euphemeite,"* the injunction to avoid any word that does not pertain to the festival. He is accompanied by his daughter as *kanephoros*, bearer of the sacrificial basket, by his wife, and by several slaves, one of whom is named Xanthias.

DIKAIOPOLIS: Let the basket-bearer come forward, and thou, Xanthias, hold the phallus well upright. Daughter, set down the basket and let us begin the sacrifice.

DAUGHTER: Mother, hand me the ladle, that I may spread the sauce on the cake.

DIKAIOPOLIS: It is well! Oh, mighty [Dionysos], it is with joy that, freed from military duty, I and all mine perform this solemn rite and offer thee this sacrifice; grant that I may keep the rural Dionysia without hindrance and that this truce of thirty years may be propitious for me.[195]

195 Aristophanes, *Acharnians* 241–67; English translation in Oates and O'Neill, eds., *The Complete Greek Drama*, II, 438.

He had concluded a thirty-year peace: a utopia, product of wishful exaltation, that had not yet found its name. Here we have in germ the squaring of the circle that will be made explicit in the *Birds*.[196] Dikaiopolis, as the *Acharnians* continues, now celebrates the feast of Dionysos in the country, the Lesser Dionysia, but at a time when Athenians were forbidden to visit their country estates. The festival of the peasants preceded the city Lenaia at which this play was performed, but in the comedy itself the calendar is of no importance. Time is suspended. At the end Dikaiopolis will celebrate the drinking contest of Choës Day, which would not take place in the city until the following month. Now he turns again to his daughter.

> DIKAIOPOLIS: Come, my child, carry the basket gracefully and with a grave, demure face. Happy he who shall be your possessor and embrace you so firmly at dawn, that you fart like a weasel. Go forward, and have a care they don't snatch your jewels in the crowd.

The dividing line between the area of illusion, Dikaiopolis' country estate where the procession takes place in time of peace, and the real scene in the theater, where anything can happen in the crowd, is broken by this reference to the possibility of a thief's robbing one of the characters during the performance. Dikaiopolis now gives his orders to one of the two slaves playing the role of *phallophoros*, bearer of the wooden implement. The implement is regarded as a person and addressed by the name of Phales.

> DIKAIOPOLIS: Xanthias, walk behind the basket-bearer and hold the

---

196 *Birds* 1005: ὁ κύκλος γένηταί σοι τετράγωνος. See also Kerényi, "Ursinn und Sinnwandel des Utopischen," pp. 11 ff.

phallus well erect; I will follow, singing the Phallic hymn; thou, wife, look on from the top of the terrace. Forward! *(He sings:)*

Oh, Phales, companion of the orgies of Bacchus, night reveller [merry companion in the *komos*], god of adultery and of pederasty, these past six years I have not been able to invoke thee. With what joy I return to my farmstead. . . .[197]

The atmosphere is one of phallic intimacy, not confined to the song in which Dikaiopolis addresses the tangible symbol, but embracing the whole audience. This was the foundation of Attic comedy—its specific element, to which the audience opened itself—but not its only characteristic. The setting aside of all barriers and inhibitions in the ecstasy of the *komos* and still more in the higher unrestraint of the Old Comedy goes far beyond the phallic liberties of a Dikaiopolis. *Komos* and comedy were phallic in spirit even without the display of the impudent cult implement. It is characteristic of Attic comedy that a scene such as that cited above involved no break in style. To be sure, leather phalli tied on by the actors were among its original accessories, but they became mere vestiges of its beginnings and were only *sometimes* used.[198] All this and much more was made possible by the *universality of comic unrestraint*. By "comic" we should understand not what modern aesthetics has abstracted from comedy, but what was essential to Attic comedy as a whole. This common element left room for every development and intensification characteristic of comedy as opposed to *komos*.

The original restriction to the male sex was already breached in the *komos*. A *komos* was a "chorus of men." But the question cannot

197   *Acharnians*, 267–70; in Oates and O'Neill, loc. cit.
198   See Pickard-Cambridge, *Dramatic Festivals*, pp. 220 ff.

be dismissed: Did the *komoi* in Attica not replace earlier choruses of women, the *lenai*, in this month? It is certain that they did not do so through the appearance of men in feminine roles, as was customary in crude farces known to us elsewhere in Greece, especially among the Dorians.[199] The imitation of women by design should probably be distinguished from that freedom from inhibition which enabled the men, in the ecstasy of *their komos*, to assimilate themselves in an otherwise forbidden manner to *Dionysian* women. Here the exclusivity of the processions and throngs of women was breached.[200] The same freedom from inhibition enabled women in the roles of men to share in the masculine pleasure of the *komos*.[201] This seems to be the most plausible explanation of paintings on Attic vases, not only of the Archaic period [104], but also of the Classical period [105], showing male choruses in women's dress. They were *komoi* and nothing else.[202]

This freedom from inhibition had far-reaching consequences for comedy. The choruses of the comedies were male choruses. Women appeared on the comic stage only as mute persons displaying their physical beauty. In the *Thesmophoriazusae* of Aristophanes, the chorus of women consisted of men. In the *Lysistrata*, half the chorus was made up of men in women's dress; the other half, of men as men. Quite strange—"comic" in the strictest sense of the word—is the situa-

199   See Pickard-Cambridge, *Dithyramb*, p. 165.

200   The participants in a *komos* could also insist on such exclusivity; see Lucian, *Calumniae* XVI. For vase paintings from the Archaic period, see Pickard-Cambridge, *Dithyramb*, pl. VIA/B.

201   This has been attested by Philostratos, *Imagines* I 2 (in Kayser, ed., I, 298); Aristides, *Rhetorica* XLI 9.

202   See Nilsson, "A Krater in the Cleveland Museum of Art with Men in Women's Attire," p. 84: "This is sufficient for the explanation of our vases; they represent a *komos*." The question (also raised by Beazley, *Attic Vase Paintings in Boston*, II, 55 f.) as to whether this was done publicly or at private banquets is irrelevant to a psychological judgment of the matter.

tion in the *Ecclesiazusae,* or *Assembly of Women.* Here the men play the roles of women disguised as men: a double masking and costuming that goes still further than the *Thesmophoriazusae,* in which Euripides and his companion disguise themselves as women in order to mingle with women who are themselves men disguised. In the Old Comedy, illusion was at all times counterbalanced by the crassest reality which could break through at any moment. Thus, the world of the Old Comedy was a world without limits.

In comedy the world of men was not even distinct from that of animals. Here we perceive most clearly the universality of what we have called comic unrestraint, and here again comedy probably inherited from *komos.* Some seventy years before the performance of Aristophanes' *Birds,* at a time when there were as yet no officially contesting comic choruses, vase paintings represented persons disguised as birds.[203] In this Dionysian area of suspended boundaries, where the world was not the limited world of men but a *world of life shot through with spirit,* Aristophanes was at his greatest. As one of his precursors, he mentions the little-known poet Magnes of Ikarion, whence also came Sousarion, the first known author of comedies. But it was Magnes

> *Who first won the trophies of victory for the choruses he*
>> *led in contest,*
> *For he offered you sounds of every kind, such as harps and*
>> *whirring plumage,*
> *The song of Lydians, the buzzing of gnats and the croaking*
>> *of tree-frog masks.*[204]

203 Herter, "Vom dionysischen Tanz," p. 8; Pickard-Cambridge, *Dithyramb,* pl. IXA/B.

204 Aristophanes, *Knights* 521-23; also see in Oates and O'Neill, II, 501.

Since the plays usually took their titles from their choruses, we know that in the Old Comedies there were frogs and fishes; ants and griffons; wasps, gall flies, and bees; nightingales, storks, and birds; goats, and simply "animals." For this very reason, however, unrestraint was of the highest order. The animal choruses did not lead to a world of bestiality, not at least in those examples of which we are able to form an opinion; they led to a fairy-tale world, the better world of wishes. This was particularly the case in the *Animals* of Krates. An animal, surely an edible one, probably a bull, is appointed by the gods to be ruler of the world. His orders to mankind suggest the rules of Pythagoras.

"You may eat boiled radishes / And fish, baked and pickled, but leave us in peace." The representative of mankind asks in horror: "Do you mean that from now on we shall have no meat / That there will be no meat pasty or sausages for sale at the market?" The animals, who apparently govern the world, also abolish slavery. Men are still more horrified. Their question is: "What's this? No one is to buy a man servant or maid servant from now on? / A feeble old man will have no one to care for him and wait on him?" Then the new ruler of the world explains the new state of affairs:

HE: No! At my bidding everything you see will come alive.
THE MAN: What if it does? What good will that do *us*?
HE: You need only cry out and every household utensil will obey you. For instance: Table, come here. Kettle, warm up the soup. Hola! Where's my cup? I want it to come here and rinse itself on the way. Come along now, you rolls. Pot, pour out your vegetables. Hurry up, carp! "Oh, wait please, my right side isn't done yet." Then turn over, salt yourself and put on some oil.[205]

205 Krates, Τὰ Θήρια, frs. 14, 17. The English translation quoted here is

Everything fabulous was appropriate to the birthday of Dionysos, anything that could provoke the wildest ideas about the return of the Golden Age. The most recent editor of the fragments of Attic comedy prefaced his collection with the quotation: "I will go back to the Country of the Young."[206] The comedy that was born at the Lenaia in Athens is the *most youthful* of all literature. The Athenian democracy was an element in the youth that produced it. When it died out, the Old Comedy, uniquely characterized by Hofmannsthal in his Prologue to the *Lysistrata*, died with it. It burst like a soap bubble and was gone. It gave way to the crudeness of the so-called Middle Comedy, and in a still later day a masculine sobriety, one might say a premature old age, reduced the festive play to the greatest simplicity. These plays too revolve around an element that is made understandable by the character of the festival.

After Aristophanes, the most important author of Greek comedies was Menander. In *The Arbitration*, which has come down to us only in fragmentary form, we see figures who strike us almost as old acquaintances. One of these is a woman with a child in her arms, similar to the Dionysian woman shown in a vase painting holding her child at her breast at the Lenaia.[207] But the woman in the Menander play is the wife of a simple charcoal burner. To one side of her stands her husband; to the other, a goatherd. They have come to the village from a wild region of Attica and are now quarreling in the street.

SYRISCUS (A CHARCOAL BURNER): You're afraid of a fair trial.

---

based on the German version of T. Zielinski, in *Die Gliederung der altattischen Komödie*. For the Greek text and an English translation of the fragments, see Edmonds, *The Fragments of Attic Comedy*, I, 158–61.

206 John Maxwell Edmonds, loc. cit., p. [v].

207 See [86A].

DAVUS (A GOATHERD): You've no honest claim, curse you.

SYRISCUS: You've no right to keep what's not yours. We must get someone to arbitrate.

DAVUS: I'm willing; let's argue it out.

SYRISCUS: Who's to decide it?

DAVUS: Anyone will do for me. It serves me right though. Why did I give you anything?

SYRISCUS (*indicating* SMICRINES, *an old man*): How about that man? Does he suit you as a judge?

DAVUS: Yes, good luck to it.

[Smicrines, the rich man coming down the street, does not suspect that the child in the arms of the charcoal burner's wife is his own grand-child, the reason for the quarrel between his daughter and her husband, who have separated. In approaching him, the contestants are also un-aware of this. The spectators are in for less of a surprise, for they know how often the whole action of a New Comedy revolves around a child.]

SYRISCUS (*to* SMICRINES): If you please, sir, could you spare us a minute?

SMICRINES (*testily*): You? What for?

SYRISCUS: We have a disagreement about something.

SMICRINES: Well, what's that to me?

SYRISCUS: We are looking for someone to decide it impartially. So if nothing prevents, do settle our dispute.

SMICRINES: Confound the rascals. Do you mean to say that you go about arguing cases, you fellows in goatskins?

SYRISCUS: Suppose we do. It won't take long and it's no trouble to understand the case. Grant the favour, sir. Don't be contemptuous, please. Justice should rule at every moment, everywhere. Whoever happens to come along should make this cause his own concern, for it's a common interest that touches all men's lives.

DAVUS (*alarmed at this burst of eloquence*): I've got quite an orator on my hands. Why did I give him anything?

SMICRINES: Well, tell me. Will you abide by my decision?

SYRISCUS: Absolutely.

SMICRINES: I'll hear the case. Why shouldn't I? (*Turning to the sullen* DAVUS) You speak first, you that aren't saying anything.

DAVUS (*sure of his case but not very sure of his words . . .*): I'll go back a bit first—not just my dealings with this fellow—so you'll understand the transaction. In the scrubland not far from here I was watching my flocks, sir, perhaps a month ago to-day, all by myself, when I found a baby left deserted there with a necklace and some such trinkets as these. (*He shows some trinkets.*)

SYRISCUS: The dispute is about them.

DAVUS: He won't let me speak.

SMICRINES (*to* SYRISCUS): If you interrupt, I'll take my stick to you.

DAVUS: And serve him right too.

SMICRINES: Go on.

DAVUS: I will. I picked it up and went back home with it and was going to raise it. That's what I intended then. In the night, though, like every one else, I thought it over to myself and argued it out: "Why should I bring up a baby and have all that trouble? Where am I to get all that money to spend? What do I want with all that worry?" That's the state I was in. Early next morning I was tending my flock again, when along came this fellow, he's a charcoal burner, to this same spot to get out stumps there. He had made friends with me before that. So we got talking together and he saw that I was gloomy and said: "Why so thoughtful, Davus?"

"Why indeed," said I, "I meddle with what doesn't concern me." So I tell him what had happened, how I found the baby and how I picked it up. And he broke in at once, before I had finished my story, and began entreating me: "As you hope for luck, Davus," he kept saying every other thing, "do give me the baby, as you hope for fortune, as you hope for freedom. I've a wife, you see," says he, "and she had a baby, but it died." Meaning this woman who is here now with the child. Did you entreat me, Syriscus?

SYRISCUS: I admit it.

DAVUS: He spent the whole day at it. Finally I yielded to his coaxing and teasing, promised him the child and gave it to him. He went off wishing me a million blessings. When he took it too, he kissed my hands. Didn't you, Syriscus?

SYRISCUS: Yes, I did.

DAVUS: He took himself off. Just now he and his wife happened on me and all of a sudden he claims the objects that I found with the child—it was some small matters, tomfoolery, nothing really—and says he's cheated because I don't consent and lay claim to them myself. I say, though, that he ought to be thankful for the share he did get by his entreaties. Though I don't give him all of it, that's no reason why I should have to stand examination. Even if he had found it while we were going about together and it had been a case of share-your-luck, why he would have got part and I the rest. But I was alone when I found it and you weren't even there and yet you think you ought to have all and I nothing.

To conclude, I have given you something of mine. If you are satisfied with it, you may still keep it; but if you aren't satisfied and have changed your mind, then give it back again to me and take neither more nor less than your due. But for you to have the whole business, part with my consent, the rest forced from me, is not fair. That's all I have to say.

SYRISCUS (*keeping a respectful eye on the stick*): Is that all?

SMICRINES: Didn't you hear what he said? He has finished. . . .

SYRISCUS: Good. Then I'll take my turn. He was alone when he found the baby. He is right about everything he has mentioned. The facts are as stated, sir. I dispute nothing. I got the child from him by entreating and imploring him. For his story is true.

Information came to me from a certain shepherd that he had been talking to, one of his fellow-workmen, to the effect that he had also found at the same time some trinkets. (*With a dramatic gesture toward the infant.*) To claim these has come, sir, in person, my client here. Give me the child, wife. (*Taking the baby from his wife's arms.*) This infant claims from you his necklace and his tokens, Davus.[208]

Syriscus, the charcoal burner, stands there with the child in his arms and demands the *child's* property. And the child will obtain not only his property but his parents as well, who, after a number of dramatic misunderstandings among all, will be reconciled.

This is not the place to speak of the dramatist's art, his knowledge of human character, nor of the central theme of this comedy. Such scenes, characteristic of the New Comedy, show us how very concretely the play revolved *around a child*. And in this connection still other plays of Menander might be cited. The abandoned child whose lot it is to be found again became the basic and to our taste tedious

208 Menander, Οἱ ἐπιτρέποντες, fr. 172H (in Edmonds, III, B, pp. 1000–1009). For the English version quoted here, see Oates and O'Neill, II, 1148–51.

theme of the whole genre.[209] In *The Arbitration*, the charcoal burner himself evokes mythical examples from tragedy.[210] The poet's intention, however, was not to enhance the credibility of his invention, for with his audience there was no need to. In the light of the law of *patria potestas* over the life and death of children, which was reinforced by Solon,[211] the exposure of infants was a distinct possibility in Athens and quite common in the case of girls. It is not inconceivable, though it cannot be proved, that the harshness of the patriarchal law was directed against the excessive power of women resulting from the Dionysian religion of earlier times. Nevertheless, in Athens it never required an unbridled imagination to identify plain human foundlings with the children of heroes or with the little Dionysos, and thus as it were to secularize the Divine Child.

The universality of comic unrestraint was a thing of the past. Instead we encounter in Menander a universality of *philanthropeia*, human sympathy, which in the New Comedy is inseparable from the Dionysian aura. The resulting transformation of comedy is among the most miraculous events in the history of European culture. Here the religion of Dionysos disclosed its finest, most humane possibility, foreshadowing the possibility of a true humanism.[212]

209 The word "tedious" (*ermüdend*) is from A. Körte, *Die hellenistische Dichtung*, p. 32.

210 Loc. cit., lines 149–57 (in Edmonds, III, B, p. 1008; in Oates and O'Neill, II, 1151).

211 See R. Tolles, "Untersuchungen zur Kindesaussetzung bei den Griechen," pp. 37 ff.

212 See "Humanismus und Hellenismus," in Kerényi, *Apollon*, pp. 232 ff.

The Greek Dionysian Religion of Late Antiquity

TRAGEDY and New Comedy were high spiritual forms of the Dionysian religion. Starting from the Great Dionysia and the Lenaia, they conquered the world. Perhaps it would not be correct to say that a world conquest also started from the Anthesteria, but the Dionysian religion whose monuments we encounter in later antiquity, from the Hellenistic period on—and I am not referring to the monuments of the theater—is most readily understood through the Anthesteria. This religion concerned *bios*, the life of the individual, which derived its existence and hope of survival after death from *zoë* itself. If we wished to obtain a complete view of its radiation, we should have to go back to still earlier times and to the Etruscans; in this book, this is possible only in a very limited degree. "Fair Italia's guardian Lord," cries the chorus in Sophokles' *Antigone*.[213] An account of the Dionysian religion in East and West would exceed our aims. We wish merely to give some idea of the consistency and coherence of the Greek religion of *zoë* down to the period of the Antonines.

A myth had to be consistent and coherent if for almost a thousand years men were to live and die by it in countries and cities where it was not a state myth—not even in a special sense as in Athens. Men lived and died by the myth, for the god himself lived and died, again in a special way—not like the gods of vegetation who can mean something to man only by *analogy*. Men and women experienced Dionysos in themselves, in the most intimate life of their own sex, and they had no experience of the cessation of this experience. What death might

213 Line 1119: κλυτὰν ὃς ἀμφέπεις 'Ιταλίαν.

be they experienced at the high points of enhanced life, and what is *almost* death they experienced in the sexual exhaustion that is so close to the exhaustion of *zoë*. In the myth of Dionysos *zoë* expressed itself. Through the myth men trusted in *zoë* as they went to their graves, but they did not express *zoë*; it expressed itself. The tombs give evidence of this trust in images that make no distinction between god and man.

There is no reason to suppose that any essential change occurred in the content of the Dionysian religion, in its living myth, after Onomakritos gave his philosophical interpretation of the aggressive, death-bringing element in the vital urge itself.[214] The new features we perceive are: a modified social setting, a greater freedom in the artistic representation of the cult, and perhaps certain excesses of concretization. We do not know how much may have been crudely concretized even in earlier times. Wherever the Dionysian religion remained, within the old social order, a partly secret cult of women, supervised and to some extent shared by the men, such innovations did not even make their appearance! At most there were amplifications or reforms in organization as were required by the change in the times. It was very much the same with the Mysteries of Eleusis. Only where there was no set place for the mysteries—no setting hallowed from time immemorial as was the Boukoleion in Athens—a place had to be sought and the setting created.

214 Nilsson, in *The Dionysiac Mysteries of the Hellenistic and Roman Age*, fails to take note of the basic unity of the religion of Dionysos. See the review by F. Matz, *Gnomon*, XXXII (1960), 542: "In regard to the later period Nilsson's method does not do justice to the complexity of the sources, nor in regard to the early period to the abundance of clear statements they offer." By benevolent interpretation Matz tries to save something out of the book, but he shares Nilsson's basic misunderstanding as to the role of the "horrors of the Underworld" in the Dionysian mysteries; see further in ch. VI, the text at note 282, below.

A "cowherd" (*boukolos*) as sayer of prayers, singer, and offerer of sacrifices was already known from the Orphic Hymn Book,[215] and as long as there was no thought of organized mysteries it was possible to regard him merely as a pious cowherd. But it was not difficult to recognize in him the bearer of an office in the mysteries of Dionysos, the representative of their setting. This is proved by a number of inscriptions that even record the rank of a "chief cowherd" (*archibouko-los*). Surrounded and served by their own *boukoloi*, the divine Dionysian pair, Sabazios and his lady, came from Asia Minor to Athens at a time when they could not hope to be admitted to the state Boukoleion.[216] The chorus of *boukoloi* in a play by Kratinos, a representative of the Old Comedy, probably related to the new cult. It began with a dithyramb.[217] The Sybilline oracle according to which a Dionysos cult was to be founded in Perinthos on the Hellespont with the mystic sacrifice of a kid was cut in stone by an *archiboukolos* represented by a chief initiate (*archimystes*).[218]

We learn more from inscriptions in Pergamon, dating from the rule of Attalos I and his successors in the third and second centuries B.C.[219] These inscriptions mention an *archiboukolos*, *boukoloi*, hymn teachers (*hymnodidaskaloi*) and sileni (*seilenoi*) in the cult of Dionysos Kathegemon, probably founded in honor of the tutelary deity of the royal

215 Quandt, *Orphei hymni* I 10 and XXXII 7. See A. Dieterich, "De hymnis orphicis," pp. 70 ff.; his reference to the Boukoleion of Athens is on p. 77.

216 See Aristophanes, *Wasps* 10: τὸν αὐτὸν ἄρ' ἐμοὶ βουκολεῖς Σαβάζιον.

217 Kratinos, fr. 18 (in Edmonds, I, 28–29). See also Dieterich, "De hymnis," p. 76.

218 Dieterich, "De hymnis," p. 72: Σπέλλιος Εὐῆθις ἀρχιβουκόλος Ἡρακλείδου Ἀλεξάνδρου ἀρχιμυστοῦντος.

219 See Quandt, "De Baccho ab Alexandri aetate in Asia Minore culto," pp. 123 f.

family.[220] It would seem that wherever a Dionysos cult with mysteries was introduced, sacral "cowherds" took over the function performed in Athens by the Boukoleion and presided over by the *archon basileus*. They created a symbolic *boukoleion* for the god and his consort. In Pergamon they performed dances when the "divine *pregma*" was celebrated—every second year in accordance with the trieteric order.[221]

In view of the scantiness even of these inscriptions, it remains hypothetical whether the *pregma*, or mysteries, were of the same kind as in Athens. The traces of the cult, however, lead into the halls of the royal palace. Though the Dionysos cult of the Pergamene kings seems to have been a private family cult,[222] it nevertheless required *boukoloi*. The role of the queen is not mentioned and one would not expect it to be mentioned, for it must have been self-evident. The failure to mention women in a Dionysos cult can only signify a gap in the tradition. This gap is bridged in a sense by two large Dionysian monuments in Italy. One is an inscription near Rome; the other, murals in the Villa dei Misteri at Pompeii. They show a *matrona* or *domina* in the same position as that of the Athenian queen in the state Dionysos cult.

A good deal can be learned from the first of these monuments, the inscription of a priestess of Dionysos in the vicinity of Rome. This priestess was a lady of high degree, whose consular family had an estate in the Alban mountains in the second century A.D. Her name has been reconstructed very probably as "Agripinilla,"[223] and her con-

---

220 E. Ohlemutz, *Die Kulte und Heiligtümer der Götter in Pergamon*, pp. 90 ff.

221 This appears twice in the inscriptions cited by Quandt, "De Baccho," loc. cit.: οἱ χορεύσαντες βουκόλοι τὴν ἐπ' αὐτοῦ τριετηρίδα.

222 Ohlemutz, *Die Kulte*, p. 96.

223 A. Vogliano, "La Grande Iscrizione Bacchica del Metropolitan Museum," pp. 218 ff.

nections with Lesbos have been disclosed. Her father Marcus Pompeius Macrinus, eloquently surnamed Theophanes, came from that large Greek island. He and Neos Theophanes, Agripinilla's brother, to judge by their surnames must have had something to do with apparitions of gods, personal religious experiences. Agripinilla herself was surrounded by a Dionysian *thiasos*, probably composed of her *familia* in the extended sense, comprising relatives, clients, and slaves. Five hundred initiates (*mystai*) set up the statue for her; the statue itself was not preserved but only the Greek inscription giving the names and dignities of the members of the Dionysian community. In all likelihood Agripinilla was its founder.

The *thiasos* consisted of men and women, as it happened, more men than women. Their functions in the mysteries are indicated by their dignities, though these are not always intelligible to the profane. There is a wide range of degrees and offices. In addition to Agripinilla, two priestesses are named, both from the noble family of the Manlii. There were three *archiboukoloi*, seven "holy *boukoloi*" (*boukoloi hieroi*), and eleven plain *boukoloi*. The *hierophantes*, who probably proclaimed the events of the mysteries after the manner of the hierophant in Eleusis, bore the name of a slave: Agathopous. More noteworthy are two other persons, a man and a woman, in two different functions.

A *heros* by the name of Macrinus is first on the long list of initiates given in the inscription. According to the known genealogy, he may have been Agripinilla's brother, but it seems more likely that he was an otherwise unknown nephew.[224] The men of the family old enough to possess authority, probably including Agripinilla's brother, formed

224 Vogliano, p. 223. F. Hiller von Gaertringen, "Neue Forschungen zur Geschichte der Epigraphik von Lesbos," p. 112, is mistaken. *Heros* in this list cannot refer to any deceased.

the college of priests. The *heros*, however, it may be assumed, took the role of the expected god, the "Heros Dionysos." The god himself is designated in inscriptions relating to the mysteries of Dionysos as "Theos Dionysos."[225] Ordinarily a god mentioned by name is not termed *theos* without some special reason.[226] Such a reason was present when someone played the part of Dionysos in the mysteries; then the true Dionysos had to be called Theos Dionysos. The most detailed inscription concerning a Dionysian *thiasos* of a still later period, the third century A.D., names Dionysos without *theos*, and in this case he was definitely a man appearing in costume.[227] Agripinilla was surrounded by *bakchoi* and *bakchai* of various degrees; a Dionysos Archebakchos, "a Dionysos who leads the *bakchoi*," is known to us from another inscription.[228] Here the only possible mortal Dionysos is the *heros*, and he, as we have seen, heads the list of initiates.

The most striking person of all on the list given in the inscription is a woman who, coming after three *liknon* bearers (*liknophoroi*), apparently in the order of the procession, bore the phallus and is designated as *phallophoros*. The role of the phallus in the mysteries, which were presided over by priestesses—two Manliae in addition to Agripinilla—is not concealed. More veiled is the role of the *heros*, the human manifestation of Dionysos. The Athenians trusted in the visionary power of their queen and her contact with the phallic idol. There is no reason to suppose that a notorious incident, recorded in Roman history, was imitated in the mysteries of Agripinilla, supervised as they were by a worthy college of priests drawn from her family. There were

225 Quandt, "De Baccho," pp. 153, 161; Nilsson, *Dionysiac Mysteries*, p. 53, note 47.
226 See Kerényi, *Griechische Grundbegriffe*, p. 19, note 75.
227 Nilsson, *Dionysiac Mysteries*, p. 60.
228 Ibid., p. 9.

assuredly gradations between a visionary *symmeixis* and a *consummatio matrimonii* with a young representative of the god.

The famous incident led in the year 186 B.C. to the prohibition in Rome of the mysteries of Dionysos that had been making their incursion from Etruria. The gist of the story told at excessive length and none too clearly by Livy is that for the secret cult of Dionysos the women needed a young man of no more than twenty.[229] The mysteries took place by the Tiber, in the grove of "Stimula," a cover figure who was interpreted as "Semele,"[230] but whose name is a feminine form of *stimulus*, "goad" or "spike." The young man was needed for abuse by the bacchantes. His mother was willing, but his beloved prevented it. The case finally came before the Senate which then handed down its decision against the Bacchanalia. Such excess, as the last form of decadence, is a part of the over-all picture. The unique monument in Pompeii, however, gives a much clearer picture of the true *matronae* and *dominae* of dignified mysteries.

This monument consists of the painted walls of a large room in the so-called Villa dei Misteri in Pompeii, which, through great art that is a far cry from copying, convey the dignity of the secret cult. The murals show the *matrona*, or *domina*, of the house observing the preparations for the mysteries. Her meaningful presence dominates the painted frieze which has preserved its radiant colors since roughly 60 A.D. To us her person is in every respect a connecting link, both historically and in terms of place. Historically, she points back to the queen of Athens who received the god, though not in her own house like the *matrona*, but in the "bull stable" of her husband, the king.

229 Livy XXXIX 18 3 ff.

230 Ibid., 12 4. See also Ovid, *Fasti* VI 503 (*dubium Semelae Stimulaene vocetur*); *CIL* VI 9897 (*ab luco Semeles*).

As in the official Athenian rite, there was no need in the *matrona*'s situation for the *boukoloi* we encounter in a later day on Agripinilla's country estate. The room at Pompeii, wide open in two directions, could not have served for mystery ceremonies to be participated in by persons of various ranks but nevertheless to be kept secret. This room could serve only for preparations. It was permissible to depict the preparations, not the mysteries themselves.

The lady is sitting at the head end of a bed, but only half the bed extends into the picture, that is, into the room where the preparations were being made [106]. This signifies a connection between the room and the adjoining *cubiculum*, the bedroom of the *domina* and *dominus*.[231] The connection exists not only in physical fact but also on the higher plane of mystic events, which the painting introduces into both rooms. To quote the words of the archaeologist who has observed the scene most closely: "The *cubiculum* is the only room in the whole house whose painting corresponds, both in form and content, to that of the large room with the frieze: here too the figures and groups of the *thiasos*, mingled with mortal women, move before the red wall mirrors like living images before the beholder, while discreet little priapic sacrificial scenes are embedded in the upper part of the wall of the one bed niche."[232] These scenes are painted windows which open out on such views in the landscape; one is crude and rustic, the other, more fanciful [107, 109].

"Here everything is naturally adapted in size, composition and rhythm to the small size of the room, but may, if we choose, be taken as a kind of prologue to the larger and more magnificent painting of

231 See R. Herbig, "Neue Beobachtungen am Fries der Mysterien-Villa in Pompeji," pp. 39 f.
232 Ibid., pp. 51 f.

the frieze. Or, if we prefer to reverse the relationship, we may regard the painting of the bedroom as a kind of condensation, a transposition of the great symphony into a more intimate chamber music. In any case it is evident that the two go together; the two rooms form a unit, not only architecturally but also from the standpoint of decoration and utility: a marriage chamber with its ceremonial vestibule." And, our observer adds, "women must have played the leading role both in the conception and in the utilization of these rooms."[233]

Indeed, we must go further and observe that apart from Dionysos and a boy, the male sex is represented in the murals of both rooms only by mythical Dionysian figures. In these rooms any other man could be only a representative of the god, not a person in his own right and surely not a representative comparable to the youth in Rome who caused the prohibition of the Bacchanalia. Accordingly, the question of where these preparations were taking place assumes a special importance and cannot be answered on the basis of purely archaeological considerations.

The large room is intended for all the preparations; this at least is the only hypothesis that makes it fully intelligible. The lady's gaze rests thoughtfully on the bride, who is separated from her by a wide door and from the continuous frieze by a large window. It is not the *domina*, a woman of indeterminate age, who is preparing herself, but the bride, who is decking herself out for the wedding [108]. The *domina* is merely thinking back to the days before she was initiated, and to the day of her initiation.[234] She herself is in a sense the bride. The art of the painter—who may have had a great model before him but, as we said, did much more than copy—does not clearly express any in-

233 Ibid., p. 52.
234 A. von Salis, "Pompejanischer Beitrag," p. 92.

dividuality yet does not exclude it. The bride's gaze rests on a young woman in an advanced state of pregnancy in the opposite frieze [110B], who, holding a tray to be used in a sacred action, is approaching a group of three women who are engaged in preparations for the rite. One of them, who is seated, might be the *domina* again. Pregnancy will follow marriage and the boy this young woman is carrying in her womb might, even in this state, be a little Dionysos. In the first group of the frieze he is a nude boy standing between two women, reading in preparation for his initiation [110A]—to judge by his face, a terrible initiation, the outcome of which is not contained in the scroll he is holding. Probably the dark-clad woman, the first figure in the frieze (she may be the *domina*), will direct the initiation ceremony. The other woman, affectionately stroking the back of the boy's neck, is holding a second scroll, which probably contains an account of the happy outcome.

All this could have taken place, in this room, perhaps over and over again, but strangely enough something else enters in, as though the whole scene were being enacted on a stage. Ordinarily Pompeiian painting opens up the houses: the eye looks through into the open countryside.[235] Here the red squares (in Herbig's description, "mirrors") of the background, separated by greenish-black borders, are opaque [110B]. In front of them, like stage props, stand boulders on one of which a pair of shepherd children, half human, half satyr, are seated. The boy is playing the syrinx; the girl is nursing a goat at her breast—a sign of the Dionysian state. Also in this state and likewise seated on boulders, two aged sileni are instructing young satyrs and initiating them into satyr manhood [110B/110C]. One silenus is their teacher in

235 See Kerényi, "Pompeji und der Zauber der Malerei," *Werke*, II, 209–212.

lyre playing and song; the other is performing the initiation ceremony. The content of the ceremony is that in a silver bowl, serving as a concave mirror, the boy to be initiated sees a reflection not of his own face but of a crude silenus mask which is being held aloft by another boy, probably already initiated.[236] The initiate is being prepared for the *thiasos* with Dionysian women.

His preparation corresponds to that of the bacchantes. That it is no simple matter may be inferred from this series of representations. The phallus, set up in a *liknon*, is not unveiled, but the goddess Aidos (Shame), with dark wings like the night,[237] strikes a blow [110D]. One of the candidate bacchantes runs away [110B]; she does not accept the Dionysian world. Behind her the youthful satyrs make their preparations in vain. Another bacchante, with the devotion of a novice, receives the goddess' blow on her bared back [110E]. This is the mystery beating that the maenads received at their initiation as advance punishment for a cruel deed. Kneeling, the novice buries her head in the lap of one of three Dionysian women, a group of noble young feminine figures who as bacchantes occasionally became maenads in their mysteries. The seated woman lays her hand on the head of the one who is being beaten. The second brings her the *thyrsos* which she, having been beaten and initiated, will bear. The third, nude, holding cymbals over her head and striking them, summons an invisible band to the dance. This too is a gesture of preparation. But the gesture with which she takes the first dance step is that of one who has been fully liberated, unveiled in her perfection.

236   See Kerényi, "Man and Mask," pp. 151 ff.; Herbig, p. 43.

237   Aidos can be conceived of as a daughter of Night, like Nemesis in Hesiod, *Theogony* 23–24, with whom she is also closely connected in *Works and Days* 200. She guards the secrets that belong to the night.

One archaeologist interprets these paintings as a representation of "the life of Greek women in its mysterious tenderness";[238] and another, of "the life of women in the upper-class society of Magna Graecia."[239] It would be more correct to speak of a feminine society molded by the mysteries of Dionysos, a society whose ideal is represented by the divine pair in the center, dominating the room [110c]. They too are in a state of preparation. The truly central figure (though the painting here is badly preserved) is the enthroned woman and not the ivy-wreathed boy reclining, rather than sitting, on a narrow chair placed beside the throne. He is *her* Dionysos, characterized as the *heros*.[240] He is wearing only one sandal. Thus, he is a *monosandalos* in the manner of daring heroes and warriors, who established communication with the underworld by going into battle with one bare foot.[241] The right sandal of the long-haired young Dionysos lies below the step of his mistress' throne. It is not entirely certain what mythological name she should be given. Ariadne would require a different arrangement, for in relation to Ariadne, Dionysos should occupy the higher level, to which she would first be raised by her divine husband. The name "Semele" is quite possible for the enthroned woman,[242] but then she would be a Semele *combining the dignity of the mother—* the primordial image of the mother as Great Goddess and mother of Dionysos—*with the happiness of the wife.* The myth relating that under the name "Thyone," Semele became her son's bacchante[243] points

238   L. Curtius, *Die Wandmalerei Pompejis*, p. 370.
239   Herbig, p. 39.
240   This characterization was noted by Curtius, p. 336.
241   See Frazer's edition of Apollodoros, *The Library*, I, p. 94, note 1.
242   Suggested by P. Boyancé, "Le disque de Brindisi et l'apothéose de Sémélé," p. 202. Opposed is F. Matz, "Ariadne oder Semele?" pp. 110–11.
243   Diodorus Siculus IV 25 4; and Apollodoros III 5 3. See also *Homeric Hymns* I 21.

to the dual quality of the Dionysian woman initiated as queen of Athens or as priestess: she was at once the god's mother and his bride, in a transcendent dual relationship. The woman on the throne seems to meet this requirement. Might the picture not disclose the features of the *domina* if this part of the painting had not been destroyed? The question is justified, but cannot be answered.[244]

The picture of the divine pair points to a higher marriage, like the *symmeixis* of the Athenian queen. Was theirs the marriage in the adjoining room? Perhaps the narrowness of the door leading into this room is significant [111].[245] The legitimacy of the marriage between the lord and lady of the house is itself expressed in the paintings. The marriage document, a double tablet, is standing beside the lady on the bed[246] which extends into the *cubiculum* [106]. And in the *cubiculum*, the lady, wreathed and looking grave but in rather informal dress that leaves her shoulders bare, stands holding a document in her left hand [112F].[247] Here—as [112A–112F] will show—in her quality of *matrona*, she is joining a dispersed Dionysian *thiasos*. In the room of preparations there is no hint of drunkenness. It is otherwise in the *cubiculum*, but not with the *domina* herself.

In Athens the drunkenness of the men at the Anthesteria and the reception of a drunken Dionysos by a woman left at home alone, even the staggering of another Dionysos supported by a silenus [113],[248] were lesser mysteries compared to the "divine *pregma*" that took place

244 Also destroyed are: two slender feminine figures and a large pole which the woman who uncovers the *liknon* carries over her shoulder. A possible —perhaps the only possible—interpretation is a frame such as that used for the mask and garment of the Dionysos idol; see above, ch. VI, at note 102.

245 Herbig (p. 14, note 1) calls this narrow door a *"Schlupfpforte."*

246 Herbig, p. 39.

247 A. von Salis, "Pompejanischer Beitrag," pp. 90 ff.

248 Deubner, *Attische Feste*, p. 97. See also [100].

in the Boukoleion. Presumably the same situation prevailed in the Greek cities of southern Italy. A bell krater from Thurii clearly shows the division between the higher and the somewhat lower mysteries [114]. This painting shows, sitting enthroned to one side of an Ionic column, a nude Dionysos with horns; he is the divine bridegroom in his *boukoleion*. The woman who crowns him takes the place of the *basilinna*. Outside, on the other side of the column, stands a young man in conversation with a woman who seems to be calling him back to her.[249]

The dispersed *thiasos* which the *domina* of the Villa dei Misteri joins is characterized by drunkenness. It is "dispersed" because its members are situated in different fields of the mural. It is headed by a fat old silenus,[250] who is trying to look potent but is unable even though a satyr is helping him [112A]. After him comes Dionysos as a nude drunken youth, supported by a silenus [112B]. There follow two maenads in loose garments with dance movements that are anything but wild [112C/112D]. The painting of a third maenad is in a poor state of preservation. She seems, however, to be only lightly veiled and is perhaps conceived as a pendant to the young Dionysos.[251] The next to last figure in the murals is a naked young satyr, his foot raised in a long stride [112E]. Then finally comes the lady, who hesitantly and looking somewhat surprised is following the *thiasos* [112F]. Her marriage will be the fulfillment of Dionysian mysteries, but surely only of substitute mysteries, accessible by a back door. From the state of the male figures it can be inferred that there was drinking in the

249 See E. M. W. Tillyard, *The Hope Vases*, pp. 115 ff.

250 This is the order according to Von Salis, "Pompejanischer Beitrag," p. 89.

251 See A. Maiuri, *La Villa dei Misteri*, p. 178.

larger room, probably from a krater placed in the center. The *krateri-zein* was a sacred Dionysian action, and since it was no secret it is known to us from many representations as a preparation for the greater mysteries. The word itself is attested in Athens in connection with the mysteries of Sabazios.[252] The reality is represented on Attic sarcophagi, with children imitating the Dionysian action [115].[253] Over *all these* preparations hovered the great mysteries.

The influence of the Anthesteria in southern Italy can be followed, as though by fossile traces, with the assistance of the choës that were manufactured there.[254] To these are related other painted vases, such as the one from Thurii [114]. The two great Italian monuments of *bios*, the murals in the Villa dei Misteri and the inscription of Agripi-nilla, show how little account life—not only naked *zoë*, but also the simplest human manifestations of life and especially the *life of women* —took of the prohibition of the Bacchanalia in Italy. Under Julius Cae-sar this prohibition had been explicitly lifted.[255] The great number of Dionysian sepulchral monuments also bears witness to Dionysian *bios*. Such monuments include the vases for burial with the dead. Many of these provide pictorial texts which, once we sense that they are texts,

252 Demosthenes XVIII (*De corona*) 259.
253 A krater is at the center of a band of Dionysian boys on one of these sarcophagi, the sarcophagus with the so-called children's *komos*. This, however, is not a *komos* but a deceased boy's first initiation, which is to be followed by another. A list of these sarcophagi was compiled by F. Matz, *Ein römisches Meisterwerk*, pp. 82–84. Clear examples are nos. 2, 10, and 29. Compare the details that are common to the sarcophagi and the choës (Matz, p. 101). Matz goes too far, however, when he expresses the opinion that the "children's *komos* of the Attic sarcophagi finds its explanation as a representation of the Choës feast."
254 Van Hoorn, *Choes and Anthesteria*, pp. 30 ff.
255 Servius' commentary on Virgil's *Eclogues* V 29. See also F. Cumont, *Les religions orientales dans le paganisme romain*, p. 198.

can be read. They are purer texts of the Dionysian religion in regard to the state after death than are the representations on the plaques or disks found in the tombs of Crete and southern Italy. These last combine the Dionysian apotheosis, attained through the Orphic use of the mystic kid sacrifice, with conceptions of the afterlife that originally had nothing to do with the religion of Dionysos.[256] In the pictorial text of countless vases, the Dionysian religion stands by itself.

The pitchers used at the Choës, however, do not take us beyond Naples. It is interesting to note that there are very few such pitchers among the archaeological finds of Etruria or in the Naples Museum.[257] Vases with other forms of Dionysian representation were distributed over a much larger territory. This means that in Italy as well as in Greece these pitchers pertained only to a particular festival and that this festival was celebrated only in certain Greek cities of southern Italy. It must have been a feast of all-souls related to the Athenian Anthesteria. One of these choës from Italy shows—through a siren approaching the sacrificial altar—a connection with the realm of souls, and the picture on a larger vase even indicates that this form of vessel was used in the funeral sacrifice.[258] The conception of the departure of the youthful dead, especially women, as an exodus from the city to Dionysian nuptials—such an exodus is represented on innumerable south Italian vases—was based on actual departures to private mysteries during the Anthesteria. An Italic chous bears the image of a characteristic figure in this nocturnal exodus: a boy satyr with torch and *situla* [116].[259] A chous from near Brindisi shows Dionysos and

256 Such conceptions, for example, are those regarding the sources of forgetfulness and of memory. See Kerényi, "Mnemosyne-Lesmosyne," *Werke*, I, 311–22. / On the *dischi sacri*, see further ch. VI, at note 322.

257 See Van Hoorn, *Choes and Anthesteria*, pp. 51 f.

258 Ibid., figs. 403, 406.   259 Ibid., fig. 404.

his female companion on a couch served by a boy satyr [117].[260] The vases with these scenes were found in tombs, and it was for this purpose no doubt that they were manufactured in such quantity. The spread of this conception required vases for burial with men as well as women; or better still, vases with pictures of two kinds that could be buried with persons of either sex.

A happy and unique find is a krater in the Naples Museum, because the painting is clarified by an inscription [118].[261] A winged youth throws a colorful embroidered ball to a hesitant woman. Looking outward but at the same time inward, she is resting one hand on a stele which bears the inscription. This stele is a *horos*, a boundary stone, and here it probably marks the boundary of the hesitant woman's home country, which she, wearing no ornament and lightly clad, must now leave. She does not reach for the ball, but looks with the shadow of a sly smile at the messenger who has thrown it to her. She *will* go. On the other side stands a woman with a grave expectant face, holding out to her a mirror and a *tainia*, a festive ribbon. The woman who thus hesitates is not a hetaira; she is a bride-to-be, but one who already knows. She would prefer not to travel this road.

Who the winged youth is and what the ball means we are told in a well-known poem by Anakreon:

> *Eros with the golden curls*
> *Throws me the purple ball*
> *And calls me to play with*
> *The girl with the bright-colored sandals.*[262]

260 See G. Marzano, *Il Museo Provinciale: Guida*, pl. XXVII; *RM*, LXX (1963), pl. XLIII.

261 The importance of this monument was recognized by J. J. Bachofen, *Gesammelte Werke*, VII, 64. See also Kerényi, *Bildtext einer italischen Vase in Giessen*, pp. 334–48.

262 Anakreon, fr. 5, in Diehl, *Anth. lyr.*; see also Kerényi, *Bildtext*, p. 337.

It is Eros—golden-curled in Anakreon, here dark-haired—who summons the girl to the game of love with his ball. The ball is an erotic message. Whence and whither? Eros is only the intermediary. What the hesitant woman thinks we are told by the inscription on the boundary stone: "They have thrown me the ball"[263]—"they" in the plural, not any definite individual, even if the bridegroom is waiting in the background. The plural does not befit the language of ancient erotic poetry, but it does that of sepulchral epigrams: "The goddesses of fate . . . led me down to Hades."[264] Ordinarily they sent a messenger to act as guide, in this case, Eros. Often it was Hermes, the guide of souls. The woman to whom the *daimon* of love has been sent as messenger and guide still hesitates to accept death fully, though it has already taken possession of her. She is unwilling, but she goes nevertheless to the great erotic adventure. For such *was* death in the atmosphere of the Anthesteria. Eros with the ball is an aspect of death.

A series of vase paintings shows us the rest of the story as—so we must assume—it was set before the painters of the pottery works, in model books.[265] The painters were free and at the same time restricted. Although they never copied their models exactly, they nevertheless followed the main lines of a coherent pictorial text representing a story with its own inner logic. If the deceased woman was lightly dressed and without ornament in starting on her way to the Dionysian nuptials, it meant, according to *this* conception, that her adornment—which in the picture with the inscription is suggested by the woman waiting with mirror and *tainia*—would follow. The painting on a bell

263 The inscription was read correctly by J. Millingen, who first published the vase; see his *Ancient Unedited Monuments*, I, 30: ἵεσάν μοι τὰν σφαῖραν.

264 Kerényi, *Bildtext*, p. 338.

265 See K. Schefold, "Buch und Bild im Altertum," pp. 104 ff.; E. Bielefeld, "Zum Problem der kontinuierenden Darstellungsweise," pp. 30 ff.

krater in Lecce shows a woman who is no longer hesitant but willing [119]; already in festive garments, she is washing her hair in the presence of two delicate nude Dionysian youths. The one, with a festive band round his head (he is thus a *mitrephoros*) holds the *thyrsos* and the burning torch for the night journey. The other holds a basket, the contents of which are destined for the impending sacrificial banquet, and a strigil, the brush with which athletes cleansed themselves; in this context it identifies him as the other's younger companion. Are they ordinary youths? Or rather does not the *mitrephoros* with the *thyrsos* represent Dionysos as bridegroom? Here we have already passed the boundary stone dividing "mortal" and "immortal."

Though the willing woman on another krater in Lecce is also making use of a mirror and arranging her hair, there can be no doubt that two divine beings are visible beside her [120]. One is a silenus from the Dionysian sphere. He holds out to her a perfume bottle and an apple, evidently sent by the waiting bridegroom to whose retinue he belongs. On the other side of her, Hermes is on the point of leaping away, impatient to escort the bride. He is carrying a folded sheet for the marriage bed; such a sheet is included in the bride's dowry on the votive tablets from the sanctuary of Persephone in Lokroi in southern Italy.[266] This sheet lends the *psychopompos* a double meaning; Hermes is a guide both to souls and to brides. The basin in the center alludes to the bridal bath, and the objects to the right of Hermes are probably *krotaloi*, Dionysian instruments which the bride will hold in each hand in her maenadic dance before the god. After the dance she will probably rest on the bed with Dionysos and refresh herself from the bowl that the satyr boy gave to her on the Brindisi chous [117].

266   See P. Zancani Montuoro, "Il corredo della sposa," pp. 37 ff.

Bearing another instrument characteristic of Dionysian dancing girls, a large *tympanon*, she is shown following the winged Eros in the passionate representation on an Apulian amphora in Bonn. It is on the basis of this painting that an erotic Dionysian abduction was for the first time recognized to be a journey to death [121].[267] With the gesture of his left hand, Eros is drawing her after him—and the resisting gesture of her right hand is unmistakable.

A bride such as this one with the tense, frightened face, followed by the escorting boy with a wreath—the wreath of Ariadne!—is not being led to an ordinary wedding. With this escort and this expressive face she can only be going to a mystery. With his right hand the winged Eros beckons to those who have remained far behind; it is a gesture of farewell, farewell to the *thiasos*. In the vase paintings of the south Italian group from which all the examples cited here are taken, we can also discern the details of the exodus in which only a few persons participate, the executants of a particular ceremony separate from the general *thiasos* in the open. The two possibilities presented by this ceremony—"earthly love" with a mortal silenus and "heavenly love" with the god—are indicated in exemplary manner by a work of the Meidias painter.[268] The exodus to the "earthly marriage" is represented on a krater in Barletta [122].[269] The little procession consists of the couple—a mortal silenus and his torch-bearing bride, hand in hand—and those who will take part in the ceremony. They are going out of the city, as is shown by the fact that the wine is carried in a wineskin with a light *situla*, a kind of pail, rather than in a krater which is hard

267 See E. Langlotz, "Eine apulische Amphora in Bonn," pl. IV.
268 See [96], also [97A/97B].
269 Published by F. Bartocchi, "Un nuovo cratere a campana del pittore di Amykos," pp. 193 ff.

to carry and rarely occurs in these scenes. The none too decorative *situla*, from which the wine is perhaps drawn with a drinking horn, is also characteristic of the "heavenly nuptials."

People do not go to "heavenly nuptials" hand in hand. To a divine encounter one is called, seduced by a superior power. Where a living person is concerned, this person will achieve the *telos* in a mystery ceremony through the *gamos*. Just this happens in the death of young people. Dionysos lured them and also summoned them with a bell; he is shown thus luring a woman on a krater in Ruvo [123].[270] She follows him with the *tympanon* which will accompany her dance when she sues for the god's love. Her face expresses the magic spell that has come over her. One of the two sileni, representing the servants who accompany her, bears both torch and *situla*. On a bell krater in Lecce a youth, naked except for the cloak thrown lightly over his shoulders, is standing before a seated woman; she is the divine maenad from whom he desires fulfillment [124]. He has arrived as though from a journey, and the egg he brings her is the egg that is buried with the dead.[271] She is awaiting him with a large *thyrsos*; a silenus holds another behind her. He also holds a wreath in preparation for the marriage which is to resemble that of Dionysos to Ariadne.

Throughout southern Italy the name "Ariadne" suggests itself for Dionysos' divine partner, into whom the female deceased are transformed, while the males are transformed into Dionysos. On a large bowl in Ruvo she is borne heavenward by two winged Erotes [125].[272] One holds the torch. The other holds the *situla*, a certain indication

270 See H. Sichtermann, *Griechische Vasen in Unteritalien. Aus der Sammlung Jatta in Ruvo*, pp. 36 f.
271 See Juvenal, *Satires* IV 84.
272 Sichtermann, *Griechische Vasen*, p. 54.

that the subject was originally a mortal, just as Ariadne in the classical myth was the mortal daughter of a king. Mortal men are awaited by immortal maenads. On a krater in Lecce a stately seated feminine figure, holding a *tympanon* in her left hand as a sign that she is a maenad, welcomes a timid youth and hands him a bowl of the wine which a silenus is pouring from a wineskin into a *situla* [126]. The youth already bears a branching, flowering *thyrsos*, but the mystery of his transformation into a true Dionysos is still to come. In other paintings a maenad lures and leads a youth who is already fully equipped as a young Dionysos. On a krater in Barletta he holds not only the *thyrsos* but also a kantharos in the manner of a Heros Dionysos [127]; on a krater in Bari he holds a cluster of grapes [128]. On a large bowl similar to that showing the erotic ascension of an Ariadne,[273] the ways of initiation of both a man and a woman are indicated. On one side the woman, already holding the *tympanon*, is being lured by a torch-bearing Eros and a maenad [129A].[274] On the other side, the youth is sitting beside his tomb as heroified dead sit beside their monuments in vase paintings [129B]. Behind the tombstone—it is at the same time a boundary stone, as always in this type of representation—stands the luring maenad with a *tympanon*; behind her stands an already initiated youth bearing clusters of grapes. Both sexes achieve the same Dionysian apotheosis in death.[275]

The luckiest find among these relatively early sepulchral relics of the Dionysian religion is the pointed amphora with continuous paint-

273 See [125].

274 The appended name was read by J. Thimme; see note 275, below.

275 The fish in the painting on the inside of the bowl [129c] can be related to another kind of apotheosis, *Urwasserseligkeit* (the term is mine). See J. Thimme, "Rosette, Myrte, Spirale und Fisch als Seligkeitszeichen," pp. 156 ff.

ings in Giessen [130A–130E],²⁷⁶ probably dating from the third century B.C. (The south Italian vases we have been discussing up to now are from the fourth century.) We know for sure that the Giessen amphora was found in Italy, though we do not know exactly where. Its sepulchral use is certain. The handles are two double snakes which seem to be tasting the liquid that was contained in the vessel and served as a libation for the dead. This pointed amphora was set on a stand or buried in the ground up to the bottommost stripe. The tomb in which it was found may have been near Rome. In any event, as the realistic treatment of the nude female body and of the phallus affixed to the pillar indicate, it must have been situated in a region where Etruscan art prevailed.²⁷⁷ The nude woman leaning against the pillar has been mistakenly interpreted as Aphrodite. An Aphrodite with such an attribute would be incompatible with this series of figures, all the rest of which are fully consonant with Greek artistic conceptions. The fact that there is a series of figures makes this a very unusual instance of a single vessel bearing a continuous pictorial text. The painting has been rightly compared to the frieze in the hall of preparations in the Villa dei Misteri.²⁷⁸

We must regard as the front of the vase the side on which the end and the beginning of the way of initiation came together.²⁷⁹ The end of the initiation is represented by a nude, wreathed woman leaning against the phallus pillar; she turns toward the viewer and is holding out her right hand [130E]. An almost wholly covered woman with an ineffably sad facial expression stands for the beginning [130A]; her

276 Published by W. Zschietzschmann, "Die Giessener Spitzamphora," pp. 115 ff.; also see Kerényi, *Bildtext*, pp. 344 ff.

277 See *Bildtext*, pp. 347 f.

278 Zschietzschmann, "Die Giessener Spitzamphora," pp. 119, 120.

279 See Kerényi, *Bildtext*, pp. 344, 347.

sadness is that of one who has died young. She is being lured by a
little Eros who is holding out a bird to her and by a girl flute player
who is to accompany her on the way. On the back of the amphora,
another sphere is delimited by two trees. The first figure behind the tree
can only be the woman who was so sad before [130B]. Her head is no
longer covered; beside her a swamp bird denotes an atmosphere of love,
as did the Eros with his bird. Naked and wreathed in ivy, Dionysos is
awaiting her on his couch [130C]. A serving woman hangs a garland
over the couch; only the preparation for the marriage is represented.
On the Brindisi chous, the bride is welcomed by a Dionysos lying on
a couch in very much the same way [117].[280] Later, as mistress,
wreathed in ivy, she sits on a special chair or on the end of the bed
[130D]. In the model books she may have held a *thyrsos* or more probably a scepter. In this painting she merely holds her right hand upward, but the similarity to the *domina* of the Pompeiian frieze is
striking.

Here again, on the Giessen amphora, the unveiled perfect bacchante
is not absent. She stands in front of the tree delimiting the scenes on
the back of the vessel, revealing herself with a gesture that seems to
say: "Here I am again, look at me!" [130E]. She is nude and wreathed
in ivy. Her garment lies on the pillar, the nature of which is emphasized by the phallus. She can be no other than the sad woman who,
having been lured away from *bios*, has experienced a Dionysian marriage and become the ivy-wreathed mistress on the other side. The
painting on a vase from Adernò in Sicily shows a similarly covered
or veiled bride—or dead woman—enthroned, with a little Eros in the

280 This chous—from the Canessa collection—is, according to Van Hoorn,
p. 158, in the "early Kertsch style," surely not designed for the Attic usage.

background [131A].²⁸¹ On the other side of the same vase, we see the more-than-half-naked bacchante sitting on a stone and looking back at her former veiled state [131B]. On the pointed Giessen amphora the pillar with the phallus, which was likewise unveiled for the viewer, hints so openly at the "divine *pregma*" that it is probably an indirect, innocent, and involuntary disclosure of the mysteries of the Boukoleion in Athens. In all this the mystery of death is presented as a mystery of enhanced life in a divine marriage.

With such a conception of death the Dionysian religion of late antiquity divested itself almost entirely of the ethical philosophy of the Orphics. The terrors of death were overcome by the identification of a deceased man with Dionysos and by the belief that a deceased woman gave herself in love to the god. In all ancient literature it has been possible to find only a single, very late testimony stating that something was done to frighten the initiand before he was admitted to the Bacchic mysteries.²⁸² This was a common feature of secret cults and had no bearing on torments in the underworld. It may have been introduced into the Dionysian mysteries from elsewhere—from lower, cruder initiations. In its original significance as a proof of the indestructibility of life, the myth of the killing of the child Dionysos re-

281   See A. D. Trendall, "Two skyphoid-pyxides in Moscow," pp. 32 ff.

282   Origen, *Contra Celsum* IV 10: τοῖς ἐν ταῖς Βακχιταῖς τελεταῖς τὰ φάσματα καὶ τὰ δείματα προεισάγουσι. Nilsson, *Dionysiac Mysteries*, p. 122, misread the passage (παρεισάγουσι for προεισάγουσι), connected it with Plutarch's polemic against the Epicureans (*Consolatio ad uxorem* 611 D), which he misunderstood, and on this double error based his view that "the belief in the punishments and horrors of the Underworld were integral elements of the Bacchic mysteries." His mistake was taken over by Matz, and by Boyancé ("Dionysiaca," p. 44, note 4), among others, without examination of the texts. The monuments invoked by Nilsson refer to the blow in initiation; see my comment in the text at note 304, below.

tained enormous importance. The undergoing of the mystic sacrificial rite was looked upon as a necessary phase in Dionysian *bios*, as a symbolic act of self-sacrifice whose purpose it was to bring about early identification with the god.[283] The reading boy in the Villa dei Misteri is being prepared for it, for an act which in the Dionysian calendar was to follow the mysteries of Choës Night. The performance of this rite was probably a duty of the Dionysian women, including the youth's mother.

Athenian boys, whose festival Choës Day was, required no initiation ceremonies in order to appear as manifestations of the god who would be present in another form on the Night of the Queen. If they died at this age, they went down to the underworld as little Dionysoi. They needed no initiation other than a sip of wine—probably their first —from a small chous which, if they lived not much longer, was put into the tomb with them as an identification. (This explains the large number of these vessels in the museums. The child mortality rate was not inconsiderable in antiquity.) Where the Dionysian religion prevailed as a mystery cult, the mystic sacrifice that served the Orphics as an apotheosis was taken over, even if the philosophical interpretation of Onomakritos might not be. As in other mysteries, the sacrifice and the identification of the *mystes* with the sacrificial animal were not represented; the representations show only the preparations for the mystic rite. Only in one work—a relatively late one, as we shall see —does a whip stroke give an intimation of the symbolic sacrifice. The entire happening, everything that was done visibly or invisibly on the way of initiation, was transferred to the child Dionysos with whom the

283 It is not excluded that Theokritos XXVI 27–29 justifies an excess of concretization which occurred in Egypt under the Ptolemies, or it may refer to a mere rumor of a "ritual child murder."

initiate shared an immanent identity, especially in the grave where the separation between mortal and immortal ceased to exist.

In a large tomb on Isola Sacra, the cemetery of the harbor of Rome, we find, along with other mythological scenes, representations of the initiation of the boy Dionysos. This is shown in four scenes adorning four wall niches.[284] Although these murals were done in the second or third century A.D.,[285] a procession is shown going out of doors as in the mysteries of the Dionysian couples in the south Italian vase paintings discussed earlier. The procession is led by a panther and a slender, fine-footed figure, surely not "Hercules" as the ignorant painter wrote over it, but Hermes [132A].[286] There follow, according to the inscriptions, Silenus and then the *sacra*, the holy accessories, borne by an ass as was already customary in the itinerant mysteries in Aristophanes' day.[287] The last figure in this niche is a Pan-like being, named "Aegypas" instead of Aegipan. These figures represent an excerpt from the procession.

In the next niche Liber Pater, the Latin name for the child Dionysos, stands wreathed and bearing a *thyrsos* before an altar [132B]; behind him stands one of his nurses, here named "Nysis oros," Mount Nysis. Behind the two an *arca*, or ark, containing the *mysteria* (as the inscription says), is lying on the ground after having been unloaded from the ass. The paintings in this niche also include a Dionysian female double-flute player named "Antiope," and Satur, a satyr. In

---

284   See G. Calza, "Rinvenimenti nell'Isola Sacra," pp. 156–61.

285   See G. Becatti, "Rilievo con la nascita di Dioniso e aspetti mistici di Ostia pagana," pp. 14, 36.

286   The figure is interpreted as "Hercules" by U. von Wilamowitz-Moellendorff, "Sepulchri Potuensis imagines," p. 95. "Hercules" occurs again instead of Hermes in *Laudamia*; see Wilamowitz, p. 90. The painter probably did not know the Greek name but only "Mercurius."

287   Aristophanes, *Frogs* 159: ὄνος ἄγων μυστήρια.

the next niche Satur is leading the panther; an animal with the *thyrsos* is following "Liber Pater Consacratus," Dionysos who has received the initiation (*consecratio*);[288] and behind him follows Silenus, all under tall vines. As for the fourth niche, we are told that only feeble traces of its tree and leaf ornament have been preserved.[289] After the consecration, began the periodic existence of Dionysos in the open with the maenads[290] who were prepared for his coming. To the Dionysian *consecratio* corresponded the maenadic *consecratio* hinted at in the Villa dei Misteri.

We can only guess at the secret contents of the ark, the *arcana* (as they were called in Latin after their container), and in this broad historic canvas we must confine ourselves to essentials. In all likelihood the *arcana* were essentially the same as the contents of the *liknon*, which was often covered with fruits and cakes. The stucco ornament of a patrician house, which was excavated near the Villa Farnesina in Rome and is consequently called "La Farnesina,"[291] reveals a few more details concerning the preparation of the initiates, or *mystai* [133]. The little initiand, with wholly covered head and holding a *thyrsos*, is facing a silenus, the male initiator who is busy with the *liknon* which he seems to be covering rather than opening.[292] On an ointment jar in the Florence Archaeological Museum, we see a boy bearing a covered *liknon* on his veiled head and approaching a no-longer-young female initiator who is holding a kantharos, the vessel

288 See Kerényi, *Eleusis*, p. 198, note 42.
289 Calza ("Rinvenimenti," p. 156) regarded this niche as the first: "La prima nicchia di fronte all'ingresso doveva contenere anch' essa delle figure, ma sull'intonaco rosso son rimaste soltanto debilissime traccie di alberi e fogliami."
290 See Kerényi, *The Gods of the Greeks*, p. 258 (Pelican edn., p. 227).
291 See F. Matz, ΔΙΟΝΥΣΙΑΚΗ ΤΕΛΕΤΗ, pp. 1394 ff.
292 This action is misinterpreted by Matz, p. 1402.

characteristic of the young Dionysos, in readiness for him [134].[293] The boy's proportions liken him to a small god.

The relation of the Dionysian boys and the male sex in general to the contents of the *liknon* is different from that of the Dionysian women.[294] The two architectonic terra-cotta reliefs facing one another in Hanover show the difference. For the female initiands the contents are disclosed; the male initiand approaches with eyes covered and the *liknon* with phallus is placed on his head [135].[295] The *liknon* on the head of the boy initiand expresses an identification: the bearer is identified with the contents of the carried basket. On the stucco relief in La Farnesina, the *liknon* is brought in for the initiation of girls, one of whom is shown caressing a panther in the next scene [136].[296]

The art of the sarcophagi, which began to flower in the period of the Isola Sacra paintings (the second or third century A.D.), carries us further than the smaller monuments showing the exodus to private mysteries.[297] If we could lay hands on the model books used by the artists, we would have overpowering testimony to the consistency and

293   See E. Simon, "Drei antike Gefässe aus Kameoglas in Corning, Florenz und Besançon," pp. 21 ff.

294   The parallelism in the stucco figures of La Farnesina was pointed out by Matz, in ΔΙΟΝΥΣΙΑΚΗ ΤΕΛΕΤΗ, but he, however, did not understand the difference between them.

295   For representations in codices, see Matz, pls. 20 and 21.

296   Ibid., pl. 11; see also [132A].

297   An example is the so-called Morgan Cup (see Simon, "Drei antike Gefässe") showing an ass on whose back the *mysteria* are loaded; also represented is the preparation of a cult action behind a curtain. The reason for the curtain is not, as Simon believes, that the contents of the *liknon* might not be revealed under the open sky. Horace, *Odes* I 18 11–13, speaks of his own reserve in the face of the ecstatic behavior of the bacchantes who swung the *liknon* and freely displayed its contents, as they were permitted to do and as, in a way, is shown in the Morgan Cup representation; also see [71]. For other examples of the use of the curtain, see [139], [140], [142].

coherence of the Dionysian religion as imprinted in Attica. Even in their fortuitous selection, the works that have come down to us present a picture of extraordinary richness. And despite their lack of coherence, they throw additional light on the Dionysian calendar of the Athenians.

The central scene on a luxurious marble sarcophagus in Baltimore is the triumphal procession of Dionysos, a motif which after the famous *pompe* of Ptolemy II pertains more to the history of culture than to that of religion.[298] The lid bears a frieze in three parts, showing the two births of Dionysos. The first scene shows the "labor of Semele";[299] the second shows Zeus, whose thigh an Eileithyia is tending like a midwife, while Hermes is hurrying off with the child. In the third scene, Dionysos is represented with his four nurses, one of whom holds him on her lap [137]. An aged silenus with a very earnest face approaches him, bowing low. He is bringing the child the mysterious cruciform structure that was carried about in Athens at the feast of the Anthesteria, an intimation of Dionysos' impending stay in the underworld, during which time the mask and garment hanging on the structure will represent the god.[300]

Three other reliefs on sarcophagi show Dionysos in the last phase of his childhood, and two of these suggest the mystic happening that has been enacted with the nurses since the child's infancy. On a sarcophagus in Munich the central motif is the preparation for the child's

298   For the Baltimore sarcophagus, see pl. 47 in Simon, "Dionysischer Sarkophag in Princeton." / The *pompe* of Ptolemy II is described by Kallixeinos of Rhodes, in Athenaios V 197 CD.

299   See [65A/65B] also.

300   For the "mysterious cruciform structure," see [93]. Simon, "Dionysischer Sarkophag," p. 145, calls it a "staff adorned with a large bow."

bath [138].[301] A half-naked maenad is pouring something into the boiling water in a kettle. The boiling itself is indicated by the surface of the water. Another maenad is preparing to immerse the child, who is lying on her lap, in the hot water. The viewer can only infer that the child is to be cooked. Beside this scene the mystic sacrifice is indicated in another way: the naked boy is riding on a ram and bearing the *liknon* on his head.[302] This animal, which replaces the he-goat for the sake of secrecy, is being led to the sacrifice by a youth with a *thyrsos*; the two women accompany him. In the third scene, as on the two other sarcophagi, the little *consecratus* is standing there.

A sarcophagus in the Capitoline Museum provides, in addition to the bath, another important hint. A silenus is beating a boy satyr as though to punish him [139].[303] Thus, the symbolic sacrifice would seem to have involved blows. The instrument employed was a folded strap.[304] The whip in the hand of the winged goddess in the Villa dei Misteri seems to betoken a similar mystery blow in the initiation of the maenads. On the Capitoline sarcophagus, there are two additional scenes along with the two allusive mystic scenes. In the scene on the far left, the *consecratus* is standing in his hunting boots; on the far right, a half-naked maenad is standing before a curtain awaiting the loving visitor.

The last sarcophagus in this series, one in Princeton, shows three scenes that may correspond to the Attic Elaphebolion, the "Dionysian March" which took place in the latter half of our March and the first

301 Simon, p. 137.

302 So also N. Himmelmann-Wildschütz, "Fragment eines attischen Sarkophags," p. 28.

303 See Matz, ΔΙΟΝΥΣΙΑΚΗ ΤΕΛΕΤΗ, p. 1452.

304 Two other examples of this usage are cited by Matz, p. 1452, note 3.

part of our April [140].[305] Evidently the three events represented take place simultaneously. In the scene on the right, the attendants have almost finished dressing the consecrated little god; in a raised position he is standing and receiving his insignia. He is already clothed in the *nebris*, a small deerskin. A youthful satyr is fastening a hunting boot on the god's right foot, while two Dionysian women and a satyr are busy with the bands he will wear on his head and hands. Apparently his *thyrsos*, a branching narthex stalk, is being tied to his hand. In the center scene, according to an archaeological description, two nude youths sitting on a panther skin are being served by two girls "with fruits or cakes [probably cakes at this time of year] for refreshment or as a pastime."[306] This description takes no account of the *velum* hanging behind the two couples, a sure sign that the entertainment will have an erotic continuation. In the scene on the left of the relief, something is being set up by three powerfully built satyr youths: the aged Dionysos in the form of a herm.

This herm has been defined more closely by Erika Simon: "It developed from the idol of the mask god familiar to us from Attic vases of the fifth century. Wooden pole, garments, and mask are here transposed into durable material, stone. The arms, mere stumps on the Attic vases, are here rendered in their natural form in accordance with the Hellenistic tradition. The god holds the kantharos in his right hand."[307] We know that on Spartan sepulchral steles this two-handled drinking vessel (the kantharos) was represented as an attribute of the *heros*.[308] Thus, as shown in the Princeton relief, the god is again divided into

305   See Simon, "Dionysischer Sarkophag," p. 137.
306   Matz, p. 1447.   307   Simon, p. 143.
308   On the *heros*, see above in ch. VI; see also G. W. Elderkin, *Kantharos*, pp. 1 ff.

two, the emasculated "lord of the dead" and the young hunter, and he remained with the men in their virility. This was a secret happening in the month of Elaphebolion in Athens, in the background of the public celebration of the Great Dionysia.

The Athenian tradition which the Attic sarcophagus workshops passed on to the Romans through models and model books can be followed up to this Princeton sarcophagus from the early Antonine period, the first half of the second century A.D. The tradition would not have lasted if the corresponding religion in the form of Greek mysteries had not also subsisted up to this time—not, to be sure, in its old style but as a kind of mixture of religious archaism and classicism, such as marks the style of the so-called neo-Attic reliefs. Thus, we have come to the end of the field that this book set out to explore: the religion of *zoë* in its Greek form. An account of the cosmic, cosmopolitan Dionysian religion, whose last religious book was the Dionysian epic of Nonnos in the fifth century A.D., would require a separate work. Here we can merely sketch in the main features of this development. One is that the Attic structure was replaced by a so-called syncretism, a Dionysian baroque, whose devotees may not even have understood the ancient mysteries. The myths of the god's childhood and his division into two, for example, take on a new form. The division takes on a static universality, reflected in a dual view of the world.

Ten important sarcophagi dating from the latter half of the second century to the beginning of the third century A.D. were found in the burial ground of the distinguished and wealthy family of the Calpurni Pisones in Rome.[309] The works include several Dionysian representations, which are not, however, sufficient grounds for regarding the

309 See K. Lehmann and E. C. Olsen, *Dionysiac Sarcophagi in Baltimore*, p. 10.

family as a Dionysian community, a sect of initiates as it were.[310] Rather, they indicate the spread of the Dionysian religion and provide magnificent examples of what I have just called "Dionysian baroque." One of these works is the sarcophagus with the Indian triumphal procession of Dionysos; its lid represented the birth myth in accordance with an old model book.[311] A second fine example of this baroque shows the arrival of Dionysos on Naxos [141].[312] Along with Dionysos (shown here arriving with his divine companions), Ariadne, whom he finds asleep, will dominate the Dionysian view of the world. These sarcophagi are now in Baltimore.

On another of these sarcophagi, the rearing of the child is represented in a "humane" manner that no longer implies any allusion to the mythical sacrifice [142]. The infant has already been bathed and placed in the lap of one of the nurses, who is holding him to her breast. The broad basket on the head of a serving woman points only in a very general sense to the mystery rites. The second half of the representation has been described as follows: "The remaining part of the relief is dominated by a fat, bearded old man, who in his drunkenness is supported by two satyrs. He wears long feminine garments and boots, and his fat body is distinguished by the feminine character of the breasts."[313] The old man's noble features ought to have suggested to the archaeologist who wrote this description that here the return of the emasculated Dionysos to the underworld is not indicated by the setting up of an idol, but finds a new artistic and wholly human ex-

---

310 Lehmann and Olsen, pp. 20 ff.
311 On the model books, see above, note 265. For the sarcophagus itself, see Lehmann and Olsen, fig. 7 and pp. 12 ff.
312 Lehmann and Olsen, fig. 9 and pp. 14 f.
313 Lehmann and Olsen, fig. 2 and pp. 11 f.

pression. The lid of the sarcophagus is decorated by a frieze showing erotic banquets before lowered curtains; the couples are seen not from outside but from within. This motif, too, is treated in such a way that one can think only of a profane ceremony. The *cista mystica* from which a snake raises its head at the bottom right corner of the sarcophagus itself clearly points to erotic mysteries. It also did so in the Villa dei Misteri murals [143], although not in the festive hall of preparations or in the *cubiculum*.[314] This is the motif that achieved its widest popularity in Athens with Sabazios. This same Sabazios was now very much favored by the tendency to "syncretism."[315]

In an ancient scholarly compendium of writings on Dionysos, Diodorus Siculus wrote: "He seems to be dual in form because there are two Dionysoi: the bearded Dionysos of the old times, since the ancients wore beards, and the younger, beautiful and exuberant Dionysos, a youth."[316] On Roman sarcophagi the old and the young Dionysoi appear quite openly in the same scene. The archaeological finds provide firm grounds for the observation "that the later Imperial Age was familiar with the dual nature of the god" and that only the iconographical forms were Roman.[317] These finds are not copious. A single composition is varied, but it does yield a view of the world, a static view that was more directly connected with the Attic tradition than the mobile view, shifting with the calendar, that was discernible in the

314 See A. Maiuri, *La Casa del Menandro*, fig. 88.

315 See Lehmann and Olsen, pp. 21 ff.

316 Diodorus Siculus IV 5 2: δίμορφον δ' αὐτὸν δοκεῖν ὑπάρχεις διὰ τὸ δύο Διονύσους γεγονέναι, τὸν μὲν παλαιὸν καταπώγων διὰ τὸ τοὺς ἀρχαίους πάντας πωγωνοτρόφειν, τὸν δὲ νεώτερον ὡραῖον καὶ τρυφερὸν καὶ νεόν. See also R. Turcan, "Dionysos Dimorphos," p. 293.

317 Matz, ΔΙΟΝΥΣΙΑΚΗ ΤΕΛΕΤΗ, p. 1426. Only five pieces comprise the finds; see Matz, p. 1421.

earlier Dionysian sarcophagi. In the last analysis, however, both views derive from the ancient myth of Dionysos.

The new, static view of the world was represented on sarcophagi of a particular type in the form of a *lenos*, the pressing vat where the new wine was kept. The lion's heads in the marble reproductions seem to have taken the place of the taps. This view of the world shows the earthly and heavenly nature of the wine god. In both the examples shown [144, 145], the composition is divided into two parts. In the lower part an emasculated old man lies beside an open vat in which the grapes are being trodden by satyrs. As a pendant—on the sarcophagus in Salerno [144][318]—he has a drunkenly dancing maenad, or—on the one in the Museo Chiaramonti in Rome [145][319]—a sleeping Dionysian woman. When a sarcophagus was adorned only with *thiasoi* of dancing maenads and satyrs, these groups of figures represented the happiness that arises when *zoë* is enhanced by wine. Such representations expressed the possibility of a supraterrestrial existence, free from crude conceptions of the afterlife. But though such a possibility finds expression on many sarcophagi, it is not taken into account in these two examples. In the upper part of these reliefs, we have an example of a higher beatitude, far above the earthly enjoyment of wine: Dionysos and Ariadne are joined in a "higher marriage." It is a heavenly marriage, to be sure, but not without sensuality—here again a mystery aim growing out of the Cretan myth.

We know the myth's itinerary, which led through Naxos. From this itinerary the great artistic composition of the "goddess with the bowl"

318   This is an example of the more recent type according to Matz, p. 1422, but it is not proved.

319   The Museo Chiaramonti sarcophagus is one of the older type according to Matz, who places it in the nineties of the second century A.D.

entered into Roman *bios* and was recorded on a magnificent sarcophagus found near the Porta Latina, not far from the house that contained this composition.[320] It is one more testimony to the closeness
of Dionysian life to Dionysian death. The connection between the
myth and the astronomical heavens has left us a more modest monument in southern Italy. This medium-sized terra-cotta disk, found in
Brindisi, is adorned with a relief of the cosmos [146].[321] Smaller disks
shaped like cakes, and marked with the attributes of many gods, served
as symbolic sacrificial offerings in this region. The large number of
such *dischi sacri* found not only in and around Taranto but also in
almost all of Magna Graecia[322] permits us to infer that they were
buried with the dead. But the sepulchral use of the Brindisi disk is only
secondary. A mythological representation such as this ascension of
a divine pair served primarily for the worship of the represented deities in their temple. This disk, however, like the smaller *dischi* without
mythological representations, may also have been found in a tomb.

The Brindisi disk includes the earliest known representation of
the zodiac on Greek or Italian soil. To the artisan who fashioned it,
the zodiac was still new. He inscribed it on the edge of the disk but
he did not understand its figures. His Capricorn, originally an Oriental
hybrid with horns and a fish's tail, has no tail; his Virgo is holding a

320   See Kerényi, "Die Göttin mit der Schale," *Niobe*, pp. 208–30, pls. III,
IV, and VI.
321   The diameter is 35 cm. See Kerényi, "Anodos-Darstellung in Brindisi,"
pp. 271–307, and "Die religionsgeschichtliche Einordnung des Diskos von Brindisi," pp. 93–99.
322   F. T. Elworthy (see his "Dischi Sacri," pp. 51 ff.) found in the museum
of Tarentum fifty-six more pieces which I was unable to find. I did, however,
find various pieces and fragments in Brindisi, Bari, and Potenza; and in Pali-
nuro, a well-preserved mold for such "cakes." See Kerényi, *Werke*, III, in the
index s.v. *foccaccie sacre* ("holy cakes").

slender vessel and is so low-waisted that the artisan's model may have stemmed from as early as the fourth century B.C. He also changed the order of the constellations but surely followed a very early model, for like the original Babylonian zodiac his has only eleven signs and a double-length Scorpio.[323] From this it may be inferred that the Brindisi disk was fashioned between the fourth and the first century B.C.

The divine pair at the center of the disk, in a chariot drawn by four horses, guided by Hermes and driven by Eros, show the same order of importance as do Dionysos and his enthroned beloved in the Villa dei Misteri frieze, but here it is expressed by other means. Here the feminine figure is on the right, and she is larger and holds the scepter. The man, though somewhat more in the foreground, is smaller and bears no scepter but a magnificent *thyrsos*. Here again the idea of an apotheosis of Semele has been suggested,[324] but the presence of Eros in the center of the zodiac marks this journey as an erotic ascension and argues in favor of Ariadne. Moreover, no cult monument of Semele has been found in southern Italy. Dionysos and Ariadne, however, appear on the gable of a Pompeiian sanctuary on the outskirts of the city, evidence that the Greek Dionysos cult was taken over by the Oscan-speaking inhabitants.[325]

The vessel by which, in addition to the *thyrsos*, the male figure in the chariot is distinguished can hardly, to judge by its shape, be anything but a chous. The chous found near Brindisi—and reproduced here [117]—shows Dionysos and his companion on their couch. On the

323 See F. Boll, C. Bezold, and W. Gundel, *Sternglaube und Sterndeutung*, pp. 7, 52.

324 See P. Boyancé, "Le disque de Brindisi et l'apothéose de Sémélé," and also ch. VI, above, at notes 242 ff.

325 At the sanctuary entrance there is an Oscan inscription.

disk Dionysos himself is carrying the vessel as he rides heavenward with Ariadne after their marriage at the Choës festival.[326] Around them the cosmos unfolds, surrounded in the outermost zone by the zodiac. The upper segment of the relief shows the background of the ascension, the firmament, characterized by the two Atlantes which support it, by the sheaf of lightnings, by sun, moon, and stars, by the star on the caps of the Dioskouroi, and the distaff of the Moirai. The symbols of the lower segment indicate the deities and cults relating to existence on the earth and sea: the wheel of Tyche, the crosstorch of Demeter and Persephone, a cornucopia, a covered *liknon* and its contents, three cakes and a phallus set down in a particular way, Hekate's torch, a *thyrsos* with band, the sickle of Kronos, Poseidon's trident, and a sign that is not clear. The ladder, obviously leading to the upper sphere (which the chariot bearing the bridal pair has already reached), points to the cult of Adonis. It was in this cult that the women went out on the roof terraces to celebrate the god of youth.[327]

By this combination of divine attributes, the *dischi sacri* of Magna Graecia bear witness to a tendency to universalism, a cult of *pantes theoi*, all the gods. This feature is stressed by the use of the zodiac. It points to a Dionysos-dominated universalism rising above all ties with any particular city or state, a universalism latent in the pre-Greek and extra-Greek Dionysian religion and in a very special way inherent in it. The widespread use of Dionysian images in tombs, as disclosed in vase paintings and sarcophagus reliefs, implies such a tendency, for it was in connection with the burial of the dead that the need to celebrate indestructible life was most absolute and universal. This is as true of the Dionysian religion as it is of Christianity. The amplifica-

---

326   See Kerényi, *The Gods of the Greeks*, p. 269 (Pelican edn., p. 237).
327   See Kerényi, "Der entschwebende Adonis," *Werke*, II, 226–32.

tion of the Dionysos cult in late antiquity to a cosmic, cosmopolitan religion was a very natural development, but such a development was possible only insofar as *zoë* could exert a spontaneous religious influence. This influence, in the mythological and cultic forms here described, had a historical limit.

ILLUSTRATIONS

*1. The Great Goddess on a mountain. Transcript
of a seal from Knossos: reconstruction*

*2. Bull game. Fresco from the palace of Knossos: reconstruction.
Heraklion, Archaeological Museum*

*3. Capture of a wild bull. Detail
of a Minoan ivory pyxis (with
transcript). Heraklion, Archaeological Museum*

4. *Persephone with two companions and a flower, in a cup from the first palace at Phaistos. Heraklion, Archaeological Museum*

5. *Dancing women, in a "fruit bowl" from Phaistos: reconstruction. Heraklion, Archaeological Museum*

6. *The cave of Eileithyia, near Amnisos. Detail of the interior showing a stalagmite suggesting two goddesses joined at the back*

7. *Man setting down a sacrifice in front of a mountain shrine, on a Minoan vase from Knossos. Heraklion, Archaeological Museum*

8. *Mountain shrine with goats and birds of prey, on a Minoan vase from Kato Zakros. Heraklion, Archaeological Museum*

9. *Two male gesture figures among crocuses. Transcript of a drawing on a small Minoan amphora from the first palace at Phaistos. Heraklion, Archaeological Museum*

10. *Epiphany scene among flowers, on the seal disk of a gold ring from Isopata. Heraklion, Archaeological Museum*

11. *Epiphany scene, on a gold ring from Knossos. A woman with half-open hand greets a small male apparition. Oxford, Ashmolean Museum*

12. *Epiphany scene, on a Minoan ring. Two female figures greet each other with upraised hands. Heraklion, Archaeological Museum*

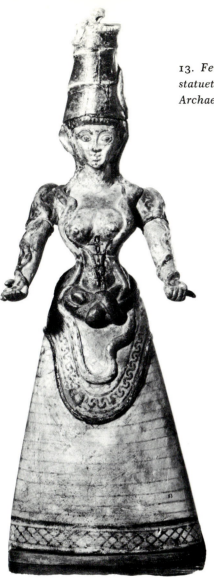

13. *Female figure with coiled snakes. Faience statuette from the palace of Knossos. Heraklion, Archaeological Museum*

14. *Female figure holding snakes. Faience statuette from the palace of Knossos. Heraklion, Archaeological Museum*

15. *Idol of a poppy goddess. Clay statuette from Gazi. Heraklion, Archaeological Museum*

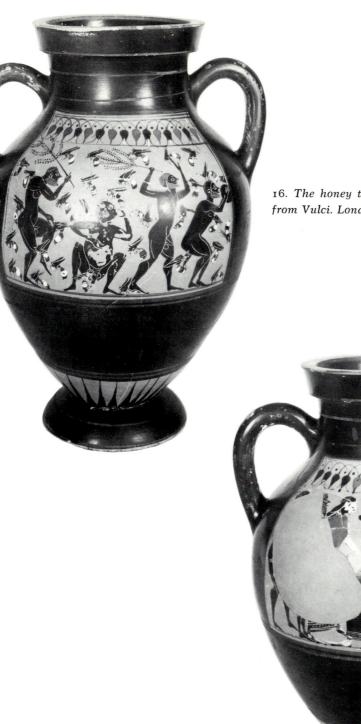

16. *The honey thieves, on an amphora from Vulci. London, British Museum*

17. *Enthroned maenads with satyrs, on the other side of the Vulci amphora*

18. *Hunt scenes and scorpion, on a black-figure vase by Nikosthenes. London, British Museum*

19. *Youth bearing a rhyton. Fresco from the palace of Knossos. Heraklion, Archaeological Museum*

20. *Bull's head rhyton from the fourth royal tomb of Mycenae. Athens, National Museum*

21A. *Sacrifice scene, on a Late Minoan painted sarcophagus from Hagia Triada. Two spotted calves are brought as gifts for the dead. Heraklion, Archaeological Museum*

21B. *On the other side of the same sarcophagus from Hagia Triada, a large, motley bull lies bound on the sacrificial altar*

22. *Scenes of maenads with snakes, on a Tyrrhenian amphora. Paris, Louvre*

23. *Silenus treading out grapes, on an Archaic vase decorated by the Amasis painter. Würzburg, Martin v. Wagner-Museum der Universität*

24. *Mask between two goats. Transcript of a stone seal from a tomb near Phaistos. Heraklion, Archaeological Museum*

25. *A "lord of the wild beasts," on a Minoan seal from Kydonia. Oxford, Ashmolean Museum*

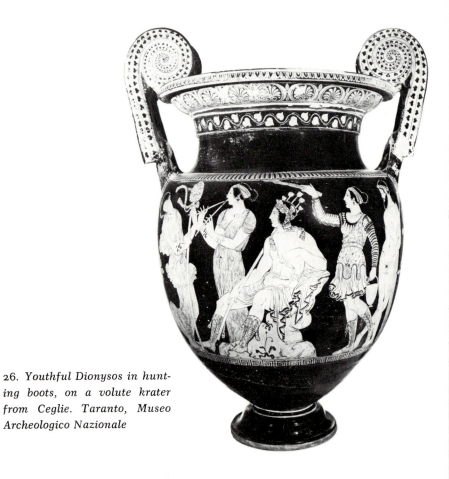

26. *Youthful Dionysos in hunting boots, on a volute krater from Ceglie. Taranto, Museo Archeologico Nazionale*

27. *Meander pattern on stairwells in the temple of Apollo at Didyma near Miletos*

28. *Pallas Athena, Theseus, and the Minotaur, on a bowl painted by Aison. Madrid, Museo Arqueologico Nacional*

29. *Pallas Athena, Theseus, and the labyrinth, on a black-figure cup from the Akropolis in Athens. Athens, National Museum*

30. *Symbolic labyrinth, on a small oil bottle from Attica*

31. *A late, complicated representation of the labyrinth, framed by meander patterns. Mosaic from a family tomb in Hadrumentum in North Africa*

32A. *The labyrinth fresco from the ground-floor corridor of the palace of Knossos: reconstruction*

32B. *Drawing of the path in the labyrinth fresco*

33. *Labyrinth graffito scratched into a tile on the left gable of the Parthenon, Athens*

34. *Labyrinth on a clay tablet (Cn 1287) from Pylos*

35. *Ariadne's thread, on a seventh-century relief pithos. Basel, Antikenmuseum*

36. Dionysos, Ariadne, and Theseus, on a cup
krater. Taranto, Museo Archeologico Nazionale

37. *Dionysos accompanied by the three Horai. Transcript of the painting on the François Vase, a krater by Ergotimos and Klitias. Florence, Museo Archeologico*

38. *Two maenads with a sacrificial animal, on a pyxis in the Archäologisches Institut, Heidelberg*

39A/39B. *Arrival of Dionysos, probably at the house of Semachos, on a sixth-century vase. Orvieto, Museo Archaeologico*

40. *Arrival of Dionysos, accompanied by Hermes, perhaps at the house of Ikarios, on an Attic amphora from the circle of the Edinburgh painter. Agrigento, Museo Archeologico Nazionale*

41. *Scene of the arrival of Dionysos, probably at the house of Ikarios and his daughter, Erigone. Orvieto, Museo Etrusco Faina*

42A. *Athenian lady escorted to a festival by a silenus. Skyphos decorated by the Penelope painter. Berlin, Staatliche Museen*
42B. *Girl swinging, pushed by a silenus, on the other side of the same skyphos*

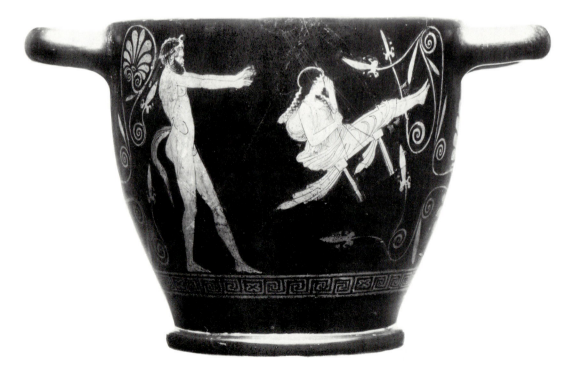

43. *Girl swinging. Terra cotta from Hagia Triada: reconstruction. Heraklion, Archaeological Museum*

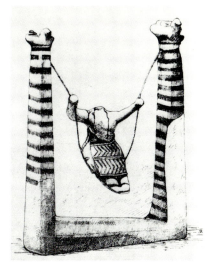

44. *Erigone mounting a chariot, with Dionysos in front of her, on an Attic krater. The he-goat with a man's head is a representation of the Dionysian afterlife. Palermo, Museo Archeologico Nazionale*

45. *Maenad between the bearded Dionysos and a nude man, on the other side of the same krater*

Stackelberg del.

46. Ascension scene in a variation of the "goddess mounting her chariot" theme. Transcript of the painting on an Attic lekythos

47. Vase painting of a scene in the underworld. Dionysos mounting a chariot is about to leave his mother, Semele, and ascend

48. *Dionysos, accompanied by two ithyphallic sileni, is received by a royal woman, on a neck amphora. Orvieto, Museo Etrusco Faina*

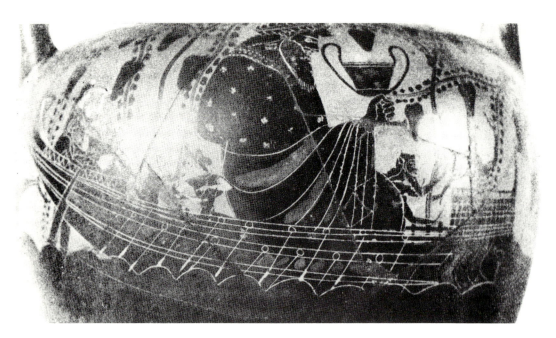

49. *Arrival of Dionysos on shipboard, accompanied by sileni and women, on an Attic amphora. Tarquinia, Museo Nazionale Tarquiniese*

50. *Variation of the "arrival of Dionysos on shipboard" theme, on an Attic amphora. Tarquinia, Museo Nazionale Tarquiniese*

51. *Dionysos on shipboard, on a cup from Vulci painted by Exekias. Munich*

52A. *Dionysos with a rhyton on board a ship with a mule's head prow, on the inside of a black-figure Attic cup. Berlin. Staatliche Museen*

52B. *Maenads riding on mules surrounding Dionysos, on the outside of the same cup*

53. *Maenads arriving at a banquet on ithyphallic mules. Transcript of the painting on an Attic lekythos*

54A. *Dionysos with kantharos on an ithyphallic mule, on an Attic amphora. Museo Nazionale di Villa Giulia, Rome*

54B. *Ithyphallic mule dancing among drunken sileni. Fragment of an amphora, by the Amasis painter, that was found on Samos and later lost in the sack of the museum*

55. *Love play between mules with painted hides, on an Attic chous in Munich*

56. *Dionysos in a ship car, with masked men as sileni. Painting (with transcript) on an Attic skyphos. Bologna, Museo Civico Archeologico*

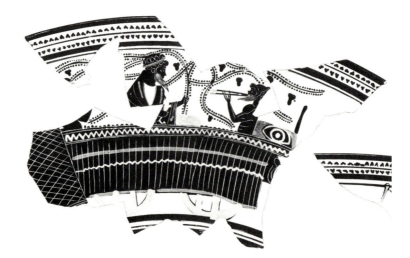

57. *Dionysos in a ship car. Transcript of a fragmentary skyphos in Athens*

58. *Procession with a sacrificial animal, on an Attic skyphos. London, British Museum*

59A. *Dionysos in a ship car with a dog's head prow, on an Attic skyphos. London, British Museum*

59B. *Transcript made when the skyphos was in better condition*

60. *Arrival of Dionysos and a companion at the house of Ikarios and Erigone with the she-dog Maira. Relief from the Bema of Phaidros. Athens, Ancient Theater*

61A. *Motley bull in procession, on a sixth-century Attic lekythos. London, British Museum*

61B. *Procession led by a salpinx. Transcript of the painting on the same lekythos*

62. *Stone slab with traces of the tripod from the temple of Apollo, Delphi*

63. *Apollo sitting on a tripod and resting his feet on a* bathron. *Late fifth-century Attic votive relief. Athens, National Museum*

64. *Scenes of preparations for a Dionysian sacrificial rite: the visit of Dionysos, the burning of Psyche by two weeping Erotes, the suckling fawn, and the milking of the goat. Reliefs on a neo-Attic marble pedestal in the Vatican*

65. *The dying Semele, on a silver vessel from Pompeii (with transcript). Naples, Museo Archeologico Nazionale*

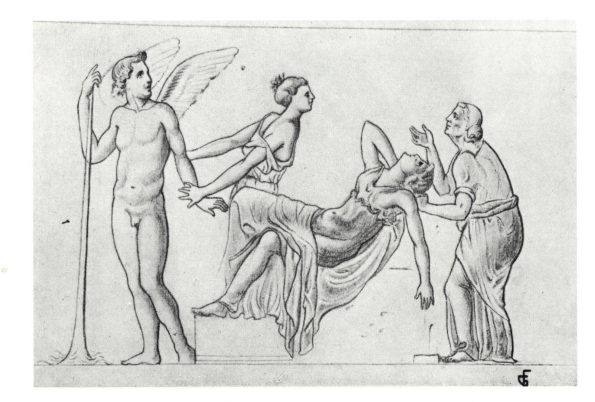

A

66A–E. *Scenes from the life of Dionysos: birth, enthronement, the boy riding away on a he-goat, and the youth driving a team of panthers to his marriage with Ariadne. Relief on an ivory pyxis. Bologna, Museo Civico Archeologico*

B

66c

66d

66E

67. *Epiphany of the Divine Child out of a vine. Terra-cotta relief from a Roman building. London, British Museum*

68. *Dancing satyrs and flute-playing maenad. Terra-cotta relief from a Roman building. Paris, Louvre*

69. *Satyr with mirror, and a dancing maenad. Terra-cotta relief from a Roman building. New York, The Metropolitan Museum of Art*

70. *Maenad with snake and satyr with panther.*
Terra-cotta relief from a Roman building. New
York, The Metropolitan Museum of Art

71. *The child awake in the* liknon, *swung by a*
maenad and a satyr. Terra-cotta relief from a
Roman building. London, British Museum

72. *The uncovering of the phallus. Terra-cotta relief from a Roman building. Paris, Louvre.*

73. *Birth of Dionysos from the thigh of Zeus, on an amphora by the Diosphos painter. Paris, Bibliothèque Nationale*

74. *Birth of Dionysos from the thigh of Zeus, on a volute krater from the late fifth or early fourth century. Taranto, Museo Archeologico Nazionale*

75. *Dionysos with his mystic alter ego, on a krater by the Altamura painter. Ferrara, Museo Archeologico Nazionale*

76A. *Dionysos idol with an ithyphallic satyr and a maenad, on an Attic skyphos with black figures on a white ground. Athens, National Museum*

76B/76C. *In the same scene, two men approach the idol, leading a half-naked hetaira and a he-goat*

77. *Dance around the Dionysos idol in the Lenaion, on an Attic cup from Vulci by Makron. Berlin, Staatliche Museen*

78. *Cult around the Dionysos idol in the Lenaion, on an Attic stamnos from Vulci. London, British Museum*

79. *Marble mask of Dionysos from his temple in Ikarion. Athens, National Museum*

80. *Kantharos in the right hand of the enthroned Dionysos from Ikarion. Athens, National Museum*

81. *Torso of the enthroned Dionysos statue from Ikarion. Athens, National Museum*

82. *Double mask of Dionysos worshiped by maenads, on an Attic lekythos. Athens, National Museum*

83. *Variation of the double mask of Dionysos worship. Athens, National Museum*

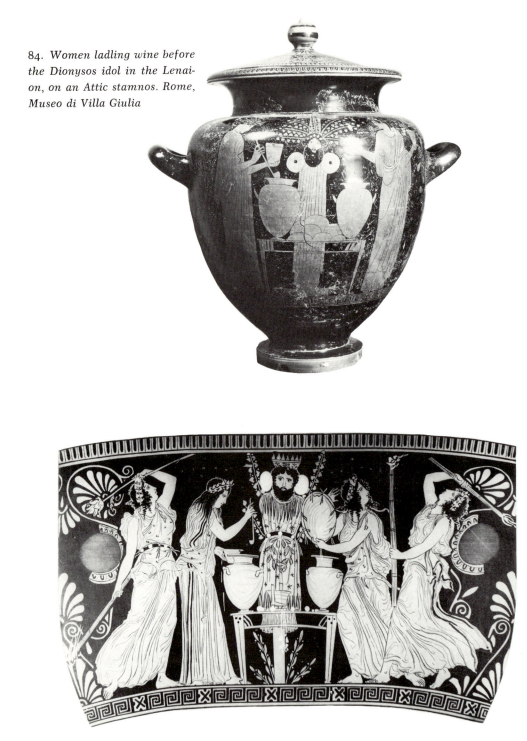

84. *Women ladling wine before the Dionysos idol in the Lenaion, on an Attic stamnos. Rome, Museo di Villa Giulia*

85. *Variation of 84 with dancing women, on an Attic stamnos. Naples, Museo Archeologico Nazionale*

86A. *The child Dionysos at the Lenaia, on an Attic stamnos. Warsaw, National Museum*

86B. *Dionysian women with wine at the Lenaia, on the other side of the Warsaw stamnos*

87. *Comic* phallophoriai, *on a black-figure Attic cup. Florence, Museo Archeologico*

88A. *Sabazios and the Great Goddess of Asia Minor enthroned, on a krater painted by Polygnotos. Ferrara, Museo Archeologico Nazionale*

88B/88D. *Ecstatic dance by the initiates in honor of the divine pair on the Polygnotos krater*

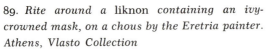
89. *Rite around a liknon containing an ivy-crowned mask, on a chous by the Eretria painter. Athens, Vlasto Collection*

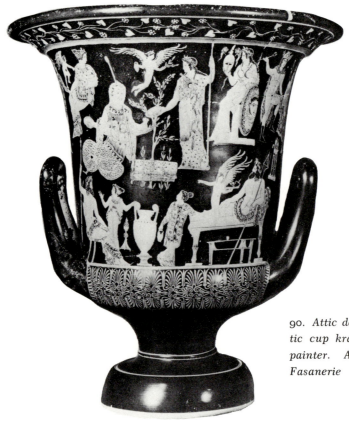

90. *Attic deities, on a large Attic cup krater by the Kekrops painter. Adolphseck, Schloss Fasanerie*

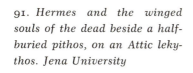

91. *Hermes and the winged souls of the dead beside a half-buried pithos, on an Attic lekythos. Jena University*

92A. *Singers of the dithyramb, on a fifth-century Attic krater. Copenhagen, National Museum*

92B. *Cloaked man being abducted by two women with* thyrsoi, *on the other side of the same krater*

93. *Children miming the rites on Choës Day on an Attic chous. New York, The Metropolitan Museum of Art*

94. *Girl swinging over an open pithos, on an Attic hydria. Berlin, Staatliche Museen*

95. *Swing game over an open pithos, on a chous by the Eretria painter. Athens, Vlasto Collection*

96. *Festive preparations of a distinguished woman, on a chous by the Meidias painter. New York, The Metropolitan Museum of Art*

97A. *Athenian lady guided by a torch-bearer in silenus costume and hunting boots, on a skyphos by Polygnotos, in the possession of Oskar Kokoschka*

97B. *A less distinguished couple, on the other side of the same skyphos*

98. *Enthronement of a youth as Dionysos, on an Attic cup krater of the Classical period. Copenhagen, National Museum*

99. *Reception of a Mitrephoros at night, on an Attic chous. New York, The Metropolitan Museum of Art*

100. *Visit of Dionysos to Althaia, on an Attic krater. Tarquinia, Museo Nazionale Tarquiniese*

101. *Dionysian boys after death, on an Attic pitcher. Baltimore, Walters Art Gallery*

102. *Boy playing with a fawn, on an Attic chous. Athens, National Museum*

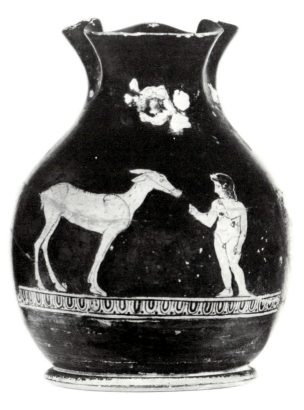

103. *Figures of the month of Elaphebolion. Calendar frieze built into the Small Mitropolis in Athens*

104. *Archaic* komos *of* men dressed as women, *on an Attic cup. Amsterdam, Allard Pierson Museum*

105. *Classic* komos *of* men dressed as women, *on an Attic krater. Cleveland, Museum of Art*

106. *The* domina, *the door to the* cubiculum, *and the first figure of the preparations, from murals in the hall of preparations in the Villa dei Misteri, Pompeii*

107. *View of a rustic ritual scene, from murals in the* cubiculum *in the Villa dei Misteri*

108. *The adorning of the bride, from murals in the hall of prep-arations in the Villa dei Misteri*

109. *View of a fantastic ritual scene, from murals in the* cubiculum *in the Villa dei Misteri*

110A. *A boy, standing between two women, reading in preparation for his initiation, from murals in the hall of preparations in the Villa dei Misteri*

110B. *Pregnant young woman holding a tray* (left); *candidate bacchante running away* (right). *Continuation of hall of preparations murals in the Villa dei Misteri*

110C. *Initiation by mirroring the mask, and the divine pair. Continuation of hall of preparations murals in the Villa dei Misteri*

110D. *Before the uncovering of the phallus. Continuation of hall of preparations murals in the Villa dei Misteri*

110E. *The novice, initiates, and the initiated maenad. Continuation of hall of preparations murals in the Villa dei Misteri*

111. *View from the* cubiculum *into the hall of preparations. Villa dei Misteri*

112A. *Old silenus, from murals
in the* cubiculum *in the Villa
dei Misteri*

112B. *Young Dionysos, from
murals in the* cubiculum *in the
Villa dei Misteri*

112C/112D. *Dancing maenads, from murals in the* cubiculum *in the Villa dei Misteri*

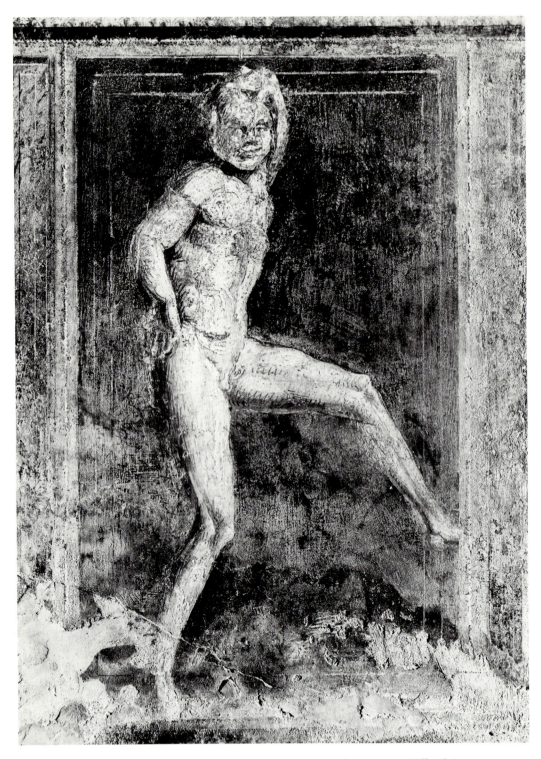

112E. *Young satyr, from murals in the* cubiculum *in the Villa dei Misteri*

112F. *The* domina *holding a document, from murals in the* cubiculum *in the Villa dei Misteri*

113. A drunken Dionysos being brought home at night by a
silenus, on an Attic chous.
Athens, National Museum

114. A horned Dionysos as bridegroom
in his Boukoleion, on a bell krater from
Thurii, one of the Hope Vases

115. Deceased boys playing around a krater, on an Attic sarcophagus.
Ostia, Museo Archeologico

116. *Boy satyr with torch and situla, on an Italic chous.* Vienna, Kunsthistorisches Museum

117. *Dionysos and his beloved, served by a boy satyr, on an Italic chous.* Brindisi, Museo Provinciale

118. *Eros throws the ball to a hesitant woman, on an Italic krater with a Greek inscription. Naples, Museo Archeologico Nazionale*

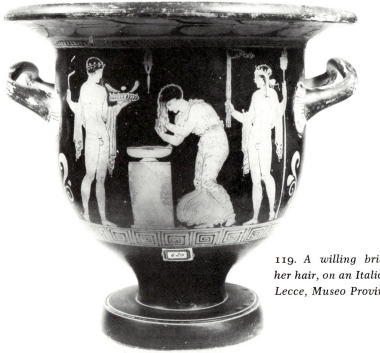

119. *A willing bride washing her hair, on an Italic bell krater. Lecce, Museo Provinciale*

120. *Bride with a mirror, pre-*
paring to go with Hermes, on
an Italic krater. Lecce, Museo
Provinciale

121. *A deceased woman as a*
maenad led by Eros, on an Apu-
lian amphora. Bonn, Antiken-
sammlung

122. *Exodus to the Dionysian nuptials. Transcript of the painting on an Italic krater. Barletta, Museo Civico*

123. *Dionysos with a bell summoning a woman, on an Apulian krater. Ruvo, Museo Jatta*

124. *Youth with an egg before an Ariadne, on an Apulian bell krater. Lecce, Museo Provinciale*

125. *Ascension of an Ariadne, on an Apulian bowl. Ruvo, Museo Jatta*

126. *A Dionysos before a divine maenad, on an Apulian krater. Lecce, Museo Provinciale*

127. *Dionysian exodus, on an Apulian krater. Barletta, Museo Civico*

128. *Another version of the Dionysian exodus, on an Apulian krater. Bari, Museo Archeologico*

129. *The ways of initiation of a woman and a man, on the sides of an Apulian bowl, in the possession of an art dealer*

130. *Continuous pictorial text of the initiation of a woman, on an Italic pointed amphora (with transcript). Giessen, Antiken-sammlung*

131. *Deceased woman as bride and maenad, on a skyphoid pyxis from Adernò, Sicily, Moscow, State Museum of Decorative Arts*

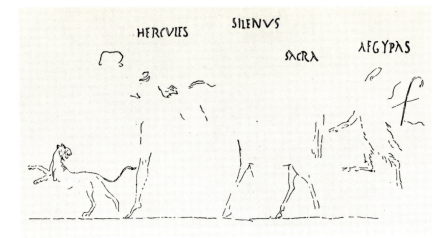

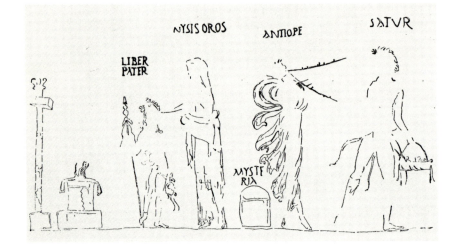

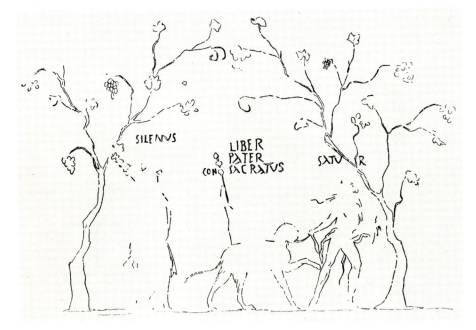

132. *Scenes of the initiation of Dionysos. Traces of murals in a tomb near Ostia. Ostia, Museo Archeologico*

133. *Scene from the initiation of a boy. Stucco ornament from La Farnesina in Rome. Museo Nazionale delle Terme*

134. *Scene from the initiation of a boy. Transcript of an ointment jar. Florence, Museo Archeologico*

135. *Scene from the initiation of a man. Terracotta relief. Hanover, Kestner Museum*

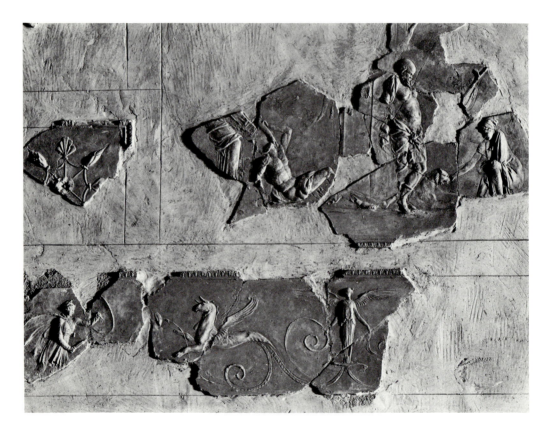

136. *Scene from the initiation of a maenad. Stucco relief from La Farnesina. Rome, Museo Nazionale delle Terme*

137. *The child Dionysos with his nurses. Detail of lid frieze of a marble sarcophagus in Baltimore, Walters Art Gallery*

138. *Scenes from the childhood of Dionysos, with preparation for the bath. Sarcophagus in Munich, Glyptothek*

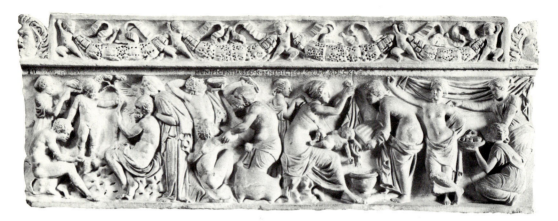

139. *Further scenes from the childhood of Dionysos, with silenus beating a boy satyr. Sarcophagus in Rome, Museo Capitolino*

140. *Scenes showing the setting up of a Dionysian idol. Sarcophagus in Princeton, The Art Museum of Princeton University*

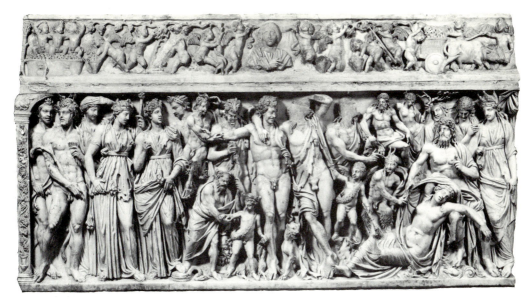

141. *Dionysos and Ariadne on Naxos. Sarcophagus in Baltimore, Walters Art Gallery*

142. *A later version of the childhood of Dionysos. Sarcophagus in Baltimore, Walters Art Gallery*

143. *The* domina *and basket with snake. Villa dei Misteri, Pompeii*

144. *Dionysian cosmos. Sarcophagus in Salerno*

145. *Another version of the Dionysian cosmos. Sarcophagus in Rome, Museo Chiaramonti*

146. *Cosmos and zodiac, with the ascension of Dionysos and Ariadne. Terra-cotta disk found in Brindisi. Brindisi, Museo Provinciale*

LIST OF WORKS CITED

These are used in the footnotes and in the List of Works Cited. Shortened titles readily identified in the List of Works Cited are not included.

AJA   *American Journal of Archaeology*. Princeton, New Jersey.

AM   *Athenische Mitteilungen (Mitteilungen des deutschen archäologischen Instituts, Athenische Abteilung)*. Berlin.

ARW   *Archiv für Religionswissenschaft*. Freiburg im Breisgau and Berlin.

BCH   *Bulletin de correspondance hellénique*. Athens.

BSA   *Annual of the British School of Archaeology at Athens*.

CIL   *Corpus inscriptionum latinarum*. Berlin.

CVA   *Corpus vasorum antiquorum*.

Diehl, *Anth. lyr.*   *Anthologia lyrica graeca*. Edited by Ernst Diehl. 3d edn. Leipzig, 1949–54.

GCS   Die griechischen christlichen Schriftsteller der ersten drei Jahrhunderte. Leipzig.

IG   *Inscriptiones Graecae*. Berlin.

Jacoby, *FGrHist*   *Die Fragmente der griechischen Historiker*. Edited by Felix Jacoby. Berlin and Leiden, 1923–59.

JDAI   *Jahrbuch des deutschen archäologischen Instituts*. Berlin.

JHS   *Journal of Hellenic Studies*. London.

JÖAI   *Jahreshefte des österreichischen archäologischen Institutes in Wien*. Vienna.

LCL   Loeb Classical Library. London and Cambridge, Mass.

MonAnt   *Monumenti Antichi pubblicati per cura dell'Accademia dei Lincei*. Rome.

Nauck, *TGF*   *Tragicorum graecorum fragmenta*. Edited by August Nauck. 2d edn. Leipzig, 1889.

OCT   Oxford Classical Texts.

Praktika   Πρακτικὰ τῆς ἐν ᾿Αρχαιολογικῆς ῾Εταιρείας. Athens.

RE   G. Wissowa et al. (eds.). *Paulys Real-Encyclopädie der classischen Alter-tumswissenschaft.* Stuttgart, 1894– . (References are to columns, not pages.)

RM   *Römische Mitteilungen* (*Mitteilungen des deutschen archäologischen Instituts, Römische Abteilung*). Berlin.

SymbO   *Symbolae Osloenses.* (Societas graeco-latina; Klassisk forening.) Oslo.

In general, classical texts are unlisted except when an edition or translation has been cited. Unless noted to the contrary, English versions of quoted passages are the author's and translator's own.

ABRAMS, MEYER H. *The Milk of Paradise.* Cambridge, Mass., 1934.

AELIAN. *De natura animalium.* Edited by Rudolf Hercher. Leipzig, 1864–66. 2 vols.

AISCHYLOS. [Fragments.] In: METTE, HANS J. (ed.), q.v.

————. [*Works.*] With an English translation by Herbert Weir Smyth. (LCL.) 1922–26. 2 vols. (Including *Eumenides, The Persians,* and *The Suppliant Women.*)

AKURGAL, EKREM. *Die Kunst der Hethiter.* Munich, 1961.

————. *Späthethitische Bildkunst.* Ankara, 1949.

ALEXIOU, STYLIANOS. *Guide to the Archaeological Museum of Heraclion.* Athens, 1968.

————. Ἡ μινωϊκὴ θεὰ μεθ' ὑψωμένων χειρῶν. *Kretika Chronika,* XII (1958).

————. Νέα παράστασις λατρείας ἐπὶ μινωϊκοῦ ἀναγλύφου ἀγγείου. *Kretika Chronika,* XIII (1959).

————. Ὑστερομινωϊκοὶ τάφοι λιμένος Κνώσου. Athens, 1967.

ALFIERI, NEREO, PAOLO E. ARIAS, and MAX HIRMER. *Spina.* Munich, 1958.

ALTHEIM, FRANZ. *Griechische Götter im alten Rom.* Giessen, 1930.

AMANDRY, PIERRE. *La mantique apollinienne à Delphes.* Paris, 1950.

ANDREAE, BERNARD. *Studien zur römischen Grabkunst.* Heidelberg, 1963.

Anthologia Graeca and *Anthologia Palatina.* In: *The Greek Anthology.* Translated by W. R. Paton. (LCL.) 1946–53. 5 vols.

ANTIGONUS CARYSTIUS. *Historiae mirabiles.* In: Παραδοξογράφοι. *Scriptores rerum mirabilium Graeci.* Edited by Anton Westermann. Brunswick, 1839.

ANTONINUS LIBERALIS. Μεταμορφώσεων συναγωγή. In: *Mythographi Graeci,* II:1. Edited by Edgar Martini. Leipzig, 1896.

APICIUS, CAELIUS. *De re coquinaria.* Edited by C. Giarratano and F. Vollmer. Leipzig, 1922.

APOLLODOROS. *The Library.* With an English translation by James George Frazer. (LCL.) 1912–21. 2 vols.

APOLLONIUS RHODIUS. *The Argonautica*. With an English translation by R. C. Seaton. (LCL.) 1912.

———. Scholia. In: *Scholia in Apollonium Rhodium vetera*. Edited by Carl Wendel. Berlin, 1935.

ARATOS. *Arati Phaenomena*. Edited by Ernst Maass. Berlin, 1893.

———. Scholia. In: *Commentariorum in Aratum reliquiae*. Edited by Ernst Maass. Berlin, 1898.

ARISTIDES, AELIUS. *Rhetorica*. Edited by Wilhelm Dindorf. Leipzig, 1829. 3 vols.

ARISTOPHANES. *Acharnians*. In: OATES, W. J., and E. O'NEILL, JR. (eds.), q.v.

———. Scholia. In: *Scholia graeca in Aristophanem*. Edited by Friedrich Dübner. Paris, 1842.

———. [*Works*.] With an English translation by Benjamin Bickley Rogers. (LCL.) 1924. 3 vols. (Including *Frogs, Knights, Peace, Plutus*, and *Wasps*.)

ARISTOTLE. *Anecdota problemata*. Edited by U. C. Bussemaker. In: *Opera Omnia*, IV:1. Paris, 1857.

———. *Works*. Translated into English under the Editorship of W. D. Ross. Oxford, 1908–52. 12 vols.

ARNOBIUS. *Adversus nationes*. Edited by A. Reifferscheid. Vienna, 1875.

ASTOUR, MICHAEL C. *Hellenosemitica*. Leiden, 1965.

ATHENAGORAS. *Libellus pro Christianis*. Edited by E. Schwartz. Leipzig, 1891.

ATHENAIOS. *The Deipnosophists*. With an English translation by Charles Burton Gulick. (LCL.) 1927–41. 7 vols.

BACHOFEN, JOHANN JAKOB. *Gesammelte Werke*, VII. Edited by Karl Meuli. Basel, 1958.

———. *Myth, Religion, and Mother Right: Selected Writings of J. J. Bachofen*. Translated by Ralph Manheim. (Bollingen Series LXXXIV.) Princeton, 1967.

BARTOCCHI, FERNANDA. "Un nuovo cratere a campana del pittore di Amykos." *Bollettino d'Arte*, XLIII (1958).

BAUDELAIRE, CHARLES. "Le Poison," in *Les Fleurs du Mal*. Edited by Jacques Crépet. (*Oeuvres Complètes*, I.) Paris, 1917.

———. *Les Paradis artificiels*. Edited by Jacques Crépet. (*Oeuvres Complètes*, III.) Paris, 1917.

BAYARD, L. "Pytho-Delphes et la légende du serpent." *Revue des études grecques*, LVI (1943).

BEAUFORT, FRANCIS. *Karamania.* London, 1817.

BEAZLEY, JOHN DAVIDSON. *Attic Black-Figure Vase-Painters.* Oxford, 1956.

——. *Attic Red-Figure Vase-Painters.* 2d edn. Oxford, 1963. 3 vols.

——. and L. D. CASKEY. *Attic Vase Paintings in the Museum of Fine Arts, Boston,* II. Oxford, 1954.

BECATTI, GIOVANNI. "Rilievo con la nascita di Dioniso e aspetti mistici di Ostia pagana." *Bollettino d'Arte,* XXXVI (1951).

BEKKER, IMMANUEL (ed.). *Anecdota Graeca.* Berlin, 1814–21. 3 vols.

BENDINELLI, GOFFREDO. *La vite e il vino. Monumenti antichi in Italia.* Milan, 1931.

BENTON, SYLVIA. "The Date of the Cretan Shields." *BSA,* XXXIX (1938–39).

BERTHELOT, M. *Collection des anciens alchimistes grecs,* III. Paris, 1888.

BETHE, ERICH. "Programm und Festzug der grossen Dionysien." *Hermes,* LXI (1926).

BIEBER, MARGARETE. "Die Herkunft des tragischen Kostüms." *JDAI,* XXXII (1917).

BIELEFELD, ERWIN. "Zum Problem der kontinuierenden Darstellungsweise." *Archäologischer Anzeiger,* LXX (1956).

BISCHOFF, E. "Kalender." *RE,* X:2.

BLEGEN, C. W., and M. RAWSON. *The Palace of Nestor in Western Messenia,* I: *The Buildings and Their Contents.* Princeton, 1966. 2 vols.

BODE, GEORG HEINRICH (ed.). *Scriptores rerum mythicarum . . . .* Celle, 1834. 2 vols. in 1. (Including *Mythographi Vaticani.*)

BOEHM, FRITZ. "Das attische Schaukelfest." In: *Festschrift für Eduard Hahn.* Stuttgart, 1917.

BOËTHIUS, AXEL. *Die Pythaïs.* Uppsala, 1918.

BOLL, FRANZ. *Griechische Kalender,* III. (Sitzungsberichte der Heidelberger Akademie der Wissenschaften, Phil.-hist. Kl., 3.) Heidelberg, 1913.

——. "Zu Holls Abhandlung über den Ursprung des Epiphanienfestes." *ARW,* XIX (1916–19).

——, CARL BEZOLD, and WILHELM GUNDEL. *Sternglaube und Sterndeutung.* 4th edn. Leipzig, 1931.

BOURGUET, ÉMILE. "Inscriptions de l'entrée du Sanctuaire au Trésor des Athéniens." In: *Fouilles de Delphes* (École française d'Athène), III: 1. Paris, 1929.

BOURGUET, "ΘΥΙΑΙ-ΘΥΣΤΙΟΝ." In: *Mélanges Perrot*. Paris, 1903.

BOWRA, C. M. (ed.). See under PINDAR.

BOYANCÉ, PIERRE. "Dionysiaca." *Revue des études anciennes*, LXVIII (1966).

―――. "Le disque de Brindisi et l'apothéose de Sémélé." *Revue des études anciennes*, XLIV (1942).

BOZZANO, ERNESTO. *Übersinnliche Erscheinungen bei Naturvölkern*. Translated into German by Ernst Schneider. Bern, 1948.

BRITISH MUSEUM. *Catalogue of the Greek Coins of Crete and the Aegean Islands*. See WROTH, WARWICK.

―――. *Catalogue of the Greek Coins of Troas, Aeolis, and Lesbos*. See WROTH, WARWICK.

―――. *Catalogue of the Greek and Etruscan Vases in the British Museum*, II. London, 1893.

―――. *A Description of the Collection of Ancient Terracottas in the British Museum*. London, 1810.

BROMMER, FRANK (ed.). *Schloss Fasanerie (Adolphseck)*. (*CVA*: Deutschland, XI.) Munich, 1956–59. 2 vols.

BRUECKNER, ALFRED. "Athenische Hochzeitsgeschenke." *AM*, XXXII (1907).

BRUEL, RENÉ. *Essai sur la confrérie religieuse des Aissâoua au Maroc*. Paris, 1926.

BRUGSCH, HEINRICH KARL. "Das Osiris-Mysterium von Tentyra." *Zeitschrift für ägyptische Sprache und Altertumskunde*, XIX (1881).

BUBER, MARTIN (ed.). *Chinesische Geister- und Liebesgeschichten*. (Manesse Bibliothek der Weltliteratur.) Zurich, 1948.

BURKERT, WALTER. "Greek Tragedy and Sacrificial Ritual." *Greek, Roman, and Byzantine Studies*, VII (1966).

BUSCHOR, ERNST. "Ein choregisches Denkmal." *AM*, LIII (1928).

―――. *Griechische Vasen*. Munich, 1940.

―――. *Die Tondächer der Akropolis*, I. Berlin and Leipzig, 1929.

CALZA, GUIDO. "Rinvenimenti nell'Isola Sacra." *Notizie degli Scavi*, 6th Ser., IV (1928).

CANTARELLA, RAFFAELE. *Euripide, I Cretesi. Testi e commenti*. Milan, 1963.

CASKEY, JOHN L. "Excavations in Keos, 1964–65." *Hesperia*, XXXV (1966).

―――. "Investigations in Keos, 1963." *Hesperia*, XXXIII (1964).

CHADWICK, JOHN, and J. T. KILLEN (eds.). *The Knossos Tablets: Third Edition.* (Bulletin of the Institute of Classical Studies of the University of London, Supplement 15.) London, 1964.

CLEMENT OF ALEXANDRIA. [*Works.*] Edited by Otto Stählin. (GCS.) Leipzig, 1905–36. 4 vols. (Including *Protrepticus* and *Stromateis.*)

COCTEAU, JEAN. "L'opium." In: *Oeuvres complètes.* Edn. Marguerat. Geneva, 1946–51. 11 vols.

COLLITZ, HERMANN, and F. BECHTEL. *Sammlung der griechischen Dialekt-inschriften,* II and III. Göttingen, 1899, 1905.

COOK, ARTHUR BERNARD. *Zeus: A Study in Ancient Religion.* Cambridge, 1914–40. 3 vols. in 5.

CORNUTUS. *Theologiae graecae compendium.* Edited by C. Lang. Leipzig, 1881.

Corpus medicorum graecorum, II. Edited by K. Hude. Berlin, 1923.

COURBY, FERNAND. "La Terrasse du Temple." In: *Fouilles de Delphes* (École française d'Athène), II:1. Paris, 1927.

CUMONT, FRANZ. *Études syriennes.* Paris, 1917.

——. *Les religions orientales dans le paganisme romain.* 4th edn. Paris, 1929.

CURTIUS, LUDWIG. "Zur Aldobrandinischen Hochzeit." In: *Vermächtnis der antiken Kunst.* Heidelberg, 1950.

——. *Pentheus.* (Winckelmannsprogramm der archäologischen Gesellschaft zu Berlin, 88.) Berlin and Leipzig, 1929.

——. *Die Wandmalerei Pompejis.* Leipzig, 1929.

DAKARIS, SOTIRIS J. "Neue Ausgrabungen in Griechenland." *Antike Kunst,* Supplement 1. Basel, 1963.

DAUX, GEORGES, and JEAN BOUSQUET. "Agamemnon, Télèphe, Dionysos Sphaleôtas et les Attalides." *Revue Archéologique,* 6th Ser., XIX (1942–43).

DAWKINS, R. M. "The Modern Carnival in Thrace." *JHS,* XXVI (1906).

DELAMARRE, JULES. "Location du domaine de Zeus Temenites." *Revue de Philologie,* 2d Ser., XXV (1901).

DELVOYÉ, CHARLES. "Rites de Fécondité dans les religions préhelléniques." *BCH,* LXX (1946).

DEMARGNE, PIERRE. "Deux représentations de la déesse Minoenne dans la nécropole de Mallia." In: *Mélanges Gustave Glotz,* I. Paris, 1932.

DEMOSTHENES. [The Orations of Demosthenes.] (LCL.) 7 vols. II, *De Corona and De Falsa Legatione.* Translated by C. A. and J. H. Vince. 3d rev. edn.,

1953. VI, *Private Orations and In Neaeram*. Translated by A. T. Murray. 1956.

DEUBNER, LUDWIG. *Attische Feste*. Berlin, 1932.

Didyma. See under WIEGAND, THEODOR (ed.).

DIEHL, ERNST. *Anth. lyr*. See the abbreviations preceding this List of Works Cited.

DIELS, HERMANN (ed.). *Die Fragmente der Vorsokratiker*. 6th edn. Edited by Walther Kranz. Berlin, 1951–52. 3 vols.

DIETERICH, ALBRECHT. "De hymnis orphicis." In: *Kleine Schriften*. Leipzig and Berlin, 1911.

———. *Eine Mithrasliturgie*. 3d edn. Leipzig and Berlin, 1923.

DIODORUS SICULUS. *The Library of History*. With an English translation by C. H. Oldfather and others. (LCL.) 1933–57. 11 vols.

DIOGENES LAERTIUS. *Lives of Eminent Philosophers*. With an English translation by R. D. Hicks. (LCL.) 1950. 2 vols.

DION CHRYSOSTOMOS. *Dio Chrysostom*, II. With an English translation by J. W. Cohoon. (LCL.) 1939.

DODDS, E. R. *The Greeks and the Irrational*. Berkeley and Los Angeles, 1951.

DÜMMLER, FERDINAND. "Skenische Vasenbilder." In: *Kleine Schriften*, III. Leipzig, 1901.

EBERT, MAX (ed.). *Reallexikon der Vorgeschichte*, VII. Berlin, 1926.

EDMONDS, JOHN MAXWELL (ed.). *The Fragments of Attic Comedy*. Leiden, 1957–61. 3 vols. in 4.

EDWARDS, MARK W. "Representation of Maenads on Archaic Red-Figure Vases." *JHS*, LXXX (1960).

EILMANN, RICHARD. *Labyrinthos*. Athens, 1931.

EISELE, T. "Sabazios." In: Roscher, *Lexikon* (q.v.), IV:1.

EISLER, ROBERT. "Nachleben dionysischer Mysterienriten." *ARW*, XXVII (1929).

ELDERKIN, GEORGE W. *Kantharos: Studies in Dionysiac and Kindred Cult*. Princeton, 1934.

ELWORTHY, FREDERIC THOMAS. "Dischi Sacri." *Proceedings of the Society of Antiquaries of London*, XVII (1897).

ERATOSTHENES. *Eratosthenis Catasterismorum reliquiae*. Edited by Carl Robert. Berlin, 1878.

ERMAN, ADOLF. *Aegypten und aegyptisches Leben im Altertum*. Reworked by Herman Ranke. Tübingen, 1923. (Original edition, Tübingen, 1885.)

Etymologicum Gudianum. Edited by F. G. Sturz. Leipzig, 1818.

Etymologicum Magnum. Edited by T. Gaisford. Oxford, 1848.

EURIPIDES. *Fabulae*, III. Edited by Gilbert Murray. Oxford, 1913.

——. [*Plays.*] With an English translation by Arthur S. Way. (LCL.) 1912. 4 vols. (Including *Alcestis, Antiope, Bacchae, Cretan Men, Cyclops, Helen, Hippolytus, Ion, Iphigenia in Tauris, Orestes, Phoenissae*, and *Rhesus*.)

EUSEBIOS. *Chronicon*. In: *Die Chronik des Hieronymus*, I. Edited by Rudolf Helm. (GCS.) Leipzig, 1913.

——. *Chronicorum Libri Duo*, II. Edited by Alfred Schoene. Berlin, 1875.

——. *Praeparatio Evangelica*. Edited by Karl Mras. (GCS.) Berlin, 1954–56. 2 vols.

EUSTATHIUS. See under HOMER.

EVANS, ARTHUR J. "The Palace of Knossos." *BSA*, VII (1900–1901).

——. *The Palace of Minos at Knossos*. London, 1921–36. 4 vols. in 6.

FALLMERAYER, J. P. *Fragmente aus dem Orient*. Stuttgart, 1877.

FARNELL, LEWIS RICHARD. *The Cults of the Greek States*. Oxford, 1896–1909. 5 vols.

FAURE, PAUL. "Cavernes et sites aux deux extrémités de la Crète." *BCH*, LXXXVII (1963).

——. *Fonctions des cavernes crétoises*. Paris, 1964.

FAUTH, WOLFGANG. "Pythia." *RE*, XXIV.

——. "Zagreus." *RE* (2d Ser.), IX:2.

FIRMICUS MATERNUS. *De errore profanarum religionum*. Edited by K. Ziegler. Leipzig, 1907.

FONTENROSE, JOSEPH. *Python*. Berkeley, 1959.

FORSDYKE, JOHN. "The 'Harvester' Vase of Hagia Triada." *Journal of the Warburg and Courtauld Institutes*, XVII (1954).

FOUCART, PAUL. "Sur l'authenticité de la loi d'Evégoros." *Revue de Philologie*, 2d Ser., I (1877).

FOUCHER, LOUIS. *Inventaire des Mosaïques*. Institut National d'Archéologie et d'Art. Tunis, 1960.

FOWLER, W. WARDE. "Mundus Patet." In: *Roman Essays and Interpretations*. Oxford, 1920.

FRAZER, JAMES GEORGE. *The Golden Bough*. 3d edn. London, 1911–15. 12 vols. See also under APOLLODOROS, OVID, and PAUSANIAS.

FREUD, SIGMUND. *Beyond the Pleasure Principle*. In: *Complete Psychological Works*, XVIII. Translated by James Strachey. London, 1955.

———. *Three Essays on the Theory of Sexuality*. In: *Complete Psychological Works*, VII. Translated by James Strachey. London, 1953.

FRICKENHAUS, AUGUST. *Lenaënvasen*. (Winckelmannsprogramm der archäologischen Gesellschaft zu Berlin, 72.) Berlin, 1912.

———. "Der Schiffskarren des Dionysos in Athen." *JDAI*, XXVII (1912).

FRISK, HJALMAR. *Griechisches etymologisches Wörterbuch*. Heidelberg, 1960. 2 vols.

FUCHS, WERNER. *Die Vorbilder der neuattischen Reliefs*. *JDAI*, Supplement 20. Berlin, 1959.

FUHRMANN, HEINRICH. "Athamas." *JDAI*, LXV–LXVI (1955–56).

FURLANI, GIUSEPPE. *La Religione degli Hittiti*. Bologna, 1936.

FURTWÄNGLER, ADOLF. *Meisterwerke der griechischen Plastik*. Leipzig, 1893.

———, and KARL REICHHOLD. *Griechische Vasenmalerei*. Munich, 1900–32. Ser. 1–3. 21 vols.

GALEN. In: *Medicorum Graecorum Opera*. Edited by C. G. Kühn. Leipzig, 1821–33. (Including *De antidotis*, *Ad Glauconem de medendi methodo*, and *Ad Pisonem de theriaca*.)

GARSTANG, JOHN. *The Hittite Empire*. London, 1929.

GASTER, THEODOR H. *Thespis*. New York, 1950. (New and revised edn., Anchor Books, 1961.)

GERHARD, EDUARD. *Etruskische und kampanische Vasenbilder des königlichen Museums zu Berlin*. Berlin, 1843.

GJERSTAD, EINAR. "Tod und Leben." *ARW*, XXVI (1928).

GOETZE, ALBERT. *Kleinasien*. (*Handbuch der Altertumswissenschaft*, III: 1 : iii.) Munich, 1933.

GRAEF, BOTHO, and ERNST LANGLOTZ. *Die antiken Vasen von der Akropolis zu Athen*, I : iv. Berlin, 1925.

GRAEVEN, HANS. *Antike Schnitzereien*. Hanover, 1903.

GROENEWEGEN-FRANKFORT, HENRIETTA A. *Arrest and Movement: An Essay on Space and Time in the Representational Art of the Ancient Near East.* London, 1951.

GUARDUCCI, MARGHERITA (ed.). *Inscriptiones Creticae*, II. Rome, 1939.

HALLIDAY, W. R. *The Greek Questions of Plutarch.* Oxford, 1928.

HANSLIK, RUDOLF. "Panopeus." *RE*, XVIII:3.

HARPOKRATION. *Lexicon in decem oratores Atticos*, II. Edited by Wilhelm Dindorf. Oxford, 1854.

HARRISON, JANE ELLEN. "Pandora's Box." *JHS*, XX (1900).

——. *Prolegomena to the Study of Greek Religion.* Cambridge, 1903.

——. *Themis.* 2d edn. Cambridge, 1927.

HASPELS, C. H. EMILIE. *Attic Black-Figured Lekythoi.* Paris, 1936.

HASTINGS, JAMES. *Encyclopaedia of Religion and Ethics.* Edinburgh and New York, 1908–27. 12 vols.

HAUSER, FRIEDRICH. "Ein neues Fragment des Mediceischen Kraters." *JÖAI*, XVI (1913).

HEAD, BARCLAY V. *Historia Numorum.* 2d edn. Oxford, 1911.

HEGEL, FRIEDRICH. *Logik.* In: *Sämtliche Werke*, IV. Edited by Hermann Glockner. Stuttgart, 1930.

HELBIG, WOLFGANG. *Führer durch die öffentlichen Sammlungen klassischer Altertümer in Rom*, I. 4th edn. Edited by Hermine Speier. Tübingen, 1963.

HELIODOROS. *Aethiopica.* Edited by R. M. Rattenbury and others. (Collection Budé.) Paris, 1935–43. 3 vols.

HELLER, JOHN L. "A Labyrinth from Pylos?" *AJA*, LXV (1961).

——. "Labyrinth or Troy Town?" *Classical Journal*, XLII (1946).

HEPDING, HUGO. *Attis, seine Mythen und sein Kult.* (Religionsgeschichtliche Versuche und Vorarbeiten, 1.) Giessen, 1903.

HERBIG, REINHARD. *Neue Beobachtungen am Fries der Mysterien-Villa in Pompeji.* (Deutsche Beiträge zur Altertumswissenschaft, 10.) Baden-Baden, 1958.

HERODOTOS. *The Histories.* Translated by Aubrey de Sélincourt. (Penguin Classics.) Harmondsworth, 1955.

HERRMANN, ALBERT. "Nysa." *RE*, XVII:2.

HERTER, HANS. "Vom dionysischen Tanz zum komischen Spiel." *Darstellung und Deutung*, I (1947).

———. "Phallos." *RE*, XIX:2.

HESIOD. *Fragmenta Hesiodea*. Edited by Reinhold Merkelbach and M. L. West. Oxford, 1967.

———. *Hesiodi Carmina*. Edited by Aloisius Rzach. 3d edn. Leipzig, 1913. (Including *Works and Days* and *Theogony*.)

HESYCHIOS. *Hesychii Alexandrini Lexicon post Joannen Albertum*. Edited by Moritz Schmidt. Jena, 1858–68. 5 vols.

HILLER VON GAERTRINGEN, FRIEDRICH. "Aristaios." *RE*, II:1.

——— (ed.). *Inschriften von Priene*. Berlin, 1906.

———. *Neue Forschungen zur Geschichte der Epigraphik von Lesbos*. (Nachrichten von der Gesellschaft der Wissenschaften zu Göttingen, Phil.-hist. Kl. N.S., 1.) Göttingen, 1936.

HIMERIOS. *Declamationes et orationes*. Edited by Aristide Colonna. (Scriptores graeci et latini.) Rome, 1951.

HIMMELMANN-WILDSCHÜTZ, NIKOLAUS. *Zur Eigenart des klassischen Götterbildes*. Munich, 1959.

———. "Fragment eines attischen Sarkophags." *Marburger Winckelmann Programm* (1959).

HIPPARCHOS. *Hipparchi in Arati et Eudoxi Phaenomena commentarii*. Edited by Karl Manitius. Leipzig, 1894.

HIPPOKRATES. "Aphorisms." In: *Works*. With an English translation by W. H. S. Jones and E. T. Withington. (LCL.) 1923–31. 4 vols.

HÖFER, O. "Orion." In: Roscher, *Lexikon* (q.v.), III:1.

———. "Semele." In: Roscher, *Lexikon* (q.v.), IV:1.

HOFMANNSTHAL, HUGO VON. "Prolog geschrieben für die erste Aufführung der *Lysistrata* des Aristophanes im deutschen Theater." In: *Das deutsche Theater in Berlin*. Munich, 1909.

HOLLAND, LEICESTER B. "The Mantic Mechanism at Delphi." *AJA*, XXXVII (1933).

HOMER. *The Iliad*. Translated by E. B. Rieu. (Penguin Classics.) Harmondsworth, 1956.

———. *The Odyssey*. Translated by W. H. D. Rouse. (Mentor Classics.) New York, 1937.

————. Scholia. In: EUSTATHIUS. *Eustathii commentarii ad Homeri Iliadem et Odysseam ad fidem exempli Romani editi.* Leipzig, 1827–30. 4 vols.

Homeric Hymns, The. Edited by Thomas W. Allen and others. 2d edn. Oxford, 1936.

HOOKE, S. H. *Myth and Ritual.* Oxford, 1933.

HOORN, GERARD VAN. *Choes and Anthesteria.* Leiden, 1951.

HOPFNER, THEODOR. *Plutarch über Isis und Osiris,* I. Prague, 1940.

HUMBOLDT, WILHELM VON. "Über das vergleichende Sprachstudium in Beziehung auf die verschiedenen Epochen der Sprachentwicklung," [1820]. In: *Gesammelte Schriften,* IV. Berlin, 1905.

HYGINUS. *De astronomica.* Edited by Bernhard Bunte. Leipzig, 1875.

————. *Fabulae.* Edited by H. J. Rose. Leiden, 1934.

ISLER, HANS PETER. *Acheloos. Eine Monographie.* Bern, 1970.

JACOBY, FELIX. *FGrHist.* See the abbreviations preceding this List of Works Cited.

JACOLLIOT, LOUIS. *Occult Science in India.* Paris, 1927.

JEANMAIRE, HENRI. *Dionysos: Histoire du Culte de Bacchus.* Paris, 1951.

JENSEN, ADOLF ELLEGARD. "Beschneidung und Reifezeremonie bei Naturvölkern." In: *Studien zur Kulturkunde,* I. Stuttgart, 1933.

JOHANSEN, K. FRIIS. *Eine Dithyrambosaufführung.* (Arkaeologisk-kunsthistoriske Meddelelser, Danske Videnskabernes Selskab, IV:2.) Copenhagen, 1959.

JULLIEN, A. *Topographie der Weinberge,* II. Leipzig, 1933. (Originally published in French, Paris, 1822.)

JUNG, C. G., and C. KERÉNYI. *Essays on a Science of Mythology: The Myth of the Divine Child and the Mysteries of Eleusis.* Translated by R. F. C. Hull. (Bollingen Series XXII.) New York, 1950. Princeton/Bollingen Paperback, 1969. (London, 1951; titled *Introduction to a Science of Mythology.*)

KÄHLER, HEINZ. *Der griechische Tempel: Wesen und Gestalt.* Berlin, 1964.

KAKOURE, KATERINA I. *Death and Resurrection: Concerning Dramatized Ceremonies of the Greek Popular Worship.* Athens, 1965.

KALLIMACHOS. *Callimachus.* Edited by Rudolf Pfeiffer. Oxford, 1949–53. 2 vols. (Including the scholia.)

KAROUZOU, SEMNI. *The Amasis Painter.* Oxford, 1956.

KEES, H. "Senyes." *RE* (2d Ser.), II:2.

KEIL, JOSEF. "Inschriften aus Smyrna." *Anzeiger der öster. Akademie, Phil.-hist. Kl.*, XC (1953).

KEKULÉ VON STRADONITZ, REINHARD. See under ROHDEN, H. VON, and H. WINNEFELD.

KELLER, GOTTFRIED ALBERT. *Eratosthenes und die alexandrinische Sterndichtung.* Zurich, 1946.

KENNA, V. E. G. *Cretan Seals. With Catalogue of the Minoan Gems in the Ashmolean Museum.* Oxford, 1960.

KERAMOPOULLOS, ANTONIOS D. Ἡ οἰκία τοῦ Κάδμου. In: Ἐφημερὶς Ἀρχαιολογική, 1909. Athens, 1910.

———. Θηβαϊκά. *Archaiologikon Deltion*, III:2 (1917).

KERÉNYI, CARL (in some publications KARL). "Anodos-Darstellung in Brindisi." *ARW*, XXX (1933).

———. *Die antike Religion.* Amsterdam and Leipzig, 1940. 3d edn. Düsseldorf, 1952.

———. *Apollon: Studien über antike Religion und Humanität.* 3d edn. Düsseldorf, 1953.

———. *Asklepios: Archetypal Image of the Physician's Existence.* Translated by Ralph Manheim. New York (Bollingen Series LXV.3) and London, 1959. (Originally published in German as *Der göttliche Arzt*, 1947.)

———. *Bachofen und die Zukunft des Humanismus.* Zurich, 1945.

———. *Bildtext einer italischen Vase in Giessen.* (Collection Latomus, 70.) Brussels, 1964.

———. "Die Blume der Persephone." *Der weisse Turm*, I:10 (1967).

———. "Il dio cacciatore." *Dioniso*, XV (1952).

———. "Dionysos am Alpheios." *Giessener Hochschulblätter*, VI:3 (1959).

———. "Dionysos le Crétois." *Diogène*, XX (1957).

———. *Dionysos und das Tragische in der Antigone.* (Frankfurter Studien zur Religion und Kultur der Antike, 13.) Frankfurt am Main, 1934.

———. *Eleusis: Archetypal Image of Mother and Daughter.* Translated by Ralph Manheim. New York (Bollingen Series LXV.4) and London, 1967.

———. *Der frühe Dionysos.* Oslo, 1961.

———. "Geburt und Wiedergeburt der Tragödie." In: *Streifzüge eines Hellenisten.* Zurich, 1960.

————. "Gedanken über Dionysos." *Studi e materiali di storia delle religioni*, XI (1935).

————. *The Gods of the Greeks*. Translated by Norman Cameron. London and New York, 1951. (Published simultaneously in German as *Die Mythologie der Griechen*; English version reprinted with different pagination in Pelican Books, Harmondsworth, 1958.)

————. *Griechische Grundbegriffe*. (Albae Vigiliae, N.S., 19.) Zurich, 1964.

————. "Hegel e gli Dei della Grecia." *Sicilia Archeologica*, I.

————. *Die Herkunft der Dionysosreligion nach dem heutigen Stand der Forschung*. (Arbeitsgemeinschaft für Forschung des Landes Nordrhein-Westfalen, 58.) Cologne and Opladen, 1956.

————. *The Heroes of the Greeks*. Translated by H. J. Rose. London, 1959, and New York, 1960. (Originally published in German as *Die Heroen der Griechen*, 1958.)

————. Ἱερὸς γάμος. In: *Archeion Kalitsounakis*. Athens, 1970.

————. "Johann Jakob Bachofens Porträt." In: *Tessiner Schreibtisch*. Stuttgart, 1963.

————. "Labyrinthos: Der Linienreflex einer mythologischen Idee." In: *Laureae Aquincenses memoriae Valentini Kuzsinszky dicatae*, II. Budapest, 1941.

————. "Leben und Tod nach griechischer Auffassung." In: *Mensch, Schicksal und Tod*. (Beihefte zur Schweizerischen Zeitschrift für Psychologie, 46.) Bern, 1963.

————. "Man and Mask." In: *Spiritual Disciplines*. (*Papers from the Eranos Yearbooks*, 4.) Edited by Joseph Campbell. New York (Bollingen Series XXX.4) and London, 1960.

————. "Mescalin-Perioden der Religionsgeschichte." *Wege zum Menschen*, XVIII (1965).

————. "Miti sul concepimento di Dioniso." *Maia: Rivista di letterature classiche*, IV (1951).

————. "Möglicher Sinn von *di-wo-nu-so-jo* und *da-da-re-jo-de*." In: *Atti e memorie del 1. Congresso Internazionale di Micenologia*, II. Rome, 1967.

————. "Die Münzen des Onomakritos." In: *Mythos: Raccolta Mario Untersteiner*. Genoa, 1970.

————. "The Mysteries of the Kabeiroi." In: *The Mysteries*. (*Papers from the Eranos Yearbooks*, 2.) Edited by Joseph Campbell. New York (Bollingen Series XXX.2) and London, 1955.

KERÉNYI. *Nietzsche an der Schöpfung seines Romans.* (Beihefte zur Schweizeri-schen Zeitschrift für Psychologie, 47.) Bern, 1964.

———. "Nietzsche zwischen Literatur- und Religionsgeschichte." *Neue Zürcher Zeitung,* May 2, 1965.

———. *Niobe: Neue Studien über antike Religion und Humanität.* Zurich, 1949.

———. "Parva realia." *SymbO,* XXXVI (1960).

———. "Persephone und Prometheus: Vom Alter griechischer Mythen." In: *Festschrift für Hans Oppermann* (a special issue of *Jahrbuch der Raabe-Gesellschaft*). Brunswick, 1965.

———. Preface to *Antigone.* Munich, 1966. Preface to *Orpheus und Eurydike.* Munich, 1963. In the series, *Theater der Jahrhunderte.*

———. *Prometheus: Archetypal Image of Human Existence.* Translated by Ralph Manheim. New York (Bollingen Series LXV.1) and London, 1963. (Originally published in German as *Prometheus: Die menschliche Existenz in griechischer Deutung,* 1959.)

———. *Prometheus: Das griechische Mythologem von der menschlichen Exis-tenz.* (Albae Vigiliae, N.S., 4.) Zurich, 1946.

———. *Pythagoras und Orpheus: Präludien zu einer Zukünftigen Geschichte der Orphik und des Pythagoreismus.* (Albae Vigiliae, N.S., 9.) 3d edn. Zurich, 1950.

———. *The Religion of the Greeks and Romans.* London, 1962. (A translation by Christopher Holme of *Die Religion der Griechen und Römer,* Munich, 1963. Both versions are based on *Die antike Religion,* originally published in 1940.)

———. "Die religionsgeschichtliche Einordnung des Diskos von Brindisi." *RM,* LXX (1963).

———. "Satire und Satura." *Studi e materiali di storia delle religioni,* IX (1933).

———. "Die Schichten der Mythologie und ihre Erforschung." *Universitas,* IX (1954).

———. "Der spiegelnde Spiegel." In: *Festschrift für A. E. Jensen.* Munich, 1964.

———. *Streifzüge eines Hellenisten; von Homer zu Kazantzakis.* Zurich, 1960.

———. "De teletis mercurialibus observationes, II." *Egyetemes Philologiai Köz-löny,* XLII (1923).

———. *Umgang mit Göttlichem.* 2d edn. Göttingen, 1961.

———. "Ursinn und Sinnwandel des Utopischen." *Eranos Jahrbuch,* XXXII (1963).

———. *Werke in Einzelausgaben.* Munich, 1966 ff. (I, *Humanistische Seelen-forschung*; II, *Auf Spuren des Mythos*; III, *Tage- und Wanderbücher, 1953–1960*; VII, *Die antike Religion.*)

———. "Das Wesen des Mythos und seine Gegenwärtigkeit" [1964]. In: *Die Eröffnung des Zugangs zum Mythos: Ein Lesebuch.* Edited by Karl Kerényi. Darmstadt, 1967.

———. *Zeus and Hera: Archetypal Image of Father, Husband, and Wife.* Translated by Christopher Holme. Princeton (Bollingen Series LXV.5) and London, 1975.

———. "Zeus und Hera." *Saeculum*, I (1950).

———, and HELLMUT SICHTERMANN. "Zeitlose Schieferbauten der Insel Andros." *Paideuma*, VIII (1962).

KERN, OTTO. "Die Herkunft des orphischen Hymnenbuchs." In: *Genethliakon.* Edited by Carl Robert. Berlin, 1910.

———. *Orpheus.* Berlin, 1920.

——— (ed.). *Orphicorum fragmenta.* Berlin, 1922.

———. "Orphiker auf Kreta." *Hermes*, LI (1916).

KINKEL, GOTTFRIED (ed.). *Epicorum Graecorum fragmenta.* Leipzig, 1877.

———. See also under LYKOPHRON.

KLAUSER, THEODOR. *Die Cathedra im Totenkult der heidnischen und christlichen Antike.* Münster, 1927.

KNACKFUSS, HUBERT. *Die Baubeschreibung.* Part I of THEODOR WIEGAND's *Didyma*, q.v.

KÖRTE, ALFRED. *Die hellenistische Dichtung.* Leipzig, 1925.

KONDOLEON, ALEXANDROS EMMANUEL. Ὁδηγὸς τοῦ Κωρυκίου Ἄντρου. Athens, 1911.

KONTOLEON, N. M. Publications in *Kykladika*, II (1956); and *Kretika Chronika*, XV–XVI (1961–62), Part 1.

KOUKOULES, PHAIDON. Βυζαντινῶν βίος καὶ πολιτισμός, V. Athens, 1952.

KOUROUNIOTES, KONSTANTINOS. Ἐλευσινιακά. *Archaiologikon Deltion*, VIII (1923).

KRETSCHMER, PAUL. "Dyaus, Ζεύς, Diespiter und die Abstrakta im Indogermanischen." *Glotta*, XIII (1924).

———. "Semele und Dionysos." In: *Aus der Anomia.* Berlin, 1890.

KRITIKOS, P. G., and S. P. PAPADAKI. "The History of the Poppy and of Opium and Their Expansion in Antiquity in the Eastern Mediterranean Area."

Translated from Greek by George Michalopoulos. *Bulletin on Narcotics* (United Nations, New York), XIX:3 (1967).

KRUEGER, ADOLF. "Quaestiones Orphicae." Halle diss., 1934.

KUNZE, EMIL. *Kretische Bronzereliefs.* Stuttgart, 1931.

LACROIX, LOUIS. *Iles de la Grèce.* Paris, 1853.

LAMBERT, WILFRED G. "The Reading of a Seal Inscription from Thebes." *Kadmos,* III (1964).

LANDAU, OSCAR. *Mykenisch-griechische Personennamen.* Göteborg, 1958.

LANG, MABEL. "The Palace of Nestor Excavations of 1957, Part II." *AJA,* LXII (1958).

LANGLOTZ, ERNST. "Eine apulische Amphora in Bonn." In: *Anthemon: scritti in onore di Carlo Anti.* Florence, 1955.

——. "Dionysos." *Die Antike,* VIII (1932).

——. See also under GRAEF, BOTHO.

LAWRENCE, D. H. *The Apocalypse.* London, 1932.

LAWSON, JOHN C. *Modern Greek Folklore and Ancient Greek Religion: A Study in Survivals.* Cambridge, 1910.

LEHMANN, KARL. *Samothrace. A Guide to the Excavations and the Museum.* 2d edn. New York, 1960.

——, and ERLING C. OLSEN. *Dionysiac Sarcophagi in Baltimore.* Baltimore, 1942.

LEIPOLDT, JOHANNES. "Dionysos." Ἄγγελος, Supplement 3. Leipzig, 1931.

LENSCHAU, T. "Peiraios." *RE,* XIX:1.

LEPSIUS, KARL RICHARD. *Denkmäler aus Ägypten und Athiopien.* Leipzig, 1892–1913.

LERAT, L. "Fouilles de Delphes (1934–35)." *Revue Archéologique,* 6th Ser., XII (1936).

LESKY, ALBIN. "Dionysos und Hades." *Wiener Studien,* LIV (1936).

——. *Die tragische Dichtung der Hellenen.* Göttingen, 1956.

LEVI, DORO. "Attività della Scuola Archeologica Italiana di Atene nell'anno 1955." *Bollettino d'Arte,* XLI (1956).

——. "The Italian Excavations in Crete and the Earliest European Civilisation." *Quaderni dell' Istituto Italiano di Cultura in Dublino,* I (1963).

————. *The Recent Excavations at Phaistos.* (Studies in Mediterranean Archaeology, XI.) Lund, 1964.

LEWIS, DAVID M. "The Deme Ikarion." *BSA*, LX (1956).

LHOTE, HENRI. *The Search for the Tassili Frescoes.* Translated by Alan Houghton Brodrick. London and New York, 1959.

LIDDELL, H. G., R. SCOTT, and H. S. JONES. *A Greek-English Lexicon.* 9th edn. Oxford, 1940.

LINDEMANN, F. O. "Grec βείομεν ἐρίων." *SymbO*, XXXIX (1963).

LOBECK, CHRISTIAN AUGUST. *Aglaophamus.* Königsberg, 1829. 2 vols.

LOBEL, EDGAR, and DENYS PAGE (eds.). *Poetarum Lesbiorum Fragmenta.* Oxford, 1955.

LORIMER, H. L. *Homer and the Monuments.* London, 1950.

LUCIAN. [*Works.*] With an English translation by A. M. Harmon et al. (LCL.) 1913–67. 8 vols.

LYKOPHRON. *Lycophronis Alexandra.* Edited by Gottfried Kinkel. Leipzig, 1880. (Including the scholia. See also under TZETZES, J.)

MAASS, ERNST. *Analecta Eratosthenica.* Berlin, 1883.

———— (ed.). See ARATOS.

MACROBIUS. [*Saturnalia.*] Edited by Franz Eyssenhardt. Leipzig, 1893.

MACURDY, GRACE M. "Basilinna and Basilissa, the Alleged Title of the 'Queen Archon' in Athens." *American Journal of Philology*, XLIX (1928).

MAIURI, AMEDEO. *La Casa del Menandro e il suo tesoro di argenteria.* Rome, 1933.

————. *La Villa dei Misteri.* Rome, 1931. 2 vols.

MARINATOS, SPYRIDON. Ἀνασκαφαὶ ἐν Βαθυπέτρωι Κρήτης. *Praktika . . . 1952.* Athens, 1955.

————. Τὸ δελφικὸν χάσμα καὶ τὸ "πνεῦμα" τῆς Πυθίας. Athens, 1959.

————. Τὸ σπέος τῆς Εἰλειθυίας. *Praktika . . . 1929.* Athens, 1931.

————. θέατρα καὶ θεάματα τοῦ Μεσογειακοῦ Πολιτισμοῦ: Δώδεκα διαλέξεις. In: Βιβλιοθήκη Ἐθνικοῦ Θεάτρου, I. Athens, 1961.

————. "Zur Orientierung der minoischen Architektur." In: *Proceedings of the First International Congress of Prehistoric and Protohistoric Sciences.* Oxford, 1934.

————, and MAX HIRMER. *Crete and Mycenae.* New York, 1960.

Marmor Parium. In: *Das Marmor Parium.* Edited by F. Jacoby. Berlin, 1904.

MARZANO, G. *Il Museo Provinciale Francesco Ribezzo di Brindisi: Guida.* Fasano, 1961.

MATTON, R. *La Crète antique.* Athens, 1955.

MATZ, FRIEDRICH. "Arge und Opis." *Marburger Winckelmann Programm* (1948).

———. "Ariadne oder Semele?" *Marburger Winckelmann Programm* (1968).

———. ΔΙΟΝΥΣΙΑΚΗ ΤΕΛΕΤΗ. Wiesbaden, 1964.

———. "Göttererscheinungen und Kultbild im minoischen Kreta." In: *Abhandlungen der Mainzer Akademie der Wissenschaften und der Literatur, Geistessozial. Kl.,* VII (1958).

———. "Minoischer Stiergott?" *Kretika Chronika,* XV–XVI (1961–62), Part 1.

———. Review of M. P. Nilsson's *The Dionysiac Mysteries.* In: *Gnomon,* XXXII (1960).

———. *Ein römisches Meisterwerk.* Berlin, 1958.

MELA, POMPONIUS. *De chorographia.* Edited by C. Frick. Leipzig, 1880.

MELLEN, CHASE, III. "Reflections of a Peyote Eater." *The Harvard Review,* I:4 (1963).

MENANDER. *The Arbitration.* In: OATES, W. J., and E. O'NEILL, JR. (eds.), q.v.

———. [Fragments.] In: EDMONDS, J. M. (ed.), q.v.

MERKELBACH, REINHOLD. "Die Erigone des Eratosthenes." In: *Miscellanea . . . Augusto Rostagni.* Turin, 1963.

———, and M. L. West (eds.). See under HESIOD.

METTE, HANS J. (ed.). *Die Fragmente der Tragödien des Aischylos.* Berlin, 1959.

MEYER, EDUARD. *Geschichte des Altertums,* I:2. 5th edn. Stuttgart and Berlin, 1926.

MILANI, LUIGI ADRIANO. *Museo Topografico dell'Etruria.* Florence and Rome, 1898.

MILCHHOEFER, ARTHUR. *Karten von Attika,* III–IV. Berlin, 1889.

MILLINGEN, J. *Ancient Unedited Monuments,* I. London, 1822.

MITTELHAUS, K. "Kanephoroi." *RE,* X:2.

MOMMSEN, AUGUST. *Heortologie.* Leipzig, 1864.

MONTUORO, PAOLA ZANCANI. See ZANCANI MONTUORO, PAOLA.

MOORTGAT, ANTON. *Tammuz.* Berlin, 1949.

MÜLLER, CARL F. W. (ed.). *Fragmenta Historicorum Graecorum.* 1841–70. 5 vols.

———. *Geographi Graeci Minores.* Paris, 1855–61. 2 vols.

MÜLLER, KARL OTFRIED. *Handbuch der Archäologie der Kunst.* 3d edn., with additions by F. G. Welcker. Breslau, 1848. (English version, *Ancient Art and Its Remains; or A Manual of the Archaeology of Art*, translated by J. Leitch. London, 1850.)

———. *Prolegomena zu einer wissenschaftlichen Mythologie.* Göttingen, 1825. New edn. edited by C. Kerényi. Darmstadt, 1970.

———, and WILHELM DEECKE. *Die Etrusker.* 2d edn. Stuttgart, 1877.

MÜLLER, WERNER. *Die Religionen der Waldlandindianer Nordamerikas.* Berlin, 1956.

Mythographi Vaticani. In: BODE, GEORG H. (ed.), q.v.

NAUCK, AUGUST. *TGF.* See the abbreviations preceding this List of Works Cited.

NEWTON, C. T. *Travels and Discoveries in the Levant.* London, 1865.

NICANDER. *Theriaca.* In: *Nicander.* Edited by A. S. F. Gow and A. F. Scholfield. Oxford, 1953.

NIETZSCHE, FRIEDRICH. *Basic Writings of Nietzsche.* Translated and edited by W. Kaufmann. New York, 1968.

NILSSON, MARTIN PERSSON. *The Dionysiac Mysteries of the Hellenistic and Roman Age.* Lund, 1957.

———. "Dionysos im Schiff." In: *Opuscula selecta*, I. Lund, 1951.

———. *Geschichte der griechischen Religion.* (*Handbuch der Altertumswissenschaft*, V:2:i, ii.) Munich, 1941–50. 2d edn. Munich, 1955–61. 2 vols. (Unless otherwise indicated, the second edition is referred to.)

———. "A Krater in the Cleveland Museum of Art with Men in Women's Attire." In: *Opuscula selecta*, III. Lund, 1960.

———. *The Minoan-Mycenaean Religion and its Survival in Greek Religion.* 2d edn. Lund, 1950.

NOGARA, BARTOLOMEO. "Una base istoriata di marmo nuovamente esposta nel Museo Vaticano." *Ausonia*, II (1907).

NONNOS. *Dionysiaca.* Edited with an English translation by W. H. D. Rouse. (LCL.) 1940. 3 vols.

NORDEN, EDUARD. *Die Geburt des Kindes.* Leipzig and Berlin, 1924.

OATES, WHITNEY J., and EUGENE O'NEILL, JR. (eds.). *The Complete Greek Drama.* New York, 1938. 2 vols.

OELLACHER, H. In: *Mitteilungen aus der Papyrussammlung Rainer*, N.S., I (1932).

OHLEMUTZ, ERWIN. *Die Kulte und Heiligtümer der Götter in Pergamon.* Würzburg, 1940.

OIKONOMOS, GEORGIOS P. "Eine neue Bergwerksurkunde aus Athen." *AM*, XXXV (1910).

OLYMPIODOROS. *In Platonis Phaedonem commentarii.* Edited by W. Norvin. Leipzig, 1913.

Orphic Hymns. In: O. KERN (ed.); and W. QUANDT (ed.), qq.v.

ORTEGA Y GASSET, JOSÉ. *Meditaciones del Quijote.* Madrid, 1957.

OTTO, EBERHARD. *Osiris und Amun.* Munich, 1966.

OTTO, WALTER FRIEDRICH. *Dionysos: Myth and Cult.* Translated by R. B. Palmer. Bloomington, Indiana, and London, 1965.

———. *Das Wort der Antike.* Stuttgart, 1962.

OVID. *The Fasti of Ovid.* Edited by James George Frazer. London, 1929. 5 vols.

———. *Metamorphoses.* Translated by Rolfe Humphries. Bloomington, Indiana, 1957.

PALMER, LEONARD R. *The Interpretation of Mycenaean Greek Texts.* Oxford, 1963.

———. *Mycenaeans and Minoans.* 2d edn. London, 1965.

PANOFSKY, ERWIN. *A Mythological Painting by Poussin in the Nationalmuseum Stockholm.* Stockholm, 1960.

PARIBENI, ROBERTO. "Ricerca nel sepolcreto di Haghia Triada presso Phaestos." *MonAnt*, XIV (1904).

PARROT, ANDRÉ. "Les fouilles de Mari." *Syria*, XXI (1940).

PATITUCCI, STELLA. "Osservazioni sul cratere polignoteo della tomba 128 di Valle Trebba." *Arte antica e moderna*, V (1962).

PAUSANIAS. *Pausanias's Description of Greece.* Translated with a commentary by James George Frazer. London, 1898. 6 vols.

PENDLEBURY, J. D. S. *A Handbook to the Palace of Minos at Knossos.* 2d edn. London, 1954.

PFUHL, ERNST. *De Atheniensium pompis sacris.* Berlin, 1900.

PHILODEMOS. *De pietate*. Edited by T. Gomperz. (Herkulanische Studien, II.) Leipzig, 1866.

PHILOSTRATOS. [*Works*.] Edited by K. L. Kayser. Leipzig, 1870–71. 2 vols.

PHOTIOS. *Bibliotheca*. Edited by I. Bekker. Berlin, 1824–25.

——. *Lexicon*. Edited by S. A. Naber. Leiden, 1864–65. 2 vols.

PHRYNICHOS. In: I. BEKKER (ed.). *Anecdota Graeca*, I. Berlin, 1814.

PICARD, CHARLES. *L'Acropole*. Paris, 1929.

——. Διόνυσος Μιτρηφόρος. In: *Mélanges Gustave Glotz*, II. Paris, 1932.

——. "Dionysos Psilax." In: *Mélanges Navarre*. Paris, 1935.

——. "Observations sur la date et l'origine des reliefs dits de la 'Visite chez Ikarios.'" *AJA*, XXXVIII (1934).

——. "Les Origines du polythéisme hellénique." In: *L'art crétomycénien*. Paris, 1930.

——. "Phèdre à la balançoire et le symbolisme des pendaisons." *Revue Archéologique*, 5th Ser., XXVIII (1928).

PICKARD-CAMBRIDGE, ARTHUR. *Dithyramb, Tragedy and Comedy*. 2d edn. Revised by T. B. L. Webster. Oxford, 1962.

——. *The Dramatic Festivals of Athens*. 2d edn. Edited by John Gould and D. M. Lewis. Oxford, 1968.

——. *The Theatre of Dionysus in Athens*. Oxford, 1946.

PINDAR. *The Odes, Including the Principal Fragments*. With an English translation by John Sandys. (LCL.) 1957.

——. *Pindari Carmina cum fragmentis*. Edited by Cecil Maurice Bowra. (OCT.) 2d edn. Oxford, 1947.

——. Scholia. In: *Scholia Vetera in Pindari Carmina*, II. Edited by A. B. Drachmann. Leipzig, 1910.

PLATAKIS, ELEFTHERIOS. Τὸ Ἰδαῖον ἄντρον. Heraklion, 1965.

PLATO. *Euthydemus*. Translated by W. H. D. Rouse. In: *The Collected Dialogues*. Edited by Edith Hamilton and Huntington Cairns. New York (Bollingen Series LXXI) and London, 1963.

——. *Euthyphro, Apology, Crito, Phaedo, Phaedrus*. With an English translation by H. N. Fowler. (LCL.) 1953.

——. *Phaedrus, Ion, Gorgias, and Symposium, with Passages from the Republic and the Laws*. Translated by Lane Cooper. London and New York, 1938.

PLATON, NIKOLAOS. *A Guide to the Archaeological Museum of Heraclion.* Heraklion, Crete, 1955.

——. Τὸ Ἱερὸν Μαζᾶ καὶ τὰ μινωικὰ Ἱερὰ Κορυφῆς. *Kretika Chronika*, V (1951).

——. "Kato Zakros." In: Τὸ ἔργον τῆς Ἀρχαιολογικῆς Ἑταιρείας κατὰ τὸ *1961* and *1963.* Athens, 1962 and 1964.

——. Περὶ τῆς ἐν Κρήτηι λατρείας τῶν σταλακτίτων. *Ephemeris Archaiologike*, 1930.

——. "Sir Arthur Evans and the Creto-Mycenaean Bullfights." *Greek Heritage*, I:4 (1965).

——. Ὁ τάφος τοῦ Σταφύλου. *Kretika Chronika*, III (1949).

PLAUMANN, GERHARD. *Ptolemais in Oberägypten.* (Leipziger historische Abhandlungen, 18.) Leipzig, 1910.

PLINY. *Natural History.* With an English translation by H. Rackham and W. H. S. Jones. (LCL.) 1938 ff. 10 vols.

PLUTARCH. *Moralia.* Edited, with an English translation, by Frank Cole Babbitt and H. N. Fowler. (LCL.) 1927 ff. 14 vols. (Including *De cupiditate divitiarum, De defectu oraculorum, De E apud Delphos, De Iside et Osiride, Mulierum virtutes, De primo frigido, Quaestiones conviviales, Quaestiones Graecae,* and *Quaestiones Romanae.*)

——. *Parallel Lives.* With an English translation by Bernadotte Perrin. (LCL.) 1914–26. 11 vols. (Including *Alexander, Solon, Themistocles,* and *Theseus.*)

POLLUX. *Onamasticon.* In: *Lexicographi graeci.* Edited by E. Bethe. Leipzig, 1900–37. 3 vols.

POMTOW, HANS. "Delphoi." *RE*, IV:2.

PORPHYRY. *Selected Works.* Edited by A. Nauck. 2d edn. Leipzig, 1886.

POTTIER, EDMOND. *Vases antiques du Louvre.* Paris, 1901.

POWELL, JOHANNES U. *Collectanea Alexandrina.* Oxford, 1925.

—— (ed.). *New Chapters in the History of Greek Literature, Third Series.* Oxford, 1933.

PREISENDANZ, KARL. "Zum Thyiafest." *ARW*, XXI (1922).

PRELLER, LUDWIG. *Ausgewählte Aufsätze.* Berlin, 1846.

PRIVITERA, G. AURELIO. "I rapporti di Dioniso con Posidone in età micenea." *Studi Urbinati*, XXXIX (1965).

PROKLOS. *In Platonis Rem publicam commentarii.* Edited by Wilhelm Kroll. Leipzig, 1899–1901. 2 vols.

PROPERTIUS. [*Works.*] Edited by J. S. Phillimore. (OCT.) 2d edn. 1907.

PROTT, HANS VON. "MHTHP. Bruchstücke zur griechischen Religionsgeschichte." *ARW*, IX (1906).

PSELLOS, MICHAEL. *Graecorum opiniones de daemonibus.* In: *De operatione daemonum.* Edited by J. F. Boissonade. Nuremberg, 1838.

PSEUDO-DEMOSTHENES. See DEMOSTHENES.

PUHVEL, JAAN. "Eleuther and Oinoatis: Dionysiac Data from Mycenaean Greece." In: *Mycenaean Studies, Wingspread, 1961: Proceedings of the Third International Colloquium for Mycenaean Studies held at "Wingspread," 4-8 September 1961.* Edited by E. L. Bennett, Jr. Madison, 1964.

QUANDT, WILHELM. "De Baccho ab Alexandri aetate in Asia Minore culto." Halle diss., 1915.

——— (ed.). *Orphei hymni.* 2d edn. Berlin, 1955.

RADIN, MAX. "The Kid and Its Mother's Milk." *American Journal of Semitic Languages and Literatures*, XL (1923–24).

RADKE, GERHARD. *Die Götter Altitaliens.* Münster, 1965.

RANSOME, HILDE M. *The Sacred Bee in Ancient Times and Folklore.* London, 1937.

REHM, ALBERT. *Die Inschriften.* Part II of THEODOR WIEGAND's *Didyma*, q.v.

REINACH, SALOMON. *Cultes, mythes et religions*, II and V. Paris, 1906, 1923.

RICHTER, GISELA. "An Ivory Relief in the Metropolitan Museum of Art." *AJA*, XLIX (1945).

RILKE, RAINER MARIA. *Sämtliche Werke.* Wiesbaden, 1956.

RODENWALDT, GERHART. "Der Klinensarkophag von S. Lorenzo." *JDAI*, XLV (1930).

ROHDE, ERWIN. *Psyche.* Translated by W. B. Hillis. London and New York, 1925.

———. "Die Religion der Griechen." In: *Kleine Schriften.* Tübingen, 1901.

ROHDEN, HERMANN VON, and HERMANN WINNEFELD. *Architektonische römische Tonreliefs der Kaiserzeit.* (*Die antiken Terrakotten*, IV:1, edited by Reinhard Kekulé von Stradonitz.) Berlin and Stuttgart, 1911.

ROSCHER, W. H. (ed.). *Ausführliches Lexikon der griechischen und römischen Mythologie.* Leipzig, 1884–1937. 6 vols. in 9 parts with 2 supplements.

RUMPF, ANDREAS. "Attische Feste–Attische Vasen." *Bonner Jahrbücher*, CLXI (1961).

SALIS, ARNOLD VON. "Pompejanischer Beitrag." *JÖAI*, XXXIX (1952).

SARIDAKIS, STYLIANOS. "Inschriften von . . . Rhodos." *JÖAI*, VII (1904).

SAVIGNONI, L. "Scavi e scoperte nella necropoli di Phaestos." *MonAnt*, XIV (1904).

SCHAEFER, J. "Sabazios." *RE* (2d Ser.), I:2.

SCHEFOLD, KARL. "Buch und Bild im Altertum." *Stultifera Navis, Mitteilungsblatt der Schweizerischen Bibliophilen Gesellschaft*, VII (1950).

SCHNEIDER, ELISABETH. *Coleridge, Opium and Kubla Khan*. Chicago, 1953.

SCHOTT, S. "Das blutrünstige Keltergerät." *Zeitschrift für ägyptische Sprache und Altertumskunde*, LXXIV (1938).

SCHWEITZER, BERNHARD. "Altkretische Kunst." *Die Antike*, II (1926).

———. *Herakles*. Tübingen, 1922.

SCHWYZER, ROBERT. "Facetten der Molekularbiologie." *Neue Züricher Zeitung*, July 17, 1966.

SEGALL, BERTA. "Sculpture from Arabia Felix." *AJA*, LIX (1955).

SERVIUS. *Commentarii in Vergilium* . . . . Edited by H. Albertus Lion. Göttingen, 1826. 2 vols.

———. *Servii Grammatici qui feruntur in Vergilii carmina commentarii*. Edited by Georg Thilo and Hermann Hagen. Leipzig, 1881–1902. 3 vols.

SICHTERMANN, HELLMUT. *Griechische Vasen in Unteritalien aus der Sammlung Jatta in Ruvo*. Tübingen, 1966.

———. See also under KERÉNYI, CARL.

SIMON, ERIKA. "Ein Anthesterien-Skyphos des Polygnotos." *Antike Kunst*, VI (1963).

———. "Dionysischer Sarkophag in Princeton." *RM*, LXIX (1962).

———. "Drei antike Gefässe aus Kameoglas in Corning, Florenz und Besançon." *Journal of Glass Studies*, VI (1964).

———. *Opfernde Götter*. Berlin, 1953.

———. "Zagreus." In: *Hommages à Albert Grenier*. (Collection Latomus, 58.) Brussels, 1962.

SMITH, WILLIAM ROBERTSON. *Lectures on the Religion of the Semites*. London, 1894.

SOKOLOWSKI, FRANCISZEK. *Lois sacrées de l'Asie Mineure*. Paris, 1955.

SOPHOKLES. *The Fragments of Sophocles.* Edited by A. C. Pearson. Cambridge, 1917.

———. [*Plays.*] With an English translation by F. Storr. (LCL.) 1912–13. 2 vols. (Including *Ajax, Antigone,* and *Oedipus at Colonus.*)

SPENCER, BALDWIN, and F. J. GILLEN. *The Arunta.* London, 1927. 2 vols.

STACKELBERG, O. M. VON. *Die Gräber der Hellenen.* Berlin, 1837.

STAUDACHER, WILLIBALD. "Die Trennung von Himmel und Erde." Tübingen diss., 1942.

STELLA, LUIGIA ACHILLEA. *La civiltà micenea nei documenti contemporanei.* Rome, 1965.

———. "La religione greca nei testi micenei." *Numen,* V (1958).

STEPHEN OF BYZANTIUM. *Ethnicorum quae supersunt.* Edited by August Meineke. Berlin, 1849.

STOBAEUS, JOANNES. *Anthologium.* Edited by K. Wachsmuth and Otto Hense. Berlin, 1884–94. 5 vols.

STOLPE, SVEN. *Från stoicism till mystik.* Stockholm, 1959.

STRABO. *The Geography.* With an English translation by Horace Leonard Jones. (LCL.) 1917–32. 8 vols.

Suidae Lexicon. Edited by Ada Adler. (Lexicographi graeci recogniti et apparatu critico instructi, I.) Leipzig, 1928–35. 5 vols.

SVORONOS, J. N. *Das Athener Nationalmuseum,* I. Athens, 1908.

———. *Numismatique de la Crète Ancienne,* I. Macon, 1890.

THIELE, G. *Antike Himmelsbilder.* Berlin, 1898.

THIMME, JÜRGEN. "Rosette, Myrte, Spirale und Fisch als Seligkeitszeichen." In: *Opus nobile: Festschrift Ulf Jantzen.* Mainz, 1969.

THOMSON, GEORGE. "The Greek Calendar." *JHS,* LXIII (1943).

TILLYARD, E. M. W. *The Hope Vases.* Cambridge, 1923.

TOD, M. N., and A. J. B. WACE. *A Catalogue of the Sparta Museum.* Oxford, 1906.

TOEPFFER, JOHANN. *Attische Genealogie.* Berlin, 1889.

TOLLES, RUDOLF. "Untersuchungen zur Kindesaussetzung bei den Griechen." Breslau diss., 1941.

TOULOUPA, EVI. "Bericht über die neuen Ausgrabungen in Theben." *Kadmos,* III (1964).

TRENDALL, A. D. *Frühitaliotische Vasen*. (Bilder griechischer Vasen, 12.) Leipzig, 1938.

———. "Two Skyphoid-pyxides in Moscow." *Bulletin van de Vereeniging tot bevordering der kennis van de antike beschaving*. 1951.

———. "A Volute Krater at Taranto." *JHS*, LIV (1934).

TURCAN, ROBERT. *Dionysos Dimorphos*. (Mélanges d'archéologie et d'histoire, 70.) Paris, 1958.

TZETZES, J. [Scholium on Lykophron, *Alexandra*.] In: E. Scheer (ed.). *Lycophronis Alexandra*, II. Leipzig, 1908.

USENER, HERMANN. *Der Heilige Tychon*. Leipzig and Berlin, 1907.

———. *Kleine Schriften*, IV. Leipzig and Berlin, 1913.

———. *Die Sintflutsagen*. Bonn, 1899.

VARRO. *De re rustica*. Edited by G. Goetz. Leipzig, 1929.

VENTRIS, MICHAEL. *Glossary of 1556 Linear B Sign-groups*. [Privately circulated], 1953.

———, and JOHN CHADWICK. *Documents in Mycenaean Greek*. Cambridge, 1959.

VERMEULE, CORNELIUS C. "The Colossus of Porto Raphti in Attica." *Hesperia*, XXXI (1962).

VIRGIL. [*Works*.] With an English translation by H. Rushton Fairclough. (LCL.) 1929. 2 vols. (Including *Eclogues* and *Georgics*.)

VOGLIANO, ACHILLE. "La grande Iscrizione Bacchica del Metropolitan Museum." *AJA*, XXXVII (1933).

WAGENVOORT, H. "Phaedra op de schommel." *Hermeneus*, II (1930).

WATZINGER, CARL. "Theoxenia des Dionysos." *JDAI*, LXI–LXII (1946–47).

WEBSTER, T. B. L. *From Mycenae to Homer*. London, 1958. (Reprinted with corrections, 1964.)

WEINREICH, OTTO. *Einleitung* to Aristophanes, *Sämtliche Komödien*, I. Translated into German by L. Seeger. Zurich, 1952.

WELCKER, FRIEDRICH GOTTLIEB. *Griechische Götterlehre*, I. Göttingen, 1857.

WELTER, GABRIEL. "Altionische Tempel I. Der Hekatompedos von Naxos." *AM*, XLIX (1924).

WENIGER, LUDWIG. "Feralis exercitus." *ARW*, IX (1906).

———. "Das Hochfest des Zeus in Olympia." *Klio*, V (1905).

————. *Das Kollegium der Sechzehn Frauen und der Dionysosdienst in Elis.* Weimar, 1883.

————. "Theophanien, altgriechische Götteradvente." *ARW*, XXII (1923–24).

WHITMAN, WALT. "From Pent-up Aching Rivers." In: *Leaves of Grass.* Philadelphia, 1891.

WHITMAN, WILLIAM. *The Oto.* New York, 1937.

WIEDMANN, ALFRED. *Herodots zweites Buch mit sachlichen Erläuterungen.* Leipzig, 1890.

WIEGAND, THEODOR (ed.). *Didyma.* Part I, *Die Baubeschreibung.* Edited by Hubert Knackfuss. Berlin, 1941. Part II, *Die Inschriften.* Edited by Albert Rehm. Berlin, 1958.

————. *Sechster vorläufiger Bericht über Ausgrabungen in Milet und Didyma.* (Abhandlungen der Berliner Akademie, Phil.-hist. Kl.) Berlin, 1908.

WIESNER, JOSEPH. "Die Hochzeit des Polypus." *JDAI*, LXXIV (1959).

WILAMOWITZ-MOELLENDORFF, ULRICH VON. *Der Glaube der Hellenen.* Berlin, 1931–32. 2 vols.

————. *Sappho und Simonides.* Berlin, 1913.

————. "Sepulchri Potuensis imagines." *Studi italiani di filologia classica,* VII (1929).

WILHELM, ADOLF. "Symmeixis." *Anzeiger der Akademie der Wissenschaften in Wien, Phil.-hist. Kl.,* LXVIII (1930).

WILLEMSEN, FRANZ. "Der delphische Dreifuss." *JDAI*, LXX (1955).

WISSOWA, GEORG. *Religion und Kultus der Römer.* 2d edn. Munich, 1912.

WITTE, JEAN JOSEPH. *Description des Collections d'antiquités conservées à l'Hôtel Lambert.* Paris, 1886.

WOLTERS, PAUL. *Archäologische Bemerkungen.* (Sitzungsberichte der bayerischen Akademie der Wissenschaften, Phil.-hist. Kl.) Munich, 1913.

————. *Darstellungen des Labyrinths.* (Sitzungsberichte der bayerischen Akademie . . . .) Munich, 1907.

WREDE, WALTHER. "Der Maskengott." *AM*, LIII (1928).

WROTH, WARWICK. *Catalogue of the Greek Coins of Crete and the Aegean Islands.* (British Museum.) London, 1886.

————. *Catalogue of the Greek Coins of Troas, Aeolis, and Lesbos.* (British Museum.) London, 1894.

ZANCANI MONTUORO, PAOLA. "Il corredo della sposa." *Archaeologia Classica,* XII (1960).

ZIEGLER, KONRAT. "Orphische Dichtung." *RE,* XVIII:2.

ZIEHEN, LUDWIG. "Panathenaia." *RE,* XVIII:3.

ZIELINSKI, TADEUSZ. *Die Gliederung der altattischen Komödie.* Leipzig, 1885.

ZIMMERMANN, HERBERT. "Das ursprüngliche Geschlecht von *dies.*" *Glotta,* XIII (1924).

ZSCHIETZSCHMANN, WILLY. "Die Giessener Spitzamphora." *Nachrichten der Giessener Hochschulgesellschaft,* XXIX (1960).

INDEX

A superior figure following a page number indicates a footnote. A number followed by an asterisk indicates an illustration in the section after page 388.

A

Abrams, M. H., 26 [41]
Achilles, 74; shield of, 65, 86
Adonis, cult of, 387
Adrasteia, 44
Aelian, 55 [11], 77 [83], 179 [150], 185 [171], 186 [173], 189 [1], 190 [4], 191 [67]
agalma, 308, 311
Agamemnon, 236
Aglaosthenes/Aglosthenes, 123 [245]
Agrai, Lesser Mysteries, 278, 295
Agrania/Agriania/Agrionia, 178, 185
Agripinilla (priestess), 352–354, 356, 363
Aidos, 359
Aigipan, 48, 375
Aigisthos, 155
Aigle, 102, 103, 104
Aigosthena, 165, 166
Aiora, 156, 157, 307
Aischylos, 83, 219, 233, 328, 329, 330; Eumenides, 89, 174 [132], 207 [48], 210, 213 [69], 217 [86], 234 [144]; Semele, 181 [155]; The Suppliant Women, 36 [33]
Aison (vase painter), 91, 92
Aissaoua, 85
Aitolia, 75
Aix (son of Python), 48
Akademeia/Akademos, 166
Akousilaos, 187 [176]
Aktaion, 248
Akurgal, E., 256 [198]
Aletis (Erigone), 154, 158
Alexiou, S., 9 [7], 12 [13], 20 [25], 21 [28], 23 [31]
Alfieri, N., 280 [26]
Alkaios, 84 [115], 187, 205 [43]
Alkmeonis, 83
Alkyonic Sea, 311
all-souls, feast of, 364
Alpha canis, 73
Alphaeios River, 181, 182, 184
Altamura painter, 280, 290
Althaia, 76, 314, 100 *

Altheim, F., 122 [240]
Amandry, P., 207 [49], 226 [111], 227 [114 115], 228 [121], 229 [124 128], 234 [145]
Amasis painter, 88, 169–170
amniotic fluid, 34
Amorgos, 298
Ampelos (epithet), 63
Amphietes, 198, 199, 213
Amphiktyon, 143, 144, 164
Amphissa, 220
Amphitrite, 9
Anakreon, 66 [43], 365–366
Ananios, 65 [38]
Andreae, B., 123 [243]
Andromachos, 60–61
Andros, 166 [104], 299
animals: caught alive, 82–89; caught in net, 87–88; in comedies, 341–342; imaginary, 81; raw meat of, eaten, 84–89, 115, 203; torn in pieces, 84, 85, 88, 115, 142, 147, 203, 235, 247
Anthedon, 184
Anthesteria, 157, 168, 170, 199, 200, 201, 234, 292, 295, 300–302, 303 [91 92], 315, 324, 325, 349, 361, 378; influence in Italy, 363, 364, 366; tragedy related to, 316, 317
Anthesterion (month), 296, 300, 304
Anthologia Graeca, 333 [184]
Anthologia Palatina, 54 [9], 103 [182], 185 [170], 249 [180], 323 [156]
Antigonus Carystius, 45 [63]
Antinoë, 248
Antonines, 349, 381
Antoninus Liberalis, 30 [7], 44 [59], 179 [149], 245 [171]
Apellaios (month), 205
Aphrodite, 109 [209], 186, 371; Ariadne as, 106–107; Urania, 197 [25]
apodemia, 209, 216
Apollo, 48–49, 103, 106, 108, 150, 219, 224, 328; birth, 106 [197]; birthday, 206, 216; at Delphi, 205–213, 216, 217, 230,

Apollo (*cont.*)
231, 238; and Delphic oracle, 229, 232; Dionysos connected with, 233, 261; epiphany of, 140; Phoibos, 210; Pythios, 213, 229, 230; on tripod, 232, 63 *

Apollodoros, 47[76], 105[192 193], 152[63], 153[69], 165[100], 176[139], 185[170 171 172], 186[173 175], 187[176], 188[183], 246[172], 360[241 243]

Apollonius Rhodius, 31[12], 39[44], 57[23], 256[196]

aporrheton, 226, 247

aporrhetos thysia, 33

Arabs, 85, 256, 257

Araña, cave painting, 35

Aratos, 42[53 54], 88, 109[208]

arcana, 376

Archebakchos, 354

Archelaos, 39–40

archiboukolos, 351, 353

Archilokos, 305–306

archimystes, 351

archon basileus, 312, 353; drama and, 332, 335; wife of, *see* queen of Athens

Arcturus, 74

Aretaios, 273–274, 309

Argonauts, 57, 256

Argos, 180, 197[25]; Dionysian religion in, 174, 176, 177, 178, 180, 181, 184–188, 203

Ariadne, xxv, 89–125, 136, 197[25], 360, 382, 35 *, 36 *, 141 *; as Aphrodite, 106–107; archetype of soul, 124–125; child or children of, 108; death of, 103, 106–107, 157, 277; Dionysos and, 101–103, 107–125; elevation to heavens, 123–124, 270, 385–387, 146 *; Erigone as, 155, 307; festivals of, 192; in heavenly marriage, 369–370, 124 *, 125 *; marriage with Dionysos, 109–110, 114, 121–123, 384; mistress of the labyrinth, 90, 95, 98–99, 101, 102, 105, 106, 107, 118; mother of Dionysos, 108, 114, 119; names and epithets, 99, 103–104; Theseus and, 98, 101–103, 107, 108, 109, 120, 123; tomb of, 103, 180, 194; wreath of, 109–110, 368, 369

Arias, P. E., 280[26]

Aridela (Ariadne), 104, 113, 116, 124

Arion, 317[137]

Aristaios, 39, 40, 77

Aristides, 168[109], 340[201]

Aristonous Corinthius, 45[64], 214[75]

Aristophanes, 333; *Acharnians*, 71[56], 164[96 97], 274[5], 296[73], 303[92], 304[95], 312[126 128], 334[186], quoted, 337–339; *Birds*, 338, 341; *Ecclesiazusae*, 341; *Frogs*, 79, 279[23], 292, 304[98], 336[193], 375[287]; *Knights*, 341; *Lysistrata*, 331, 340, 343; *Peace*, 151, 152[61]; *Plutus*, 229[123 126]; *Thesmophoriazusae*, 340–341; *Wasps*, 328[174], 336[194], 351[216]

Aristotle, 158, 299–300, 311; *Anecdota problemata*, 246–247, 250[181]; *Atheniensium Respublica*, 308[113], 309–310; *De generatione animalium*, xxxiii[4]; *Historia animalium*, 34; *Metaphysics*, 37; *Poetics*, 318, 321, 325–326, 332; *Politics*, 300[82]

ark/*arca*, 375, 376

Arnobius, 117[229], 276[14], 311[122]

arrheta hiera, 293, 310

arrheton, 226, 247, 261

arrival of a god, *see* *epidemia*

Artemis, 15, 107, 133, 184, 209; Apanchomene (hanged), 106, 157; Ariadne and, 98, 101, 103, 106, 108–109; sanctuary at Brauron, 151, 155

Asia Minor, 50, 209, 277; Great Mother religion, 275–276; myth of grapevine, 58–60

Asine, 187

Asklepios, birth of, 103, 104, 106

askoliasmos, 312, 324

askos, 38

Asterios/Asterion, 105

Astour, M. C., 146[44], 153[65]

Athamas, 246

Athena, 259, 260; born from head of Zeus, 278; Salpinx, 174[130]; with Theseus and Dionysos, 102, 36 *; with Theseus and Minotaur, 91, 28 *, 29 *

Athenagoras, 111, 112

Athenaios, 33[20], 60[26], 123[245], 144[35], 146[42], 158[82], 163[92], 166[104], 181[158], 192[9], 250[181], 287[42], 291[51], 306[104], 312[127], 316[135], 324[160], 378[298]

Athens, 30, 76; Akademeia, 166, 173, 175, 182[161], 320; Akropolis, 92; Boukoleion,

307–311, 313, 314, 315, 350, 351, 352, 362, 373; Dionysian festivals, *see* festivals; Dionysian religion in, 141, 143–144, 193, 199, 201, 278, 279; Dionysos arrives in, 144, 146, 160–175; Gerairai, *see* Gerairai; image of Dionysos brought to, 163–164, 166–167, 172, 175; images (idols) of Dionysos used in, 281–286, 76A*–84*; Lenaion, 162, 283, 298–299, 336; Panathenaia, 167; Parthenon graffito, 97, 33*; participation in Delphic rites, 141, 213, 219; procession before Eleusinian Mysteries, 78–79; processions of Dionysos, 166–175, 296; Pythion, 213; Sabazios cult in, 275; Small Mitropolis, 319, 103*; springs, 291, 292; swamps, 291, 292; temple of Dionysos Lemnaios, 291–293, 302; theater, 171, 172, sacrifice in, 319–320, 325; Thesmothetion, 312

Atlantes, 387
Atthidographes, 143 [32]
Attica, Dionysian religion in, 141–160, 200, 201
Attis, 275, 277
ax, double, 190–193

B

Bacchanalia, 355, 357, 363
bacchantes, *see* maenads
Bachofen, J. J., 129–130, 132, 134, 254 [191], 290 [48], 365 [261]
Bakcheia, 200
Bakcheutas (epithet), 291, 294
bakchoi/bakchai, 354
Bakchos/Bacchos/Bakcheus/Bakchios, 67, 123, 233, 251
Bakchylides, 187 [176]
barley, 24, 53
Bartocchi, F., 368 [269]
basilinna, 362
basket, see *cista mystica; liknon*
Bassarai, 233
Bassus, Cassianus, 40
bathron, 232, 63*
Baudelaire, C., 25–26
Bayard, L., 208 [54]
bears, 48

bearskin, 48
Beaufort, F., 46 [71]
Beazley, J. D., 61 [29], 75 [73], 91 [140], 102 [177], 284 [35], 340 [202]
Becatti, G., 375 [285]
Bechtel, F., 113 [223], 224 [105]
beer, 36, 53
bees, 42–43; awakening of, 38–41, 43, 50; in cave, 30–31; prophetesses as, 49
Beethoven, L. van, 135
beetle, sacred, 9
Bekker, I., 94 [151], 145 [41], 308 [113]
Bema of Phaidros, 171
Bendinelli, G., 66 [39]
Benton, S., 84 [112]
Berthelot, M., 242 [164]
Bethe, E., 172 [124]
Bezold, C., 386 [323]
Bible, *see* New Testament; Old Testament
Bieber, M., 328 [173]
Bielefeld, E., 366 [265]
biologos, xxxiii
bios, 190 [4], 349, 363, 374; *zoë* distinguished from, xxviii, xxxi–xxxvii
birds, 372; persons disguised as, 341
birth: in death, 107–108; premature, 106, 106 [197], 108, 294–295
Bischoff, E., 30 [4], 206 [44]
Blegen, C. W., 263 [217]
blood, overflowing of, 30, 33, 34, 38
Boehm, F., 156 [74]
Boeotia, 141, 178, 179, 185, 192, 218
Boëthius, A., 213 [70]
boiled meat, 246–247, 250; in milk, 252–256
Boll, F., 215 [77], 386 [323]
Bougenes (epithet), 55
Bougonia, 40
Boukoleion, *see* Athens, Boukoleion
boukouloi, 351–353, 356
bouplex, 176–177
Bourguet, É., 194 [17], 197 [26], 217 [87]
Bousquet, J., 236 [153]
Bowra, C. M., 74 [72], 190 [4], 305 [106], 318 [189]
boy/boys: fawn with, 319, 102*; in festivals, 305–309, 314, 93*, 98*; goats with, 318–319, 101*; initiation, 268–269, 358, 359, 373–377; in mysteries, 357, 358, 360

Boyancé, P., 360[242], 373[282], 386[324]

Bozzano, E., 227[117]

Brasiai, 183

Brauron, 151, 152, 155

Brindisi disk, 385–387, 146 *

Brindisi pitcher, 364–365, 367, 372, 386, 117 *

Britomartis, 82, 84, 87

Bromios (epithet), 291, 294

Brommer, F., 297[74]

Brueckner, A., 300[83]

Bruel, R., 85[118]

Brugsch, H., 293[60]

Buber, M., 304[94]

bull/bulls, 52, 54–55; "bull's foot," 182, 183, 308; caught in nets, 87; Dionysos as bull god, 52, 54–55, 86–87, 308; as prize, 315–316; raw meat of, eaten, 84, 86, 115; religious significance of, 55, 115–118; as sacrifice, 173, 180, 182, 190, 203, 213, 236, 315–316, 318, 61A *; snake and, 117; torn in pieces, 84, 115, 142, 203; on wine vessels, 53–55, 20 *

bull game, 12, 84, 2 *, 3A, 3B

Burkert, W., 318[141], 320[150]

Buschor, E., 97[162], 167[105], 288[43], 307[112]

butterfly, 254

Bysios (month), 206, 216, 217, 222, 233, 235

C

Caelius Apicius, 253[187]

calendar: Athenian, 278, 294, 295, 319, 378; Delphic, 205–206; Egyptian, 29; Greek, 30, 37; Julian, 29, 299

calf, 54–55, 119, 190–191, 270

Calpurni Pisones family, 381–382

Calza, G., 375[284], 376[289]

Canaanites, 255

Cantarella, R., 84[116]

Carian/Karios, 153

Caskey, J. L., 191[8]

cattle: sacrifice of, 40–41, 54, 55, 115–116, 190–191, 270; wild, 87; *see also* bull

caves, 17–19, 46, 110, 113, 114, 118, 223–224; bees in, 30–31; stalactites and stalagmites in, 18–19

Ceglie, 88

centaurs, 254

Chadwick, J., 23[33], 53[2], 54[8], 56[18], 71[57], 100[169], 264[220]

Chamaileon, 330

Charites (Graces), 182–183; terrible (*phoberai*), 333

child: bull as, 116–120; Divine, *see* Divine Child; horned, 114, 115, 245, 270; sacrifice of, 179, 189, 269–270, 379

childbirth, 132, 133

children: exposure of, 348; in festivals, 305–307, 317, 93 *; in New Comedy, 344, 347; on sarcophagus, 363, 115 *

choës (sing.: chous), 156, 170, 289, 290, 292, 295[69], 303, 305–308, 314, 318; buried with the dead, 363–365, 374

Choës Day, 156, 169, 170, 174, 292, 293, 300, 303–315, 374, 387; drinking contest, 312, 338; marriage ceremony, 308–312; preparations for, 307–308; women in, 312–315

Choreia, 177

choruses, 321; in comedy, 332, 333, 334, 339–342; dithyrambic, 305, 92A *; of satyrs, 325; tragic, 317, 331

Christianity, 387; Jesus as true vine, 257–258; wine, significance of, 258

Christmas, 299

Chthonios (epithet), 199

Chytroi, 304, 315

Cilicia, 46, 47

circumcision, 270

cista mystica, 260, 383

Clement of Alexandria, 66[42], 181[157], 196[22], 202[37], 267, 276–277, 311[124]

Cocteau, J., 26

Cocullo, 61

Codex Theodosianus, 294

Colchians, 270

Collitz, H., 113[223], 224[105]

Columella, 39–40

column, 17; as idol, with mask, 281–284, 76A *–76C *; phallic, 371–373

comedy, 168, 288, 297, 330–348; Middle, 343; New, 319, 335, 344, 347, 348,

349; Old, 335, 336–337, 339, 341, 342, 343, 351; satyr plays, 324–325, 330

Cook, A. B., 31 [8], 123 [246], 231 [131], 232 [137 138]

Cornutus, 67

corona borealis, 109

cortina, 230–231

cosmos, 384–388, 144 *–146 *

Council of Constantinople, Second (Trullianum), 67

Courby, F., 228 [120]

Cretan-Minoan art, 5–9, 62, 65, 115; gesture in, 10–14, 20–22

Cretan-Minoan culture and religion, 50, 77, 261, 269; Apollo in, 212; bulls in, 54–55, 115–118; Dionysos in, xxvi–xxvii, 27–28, 50, 52–56, 67–68, 103, 107, 110, 113, 115, 117, 119, 138, 190, 191, 193, 198, 262–263; languages, 208; visions in, 14–20; wine in, 53–58

Cretan writing, 11, 68–69; Linear B, xxvi, 34, 56

Crete, 49, 184, 252, 276; Delphic cult from, 50; enthronement ritual in, 263, 264; hunting in, 82–83; Orion associated with, 41–43; viticulture in, 55–58; Zeus born in, 30–33, 113, 119, 266

cruciform structure, cult object, 305, 361 [244], 378

Cumae, xxv

Cumont, F., 256–257, 363 [255]

cupids, *see* Erotes

Curtius, L., 147 [47], 314 [133], 360 [238 240]

Cyprus, 298, 299

D

Dadophoriae, 294

Dadophorios (month), 215, 217

Dadouchos, 279

Daidalidai, 100

Daidalos, 98–101

Dakaris, S. J., 230 [129]

Danaos, 178, 184

dance, 13, 16; in Dionysian religion, 146, 214, 271–272, 352, 367; in drama, 321, 332, 333; in Eleusinian Mysteries, 93; of Korybantes or Kouretes, 264–266, 269; in labyrinth, 94, 97–101, 107, 118;

in Sabazios mysteries, 288, 88B *–88D *; of Thyiades on Parnassos, 218–219, 222

Daphni, 213

Daux, G., 236 [153]

Dawkins, R. M., 106 [197]

death, 349–350; birth in, 107–108; life after, 349, 364–373, 118 *–131B *; life contrasted with, xxxiv, xxxv; struggle with, 8; vases buried with the dead, 363–365, 374

Deecke, W., 174 [130]

deerskin, 147, 218, 380

Delamarre, J., 298 [75]

Delos, 150, 151, 166 [104]

Delphi, 30, 141, 188, 197, 261; Apollo at, 205–213, 216, 217, 230, 231; calendar, 205–206; Dionysian religion, 141–142, 204–237, 238, 316; Dionysion, 223, 236; dragon, *see* Python; *omphalos*, 207, 228; oracle, 207–208, 210, 211, 212, 216, 224, 228–230, 232–236; temple of Apollo, 226, 228; Thyiades, *see* Thyiades; Thyiai, 217–218; tomb of Dionysos, 49, 232–233; tripod, 211, 223, 226, 228–232, 233 [138], 235, 261, 62 *, 63 *

Delphyne, 48, 211

Delvoyé, C., 160 [87]

Demargne, P., 72 [60]

Demeter, 82–83, 104, 110–112, 114, 116, 124, 150, 194, 248, 249, 387

Demokritos, 40

Demosthenes, *De corona*, xxxiii [5], 60 [26], 363 [252]

Deo (Demeter), 111

de Quincey, Thomas, 25

Deubner, L., xxvii, 145 [38 41], 170 [116], 171 [118], 279 [23], 284 [34], 300 [84 85], 302 [88], 304 [96], 306 [108], 312 [125], 319 [147], 335 [189], 336 [191], 361 [248]

Deukalion, 75, 235

Dia, 101, 109, 121–122

diadoche, 210

Didyma, 90–91

Diehl, E., 45 [64], 65 [38], 66 [43], 192 [10], 365 [262]

Diels, H., 60 [27], 94 [152], 110 [210], 240 [158]

Dieterich, A., 117 [229], 251 [183], 268 [241], 351 [215 217 218]

Dikte Cave, 33, 266

Dikte mountains, 87
Dimetor (epithet), 277
Dindorf, W., 168 [109]
Dindymion, Mt., 57, 256
Diodorus Siculus, xxxiv [9], xxxv [16], 8 [4], 39 [42], 45 [67], 53 [5], 83 [109], 87 [124], 102 [175], 106 [197], 110, 111, 120 [237], 121 [239], 124 [247], 138 [19], 186 [175], 197, 200, 233 [142], 248–249, 270 [250], 360 [243], 383
Diogenes Laertius, 25 [38]
Dion Chrysostomos, 243 [165]
Dionysia, Great, 168, 172, 173, 199, 296, 309, 312, 316, 381; drama in, 335, 349; tragedy originated in, 316–318, 322, 325–326
Dionysia, rural, 296–297, 321, 335–336, 338
Dionysian, the, 134, 138
Dionysian religion, 45, 50–51, 52–68; Cretan origin, *see* Cretan-Minoan culture and religion; Dionysian baroque, 381, 382; historical interpretations of, 129–139; of late antiquity, 349–388; mysteries, *see* mysteries, Dionysian; names in, 68–71; Orphism and, 240–245, 262–272; resistance to, 175–179, 184–188; sarcophagi representing, 377–385, 137 *–142 *, 144 *, 145 *; Semitic, 256–257; signs of, 52; syncretism, 381, 383; universalism, 387–388
Dionysios of Argos, 318 [142]
Dionysios Perigetes, 231 [131]
Dionysios Thrax, 334 [185]
Dionysius of Halicarnassus, 310 [120]
Dionysodoros, 195 [20]
Dionysodotes (Apollo), 212
Dionysos, xxvi–xxviii; absent for twelve months, 198–199; with alter ego, 280, 290, 75 *; Apollo connected with, 233, 261; archetype of *zoë*, 124–125; Ariadne and, 101–103, 107–125; Ariadne his mother, 108, 114, 119; arrivals of, 139–188, 39A *, 39B *, 40 *, 41 *; awakening of, 44, 49, 199–202, 212, 217, 222–223, 226; birth in Eleusinian Mysteries, 278, 279, 295; birthday of, 279, 299, 336, 343; born from thigh of Zeus, 75, 273–280, 295, 378, 73 *, 74 *; born in Ikaros, 152; born in Thebes, 143; as bull god, 52, 54–55, 86–87, 308; as child: initiation, 374–376, 132A *–132C *, killed by guardians, 240–246, 259, 263, 265–269, 373–374, riding on goat, 265, 270, 66C *, in vine, 270–272, 67 *, *see also* Divine Child; of Crete (Kresios), 103, 107, 110, 119, 180; "crusher of men," 190; Demeter his mother, 249; dismemberment, 66, 67, 110–111, 212, 213, 217, 223, 231, 235, 245, 248, 256, 261, 263; dual nature, 381–384; elevation to heavens, 123–124, 270, 385–387, 146 *; enthronement, 262–272, 80 *, 81 *, 98 *; Erigone and, 155, 158, 44 *; and female companion, 364–365, 386, 117 *; flight and pursuit of, 178; heavenly marriage of women with, 366–373; as herm, 307, 380–381, 140 *; honey associated with, 31, 49; Horai with, 144, 250, 37 *; as hunter, 87–89, 26 *; image of, brought to Athens, 163–164, 166–167, 172, 175; images (idols) used in Athens, 281–286, 305, 361 [244], 76A *–84 *; ivy associated with, 62–64, 196; kid identified with, 245, 246, 256; light associated with, 74, 75, 77–78, 279; as "lord of the wild beasts," 81–82, 84, 203, 25 *; marriage with Ariadne, 109–110, 114, 121–123, 384; marriage with queen of Athens, 293, 300, 301, 307–312, 361; in mysteries, impersonated, 354–355, 357, 360–362; names and epithets, 63, 67, 69, 83, 84, 85, 123, 163, 198, 203, 231, 245, 277, 291, 294, 301; Nietzsche's view of, xxiii–xxiv, 324, 329; as old man, 382–384, 142 *, 144 *, 145 *; Oriental, 81; Persephone his mother, 83, 110–114, 248, 256, 265, 279; pirates capture him, 152, 167; Poseidon and, 297, 90 *; as ruler of world (Dionysian era), 242, 244–245, 263, 265; as sacrificial victim, 203, 241–261, *see also* suffering god; scenes from life of, 66A *–66E *; second birth, 259; Semele his mother, 106–108, 110, 120, 161 [88], 181, 184, 185, 194, 256, 279, 295, 306, 378; statues of, at Thebes, 195–196; third birth of, 270; three

phases of his myth, 119–121; tomb at Delphi, 49, 232–233; in underworld, 180–182, 199–200, 256, 292, 303, 304, 311; as wine god, *see* wine; wine-making invented by, 57–60, 142–143; year of, see *trieteris*; Zeus his father, 69, 83, 106, 110–114

Dioskorides, 323 [156]

Dioskouroi, 387

Diosphos painter, 75 [73], 279, 280

dischi sacri, 385–387, 146 *

dithyramb/*dithyrambos*, 198–199, 215, 216, 301, 305–306, 315–316; singers, 305, 92A *; tragedy related to, 317–318, 321–322, 326

Dithyrambos (epithet), 218, 291, 294, 301, 305, 306

Divine Child, 45, 84; Dionysos, 55, 58, 244, 245, 246, 263, 265–272, 284, 299, 336, 348; in Eleusinian Mysteries, 78, 118, 278, 295; Liknites, *see* Liknites; Zeus, 30–33

Dodds, E. R., 85 [118], 138 [21], 139 [22], 158 [80], 176 [138], 227 [114]

Dodona, 208, 230 [129]

Doliche, 256

Dolukbaba, 256

domina/matrona, 352, 355–358, 361, 362, 372

Dominic, St., 61

Donus/Donusia, 122

Dorians, 332, 340

double ax, 190–193

Drachmann, A. B., 211 [62]

drama, 197; Dionysos and, xxiv, xxv, 296, 327–330, 331, 333, 334, 336, 348; systole and diastole in, 332, 333; *see also* comedy; tragedy

Drios, Mt., 123

drinking, 35, 36, 131, 135–137, 317; contest on Choës Day, 312, 338; in mysteries, 361–363

Dümmler, F., 167 [107]

Dusares, 256–257

E

Earth Goddess, *see* Gaia

Ebert, M., 35 [26]

Edmonds, J. M., xxxii [3], 168 [11], 300 [85], 343 [205 206], 347 [208], 348 [210], 351 [217]

Edwards, M. W., 27 [46], 61 [29]

egg as offering, 369

Egger, R., 222 [94]

Egypt, 43, 67, 72, 73, 77, 167, 270; beer, 36; festival of light, 299; viticulture, 56–57; year, beginning of, 29, 73

Eileithyia, 32, 133, 378; cave of, 18

Eilmann, R., 92 [143]

Eiraphion (month), 298

Eiraphiotes (epithet), 275, 277, 298

Eisele, T., 275 [10]

Eisler, R., 85 [120]

Elaphebolion (month), 296, 316, 319, 379, 381

Elderkin, G. W., 380 [308]

Eleusinian Mysteries, 33, 108, 118, 124, 187, 295, 350; dances, 93; Divine Child, 78, 118, 278, 279, 295; drink (*kykeon*), 24, 53; poppies as symbols, 24; procession before, 78–79

Eleusis, 213

Eleuther/Eleutheros/Eleuthereus (Dionysos), 69, 163, 172, 175, 296, 319, 320

Eleuther, daughters of, 163, 165

Eleutherai (place), 163, 165, 172, 175, 201, 317

Elis, 183, 190, 197, 293; Sixteen Women, 69, 181, 184, 190 [2], 197, 217, 293, 308, 327; song of women, 141, 181–182

Elworthy, F. T., 385 [322]

emasculation, 275–277, 285, 286

Enorches (epithet), 286

enthousiasmos, 200

enthronement, 262–272, 80 *, 81 *, 98 *

epheboi, 145, 162, 173

Ephyra, 230

Epicharmos, 332

Epidauros, 30

epidemia, 139, 140, 141, 170–171, 205, 209

Epikrates, xxxii [3]

Epimenides, 25, 110 [210]

Epiphany (Christian), 299

epiphany, 9, 13, 14 [16], 16, 17, 140, 159; of Dionysos, 124, 139, 140–141, 168, 200, 202; in Eleusinian Mysteries, 278; gestures and, 21–22, 9 *–12 * *epithema*, 229, 232

Eratosthenes, 41[51], 42[53], 149, 152, 153, 155, 323, 324[158]

Erigone, 148, 149, 154–161, 307, 323, 44 *

Eriphos (epithet), 245

Erman, A., 56[19], 167[107]

Eros, 297, 386; as guide of souls, 366, 368, 369, 370, 372, 121 *, 125 *; throwing ball, 365–366, 118 *

Erotes (cupids), 66, 123[233], 254, 64B *

Etruria, 355, 364

Etruscans, 174, 267, 371

Etymologicum Gudianum, 82[100], 195[20], 319[148]

Etymologicum Magnum, 83[110]

Euanthes (epithet), 291, 294, 301

Eudocia, 228[121]

Euenos, 249[180]

Euhemerism, 259

Euhemeros, 232[188]

Euhias, 219

Euios (epithet), 67

Euoi (cry), 59, 251

Euphorion, 248[176], 268

Euripides, 33[19], 233, 331, 341; *Antiope*, 196[22]; *Bacchae*, 31[10 11], 78[88], 89, 131[6], 136, 158[80], 192–193, 194, 203, 237, 306[105], 329; *Cretan Men*, 84, 85, 86, 243[167]; *Cyclops*, 131[6], 314[133]; *Helen*, 112[221]; *Heraclidae*, 174[132]; *Hippolytus*, 109; *Hypsipyle*, 218[89]; *Ion*, 214[75], 222, 226, 227[115]; *Iphigenia in Tauris*, 210, 211[61 62]; *Lykymnios*, 233; *Orestes*, 37[26]; *Phoenissae*, 174[132], 196[23 24]; *Rhesus*, 132

Europa, 105, 116

Euryale, 41–42

Eusebios, 143[32], 187[177]

Eustathius, 41[50]

Evans, Sir A. J., 5, 7[3], 8[4], 17[20], 53, 62, 81[98], 95, 101[173], 152[64], 159[85], 263[217]

Exekias, 167

F

Fallmerayer, J. P., 58[24]

Farnell, L. R., 113[222], 119

Faure, P., 18[21 22], 19[24], 101[172]

Fauth, W., 228[121], 262[212]

fawn, 254, 319, 64c *, 102 *

fermentation, 34, 38

festivals, 290–315; Agrionia, 178, 185; Aiora, 156, 157, 307; all-souls, 364; of Ariadne, 192; Chytroi, 304, 315; of new wine, 291–294, 296, 297, 302[89]; Oschophoria, 102, 144–146, 162; Panathenaia, 167, Panegyreis, 197; of *pentaeteris*, 151–152; Pithoigia, 302–303; Thyia, 183, 184[169], 190; of *trieteris*, 141–142, 199–202; *see also* Anthesteria; Choës Day; Dionysia; Lenaia

fig tree or wood, 260, 274, 282

fire in ceremonies, 33, 77, 78

Firmicus Maternus, 83[109], 84[113], 117[229], 253[186], 260[207]

five-year cycle/*pentaeteris*, 37, 38, 151–152

flute-playing, 66–67, 271, 305, 68 *–70 *, 92A *

Fontenrose, J., 211[63]

Forsdyke, J., 72[62]

Foucart, P., 144[37]

Foucher, L., 94[149]

Fowler, W. W., 300[86]

François Vase, 144, 37 *

Frazer, Sir J. G., xxvii, 35[27], 40[49], 45[70], 61[28], 157[76], 183[167], 360[241]

Freud, S., 157[80], 204[41]

Frickenhaus, A., 166[104], 167[105], 170[116], 171[119], 172[123], 173[126], 174[133], 281[28], 282[29], 283[33 34], 284[35]

Frisk, H., 99[165]

Fuchs, W., 254[188]

Fuhrmann, H., 75[73], 280[27]

Furlani, G., 47[75]

Furtwängler, A., 144[34], 157[80], 263[218]

G

Gaia/Ga/Ge, 83, 207, 210

Galen, 52[1], 60[27]

Gamelion (month), 296, 298–299

gamos, 309–310, 311, 369

Garstang, J., 46[73], 257[198]

Gaster, T. H., 255

Gerairai, 69, 217, 284, 293, 298, 301, 307, 308, 309, 336

gesture, 10–14, 20–22

ghosts, 303–304

Giessen amphora, 371–373, 130A *– 130F *

Gillen, F. J., 35 [27]

girls, initiation of, 377; *see also* children

Girodet, A.-L., 158 [83]

Gjerstad, E., 304 [97]

goat/kid, 76, 80, 87–88, 24 *; children with, 318–319, 101 *; Dionysos as kid, 245, 246, 256; Dionysos riding on, 265, 270, 66c *; kid boiled in milk, 252–256; male organ in sacrifices, 260; as prize, 320, 323; sacrifice of, 202 [37], 203, 233–235, 249, 250, 252–256, 270, 281, 318–324, 333, 351, 364, 76B *, 76C *, 103 *; tragedy related to, 318–324, 333; wild, 87

"goddess mounting her chariot," 161, 161 [88], 44 *, 46 *, 47 *

Goethe, J. W. von, 225 [108]

Goetze, A., 47 [75]

Graef, B., 92 [141 142], 171 [120]

Graeven, H., 265 [224]

grapes/grapevines, 64–65; Arabic cult of, 257; Dionysos as child in vine, 270–272, 67 *; harvest, 65, 74; Jesus as true vine, 257–258; mother of grape or wine, 256, 257; myths of origin, 58–60, 75–76; sacrifice for vines, 249–252; seeds found in excavations, 51; treading, 59–60, 65–66; viticulture, 50, 51, 55–60

Great Goddess, 7–8, 57–58, 111, 133, 207, 214, 256, 360; Ariadne as, 90, 99, 106, 107, 124; Artemis as, 155; bull game and, 12–13; Hera as, 184, 187; in Sabazios mysteries, 288, 88A *; on seal, 7, 13, 16, 1 *

Great Mother, 8, 24, 264, 269, 275–276

Groenewegen-Frankfort, H. A., 10 [8]

Guarducci, M., 45 [66]

Gundel, W., 386 [323]

H

Hades (god), *see* Plouton

Hades (place), *see* underworld

Hadrumentum, mosaic, 94, 31 *

Hagia Triada, 159; frescoes, 62; Harvester Vase, 72; sarcophagus, 54, 21A *, 21B *

Haliai, 177

Halliday, W. R., 182 [100]

hanging, 106, 157, 158

Hanslik, R., 103 [182]

hares, 88–89

Harmonia, 196 [25]

Harpokrates, 284

Harpokration, 147 [47]

Harrison, J. E., 85 [118], 266 [229], 268 [242], 303 [91]

Haspels, C. H. E., 75 [73], 92 [143], 161 [88]

Hastings, J., 255 [192]

Hauser, F., 229 [127]

Head, B. V., 192 [11]

head, severed, 267

headbands, 280, 314, 367

heart, 261; in sacrifices, 231, 259–260

Hebe, 116

Hegel, G. W. F., 204

Hekataios, 45 [68], 75–76

Helbig, W., 97 [161], 122 [243], 254 [190]

Helen, 157

Heliodoros, 213 [69]

Heller, J. L., 96 [157], 97 [162]

Helm, R., 143 [32]

Hepding, H., 275 [13]

Hephaistos, 65, 98

Hera, 116, 133, 181, 184, 242; Dionysos and, 187, 246, 267, 279; marriage with Zeus, 300; punishes daughters of Proitos, 186–187

Herakleion, Archaeological Museum, 5, 19, 53 [7]

Herakleitos of Ephesos, 239–240

Herakleotic knot, 112

Herakles, 180, 213 [70], 295 [69], 318

Herbig, R., 356, 356 [231], 357, 358, 359 [236], 360 [239], 361 [245 246]

herm, 307, 380–381, 140 *

Hermes, 48, 195, 246, 375, 378, 386; guardian of the dead (Chthonios), 303, 304, 307, 327, 366, 367, 120 *; as infant, 44; staff of, 112–113

Hermippos, 168

Herodotos, 43, 72, 73, 164–165, 167, 188, 218 [87 88], 224 [102], 238 [157], 257, 268 [239], 270 [247], 274 [4], 317 [137]

heros, 353, 354, 360, 370, 380

Herrmann, A., 57 [21]

Herter, H., 311 [123], 325 [162], 341 [203]

Hesiod, 65, 74, 109[206], 111[218], 165[99], 186[174 175], 300[85], 303[92], 319[149], 335, 359[237]

Hesychios, xxxiv[12], 42, 43, 78, 82[101], 86[121], 99[165], 104[183], 145[39], 153[68], 185[172], 203[40], 245[171], 264[219], 286[40], 298[76]

hetaira, 281, 312, 76B *, 76C *

Hieronymus, 143[32]

hierophantes, 353

Hieros gamos, 300

Hiller von Gaertringen, F., 39[41], 202[35], 353[224]

Himerios, 110, 113, 205[43], 251

Himmelmann-Wildschütz, N., 314[131], 379[302]

Hipparchos, 29[2]

Hippokrates, 37

Hipponax, 65[38]

Hipta, 260, 274–275

Hirmer, M., 12[12], 53[7], 56[15], 72[62], 87[125], 280[26]

Hittites, 255, 256, 257[198], 261; weather god, story of, 46–47, 49

Höfer, O., 88[128], 161[88]

Hofmannsthal, H. von, 343; quoted, 330–331

Holland, L. B., 223[99], 228[120], 229[125]

holmos, 229[124], 232

"holy open secret," 225, 226

Homer, xxxiii, xxxiv, 54, 55, 65, 67, 73, 99, 100, 106, 109, 174, 214, 251, 257; Iliad, xxiii[6 7 8], xxxiv[10], 34, 42[56], 54[9], 55[13 14], 65[37], 74[68 69], 98, 105[193], 131[3 5], 174[130], 176, 177, 178[145], 179[151], 192[11], 208[52], 212[67], 240[159], 275[12], 328[176]; Odyssey, xxxiii[7], 15–16, 18, 25, 37, 41[50], 54[9], 57[22], 65, 70[59], 98, 101, 103, 214[72], 239, 263[216]

Homeric Hymns, 152, 181, 198[28], 277[19], 360[243]; to Apollo, 45[68], 50, 207[48], 208[53], 210, 212; to Demeter, 112, 149; to Dionysos, 88–89, 167; to Hermes, 44, 49

honey, 31, 34–35, 36, 38, 42, 44, 48, 50, 52, 118, 225; Dionysos and, 31, 49; mead from, 35–38, 43, 49–50, 90, 98; thieves, 30–31, 33, 44, 16 *

Hooke, S. H., 255[192]

Hoorn, G. van, 289[46], 292[53], 306[107], 307[111], 318[143], 363[254], 364[257], 372[280]

Hopfner, T., 248[175], 284[37], 294[66]

Horace: *Carmina* (*Odes*), 219, 377[297]; *Epistolae*, 327[167], 328[175]

Horai, 163, 250, 286; Dionysos with, 144, 37 *

horned child, 114, 115, 245, 270

horned Dionysos, 362, 114 *

Horus, 294

Hosioi (holy men), 49, 223, 229, 235–236

hosion (commandment), 30, 31, 33, 44

hosioter (sacrifice), 236

humanism, 348

human race, creation of, 242

Humboldt, W. von, xxxi[1]

hunters/hunting: animals caught alive, 82–89; Dionysos, 87, 88–89, 26 *; Orestheus, 75–76; Zagreus, 80–89

hunting boots, 55, 88, 190, 270, 313, 379, 380

Huxley, A., 139

Hydra, 180

hydromeli, 36, 37

Hyginus, 76[77], 106[197], 109[209], 110[210], 120[235], 154[70 72], 155[73], 157[78], 185[170], 230[130], 259[206], 314[133], 324[158]

hymnodidaskaloi, 351

Hyperboreans, land of, 205[43], 206, 209, 217

Hyria, 42–43

Hyrieus, 42

hysteria, collective, 138–139

I

Iachen/Iachim, 77

iachron, 78

Iakar, 73, 77

Iakchos/Iakos/Iachos, 73, 77, 78–79, 279, 280

Iasion/Iasios, 83

ichor, 34

Ida, Mt., 275

Idaean Cave, 33, 84, 86, 266

Ikarion (deme), 148, 149, 152, 155, 160, 172, 296, 307; idols of Dionysos in, 282–283, 322–323, 328, 79 *, 80 *, 81 *; tragedy originated in, 322, 323, 324, 326

Ikarios, 149, 151–156, 162, 163, 164, 323; Dionysos visits, 148, 171, 41 *, 60 *

Ikaros/Ikaria (island), 151, 152, 153
Iliad, *see* Homer
Illuyankas, 46–47
Inachos River, 180, 181, 184
Inatos, cave sanctuary, 19
incest in birth of Dionysos, 110–114
Indians, American, visions, 15, 26
initiation: of boys, 268–269, 358, 359,
 373–377; of child Dionysos, 374–376,
 132A *–132C *; in Dionysian mysteries,
 358–361, 373–377; enthronement as,
 263, 264; of girls, 377; murder simu-
 lated in, 267; whitened faces in, 268
Ino, 246, 248
Ion (poet), 108 [204]
Ionia, 298
Iphigeneia, 155
Isis, 154, 247, 282, 284, 310–311
Isler, H. P., 161 [88]
Isodaites (epithet), 231
Isola Sacra, murals, 375–376, 132A *–
 132C *
Israelites, 255
Italy, Dionysian religion in, 360, 362, 363,
 371, 385–388; *see also* Bacchanalia;
 mysteries of Dionysos
ivy, 61–64, 187, 196, 305

J

Jacoby, F., 45 [78], 49 [81], 75 [75], 102 [176 178],
 123 [245], 143 [32], 180 [152], 185 [171], 192 [11],
 195 [20], 232 [136], 291 [51], 317 [138]
Jacolliot, L., 227 [117]
Jeanmaire, H., 85 [118 119], 138 [21]
Jensen, A. E., 270 [246]
Jesus Christ as true vine, 257–258
Johansen, K. F., 305 [101 102], 314 [130]
Julius Caesar, 363
Jullien, A., 298 [77]
Jung, C. G., 208 [54], 262 [214]
Jupiter Dolichenus, 256
Juvenal, 369 [271]

K

Kabeiroi, 195 [20], 269, 276
Kadmos, 143; daughters of, 185; palace of
 (Kadmeia), 194–197

Kadmos/Kadmeios (epithet), 195
Kähler, H., xxiv [3]
Kakoure, K. I., 23 [35]
Kallimachos, 32, 44, 83 [110], 140, 216 [82],
 232 [135]
Kallixeinos of Rhodes, 60 [26], 66 [41], 378 [298]
kanephoros, 173
kantharos, 327, 376–377, 380
Karouzou, S., 66 [39], 170 [115]
Kasion, Mt., 46, 47
Kastalia spring, 207
Kastor of Rhodes, 143 [32]
Kathegemon (epithet), 351
Kato Zakros, 53 [6 7], 56
Kees, H., 77 [84]
Keil, J., 295 [68]
Kekrops painter, 297
Keller, G. A., 153 [67]
Kenna, V. E. G., 22 [30], 81 [98]
Keos, 39, 77, 191–192
Kephaisodotos, 195
Keramopoulos, A. D., 194 [14], 196 [21]
Keres, 304, 304 [96]
Kern, O., 35 [28], 36 [30], 111 [215], 112 [220], 231 [134],
 242 [162 163], 244 [169], 248 [176], 249 [179], 251 [184],
 253 [185], 259 [205 206], 260 [207 208], 261 [210], 264 [221],
 269 [244], 270 [249], 274 [7], 275 [8]
kid, *see* goat
Killen, J. T., 71 [57]
Kinkel, G., 83 [107]
Kissos (Dionysos), 63, 196
Kithairon, Mt., 179 [149 150], 192
Klauser, T., 263 [215]
Klea, 222–223, 226
Kleidemos, 102
Klitias and Ergotimos, Krater of, 144, 37 *
Klytaimnestra, 155
Knackfuss, H., 91 [137]
Knossion (pattern), 96–98, 34 *
Knossos, 5, 8, 53, 54, 72 [61], 193, 212; coins,
 96–97, 104–106; frescoes, 12 [12], 62, 94,
 101 [73], 2 *, 32A *, 32B*; labyrinth, *see*
 labyrinth; mysteries, 79, 118; palace,
 17, 263; tablets, 69, 71, 77 [81], 89, 98,
 100, 212 [67]
koinonia, 310
komodia, 333, 334
komos, 72, 333–337, 339–340, 341, 104 *,
 105 *; children's, 363 [253], 115 *

Kondoleon, A. E., 237 [155]
Kontoleon, N. M., 81 [97]
Kore, 116
Korgos, 46
Korkyne, 122 [243]
Koronis, 103, 104, 106–108, 120
Körte, A., 348 [209]
Korybantes, 264, 267, 269
Korykion antron (cave), 48, 49, 210, 223–224, 255, 261
Korykos (localities), 43, 45–46
korykos, 43, 45, 225; *see also* sack, leather
Koukoules, P., 67 [46 47]
Kouretes, 264, 265, 266, 269
Kourouniotes, K., 278 [21]
Kouros, 266
Kradiaios Dionysos, 260, 274
Krates, 332; *Animals*, quoted, 342
Kratinos, 351
Kretschmer, P., 32 [13], 107 [203]
Kritikos, P. G., 24 [37]
Kronos, 35, 113, 242, 266, 275, 387; castration of, 36
krotaloi, 367
Krueger, A., 241 [161], 243 [165]
Kühn, C. G., 52 [1], 60 [27]
Kunze, E., 84 [112]
Kybele, 150, 264
Kydonia, 45; seal from, 81, 25 *
kykeon, 24, 53
Kyllenian grotto, 44
Kynaithai, 54

L

labyrinth, 90–107, 110, 117–118, 28 *–35 *; dance in, 94, 97–101, 107, 118; mistress of, 90, 95, 98–99, 101, 102, 105, 106, 107, 118
Lacroix, L., 191 [5]
Lambert, W. G., 193 [13]
Landau, O., 71 [58 59]
Lang, M., 97 [163]
Langlotz, E., 81 [99], 92 [141 142], 171 [120], 368 [267]
Latte, K., 104 [183]
Lawrence, D. H., 61 [30]
Lawson, J. C., 148 [50]
Learchos, 246, 248
leather sack, *see* sack, leather

Lehmann, K., 264 [222], 381 [309], 382 [310–313], 383 [315]
Leipoldt, J., 140 [26]
Leitch, J., 27 [45]
Lenai (bacchantes), 296, 298, 340
Lenaia, 199, 279, 283–284, 296–300, 316, 317, 327; drama in, 335, 336, 338, 343, 349
Lenaion (month), 298, 299
lenos, 65, 66, 298, 299, 384
Lenschau, T., 144 [36]
Leonidas of Tarentum, 249
Lepsius, K. R., 167 [107]
Lerat, L., 207 [49]
Lerna, 174, 178, 183, 201, 207, 292, 293, 311; lake of, 179–181
Lesbos, 286, 353
Lesky, A., 240 [158], 326 [165 166]
Leto, 209, 211, 214
Levi, D., 6 [2], 20 [27], 51 [86], 53 [7], 119 [231]
Lewis, D. M., 148 [49]
Lhote, H., 57
Liber Pater, 375, 376
Liddell, H. G., 34 [24]
life: after death, 349, 364–373, 118 *–131B *; and death in Dionysian religion, 52, 179–181, 183, 192, 197, 200, 204–205, 261, 317; indestructibility of, 115, 200, 241, 373, 387; *zoë* and *bios* distinguished, xxviii, xxxi–xxxvii
light: Apollo as god of, 209, 233; and birth of Zeus, 30–35; Dionysos associated with, 74–75, 77–78, 279; festival of, 118; and new year, 43; of Zeus, 32, 75, 78
Liknites (Dionysos), 44, 49, 215 [77], 218; awakening of, 222–226, 235, 260, 272, 288, 310
liknon (winnowing basket), 44–45, 218, 222, 223, 225, 379, 387; child in, 272, 274, 71 *; mask in, 289, 89 *; in mysteries, 354, 359, 361 [244], 376, 377; phallus in, 260, 273, 276, 288, 359, 377, 72 *
Lindemann, F. O., xxxii [2]
linos song, 65
lion, 84
Lipari, 252
Livy, 45 [68], 355

Lobeck, C. A., 268 [241]
Lobel, E., 84 [115], 187 [180], 205 [43]
Locrians, Ozolian, 76
Lokroi, 367
"lord of the wild beasts," 81–82, 84, 203, 25 *
Lorimer, H. L., 174 [130]
Lucan, 219–220
Lucian, 78, 106 [197], 161 [90], 164 [97], 340 [200]
Luschey, H., 283 [32]
Lycia, 209
Lydia, 275
Lykaion, Mt., 32
Lykophron, 181 [156], 195 [20], 224 [106], 236, 261 [209], 286 [40]
Lykourgos, 176–178, 219, 233, 329

M

Maass, E., 153 [67], 154 [71]
Macrinus, Marcus Pompeius (Theophanes), 353
Macrobius, 233 [141], 237, 303 [93], 325 [161]
Macurdy, G. M., 310 [121]
madness, 131-134, 163, 165, 176, 179, 186, 188
maenads, 31, 52, 78, 88–89, 176, 179, 197, 202–203, 217, 227, 231, 254, 266, 271–272, 281, 17 *, 64C *, 68 *–71 *; in heavenly marriage after death, 370; maenadism, 138–139, 176, 189; on mules, 169, 52B *, 53 *; in mysteries, 359, 362, 110B *, 110D *, 110E *, 112C *, 112D *; as nurses of Dionysos, 379, 138 *; on Parnassos (Thyiades), 218–224, 235, 237; snakes used by, 60–61, 64, 22A *, 22B *; Thracian bacchantes, 219–220, 233, 329
Magna Graecia, *see* Italy
Magnes, 341
Mago, 40
Maimakterion (month), 295, 296
Maimonides, Moses, 255 [192]
Maira (dog), 153, 154, 171–172
Maiuri, A., 265 [225], 362 [251], 383 [314]
mankind, creation of, 242
Mari, 159
Marinatos, S., 12 [12], 18 [22], 30 [5], 53 [7], 56 [15], 72 [62], 87 [125], 208 [51]

Marmor Parium, 320 [151], 323 [155]
marriage: in Dionysian mysteries, 355, 357–358, 360–362, 110C *, 112F *, 114 *; of Dionysos and Ariadne, 109–110, 114, 121–123, 384; of Dionysos and queen of Athens, 293, 300, 301, 307–312; heavenly, after death, 366–373; of Poseidon and Amphitrite, 9; significance of, *symmexis* and *gamos*, 309–310, 311; of Zeus and Hera, 300
Marzano, G., 365 [260]
masks, 80, 166, 24 *; of actors, 327, 332; of Dionysos, 123, 192, 281–284, 76A *–79 *, 82A *–85 *; of grape treaders, 67; in Great Dionysia, 317; in *liknon*, 289, 89 *; in mysteries, 359
matrona, see *domina*
Matton, R., 62 [33]
Matz, F., 14 [16], 18 [23], 116 [227], 350 [214], 360 [242], 363 [253], 373 [282], 376 [291 292], 377 [294 295], 379 [303 304], 380 [306], 383 [317], 384 [318 319]
mead, 35–38, 43, 49–50, 52
meander (pattern), 90–92, 94–96, 104
meat, boiling and roasting, 246–247, 250, 252–256
Megapenthes, 70, 72, 185
Meidias painter, 307–308, 368
Meilichios (epithet), 123
Meineke, A., 149 [51]
meixis, 310
Melampous, 72, 164–165, 167, 187, 239, 240, 285
Melanaigis (epithet), 163, 319
Melikertes, 246
melikratos, 37
Mellen, C., 26 [44]
Melpomenos, 161 [88]
men: in Choës Day celebration, 312–315; in choruses, 325, 339–341; in Dionysian mysteries, 353–355; in Dionysian religion, 164, 202–203, 226, 235–237, 240, 297, 307, 309, 350; in Great Dionysia, 317; heavenly marriage after death, 370; holy, *see* Hosioi; in *komos*, 333–336, 339–340; in women's parts on stage, 340–341, 104 *, 105 *
Menander, 300 [85], 348; *The Arbitration*, 348, quoted, 343–347
Menelaos, 70 [54]

Merkelbach, R., 154

mescalin, 26

Mette, H. J., 181 [155], 233 [140], 329 [177]

Meuli, K., 254 [191]

Meyer, E., 29 [1]

Milani, L. A., 159 [84]

Milchhoefer, A., 149 [53], 150 [55]

milk, kid boiled in, 252–256

Millingen, J., 366 [263]

Minoan culture, *see under* Cretan-Minoan

Minos, 41, 82, 98, 102, 109, 263

Minotaur, 86, 91, 104, 105, 109, 117–120; in labyrinth, 91, 94, 99, 28 *, 31 *

Minyas, daughters of, 179, 184, 185, 186, 188 [183], 192

mirror, 365, 366, 367; of child Dionysos, 265, 267, 269, 271; in initiation, 359

Mitrephoros (epithet), 280, 314

mitrephoros, 367

Mittelhaus, K., 173 [125]

Mnaseas, 196 [23 24]

Moirai, 387

Mommsen, A., 298 [77]

moon: Ariadne associated with, 104, 105–106, 116, 124; Erigone associated with, 155

moon goddess: Artemis, 155; Hera, 184

Moortgat, A., 257 [200]

Morgan Cup, 377 [297]

Mother Goddess, *see* Great Mother

mountains, shrines on, 7, 13, 16, 19–20, 1 *, 7 *, 8 *

mules, 169–170, 290, 52A *–55 *

Müller, C. F. W., 138 [19], 231 [131]

Müller, K. O., 27, 28, 129, 174 [10], 268 [240]

Müller, W., 15

mundus patet, 300, 306, 315, 316, 317

Murray, G., 203 [38]

Muses, 178, 179

Mycenaean culture, 11, 138, 184, 187, 191, 194, 195, 198, 269

mysteries, Dionysian, 350–363, 381–383; Dionysos impersonated in, 354–355, 357, 360–362; initiation, 358–361, 373–377; Villa dei Misteri murals, 352, 355–363, 371, 374, 376, 379, 383, 386, 106 *–112F *, 143 *

mysterion, 309, 310

Mythographia Vaticani, 76 [76], 116 [228], 245 [171]

N

Naples, 364

Nauck, A., 83 [108], 84 [116], 86 [121], 218 [89], 233 [140], 328 [176]

Naxos, 120–123, 151, 152; Dionysos in, 382, 141 *; festivals of Ariadne, 192

Neoplatonism, 241, 242

Neos Theophanes, 353

Neraides, 237

Nestor, palace of, 69

net, animals caught in, 87–88

New Testament: John, xxv [18], 257 [203], 258; Luke, xxv [18]; Mark, xxv [18], 257 [202]; Matthew, xxv [18]

Newton, C. T., 191 [5]

New Year's festival, 41, 43, 50

Nicander, 42 [56]

Nietzsche, F. W., xxiii–xxv, 129, 132, 134–138, 324, 329

Nikias of Elea, 264

Nikomachos, 124 [249]

Nikosthenes, 42

Nile, 167, 184; rising of, 29, 73

Nilsson, M. P., xxvii, 30 [6], 60 [27], 118 [231], 138 [20], 159 [86], 169 [112], 203 [39], 261 [211], 285 [38 39], 295 [68], 340 [202], 350 [214], 354 [225 227], 373 [282]

Nilus, 85 [118]

Nogara, B., 254 [188]

Nonnos, 57, 60 [25], 114, 245, 265, 267, 270, 381; myth of grapevine, quoted, 58–60

Norden, E., 215 [77], 295 [70], 299 [80]

Norvin, W., 242 [162]

numbers: three, 37; four, 40; seven, 106 [197], 261

nurses of Dionysos, 120–121, 178, 179, 246, 265, 270, 276, 284, 288, 289, 291, 378–379, 382

Nyktelios (epithet), 231

nymphs, 199, 210, 246, 291

O

Oates, W. J., 337 [195], 339 [197], 348 [210]

Odyssey, *see* Homer

Oellacher, H., 199 [30]

Ohlemutz, E., 352 [220 222]

Oikonomos, G. P., 147 [45]

Oineus, 75, 76, 314
Oinioe (place), 213
Oinoa (place), 69
Oinoë (place), 152
Oinopion, 76–77
Oinops (epithet), 54, 63
Oinos (epithet), 270, 271
Old Testament: Deuteronomy, 255 [192]; Exodus, 255 [192]; Isaiah, 67, 140; Jeremiah, 257–258; Psalms, 257 [202]
Olsen, E. C., 381 [309], 382 [310–313], 383 [315]
Olympia, 30, 181, 184
Olympias, 60
Olympic Games, 37
Olympiodoros, 212 [65], 242
Olympos, Mt., 267, 270
Omadios (epithet), 84, 203
Omestes (epithet), 84, 203
Onasimedes, 195
O'Neill, E., Jr., 337 [195], 339 [197], 348 [210]
Onomakritos, 231, 238, 240–245, 247, 261, 262, 263, 268, 269, 278, 326, 350, 374
opium, 24–27
opora, 73, 74
oracle at Delphi, *see* Delphi, oracle
Oracula Sibyllina, 263 [215]
Orchomenos, 179 [148 149], 192
Orestheus, 75, 76
Origen, 373 [282]
Orion, 76–77, 82, 87, 88, 103; birth of, 41–43, 76; constellation, 73–74; scorpion associated with, 42, 18 *; Sirius his dog, 41, 73–74, 75
Orista, 76 [76]
Orpheus, 239, 262, 264; killed by bacchantes, 233, 267, 329
Orphic Hymns, 198, 202 [35], 243, 277, 351; to Amphietes, 198, 199, 200 [32]; to Hipta, 275; to Perikionios, 196; to the Titans, 268
Orphic literature, 110, 239–245, 249, 260, 269, 274–275
Orphic religion, 35–36, 93 [148], 110–112, 118, 231, 256, 259, 261, 276, 277–278, 364, 373, 374; Dionysian religion and, 240–245, 262–272; gold leaves used in, 252–253
Ortega y Gasset, J., 331; quoted, 315

Orthos (Dionysos), 144, 163, 286
Oschophoria, 102, 144–146, 162
Osiris, 154, 247, 247 [175], 274, 282, 284, 293, 294, 310–311; mysteries of, 223, 226
Otto, E., 247 [175]
Otto, W. F., xxv, xxvi, xxviii, 55 [13], 64 [36], 85, 89 [133], 103 [181], 106 [195], 107 [201], 120 [238], 131–134, 138, 139, 176 [138], 190 [3 4], 204 [42], 206 [47]; quoted, 63–64, 131–134
Ouranos, 242
Ovid: *Fasti*, 31 [9], 35 [27], 36, 40 [49], 42 [56], 355 [230]; *Metamorphoses*, 106 [197], 111, 158, 177 [140], 179 [149], 243 [165], 245 [171]

P

paean/*paian* (song), 79, 212, 214–217, 233
Pagasai, 192
Page, D., 84 [115], 187 [180], 205 [43]
Paian/Paieon (god), 212, 215
Pallas Athena, *see* Athena
Palmer, L. R., 208 [55], 257 [198], 303 [90]
Palmer, R. B., xxv [4]
Pan, 266
Panathenaia, 167
Panegyreis, 197
Pangaion mountains, 219
Panofsky, E., 158 [83]
Panopeus, 103, 213–214
panthers, 266, 271, 376, 377, 66D *, 70 *
Papadaki, S. P., 24 [37]
Papadimitriou, I., 151 [58]
Paribeni, R., 159 [85]
Parmenides, 94
Parnassos, Mt., 44, 208, 210–214, 217, 231, 235; secret ceremonies on, 236–237; Thyiades on, 218–224, 235, 237
parousia, 202, 278, 310, 317
Parrot, A., 160 [88]
Pasiphaë, 86, 116, 117
Patara, 209
pateterion, 65, 66
Patitucci, S., 288 [45]
Pausanias, 32 [16], 49 [81], 54 [10], 63 [34], 76 [78], 103 [179], 105 [192], 111 [219], 113 [222], 137 [16], 141 [30], 143 [33], 145 [40], 150 [54], 157 [79], 161 [88], 164 [94], 165, 166, 174 [130], 177 [143], 178 [144],

Pausanias (*cont.*)
180[154], 181[156][159], 183[167], 184[169], 194, 195,
196[24][25], 202[37], 207[48], 214, 224, 229[125],
241, 268[239], 311[122], 327[171]
Pearson, A. C., 94[150], 99[167]
Pegasos, 163–166
Peisistratos, 164
Pelekys (epithet), 192
Pendlebury, J. D. S., 95[156]
Penelope painter, 157
pentaeteris, 37, 38, 151–152
Pentelikon, Mt., 148
Pentheus, 69–71, 89, 185, 193, 203, 210,
217, 329
Pergamon, 351–352
Perikionis (epithet), 198
Perinthos, 250–251, 351
Persephone, 103, 104, 106, 116, 120, 124,
199, 301, 387; Ariadne as, 107, 113,
116; with dancers and flower, 13, 16,
4 *; in Eleusinian Mysteries, 278; moth-
er of Dionysos, 83, 110–114, 248, 256,
265, 279
Perseus, 176, 177, 179, 180, 184
Persius, 67
peyote, 26
Pfuhl, E., 172[122]
Phaidra, 102, 109
Phaistos, 51, 53[7]
Phaleron, 102, 144, 145, 162, 170
Phales, 71
phallophoriai/phallagogiai, 71–73, 239,
260, 285–288, 297, 335, 338, 354, 87A *,
87B *
phallus, 19, 71–73, 144, 195, 387; artificial, 285, 339; in basket (*liknon*), 225,
267, 276, 288, 359, 377; ithyphallic
state, significance of, 273–274; in mysteries, 354, 359; of Osiris, 247, 247[175];
phallic element in comedy, 332, 336–
339; on pillar, 371–373; in sacrifices,
260–261; symbol of Dionysos, 163, 164,
165, 181, 285–290, 311; uncovering of,
273, 72 *
Phanodemos, 291, 292
Phanokles, 291
pharmaka, 24, 25
Pherakydes, 185[171]
philanthropeia, 348

Philistines, 53
Philo, 202[36]
Philochoros, 49[81], 232, 250, 317[138]
Philodamos, 216–217
Philodemos, 248[176]
Philostratos, 101[171], 164[98], 168[109], 340[201]
Phoebe, 210
Phoenicians, 255
Phokians, 268
Phorbas, 328
Phormis, 332
Photios, 145[41], 147[47], 300[84], 305[99]
Phrygia, 36, 275, 276
Phrynichos, 94[151], 305, 330
Physios (Bysios, month), 217
physis, xxxii, 7
Phytios, 75
phytou bios, xxxiii
Picard, C., xxvi, 81[99], 88[130], 159[85], 171[121],
254[189], 280[25]
Pickard-Cambridge, A., 146[43], 164[95],
284[34], 288[44], 290[49], 296[72], 299[78], 319[148],
333[183], 335[189][190], 339[198], 340[199][200], 341[203]
pillar, *see* column
Pindar, 49[84], 74, 106[196], 183[163], 211[62],
216[82], 306, 316[135]
Piraeus, 144
pirates, Dionysos captured by, 152, 167
Piskokephalo, 9
Pithoigia, 302–303
Platakis, E., 86[123]
Plato: *Euthydemus*, 92, 93[144], 264–265;
Laws, 74, 131, 269[245]; *Phaedo*, xxxiv,
93, 242; *Symposium*, 289; *Timaeus*,
xxxiv[13]
Platon, N., 6, 7, 8, 12, 18[22], 19[24], 20[26],
53[67], 56[16], 72[61], 138[18]
Plaumann, G., 295[68]
Pleiades, 84, 215[77]
Pliny the Elder, 36[34], 37, 38, 39[43], 43[57],
50, 57[23], 65[38], 280[25], 299[81]
Plotinos, xxxv
Plouton/Pluto/Hades, 83, 113, 297; Di-
onysos identified with, 239–240
Plutarch, xxxv, 93, 181, 183, 214–215,
218, 222–223, 228, 231, 234; *Alexan-
der*, 60[26], 61[31], 216[81]; *Consolatio ad
uxorem*, 373[282]; *De cohibenda ira*, 84[114];
De cupiditate divitiarum, 285; *De defec-*

tu oraculorum, 222 [96], 227 [116], 234 [146 148];
De E apud Delphos, 215 [76 79], 217 [86],
223 [100], 226, 229 [122], 231 [133]; *De Iside et
Osiride*, xxxv [17], 44 [62], 49 [82], 180 [152],
223 [98 99], 231 [133], 248 [175], 282, 294 [66]; *De
primo frigido*, 220 [93]; *Moralia*, xxxiv [14];
Mulierum virtutes, 220 [92]; *Quaestiones
conviviales*, 64 [36], 122 [241], 178 [146], 179 [148],
234 [147], 302 [89], 330; *Quaestiones Graecae*,
32 [17], 48 [79], 55 [12], 178 [146 147], 182 [160 162],
183 [164], 206 [46], 216 [80], 217 [85], 233 [143],
235 [150], 236 [151]; *Quaestiones Romanae*,
62 [32], 187 [178]; *Solon*, 327 [167]; *Themistocles*,
84 [114], 202 [37]; *Theseus*, 102 [174-176 178],
106 [195 198], 107 [199], 108 [204], 122 [243], 123 [244],
277 [17]
Pollux, 67 [44], 174 [131], 229 [124], 293 [59], 319 [149],
325 [163]
Polyanos, 268 [239]
Polydoros, 195
Polymnos, 311
Pompeii: graffito, 96; Villa dei Misteri,
murals, 352, 355-63, 371, 374, 376,
379, 383, 386, 106 *-112F *, 143 *
Pomponius Mela, 45 [70], 46
Pomtow, H., 206 [46], 215 [79]
poppy/poppy seed, 23-24
poppy goddess, 23, 24, 15 *
Porphyry, 84 [115], 86 [123], 202 [37], 232 [138], 266 [231],
Porto Raphti, 148-151
Poseidon, xxxiii, 9, 41, 111, 122 [241], 387;
Dionysos and, 297, 90 *
Poseidon (month), 296
Pottier, E., 61 [29]
Poussin, N., 158 [83]
Powell, J. U., 149 [51], 199 [30], 214 [75], 217 [84],
248 [176], 268 [238], 301 [87], 323 [157]
Pozzo di Santulla, 46
Prasiai, 149-152, 183-184
Pratinas of Phleious, 324
pregma, 274, 309, 310, 352, 361, 373; *see
also* mysteries, Dionysian
pregnancy, 358; interrupted, 295
Preisendanz, K., 183 [165]
Preller, L., 103 [181]
premature birth, 106, 108, 294-295
Priene, 201
Privitera, G. A., 240 [158]
Probos, 76 [76], 186 [174]

processions of Dionysos, 166-175, 285-
288, 296
Proitos, daughters of, 165, 184-188
Proklos, 93 [144], 145 [41], 260 [208], 261 [209]
Prometheus, 142
Propertius, 154 [70]
Prosymnos, 311
Protrepticus, 277 [16]
Prott, H. von, 183 [165]
Psellos, M., 230 [129]
Pseudo-Demosthenes, 292 [57], 293 [61], 302 [88],
308 [114], 309 [116 117]
psyche, xxxiv, 354
Ptolemaios Philadelphos, 60 [26], 66
Ptolemy II, 378
Puhvel, J., 69 [51], 165 [101]
Pylaochos, 180
Pylos, xxvi, 23, 28, 71, 165, 188, 263;
tablets, 68-69, 71 [58], 77 [81], 82, 97, 98,
137, 264, 303, 34 *
Pythagoras, 342
Pythais (procession), 213, 236
Pythia (prophetess), 49, 206, 210, 211,
232, 234; duties of, 226-229
Pythian games, 230
Pytho (Delphi), 208
Python, 48, 210, 211-212, 230-231

Q

Quandt, W., 84 [115], 196 [24], 198 [28 29], 199 [31],
225 [107], 243 [167 168], 268 [238], 275 [9], 276 [15],
277 [20], 351 [215 219], 352 [221], 354 [225]
queen of Athens, 76, 160, 162, 169, 170,
290, 352, 354, 355; marriage with Dionysos, 293, 300, 301, 307-312, 361

R

Radin, M., 255 [192]
Radke, G., 122 [240]
ram, 180, 379
Ramsay, W. M., 255 [192]
Ransome, H. M., 35 [26]
Ras Shamra, 46, 255
Rawson, M., 263 [217]
Rehm, A., 90 [136]
Reichhold, K., 144 [34], 157 [30]
Reinach, S., 247 [173], 250 [181], 255 [192]

Reni, G., 158 [83]

rhamnus leaves, 305

Rhea, 8, 24, 30, 57–58, 59, 60, 111–112, 114, 116, 119, 124, 256, 264, 275; and birth of Zeus, 266; restores Dionysos to life, 248, 256

Rhodes, 201

Rhodope mountains, 219

rhyton/rhyta, 53, 54, 55, 60, 19 *, 20 *

Richter, G., 18 [23]

Rieu, E. V., 74 [68]

Rilke, R. M., 287

roasted meat, 246–247, 250

Robert, C., 153 [67]

Rodenwaldt, G., 66 [40]

Rohde, E., xxv, 137, 138, 158 [60], 175, 176 [135], 202 [36], 305 [99]

Rohden, H. von, 254 [189], 271 [252], 272 [253], 273 [1]

Rome: Bacchanalia forbidden in, 355, 357, 363; Farnesina, ornament, 376, 133 *; house of Pammachius, 122 [243]

Ross, W. D., xxiii [4], 308 [113]

Rouse, W. H. D., 16 [18]

Rumpf, A., 290 [48]

S

Sabazios, 60 [26], 117, 275, 276; mysteries of, 288–289, 351, 363, 383, 88A *–88D *

sack, leather, 38, 40–41, 44–51, 211, 212, 225, 256 [198], 277; in birth of Orion, 42–43, 76

sacrifice, 39, 120, 238–261; as atonement for sin, 320–321, 323; of bull, 173, 180, 182, 190, 203, 213, 236, 315–316, 318; of cattle, 40–41, 54, 55, 115–116, 190–191, 270; of child, 179, 189, 269–270, 379; Dionysos as victim, 203, 244–261; of enemy of Dionysos, 324–326, 329, 333; of goat or kid, 202 [37], 203, 233–235, 249, 250, 252–256, 270, 318–324, 333, 351, 364, 76B *, 76c *, 103 *; human, 202; in Lenaia, 335; preparations for, 64A *–64D *; of ram, 180; secrecy in, 259–261

St. Martin's Day, 294

Salis, A. von, 357 [234], 361 [247], 362 [250]

salpinx/salpinges, 173–174, 180, 312, 61B *; Dionysos called with, 201–202

Samos, 286

Samothrace, 264; mysteries, 118, 267, 269

sandal, one only, 360

Sannion, 71, 73

Sappho, 187

sarcophagi, Dionysian scenes on, 377–385, 137 *–142 *, 144 *–145 *

Saridakis, S., 201 [34]

satyr plays, 324–325, 330

satyrs, 271–272, 281, 285, 364–365, 375, 376, 379, 380, 384, 68 *–71 *, 116 *, 117 *; as grape treaders, 59–60, 66, 68 *; men impersonating, 237, 325; in mysteries, 358, 359, 362

Savignoni, L., 80 [94]

Schaefer, J., 275 [10]

Schefold, K., 366 [265]

Schelling, F. W. J. von, 133, 134

Schneider, E., 26 [41]

Schoene, A., 143 [32]

Schopenhauer, A., 137

Schott, S., 67 [48]

Schweitzer, B., 28, 177 [141]

Schwyzer, R., xxviii [11]

Scorpio, 42

scorpion, 42, 82, 18 *

Scott, R., 34 [24]

Segall, B., 81 [99]

Selloi, 208

Semachidai, 146, 149

Semachos, 161, 163; Dionysos visits, 146–149, 162, 39A *, 39B *

Semele, 196, 196 [25], 248, 265, 277, 355, 386, 65A *, 65B *; bridal chamber (sanctuary) of, 194; mother of Dionysos, 55, 106–108, 110, 120, 161 [88], 181, 184, 185, 256, 259, 279, 295, 306, 378; in mysteries, 360

Semites, 261, 270; Dionysian religion, 256–257

Semitic languages, 208, 211, 255

Semos, 287

Senyes, 77

Servius, 42 [56], 76 [76], 174 [129], 185 [171], 209 [56], 231 [131 132], 261 [209], 363 [255]

sheep as prize, 318

ship (car) of Dionysos, 141, 144, 166–172, 309, 49 *–52A *, 56A *, 56B *, 57 *, 59A *, 59B *

Sichtermann, H., 17 [20], 369 [270 272]

Sicily, 332

sileni, 71, 147, 148, 158, 162, 169, 266, 285, 367–370, 375, 376, 378, 379; as grape treaders, 66, 67, 23 *; men impersonating, 171, 313, 314; in mysteries, 351, 358–359, 361, 362

Simon, E., 271 [252], 272 [253], 288 [45], 307 [110], 313 [129], 377 [293 297], 378 [298 300], 379 [301], 380

Simonides, 191–192

Sirius, 75, 172; dog of Orion, 41, 73–74, 75: in Ikarios myth, 153, 154; protective magic against, 77; rising of, 29, 30, 34, 37, 39, 40, 41, 43, 50, 73, 74, 77, 118, 206; year of, 38, 41, 78, 205

sistrum, 72

situla, 364, 368–370

Skopelos, 138

Smith, W. R., 257 [201]

Smyrna, 168, 295

snake/snakes, 21, 52; in birth of Dionysos, 111–114, 263; bull and, 117; in Dionysian rites, 60–62, 64, 383, 22A *, 22B *; Dionysos as, 123; as god, 113; grapevines associated with, 57, 58–60; ivy associated with, 61–62, 64; poisonous, 60–61; in Sabazios mysteries, 288–289; symbolism of, 114–115, 117, 119

snake goddess, 13, 16, 22, 52, 4 *, 13 *, 14 *

Sokolowski, F., 202 [35]

Sokrates, 92, 93, 264–265

Sokrates (historian), 180, 182 [162]

Solon, 317 [137], 326–327, 348

Sophokles, 94, 99, 328; *Ajax*, 174 [132], *Antigone*, 78, 224 [104], 349; *Oedipus at Colonus*, 63 [35]

Sosipolis, 113 [222], 119

soul, the, Ariadne as archetype, 124–125

souls, wine for, 303–304, 91 *

Sousarion, 341

sparagmos (dismemberment), 245, 247

Spencer, B., 35 [27]

spiral pattern, 91, 92, 94–96, 99

Stackelberg, O. M. von, 161 [89], 169 [113], 173 [126]

Staphylos, 76 [76], 108, 138

stars, 105–106, 117–118

Staudacher, W., 47 [77]

Stella, L. A., 54 [8], 56 [17], 82 [103]

Stephen of Byzantium, 43 [57], 122 [242], 143 [32], 245 [171]

Stimula, 355

Stobaeus, 93 [145]

Sto Dionyso, 148

Stolpe, S., 267 [235]

Strabo, 35 [27], 43 [57], 45 [65 69 70], 75 [74], 275 [11], 292

suffering god, 70–71, 116, 179, 190, 193, 213, 329

Suidae Lexicon, 77 [83], 151 [60], 163 [93], 228 [121], 241 [161], 304 [96], 308 [113], 317 [137], 324 [160], 326 [166], 327 [169], 328 [176], 330 [179]

summer solstice, 29

Svoronos, J. N., 88 [130], 97 [160], 104 [185 186], 105 [187–189 191], 232 [137]

swaddling clothes of Zeus, 30, 44

swinging, 156–159, 160, 301, 307, 312, 42B*, 43 *, 94 *, 95 *

Sybaris, 252

Sybil, 188 [182]

Sybilline oracle, 351

symmeixis, 309–310, 311, 355, 361

Syria, 46, 47, 50

T

Tabulae Heracleenses, 141 [30]

Tacitus, 67 [47], 158 [80]

tainiai, 44, 365, 366

Tarquinius Priscus, 188 [182]

Tenedos, 54–55, 190, 191, 270

Teos, 45

thanatos, xxxiv, 132

theaters, 296; *see also* comedy; drama; tragedy

Thebes, 179 [149], 184, 185, 188, 213; Dionysian cult, 192–197, 278, 329; Dionysos born in, 143; Kadmeia (palace), 194–197

Themis, 210, 211, 211 [62]

Themistios, 326 [165]

Theodoros of Kolophon, 158 [82]

Theogamia, 300

Theokritos, 23, 374 [283]

Theopompos, 181, 192 [11]

Theoxenios (month), 206, 217

Theseus, 94, 145; Ariadne and, 98, 101–103, 107, 108, 109, 120, 123; in labyrinth, 91, 98–99, 28 *, 29 *

Thesiger, E., 85[118]

Thespis, 317[137], 320, 322, 326–330; plays of, 328–329

Thesprotian oracle, 230

Thetis, 178, 179

thiasos, 123, 313, 319, 368; in mysteries, 353, 354, 356, 359, 361, 362

Thiele, G., 88[128]

Thimme, J., 370[274][275]

Thomson, G., 37[40]

Thorikos, 149

Thrace, 137–138, 176; bacchantes (maenads), 219–220, 233, 329; mysteries, 118; Shrovetide play, 295

Thukydides, 292, 302, 316[136]

thunderstone, 86

Thurii, krater from, 362, 363, 114 *

thyein (raving), 182, 183, 189, 220

Thyia, 183, 184[169], 190

Thyiades, 49, 69, 212, 213, 214, 217, 222, 223, 227, 228, 231, 236, 298; on Parnassos, 218–224, 235, 237

thyiadic state, 189–190, 217, 222

thymaterion, 173

Thyone, 360

thyrsos, 180, 200, 201, 218, 280, 313, 359, 367, 369, 370, 379, 380, 386, 387

Tillyard, E. M. W., 362[249]

Timarchos, 195

Titans, 110–111; Dionysos killed by, 231, 240–246, 259, 267–268; killed by Zeus, 242–245; mankind descended from, 242; white faces of, 267–268

Tityos, 214

Tmolos, Mt., 275

Tod, M. N., 327[172]

Toepffer, J., 100[168]

Tolles, R., 348[211]

torchbearers/torchlight, 78, 215, 218, 222

Touloupa, E., 193[13], 194[14]

tragedy/tragedies, 163, 166, 331, 333, 349; beginnings of, 315–330

Tragliatella, wine pitcher, 97

tragodia, 334; meaning of, 318, 333

transmigration of souls, 243[167]

trees, bending, 237

Trendall, A. D., 75[73], 86[130], 280[24], 373[281]

Trieterikos, 198, 213

trieteris (year of Dionysos, two-year period), 141–142, 192, 197, 205, 213, 214–215, 217, 218, 222, 231, 235, 238, 249, 283, 323; dialectic of, 198–204

Trigonos (epithet), 277

tripod: at Delphi, *see* Delphi, tripod; as prize, 320

Troglodytes, 35[27]

tropeion, 65, 66

Troy, J.-F. de, 158[83]

trygodia, 334

tuba, Roman, 174

Turcan, R., 383[316]

Tyche, 387

tympanon, 368, 369, 370

Typhon, 46, 47–48

Tzetzes, J., 286[40]

U

Ugarit, 46, 255, 261

underworld, 118, 236[151]; Ariadne in, 107, 108; Dionysos in, 180–182, 199–200, 256, 292, 303, 304, 311; Journey to, 93, 181, 239, 318; oracle connected with, 230, 232

unlucky days, 216

Usener, H., 168[110], 235[150], 294[63]

V

Varro, Marcus Terentius, 39–40, 174[129], 249, 303[93]

Vathypetro, 56

Ventris, M., xxvi, 23[33], 53[2], 54[8], 56[18], 71, 100[169], 264[220]

Vermeule, C. C., 150[66]

Virgil: *Aeneid*, 42[56], 209[56], 231[131][132], 261[209]; *Eclogues*, 185[171], 186[174], 295[70], 363[255]; *Georgics*, 40[47], 76[76], 322[154]

visions, 14–20, 52; gestures and, 20–22, 9 *–13 *; opium and, 24–27

vita, xxxi

viticulture, 50, 51, 55–58; myth of origin, 58–60

Vogliano, A., 352[223], 353[224]

W

Wace, A. J. B., 327 [172]
Wagenvoort, H., 157 [77]
Wagner, R., 135, 137
Watzinger, C., 254 [189]
weather god, Hittite, 46–47
Webster, T. B. L., 80 [96]
Weinreich, O., 335 [187]
Welcker, F. G., 191
Welter, G., 122 [241]
Weniger, L., 30 [3], 139 [24], 181 [159], 268 [239 241]
Westermann, A., 45 [63]
Whitman, Walt, 286–287
Whitman, William, 15 [17]
Wiedmann, A., 72 [63]
Wiegand, T., 91
Wiesner, J., 9 [6]
Wilamowitz-Moellendorf, U. von, 137, 218 [87], 281 [182], 375 [286]
wild strawberry tree, 327
Wilhelm, A., 310 [119 120]
Willemsen, F., 228 [118 119], 233 [139]
wine: Christian significance of, 258; Dionysos as god of, xxiv–xxv, 35, 52, 55, 76, 142–146, 249, 270; Ikarios as discoverer of, 152–156, 323; lees of, for painting faces, 327, 334, 336; mead related to, 36–37, 50; in Minoan culture, 53–58; myths of origin, 58–60, 75–77; new wine festival, 291–294, 296, 297, 302 [89]; water transformed into, 299
wine-making, 65–68; Dionysos teaches, 142–143, 152; invention of, 57–60
wine press, 66–67
wineskin, jumping on, 312, 324
Winnefeld, H., 254 [189], 271 [252], 272 [253], 273 [1]
winnowing basket, see *liknon*
winter, Dionysian festivals and rites, 217–222, 290–291, 296–300
winter solstice, 299
Wissowa, G., 188 [182], 302 [89]
Witte, J. J., 284 [36]
Wolters, P., 91, 92 [141 142]
women: in Choës Day celebration, 312–315; at Delphi in Dionysian rites, 213, 214, 217–219; in Dionysian religion, 52, 55, 69, 121, 130–133, 145, 146, 160–162, 176–179, 187, 190, 191, 200–203, 288–290, 293, 296, 298, 317, 348; forbidden to approach tripod, 226, 228, 235; heavenly marriage after death, 366–370; in labor, youths imitating, 277; in mysteries, 352–355, 357–363; as nurses of Dionysos, 178, 179, 276, 284, 288, 289; in Orphism, 262; sacrificial ceremonies, 244, 246, 258–259, 261; secret rituals, 189–190, 192–193, 197, 214, 235, 240, 241, 261, 288–289, 302, 350; on stage, 340; *see also* maenads; Thyiades
women's clothes, boys or men in, 145, 145 [41], 150, 170, 335; men in, on stage, 340–341, 104 *, 105 *
Wrede, W., 283 [81]
Wroth, W., 97 [160], 104 [185 186], 105 [188 189 191], 191 [6], 192 [11]

Y

year: Athenian, 278; beginning of, 29–30, 41, 43, 73, 78; of Dionysos, see *trieteris*; of Sirius, 38, 41, 78, 205; solar, 215–216

Z

Zagreus, 80–89, 110, 114, 190, 193, 231, 267, 270
Zancani Montuoro, P., 367 [266]
zein, 33, 34
Zeus, xxxiii, 35, 38, 50–51, 55, 86, 105, 109, 116, 119, 187, 210, 247, 259, 260, 261; Athena born from his head, 278; birth of, 30–33, 113, 266; Dionysos as son of, 69, 83, 106, 110–114, 246; Dionysos born from his thigh, 75, 273–280, 295, 378, 73 *, 74 *; emasculates himself, 275–276; as his own son, 114; Idaios, 85, 86; Ikmaios, 39; as infant, 44; Kronos castrated by, 36; light associated with, 32, 75, 78; marriage with Hera, 300; Persephone seduced by, 110–114; Semele and, 106, 194; swaddling clothes of, 30, 44; Titans killed by, 242–245; Typhon's battle with, 46, 47–48; of the underworld, 83
Ziegler, K., 241 [161], 243 [166]

Ziehen, L., 167[108]
Zielinski, T., 343[205]
Zimmermann, H., 32[13]
zodiac, 385–387, 146 *
zoë, 7, 52, 64, 80, 132, 190, 204–205, 218, 278, 285, 286, 322, 324, 349, 350, 363, 381; *bios* distinguished from, xxviii, xxxi–xxxvii; Dionysos and, 119, 120, 124, 179, 200, 202, 238, 288, 289, 294, 295, 321; myth of fermentation and, 38, 41; snake as symbol of, 114–115, 117; soul and, 124; symbols of, 95, 116–117
Zschietzschmann, W., 371[276][278]

Index by Delight Ansley

C. Kerényi

Kerényi Károly (the Hungarian form of his name) was born on January 19, 1897, in Temesvár, in the southeastern part of the Austro-Hungarian Empire (now Timisoara, Romania). He grew up in a family of Roman Catholic small landowners, and was drawn to language study as a boy, when he learned Latin. At the University of Budapest, he studied classical philology and read widely in world literature. He earned his doctorate in 1919 with a dissertation on "Plato and Longinus, Investigations in Classical Literary and Aesthetic History." For several years, Kerényi was a secondary-school teacher; he traveled in Greece and Italy, and studied intermittently at the German universities of Greifswald, Heidelberg, and Berlin. He was a pupil of Diels, Wilamowitz-Moellendorff, Eduard Norden, Eduard Meyer, and Franz Boll, to whom he dedicated his first book, *Die griechisch-orientalische Romanliteratur in religionsgeschichtlicher Beleuchtung* (The Greek-Oriental Romances in the Light of the History of Religions) (Tübingen, 1927). On the strength of this book he was appointed privatdocent in the history of religions at the University of Budapest. In 1934 he became professor of classical philology and ancient history at Pecs and in 1941 at Szeged (both in southern Hungary), all the while retaining his docentship at Budapest.

Kerényi traveled extensively, and in Greece in 1929 he met W. F. Otto, whose approach to the history of religions influenced him profoundly. He now saw the necessity of combining the "historical" with the "theological" method. His first deliberate steps beyond the limits of official philology were his *Apollon*, a collection of essays (1937), and *Die antike Religion* (1940).

In 1943 Kerényi emigrated to Switzerland to lead the life of an independent humanist. His choice was determined in part by his close connection with C. G. Jung, in collaboration with whom he had published *Einführung in das Wesen der Mythologie* in 1941 (*Essays on a Science of Mythology*, Bollingen Series, 1949). He was a co-founder of the C. G. Jung Institute in Zurich, at which he also lectured. It was in the course of his work with Jung that Kerényi conceived the idea of a series of monographs on the Greek gods, of which the present work is part. Perceiving that in the study of religions mythology has been increasingly overshadowed by cult, he wished, in agreement with W. F. Otto, to develop a view of the Greek gods that would be accessible to modern man. To this end he found it necessary to take the findings of psychology into consideration.

Kerényi's numerous publications on the history of ancient religion, including *Die Mythologie der Griechen* (1951), which has been translated into nine languages and is generally regarded as a standard work, won him visiting professorships and invitations to lecture at many European universities. In 1961 he became a member of the Norwegian Royal Academy of Sciences. His awards include an honorary doctorate from the University of Uppsala, the gold medal of the Humboldt Society, and the Pirckheimer Ring of the City of Nuremberg.

After 1943, Kerényi made his home at Ascona, in the Italian-speaking Swiss canton of Ticino, and was often a lecturer at the Eranos conferences. His literary language was German, in which he used the name Karl; he also used Carlo and Charles, as appropriate.

Karl Kerényi died on April 14, 1973.

As Kerényi saw it, every view of mythology is a view of man. Thus every "theology" is at the same time an "anthropology." His basic method is to test the "authenticity" of mythological tradition by stylistic traits. To his mind, the essence of his work consisted in establishing a science of ancient religion and mythology, based not only on a detailed knowledge of the relevant literature and archaeology but also on a reciprocal sympathy between the interpreter and his material, and in this way to broaden the field of knowledge already laid bare by the traditional historical methods.

Kerényi's scholarly and literary accomplishment was prodigious; it is being published in a collected edition in German. Many of his chief works have been translated not only into English, but into French, Italian, and Swedish. His principal publications in English, besides those included in Bollingen Series (*Essays on a Science of Mythology*, with C. G. Jung, and the series of studies of Archetypal Images in Greek Religion: *Prometheus, Dionysos, Asklepios, Eleusis*, and *Zeus and Hera*), are *The Gods of the Greeks* (tr. 1951), *The Heroes of the Greeks* (tr. 1959), *The Religion of the Greeks and Romans* (tr. 1962). His correspondence with Thomas Mann, entitled *Mythology and Humanism: The Correspondence of Thomas Mann and Karl Kerényi*, was translated and published in 1975.

A Bibliography of C. Kerényi

compiled by Magda Kerényi

This listing excludes publications in periodicals and writings in Hungarian, except for translations made by others from original German works into Hungarian. The arrangement is alphabetical within years. When no translator is named, one was not mentioned in the publication. Abbreviations: AV = Albae Vigiliae. Series I: Amsterdam/Leipzig: Pantheon Akademische Verlagsanstalt. Series II: Zurich: Rhein-Verlag. / BS = Bollingen Series. New York: Pantheon Books; after 1967, Princeton University Press. / EJ = Eranos-Jahrbuch. Zurich: Rhein Verlag. / K. K. = the author.

1927

Die griechisch-orientalische Romanliteratur in religionsgeschichtlicher Beleuchtung. Ein Versuch. Tübingen: J.C.B. Mohr; Paul Siebeck. (= 1962d, 1973b.)

1935

Dionysos und das Tragische in der Antigone. Frankfurter Studien zur Religion und Kultur der Antike 13, ed. Walter F. Otto. Frankfurt a. M.: Vittorio Klostermann.

1936

a. *La Filologia latina nell'Ungheria del dopoguerra.* (Tr. from Hung., Angelo Brelich.) Gli Studi Romani nel mondo. Rome: Istituto di Studi Romani. (Parts integrated in 1937a 10; = 1941b 13, 1953b 12.)

b. "Orphische Seele." In *Gedenkschrift für Akos von Pauler.* Berlin/Leipzig. (Rev. and enl. 1937b, 1940d, 1950g 1, 1966e 1.)

c. "Die Papyri und das Wesen der alexandrinischen Kultur." In *Atti del IV Congresso internazionale di papirologia a Firenze, Primavera 1934.* Milan. (With small additions = 1937a 9, 1941b 11, 1953b 10.)

1937

a. *Apollon. Studien über antike Religion und Humanität.* 7 pl. Vienna/Amsterdam/Leipzig: Franz Leo & Co. (Enl. = 1941b; further enl. = 1953b.)

   1. Antike Religion und Religionsgeschichte.

2. Unsterblichkeit und Apollonreligion.
3. Hippolytos.
4. Ergriffenheit und Wissenschaft.
5. Landschaft und Geist.
6. Der antike Dichter.
7. Korfu und die Odyssee.
8. Sophron und der griechische Naturalismus.
9. Die Papyri und das Wesen der alexandrinischen Kultur. (Enl. from 1936c; = 1941b 11, 1953b 10.)
10. Der Geist der römischen Literatur. (= 1962b.) (Parts integrated from 1936a; = 1941b 13, 1953b 12, 1962b.)
11. Horatius–Horationismus.
12. Humanismus und Hellenismus.

b. "Pythagoras und Orpheus." In: *Aufsätze zur Geschichte der Antike und des Christentums. Essays.* Berlin: Die Runde. (Rev. and enl. from 1936b; = 1940d, 1950g 1, 1966e 1.)

1938

a. *Die Göttin Diana im Römischen Pannonien.* 6 ill. Pécs: Pannonia-Könyvtár, no. 49. University Edition.
1. Ein ländliches Heiligtum bei Csákvár.
2. Spuren des Diana-Kultes an der militärischen Grenze.
3. Denkmäler des Balaton-Gebietes.

b. "Die Papyri und das Problem des griechischen Romans." In: *Actes du Ve Congrès International de Papyrologie, Oxford, 30.8–3.9.1937.* Brussels. (= 1941b 12, 1953b 11, 1962d 1.)

c. *Religio Academici.* Pécs: Pannonia-Könyvtár, no. 52. University Edition. (Integrated in every ed. and tr. of 1940b 4.II, 1963j 4.II, 1971a 5.II.)

1940

a. Editor of *Albae Vigiliae* I, Series I–XV, 1940–1943. Amsterdam: Pantheon Akademische Verlagsanstalt. II, New Series I–XIX, 1944–1964. Zurich: Rhein-Verlag.

b. *Die Antike Religion. Eine Grundlegung.* Amsterdam: Pantheon Akademische Verlagsanstalt [Printed in Germany]. (= 1942a, 1952a, 1971a 1, 3–8; tr. = 1940a, 1951h, 1957e, 1972h; revision = 1963j; tr. of rev. = 1962c, 1962i, 1972i, 1973f.)
1. Die antike Religion als mythologische Religion.
2. Die antike Religion als Festreligion.
3. Griechischer und römischer religiöser Stil.

4. Höhepunkte der griechischen und römischen religiösen Erfahrung.
    I. θεορία.
    II. *religio.*

5. Mensch und Gott nach Homer und Hesiod.
    I. Die griechische Idee des Opfers.
    II. Vom Lachen der Götter.

6. Mensch und Gott nach römischer Auffassung.
    I. Das Leben des Flamen Dialis.
    II. Von den Arten des Mythos.

Nachwort. Die religiöse Idee des Nichtseins.

c. Intro. to *Das griechische Antlitz in Meisterwerken der Münzkunst*, with L. M. Lanckoroński. AV III. (Summary of 1941c.)

d. *Pythagoras und Orpheus.* 2nd ed. With an appendix on Ennius' Doctrine of Metempsychosis. AV II. (= 1937b, 1950g 1, 1966e 1.)

e. *La Religione antica nelle sue linee fondamentali.* Tr. of 1940b, Delio Cantimori. Bologna: Zanichelli.

f. "Das Urkind in der Urzeit." In: C. G. Jung and K. K.: *Das göttliche Kind in mythologischer und psychologischer Beleuchtung.* 5 pl. AV VI/VII. (= 1942b 2, 1951c 2, 1966e 3; tr. = 1948d 2, 1949b 2, 1951c, 1953e 2, 1963a 2, 1964g 2, 1969c 2, 1970f 2, 1972g 2, 1974c 2.)

1941

a. *Das Aegäische Fest. Die Meergötterszene in Goethes Faust II.* AV XI. (= 1949a; enl. = 1950a, 1966e 4.)

b. *Apollon. Studien über antike Religion und Humanität.* 2nd ed., enl. 7 pl. Amsterdam/Leipzig: Pantheon Akademische Verlagsanstalt.
    1-4. (= 1937a 1-4, 1953b 1-4.)
    5. Unsinnliche und sinnliche Tradition. (= 1953b 5, 1970m.)
    6. Landschaft und Geist. (= 1937a 5, 1953b 6.)
    7. Der antike Dichter. (= 1937a 6, 1953b 7.)
    8. Korfu und die Odyssee. (= 1937a 7, 1953b 8.)
    9. Sophron und der griechische Naturalismus. (= 1937a 8, 1953b 9.)
    10. Platonismus. (= 1966j.)
    11. Die Papyri und das Wesen der alexandrinischen Kultur. (= 1936c, 1937a 9, 1953b 10.)
    12. Die Papyri und das Problem des griechischen Romans. (= 1938b, 1953b 11.)
    13. Der Geist der römischen Literatur. (Parts integr. from 1936a; = 1937a 10, 1953b 12, 1962b.)

14. Catullus. (= 1953b 15.)

15. Horatius–Horationismus. (=1937a 11, 1953b 14.)

16. Humanismus und Hellenismus. (= 1937a 12, 1953b 15.)

c. "Arethusa. Über Menschengestalt und mythologische Idee." In *Mythos der Hellenen in Meisterwerken der Münzkunst*, with L. M. Lanckoroński. Amsterdam: Pantheon Akademische Verlagsanstalt. (Compl. vers. of 1940c; = 1966e 6.)

d. *Hölderlins Mysterien*. Nachbemerkung zu Hölderlins *Hyperion* oder der Eremit in Griechenland. Amsterdam: Pantheon Akademische Verlagsanstalt. (= 1953b 16.)

e. "Kore." In C. G. Jung and K. K. *Das göttliche Mädchen*. Die Hauptgestalt der Mysterien von Eleusis in mythologischer und psychologischer Beleuchtung. AV VIII/IX. (Enl. = 1942b.)

f. "Labyrinthos. Der Linienreflex einer mythologischen Idee." In *Laureae Aquincenses memoriae Valentini Kuzsinszky dedicatae* II. Budapest, 1941.

g. *Labyrinthstudien*. 30 ill. AV XV. (= 1950d, 1966e 8.)

1942

a. *Die antike Religion*. 2nd edn. [Printed in Holland]: Pantheon Akademische Verlagsanstalt. (= 1940b, 1952a, 1971a 2–8; tr. = 1940e, 1957d, 1972h; revision = 1963j; tr. of revision = 1962c, 1962i, 1972i, 1973f.)

b. In C. G. Jung and K. K.: *Einführung in das Wesen der Mythologie*. Gottkindmythos–Eleusinische Mysterien. 5 pl. Amsterdam: Pantheon Akademische Verlagsanstalt, n.d. Contributions of K. K.:

1. Über Ursprung und Gründung in der Mythologie. (= 1951c 1, 1966e 5.I; tr. = 1942c 1, 1948d 1, 1949b 1, 1951c 1, 1953e 1, 1963a 1, 1964g 1, 1969c 1, 1970f 1, 1972g 1.)

2. Das Urkind in der Urzeit. (= 1940f, 1951c 2, 1966e 3; tr. = 1948d 2, 1949b 2, 1951e 2, 1953e 2, 1963a 2, 1964g 2, 1969c 2, 1970f 2, 1972g 2, 1974c 2.)

3. Kore. (Enl. from 1941e; = 1951c 3; tr. = 1948d 3, 1949b 3, 1951h 3, 1953e 3, 1963a 3, 1964g 3, 1969c 3, 1970f 3, 1972g 3, 1974c 3.)

4. Über das Wunder von Eleusis. (= 1951c 4; tr. = 1948d 4, 1949b 4, 1951h 4, 1953e 4, 1963a 4, 1969c 4, 1970f 4, 1972g 4, 1974c 4.)

c. *Der grosse Daimon des Symposion*. AV XIII. 1 pl. (= 1966e 10.)

d. "Mythologie und Gnosis." In *EJ* 1940/41.

1. Über Ursprung und Gründung in der Mythologie. (= 1942e 1, 1942b 1.)

2. Das Wissen vom Wege. (= 1942e 2, 1966e 5.II.)

e. *Mythologie und Gnosis*. AV XIV [Printed in Switzerland].
  1. Über Ursprung und Gründung in der Mythologie. (= 1942b 1, 1942d 1.)
  2. Das Wissen vom Wege. (= 1942d 2, 1966e 5.II.)

1943

a. "Hermes der Seelenführer. Das Mythologem vom männlichen Lebensursprung." In *EJ* 1942. (= 1944b; tr. = 1950e 2.)

1944

a. *Der Geist*. Budapest: Officina. 120 num. copies. Budapest: Taurus. (= 1945b 2.)

b. *Hermes der Seelenführer. Das Mythologem vom männlichen Lebensursprung*. AV, n.s. I. (= 1943a; tr. = 1950e 2.)

c. *Töchter der Sonne. Betrachtungen über griechische Gottheiten*. With a genealogical tree of the sun-kinship. 7 pl. Zurich: Rascher. (= 1947c, 1949c.)
Der Vater und König.
  1. Der an jedem Tag Neue.
  2. Der Titan.
Die Suche nach der Königin.
  3. Die Zauberin (Kirke).
  4. Die Mörderin (Medeia).
  5. Die Hälfte (Hera).
  6. Die Güldene (Aphrodite).
Finis Initium.
  7. Die kretische Sonnentochter.

d. "Vater Helios." In *EJ* 1943. (= 1944c 1–2; tr. = 1947c 1–2, 1949c 1–2.)

1945

a. *Bachofen und die Zukunft des Humanismus*. With an Intermezzo on Nietzsche and Ariadne, Zurich: Rascher. (= 1971e 1.)

b. *Die Geburt der Helena. Samt humanistischen Schriften aus den Jahren 1943–1945*. AV, n.s. III.
  1. Die Geburt der Helena. (= 1966e 2; tr. = 1950e 1.)
  2. Der Geist. (= 1944a.)
  3. Mysterien der Kabiren. Einleitendes zum Studium antiker Mysterien. (= 1945d; tr. = 1950e 3, 1955e.)
  4. Castello di Tegna. Eine archäologische Parallele zu einem Heiligtum in der Gegend von Theben. (= 1945d; tr. = 1955e.)

5. Die Heiligkeit des Mahles im Altertum. (= 1971a 11; tr. = 1950e 4.)

6. Mnemosyne-Lemosyne. Über die Quellen "Erinnerung" und "Vergessenheit" in der griechischen Mythologie. (= 1966e 11.)

7. Selbstbekenntnisse des Livius. (= 1966e 15.)

8. Über das Klassische. Aus Anlass einer Sophokles-Übersetzung.

9. Grundbegriffe und Zukunftsmöglichkeiten des Humanismus. (= 1966e 16, 1970a.)

c. "Heros Iatros–Über Wandlungen des ärztlichen Genius in Griechenland." In *EJ* XII: *Studien zum Problem des Archetypischen*. Festschrift for C. G. Jung.

d. "Mysterien der Kabiren." With appendix: "Castello di Tegna." In *EJ* 1944. (= 1945b 3–4; tr. = 1950e 3, 1955e.)

e. *Romandichtung und Mythologie–ein Briefwechsel mit Thomas Mann, 1934–1945*. AV, n.s. II. (= 1960c 1, 1967c 1, 1972b 1; tr. = 1947d, 1960j, 1973a 1, 1975d 1.)

1946

a. "Apollon-Epiphanien." In *EJ* 1945. (= 1949e 6; tr. = 1954b.)

b. *Prometheus. Das griechische Mythologem von der menschlichen Existenz.* AV, n.s. IV. (Rev. and enl. = 1959d; tr. = 1950e 5; tr. of enl. = 1963i.)

c. "Zur Einführung in das Lesen Platonischer Werke." In *Über Liebe und Unsterblichkeit*. Die Sokratischen Gespräche Gastmahl, Phaidros, Phaidon. Zurich: Rascher.

1947

a. "Die Göttin Natur." In *EJ* 1946. (= 1949e 4; tr. = 1950e 8.)

b. "Hombre primitivo y mysterio." In *Anales de Arqueologia y Etnologia*. Mendoza: Universidad. (Tr. of 1948f, M. de Ferdinandy.)

c. *Napleányok.* (Hungarian tr. of 1944c, V. Zolnay.) Budapest: Bibliotheka. Without ill. and genealog. tree.

d. *Thomas Mann és Kerényi Károly levélváltása regényröl és mitológiáról.* (Hungarian tr. of 1945e, M. Petrolay.) Budapest: Officina.

1948

a. *Der Göttliche Ärzt. Studien über Asklepios und seine Kultstätten.* 57 ill. Basel: Ciba AG. (= 1956a, 1964c, 1975c; tr. = 1948b, 1959b, 1960a.)

b. *Le Médecin divin. Promenades mythologiques aux sanctuaires d'Asklepios.* (Tr. of 1948a, V. Baillods.) 57 ill. Basel: Ciba S.A.

c. "Der Mensch in griechischer Anschauung." In *Proceedings of the Xth International Congress of Philosophy*, Amsterdam, 11–18 August 1948. Amsterdam: North-Holland Publishing Co. (= 1949e 10; tr. = 1950e 15.)

d. In C. G. Jung and K. K.: *Prolegomeni allo studio scientifico della mitologia.* (Tr. of 1942b, Angelo Brelich.) Turin: Einaudi. (= 1964g, 1972g.)

e. "Prometeo e Niobe: Due archetipi del modo d'esistere umano." In *Atti del Congresso internazionale di filosofia*, Rome 1946. Milan: Castellani, Vol. II. "L'Esistenzialismo." (Tr. of 1949e 2; = 1950e 7.)

f. "Urmensch und Mysterium." In *EJ* 1947. (= 1949e 3; tr. = 1947b, 1950e 11.)

g. "Wolf und Ziege am Fest der Lupercalia." In *Mélanges de philologie, de littérature et d'histoire anciennes*. Festschrift for J. Marouzeau. Paris: Les Belles Lettres. (= 1949e 5; tr. = 1950e 9.)

1949

a. "Das Aegäische Fest. Erläuterungen zur Szene 'Felsbuchten des Aegäischen Meeres' in Goethes Faust II." In *Spiegelungen Goethes in unserer Zeit*. Wiesbaden: Limes. (= 1941a; enl. = 1950a, 1966e 4.)

b. In C. G. Jung and K. K.: *Essays on a Science of Mythology. The Myth of the Divine Child and the Mysteries of Eleusis*. (Tr. of 1942b, R. F. C. Hull.) 5 ill. BS XXII. (= 1951e; rev. = 1963a, 1969c.)
   1. Prolegomena.
   2. The Primordial Child in Primordial Time.
   3. Kore.
   4. Epilegomena: The Miracle of Eleusis.

c. *Figlie del sole*. (Tr. of 1944c, Francesco Barberi.) 7 ill. Torino: Einaudi.

d. "Mensch und Maske." In *EJ* 1948. (= 1966e 13; tr. = 1950e 14, 1960h.)

e. *Niobe. Neue Studien über Religion und Humanität*. 6 pl. Zurich: Rhein-Verlag.
   1. Niobe. (tr. = 1950e 6.)
   2. Bild, Gestalt und Archetypus. (tr. = 1948e, 1950e 7.)
   3. Urmensch und Mysterium. (= 1948f; tr. = 1947b, 1950e 11.)
   4. Die Göttin Natur. (= 1947a; tr. = 1950e 8.)
   5. Wolf und Ziege am Lupercalienfest. (= 1948g; tr. = 1950e 9.)
   6. Apollon-Epiphanien. (= 1946a; tr. = 1954b.)
   7. Das Mythologem vom zeitlosen Sein im alten Sardinien. (tr. = 1950e 12.)
   8. Die Göttin mit der Schale. (tr. = 1950e 13.)
   9. Arbor Intrat. (tr. = 1950e 10.)
   10. Der Mensch in griechischer Anschauung. (= 1948c; tr. = 1950e 15.)

f. "Il segreto delle città alte." In *Mediterranea: Almanacco di Sicilia*. Palermo: IRES. (Tr. of 1953b 17.)

g. "Ziegenfell und Gorgoneion." In *Mélanges Grégoire*. Festschrift for Henri Grégoire. Annuaire de l'Institut de philologie et d'histoire orientales et slaves, IX. Brussels.

1950

a. "Das Aegäische Fest. Erläuterungen zur Szene 'Felsbuchten des Aegäischen Meeres' in Goethes Faust II." In *Spiegelungen Goethes in unserer Zeit*. 3rd ed., enl. Wiesbaden: Limes. (= 1941a, 1949a, 1966e 4.)

b. "Aidos und Themis." In *Pro regno pro sanctuario*. Festschrift for Gerardus van der Leeuw. Nijkerk: Callenbach.

c. "Die Entstehung der olympischen Götterfamilie." In *Mythe, Mensch und Umwelt*. For the 50th Jubilee of the Frobenius Institute. Ed. A. E. Jensen. Bamberg: Meisenbach & Co. (= 1972n 3.)

d. Labyrinth-Studien. 30 ill. New edition (reprint) for the 70th birthday of C. G. Jung. AV, n.s., X. (= 1941f, 1966e 8.)

e. *Miti e misteri*. (Tr. Angelo Brelich.) 10 ill. Turin: Einaudi.
    1. La nascita di Helena. (Tr. of 1945b 1.)
    2. Hermes, la guida delle anime. (Tr. of 1943a.)
    3. I misteri dei Kabiri. (Tr. of 1945b 3.)
    4. La sacralità del pasto. (Tr. of 1945b 5.)
    5. Prometeo: il mitologema greco dell'esistenza umana. (Tr. of 1946b.)
    6. Niobe. (Tr. of 1949e 1.)
    7. Immagine, figura e archetipo. (= 1948e.)
    8. La dea Natura. (Tr. of 1947a.)
    9. Lupo e capra nella festa dei Lupercalia. (Tr. of 1948g.)
    10. Arbor intrat. (Tr. of 1949e 9.)
    11. L'uomo dei primordi e i misteri. (Tr. of 1948f.)
    12. Il mitologema dell'esistenza atemporale nell'antica Sardegna. (Tr. of 1949e 7.)
    13. La dea con la coppa. (Tr. of 1949e 8.)
    14. Uomo e maschera. (Tr. of 1949d.)
    15. La concezione greca dell'uomo. (Tr. of 1948c.)

f. "Die orphische Kosmogonie und der Ursprung der Orphik." In *EJ* 1949. (= 1950g, 1966e 12.)

g. *Pythagoras und Orpheus*. 1 pl. 3rd ed., enl. AV, n.s., IX.

1. Pythagoreische und orphische Seele und Seelenlehre im VI. Jh. (Rev. and enl. ed. of 1936b; = 1937b, 1940d, 1966e 1.)
2. Die orphische Kosmogonie und der Ursprung der Orphik. Ein Rekonstruktionsversuch. (= 1950f, 1966e 12.)
3. Die pythagoreische Seelenwanderung im II Jh. v. Chr. (= 1940d.)

1951

a. "Archetypisches und Kulturtypisches in den Grundlinien der griechischen und römischen Religion." Summary in *Proceedings of the 7th Congress for the History of Religions*, Amsterdam, 4–9 Sept. 1950. Amsterdam: North-Holland Publishing Co.

b. "Dramatische Gottesgegenwart in der griechischen Religion." In *EJ* XIX.

c. In C. G. Jung and K. K.: *Einführung in das Wesen der Mythologie. Gottkindmythos—Eleusinische Mysterien.* 4th ed., rev. 2 fig., 6 pl. Zurich: Rhein-Verlag. (= 1942b.)

d. *The Gods of the Greeks.* (Tr. of 1951g, Norman Cameron.) 52 ill. London: Thames & Hudson. Reprint, 1961. (= 1958a, 1960d, 1974a.)

e. In C. G. Jung and K. K.: *Introduction to a Science of Mythology. The Myth of the Divine Child and the Mysteries of Eleusis.* London: Routledge & Kegan Paul. (= 1949b [identical, with variant title], 1970f.)

f. *La Mitologia dei Greci. I Racconti sugli dèi e sull'umanità.* (Tr. of 1951g, Angelo Brelich.) Rome: Astrolabio.

g. *Die Mythologie der Griechen. I. Göttergeschichten.* 66 ill. Zurich: Rhein-Verlag. (= 1966h I; tr. = 1951d, 1951f, 1952c, 1955b, 1958a, 1960d, 1960f, 1963c 1, 1968b, 1972c I, 1973c, 1974a, 1974d I, 1975d I.)

h. *La Religione antica.* (Tr. of 1940b, Delio Cantimori, Angelo Brelich.) Rome: Astrolabio.

1952

a. *Die antike Religion.* 3rd ed., rev. Düsseldorf: Eugen Diederichs. (= 1940b, 1942a.)

b. *Die Jungfrau und Mutter der griechischen Religion.* Eine Studie über Pallas Athene. AV, n.s., XII.

c. *La Mythologie des grecs.* Histoires des dieux et de l'humanité. (Tr. of 1951g, Henriette de Roguin.) Paris: Payot.

d. *Stunden in Griechenland–Horai Hellenikai.* 12 pl. Zurich: Rhein-Verlag.

1. "Neugriechen" ("Der Mann mit dem Gritza"). (= 1967a 1.)
2. Griechisches Stundenbuch 1952. (= 1967a 5.)
3. Fragmente aus Griechenland 1929. (= 1967a 2.)
4. Reisetagebuch aus Lesbos 1935. (= 1967a 3.)

1953

a. Answer to the inquiry about three favorite poems. In *Trunken von Gedichten. Eine Anthologie*. Ed. Georg Gerster. Zurich: Arche.

b. *Apollon. Studien über antike Religion und Humanität*. New ed. 1 pl. Düsseldorf: Eugen Diederichs.

    1–9. = 1941b 1–9.
  10–15. = 1941b 11–16.
      16. Hölderlins Mysterien. (= 1941d.)
      17. Mysterien der Hohen Städte. (= 1966e 7; tr. = 1949f.)
      18. Mythologisches Mädchenbildnis. (= 1971a 12; tr. = 1969h.)
      19. Das Geheimnis der Pythia. (= 1966e 14, 1975g; tr. = 1970i, 1970j.)
      20. Lob des Konkreten. (= 1966e 17.)

c. "Das 'Bevor' der Religion." In *Proceedings of the XIth International Congress of Philosophy*, Brussels, 20-26 August 1953. Amsterdam: North-Holland Publishing Co. (= part of 1955g 2.)

d. "Der erste Mensch." In *Lebendiges Wissen*. Ed. Heinz Friedrich. Wiesbaden: Dietrich'sche Verlagsbuchhandlung. (= 1955g 6.)

e. In C. G. Jung and K. K.: *Introduction à l'essence de la mythologie. L'enfant divin—La jeune fille divine*. (Tr. of 1942b, H. E. Del Medico.) 8 ill. Paris: Payot.

f. "Die Sage von der verfolgten Hinde in der ungarischen Gründungssage und 'Im 1001 Tag.'" German and Spanish. (Spanish tr., Catalina Schirber.) In *Anales de la Facultad de filosofia y letras, Instituto de historia antigua y medioeval*. Buenos Aires.

1954

a. Answer to an inquiry about love poetry. In *Verse der Liebe*. Ed. Max Niedermayer. Wiesbaden: Limes.

b. "Apollo-Epiphanies." (Tr. of 1949e 6, Ralph Manheim.) In *Spirit and Nature*. Papers from the Eranos Yearbooks. BS XXX.1. / London: Routledge & Kegan Paul.

c. "Mythologische Epilegomena" to C. G. Jung, P. Radin, K. K.: *Der göttliche Schelm*. Zurich: Rhein-Verlag. (Tr. = 1956d, 1958b, 1965h.)

d. *Unwillkürliche Kunstreisen. Fahrten im alten Europa 1952/1953*. AV, n.s., XIII/XIV. 26 ill. (= 1967a 6; tr. = 1957c.)

1955

a. Geistiger Weg Europas. Five lectures on Freud, Jung, Heidegger, Thomas Mann, Hofmannsthal, Rilke, Homer, and Hölderlin. AV, n.s., XVI.
  1. Geistiger Weg Europas.
  2. Hölderlin und die Religionsgeschichte.
  3. Die Götter und die Weltgeschichte.
  4. Hölderlins Vollendung. (= 1961c.)
  5. Das Christusbild der 'Friedensfeier.'
Anhang: Zur Entdeckung von Hölderlins 'Friedensfeier.'

b. *Grekiska Gudar och Myter*. (Tr. of 1951g, Assar Asker.) 64 pl. Stockholm: Natur och Kultur.

c. "Interpretation und Ursprung in der Wissenschaft der Religion und Mythologie." In *Studi di filosofia della religione*. German and Italian. Rome: "Bocca." (= 1955g 3.)

d. "Kadmos und Harmonia. Ein Kapitel aus der Heroenmythologie der Griechen." In *Psychologia-Jahrbuch 1955*. Ed. Willy Canziani. Zurich: Rascher. (Preprint of chap. 1 of 1958c.)

e. "The Mysteries of the Kabeiroi." (Tr. of 1945d, Ralph Manheim.) In *The Mysteries*. Papers from the Eranos Yearbooks. BS XXX.1. / London: Routledge & Kegan Paul.

f. "Perseus. Aus der Heroenmythologie der Griechen." In *Studien zur Analytischen Psychologie C. G. Jungs*. Festschrift for C. G. Jung. Zurich: Rascher. (Preprint of chap. 4 of 1958c.)

g. *Umgang mit Göttlichem. Über Mythologie und Religionsgeschichte*. Göttingen: Vandenhoeck & Ruprecht, "Kleine Vandenhoeck-Reihe" 18. (Rev. = 1961g.)
  1. Was heisst Umgang?
  2. Wo beginnt die Religionsgeschichte? (Parts of = 1953c.)
  3. Interpretation und Ursprung. (= 1955c.)
  4. Zur Charakteristik der Mythologie.
  5. Menschliches und Göttliches: ein Blick auf das Archetypische.
  6. Der erste Mensch. (= 1953d.)
  7. Das Ungeschichtliche.

h. "Varro über Samothrake und Ambrakia." In *Studi in onore di Gino Funaioli.* Festschrift. Rome: Signorelli.

1956

a. *Der göttliche Ärzt. Studien über Asklepios und seine Kultstätten.* 2nd ed. 57 ill. Darmstadt: Wissenschaftliche Buchgesellschaft. H. Gentner. (= 1948a, 1964c, 1975c; tr. = 1948b, 1959b, 1960a.)

b. *Die Herkunft des Dionysosreligion nach dem heutigen Stand der Forschung.* No. 58 der Arbeitsgemeinschaft für Forschung des Landes Nordrhein-Westfalen. Cologne: Westdeutscher Verlag.

c. "Symbolismus in der antiken Religion." In *Filosofia e simbolismo.* Archivio di Filosofia. German and Italian. (Italian tr., O. M. Nobile Ventura.) Rome: "Bocca." (= 1957a 3, 1967a 10; tr. = 1957e 7.)

d. "The Trickster in Relation to Greek Mythology." In C. G. Jung, P. Radin, K. K.: *The Trickster.* (Tr. of 1954c, R. F. C. Hull.) London: Routledge & Kegan Paul.

e. Foreword to *Griechenland.* Picturebook by H. G. Hoegler. Zurich: Europa-Verlag. (= 1966k, 1967a 7; tr. = 1957b, 1957d.)

1957

a. *Griechische Miniaturen.* 12 ill. Zurich: Rhein-Verlag.
   1. Nach einem Besuch in Samothrake. (= 1967a 8.)
   2. Pompeji oder der Zauber der Malerei. (= 1961d, 1967a 9.)
   3. Symbolismus in der antiken Religion. (= 1956c, 1967a 10; tr. = 1957e 7.)
   4. Griechische Vase aus Tischbeins Schule. (= 1967a 11.)
   5. Das neue Bild von Paestum. (= 1967a 13.)
   6. Der entschwebende Adonis. (= 1967a 12.)
   7. Sonnenkinder-Götterkinder. (= 1967a 15.)
   8. Apollons Tempeldiener. (= 1967a 14.)
   9. Die Dichterweihe auf Paros. (= 1967a 16.)
   10. Neues aus Alt-Kreta. (= 1967a 17.)
   11. Im Nestor-Palast von Pylos. (= 1967a 18.)
   12. Die Herrin des Labyrinthes. (= 1967a 19.)
   13. Ankunft des Dionysos. (= 1967a 20.)
   14. Die Bacchantinnen des Euripides. (= 1967a 21.)
   15. Werk und Mythos. (= 1967a 22.)

16. Nachwort: Perspektiven. (Die neue Deutung der Antike.—Ein Radio-vortrag.)

b. Foreword to *Det Gyllene Grekland*. (Tr. of 1956e.) Stockholm: Natur och Kultur.

c. *En Konstälskare Loggbok. Resor i det gamla Europa*. (Tr. of 1954d, Erland Rådberg.) Stockholm: Natur och Kultur.

d. Preface to *Greece in Color*. (Tr. of 1956e, Daphne Woodward.) London: Thames & Hudson.

e. *La Religion antique*. (Tr. of 1940b, enl. by chap. 7, Y. Le Lay.) Geneva: Georg & cie.

    7. Le Symbolisme dans la religion antique. (Tr. of 1956c.)

f. *Vergil und Hölderlin*. Zum 70. Geburtstag des Altertumsforschers K. K. 19 Jan. 1957. Zurich: Rhein-Verlag. (= 1963m.)

1958

a. *The Gods of the Greeks*. (Tr. of 1951g, Norman Cameron.) 52 ill. Harmonds-worth, Middlesex: Penguin Books. Pelican Book No. A 429.

b. "Le mythe du Fripon et la mythologie grecque." In C. G. Jung, P. Radin, K. K.: *Le Fripon divin*. (Tr. of 1954c, A. Reiss.) Geneva: Georg & cie.

c. *Die Mythologie der Griechen. II. Heroengeschichten*. 80 ill. Zurich: Rhein-Verlag. (= 1966h II; tr. = 1959c, 1960e, 1960g, 1962e, 1962f, 1963c II, 1972c II, 1973d, 1974b, 1974d II, 1975d II.)

d. "Orfeo, simbolo dionisiaco." In *Umanesimo e simbolismo*. (Tr. O. M. Nobile Ventura.) Atti del IV convegno internazionale di studi umanistici, Venice, 19–21 Sept. 1958. Padua: CEDAM.

e. "Das Theta von Samothrake." In *Geist und Werk*. Festschrift for Daniel Brody. Zurich: Rhein-Verlag.

1959

a. *Abenteuer mit Monumenten*. Bibliophile Ausgabe. Oltener Bücherfreunde. (= 1969j.)

    1. Asklepios in Trastevere.

    2. Laokoon, oder Odysseus und das Meerungeheuer.

    3. Sich wandelndes Paestum.

b. *Asklepios. Archetypal Image of the Physician's Existence*. (Tr. of 1948a, plus Postscript "On Snakes and Mice in the Cults of Apollo and Asklepios," Ralph Manheim.) 58 ill. BS LXV.3.

c. *The Heroes of the Greeks*. (Tr. of 1958c, H. J. Rose.) 76 pl. London: Thames & Hudson.

d. *Prometheus. Die menschliche Existenz in griechischer Deutung*. (Rev. and enl. ed. of 1946b.) Reinbek bei Hamburg: Rowohlt. "rowohlts deutsch enzyklopädie." (Reprint 1962.) (Tr. = 1963i.)

e. "Walter Friedrich Otto: In Memoriam." In *Jahresring 1959/60*. Beiträge zur deutschen Literatur und Kunst der Gegenwart. Stuttgart: Deutsche Verlagsanstalt.

1960

a. *Asklepios. Archetypal Image of the Physician's Existence*. London: Thames & Hudson. (= 1959b, identical.)

b. *Eleusis. De heiligste mysterien van Griekenland*. (Tr. from the German ms, J. A. Schroeder.) 29 pl. 7 fig. The Hague: Servire. (Rev. and enl. = 1962h; tr. of revision = 1967b.)

c. *Gespräch in Briefen*. With Thomas Mann. Zurich: Rhein-Verlag.
    1. Romandichtung und Mythologie, 1934–1945. (= 1945e, 1967c 1, 1972b 1; tr. = 1947d, 1960j, 1973a 1, 1975d 1.)
    2. Humanismus—schweres Glück, 1945–1955. (= 1967c 2, 1972b 2; tr. = 1963b 2, 1973a 2, 1975d 2.)

d. *The Gods of the Greeks*. (Tr. of 1951g, Norman Cameron.) 52 ill. Paperback, Evergreen ed. New York: Grove Press.

e. *Grekiska Hjältesagor*. (Tr. of 1958c, Alf Ahlberg.) 80 pl. Stockholm: Natur och Kultur.

f. *Griekse Mythologie*. (Tr. of 1951g, P. J. F. van Leeuwen.) 37 ill. Antwerp: W. De Haan. "Phoenix-Pocket," No. 42.

g. *The Heroes of the Greeks*. (Tr. of 1958c, H. J. Rose.) 76 pl. Hardcover ed. New York: Grove Press.

h. "Man and Mask." In *Spiritual Disciplines*. Papers from the Eranos Yearbooks. (Tr. of 1949d, Ralph Manheim.) BS XXX.4. / London: Routledge & Kegan Paul.

i. "Mythos in verbaler Form." In *Beiträge zu Philosophie und Wissenschaft*. Festschrift for Wilhelm Szilasi. Munich: A. Francke. (= 1964d 5.)

j. *Romanzo e mitologia. Un carteggio Thomas Mann-Karl Kerényi*. (Tr. of 1945e, E. Pocar.) Milan: Il Saggiatore. "Biblioteca delle Silerchie." (= 1973a I.)

k. *Streifzüge eines Hellenisten. Von Homer zu Kazantzakis*. Zurich: Rhein-Verlag.
    1. Homer und die Kampfer um seinen Gesang.

2. Geburt und Wiedergeburt der Tragödie—Vom Ursprung der italienischen Oper zum Ursprung der griechischen Tragödie.

3. Niko Kazantzakis—oder Nietzsches Forsetzung in Griechenland. Nachwort: Über den neuen Menander.

1. "Über László Németh." Afterword to L. Németh's *Wie der Stein fällt*. Stuttgart: Steingrüben. Reprint in "Fischer-Bücherei," No. 486. Frankfurt a. M. 1963.

1961

a. *Der frühe Dionysos*. Die Eitrem-Vorlesungen, gehalten an der Universität Oslo im September 1960. Oslo: Universitetsforlaget.

b. "Hercules Fatigatus." In *Dauer im Wandel*. Festschrift for C. J. Burckhardt. Munich: Georg D. W. Callwey. (= 1971a 13.)

c. "Hölderlins Vollendung." In *Hölderlin*. Schriften der Hölderlin-Gesellschaft, 3. Ed. Alfred Kelletat. Tübingen: J. C. B. Mohr (Paul Siebeck). (= 1955a 4.)

d. "Pompeji oder der Zauber der Malerei." In *Deutsche Welt in Wort*. 27 moderne deutsche Essayisten. Ed. Johannes Edfelt. Stockholm: Bonniers. (= 1957a 2.)

e. "Das Problem des Bosen in der Mythologie." In *Das Böse*. Studien aus dem Jung-Institut, Zurich: Rascher. (Tr. = 1967i.)

f. "Theos e Mythos." In *Il Problema della demitizzazione*. Atti del Colloquio internazionale sul problema della demitizzazione, Rome, 16–21 Jan. 1961. (Tr. of the German ms. of 1963l, O. M. Nobile.) Rome: Istituto di studi filosofici.

g. *Umgang mit Göttlichem. Über Mythologie und Religionsgeschichte*. Göttingen: Vandenhoeck & Ruprecht. 2nd ed., rev., of 1955g.

1962

a. "Agalma, Eikon, Eidolon." In *Demitizzazione e immagine*. Atti del Convegno a Roma, 11–16 Jan. 1962. (Italian tr. of the German ms. of 1964a.) Rome: Istituto di studi filosofici.

b. "Geist der römischen Literatur." In *Römertum*. Wege der Forschung XVIII. Ed. Hans Oppermann. Darmstadt: Wissenschaftliche Buchgesellschaft. (= 1937a 10, 1941b 13, 1953b 12.)

c. *Grekarnas och Römarnas Religion*. (Tr. of 1963j, Sten Söderberg.) 124 pl. Stockholm: Natur och Kultur.

d. *Die griechisch-orientalische Romanliteratur in religionsgeschichtlicher Be-*

leuchtung. Ein Versuch mit Nachbetrachtungen. Darmstadt: Wissenschaftliche Buchgesellschaft. (= 1927; enl. = 1973b.)

    Nachbetrachtungen:
1. Die Papyri und das Problem des griechischen Romans. (= 1941b 12, 1953b 11.)
2. Nachwort über die Methode.

e. *Griekse Heldensagen*. (Tr. of 1958c, P. J. F. van Leeuwen.) 38 ill. Antwerp: W. De Haan. "Phoenix-Pocket," No. 63. (= 1973d.)

f. *The Heroes of the Greeks*. (Tr. of 1958c, H. J. Rose.) 76 pl. Paperback, Evergreen ed. New York: Grove Press. (= 1959c, 1960g, 1974b.)

g. "Licht, Wein, Honig: Frage nach dem minoischen Festkalender." In *Kretika Chronika* 15. Proceedings of the 2nd Congress of Cretology at Heraklion, Crete, 23–26 Sept. 1961. Heraklion: Kalokairinos.

h. *Die Mysterien von Eleusis*. Enl. ed. of 1960b. 48 pl. 15 fig. Zurich: Rhein-Verlag. (Tr. = 1967b.)

i. *The Religion of the Greeks and Romans*. (Tr. of 1963j, Christopher Holme.) 124 pl. London: Thames & Hudson. New York: E. P. Dutton & Co. (= 1973f.)

j. "Vom Nutzen des Essayisten." Afterword to László Németh's *Die Revolution der Qualität*. Stuttgart: Steingrüben.

1963

a. In C. G. Jung and K. K.: *Essays on a Science of Mythology. The Myth of the Divine Child and the Mysteries of Eleusis*. Rev. ed. of 1949b, without ill. New York: Harper Torchbooks / The Bollingen Library.

b. *Felicità difficile. Un carteggio con Thomas Mann*. (Tr. of 1960c 2, E. Pocar.) Milan: Il Saggiatore. "Biblioteca delle Silerchie." No. 95. (= 1973a II.)

c. *Gli Dei e gli eroi della Grecia*: I. *Gli dei*, II. *Gli eroi*, in 2 vols. (Tr. of 1951g and 1958c, Vanda Tedeschi.) Paperback. Milan: Il Saggiatore. Reprint 1965 (= 1972c.)

d. "Martin Buber als Klassiker." In *Philosophen des 20. Jahrhundert*. Festschrift for Martin Buber. Stuttgart: Kohlhammer. (= 1963k 4.)

e. "Medea." In *Medea—Theater der Jahrhunderte*. Foreword to the texts of the plays. Munich: Langen-Müller.

f. "Nietzsche an der Schöpfung seines Romans." In *Festschrift Leopold Szondi*. Bern: Hans Huber. (= 1971e 2.)

g. "Origine e senso dell'ermeneutica." In *Ermeneutica e tradizione*. (Tr. of 1964d 3, O. M. Nobile.) Atti del Convegno a Roma, 10–16 Jan. 1963. Rome: Istituto di studi filosofici.

h. "Orpheus und Euridike." In *Orpheus und Euridike—Theater der Jahrhunderte.* Foreword to the texts of the plays. Munich: Langen-Müller.

i. *Prometheus. Archetypal Image of Human Existence.* (Tr. of 1959d, Ralph Manheim.) 18 pl. BS LXV.1. London: Thames & Hudson.

j. *Die Religion der Griechen und Römer.* 124 pl. Revision of 1940b. (= 1971a 2–8; tr. = 1962c, 1962i, 1972i, 1973f.) Munich: Droemer-Knaur. Lizenzausgabe: Zurich: Buchclub Ex Libris.

k. *Tessiner Schreibtisch. Mythologisches Unmythologisches.* Stuttgart: Steingrüben.

  1. Béla Bartóks 'Cantata Profana.'
  2. Johann Jakob Bachofens Portrait.
  3. Das Buch und die Bücher. (= 1967a 24.)
  4. Martin Buber als Klassiker. (= 1963d.)
  5. Die ungarische Madonna von Verdasio.
  6. Mythologie des Sommernachtstraum.
  7. Die goldene Parodie.
  8. Enthumanisierte Antike.
  9. Thomas Mann und der Teufel in Palestrina.
  10. Pandelis Prevelakis und die griechische Erzählung.
  11. Zauberberg-Figuren.
  12. Tibet in Ungarns Geisteswelt.
  13. Selbstbiographisches.

l. "Theos und Mythos." In *Kerygma und Mythos.* VI, 1. Hamburg: H. Reich. (= 1967k; tr. = 1961f.)

m. "Vergil und Hölderlin." In *Wege zu Vergil.* Wege der Forschung, XIX. Ed. Hans Oppermann. Darmstadt: Wissenschaftliche Buchgesellschaft. (= 1957f.)

n. "Walter Friedrich Otto: Erinnerung und Rechenschaft." In *Die Wirklichkeit der Götter.* rowohlts deutsche enzyklopädie No. 170. Reinbek bei Hamburg: Rowohlt.

1964

a. "Agalma, Eikon, Eidolon." In *Kerygma und Mythos*, VI, 2. Hamburg: H. Reich. (= 1964d 2; tr. = 1962a.)

b. "Bildtext einer italischen Vase in Giessen." In *Hommages à Jean Bayet.* Collection Latomus, LXX. 27 ill. Brussels: Latomus.

c. *Der göttliche Ärzt. Studien über Asklepios und seine Kultstätten.* 57 ill. Darmstadt: Wissenschaftliche Buchgesellschaft. Reprint of 1956a. (= 1948a, 1975c; tr. = 1948b, 1959b, 1960a.)

d. *Griechische Grundbegriffe*. Fragen und Antworten aus der heutigen Situation. AV, n.s., XIX.

    1. Theos und Mythos—Zum Problem der Entmythologisierung. (Enlarged from 1963l.)

    2. Eidolon, Eikon, Agalma—Vom heidnischen und christlichen Bildwerk. (= 1964a; tr. = 1962a.)

    3. Hermeneia und Hermeneutike—Ursprung und Sinn der Hermeneutik. (tr. = 1963g.)

    4. Moira—Vom Schicksal nach griechischer Auffassung.

    5. Mythos in verbaler Form. Zur Wortgeschichte als Geistesgeschichte. (= 1960i.)

e. "Die griechischen Götter." In *Der Gottesgedanke im Abendland*. Ed. Albert Schaefer. (Shortened from 1969k.) Urban-Bücher No. 79. Stuttgart: Kohlhammer.

f. "Dal mito genuino al mito tecnicizzato." In *Tecnica e casistica*. (Tr. of 1968i, R. Giorgi.) Atti del Colloquio Internationale a Roma, 7–12 Jan. 1964. Roma: Istituto di studi filosofici.

g. In C. G. Jung and K. K.: *Prolegomeni allo studio scientifico della mitologia*. (= 1948d.) Rev. ed. Turin: Boringhieri. (= 1972g.)

h. "Der spiegelnde Spiegel." In *Festschrift Ad. E. Jensen*. 5 ill. Munich.

i. "Ursinn und Sinnwandel des Utopischen." In *EJ* XXXII.

1965

a. "Antikes Erbe—Sinnliches Erbe." Foreword to *Antikes Erbe. Meisterwerke aus schweizer Sammlungen*. Zurich: Orell Füssli.

b. "Elektra." In *Elektra—Theater der Jahrhunderte*. Foreword to the texts of the plays. Munich: Langen-Müller.

c. "Grund zur Eleusinischen Vision." In *Spectrum Psychologiae*. Festschrift for C. A. Meier. (Preliminary version of part of the last chap. of the German ms. of 1967b.) Zurich: Rascher.

d. "Homer und seine Odyssee." In *Die Odyssee—Homers Epos in Bildern*. (E. Lessing.) Freiburg i. Br.: Herder. (= 1969d; tr. = 1965i, 1966b, 1966c, 1966d, 1969e, 1969i, 1970d, 1970e.)

e. "Il mito della 'Areté.'" In *Demitizzazione e morale*. (Tr. of 1968c, R. Giorgi.) Atti del Convegno a Roma, 7–12 Jan. 1965. Rome: Istituto di studi filosofici.

f. "Le mythe de l'Areté." In *Démythisation et morale*. (Tr. of 1968c, R. Klein.) Paris: Aubier.

g. "Persephone und Prometheus. Vom Alter griechischer Mythen." In *Jahrbuch der Raabegesellschaft*. Festschrift for H. Oppermann. Braunschweig: Waisenhaus-Verlag.

h. Preface and Epilegomena to: C. G. Jung, P. Radin, K. K.: *Il Briccone divino*. (Tr. of 1954c, N. Dalmasso, S. Daniele.) Milan: Bompiani.

i. "Ulysses." In *The Voyages of Ulysses*. (Shortened version of 1966b.) Printed for the U.S.A. in West Germany: Freiburg i. Br.: Herder.

j. "Voraussetzungen der Einweihung in Eleusis." In *Initiation. Contributions to the Study Conference of IAHR*. Strasbourg, 17–22 Sept. 1964. Leiden: E. J. Brill.

k. "Was ist der Mythos?" In *Aufruf zur Wende*. Festschrift for E. Schönwiese. (Part of 1965l.) Vienna: Österreichische Verlagsanstalt.

l. "Des Wesen des Mythos und die Technik." In *Die Wirklichkeit des Mythos*. Munich/Zurich: Knaur-Taschenbuch-Serie. (= 1967l II, 1968i; tr. = 1964f.)

1966

a. "Antigone." In *Antigone—Theater der Jahrhunderte*. Foreword to the texts of the plays. Munich: Langen-Müller.

b. "Homer and his Odyssey." In *The Voyages of Ulysses*. (Tr. of 1965d, Kevin Smyth.) London: Macmillan & Co.

c. "Homère et son Odyssée." In *L'Odyssée*. (Tr. of 1965d.) Paris: Hatier.

d. "Homeros en zijn Odyssee." In *De Odyssee*. (Tr. of 1965d, Onno Damasté.) Amsterdam: H. J. W. Becht's.

e. *Humanistische Seelenforschung*. Werke in Einzelausgaben, I. 28 ill. Munich: Langen-Müller.

 1. Pythagoras und Orpheus. (= 1936b, 1937b, 1940d, 1950g 1.)
 2. Die Geburt der Helena. (= 1945b.)
 3. Das Urkind. (= 1940f, 1942b 2, 1951c 2.)
 4. Das Aegäische Fest. (= 1941a, 1949a, 1950a.)
 5. Mythologie und Gnosis.
  I. Über Ursprung und Gründung in der Mythologie. (= 1942b 1, 1942d 1, 1942e 1, 1951c 1.)
  II. Das Wissen vom Wege. (= 1942d 2, 1942e 2.)
 6. Arethusa—Über Menschengestalt und mythologische Idee. (= 1941c.)
 7. Das Geheimnis der Hohen Städte. (= 1953b 17.)
 8. Labyrinth-Studien. (= 1941g, 1950d.)
 9. Vom Labyrinthos zum Syrtos—Gedanken über den griechischen Tanz.

10. Der grosse Daimon des Symposion. (= 1942c.)

11. Mnemosyne—Lemosyne—Über die Quellen "Erinnerung" und "Vergessenheit." (= 1945b 6.)

12. Die orphische Kosmogonie und der Ursprung der Orphik. Ein Rekonstruktionsversuch. (= 1950f, 1950g 2.)

13. Mensch und Maske. (= 1949d.)

14. Gedanken über die Pythia. Ein Fragment. (= 1953b 19; rev. = 1975f;
tr. of rev. 1970i, 1970j.)

15. Selbstbekenntnisse des Livius. (= 1945b 7.)

16. Grundbegriffe und Zukunftsmöglichkeiten des Humanismus. Ein Brief
an junge Humanisten. (= 1945b 9, 1970a.)

17. Lob des Konkreten. Aus einem Brief an einen deutschen Dichterfreund.
(= 1953b 20.)

f. "Il mito della Fede." (Tr. of 1968d, R. Giorgi.) In *Mito e fede*. Atti del Convegno a Roma, 6–12 Jan. 1966. Rome: Istituto di studi filosofici.

g. "Le mythe de la foi." (Tr. of 1968d, O. M. Nobile.) In *Mythe et foi*. Actes
du Colloque à Rome, 6–12 Jan. 1966. Paris: Aubier.

h. *Die Mythologie der Griechen*. I. *Göttergeschichten*. II. *Heroengeschichten*.
dtv-Reihe No. 392 + 397. Munich: Deutscher Taschenbuchverlag. (I = 1951g,
II = 1958c.)

i. "Der Mythos der Areté." In *Freundesgabe für Max Tau*. Festschrift. Hamburg:
Hoffmann und Campe. (= 1968c, 1971a 14; tr. = 1965e, 1965f.)

j. "Platonismus, ein phänomenologischer Versuch." In *Liber Amicorum*. Festschrift for Salvador de Madariaga. (Enl. of 1941b 10.) Bruges: De Tempel,
Tempelhof; V. Collège d'Europe.

k. Foreword to *Griechenland*. Special ed. Lucerne: C. J. Bucher. (= 1956e,
1967a 7.)

1967

a. *Auf Spuren des Mythos*. Werke in Einzelausgaben, II. 7 ill. Munich: Langen-
Müller.

1. "Der Mann mit dem Gritza." (= 1952d 1.)

2. Fragmente aus Griechenland. (= 1952d 3.)

3. Reisetagebuch aus Lesbos. (= 1952d 4.)

4. Aus dem Tagebuch eines Migränikers.

5. Griechisches Stundenbuch. (= 1952d 2.)

6. Unwillkürliche Kunstreisen. (= 1954d.)

7. Das Licht und die Götter Griechenlands. (= 1956e, 1966k.)

8. Nach einem Besuch auf Samothrake. (= 1957a 1.)

9. Pompeji oder der Zauber der Malerei. (= 1957a 2, 1961d.)
10. Symbolismus in der antiken Religion. (= 1956c, 1957a 3.)
11. Grossgriechische Wunder der Goethezeit. (= 1957a 4.)
12. Der entschwebende Adonis. (= 1957a 6.)
13. Das neue Bild von Paestum. (= 1957a 5.)
14. Apollons Tempeldiener. (= 1957a 8.)
15. Sonnenkinder—Götterkinder. (= 1957a 7.)
16. Dichterweihe auf Paros. (= 1957a 9.)
17. Neues aus Alt-Kreta. (= 1957a 10.)
18. Im Nestorpalast bei Pylos. (= 1957a 11.)
19. Die Herrin des Labyrinthes. (= 1957a 12.)
20. Ankunft des Dionysos. (= 1957a 13.)
21. Die Bacchantinnen des Euripides. (= 1957a 14.)
22. Werk und Mythos. (= 1957a 15.)
23. Heiliges Kreta.
24. Das Buch und die Bücher. (= 1963k.)

b. *Eleusis. Archetypal Image of Mother and Daughter.* (Rev. and enl. version of 1962h, tr. Ralph Manheim.) 80 ill. BS LXV.4. London: Routledge & Kegan Paul. Added:
Chap. V: A Hermeneutical Essay on Mysteries.
Appendix I: The Preparation and Effect of the *Kykeon.*
Appendix II: Concerning the Vessels That Were Carried on the Head in the Procession.

c. *Gespräch in Briefen.* With Thomas Mann. "Sonderreihe DTV," No. 61. Munich: Deutscher Taschenbuch Verlag.
1. Romandichtung und Mythologie, 1934–1945. (= 1945e, 1960c 1, 1972b 1.)
2. Humanismus—schweres Glück, 1945–1955. (= 1960c 2, 1972b 2.)

d. "Griechische Grundlagen des Sprechens von Gott." In *Weltgespräch*, 1. Weltliches Sprechen von Gott—Zum Problem der Entmythologisierung. Freiburg i. Br.: Herder.

e. "Menschsein als Mysterium in griechischer Deutung." In *Weltgespräch*, 2. Weltliche Vergegenwärtigungen Gottes—Zum Problem der Entmythologisierung. Freiburg i. Br.: Herder.

f. "Der Mythos des Glaubens." In *Studies in Mysticism and Religion*. Festschrift for Gershom Scholem. Jerusalem: Hebrew University. (= 1968d.)

g. "La peine de Prométhé." (Tr. of 1968g, A. Wieser.) In *Le Mythe de la peine*. Actes du Colloque à Rome, 7–12 Jan. 1967. Paris: Aubier.

h. "La pena di Prometeo." (Tr. of 1968g, R. Giorgi.) In *Il Mito della pena*. Atti del Convegno a Roma, 7–12 Jan. 1967. Rome: Istituto di studi filosofici.

i. "The Problem of Evil in Mythology." In *Evil*. Essays edited by the Curatorium of the C. G. Jung Institute, Zurich. Evanston: Northwestern University Press. (Tr. of 1961e, Ralph Manheim.)

j. "Ancient Greece—Mythology." In *Encyclopaedia Hebraica*, 19. (Hebrew tr. of 1971a 9.) Jerusalem.

k. "Theos und Mythos." In *Religion und Religionen*. Festschrift for Gustav Mensching. Bonn: Ludwig Rohrscheid. (= 1963l.)

l. I. "Was ist Mythologie?" II. "Wesen und Gegenwärtigkeit des Mythos." In *Die Eröffnung des Zugangs zum Mythos*. Readings, ed. and with foreword by K. K. Wege der Forschung, XX. Darmstadt: Wissenschaftliche Buchgesellschaft. (I = 1940b 1, 1942a 1, 1952a 1, 1971a 1; II rev. of 1965l; = 1968i.) Reprint 1976.

1968

a. "Möglicher Sinn von DI-WO-NU-SO-JO und DA-DA-RE-JO-DE." In *Atti e memorie del I. Congresso Internazionale di Micenologia*, Rome, 27 Sept.–3 Oct. 1967. Rome: Edizioni dell'Ateneo.

b. *I Mythologia ton Hellinon*, I. (Tr. of 1951g, Dimitri Stathopoulos.) Athens: Galaxia. (= 1975d I.)

c. "Der Mythos der Areté." In *Kerygma und Mythos* VI/3. Hamburg: H. Reich. (= 1966i, 1971a 14; tr. = 1965e, 1965f.)

d. "Der Mythos des Glaubens." In *Kerygma und Mythos* VI/4. Hamburg: H. Reich. (= 1967f, 1971a 16; tr. = 1966f, 1966g.)

e. "Ödipus." In *Ödipus—Theater der Jahrhunderte*. Foreword to the texts of the plays. Munich: Langen-Müller.

f. "Prometheus heute—und immer." In *Prometheus*. Contribution to Carl Orff's music drama after Aischylos. Tübingen: Wunderlich-Leins.

g. "Die Strafe des Prometheus." In *Opuscula Romana* (Festschrift for Gösta Säflund.) Lund: C. W. K. Gleerup. (= 1968h; tr. = 1967g, 1967h.)

h. "Strafe und Schuld des Prometheus." In *Weltgespräch* 6. Schuld und religiöse Erfahrung. Freiburg i. Br.: Herder.

i. "Vom Wesen des Mythos und der Technik." In *Kerygma und Mythos* VI/3. Hamburg: H. Reich. (= 1965l, 1967l II; tr. = 1964f.)

j. Foreword to the 2nd German ed. of James G. Frazer, *Der goldene Zweig. Eine Studie über Magie und Religion*. Cologne: Kiepenhauer & Witsch.

1969

a. "Anleitung zu Ovids 'Metamorphosen.'" In *Ovid: Metamorphosen*. Illus. by Manfred Henninger. Bibliophil. Ed. Heidenheim: E. Hoffmann.

b. Introduction to Nikos Kazantzakis' drama *Komödie-Tragödie in einem Akt.* Zurich: Propyläa. With Greek tr., Argyris Sfountouris.

c. In C. G. Jung and K. K.: *Essays on a Science of Mythology. The Myth of the Divine Child and the Mysteries of Eleusis.* (Tr. of 1942b, R. F. C. Hull.) BS XXII. First Princeton/Bollingen ed. Also: 2nd hardcover ed. (= 1963a.)

d. "Homer und seine Odyssee." In *Die Abenteuer des Odysseus.* (Volksodyssee.) Freiburg i. Br.: Herder. (Adaptation of 1966b, by W. Stadler.)

e. "Homeros och hans Odyssee." In *Odysseen.* (Tr. of 1965d, Bengt G. Söderberg.) Malmö: Allhems Förlag.

f. "Introduzione al 'Totem e Tabù' di S. Freud." In Sigmund Freud: *Totem e tabù.* (Tr. S. Daniele.) "Universale Scientifica," No. 36. Turin: Boringhieri.

g. "Il linguaggio della teologia e la teologia della lingua." (Tr. R. Giorgi.) In *Linguaggio della teologia.* Atti del Convegno a Roma, 5–11 Jan. 1969. Rome: Istituto di studi filosofici.

gg. "Le Langage de la théologie et la théologie de la langue." (Tr. O. M. Nobile.) In *L'Analyse du langage théologique—Le Nom de Dieu.* Actes du Colloque à Rome, 5–11 Jan. 1969. Paris: Aubier.

h. "A Mythological Image of Girlhood." (Tr. of 1953b 18, Hildegard Nagel.) In *Spring Publications. Contributions to Jungian Thought.* New York: Analytical Psychology Club.

i. "Omero e la sua Odissea." (Tr. of 1965d, Gianfranco Groppo.) In *L'Odissea.* Alba: Edizioni Paoline.

j. *Tage- und Wanderbücher 1953-1960.* 5 ill. Werke in Einzelausgaben, III. Munich: Langen-Müller.

    1. Tagebücher 1953–1960.
    2. Abenteuer mit Monumenten. (= 1959a.)
    3. Die andriotische Säule.

k. "Antworten der Griechen." In *Wer ist das eigentlich Gott?* Bücher der Neunzehn. Ed. H. J. Schultz. Munich: Kösel. (Enl. of 1964e; = 1971a 10, 1973g.)

l. "Wissenschaft und Sprache." In *Weltgespräch,* 7. Sprache und Wahrheit. Freiburg i. Br.: Herder.

1970

a. "Grundbegriffe und Zukunftsmöglichkeiten des Humanismus." In *Humanismus.* Wege der Forschung, XVII. Ed. Hans Oppermann. Darmstadt: Wissenschaftliche Buchgesellschaft. (= 1945b 9, 1966e 16.)

b. "Hegels Wiederentdeckung der Götter Griechenlands und der Humanismus der Zukunft." In *Beiträge zur alten Geschichte und deren Nachleben*. Festschrift for Franz Altheim. Vol. II. Berlin: Walter de Gruyter & Co. (= 1971e 3.)

c. "Hölderlin und die Philologie." In *Von der Beständigkeit*. Festschrift for Otto Heuschele. Mühlacker: Stieglitz-Verlag.

d. "Homer and His Odyssey." In *The Adventures of Ulysses*. (Adaptation of 1966b by W. Stadler.) New York: Dodd, Mead & Co.

dd. "Homero y la Odisea." In *Las Aventuras de Ulises*. (Tr. of 1966b, F. Turienzo.) Barcelona: Editorial Herder.

e. "Homeros en zijn Odyssee." In *De Avonturen van Odysseus*. (Adaptation of 1966b by W. Stadler.) Amsterdam: H. J. W. Becht's.

f. In C. G. Jung and K. K.: *Introduction to a Science of Mythology. The Myth of the Divine Child and the Mysteries of Eleusis*. (Tr. of 1942b, R. F. C. Hull.) New ed. London: Routledge & Kegan Paul. (= 1951e.)

g. "Ist die griechische Religion Erlösungsreligion?" In *Types of Redemption*. Contributions to the Study-Conference of the IAHR in Jerusalem, 14–19 July 1968. Leiden: E. J. Brill. (= 1971a 15.)

h. "Die Münzen des Onomakritos." In *Mythos*. Festschrift for Mario Untersteiner. Genoa: Istituto di filologia classica e medioevale.

i. "Problèmes sur la Pythia." In *L'Infallibilité, son aspect philosophique et théologique*. (Tr. of rev. 1966e 14.) Actes du Colloque à Rome, 5–12 Jan. 1970. Paris: Aubier.

j. "Problemi intorno alla Pythia." (Tr. of rev. 1966e 14.) In *L'Infallibilità, i suoi aspetti filosofici e teologici*. Atti del Convegno a Roma, 5–12 Jan. 1970. Rome: Istituto di studi filosofici.

k. "Satire und Satura." In *Die römische Satire*. Wege der Forschung, CCXXXVIII. Ed. Dietmar Korzeniewski. Darmstadt: Wissenschaftliche Buchgesellschaft.

l. "Über Karl Otfried Müllers Werk und Leben." Foreword to new ed. of K. O. Müller's *Prolegomena zu einer wissenschaftlichen Mythologie*. Darmstadt: Wissenschaftliche Buchgesellschaft.

m. "Unsinnliche und sinnliche Tradition." In *Humanismus*. Wege zur Forschung, XVII. Ed. Hans Oppermann. Darmstadt: Wissenschaftliche Buchgesellschaft. (= 1941b 5, 1953b 5.)

n. "Zauber und Mysterien des Buches." In *Begegnung mit Lübeck*. Zum Jubiläum der Lübecker Buchhandlung Gustav Weiland Nachf. Lübeck: G. Weiland.

1971

a. *Antike Religion*. Werke in Einzelausgaben, VII. 4 ill. Munich: Langen-Müller.
   1. Was ist Mythologie? (= 1942a 1, 1952a 1, 1967l I; tr. = 1940e 1, 1951h 1, 1957e 1, 1972h 1.)

2. Der mythologische Zug der griechischen Religion. (= 1963j; tr. = 1962c, 1962i, 1972i, 1973f.) [3–8 = ed. of 1940b.]
3. Von Wesen des Festes.
4. Zwei Stile der religiösen Erfahrung.
5. Höhepunkte der griechischen und römischen religiösen Erfahrung.
   I. Theoria.
   II. Religio.
6. Mensch und Gott nach griechischer Auffassung.
   I. Die griechische Idee des Opfers.
   II. Vom Lachen der Götter.
7. Mensch und Gott nach römischer Auffassung.
   I. Das Leben des Flamen Dialis.
   II. Rückblick.
8. Die religiöse Idee des Nichtseins.
9. Religion und Mythos in Griechenland. (= 1967j.)
10. Theos: "Gott"—auf Griechisch. (= 1969k, 1973g.)
11. Die Heiligkeit des Mahles. (= 1945b 5.)
12. Mythologisches Mädchenbildnis. (= 1953b 18; tr. = 1969h.)
13. Der müde Herakles in Olympia. (= 1961b.)
14. Der Mythos der Areté. (= 1966i, 1968c; tr. = 1965e, 1965f.)
15. Ist die griechische Religion Erlösungsreligion? (= 1970g.)
16. Der Mythos des Glaubens. (= 1967f, 1968d; tr. = 1966f, 1966g.)
17. Was ist der griechische Tempel?

b. *Der antike Roman.* Introduction and selection of texts. Series "Libelli," CCCXV. Darmstadt: Wissenschaftliche Buchgesellschaft.
   1. Romane und Mysterien—Der Hirtenroman des Longos.
   2. Mission und Unterhaltung—Xenophon von Ephesos und Chariton.
   3. Eselsroman, Romanparodie und Schelmenroman—Apuleius und Petronius.
   4. Der frivole und der fromme Prunkroman—Achilleus Tatios und Heliodoros.

c. "Che cos' è la teologia della storia presso i greci?" (Tr. O. M. Nobile.) In *La Teologia della storia. Ermeneutica e eschatologia.* Atti del Convegno a Roma, 5–11 Jan. 1971. Rome: Istituto di studi filosofici.

d. "Vom *Hieros Gamos.*" In *Économie et Développement économique.* Festschrift for D. E. Kalitsounakis. Athens: Estias.

e. *Der Höhere Standpunkt.* Zum Humanismus des integralen Menschen. List Taschenbücher No. 380. Munich: List.
   1. Bachofen—Nietzsche und Ariadne: Präludien. (= 1945a.)
   2. Der Sprung: Nietzsche zwischen seinem Roman und seinem Evangelium. (enl. of 1963f.)
   3. Hegels Wiederentdeckung der Götter Griechenlands. (= 1970b.)
   4. Humanismus des integralen Menschen.

5. Wilhelm von Humboldt und der Humanismus des integralen Menschen.

f. "Landscape and the Quest of the Historical Jesus." (Tr. of 1971g, Angela Zerbe.) Intro. to *Jesus. History and Culture of the New Testament.* Picture book by E. Lessing. New York: Herder & Herder.

g. "Landschaft und Leben Jesu-Forschung." Intro. to *Der Mann aus Galiläa.* Picture book by E. Lessing. Freiburg i. Br.: Herder.

h. "Qu'est-ce que c'est la théologie de l'histoire chez les Grecs?" (Tr. O. M. Nobile.) In *Herméneutique et eschatologie.* Actes du Colloque à Rome, 5–11 Jan. 1971. Paris: Aubier.

i. "Vom Mythos der Freimaurerei." In 200 *Jahre Modestia cum Libertate.* Festschrift (for Freemasons in Zurich). Ed. Roger Ley. Zurich: Lindenhof.

1972

a. *Briefwechsel aus der Nähe.* With Hermann Hesse. 22 facsimiles. Munich: Langen-Müller.
  1. Briefe 1939–1956.
  2. Epilog: Der vergebliche Garten.

b. *Gespräch in Briefen.* With Thomas Mann. Frankfurt a. M.: S. Fischer. (= 1960c.)
  1. Romandichtung und Mythologie, 1934–1945.
  2. Humanismus—schweres Glück, 1945–1955.

c. *Gli Dei e gli eroi della grecia.* I. Gli dei, II. Gli eroi, 3rd edn. in 1 vol. "Quality Paperback" No. 6. Milan: Il Saggiatore. (= 1963c.)

d. "Der Handschuh der Diana." In *Überlieferung und Auftrag.* Festschrift for Michael de Ferdinandy. Wiesbaden: Pressler.

e. "Homer." Encyclopedic essay in *Die Grossen der Weltgeschichte*, I. Munich: Kindler.

f. "Landschap en 'Leben Jesu-Forschung.'" In *De Man van Nazareth.* (Tr. of 1971g, N. Greitemann.) Amsterdam: H. J. W. Becht's.

g. In C. G. Jung and K. K.: *Prolegomeni allo studio scientifico della mitologia.* (= 1948d and 1964g.) Series: "Universale Scientifica." Turin: Boringhieri.

h. *La Religion antigua.* (Tr. of 1940b, Pilar Lorenzo and Mario Leon Rodriguez.) Madrid: Rivista de Occidente.

i. *The Religion of the Greeks and Romans.* [In Japanese.] 124 pl. (Tr. of 1963j, Hideo Takahashi.) Agent Charles E. Tuttle Co. Tokyo.

j. "Sophokles." Encyclopedic essay in *Die Grossen der Weltgeschichte*, I. Munich: Kindler.

k. "Traum und Mythologie." In *Was weiss man von den Träumen?* Ed. H. J. Schultz. Stuttgart: Kreuz-Verlag.

l. "Über Stefan: Tagebuchauszüge." In *Utopie und Welterfahrung.* (Gedächtnis-buch für Stefan Andrea.) Munich: Piper. (Extr. from 1969j 1.)

m. "Vergil." Encyclopedic essay in *Die Grossen der Weltgeschichte*, II. Munich: Kindler.

n. *Zeus und Hera. Urbild des Vaters, des Gatten und der Frau.* Studies in the History of Religions, XX. Leiden: E. J. Brill. (tr. = 1975h.)
   1. Das Wort "Zeus" und seine Sinnverwandten (*théos* und *daimon*).
   2. Anfangszeit der Zeusreligion: Fragen ihrer frühen Geschichte.
   3. Die Entstehung der olympischen Götterfamilie. (rev. and enl. = 1950c.)
   4. Poseidon, der "Gatte" und "Vater."
   5. Zeus, der Brudergatte.
   6. Herakulte auf der Peloponnes, auf Euboia und in Böotien.
   7. Die grosse Göttin von Samos und Paestum.

1973

a. *Dialogo: Thomas Mann-C. Kerényi.* 1960j and 1963b in 1 vol. Intro. note by Giacomo Debenedetti. Milan: Il Saggiatore. "i gabbiani," no. 111.

b. *Die griechisch-orientalische Romanliteratur in religionsgeschichtlicher Beleuchtung.* Ein Versuch mit Nachbetrachtungen. 3rd ed. Darmstadt: Wissenschaftliche Buchgesellschaft. (= 1962d.)

c. *Griekse Godensagen.* (Tr. of 1951g, P. J. F. van Leeuwen.) 22 ill. "De Haans Paperbacks." Bossum, Holland: Unieboek b.v. (= 1960f.)

d. *Griekse Heldensagen.* (Tr. of 1958c, P. J. F. van Leeuwen.) 25 ill. "De Haans Paperback." Bossum, Holland: Unieboek b.v. (= 1962e.)

e. "Pirckheimer und der Humanismus." In *Studia humanitatis.* Festschrift for Ernesto Grassi. Ed. Eginhard Hora and Eckhard Kessler. Munich: Wilhelm Fink.

f. *The Religion of the Greeks and Romans.* (Tr. of 1963j, Christopher Holme.) Reprint of 1962i. Westport, Conn.: Greenwood Press.

g. "Antworten der Griechen." In *Wer ist das eigentlich Gott?* "suhrkamp taschenbuch" 135. Frankfurt a. M.: Suhrkamp. (= 1969k, 1971a 10.)

1974

a. *The Gods of the Greeks.* (Tr. of 1951g, Norman Cameron.) 52 ill. Paperback, London: Thames & Hudson. (= 1951d, 1958a, 1960d.)

b. *The Heroes of the Greeks*. (Tr. of 1958c, H. J. Rose.) 76 pl. Paperback, London: Thames & Hudson. (= 1959c, 1960g, 1962f.)

c. In C. G. Jung and K. K.: *Introduction à l'essence de la mythologie. L'enfant divin—La jeune fille divine*. (Tr. of 1942b, H. H. Del Medico.) "Petite bibliotheque," no. 124. Paris: Payot. (= 1953e.)

d. *The Mythology of the Greeks*. [In Japanese.] I. Gods, II. Heroes, in 1 vol., ill. (Licence Thames & Hudson.) (Jap. tr. of 1951g and 1958c.)

1975

a. "Die anthropologische Aussage des Mythos." In *Philosophische Anthropologie*, Part I. Series "Neue Anthropologie," 6. Ed. H. G. Gadamer, Paul Vogler. Stuttgart: Georg Thieme Verlag.

aa. Idem in "Wissenschaftliche Reihe," WR 4074. Munich: Deutscher Taschenbuch Verlag.

b. "Bachofen und die Zukunft des Humanismus." In *Materialien zu Bachofens 'Das Mutterrecht.'* Ed. Hans-Jürgen Heinrichs. "suhrkamp taschenbuch" 136. Frankfurt a. M.: Suhrkamp. (Some paragraphs of 1971e 1.)

c. *Der göttliche Ärzt. Studien über Asklepios und seine Kultstätten*. 57 ill. Reprint of 1956a and 1964c. Darmstadt: Wissenschaftliche Buchgesellschaft. (= 1948a.)

d. *I Mythologia ton hellinon*. (Tr. of 1951g and 1958c, Dimitri Stathopoulos.) I. *Hoi theoi*. II. *Hoi heros*, in 1 vol., ill. Athens: Estias. (I = 1968b.)

e. *Mythology and Humanism. The Correspondence of Thomas Mann and K. Kerényi*. (Tr. of 1960c, Alexander Gelley.) Ithaca and London: Cornell University Press.

f. "Naissance du mythe du heros." In *Recherches poétique*, I. (Tr. of the preface to 1958c, Marie-Noelle Delorme, Louise and Brigitte du Plessis.) Paris: Editions Klincksieck.

g. "Über die Pythia." In *Kerygma und Mythos*, VI/6. Hamburg: H. Reich. (Rev. of 1953b 19, 1966e 14; tr. of rev. = 1970i, 1970j.)

h. *Zeus and Hera. Archetypal Image of Father, Husband, and Wife*. (Tr. from German ms., Christopher Holme.) BS LXV.5. London: Routledge & Kegan Paul. (= 1972n.)

LIBRARY OF CONGRESS CATALOGING IN PUBLICATION DATA

Kerényi, Károly, 1897-1973.
  Dionysos; archetypal image of indestructible life.

  (Bollingen series, 65. Archetypal images in Greek religion, v. 2)
  "Translated from the original manuscript of the author."
  Bibliography: pp. 393-420
    1. Dionysos. I. Title. II. Series: Bollingen series, 65. III. Series: Ar-
chetypal images in Greek religion, v. 2.
  BL820.B2K4713   292.'2'11   78-166395
  ISBN 0-691-09863-8